THE
ILLUSTRATED
ENCYCLOPEDIA OF
DINOSAURS
AND PREHISTORIC ANIMALS

THE
ILLUSTRATED
ENCYCLOPEDIA OF
DINOSAURS
AND PREHISTORIC ANIMALS

CONSULTANT EDITOR DR. DOUGLAS PALMER

PROFESSOR BARRY COX, PROFESSOR R.J.G. SAVAGE,
PROFESSOR BRIAN GARDINER, DR. COLIN HARRISON, DR. DOUGLAS PALMER

MARSHALL PUBLISHING • LONDON

A Marshall Edition
The Orangery
161 New Bond Street
London W1Y 9PA

This edition first published in 1999 in the UK by Marshall Publishing Ltd

10 9 8 7 6 5 4 3 2 1

ISBN 1-84028-152-9

CONSULTANTS:

This edition revised and updated by
Dr. Douglas Palmer

Consultant Editor: **Professor Barry Cox**
Department of Biology, King's College London
Fishes: **Professor Brian Gardiner**
Professor of Vertebrate Paleontology, King's College London
Contribution: Introduction to fishes
Amphibians and Reptiles: **Professor Barry Cox**
Contribution: Introduction to amphibians, reptiles, ruling reptiles,
birds and mammal-like reptiles.
Birds: **Dr. Colin Harrison**
Former Principal Scientific Officer, Sub-Department of Ornithology,
British Museum (Natural History), London.
Contribution: Text on birds .
Mammals: **Professor R. J. G. Savage**
Department of Geology, University of Bristol, UK
Contribution: Introduction to mammals

Artists:
Fishes and Amphibians: **Colin Newman**
Reptiles, Ruling Reptiles and Mammal-Like Reptiles: **Steve Kirk**
Birds: **Malcolm Ellis**
Mammals: **Steve Kirk, Graham Allen, Andrew Robinson,
Andrew Wheatcroft, Steve Hoiden**
Additional illustrations: **Vana Haggerty**

This edition designed and updated by Axis Design

Printed in Germany by Mohndruck Graphische Btriebe GMBH
Originated in Singapore by Chroma Graphics

CONTENTS

FOREWORD

This book is a natural history of times past, featuring real creatures that lived, breathed, reproduced – then disappeared from the face of the Earth. That they could be brought back to life in such convincing form is a credit to the painstaking scientific detective work of a team of paleontologists, writers and artists.

Decisions have had to be made about which animals to select. To recreate a truly valuable selection of prehistoric animals it was vital to include not only the dinosaurs and their reptile relatives but also representatives of all the other major groups of vertebrates – that is, animals with backbones. The result is a fascinating catalogue of creatures, which includes the fishes of the past; the first amphibians; the mammal-like reptiles, the ancient masters of the air, in the form of flying reptiles and the first birds and bats; and the mammals that were our predecessors.

The reconstructions were made through a combination of the knowledge of the paleontologists and the skills of the artists. The resulting creatures may look fantastic, but they are by no means the creations of the imagination. In recreating each animal the artists have held faithfully to the fossil record. From study of fossils and of animal anatomy, plus detailed observations of the appearance and behaviour of modern creatures, the artists have been able to 'clothe' the skeleton of each animal, and make realistic reconstructions of physical features, posture and coloration.

Life began on Earth about one and a half billion years ago. Though relative newcomers on Earth, the human species has done much to change its face. We have been instrumental in causing the extinction or near-extinction of many species. So as you marvel at the wonders of the life in the past it might be as well to remember that many of the living animals with whom we share our planet may in future appear only on the pages of books or as mute bones and stuffed skins in museums. In paying tribute to the beauty and diversity of the life of the past, this book reminds us of our responsibilities for our living heritage.

Barry Cox, Professor of Biology, King's College,
University of London, Consultant Editor 1st Edition

The rock and fossil record of the past has more gaps than data. New fossils are constantly being discovered and the study of these fossils continuously reveals new insights into the life and environments of the past. This book had been brought up-to-date to provide an accurate portrait of the astonishing diversity of extinct vertebrate animals which have lived on Earth for over 500 million years in the context of the changes happening all the time in scientific thinking.

Classification of fossil organisms is fraught with difficulty. Classification schemes are constantly changing to reflect new data and its interpretation. The advent of molecular classification based on DNA analysis, for example, has forced a reassessment of the traditional fossil classification based on bone morphology.

The past was a very strange country and despite over 200 years of intensive scientific investigation, the fossil record, like so much of science remains a largely unread book. Consequently, the science of fossils – paleontology – has enormous potential for future discovery. Only now do we have some idea of what we want to know and how to go about finding it.

The total of some 500,000 known fossil species is perhaps less than a 0.1% sample of the life of the past. However, we now know that much of this ancient biodiversity is unrecoverable because so many groups of organisms do not fossilize easily. Some special sites preserve the common types of fossils – shells and bones – and traces of soft tissue muscle, skin, feathers. New understanding of how such deposits form and are preserved allow paleontologists to actively prospect for such sites.

Discoveries have been made over the last decade, which have helped to revolutionize understanding of the life of the past. There have been new insights into the origin of back-boned animals (vertebrates) back as far as Cambrian times, some 530 million year ago; the origin of four-footed vertebrates (the tetrapods) and questions about the relationships of the dinosaurs and birds. Most recently the extraordinary discoveries in China of flightless, feathered dinosaurs have stunned even the paleontological professionals, who know only too well to expect the unexpected when it comes to the fossil record.

Dr. Douglas Palmer, Consultant Editor 2nd Edition

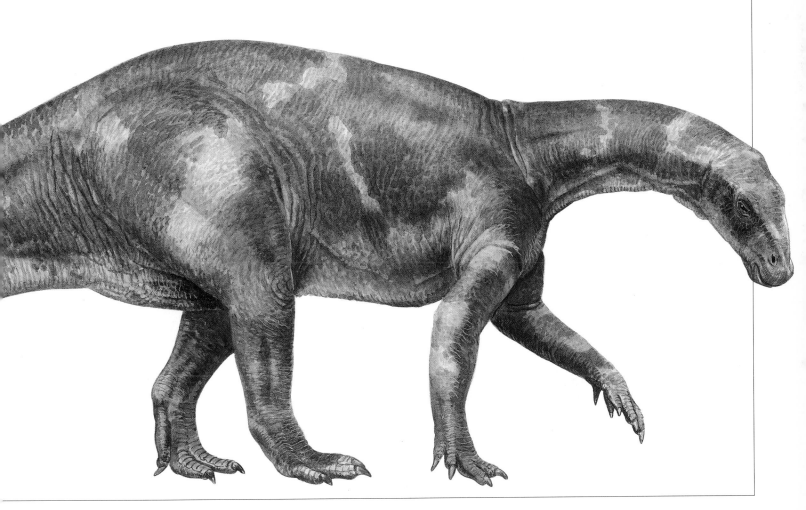

INTRODUCTION

Today, fossils are readily accepted as the remains of once living organisms. Human perceptions of the life of the past have been transformed by fossil discoveries made over the last few decades. The raw data and information on which the reconstruction of ancient creatures is based, however, is often no more than a collection of petrified, broken and distorted fossil bones.

These unpromising fossil beginnings are brought to life by paleontologists, modellers and scientific illustrators as convincing animals. This book shows the nature of fossil finds, and 'state of the art' pictorial reconstructions show how petrified fossil bones can be viewed as once living animals.

This revelatory process continues. The investigation of the fossil past is still in its infancy. Each year significant finds reveal new and often unsuspected aspects of the 'deep past'. We are still scratching the surface of the rock record of the history of life

Science and fossils

The active academic study of fossils (paleontology) and the wider context of the rocks in which they are found (geology) began in the period of the growth of the sciences in the nineteenth century.

The process of fossilization preserves only hard structures such as bones and teeth, and even then many creatures are not preserved because their bones were too small or fragile. The mammalian fossil record, for example, is poorly preserved and often the teeth are all that remain. Even these can yield some information, however. By studying the patterns of cusps, ridges and furrows on the teeth, paleontologists can identify species and their feeding habits, but to reconstruct the animals they need more complete skeletal remains.

Such remains are occasionally found, but they often result from a rapid or catastrophic burial event that has protected the cadaver from scavenging and degradation. The submarine mud avalanches that buried the Cambrian age faunas of the Burgess Shale; the sandstorms in the Cretaceous semi-arid deserts of Mongolia that buried dinosaurs, their nests, eggs and hatchlings as well as tiny mammals; and the Ice Age 'freezer' that preserved mammoths and humans for thousands of years all provided paleontologists with unusually well-preserved fossils.

Paleontology is still a 'frontier' subject and we have only sampled a very small percentage of the life that once lived on Earth. There are an estimated 10 million species of organisms alive today. Life has been abundant on Earth for at least 500 million years, and a conservative estimate of the rate of species' longevity or turnover is 10 million years. Making a rough calculation, then, the fossil record of the last 500 million years should contain the remains of 500 million species. The known fossil record contains about 500,000 species – a 0.1% sample.

Reconstructing the evidence

The science of comparative anatomy, founded by the Scottish surgeon John Hunter and the French naturalist Georges Cuvier, allowed scientists to reassemble the often fragmentary, incomplete and even mixed fossil bones of extinct creatures into anatomically viable

FOSSILIZATION OF AN ICHTHYOSAUR

Any animal is more likely to be fossilized if it is buried in soft sediments. The corpse of an ichthyosaur (illustrated above) has fallen onto soft seabed sidiment. The flesh is scavenged and the body decays, but the bones and teeth do not.

Layers of sediment pile up on top of the bony remains. Minerals from the sea water percolate through the skeleton and become deposited in the bones, filling any spaces between them. They gradually replace the material of the bones.

The fossilized skeleton is compressed and distorted by the addition of more layers of sediment and by movement of the land. Here the rock has been pushed upward so that the strata have become tilted and are exposed as dry land.

animals. Behind such reconstructions is the idea that all vertebrate animals have a common skeletal plan, inherited from their common ancestors. Cuvier made some of the most innovative reconstructions of extinct mammals from the Ice Age giant ground sloth (*Megatherium*, 1796) of South America to some of the then earliest known primitive mammals of Tertiary age from the strata of the Paris basin.

The changing interpretation of fossils

Today few people doubt the evolutionary story of life – a 3.8 billion year development from microbes to mammals. But this well-developed understanding of the fossil record is little more than 100 years old.

Early interpretation

The first large fossil bones to be discovered were generally construed as belonging to mythical beasts. However, within the Judeo-Christian tradition, the Bible provided another explanation for such remains – The Flood. The power of this explanation was so strong – even among many eminent geologists – that it was not dislodged until the early nineteenth century. When the bones of a variety of large animals, such as elephants, were found far beyond the animal's known geographical range it seemed reasonable to conclude that they had been swept there by the Flood. This view was only replaced when it was overwhelmed by contradictory geological information. Calculations based on biblical evidence put the Earth's age at about 6000 years, but as awareness of the slowness of the rates of geological processes increased, the age of the Earth had to be extended into millions of years.

Geologists were discovering that during the Earth's history there had been continuing burial of layers of sediment containing organic remains. It also became clear that the types of fossil creatures changed throughout the succession of rock layers (strata). By the early 1800s great thicknesses of rocks filled with fossil remains had been discovered and it became clear that they could not all have been produced by a single flood, however catastrophic.

At the same time, scholarship had shown that the Bible was not a simple document of fact, but a complex cumulation of historical narratives that required interpretation. For many Christian divines involved in the investigation of the natural world, these revelations were not overly problematic. The new discoveries could still be viewed as the 'wondrous works of a benevolent and munificent God'. However, cracks were soon to appear even in this liberal view.

Another problem was posed by those fossil remains that could not be identified as any known creature. In 1786, an enormous skull armed with ferocious teeth was found in a Maastricht chalk quarry. Scientists could not agree on what kind of animal it had belonged to, for it looked like a cross between a crocodile and toothed whale, so it was reconstructed as a crocodile-like animal. Although no such living animal was known at the time, it was still possible that such an animal might exist somewhere on Earth. In 1795 the 'beast' was captured by Napoleon's army and brought to Paris, where its pedigree as a mososaur, a kind of giant marine lizard, was eventually established.

Naturalists were having to face up to the possibility that some of these creatures might be extinct, but more difficult problems were to follow. There was growing evidence that individual species and groups of animals and plants appeared in the geological record at different times and there were questions over just how fixed in form species were. After all, if new varieties of life could be produced by human intervention in the interbreeding of species, perhaps one species could 'transmute' or change into another through time.

The forces of erosion wear away the land surface. The eroding action of a stream has created a sheer cliff face (right). As a result, the tail of the ichthyosaur is beginning to be exposed and bones drop into the bed of the stream.

With further erosion, more of the ichthyosaur tail becomes visible. The fossil skull can also be seen again due to erosive forces wearing away the surface of the land.

The Darwinian revolution

The publication of Charles Darwin and Alfred Wallace's joint theory of evolution in 1858, entitled 'On the Tendency of Species to form Varieties; and on the Perpetuation of Varieties and Species by Natural Selection' had far-reaching effects which are still being felt in the western world. The controversial theory provided some explanation of the role of extinction in the development of life on Earth. It also raised the expectation that evolutionary 'links' or transitional forms would be found between different groups of organisms as one evolved from another. However, Darwin realized that the fossil evidence represented such a small sample of the vast diversity of past life that it was unlikely that such intermediary forms would be preserved and discovered. However, the fossil record was growing and becoming more complete all the time and was soon to provide evidence to support his theory.

The discovery of one particular fossil in 1860 helped to make a breakthrough. A single feather was discovered in some Jurassic lithographic limestones in Bavaria, Germany. Six months later, further excavation at the site had yielded a bird skeleton, complete with the impressions of asymmetrical flight feathers around its wing bones.

Thomas Henry Huxley realised that this new find, named *Archaeopteryx* (Greek for 'ancient wing') showed a mixture of reptilian and bird characteristics. It therefore provided the first and surprisingly good fossil example of a transitional form, clearly linking one major group of animals (the birds) to the ancestral group (the dinosaur reptiles) from which it had evolved. This was further reinforced by the discovery of a small bipedal dinosaur (*Compsognathus)* from the same deposits, which had a close resemblance to *Archaeopteryx.*

In 1997-8 the picture of dinosaur-bird relationships became even more intriguing. Two small bipedal theropod dinosaurs, *Protarchaeopteryx* and *Caudipteryx,* were found in China with traces of feathers covering their bodies. However, these animals could not fly and were not birds, they were still dinosaurs.

In 1996, another Chinese specimen of similar age, called *Sinosauropteryx* , very similar to both *Compsognathus* and *Archaeopteryx,* had been discovered with a crest of small feather-like structures running down its neck, backbone and flanks. It is becoming increasingly clear that there was evolution of carnivorous dinosaurs through the coelurosaur dinosaurs (including feathered forms) into true birds, and the feathers of *Archaeopteryx* are now less problematic, since they no longer appear as if from nowhere as fully formed flight feathers without antecedents.

Another, and in some ways even better example of evidence for the process of evolution provided by the fossil record, came from the recovery by a French expedition in the 1850s of large numbers of horse leg bones from terrestrial deposits in Greece. When the fossilized horse remains were described in the 1860s by Albert Gaudry, he was able to draw up a provisional family tree describing the evolution of the horses by linking the Greek find with previous fossil discoveries from France.

Subdividing time

By the middle of the nineteenth century, geological time, as represented by great thicknesses of rock strata, was well-enough understood to allow for formal subdivision. Sequences of particular rock types with characteristic fossils could be recognized. For instance, coal-bearing strata, with their common and distinctive fossil tree ferns and club mosses came to be referred to as belonging to the Carboniferous Period (*carbon* being Latin for charcoal).

Similarly, the younger and abundant chalk rocks of Europe, with their fossil ammonites and other more familiar-looking shells, were referred to as Cretaceous (*creta* being Latin for chalk). Both Carboniferous and Cretaceous strata were seen to belong within what was called the Secondary series. Below lay the Transition series and then Primary rocks and above there were the younger Tertiary series and Diluvial and post-diluvial sediments.

Over several decades, the whole of geological time from Primary to post-diluvial, with its relatively crude subdivisions, was carved up into some 16 periods such as the Carboniferous and Cretaceous.

These formalized periods each contained characteristic fossil remains and were underlain by an earlier phase which was thought to have been devoid of life, called the Azoic (Greek for 'without life'). However, no dates could be given to the duration of these periods because no reliable method of dating rocks was available until the end of the century.

The 16 periods of fossil life were in turn grouped into three formalized versions of the old series, renamed as Palaeozoic (from the Greek *palaios,* meaning ancient, and *zoos,* meaning life), Mesozoic (*meso* meaning middle) and Cainozoic (*caino* meaning recent).

The Palaeozoic Era

Lower Palaeozoic seas were occupied by several extinct groups of invertebrates such as the arthropod trilobites and eurypterids and strange, vaguely plant-like graptolites, which were in fact colonial animals. They all look quite alien to us today but were accompanied by early representatives of the more familiar snails, clams, sea-urchins, starfish and shrimp-like arthropods.

These oceans were also home to early vertebrate animals – bizarre jawless fish whose sole surviving representatives are today's lampreys and hagfish. The latter part of the Palaeozoic also heralded one of the major developments in the history of life on Earth – the invasion of the land. The first land-living plants evolved and diversified so that, by the end of the Era, there were extensive forests of tree ferns and club mosses, occupied by a diverse fauna of four-limbed vertebrates, the early tetrapods and abundant land-living invertebrates.

The early tetrapods included the ancestors of the amphibians, reptiles and mammal-like reptiles. The invertebrate animals on which they preyed in order to survive and thrive were dominated by arthropods such as early millipedes, cockroaches, scorpions and the dragonflies (which were the first flying creatures).

THE WORLD'S CHANGING FACE

1

2

3

The series of globes shows how the face of the Earth has changed over the millennia. In these maps, areas at the 'back' of the globe have been folded out. Dotted lines indicate the coastlines of the modern continents' shallow seas are shaded light blue, deep seas dark blue.

1 In the Late Carboniferous to Early Permian, there were two great continents, Euramerica in the north and Gondwanaland in the south. Three other landmasses were the forerunners of Asia.

2. By the Late Permian, all the world's continents were united into one huge landmass called Pangaea.

3. Pangaea started to split up so that, by the Mid Jurassic, seaways spread down the eastern coast of Africa. The fledgling Atlantic appeared as North America started to separate from Europe.

4. In the Early Cretaceous sea had spread around Africa's southern tip. North and South America split apart at this time. Seaways spread northwards to separate Europe from Asia. India had split away from Gondwanaland and begun its long journey northward.

5. By the Late Cretaceous, there were two landmasses in the northern hemisphere. One, 'Asiamerica', included Asia and western North America. 'Euramerica', comprised Europe and eastern North America.

6. By the Eocene, the modern continents had nearly taken shape. India had nearly completed its northward journey and Australia and Antarctica had split from the tip of South America.

4

5

6

The Mesozoic Era

The Mesozoic retained vestiges of the ancient life forms, whilst also having some important distinctive elements and the origins of modern life forms. Cycads provided the basic food supply of the terrestrial reptiles, the dinosaurs and their reptilian relatives, some of whom also returned to the sea. The marine realm had its distinctive marine reptiles, like the ichthyosaurs and plesiosaurs, many of which fed on invertebrate ammonites and belemnites. The air was dominated by flying reptiles. These pterosaurs, though, were not alone; waiting to take off was a group of feathered dinosaurs. We now know them as birds. Two other early Mesozoic innovations were the emergence of small, warm-blooded, shrew-like hairy creatures – the mammals – and the early evolution of the flowering plants (angiosperms).

The Cainozoic Era

The Cainozoic, the most recent 65 million years of geological time, contains the most familiar fossils, many of which are extant today. The Cainozoic is often referred to as the Tertiary (third age), but the two terms are not strictly synonymous. Cainozoic is the Tertiary plus the subsequent Quaternary (fourth age). An early Cainozoic landscape would have been home to many unfamiliar mammals. More recognizable were the plants (flowering plants from herbs to trees and, for the first time, extensive grasslands), amphibians, reptiles and birds that had all survived the K/T extinction event.

The youngest part of the Cainozoic, also known as the Diluvial, had a fauna of megaherbivores and predatory carnivores. Their abundant and well-preserved remains looked superficially similar to many living animals, so were construed as victims of The Flood. In time it became clear that animals, such as the woolly mammoth and rhinoceros were adapted to the cold and had lived during an Ice Age.

Extinction events

We now know that major extinction events separated the Palaeozoic from the Mesozoic and the Mesozoic from the Cainozoic.

The Permo-Triassic Event

The Permo-Triassic extinction event, which marks the end of the Palaeozoic, is the most drastic known to have occurred in the history of the Earth. At least 57 percent of all families of marine organisms died out and perhaps as many as 95 percent of all species disappeared. Hardest hit were the common shell fossils, such as the brachiopods (lamp shells), bryozoans (moss animals) and crinoids (sea lilies). Terrestrial faunas also suffered. It is a testament to the resilience of living organisms that they recovered and continued to diversify.

The cause of this extinction is generally thought to have been environmental, although it has been suggested that the impact of an extra-terrestrial body was involved. As yet, however, no evidence for this theory has emerged in the form of a large impact crater or impact-related debris of the correct age. The extinction seems to have been drawn out over some 10 million years and there is good evidence for global cooling associated with glaciation plus a major fall in sea-level. The extensive shallow seas that surrounded the continents withdrew, and conditions for the great diversity of creatures living there were so abruptly altered that many, especially those that lived attached to the seabed and within reefs, were unable to adapt.

The K/T event

The so called K/T event (from K for *kreta,* the German word for chalk, and T for Tertiary) marks the boundary between the Mesozoic and Cainozoic. Although it killed off only some 15 percent of all marine families, it has attracted considerable attention because it is associated with an extra-terrestrial impact and has been blamed for causing the extinction of the dinosaurs.

The mystery of the disappearance of the dinosaurs has taxed scientists for many years now and over 200 different theories have been put forward, ranging from the ridiculous to the unlikely.

Although we know that the dinosaurs died out some 65 million years ago, one of the problems is that there are not enough dinosaur fossils to help pinpoint the exact time of the extinction event, and since the dinosaurs were land-living creatures, their remains occur mainly within terrestrial sediments. However, the extinction event is marked almost globally in sequences of marine strata by a thin layer of clay sediment, containing unusually high levels of rare metals. These metals are evidence of the impact of an extra-terrestrial body, such as a very large meteorite or asteroid. A 60 mi/100 km-wide crater created by the impact has been found, buried deep beneath younger sediment at Chicxulub in the Yucatan peninsula, Mexico. Scientists believe that following the impact and catastrophic blast damage, wildfires spread throughout the Americas, followed by darkening of the skies from soot and dust, causing air temperatures to fall. After several hours, coastal regions around the Caribbean were devastated by tidal waves that swept inland and drowned anything left alive after the blast and firestorms. By the end of a week, the most vulnerable species, such as the big sauropod and top carnivore dinosaurs with relatively small populations, had been wiped out. The immediate extinction effects continued for at least a year, until rain washed the dust out of the atmosphere. However, it is thought that secondary effects reverberated through the food chain and ecosystem for at least 300,000 years. At the end of this time not only were all the remaining dinosaurs extinct, but suspended dust in the atmosphere caused global temperatures to drop, seriously disturbing all ecosystems.

The question is, why was the extinction event so selective? The dinosaurs might have died out along with the last of the flying reptiles, but their other reptilian relatives, such as the crocodiles and lizards, were barely affected, nor were the birds, mammals or plants.

There undoubtedly was a major impact event, but other major events, like the lava eruptions in the Indian Deccan region changing atmospheric conditions and a rapid fall in global sea levels, could also have seriously disturbed the global ecosystem. These alternatives may not have the appeal of a meteorite, but other extinction events have had equally drastic results. The jury is still out on whether dinosaurs were on the brink of extinction or were pushed into oblivion by a meteorite.

The Ice Age 'event'

The most recent extinction has been associated with the last Ice Age. As the zone of permanently frozen ground spread south from the North Pole across northern Asia, Europe and North America, glaciers developed in the mountains and sea-ice spread into the Atlantic. The large mammals had to retreat southwards, but many of them adapted to the cold and survived on the windswept tundra and grassland steppe of Asia and North America. We know that woolly mammoth and rhinoceros, bear, wolves, wolverines, giant deer, horses and big cats and other mammals occupied these cold regions because their fossils, butchered bones and drawings of them remain. They shared these habitats with humans. The rapid climate and associated vegetation change at the end of the Ice Age was largely responsible for their demise. However, in the northern hemisphere the pressure of human hunting probably reduced stock population numbers to an unsustainable level.

Systems of classification

Since 1735, the year when Swedish naturalist Carl Linnaeus published his *System of Nature*, scientists have been using Linnaeus's method of organizing and grouping plants and animals. Linnaeus believed that species are discrete units that stay constant from one generation to another and do not show any significant ability to transmute. His hierarchical system had four levels: species being the most specific, then genus, order and class. It was Linnaeus who designated species by Latin names; the first referring to the genus, the second to the species. For the first time the genus *Homo* was grouped in the order Primates, along with the apes, monkeys and lemurs and these, in turn, were placed within the Class Mammalia, as part of the Kingdom Animalia. Criticized for this grouping, Linnaeus challenged his critics to show any physical feature that could separate the two.

The German biologist Ernst Haeckel developed the concept of the phylum, a new and high rank of classification, within which all classes of organisms descended from a common ancestor are grouped. In doing so Haeckel introduced the dimension of time and therefore the concept of evolution to the Linnaean classification. Haeckel, among others, portrayed the succession of prehistoric changes through time as an extended family tree (connected genealogy) with humans on the highest branch. (Modern scientists are less inclined to see all evolution as progress, or to consider man the finest product of such progress).

Cladistics

A recent development in classification has been cladistic analysis of morphological information from living and fossil organisms. Using this method, the importance of the time dimension is reduced. The closeness of relationship between the species being considered and their most recent common ancestor is represented by a branching diagram, called a cladogram. The diagram is constructed from an assessment of characteristics which are shared between two species but not with any others (called shared derived characters or synapomorphies). A succession of branching points (nodes) show the relative order in which synapomorphies arise. These characters are

HOW ANIMALS ARE CLASSIFIED

Animals are classified in groups of decreasing diversity. The smallest unit of classification is the species. Species that share several common characteristics are grouped together into genera, genera into families, and so on. The largest group, the animal kingdom, embraces animals of all kinds, including tribolites and other creatures without backbones. The diagram shows the classification of the imperial mammoth, Mammuthus imperator.

| MAMMUTHUS IMPERATOR (IMPERIAL MAMMOTH) | MAMMUTHUS PRIMIGENIUS (WOOLLY MAMMOTH) | ELEPHAS FALCONERI (DWARF ELEPHANT) | MOERITHERIUM (EARLY ELEPHANT) | ALPHADON (MAMMAL) | TYRANNOSAURUS (REPTILE) | TRILOBITE (INVERTEBRATE) |

KINGDOM ANIMALIA (ANIMALS)

PHYLUM VERTEBRATA (ANIMALS WITH BACKBONES)

CLASS MAMMALIA (VERTEBRATES WITH HAIR AND MAMMARY GLANDS)

ORDER PROBOSCIDEA (MAMMALS WITH A TRUNK OR PROBOSCIS)

FAMILY ELEPHANTIDAE (ELEPHANT FAMILY)

GENUS MAMMUTHUS (MAMMOTH)

SPECIES MAMMUTHUS IMPERATOR (IMPERIAL MAMMOTH)

distinguished from primitive characters which may be more widespread outside the group being studied. The distinction of which synapomorphies should be chosen as most useful for analysis can be highly contentious and lead to the development of a number of alternative cladograms, which then have to be critically assessed. Selection of synapomorphies is made by so-called 'out-group' comparison, with the out-group being closely related so that meaningful comparisons can be made.

In this book, cladistic analysis is referred to in the discussion of individual groups but phylogenetic diagrams form the basis for the representation of classification and inter-relationships through time.

CONVERGENT EVOLUTION

THE ICTHYOSAUR *MIXOSAURUS*

PECTORAL FIN

A MODERN DOLPHIN

THE SHARK *HYBODUS*

Convergent evolution takes places when different groups of animals, which are only distantly related, become independently adapted to the same environment. The illustration shows how convergent evolution has taken place in the forelimbs of three different groups of vertebrates – fish (shark), mammal (dolphin.), and reptile (ichthyosaur).

Genetic evidence

The underlying genetic 'mechanism' that caused change to occur through successive generations was not generally understood until the turn of the century. A species is determined by the ability of individuals to interbreed and produce viable offspring. So there had to be something controlling how reproductive cells were able to combine and exchange information that would determine the inheritance of parental characters in the offspring.

Experiments by the British zoologist William Bateson (1861-1926) and Dutch botanist Hugo de Vries (1848-1935) showed repeated occurrences of certain dominant characters in successive generations of offspring. Also, the ratio of dominant to recessive characters remained the same, showing that some underlying regulatory mechanism must be at work in breeding and inheritance. That mechanism was finally discovered in 1953 by American James Watson (1928–) and the Englishman Francis Crick (1916–), building on the pioneering work of other scientists, working towards a similar goal. The detailed genetic code of each body cell determines the uniqueness of every individual organism and the similarity of the genetic codes determines the ability to interbreed. The code is carried within each body cell's chromosomes and is replicated during cell division by duplication of the double helix structure of nucleic acid (DNA).

The ability to analyse and read the detailed sequences of genetic information has brought a new method of determining the closeness of evolutionary relationships amongst living organisms. In addition, the idea of a 'molecular clock' was developed. Using known rates of genetic mutation and well-established evolutionary branching points, scientists could estimate the point in time at which species diverged by measuring the amount of genetic difference between them.

Such analysis has vindicated Linnaeus' proximation of humans and chimps. In the 1960s and 1970s molecular biologists were able to show that chimp genes are closer than expected to those of humans. Until then, the fossil record was thought to show that the evolutionary split between the higher apes and humans had occurred some 15 million or so years ago. If that had really been the case then there would have been a greater genetic difference than is actually found between the two groups. According to the molecular clock for primate evolution, however, the ape/human split is only some 5 million years old. New fossil finds tend to support this idea.

The problem with genetic analysis is that, despite recent claims it is not possible to extract DNA from fossils of any great age. Most essential cell proteins break down very rapidly after the death of an organism, unless the tissue is preserved in some unusual way – for example the flesh of woolly mammoths became preserved in permanently frozen ground during the Ice Age. Their DNA has been preserved and analysed, but then the cadavers are only some tens of thousands of years old.

Genetic analysis of the inter-relationships of living organisms has revolutionized ideas about the classification of animals and has led to extensive reassessment of the fossil record. Although fossils cannot supply detailed information about relationships, they are nevertheless the only direct evidence that we have of the distribution of life through time. However, there is a major problem with the nature of this information source, because the sample of past life available in the fossil record is very small as yet. The oldest known fossil representative of a particular group does not necessarily tell us when that group originated, it only reveals the first time a specimen was fossilized. Also, the duration of fossil groups is constantly being modified by new discoveries. Nevertheless, fossils are particularly important for informing us of the extinct creatures of the past, including whole major groups like the dinosaurs.

An outline of vertebrate evolution

Fossil discoveries have changed our understanding of the history of life. The origin of life has been pushed back to at least 3.6 billion years ago and our view of the first 3 billion years of life has been transformed. The evolution of many-celled organisms is thought to have been at least 1 billion years ago and diverse soft-bodied organisms called Ediacarans (the biological relationships of which are unclear) were present in marine waters 600 million years ago. By Cambrian times, 550 million years ago, clearly identifiable groups of invertebrate animals, such as molluscs, annelid worms and arthropods had evolved.

THE EVOLUTION OF VERTEBRATES

Animals are classified in groups of decreasing diversity. The smallest unit of classification is the species. Species that share several common characteristics are grouped together into genera, genera into families, and so on. The diagram outlines the evolution of the major groups of vertebrates through time, from jawless fish (Agnatha) to mammals.

0
QUATERNARY
2
TERTIARY
65
CRETACEOUS
142
JURASSIC
205
TRIASSIC
248
PERMIAN
290
CARBONIFEROUS
354
DEVONIAN
417
SILURIAN
443
ORDOVICIAN
495
CAMBRIAN
545

Millions of Years Ago

EARLY TETRAPODS

JAWED FISH – GNATHOSTOMES

AGNATHA   CHONDRICHTHYES   PLACODERMI   ACANTHODII   OSTEICHTHYES   AMPHIBIA   REPTILIA   AVES   MAMMALIA

Vertebrate beginnings

The first known fossil animal to show the beginnings of vertebrate characteristics is *Pikaia*, which dates from mid-Cambrian times, around 535 million years ago. Thought to be similar to the living lancelet (*Branchiostoma*), the body of this small eel-like creature was stiffened and elongated by the presence of a stiff, but flexible rod called a notochord. It is thought that from such unpromising chordate beginnings all vertebrate organisms evolved – the notochord developing into a backbone from which a skeleton of shoulder and hip girdles could be hung. Eventually, paired limbs were slung from the girdles for improved steering and locomotion. The development of the front–back body axis led to the concentration of the sense organs at the front, where they encountered the environment 'head-on'.

Intriguingly the fossil record reveals another group of primitive chordates, the extinct conodont animals (see *Promissum*, p.23), which had the ability to use bone-like material in their bodies. The mineral bone-like tissue is found in their tiny arrays of teeth which intermesh as a very effective prey-catching apparatus.

The fossil record also reveals an great diversity of bizarre-looking marine fish-like animals that had neither teeth nor jaws. The jawless fish (agnathans), who had bony scales and plates embedded in their skin, fed by sucking and filtering organic debris and micro-organisms from seawater and seabed deposits. Agnathans, the stratigraphic rock record shows, were soon joined by jawed fish with teeth.

Preparing for life on land

One of the most important developments in the history of life occurred when animals were first equipped for life on land. Seawater is a relatively supportive, dense, fluid medium that generally does not change temperature quickly, is easy to swim in, obtain oxygen from, feel vibrations in and see through. By comparison, air is a light, dry gas that is unsupportive, fluctuates widely and quickly in temperature, is dehydrating and does not block harmful radiation from the sun. To faciliiate the move from sea to land a number of modifications were required and in place before the move was made.

The earliest tetrapods – the first four-limbed fossil vertebrates – were neither amphibians in the modern sense, nor were they land-going animals. It now appears that the differentiation between amphibians and reptiles, as seen in living forms, was not clearly established to begin with. The paired limbs of the early tetrapods were probably adapted from fish-type fins for continued survival in shallow water environments. It is now known that the first tetrapods had limbs with fingers and toes, although they retained fish-like gills and powerful 'fishy' tails. These pre-adaptations would have equipped their descendants for life on land.

Even by early Carboniferous times the evolutionary situation was still confusing. Recently a 334 million year old tetrapod called *Eucritta* has been described. This salamander-sized fossil incorporates features associated with the amphibians and reptiles.

Amphibians and reptiles

By later Carboniferous times true amphibians and reptiles had diverged from the ancestral tetrapods. Even so, many of these early extinct amphibians resembled reptilian crocodiles not modern amphibians. They included large predatory amphibians, well-developed for life on land except that breeding involved a return to the water. Sharing the swampy environments of Carboniferous times were the first reptiles, many of which were also probably aquatic fish-eaters. But being able to lay shelled fertile eggs, meant they were soon able to leave the water and exchange fish for insects as a food source.

The diversification of these land-living tetrapods went a step further in Permian times when the first of the so-called mammal-like reptiles evolved. They show the first differentiation of teeth for separate functions of capturing, holding, killing and cutting up prey as a means of predigestion. In addition, there are indications of early mechanisms for controlling body temperature.

Mammals

A simple definition of the mammals describes them as warm blooded and hairy vertebrates capable of bearing live young and having milk-secreting mammary glands. Unfortunately, such characteristics can only be deduced from soft tissues and are not generally preserved in the fossil record unless in exceptional circumstances. Teeth are some of the most commonly preserved skeletal remains and allow the separation of true mammal fossils from the remains of the mammal-like reptiles, from which they evolved some 225 million years ago.

Although mammals coexisted with the dinosaurs and other ruling reptiles throughout the Mesozoic, their fossil record from this long period of time (over 150 million years) is generally sparse and it was not until Tertiary times that mammals were able to diversify into the new environmental niches provided by the rapid evolution of the flowering plants and grasses. Within a few tens of millions of years, several thousand species of mammals had evolved.

Dinosaurs: the creation of an icon

In late Permian times, some 230 million years ago, a group of scaly-skinned, egg-laying reptiles, evolved and gradually came to dominate the planet for over 155 million years, These reptiles, which came to be known as dinosaurs, ruled the landscape from Alaska to Antarctica. In the history of life, no other group of large animals have been so successful for so long. There are over 6500 species of reptiles alive today, most of which are lizards. By comparison there are only 4000 mammals, nearly half of which are rodents. So far, the mammals have only been in charge for a mere 65 million years.

The word 'dinosaur' has almost taken over our world view of the past. While the dinosaurs are a nineteenth-century invention of the then newly emergent science of paleontology, there was already fossil evidence for the existence of vertebrate animals in the 'deep past'.

Early finds

Between 1811 and 1830, Mary Anning, and her family uncovered complete flattened skeletons of creatures up to 13 ft/4 m long, with toothed beaks like mammalian dolphins mixed with predominantly reptilian characteristics, in the 200-million-year-old rocks of Lyme Regis in Dorset, England. These ichthyosaurs (meaning fish-lizards) and plesiosaurs (near-lizards) as scientists called them, evidently lived in the seas of the past because they were found along with the shells of typically marine clams, starfish and cephalopods. These discoveries stirred the public imagination. They were the first large extinct animals to be illustrated in reconstructions of their environments.

In 1825, some puzzling fossil bones were found near Cuckfield, Sussex in the south of England. The fossils included peculiar leaf-shaped teeth with serrated edges and a jumble of bones, including a single conical horn-shaped bone about 6in/15 cm long. The animal was reconstructed and named *Iguanadon* by Gideon Mantell, who was the first to describe the Cuckfield fossils. He placed the conical bone, rhinoceros-like, on the end of its nose. As more fossil remains were found, competition grew between amateur Mantell (a physician more interested in fossils than patients) and a Professor Richard Owen.

Inventing dinosaurs.

In 1842, British scientist Richard Owen recognized that the fossils *Iguanodon* and *Megalosaurus* were of extinct animals; he coined the name Dinosauria, meaning 'terrible lizard' to distinguish them from the known living reptiles. His creation was to become a universal icon, eclipsing dragons and the mammoth, and its image was to undergo a number of transformations over the next 150 years.

Owen achieved perhaps the greatest scientific publicity coup of the mid-nineteenth century, redefining the concept and appearance of his new invention and transforming Mantell's 'lowly, creeping', serpent-like animals into something much more imperious. Owen calculated that his dinosaurs might be as much as six times the size of an elephant. He produced an exhibition of lifesize models at Crystal Palace in Sydenham, London, which drew crowds of thousands.

Dinosaur hunting in the USA

In 1802 an observant youth by the name of Pliny Moody uncovered some fossil footprints whilst ploughing on the family farm in Massachusetts. A local naturalist, Edward Hitchcock, eventually described them in1836. Since the tracks had been made by some large three-toed animals, Hitchcock concluded that they must have been made by giant birds. They were, in fact, dinosaur footprints and they provided the first evidence that some dinosaurs were not four-legged as everyone had at first assumed. The image of the dinosaurs was on the move again. In 1858, Joseph Leidy found a partial skeleton in New Jersey, which he reconstructed in a two-legged kangaroo-like posture, and in 1878 it emerged that *Iguanodon* was one of these three-toed bipedal monsters, when Belgian miners recovered the virtually complete skeletons of some 40 specimens.

The hunt moved west and really began to take off in the 1870s. Two school masters, Arthur Lakes and O. W .Lucas, independently found dinosaur fossils in Colorado and sent their finds to experts back east. By doing so, these two amateurs quite unwittingly fomented a bitter personal rivalry between Professor Othniel Charles Marsh of Yale and Edward Drinker Cope of New Jersey. But one positive result of the so-called 'dinosaur wars', with their competing expeditions, was the discovery and description of some 130 new species.

Giant dinosaurs

In the1880s Marsh produced the first reconstruction of a sauropod, a giant plant-eating dinosaur that he called *Brontosaurus*, meaning 'thunder lizard', with individual limb bones over 3 ft 3 in/1 m long and what seemed like endless vertebrae. It became clear that here were by far the largest animals to have lived on land. The unforgettable image of giant plant eating sauropods over 66 ft/20 m long, supported by elephantine pillar-like legs, captured the public imagination.

These dinosaur giants were so impressive that their remains were sought the world over. One of the finest discoveries was the 1907 find of a 73 ft/22 m long *Brachiosaurus* in East Africa, weighing nearly 49 tons/50 tonnes and standing some 40 ft/12m tall, with long forelegs and an enormously long giraffe-like neck.

The first indication that the dinosaurs included animals that were not just big but awesomely dangerous came in 1908, when an expedition from the American Museum of Natural History in New York found a nearly complete skeleton and skull of a new kind of dinosaur in the late Cretaceous rocks of northern Montana. Of all the dinosaurs to have captured the public imagination, this beast, the giant bipedal carnivore *Tyrannosaurus rex*, has come to epitomize all that is mean and nasty. Standing some 20 ft/6 m high, 39 ft/12 m long and weighing around 8 tons/ 7 tonnes, with a fine set of 8 in/20 cm long carving knives in its jaws, *T. rex* was something special. No modern land-living carnivore comes close.

Despite over 140 years of investigation since they were first 'invented', there are still vast gaps in our knowledge of the dinosaurs, their distant reptile relatives and all the other extinct fossil vetebrates which have inhabited the Earth for over 500 million years. Recent decades have seen a revolution in dinosaur studies, the concern now is to understand how they 'worked' as once living animals. What did they really look like? How fast could they run? How quickly did they grow? How did they communicate? Did they look after their young? And finally, why, if they were so successful, did they and many of their relatives die out?

The text of this book answers some of these questions based on our current knowledge. But paleontology, the study of past life, is still very much in its infancy compared with biology. The answers to many of these fascinating questions are still lying buried in the rocks, just waiting to be uncovered.

THE FIRST VERTEBRATES

The most primitive back-boned animals (or vertebrates as they are technically called) are the fishes, not the familiar kinds of fish such as sharks and salmon, but somewhat peculiar jawless fish, the agnathan hagfish (myxinoids) and lampreys (petromyzontiforms).

Despite their lack of familiarity, the agnathans still possess the fundamental characteristics of the vertebrates. These include an articulated stiffening rod running from head to tail with paired blocks of muscles on either side. Contraction of the muscles flexes the body in sinuous waves during swimming. A dorsal nerve cord lies above the back-bone has some enlargement at the front end associated with sense organs. This anterior 'brain' is protected within the cranium.

The 'backbone' and braincase need not be made of bone, cartilagenous fish such as the agnathans and sharks are vertebrates but their 'backbones' are stiffened with cartilage. Cartilage is more primitive than bone, although it does not generally fossilize.

Agnathans were much more common in the past. Several groups evolved and occupied ancient seas, then moved into freshwater before dying out at the end of Devonian times. Mostly, these extinct agnathans looked different from the living survivors which have rather specialized modes of life. Many fossil forms had a leathery covering of bony plates and scales, especially in the head region. But even these extinct forms are probably not the earliest vertebrates.

Conodonts

Evidence strongly suggest that conodonts were the first vertebrates. They were, for a long time, a group of marine animals without a taxonomic home. Their fossil remains consist predominantly of tiny mineralized teeth. Little was known except that they were very common and widely distributed in ancient seas.

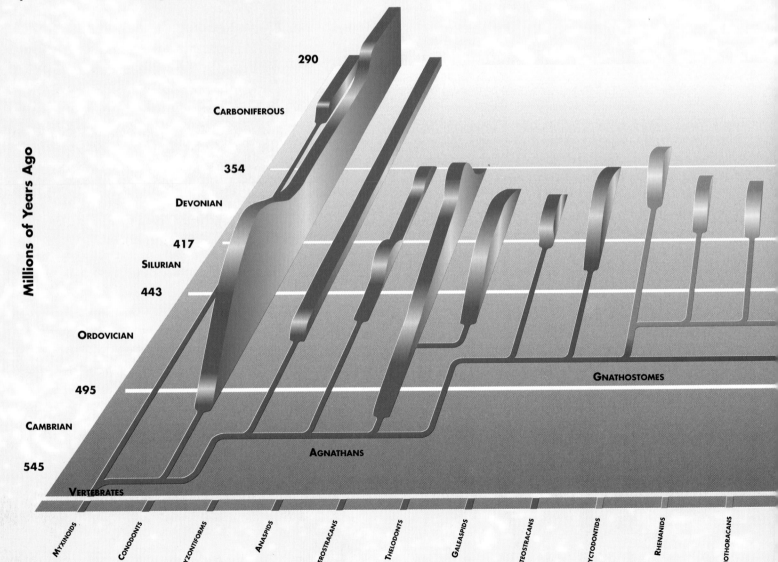

Discoveries from Scotland have shown that the tiny fossil teeth were part of a feeding apparatus in the mouth of tiny eel-shaped jawless animals. The teeth have detailed structures and a composition which ally them with vertebrate teeth. Conodonts' eyes had vertebrate type muscles and the body was flexed by paired blocks of muscles called myotomes, just like the vertebrates. The muscles flexed an axial stiffening rod into typically fish-like sinuous waves for swimming.

There is considerable debate about the relationship of the conodonts to other agnathans and which group of animals they arose from.

The backbone's template

The 'template' for the back-bone is an axial stiffening rod, called the notochord, which is found in a small group of living marine animals called the cephalochordates. The cephalochordates along with the vertebrates are placed within a larger taxonomic group called the Phylum Chordata. Until recently the cephalochordates had no known fossil record because their unmineralized notochord is

not normally fossilized. However, the Cambrian age Burgess Shale of British Columbia, Canada fossilized a creature called *Pikaia*, which is almost certainly a fossil cephalochordate.

If the diagnosis of all these extinct ancient fossils is correct then the origin of the vertebrates was much earlier than once suspected.

The jaws that revolutionized life

The development of jawed fish (the gnathostomes) meant that fish no longer had to rely for sustenance on microscopic organisms. Gnathostomes could actively pursue and seize prey. They could grow larger and specialize in particular lifestyles and diets. Jaws were an evolutionary innovation that led to an explosive radiation and diversification. The chondrichthyans (sharks, skates rays and chimaeras), kept the cartilagenous skelton of their ancestors. Bone replaced cartilage in the others to produce the bony fish (osteichthyans). Two types of bony fishes evolved from a common ancestor – the ray-finned fish (actinopterygians) and the lobe-finned fishes (sarcopterygians).

Lampreys, and their relatives the hagfishes, are the sole survivors of the first fishes to evolve, the jawless agnathans. One of their members, possibly an osteostracan, gave rise to all the jawed fishes. The Devonian period was the 'Age of Fishes', when many of the groups evolved and flourished. The cartilaginous chondrichthyans include the dominant predators of today's seas, the sharks. The bony fishes (osteichthyans) evolved into two groups. The ray-finned actinopterygians include the modern teleosts. And the lobe-finned sarcopterygians were the ancestors of the first land animals.

PLACODERMS

CHONDRICHTHYANS   OSTEICHTHYANS   SARCOPTERYGIANS   TETRAPODS

PETALICHTHYIDS   PHYLLOLEPIDS   ANTIARCHS   ARTHRODIRES   ELASMOBRANCHS   ACANTHODIANS   ACTINOPTERYGIANS   DIPNOANS   ACTINISTIANS   RHIPIDISTIANS   TETRAPODS

The most successful vertebrates

Ray-finned fishes evolved into the most successful group of fishes – the modern teleosts (see pp.38–41). The 21,000 living species make the teleosts the most successful of all living vertebrate groups in terms of abundance. (For comparison, there are about 4000 living species of mammal, 8600 species of bird, 4000 species of reptile and 2500 species of amphibian.)

In terms of diversity of form and lifestyle, teleosts surpass all other water-dwelling creatures (both freshwater and marine, vertebrate and invertebrate). They range from fast-moving predators, such as barracuda and marlin, to sluggish bottom-dwellers, such as stargazers and flatfish; from typical 'fishy' shapes, like mackerel and perch, to weird and wonderful forms like the seahorse, ocean sunfish and lionfish; from the very surface of the ocean, such as the Atlantic flying fish, to its very depths, such as the deep-sea angler fishes.

Modern teleosts are at the top of an evolutionary ladder which proceeded in a series of steps from one group of ray-finned fishes to another (see pp.34–41). This progression started in the Late Silurian, with the appearance of the paleoniscids. Their heavy scales, inflexible fins and asymmetrical tails gave way to the thinner scales of the neopterygians, with their flexible jaws and near symmetrical tails. These fishes were replaced in turn by the teleosts, with even thinner scales, symmetrical tails and highly mobile jaws and fins. Herring-like teleosts were the first to evolve. The group advanced in two major evolutionary bursts. The first occurred in about the middle of the Cretaceous Period, when the salmon/trout group appeared. The second, and final, burst came in the Late Cretaceous/Early Tertiary, when the highly advanced perch-like forms evolved. These make up some 40 percent of the teleosts species of today.

The close of the Mesozoic Era, about 65 million years ago, saw the rise of the teleosts in the waters of the world and also the rise of the mammals on the land. Major changes were occurring at this time in the world's flora and fauna. Fish-eating reptiles, such as the plesiosaurs, ichthyosaurs and mosasaurs, had become extinct. The dinosaurs disappeared and the pterosaurs vanished from the skies. Many types of small planktonic organisms in the seas disappeared without trace, possibly wiped out by the Cretaceous-Tertiary boundary impact event.

These extinctions seem to have been the signal for the teleosts and the mammals to enter their final explosive phase of evolution, and develop into the creatures that dominate the waters and the land today.

The ancestors of land animals

It may seem strange to describe the evolution of the world's most successful vertebrates – the bony ray-finned teleosts – as an evolutionary sideshow. But this, in fact, is what it was, since in the overall story of the evolution of life the ray-finned fishes were a dead-end. Their bony cousins, the lobe-finned fishes – an unspectacular assemblage by comparison – proved to be in the mainstream of evolution.

One of the members of the lobe-finned group provided the ancestor of the first four-limbed animals, the tetrapods. This transition was accomplished relatively quickly in their evolution; the first lobe-finned fishes appeared in the Early Devonian, and by the end of that period, some 20 million years later, the tetrapods had set foot on dry land.

General trends among fishes

Some general trends can be seen in the evolution of fishes, all of which led to fishes that were better adapted to finding, seizing and chewing prey, and to detecting and avoiding predators.

The earliest fishes, the ostracoderms, were protected by a heavy bony armour, developed as a plate-like head shield, and thick, square-shaped body scales. Such a covering would have

ANATOMY OF A SHARK

A shark is a typical fish. It has an anal fin and paired pectoral and pelvic fins on the ventral, or under, surface; two dorsal fins on the back; and a caudal or tail fin, in which the upper lobe is often longer than the lower lobe. All the fins are supported by stiff rays. A shark's 'backbone' is made of calcium-impregnated cartilage with a thin layer of bone. In bony fishes bone replaces cartilage.

1ST DORSAL FIN

2ND DORSAL FIN

ASYMMETRICAL TAIL

ANAL FIN

PAIRED PECTORAL FINS

PAIRED PELVIC FINS

EVOLUTION OF LUNGS AND SWIM BLADDER

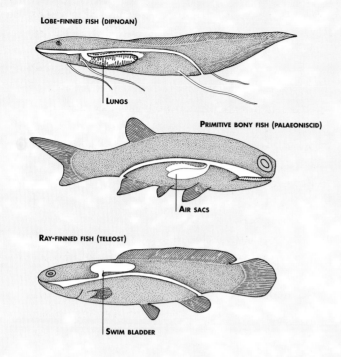

LOBE-FINNED FISH (DIPNOAN)

LUNGS

PRIMITIVE BONY FISH (PALAEONISCID)

AIR SACS

RAY-FINNED FISH (TELEOST)

SWIM BLADDER

The earliest bony fishes (the palaeoniscids), with thick, heavy scales, had paired air sacs connected to the gut. These could be inflated with air to buoy the fish up in the water. As evolution progressed, the bony fishes split into two lines. The lungfish developed air-breathing lungs (while retaining gills), their tissues infolded to increase oxygen uptake. The teleosts, the majority of today's fishes, developed a swim bladder above the throat, to control buoyancy. In the most advanced teleosts, the swim bladder is disconnected from the throat, and is able to secrete and absorb its own gases.

made swimming an energy-expensive process, and many of these fishes lived and fed on the seabed. The upper lobe of their tails was often longer than the lower lobe, which tended to drive the body down in the water, a useful feature for a bottom feeder.

Other ostracoderms developed 'fins' in the form of various spines, flaps and projections, which acted as hydrodynamic aids. These, combined with the enlarged lower lobe of the tail (which tended to drive the fish up in the water) meant that such fishes could swim and feed among the plankton in the surface waters.

The general trend among bony fishes was to develop smaller, thinner scales of a rounded, more hydrodynamic shape. The tail fin became symmetrical, with lobes of equal size, so keeping the fish on a straight course. Paired fins developed at the front of the body (the pectorals) and toward the rear (the pelvics); these not only stabilized the fish, but also worked like built-in oars, allowing it to change direction as it moved.

Accompanying these changes in the shape of the tail and the weight and extent of scales, bony fishes were also developing a more efficient means of controlling their position in the water.

Even the earliest bony fishes possessed paired air sacs on the underside of their bodies. By pumping gases in or out of these sacs, the fish became able to alter its buoyancy and change its level in the water.

In the ray-finned fishes, the air sacs evolved into a single swim bladder, placed above the throat; in most teleosts, it remains connected to the throat, but in the advanced perch-like forms the connection is broken, and the swim bladder functions independently as a sophisticated buoyancy device, secreting and absorbing its own gas.

In the lungfishes, the air sacs evolved into proper air-breathing lungs connected to the blood system, as they are in land-living animals. The walls of the lungs became highly convoluted to increase the uptake of oxygen. Living lungfishes, as well as having gills, can breathe air, and the African species can even exist for long periods out of water, curled up in a burrow in the muddy riverbank.

Feeding and breathing go together in the bony ray-finned fishes. The general trend was for their jaws to become more mobile and flexible, allowing them to be pursed together to form a tube. At the same time, the gill chambers behind the jaws became expandable, so that more water could flow through them. This increased the uptake of oxygen, and so increased the fish's capability for activity.

Since the tubular jaws acted in conjunction with the expandable gills chambers, this resulted in prey being sucked or drawn toward the fish, rather than the fish having to engulf it at close quarters. Watch a goldfish or any aquarium fish feed, and this method can be seen in action.

EVOLUTION OF JAWS

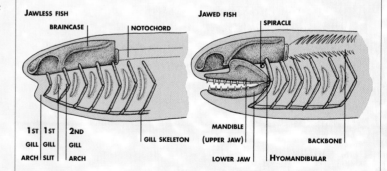

JAWLESS FISH
BRAINCASE   NOTOCHORD

1ST GILL ARCH | 1ST GILL SLIT | 2ND GILL ARCH   GILL SKELETON

JAWED FISH
SPIRACLE

MANDIBLE (UPPER JAW)   BACKBONE
LOWER JAW | HYOMANDIBULAR

The first fishes had neither jaws nor teeth. Their gills, behind the mouth, were supported by a series of arches made of cartilage, between which were the gill slits. Jaws probably evolved from the 1st gill arch on either side, which folded over and joined in the midline to form the upper and lower jaws. Teeth were developed from the skin that lined the mouth. The 2nd gill arch, the hyomandibular, moved to support the jaws from behind, and ligaments attached them to the braincase. The 1st gill slits became tiny holes, or spiracles.

JAWLESS FISHES

PHYLUM CHORDATA

The great diversity of back-boned animals (vertebrates) and some less familiar animals belong to a larger group – the chordates. They share some primitive features, of which the most obvious include an elongate axial rod, the dorsal notochord that runs from anterior to posterior. In vertebrates, the notochord is ossified to form the back-bone. The oldest chordate is the 535 million year old cephalochordate, *Pikaia*, from the Middle Cambrian Burgess Shale.

SUBPHYLUM CEPHALOCHORDATA (ACRANIATA)

From the evolutionary point of view , the most important non-vertebrate chordate group is that of the cephalochordates (also known as the acraniates), which includes the remarkable living marine lancelet – *Branchiostoma*. This tiny (2 in/5 cm) long marine creature is flattened sideways and burrows tail first in the seabed. Its anterior has a perforated pharynx through which seawater is filtered to obtain oxygen and microscopic food. The fossil record of this group is extremely poor.

NAME	*Pikaia*
TIME	Middle Cambrian
LOCALITY	Canada
SIZE	2 in/5 cm long

The quality of preservation of the 535 million year old Burgess Shale is so good that fossils of *Pikaia* even show traces of soft tissues. The axial notochord and v-shaped muscle blocks, typical of the pre-vertebrate cephalochordates can be seen. The notochord is stiff, but flexible, and can be bent into sinuous waves for swimming by pulses of contractions from the muscle blocks on either side of it. *Pikaia* is the oldest known chordate which means that it, or a similar animal is our ancestor.

SUBPHYLUM VERTEBRATA (CRANIATA)

Vertebrates as they are commonly known (or craniates) are the main subject of this book. The most important characteristics are the basic chordate ones. But there is the additional feature of 'cephalisation' in which the sense organs and their nerve connections are concentrated at the front. This forms the basis of the 'brain' (cranium) and part of the developing head region.

CLASS AGNATHA

The first backboned animals (vertebrates) to evolve were agnathans, or 'jawless fishes'. Fossil traces are found in Late Cambrian rocks, more than 510 million years old. These first fishes had no jaws. Nor did they have paired fins, to stabilize their bodies in the water. Catching prey and eating it presented problems. Consequently, these fishes tended to be small, rarely reaching more than 1 ft/30 cm long. They were restricted to sucking up microscopic food particles from the muddy seabed, or feeding on the plankton that lived in the surface waters.

The internal skeleton was made entirely of gristle or cartilage. This material – unlike bone – decays after death, so paleontologists know that these ancient fishes existed only because their bodies had an 'overcoat' of bone, which was preserved. This consisted of bony plates sometimes fused into a large head shield, and small bony scales that covered the body. This armour plating was the only protection against attack from the predatory sea scorpions that inhabited the Paleozoic seas.

The bony armour has been preserved in the rocks, and gives the fossil agnathans their collective name of ostracoderms, meaning 'shell-skins'. Despite their lack of jaws, ostracoderms dominated the seas and freshwaters of the northern hemisphere for about 130 million years, from Early Ordovician to Late Devonian times.

Two types of agnathan survive today – the worm-like, scavenging hagfishes and the eel-like, parasitic lampreys.

SUBCLASS CONODONTA

The zoological affinities of the extinct conodonts have been a puzzle for over 150 years and were only resolved in 1993 when fossilized soft tissues were found. Before that the conodonts were known as a common group of tiny tooth-like structures found mainly in Paleozoic rocks from the late Cambrian to the end of the Triassic times (540-210 million years ago). The teeth are made of calcium phosphate and were found in bilaterally symmetrical assemblages of several elements with different shapes, clearly forming some kind of small feeding apparatus.

The remarkable discovery of the first conodont animal in Carboniferous rocks in Scotland showed that the feeding apparatus was clearly positioned below a pair of well-developed eyes. The increased cephalisation beyond that seen in the cephalochordates indicates a higher degree of organization, one perhaps closer to the living agnathans the hagfish. The mineralization of the teeth has led to their being placed within the vertebrates, though some experts dispute this.

NAME *Promissum*

TIME Late Ordovician

LOCALITY South Africa

SIZE 16in/40cm

Promissum was an unusually large conodont and is found in the 500 million year old Late Ordovician cold and glacially influenced sea deposits of South Africa. In 1994 specimens of *Promissum* were found with the conodont feeding apparatus preserved below eye capsules and in front of traces of the muscle blocks and notochord. This confirmed the form of the conodont animal, seen from younger Scottish Carboniferous strata.

Order Heterostraci

The heterostracans were the first fishes, and among the earliest of all the vertebrates, to evolve. The oldest undisputed remains date from the Early Ordovician Period, some 500 million years ago. These fishes were the most abundant and diverse of all the agnathans. They reached their peak during Late Silurian and Early Devonian times, when a variety of marine forms evolved, ranging from mud-eating bottom-dwellers to free-swimming plankton-feeders. Later, the heterostracans invaded freshwaters. All had the characteristic bony head shield, which could grow throughout the life of the fish.

NAME *Arandaspis*

TIME Early Ordovician

LOCALITY Australia (Northern Territory)

SIZE possibly 6in/15cm long

In 1959, the fossilized remains of four distinct types of fish were discovered south of Alice Springs, Australia. The remains were in layers of marine sandstones, laid down in a shallow sea about 500 million years ago. It was not until the late 1960s that the remains were recognized as those of the earliest vertebrates. The name of *Arandaspis* was given to the best-preserved specimens.

Arandaspis had a streamlined, deep-bodied shape. With no fins to stabilize it in the water, it probably would have swum erratically, like a tadpole. Its lower body was covered in oblique rows of small bony scales, each of which was shaped like a cowrie shell, and decorated with pointed tubercles, giving the skin an abrasive texture.

The front of *Arandaspis'* body was encased in a head shield, made from two large plates of thin bone – a deep, rounded ventral (underside) plate and a flatter dorsal (topside) plate. The head shield had openings for the eyes, nostrils and the single pair of gill apertures on either side. Deep grooves in the shield marked the position of the lateral line canals – the organs that fishes use to sense vibrations.

Arandaspis' jawless mouth was on the underside of its head, a position that suggests that it may have fed on or near the seabed. Like other heterostracans it probably possessed small, movable plates inside its mouth equipped with ridges of dentine. These plates could have formed a pair of flexible 'lips', which would have been capable of scooping or sucking up particles of food from the mud of the seabed.

NAME *Pteraspis*

TIME Early Devonian

LOCALITY Europe (UK and Belgium)

SIZE 8in/20cm long

Pteraspis is typical of the pteraspid family of heterostracans, which became very numerous and diverse during the Late Silurian and Early Devonian Periods.

Although *Pteraspis* lacked paired fins, the feature that normally allows for greater stability in the water, it was a powerful swimmer, to judge by several hydrodynamic features of its body. Stability was provided by bony outgrowths from the back of the head shield – a large spine acted as a kind of dorsal fin, while a pair of rigid 'wings' or keels functioned as pectoral hydrofoils.

Pteraspis had a long, flexible tail that was also a hydrodynamic shape, with the lower lobe elongated in order to provide lift at the front of the body during swimming. Additional lift in the water was provided by the elongated snout, which was drawn out into a blade-like 'rostrum', below which the mouth opened.

Paleontologists think that *Pteraspis* and its relatives probably fed in mid-water or near the surface of the sea, among the shoals of planktonic, shrimp-like crustaceans.

JAWLESS FISHES CONTINUED

NAME *Doryaspis*

TIME Early Devonian

LOCALITY Spitsbergen

SIZE 6in/15cm long

This pteraspid (also called *Lyktaspis*) had a longer snout or rostrum than its relatives. There were bony spines set along its length (like the 'saw' of a modern sawfish), and the mouth opened above, rather than below, the rostrum. This strange and impressive appendage must have had some hydrodynamic function, since *Doryaspis'* shape suggests that it was an active swimmer, probably feeding on plankton near the water's surface.

An additional function of the rostrum among pteraspids could have been to stir up the bottom mud or sand, so as to root out crustacean prey.

Doryaspis had unusually long, lateral keels growing from the back of the head shield. The leading edges of the lateral keels were armed with sharp, tooth-like spines. These keels may have acted as gliding planes and, together with the elongated rostrum and downturned tail, would have provided lift at the front of the body while the creature was swimming.

NAME *Drepanaspis*

TIME Early Devonian

LOCALITY Europe (Germany)

SIZE 1ft/30cm long

A number of the heterostracans, such as *Drepanaspis*, were well-adapted bottom dwellers, and lived by scavenging in the mud of the seabed for food.

The front of *Drepanspis'* body was broad and flattened, allowing it to hug the seabed as it swam, and on either side of the large, upturned mouth, its small eyes were set wide apart to give it a wide angle of vision.

ORDER THELODONTI

The thelodonts were small jawless fishes, without head shields. Only the tiny bony scales that covered their bodies remain to testify to their existence during Late Silurian and Early Devonian times. Isolated body scales are often found in the ancient sediments that were laid down on sea beds during these periods. The scales can be very useful indicators for scientists seeking to correlate the age of the rocks.

NAME *Thelodus*

TIME Late Silurian

LOCALITY Worldwide

SIZE 7in/18cm long

The mouth of this small thelodontid was at the front of the head, suggesting that it fed from the seabed or surface. It could probably swim well. The lower lobe of the tail was elongated, and fins were gave stability – a dorsal and anal fin at the rear, and two pectoral flaps at the front.

ORDER OSTEOSTRACI

The osteostracans (also called the cephalaspids, meaning 'head shields') appeared in the Late Silurian Period, about 80 million years after the earliest heterostracan fishes. This order evolved in the sea, and then colonized freshwaters.

Osteostracans were flattened bottom-dwelling creatures that sucked up food from the seabed through a rounded mouth on the underside of the head. The head shield was a plate of undivided bone, which did not grow during adult life (unlike the individual head plates of the heterostracan fishes).

Evidently, osteostracans were also good swimmers, since many had a dorsal fin, paired scale-covered flaps where the pectoral fins are normally found, and a strong, upturned tail.

The anatomy of osteostracans is well known because of a unique development. Bone was laid down inside the body, in a thin layer over the cartilage of the skeleton. From this fossilized bone, it is possible to trace the structure of the brain, gills, mouth and even individual nerves and blood vessels.

Concentrated patches of sensory organs on both sides and on top of the head were richly supplied with nerves. They were probably used to detect vibration, or were electric organs.

NAME *Tremataspis*
TIME Late Silurian
LOCALITY Europe (Estonia)
SIZE 4 in/10 cm long

This osteostracan had an unusual extended bony head shield, nearly circular in cross-section. Its eyes and single nostril were on top of the head, near the midline. The shape is probably derived from a more usual flattened head shield and is thought to have been an adaptation to a burrowing mode of life.

Tremataspis' head shield was made of one piece of bone, so it is unlikely that it grew with the animal. Paleontologists think that osteostracans had an unarmoured larva, and that the bony shield developed only when the fish was full-grown.

NAME *Dartmuthia*
TIME Late Silurian
LOCALITY Europe (Estonia)
SIZE 4 in/10 cm long

The broad head shield is the only part of *Dartmuthia* that is known. It was a bottom-feeder, with a round, sucking mouth on the underside of the head, like its contemporary *Tremataspis*. There was a small dorsal fin halfway along its back, and the pressure-sensitive organs were well-developed on its head and behind the eyes.

NAME *Hemicyclaspis*
TIME Early Devonian
LOCALITY Europe (England)
SIZE 5 in/13 cm long

This osteostracan was a more powerful swimmer and could manoeuvre itself better in the water than either of its bottom-dwelling relatives, *Tremataspis* or *Dartmuthia*. Its hydrodynamic features included a dorsal fin, to stabilize the body in the water, and a pair of scale-covered flaps, similar to pectoral fins, which provided uplift and kept the fish on course while swimming.

The corners of *Hemicyclaspis'* head shield were drawn out into keel-like cutwaters. In addition, the upper lobe of the tail was enlarged, producing lift at the rear of the body. This feature would have helped to keep the fish's head down while it sucked up food particles from the seabed.

NAME *Boreaspis*
TIME Early Devonian
LOCALITY Spitsbergen
SIZE 5 in/13 cm long

At least 14 species of *Boreaspis* are known from Early Devonian sandstones in Spitsbergen. They differ in the width of their triangular-shaped head shields, and in the length of the bony spine that grew out from the cheek area on either side. The snout was elongated in all species into a blade-like rostrum. Beside its hydrodynamic function, the rostrum was probably used to probe on the muddy lagoon floor for prey.

ORDER ANASPIDA

The anaspids did not have heavy bony head shields. Their slender, flexible bodies were covered in thin scales and had stabilizing fins. Numerous in the seas of Europe and North America during the Late Silurian Period, they later invaded rivers and lakes during the Devonian, and survived to the end of that period.

NAME *Jamoytius*
TIME Late Silurian
LOCALITY Europe (Scotland)
SIZE 11 in/27 cm long

The *Jamoytius* had a narrow, tubular, eel-like shape, with a long fin on its back, a pair of lateral fins running along its flanks and a small anal fin. Uplift was produced by the strongly downturned tail. *Jamoytius* had a round, sucker-like mouth but it is unlikely to have been a parasite like its living descendant, the marine lamprey This jawless fish attaches itself to other fishes, rasps away their flesh and then sucks their blood.

NAME *Pharyngolepis*
TIME Late Silurian
LOCALITY Europe (Norway)
SIZE 4 in/10 cm long

Pharyngolepis must have been a poor swimmer because it lacked basic stabilizing fins. A row of crested scales ran along its back, and a pair of bony spines projected from the pectoral area. There was a well-developed anal fin, and the tail was downturned. But none of these features would have stabilized its deep body.

Pharyngolepis' probably fed by scooping up tiny food particles from the bottom sediment.

CARTILAGINOUS FISHES

CLASS CHONDRICHTHYES

What could be more evocative of 'Jaws' than sharks? In fact, sharks and their relatives – the skates and rays, and the chimaeras or ratfishes – were among the earliest vertebrates to develop jaws and bony teeth (see p.21). The mineralized teeth are normally the only part of these animals to be fossilized.

These jawed fishes also share another feature. All have skeletons made entirely of gristle or cartilage, which unites them as the chondrichthyans, or cartilaginous fishes. (Agnathans also have cartilaginous skeletons, but they have no jaws.) The skeleton is 'calcified', or strengthened by prismatic granules of calcium carbonate deposited in the outer layers of the cartilage. These granules are arranged in a mosaic pattern, unique to this group. A thin layer of bone covers the cartilage.

Cartilaginous fishes share other characteristics. For example, their fins are paired, and stiffened by horny rays of cartilage. The pelvic fins in males are modified into penis-like 'claspers', to aid in the transfer of sperm during copulation – a feature unique to these fishes. The skin bristles with tiny, teeth-like scales, which give it a rough texture like sandpaper. (In fact, 19th-century cabinet-makers used shark skin, called 'shagreen', to give a smooth finish to the wood.) Like the teeth, the body scales are constantly replaced throughout the fish's life.

Two main groups of cartilaginous fishes evolved from a common ancestor during the Early Devonian Period, 400 million years ago (see pp.18–19). Representatives of both groups – the elasmobranchs and the holocephalians – survive today, distinguished by their teeth and different feeding habits.

SUBCLASS ELASMOBRANCHII

The elasmobranchs – sharks, dogfishes, skates and rays – evolved from a common ancestor during the Early Devonian, some 400 million years ago. Sharks have changed little over this vast span of time. They diversified into many forms during the Carboniferous, and after a period of decline, underwent a second burst of evolution in the Jurassic, when most of the modern groups appeared. Then, as now, sharks were the dominant predators in the seas, ousting other creatures that attempted a marine, fish-eating lifestyle – reptiles such as the ichthyosaurs and plesiosaurs.

The skates, rays and sawfish evolved in the Early Jurassic, some 200 million years after sharks. They are essentially sharks that have become flattened for a life on the seabed.

NAME	*Cladoselache*
TIME	Late Devonian
LOCALITY	North America (Ohio)
SIZE	up to 6ft/1.8m

Remains of shark scales are known from the Late Silurian Period and teeth from the Early Devonian. But it is only in the Late Devonian that recognizable specimens are found.

Cladoselache has been remarkably well-fossilized in the Cleveland shales of Ohio, USA. The fleshy outline of its body has been imprinted in the rocks, and even traces of its skin, muscles and kidneys can be seen.

Cladoselache had a streamlined, torpedo-shaped body, with two equal-sized dorsal fins; a pair of large pectoral fins; a pair of smaller pelvic fins; a large tail shaped roughly like a half-moon, with equal-sized lobes, and a pair of horizontal keels at its base. Its head was blunt and its eyes large. Five to seven gill slits opened behind its toothed jaws.

Superficially, the description of this ancient shark that cruised the open seas 400 million years ago is strikingly similar to that of a modern oceanic shark, such as the infamous Great White. The main differences are that the modern shark has a pointed snout, a high first dorsal fin, a tail in which the upper lobe is considerably longer than the lower lobe, and an additional fin – the anal fin.

Like many early sharks, *Cladoselache* had a spine in front of each dorsal fin. The spines were made of tooth-like dentine and probably skin-covered during life, since they are not coated in the protective layer of enamel seen in later sharks. Another unusual feature of *Cladoselache* is the lack of scales on its body. The only scales were concentrated round the eyes and along the margins of the fins.

Besides being a powerful swimmer, *Cladoselache* was obviously a formidable carnivore. Its mouth was filled with sharp, pointed teeth, each with a long central cusp or projection, flanked by several smaller cusps. The seas of the Late Devonian Period teemed with suitable prey – squid, crustaceans, small jawless fishes, and early bony fishes.

NAME *Stethacanthus*

TIME Late Devonian to Late Carboniferous

LOCALITY Europe (Scotland) and North America (Illinois, Iowa, Montana and Ohio)

SIZE 2 ft 4 in/70 cm long

The remarkable feature of this early shark was the strange adaptation of the first dorsal fin. It was anvil- or T-shaped, and the flat, upper surface bristled with teeth-like denticles. The top of the head was also covered with denticles.

The function of these structures is uncertain. Some paleontologists speculate that they were part of a threat display to others of its kind, maybe giving the impression of an enormous pair of jaws. Another theory suggests that these toothy patches were were connected with sexual display, perhaps forming some sort of mating device.

NAME *Cobelodus*

TIME Middle to Late Carboniferous

LOCALITY North America (Illinois and Iowa)

SIZE up to 6 ft 6 in/2 m long

This strange-looking shark had a bulbous snout and a humpbacked profile, with only one dorsal fin on its back, set far to the rear, above the pelvic fins. It also had remarkably large eyes, which could suggest that it hunted in deep, dark waters for crustaceans and squid.

One of the cartilaginous rays that supported the pectoral fin was drawn out on each side into a whiplash, about 1 ft/30 cm long. These appendages were obviously movable, since they were jointed along their length.

NAME *Xenacanthus*

TIME Late Devonian to Middle Permian

LOCALITY Worldwide

SIZE 2 ft 5 in/75 cm long

Early in their evolution, a group of sharks invaded fresh water, spreading into rivers and lakes all over the world. These xenacanthids were specialized fishes and highly successful, since they existed from Early Devonian times to the end of the Triassic – a span of almost 150 million years. *Xenacanthus* was a typical member of the group. A thick spine grew out from the back of its skull. The dorsal fin formed a continuous ribbon along the length of the back, right around the tail, and joined up with the anal fin – like the arrangement seen in the modern Australian lungfish or the conger eel. It probably swam like these modern fishes, with sinuous movements of its long, streamlined body. Paired pectoral and pelvic fins stabilized it from below.

The dentition of these freshwater sharks was unusual; each tooth was V-shaped, and formed of two prominent cusps. Shrimp-like crustaceans were probably the chief prey, as well as the thick-scaled bony fishes, the paleoniscids (see pp.34–36).

NAME *Tristychius*

TIME Early Carboniferous

LOCALITY Europe (Scotland)

SIZE 2 ft/60 cm long

Superficially, *Tristychius* looked like a modern dogfish. It was a hybodontoid shark; this group was to dominate the seas from Carboniferous times to the end of the Cretaceous – a reign of almost 300 million years. Some fine tuning occurred in their structure during this time, but essentially sharks had 'got it right' some 40 million years earlier.

Like all its relatives, *Tristychius* had a pair of large spines in front of each dorsal fin. The pectoral and pelvic fins had much narrower bases, and were therefore more flexible swimming appendages than the broad-based, rigid fins of earlier sharks, such as *Cladoselache*. The upper lobe of the tail had developed into the powerful, propulsive, upturned fin seen in modern oceanic sharks.

CARTILAGINOUS FISHES CONTINUED

NAME Hybodus
TIME Late Permian to Late Cretaceous
LOCALITY Worldwide
SIZE 6ft 6in/2m long

Hybodus was one of the most
common, widespread and long-lived
types of fossil shark. It looked essentially
similar to a modern blue shark, although it was only half the size
and would have had a blunter snout.

Hybodus had two types of teeth in its powerful jaws,
suggesting a varied diet. The pointed teeth at the front seized
and pierced its fish prey, while the blunt, low-crowned teeth at
the back crushed the fish bones, and also the hard shells of the
bottom-dwelling snails, sea urchins, crustaceans and shellfish
that it consumed.

Hybodus and its relatives gained (and their descendants have
retained) a reproductive advantage over other fishes. Part of the
pelvic fins in the male shark were modified into erectile, penis-
like organs called 'claspers' (seen in the illustration above). These
were inserted into the female during copulation, and sperm was
transferred directly into her body – a superior method of
fertilizing eggs to the wasteful shedding of sperm
into the open sea practised by
most bony fishes.

NAME Scapanorhynchus
TIME Early to Late Cretaceous
LOCALITY Worldwide
SIZE 20in/50cm long

A final burst of evolution among the elasmobranchs in Late
Jurassic times led to the development of the modern sharks,
skates and rays – known as the neoselachians, or 'new sharks'.

Several improvements had
been made to their skeletons. For example,
the cartilaginous 'backbone' became strongly
impregnated with calcium (calcified) enabling it to
resist the powerful forces that were produced by lateral
flexure of the body while the animals were swimming.

The bones of the upper jaw became articulated with the
braincase by means of a movable joint, which allowed the jaws
to be opened wide, and even to be protruded beyond the skull.
This modification allowed large chunks of flesh to be gouged
from the neoselachians' prey.

Finally, the brain and its sensory areas became larger,
especially the olfactory lobes associated with smell.

Scapanorhynchus was an early, but not a typical, neoselachian.
It had a greatly elongated snout, and its teeth were all of the
biting and tearing kind, suitable for fish-eating.

NAME Spathobathis
TIME Late Jurassic
LOCALITY Europe (France and Germany)
SIZE 20in/50cm long

Of the elasmobranch skates, rays and sawfishes, the rays were
the first to evolve. *Spathobathis* is the earliest known ray, and it
is strikingly similar to the modern-day Guitar or Banjo fish
which occurs in the Atlantic waters off North America.

Spathobathis' body was essentially similar to that of a shark,
but it was broad and flattened to suit a life on the seabed. The
eyes and spiracles (for water intake) were repositioned on top of

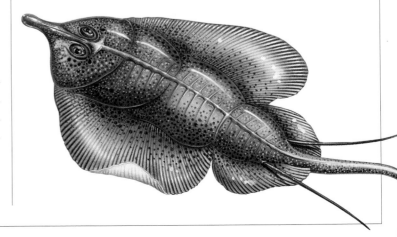

the ray's head, and the mouth and gill slits were on the underside of the body. The pair of pectoral fins were expanded into great 'wings' for swimming.

The teeth of this ancient ray were also broad and flattened, and formed effective shellfish-crushers. Its elongated snout was used to probe the seabed in search of its prey.

NAME	*Sclerorhynchus*
TIME	Late Cretaceous
LOCALITY	Africa (Morocco), Asia (Lebanon) and North America (Texas)
SIZE	3 ft 3 in/1 m long

The skates had evolved from the rays by Early Cretaceous times. *Sclerorhynchus* was an early type of skate, though it looked more like a modern sawfish. Flapping its pectoral 'wings', this flattened fish 'flew' just above the seabed, probing and sifting the mud with its long, toothy snout for hidden shrimps, shellfish and bony flatfish as it went.

SUBCLASS HOLOCEPHALI

The second major group of cartilaginous fishes are the holocephalians, or chimaeras – which are commonly known as rabbit-fishes or ratfishes. The Holocephali appeared in the Early Carboniferous when a few forms, such as *Deltoptychius*, acquired the so-called rat-like appearance and had long, thin tails. But it was not until the Jurassic, and fish such as *Ischyodus,* that the modern chimaera form became common. The males of the subclass have penis-like claspers.

Today, 25 species of this subclass inhabit the oceans of the world, usually swimming in deep water and feeding on the seabed.

NAME	*Deltoptychius*
TIME	Early to Late Carboniferous
LOCALITY	Europe (Ireland and Scotland)
SIZE	18 in/45 cm long

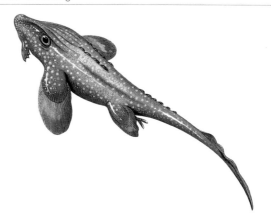

This early ratfish had practically all of the features that distinguish its modern descendants. *Deltoptychius* swam by flexing its long body and whiplash tail from side to side, and gliding along on its outstretched, wing-like pectoral fins.

The large eyes of *Deltoptychius* enabled it to see better in the gloomy ocean depths, and its large dental plates (rather than individual teeth) were used to crush its shellfish prey.

NAME	*Ischyodus*
TIME	Middle Jurassic to Paleocene
LOCALITY	Europe (England, France and Germany) and New Zealand
SIZE	5 ft/1.5 m long

Ischyodus, which lived more than 150 million years ago, was practically identical in size and shape to *Chimaera monstrosa* – the modern ratfish which is found today inhabiting the depths of the Atlantic and Mediterranean oceans. *Ischyodus* had the same large eyes, pursed lips, tall dorsal fin, fan-like pectorals and whiplash tail of its living relative. It even had a similar spine in front of the dorsal fin, which in the living species is connected to a venom gland, and is used by the creature to defend itself against predators.

SPINY SHARKS
AND ARMOURED FISHES

CLASS ACANTHODII

The acanthodians – commonly known as the 'spiny sharks' – are the earliest known vertebrates with jaws. These structures are presumed to have evolved from the first gill arch of some ancestral jawless fish which had a gill skeleton made of pieces of jointed cartilage (see p.21).

The popular name 'spiny sharks' is really a misnomer for these early jawed fishes. The name was coined because they were generally shark-shaped, with a streamlined body, paired fins and a strongly upturned tail; stout bony spines supported all the fins except the tail – hence, 'spiny sharks'. Fossilized spines are often all that remains of these fishes in ancient sedimentary rocks.

In fact, acanthodians were a much earlier group of fishes than sharks. They evolved in the sea at the beginning of the Silurian Period, some 50 million years before the first sharks appeared. Later the acanthodians colonized freshwaters, and thrived in the rivers and lakes during the Devonian and in the coal swamps of the Carboniferous. But the first bony fishes were already showing their potential to dominate the waters of the world, and their competition proved too much for the spiny sharks, which died out in Permian times.

Many paleontologists consider that the acanthodians were close to the ancestors of the bony fishes. Although their internal skeletons were made of cartilage, a bone-like material had developed in the skins of these fishes, in the form of closely fitting scales. Some scales were greatly enlarged, and formed a bony covering on top of the head and over the lower shoulder girdle. Others formed a bony flap over the gill openings (the operculum in later bony fishes).

NAME *Climatius*

TIME Late Silurian to Early Devonian

LOCALITY Europe (UK) and North America (Canada)

SIZE 3 in/7.5 cm long

The name 'spiny shark' seems particularly appropriate for this fish. Its tiny body was crowded with spines and fins. Two large dorsal fins rose from the back, each supported in front by a stout bony spine, superficially embedded in the skin. There was a large anal fin and spine at the back, and a pair of large pectoral fins with spines at the front.

The underside of *Climatius'* body bristled with spines, but had no fins. There was also a pair of pelvic spines and four pairs of sharp belly spines.

Climatius was obviously an active swimmer, to judge by its stabilizing fins and the powerful, shark-like tail, with its large, upturned upper lobe. Like many other acanthodians, it had no teeth in its upper jaw, but there were whorls of small teeth in the lower jaw, continually replaced as they were being worn – another shark-like feature. Its large eyes suggest that sight was the chief sense used for locating prey, and it probably fed on crustaceans and fish fry in mid-water and at the surface.

Its swimming agility and the tight-fitting armour of bony scales must have protected *Climatius* from attack by larger fish and predatory invertebrates, such as squid. The 15 fin spines that arrayed its body were its chief defence, making it extremely awkward to swallow.

NAME *Acanthodes*

TIME Early Carboniferous to Early Permian

LOCALITY Australia (Victoria), Europe (Czechoslovakia, England, Germany, Scotland and Spain) and North America (Illinois, Kansas, Pennsylvania and West Virginia)

SIZE 1 ft/30 cm long

Acanthodes was a member of the last group of spiny sharks to evolve. They had no teeth in their jaws, but the gills were equipped with long bony 'rakers' made of tooth-like spikes. *Acanthodes* and its relatives were probably filter-feeders, sieving tiny, planktonic animals through their gills.

Like all later acanthodians, *Acanthodes* was larger than its earlier relatives; some members of its group reached lengths of over 6 ft 6 in/2 m. *Acanthodes* was also less spiny than earlier forms. Its paired pectoral fins still had stout spines, as did the large anal fin. But there was only one spiny dorsal fin, set far back near the tail, and the pair of ribbon-like pelvic fins that ran along the belly each had a single spine. Thus, *Acanthodes* only had six fin spines on its body, compared with the 15 spines of its prickly relative, *Climatius*.

CLASS PLACODERMI

The placoderms, or 'flat-plated skins', were a strange assemblage of heavily armoured jawed fishes. Several large interlocking plates formed a bony head shield, while another series of plates encased the front part of the body in a trunk shield. The rest of the body was usually naked, with no scaly covering.

The placoderms represent a specialized offshoot from the main evolutionary line leading to the bony fishes (see pp.34–45). It was a comparatively short-lived group, which first appeared in the Early Devonian Period and had died out by the Early Carboniferous.

Many placoderms spent their lives foraging for food on the seabed, with their flattened bodies weighed down by their heavy bony armour. Others had less armour and became swimmers in the open sea. The jaws of all of these fishes were equipped with broad dental plates (rather than individual teeth), which were used for crushing hard-shelled prey.

Representatives from each of the four main groups of placoderm (rhenanids, ptyctodontids, arthrodires and antiarchs) are described.

NAME	*Gemuendina*
TIME	Early Devonian
LOCALITY	Europe (Germany)
SIZE	1 ft/30 cm long

The rounded and flattened body of this early bottom-dwelling placoderm (of the rhenanid order) was remarkably similar to that of a modern ray. The pectoral fins of *Gemuendina* were drawn out into wing-like lobes on either side of the body, and the eyes and nostrils were repositioned on top of the head. These features were

duplicated about 260 million years later in an unrelated group of fishes – the rays and skates that inhabited the seabed from Jurassic times onward. This is an excellent example of convergent evolution – in which unrelated creatures eventually evolve the same structure, and often the same habits, in response to the influence of similar environments and lifestyles (see p.14) on natural selection.

Gemuendina was not equipped with the heavy armour of its later relatives, however. Instead a mosaic of small bony plates covered its body, decorated with sharp, defensive denticles; a few large plates were developed above and below the head.

This placoderm also lacked the characteristic tooth plates of its later relatives. Instead, the jaws were equipped with star shaped tubercles, which acted like teeth. The jaws could be protruded out of the mouth in order to pick up sea urchins and shellfish from the seabed. The creatures were then crushed between the *Gemuendina's* teeth-like tubercles.

NAME	*Ctenurella*
TIME	Late Devonian
LOCALITY	Australia (Western
SIZE	5 in/13 cm long

Ctenurella was a small, naked placoderm (one of the ptyctodontids). Its only protective armour was developed on top of its head and in a band around the shoulder girdle. It had two dorsal fins, one upright and the other long and low. Large, paired pectoral and pelvic fins stabilized it from below, and the tail tapered to a whiplash.

This small placoderm was equipped with crushing tooth plates in its jaws, the upper bones of which were firmly fused to the braincase. It fed on the seabed, grinding up shellfish and sea urchins with its strong jaws. It could obviously swim, to judge by its hydrodynamic shape and paired fins.

Here again, as with *Gemuendina* (left), is an excellent example of convergent evolution. As in the case of the ray-like rhenanids, *Ctenurella* and its relatives had evolved a body design that was to appear again in a later group of cartilaginous fishes – the chimaeras or ratfishes (see p.29). These placoderms even had similar penis-like claspers to those developed in the males of the cartilaginous group of fishes.

SPINY SHARKS
AND ARMOURED FISHES CONTINUED

NAME *Groenlandaspis*

TIME Late Devonian

LOCALITY Antarctica (South Victoria Land), Australia (New South Wales), Europe (England, Ireland and Turkey) and Greenland

SIZE 3 in/7.5 cm long

This tiny armoured fish, found in sites literally poles apart, was a member of the most abundant and diverse group of placoderms – the arthrodires, or 'jointed-necked' fishes. The arthrodires account for 60 percent of all known placoderms. *Groenlandaspis* was a flattened bottom-dweller, crushing molluscs and crustaceans between its tooth plates. Since the lower jaw could not be dropped while the fish was lying flat on the seabed, this fish, like most of its relatives, evolved an ingenious hinge system to allow it to open its jaws wide to engulf large prey. The head shield was hinged to the trunk shield by a pair of ball-and-socket joints set high up on either side of the body. These hinges allowed the head to be tilted up and back, while the lower jaw dropped and the gaping mouth moved forward to seize the prey.

NAME *Coccosteus*

TIME Middle to Late Devonian

LOCALITY Europe (Scotland and former USSR) and North America (Ohio)

SIZE 16 in/40 cm long

Coccosteus was a fast-moving hunter and scavenger of the seabed. Its smooth, streamlined body (devoid of scales), whose hydrodynamic features included paired fins, upturned tail and a stabilizing dorsal fin, made it a powerful swimmer.

It must also have been an aggressive carnivore, due to improvements in the jointing system of its neck. Not only were the head and trunk shields hinged externally, as in

Groenlandaspis (above); an internal joint had also developed between the neck vertebrae and the back of the skull, enabling *Coccosteus* to tilt its head back farther. Thus, it could attain an even wider gape than its relative. Its jaws were also longer than those of *Groenlandaspis*, so extending its predatory range.

Another advantage of the jointed-neck system was that the up-and-down movement of the head would have helped to pump water through the gills, which expanded when the mouth was opened; more water flowing through the gills meant a greater uptake of oxygen and increased activity. *Coccosteus* probably supplemented its diet by swallowing mouthfuls of mud and digesting the organic matter contained in it.

NAME *Dunkleosteus*

TIME Late Devonian

LOCALITY Africa (Morocco), Europe (Belgium and Poland) and North America (California, Ohio, Pennsylvania and Tennessee)

SIZE 11 ft 6 in/3.5 m long

Some arthrodires grew to an enormous size, and these large fish may even have competed for prey with contemporary sharks such as *Cladoselache* (see p.26). *Dunkleosteus* was the giant of the group, with a skull over 2 ft/65 cm long. Some of its relatives, such as *Dinichthys* and *Titanichthys*, rivalled it in size, at 7 ft/2.1 m and 11 ft/3.4 m respectively.

The bony trunk shield in *Dunkleosteus* stopped short of the pectoral fins, so freeing them for better control of steering and braking manoeuvres. Sinuous movements of the smooth, scaleless body and the long, eel-like tail would have swept this great creature through the sea in search of its fish prey.

The jointed neck and hinged body shields endowed *Dunkleosteus* with a slow, powerful bite. Once the victim had been caught, the great dental plates got to work, with the fang-like picks at the front of the jaws holding and piercing the prey, while the sharp-edged, cutting pavements at the back broke it up.

NAME *Bothriolepis*

TIME Late Devonian

LOCALITY Worldwide

SIZE 1 ft/30 cm long

Bothriolepis was a member of the most heavily armoured group of placoderms, the antiarchs. These fishes shared a common ancestor with the arthrodires, and like many of them, were flattened bottom-dwellers – although antiarchs lived in freshwaters. The head was protected by a short bony shield, which hinged onto a long trunk shield.

The pectoral fins of *Bothriolepis* and its relatives were reduced to a pair of bony-plated spines, which could have played no role in swimming. They articulated with the front edge of the trunk shield via a complex hinge. A joint halfway along their length suggests that they could have been bent, and used like stilts to carry their heavy owner over the river bed. The upturned tail would have produced lift at the rear of the body, keeping the fish's head down while it scavenged in the mud or sand of the seabed for food particles.

NAME *Palaeospondylus*

TIME Middle Devonian

LOCALITY Europe (Scotland)

SIZE 2 in/6 cm long

This tiny creature has vexed paleontologists ever since its discovery in 1890. Hundreds of specimens have been found at the one Scottish locality. All consisted of a long 'backbone' with spines at one end, presumably supporting a tail fin, and a strangely shaped skull at the other end. This creature had no obvious jaws and no paired fins.

Over the years, *Palaeospondylus* has variously been interpreted as a jawless agnathan, a naked placoderm, a type of ratfish or even a lungfish. Some have even suggested that it represents the tadpole larva of an amphibian. To add to the enigma, paleontologists have not been able to determine whether the skeleton is made of calcified cartilage or of bone.

PRIMITIVE RAY-FINNED FISHES

CLASS OSTEICHTHYES

In terms of abundance and diversity, the 'bony fishes', or osteichthyans, are the success story of vertebrate evolution: there are more than 20,000 modern species, accounting for half of all living vertebrates. In a sense, the bony fishes are also the most successful group of vertebrates, since their descendants inherited the lands of the world in the form of the tetrapods: amphibians, reptiles, birds and mammals.

All osteichthyans, ancient and modern, are characterized by an internal skeleton which is completely 'ossified', or made of bone. The replacement of cartilage by bone happened suddenly in their evolution. It was preceded by the laying down of a thin film of bone over the skull and 'backbone' in the agnathans and cartilaginous fishes. The bony skeletons of these fishes increases their preservation potential considerably, so that their fossil record is much bettter than that of the cartilaginous fishes.

Two major groups (or subclasses) of bony fishes evolved some 400 million years ago. They are distinguished by the arrangement of the skeleton that supports their fins. The 'ray-finned' fishes, or actinopterygians, include the majority of today's bony fishes, the teleosts (see pp.38–41). The 'lobe-finned' fishes, or sarcopterygians (see pp.42–45), provided the ancestors of the first land animals.

SUBCLASS ACTINOPTERYGII

The ray-finned actinopterygians were the earliest bony fishes to appear. A great diversity, first of marine and then of freshwater types, evolved some 400 million years ago. Today, this ancient group lives on in the vast and varied assemblage of modern teleosts, as well as in the much rarer representatives – the sturgeons, paddlefishes, bowfin, garpike and birchirs.

The characteristic feature of the actinopterygians, both fossil and modern, is the skeleton of parallel bony rays that supports and stiffens each fin – hence the name, 'ray-finned' fishes. In early actinopterygians the fins were quite immovable; in later, more advanced, forms they became more flexible, culminating in the highly mobile fins of modern bony fishes.

Other improvements were made as the actinopterygians evolved toward modern teleosts. A swim bladder developed from the paired air sacs of earlier fishes, enabling the fish to control its buoyancy (see p.21). Heavy scales were replaced by a lighter, more flexible scaly covering. And the tail became symmetrical, with equal-sized lobes to provide an even, propulsive thrust.

The classification of bony fishes is extremely complex, with several dozen orders involved; five of these have been selected here to illustrate the evolution of the group (see pp.18–19).

The palaeoniscids were the earliest ray-finned fishes to appear, more than 400 million years ago. They evolved rapidly, and many groups invaded freshwaters. Toward the end of the Paleozoic, these early fishes (sometimes grouped as the chondrosteans) gave rise to many new types (the neopterygians, see p.37), from which arose the teleosts.

The typical features of the early ray-finned fishes were thick bony scales which articulated with each other; a single dorsal fin to the rear of the body; and an asymmetric, shark-like tail.

NAME	*Cheirolepis*
TIME	Middle to Late Devonian
LOCALITY	Europe (Scotland) and North America (Canada)
SIZE	up to 22 in/55 cm long

Cheirolepis was a fast-moving freshwater predator and one of the largest of the palaeoniscids. Its streamlined body was encased in a heavy coat of small, rectangular scales, arranged in diagonal rows – just like those of the spiny sharks. (The scales were covered with a unique type of enamel called ganoine, which gives the palaeoniscids their collective name of 'ganoid' fishes.) A row of large scales stiffened the top side of the tail's elongated upper lobe, enhancing its powerful flexing movements during swimming. These scales were a unique feature of all early ray-finned fishes. While the upturned tail tended to drive the fish downward in the water, paired pectoral and pelvic fins on the underside counteracted this, elevating the body at the front. Stability was provided by the large dorsal and anal fins.

Like all palaeoniscids, *Cheirolepis* had large eyes, and probably hunted by sight. Its jaws were equipped with many sharp teeth, and could be opened sufficiently wide to engulf prey two-thirds its own length.

NAME *Moythomasia*

TIME Middle to Late Devonian

LOCALITY Australia (Western Australia) and Europe (Germany)

SIZE 3.5 in/9 cm long

The palaeoniscids evolved into a great variety of forms during the Devonian, and became the most abundant and diverse of freshwater fishes in the Late Paleozoic.

A contemporary of *Cheirolepis*, *Moythomasia* had evolved a new type of ganoid scale, unique to the early ray-finned fishes. A peg on the top edge of each scale fitted into a socket on the bottom edge of the scale above. Thus all the body scales articulated with each other, to form a flexible and protective coat of armour.

NAME *Canobius*

TIME Early Carboniferous

LOCALITY Europe (Scotland)

SIZE 3 in/7 cm long

A new development had occurred in the skull of this tiny fish. The cheek bones and the hyomandibular bones, which attached the upper jaws to the braincase (see p.21), both became upright. This meant that *Canobius*' jaws were suspended vertically beneath the braincase (rather than obliquely as in other palaeoniscids). The new arrangement allowed the mouth to be opened wider, while at the same time the gill chambers behind the jaws were greatly expanded.

This innovation affected both respiration and feeding. Respiration was improved because, as the mouth was opened wide, a greater volume of water passed over the gills. More oxygen could therefore be absorbed from the water, which in turn permitted increased activity. As for feeding, *Canobius*

could now exploit a rich source of food. Tiny planktonic creatures were carried into its gaping mouth in the surge of incoming water, and were caught on the minute teeth that lined its jaws and gills.

NAME *Platysomus*

TIME Early Carboniferous to Late Permian

LOCALITY Worldwide

SIZE 7 in/18 cm long

One family of palaeoniscids became disc-shaped – rather like such modern teleosts as the reef-dwelling blue tang or the Amazon discus fish. *Platysomus*, which lived in both freshwater and the sea, is one example of this.

Its deep body was fringed toward the rear by the elongated dorsal and anal fins. The pectoral and pelvic fins were tiny. *Platysomus* must have sculled along, bending its body from side to side in a slow swimming action. A fairly straight course could have been maintained, since the tail was deeply forked and symmetrical, although the main propulsive force still came from the tail's upper lobe which, as in all the early ray-finned fishes, was stiffened by rows of stout scales.

Like *Canobius*, the jaws of *Platysomus* were suspended vertically from its braincase, giving it the advantage of a wide gape and bulging gill chambers when the mouth was open. *Platysomus* probably also ate plankton.

PRIMITIVE RAY-FINNED FISHES CONTINUED

NAME *Palaeoniscum*

TIME Late Permian

LOCALITY Europe (England and Germany), Greenland and North America (USA)

SIZE up to 1 ft/30 cm long

With its torpedo-shaped body, high dorsal fin and powerful, deeply forked tail, *Palaeoniscum* was built for speed. It must have been a ferocious predator of other freshwater bony fishes. Its jaws were set with numerous sharp teeth, which were constantly being replaced throughout its lifetime.

Like all early ray-finned fishes, *Palaeoniscum* had a pair of air sacs connected to the throat, which could be inflated to act as a primitive buoyancy device (see p.21).

NAME *Saurichthys*

TIME Early to Middle Triassic

LOCALITY Worldwide

SIZE up to 3 ft 3 in/1 m long

The long, narrow body of this freshwater palaeoniscid is reminiscent of that of the modern pike, as is the positioning of its dorsal and anal fins, which were placed well back on the body, near the symmetrical equal-lobed tail.

It is likely that *Saurichthys* also behaved rather like a modern pike. It may have ambushed its prey, lurking among the water weeds or lying still on the river bed, and seizing passing fishes in its toothed jaws.

Saurichthys' jaws were elongated into a long beak-like stucture, almost a third of the total body length, which – as well as contributing to its distinctive appearance – greatly extended the fish's predatory range. The symmetrical placing of *Saurichthys'* fins, together with its long streamlined shape and a great reduction in its bony coat of scales, would have made it a powerful swimmer.

NAME *Perleidus*

TIME Early to Middle Triassic

LOCALITY Worldwide

SIZE 6 in/15 cm long

Perleidus and its relatives evolved from the palaeoniscids, and survived throughout the 35 million years of the Triassic Period. They were all freshwater predators with strong, toothed jaws, which could be opened wide due to their vertical suspension from the braincase, a feature first developed in their predecessor, *Canobius* (see p.35).

A notable feature of this group was the flexibility of their dorsal and anal fins. This improvement was made possible by a reduction in the number of bony rays within each fin, a thickening of the bases of those rays that remained, and an alignment with their bony supports within the body. Such mobile fins, combined with an almost symmetrical tail, allowed greater swimming manoeuvrability.

NAME *Lepidotes*

TIME Late Triassic to Early Cretaceous

LOCALITY Worldwide

SIZE 1 ft/30 cm long

Toward the end of the Paleozoic Era, many new types of ray-finned fishes evolved from the marine palaeoniscids. Grouped together as the neopterygians, these fishes display many of the features that were later developed in the modern bony fishes, which descended from this group.

Lepidotes, a member of the semionotids, had evolved one such feature, a new jaw mechanism that allowed it to feed differently from earlier fishes. Its upper jaw bones were shortened and freed of their connection to the cheek bones, to which they had formerly been fused. This new mobility allowed the mouth to be formed into a tube, and prey could be sucked from a distance toward the fish, rather than engulfed at close quarters as early fishes had done.

NAME *Dapedium*

TIME Late Triassic to Early Jurassic

LOCALITY Asia (India) and Europe (England)

SIZE 14 in/35 cm long

The deep, round body of *Dapedium* (like *Lepidotes*, a member of the semionotids) was stabilized by long dorsal and anal fins at the rear. Its body was covered in heavy, protective scales with a thick outer layer of enamel.

Dapedium had long, peg-like teeth in its jaws and crushing teeth on its palate. These, combined with its body shape, suggest that it was a mollusc-eater, weaving slowly through the coral reefs of the Early Mesozoic seas.

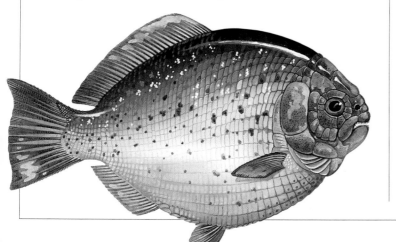

NAME *Pycnodus*

TIME Middle Cretaceous to Middle Eocene

LOCALITY Asia (India) and Europe (Belgium, England and Italy)

SIZE 5 in/12 cm long

Although belonging to a later group (the pycnodontids), *Pycnodus* had evolved the same deep-bodied shape and grinding teeth as *Dapedium*, probably in response to living in the same type of environment – calm reef waters – and eating similar food – hard-shelled molluscs, corals and sea urchins.

NAME *Aspidorhynchus*

TIME Middle Jurassic to Late Cretaceous

LOCALITY Antarctica and Europe (England, France and Germany)

SIZE 2 ft/60 cm long

Superficially, *Aspidorhynchus* looked like the modern gar, or garpike (*Lepisosteus*) of North America, although there is no evolutionary relationship between them. Like it, *Aspidorhynchus* must have been a ferocious predator. Its elongated body, protected by thick scales, was perfectly adapted for fast swimming. The symmetrical tail propelled it, the dorsal and anal fins stabilized it, and the paired pectoral and pelvic fins kept it on course. The jaws were studded with sharp, pointed teeth and the upper jaw was elongated into a toothless guard.

Aspidorhynchus and its relatives, the aspidorhynchids, are closely related to the modern teleosts (see pp.38–41), and most probably shared a common ancestry with them. Only a single species of aspidorhynchid survives today – the bowfin, *Amia calva*, of North American freshwaters.

MODERN RAY-FINNED FISHES

ORDER TELEOSTEI

By the close of the Mesozoic Era, some 65 million years ago, the teleosts were well-established as the dominant bony fishes in the seas, lakes and rivers of the world.

The teleosts had evolved more than 150 million years before the end of the Mesozoic. They first appeared in the seas of the Late Triassic Period, some 220 million years ago. Initially, they were small herring-type fishes, with symmetrical tails and flexible jaws, rather like advanced neopterygians such as *Aspidorhynchus* (see p.37). But in the middle of the Cretaceous Period, the teleosts underwent an explosive phase in their evolution, which resulted in more advanced fishes like the modern salmon and trout. These diversified rapidly, and by Late Cretaceous/Early Tertiary times, a second evolutionary burst gave rise to the highly advanced teleosts of today – the spiny-rayed, perch-like fishes (see p.41).

(rhomboid) scales. But the scales were comparatively smaller and allowed greater flexibility during swimming.

Its tail was symmetrical and halfmoon-shaped, superficially like that of a modern mackerel, although there were many more bony fin rays supporting the tail lobes than in modern teleosts.

Its fins, too, were arranged differently. Besides the long anal fin, there was only one dorsal fin. The extra large pectoral fins were low on either side (rather than high up on the flanks, behind the gills, as in more advanced bony fishes). The pelvic fins were unusually small and placed halfway down the belly.

Hypsocormus did, however, have fairly advanced jaws. They were flexible and mobile, and well-equipped with muscle attachment points to ensure a powerful bite. The upper and lower jaw bones were long, and had teeth along their length.

NAME *Hypsocormus*
TIME Middle to Late Jurassic
LOCALITY Europe (England and Germany)
SIZE up to 3 ft 3 in/1 m long

The dividing line between the advanced neopterygians (see p.37) and the primitive teleosts is unclear. *Hypsocormus* was a fast-swimming, fish-eating predator, which could have belonged to either group since it had both primitive and advanced features. For example, it had the heavy, 'old-fashioned' body armour of its palaeoniscid ancestors – thick, enamel-covered, rectangular

NAME *Pholidophorus*
TIME Middle Triassic to Late Jurassic
LOCALITY Africa (Kenya and Tanzania), Europe (England, Germany, Italy and former USSR) and South America (Argentina)
SIZE 16 in/40 cm long

Pholidophorus is one of the earliest known undisputed teleosts to appear in the sea. Superficially, it looked like a modern herring, with a symmetrical tail, a single dorsal fin placed halfway along its back, paired pectoral and pelvic fins on the underside, and an anal fin toward the tail. With large eyes and flexible jaws equipped with small, rounded teeth, it was obviously a fast-moving, predatory fish, probably feeding on crustaceans in the plankton. Some specimens of *Pholidophorus* have also been found with the remains of other bony fishes in their stomachs.

Despite their 'modern' appearance, *Pholidophorus* and its relatives were primitive bony fishes, as betrayed by two main features. Their bodies were encased in the heavy, enamelled scales of the earlier 'ganoid' fishes, the palaeoniscids (see pp.34–36). And their 'backbones' were only made of bone in places. Their successors, the leptolepids, were the first teleosts to have a backbone made entirely of bone.

NAME *Leptolepis*

TIME Middle Triassic to Early Cretaceous

LOCALITY Africa (Tanzania), Australia (New South Wales), Europe (Austria, England, France and Germany) and North America (Nevada)

SIZE 1 ft/30 cm long

Leptolepis and its relatives were herring-type fishes, like the pholidophorids. But unlike them, the leptolepids lived and moved in shoals, gaining safety in numbers as they fed on plankton in the surface waters.

This gregarious lifestyle can be deduced from the many fossil finds in which hundreds of these fishes have been preserved in the same slab of rock.

The leptolepids were also more advanced than the pholidophorids in two important respects. First, their skeletons were made entirely of bone, and second, their bodies were covered in thin, rounded scales with no enamel coat.

Both these developments made the leptolepids better swimmers. The backbone formed a strong, yet flexible, rod to resist the pressures created by the S-shaped bending of the body during swimming. The thin scales reduced the fishes' weight, and their rounded shape made the body more hydrodynamic.

NAME *Thrissops*

TIME Late Jurassic to Late Cretaceous

LOCALITY Europe (England, France and Germany)

SIZE 2 ft/60 cm long

Thrissops (above) was a streamlined predator that hunted others of its own kind in the warm, shallow seas of the Late Mesozoic, some 140 million years ago. Its tail was deeply cleft into two equal lobes, which may have increased its speed. The pelvic fins were tiny, and could have played little part in stabilizing the fish's deep body in the water. Perhaps to compensate for this, the anal fin formed a long fringe on the fish's underside.

Thrissops was small in comparison with some of its relatives, such as *Xiphactinus* (formerly called *Portheus*). This fossil fish grew to a length of 13 ft/4 m – as large as any shark that cruised Cretaceous seas. One specimen is preserved with a 6 ft/1.8 m bony fish intact within its stomach.

A modern group of freshwater fishes may be the sole survivors of *Thrissops* and its relatives. These modern fishes are called the 'bony tongues' (grouped together as the Osteoglossoformes) because of the tooth plates embedded in their stout tongues. The tongue shears against the teeth on the palate, so holding and crushing prey.

A member of this modern group, the huge bony-tongued pirarucu (*Arapaima gigas*) of the South American rivers, is the world's largest known freshwater fish. It reaches a length of 13 ft/4 m and a weight of some 440 lbs/200 kg.

MODERN RAY-FINNED FISHES CONTINUED

NAME *Protobrama*

TIME Late Cretaceous

LOCALITY Asia (Lebanon)

SIZE 6 in/15 cm long

This small relative of *Thrissops* had lost its pelvic fins. Its deep body was fringed toward the rear by a long dorsal and anal fin, in front of the deeply forked tail. The pectoral fins were placed high on the flanks, greatly improving its manoeuvrability.

The size of *Protobrama* and its body shape suggest that it may have been a reef-dweller, nipping in and out of the coral formations in pursuit of its prey.

NAME *Enchodus*

TIME Late Cretaceous to Paleocene

LOCALITY Worldwide

SIZE 7 in/18 cm long

At the very end of the Cretaceous and during the Early Tertiary, a second burst of evolution led to the advanced bony fishes. Salmon and trout are survivors of this evolutionary phase, and from their ancestors descended all the modern types of teleost.

Enchodus was one of these early, salmon-like teleosts. Its large head and big eyes, together with the lightweight, streamlined body, suggests an agile predator of the open seas. The scales were reduced to a band along each flank; the pelvic fins were set well back on the belly, directly beneath the large, stabilizing dorsal fin; and the pectoral fins were mounted higher on the flanks, giving greater control of steering and braking.

The most remarkable feature of *Enchodus*, however, was its mouthful of greatly elongated teeth. The teeth were slightly recurved and interlocked when the jaws were closed, thus forming an effective trap. *Enchodus* probably preyed on plankton-eating fishes in the surface waters.

NAME *Hypsidoris*

TIME Eocene

LOCALITY North America (Wyoming)

SIZE 8 in/20 cm long

Early in the Tertiary, a group of fishes (called the Ostariophysi) diverged from the main teleost line, and became specialized for freshwater life, though some groups later returned to the sea. More than 6000 species survive, including the carp, minnow, goldfish, loach, piranha and catfish.

With its whiskery feelers, *Hypsidoris* was strikingly similar to a modern catfish. It lived in the subtropical rivers and lakes of western North America some 50 million years ago. Many excellent specimens have been preserved in the Green River deposits of Wyoming, laid down in the Eocene.

The structure of *Hypsidoris'* backbone indicates that it had the acute hearing (especially of high-frequency sounds) characteristic of all living ostariophysid fishes.

This sensitivity to sound is due to a unique specialization of the vertebrae at the front of the backbone in these fishes. The vertebrae are modified into a chain of small, movable bones, which can transmit vibrations picked up by the swim bladder (which acts as a hydrophone and resonator) to the inner ear. There, the vibrations are interpreted by the brain as either potential prey or approaching predator.

These sound-transmitting bones in fishes are called the Weberian ossicles, and serve a similar function to the hammer-anvil-stirrup chain in the middle ear of mammals (see p.184).

Like its modern relatives, *Hypsidoris* had a stout spine at the front edge of each pectoral fin. These spines were defensive, and could be erected by powerful muscles in times of need. Prey was located, or danger sensed, by its acute hearing – a valuable asset in the often dark and murky waters of the sediment-laden rivers in which it lived.

Having homed in on the potential prey, its edibility was assessed at closer quarters by the long, sensory filaments surrounding the catfish's mouth. These 'feelers' were sensitive to touch and to chemical substances in the water. Fish were *Hypsidoris'* chief prey, but crayfish and other bottom-dwellers were also detected by the trailing feelers.

NAME *Sphenocephalus*

TIME Late Cretaceous

LOCALITY Europe (England and Italy)

SIZE 8 in/20 cm long

Two groups of advanced teleosts arose from the ancestral salmon/trout group. These were the cod/haddock-type fishes (the paracanthopterygians) and the spiny-rayed, perch-like fishes (the acanthopterygians).

Sphenocephalus seems to have been intermediate in structure between the two groups. In fact, it is remarkably similar in appearance to the living freshwater 'trout-perch' of North America, so called because it has both primitive-trout and advanced-perch characteristics.

Besides its rather large head, the distinctive feature of *Sphenocephalus* was that its pelvic fins had moved forward to lie beneath the pectoral fins, which were placed high on the sides of its body. The arrangement of these paired fins greatly enhanced the fish's manoeuvrability. In the modern cod group, the pelvic fins are actually in front of the pectorals.

NAME *Berycopsis*

TIME Late Cretaceous

LOCALITY Europe (England)

SIZE 14 in/35 cm long

Berycopsis was one of the earliest spiny-rayed teleosts (the acanthopterygians) to appear. Today, this group, with an evolutionary history of some 70 million years, is the most successful and varied of all the bony fishes, accounting for 40 percent of living species. Modern members of the group range from barracuda and swordfish, to perch, tropical reef fish, flatfish and seahorses.

Berycopsis had all the typical features of the group. The first fin ray in the dorsal and anal fin was enlarged into a stout spine, which could be erected for defence (hence the name of the group, 'spiny-rayed' fishes). Its pectoral fins were placed high on the side of the body, to better control steering and braking; the pelvic fins had moved forward, to counterbalance the pectorals. *Berycopsis'* body had a lightweight coat of thin, rounded scales, their surfaces made abrasive by tiny, comb-like teeth. Its swim bladder was no longer connected to the throat, and the fish relied on the bladder's own gas-secreting and absorbing glands to make it neutrally buoyant.

NAME *Eobothus*

TIME Middle Eocene

LOCALITY Asia (China) and Europe (England and France)

SIZE 4 in/10 cm long

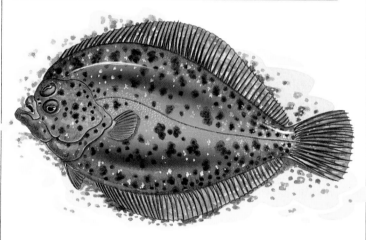

As evolutionary 'late-comers', the flatfishes, such as *Eobothus*, filled one of the few remaining niches left among the spiny-rayed fish group. They became specialized for living and feeding on the seabed. Unlike the rays and skates, which became flattened from top to bottom, the flatfish became compressed from side to side during development. Young fish look like other ray-finned fish and swim normally, but as they grow the eye, on what is to be the underside, migrates onto the top side. This is accompanied by other complex structural modifications of the skeleton, nerves and muscles.

As in all flatfish, *Eobothus'* dorsal and anal fins formed an almost-continuous fringe around its oval-shaped body. The fish glided over the seabed with an undulating motion of these fins. The success of this peculiar fish form is shown by the 570 species of flatfish, most of which are marine but three of which live in freshwater. Plaice, sole, turbot, halibut, and flounder are living relatives of *Eobothus*.

LOBE-FINNED FISHES

SUBCLASS SARCOPTERYGII

In the Early Devonian, about 390 million years ago, the first lobe-finned fishes (sarcopterygians) appeared in the sea. Only seven species survive today – a single species of coelacanth and six species of lungfish (see p.45). Some 10 million years before this, the first ray-finned fishes (actinopterygians, see pp.34–41) had evolved, and their fate was very different, with 21,000 species alive today to testify to their success.

Both these types of fishes are bony fishes (osteichthyans); both have an internal skeleton of bone and an external skeleton of bony scales. But their fins differ fundamentally.

The fins of actinopterygians are supported by numerous stiff, parallel bony rays (hence the common name for the group, 'ray-finned' fishes). There are no muscles within the fins; they are moved by muscles within the body.

In contrast, the paired pectoral and pelvic fins of sarcopterygians consist of long, fleshy, muscular lobes (hence the common name for the group, 'lobe-finned' fishes). Each lobe is supported by a central core of individual bones, which articulate with each other. The first bone of the series articulates with a sturdy shoulder (pectoral) or a hip (pelvic) girdle. Most of the bones can be directly related to the bones that make up the limbs of land animals (see p.49).

The rounded tip of each lobed fin is stiffened by bony rays, which fan out from the bony skeleton above. Muscles within each lobe can move the fin rays independently of one another.

The structure of these muscular, lobed fins was of great evolutionary importance, because some member of the lobe-finned group of fishes (and paleontologists still hotly debate which member, see pp.47, 49) was to evolve into the first tetrapod (see pp.48, 50); tetrapods, in turn, gave rise to the first amphibians.

The lobe-finned fishes are grouped into two major types, both with living, though exceedingly rare, representatives. First, there are the extinct rhipidistians (the Porolepiformes and the Osteolepiformes, see pp.42–44) and the related coelacanths, or actinistians, today represented by a single marine species. These two groups are classed as the crossopterygians. The second major group of lobe-finned fishes are the lungfishes, or dipnoans.

ORDER ONYCHODONTIFORMES

The onychodontiforms were an odd group of Devonian rhipidistians. They were undoubtedly lobe-finned fishes, possibly the most primitive of the group, and yet they did not have the characteristic muscular, lobed fins.

NAME	*Strunius*
TIME	Late Devonian
LOCALITY	Europe (Germany)
SIZE	4 in / 10 cm long

Strunius had a short body, compressed from side to side, and covered in large, rounded, bony scales. It had the characteristic jointed skull that is unique to both the rhipidistians and the coelacanths (but not the lungfishes). This design evolved as an adaptation to increase the bite-power of the jaws. This was necessary if they were to feed successfully on the chief prey of the day, the palaeoniscid ray-finned fishes, which were covered in thick bony scales (see p.34).

The bones on the roof of *Strunius'* skull were divided across the midline by a deep joint, which separated the bony skull into front and back portions. The braincase, fused to the skull roof, was presumably similarly jointed, and a large muscle probably connected both halves. (This is the arrangement seen in *Eusthenopteron* and coelacanths.) When this muscle contracted, it pulled the front half of the skull downward, and the teeth were sunk into the prey.

The arrangement of the fins on *Strunius'* body was like that of all other rhipidistians, in fact of all other lobe-finned fishes. There were two dorsal fins on its back, set near the tail, and paired pectoral and pelvic fins, plus a single anal fin, on its underside. The tail was three-pronged, with two equal lobes on either side of a central axis. The fins were not the usual muscular lobes: they were stiffened by numerous bony rays, like those of the ray-finned fishes.

ORDER POROLEPIFORMES

The porolepiforms, like the onychodontiforms, were rhipidistians that existed only during the Devonian Period. But, unlike their contemporaries, the porolepiforms had developed the muscular, lobed fins typical of the sarcopterygians. They also had the unique jointed skull, as described for *Strunius*.

NAME *Gyroptychius*

TIME Middle Devonian

LOCALITY Europe (Scotland)

SIZE 1 ft/30 cm long

Gyroptychius was a fast-moving, long-bodied predator found in Devonian rivers, with small eyes and a keen sense of smell. Like other porolepiforms, it had short jaws. This actually enhanced the bite-power of the jaws.

Gyroptychius had fleshy, muscular fins, all of which, except for the pectorals were concentrated at the rear of the body. This increased the propulsive force of the arrow-shaped tail.

NAME *Holoptychius*

TIME Late Devonian

LOCALITY Worldwide

SIZE 20 in/50 cm long

Holoptychius was a deep-bodied, streamlined fish, with a lightweight covering of thin, rounded scales which promoted fast swimming. It was a voracious predator of other bony fishes. Like all its rhipidistian relatives, it had fang-like teeth arranged around the margin of its palate, and numerous smaller, pointed teeth lined both jaws. Its victims would have been held fast between the teeth, then swallowed whole.

Holoptychius had an asymmetrical tail. The powerful thrust produced by its upper lobe during swimming would have tended to drive *Holoptychius* down in the water. To compensate for this, the muscular pectoral fins were extra-long and mounted high on the flanks. They acted as hydrofoils; their slightest movement out to the sides would have elevated the front of the body, and counteracted the down-thrust produced by the tail. The pectoral fins also stabilized the fish and steered a course by their concerted movements.

ORDER OSTEOLEPIFORMES

The osteolepiforms were the longest-lived group of rhipidistian fishes. They appeared in the Early Devonian and died out during the Early Permian, a span of some 130 million years. Many paleontologists are convinced that these rhipidistians were the ancestors of the tetrapods (see p.47, 49).

NAME *Osteolepis*

TIME Middle Devonian

LOCALITY Antarctica, Asia (India and Iran) and Europe (Latvia and Scotland)

SIZE 8 in/20 cm long

This early member of the osteolepiforms was encased in thick, square scales, which must have weighted its body in freshwater. A thin layer of bony and spongy tissue (called cosmine) covered the scales and the bones of the head.

This outer coat of cosmine was a vitally important feature in *Osteolepis* and other early lobe-finned fishes, since through it ran tiny canals that were connected to sensory cells deeper in the skin. These canals opened on the surface as tiny pores. Thus, the whole surface of the body was alive with sensory receptors. These probably detected vibrations in the water, warning *Osteolepis* of the approach of potential prey or predators, and perhaps also detected chemical substances.

LOBE-FINNED FISHES CONTINUED

NAME *Eusthenopteron*

TIME Late Devonian

LOCALITY Europe (Scotland and former USSR) and
North America (Canada)

SIZE up to 4 ft / 1.2 m long

NAME *Macropoma*

TIME Late Cretaceous

LOCALITY Europe (Czechoslovakia and England)

SIZE 22 in / 55 cm long

Large rhipidistian fish like *Eusthenopteron* are considered by many paleontologists to be closely linked to the early tetrapods on the basis of several features. The pyramidal arrangement of the bones in its paired fins is strikingly similar to the arrangement of the limb bones in land animals (see p.49). In addition, the structure of its backbone, the pattern of the skull bones and the complex, labyrinthine folding of the enamel inside each tooth all bear a remarkable resemblance to these features in the first tetrapods (see p.50–53).

Eusthenopteron was a long-bodied, predatory fish with a powerful three-pronged tail, consisting of two equal-sized lobes on either side of the bony axis of the vertebral column. Its pectoral fins were placed well forward on the body, and articulated with the shoulder girdle, which in turn articulated with the back of the skull. The pelvic fins were well to the rear, as were the two dorsal and anal fins.

INFRACLASS ACTINISTIA

The actinistians, or coelacanths, have a long evolutionary history. They arose in the Middle Devonian, and the last fossils found are from the Late Cretaceous, some 70 million years ago.

In 1938 a living coelacanth was caught in the deep waters that separate Madagascar from southern Africa. The people of the Comoro Islands had known of this fish for generations, but it was new to science. In 1998 a new population of coelacanths was found on the other side of the Indian Ocean near Sulawesi, Indonesia. The term 'living fossil' was awarded to *Latimeria chalumnae*, which has proved to be the only surviving species of a group that first evolved over 380 million years ago.

Although *Macropoma* was only about one-sixth the length of its living relative, *Latimeria*, in all other respects these two fishes, which are separated in time by almost 70 million years, are remarkably similar.

Macropoma had a short, deep body and a bulbous, three-lobed tail – a design characteristic of coelacanths. The only teeth in its mouth were concentrated at the front, but the hinge joint in the skull (the same arrangement as in the rhipidistians) ensured that the jaws could be opened wide and closed forcefully on prey. Its pectoral fins were set high on the flanks, to aid manoeuvrability, and the pelvic fins were placed midway along the belly. The first of the dorsal fins was sail-like and supported internally by long bony rays; the other fins were fleshy, muscular lobes.

The living coelacanth is one of the few bony fishes that give birth to live young. Whether this was also the case among its ancient relatives is not known, but discoveries of fossil coelacanths in Niger and Brazil may shed light on their breeding habits.

ORDER DIPNOI

The dipnoans, or lungfishes, arose in Early Devonian times and survive to this day in the form of three genera of highly specialized freshwater fishes – the Australian lungfish (*Neoceratodus*), the African lungfish (*Protopterus*) and the South American lungfish (*Lepidosiren*). The African and South American fishes live in tropical areas subject to drought. When the waters get low or become stagnant, the fish can change from its normal gill-breathing method to breathing air at the surface. Air is taken in through external nostrils, which are placed low on either side of the mouth; it then passes directly to the internal nostrils on the roof of the mouth and into the two lungs (only one in the Australian species) connected to the throat on the underside. Fossil lungfishes also had internal nostrils, so they too could breathe air in times of necessity.

Fossil lungfishes, like some modern species, could survive out of water during the dry season by 'hibernating' in watertight burrows in the mud, which were linked by tiny air vents to the surface.

NAME *Dipnorhynchus*

TIME Early to Middle Devonian

LOCALITY Australia (Western Australia) and Europe (Germany)

SIZE 3 ft/90 cm long

Even the earliest lungfishes were quite different to other lobe-finned fishes. For example, *Dipnorhynchus*' skull and braincase did not have the hinge joint that divided the skulls of coelacanths and rhipidistians into two parts. Its skull was a solid bony box, like that of the first tetrapod land animals. This early lungfish had also lost its cheek teeth; these were replaced by a crushing surface of tooth-like 'blisters' on the palate and lower jaw. Another advanced feature was that the palate was fused to the braincase (as in land animals).

NAME *Dipterus*

TIME Middle to Late Devonian

LOCALITY Europe (Germany and Scotland)

SIZE 14 in/35 cm long

The surface of raised blisters that acted as teeth in *Dipnorhynchus* had been replaced by a pair of large, fan-shaped tooth plates on the palate and on the lower jaws of *Dipterus* (above). This type of dentition was to remain practically unchanged over the next 380 million years.

The arrangement of the fins, however, has changed. The two dorsal fins of *Dipterus*, together with the tail fin and anal fin, have merged in modern species.

NAME *Griphognathus*

TIME Late Devonian

LOCALITY Australia (Western Australia) and Europe (Germany)

SIZE 2 ft/60 cm long

By the end of the Devonian Period, various specialized types of lungfish had evolved. *Griphognathus* had an elongated snout, and small, teeth-like denticles, capped with enamel, studded its palate and lower jaws. Like all the other members of the order, this lungfish was covered in large, overlapping, rounded scales, and the tail was asymmetrical.

INVADERS OF THE LAND

The modern newts and salamanders (urodeles) and frogs and toads (anurans) are the amphibian survivors of the tetrapods that first ventured out of the water and began to take advantage of the evolutionary opportunity presented by land, some 370 million years ago. Their pioneering land effort was not a total success, however, since amphibians must still return to water to breed. It was their descendants, the reptiles, that truly conquered the land.

The very word *amphibia* defines the essential quality of these animals, for it means 'both lives'. It refers to their ability to live in two radically different worlds – the world of water, which their fish ancestors still inhabit, and the world of land, which their descendants, the reptiles, eventually inherited.

The young amphibian larva that emerges from the egg is adapted to life in water – it has gills and a swimming tail. Later, there is a fairly rapid change in structure (a metamorphosis), encapsulating in a few short weeks the evolutionary development of their ancestors, when the larva loses these aquatic features and replaces them with lungs and stronger limbs to adapt it to life on land.

There are several reasons for believing that the fossil amphibians of the Paleozoic Era passed through a similar aquatic larval stage of development. In some cases, juvenile specimens have been found in which traces of the gills have been preserved, and a series of progressively larger forms link them to an adult which retains no trace of gills and must have breathed through lungs.

In other cases, such as *Seymouria* (see p.53), the head of young fossil specimens still shows traces of canals in which were located the sensory, lateral-line organs (inherited from their fish ancestors). Such organs could only have served their purpose in the aquatic environment of a larval stage.

Finally, some living amphibians, such as the mudpuppy of North America, have returned to a wholly aquatic lifestyle, retaining into adulthood the gills that previously only the larva had possessed. This is true also of some of the Paleozoic amphibians, such as *Gerrothorax*, with its three pairs of feathery gills (see p.53).

The problems of breathing on land

Amphibians' characteristic moist skin is one of the ways in which they differ most markedly from their Paleozoic ancestors. Modern amphibians supplement their normal respiratory exchange through the lungs by breathing through their moist skins. But this, in turn, limits their size and way of life. Many Paleozoic amphibious tetrapods had scales or armour covering their bodies, and many of them grew to a great size. Both these facts suggest that the early tetrapods had not evolved the skin respiration system of their living descendants. Those ancient tetrapods that did emerge from the water to live on land must, therefore, have had an impermeable, leathery or scaly skin, to prevent water loss. Such a covering would have made them rather slow and cumbersome.

Living amphibians are grouped together as the lissamphibians and their fossil record as recognizable groups only extends back as far as Triassic times. Their evolutionary relationships with the older extinct groups of early tetrapods have not been well-established. This is one of the reasons that the first land-going vertebrates are no longer regarded as amphibians but instead are given the less definite assignation of tetrapods.

A controversial lineage

Paleontologists agree that the first tetrapods must have evolved from one of the three groups of lobe-finned fishes. These are the living lungfish or dipnoans; the coelacanths or actinistians, also living; or the extinct rhipidistians (the porolepiforms/osteolepiforms).

The muscles and bony axis of the paired fleshy fins of these fishes provide a structure that could have evolved into the limbs of an early tetrapod (see p.49). Similarly, there seems little doubt that these fishes possessed lungs like those of amphibians. Living lungfish, for example, have them, and a similar structure (though single) is present in the living coelacanths (see p.44). It is, therefore, considered likely that the extinct rhipidistians also had lungs. Support for this belief comes from the fact that lungfish and the rhipidistians have openings in the palate of their mouths that are similar to the internal nostrils of amphibians.

Most paleontologists consider that the first tetrapods evolved from the rhipidistian fishes, based on the remarkable similarity in the pattern of bones in their skulls and fins/limbs. Other paleontologists, however, believe that the lungfish were ancestral to the tetrapods, since the development of the lungs, nostrils and limbs of living lungfish is strikingly similar to those of living amphibians.

Tetrapods evolved as water living animals in the lakes and rivers of late Devonian times. It was not until Carboniferous times that they successfully established themselves on land, but once there they rapidly expanded into a number of groups. Some of these developed into large crocodile-like animals, quite unlike the modern amphibians. Only three groups of amphibians have survived into modern times – frogs and toads (anurans), newts and salamanders (urodeles) and the curious leg-less caecilians (gymnophiones).

REPTILIOMORPHS

PLAGIOSAURIDS   DISSOROPHIDS   GYMNOPHIONES   URODELES   ANURANS   ANTHRACOSAURS   SEYMOURIAMORPHS   DIADECTOMORPHS   AMNIOTES

THE EARLIEST TETRAPODS

Acanthostega (above) and Ichthyostega are the most important early tetrapods known. They combine typically 'fishy' features, such as a laterally flattened tail, gills and lateral line sensory system with characteristic tetrapod features such as four limbs and a deep ribcage. They would seem to fill the evolutionary 'gap' between the fishes and land going tetrapods. However, it is now realised that the limbs were better adapted for life in shallow fast-flowing streams than for walking on land. The limbs were probably used for swimming, especially the hind ones, which point backwards.

The forelimbs could have held onto submerged plant roots and grubbed in the stream sediment for food. The recent discoveries of Acanthostega and Tulerpeton have greatly increased our knowledge of early tetrapod evolution. It used to be thought that these animals established the basic five-fingered plan for tetrapods, but this is not the case. Acanthostega had eight fingers and toes, Ichthyostega at least seven toes and an unknown number of fingers, while Tulerpeton had six fingers and toes. The so-called five-digit limb plan was not established until Carboniferous times.

An evolutionary opportunity

Whatever may have been the group from which the first tetrapods evolved, the interesting question is why did they leave their ancestral waters to brave the land, with its greater range of temperature and the dangers of desiccation? At one time, it was thought that this evolutionary change had taken place in an environment liable to seasonal drought. In such an environment, there would have been considerable advantage for any fish that was capable of leaving its drying-up pond or stream, and travelling overland in search of another home that might still contain water.

The current theory suggests that it was more likely the pressure of predation in the waters themselves that drove the first tetrapods ashore. With their lungs and stout, muscular limbs, the early tetrapods might well have moved out of the water and up the river bank, to escape larger, predatory fishes. Once on land, they would have found a rich source of food in the numerous insects, worms, snails and other invertebrates that lived in the mud and moist vegetation. Here lay the opportunity that evoked the crucial evolutionary changes that eventually produced the first land-going tetrapods.

From Carboniferous through to Triassic times, a period of more than 150 million years, the early tetrapods diversified into very many different groups and more than 70 families have been

named. The fossil remains of their skeletons furnish evidence that some of the early tetrapods evolved as true amphibians; these are generally referred to as batrachomorphs. Others evolved in the direction of the amniote reptiles, and these are generally referred to as reptiliomorphs.

Radiation of the early tetrapods

The earliest tetrapods, such as *Ichthyostega*, have been found in rocks of Late Devonian age in Greenland. At that time – some 370 million years ago – Greenland was part of a Euramerican continent that lay near the equator, and stretched from today's western North America to eastern Europe (see p.11).

A remarkable feature of the distribution of these early tetrapods, and of their relatives, the reptiles, is that until the middle of the Permian Period (about 100 million years later), nearly every one of them has been found only on this former Euramerican continent. This strongly suggests that this continent was the homebase in which they first evolved and diversified. Only after the middle of the Permian – when Asia and the southern landmass of Gondwanaland had become attached to Euramerica to form the supercontinent of Pangaea – did the amphibians and reptiles spread throughout the world.

In the Early Carboniferous (Mississippian) times that followed the Devonian, there was an increase in diversity of the

Paleozoic amphibians. Nearly all of these amphibians were aquatic or semi-aquatic.

In the Late Carboniferous (Pennsylvanian), much of the Euramerican continent was covered by low-lying, tropical swamplands. From these swamps rose tall coniferous trees, 49–130 ft/15–40 m tall, and tree ferns up to 25 ft/7.5 m tall. Seed ferns and other smaller plants abounded.

A variety of insects, spiders, millipedes and centipedes lived in the rich leaf litter that covered the forest floor. A giant dragonfly-like insect, *Meganeura*, with a wingspan of up to 2 ft 5 in/76 cm, flew among the trees, while a giant centipede-like arthropod, *Arthropleura*, up to 6 ft 6 in/2 m long, fed on the leaf litter. The thick accumulations of leaves eventually formed the rich coal deposits that have long been mined in eastern North America, Britain and central Europe.

The fresh waters of this landscape abounded with fishes, providing the amphibians with a rich food source. The total known amphibian fauna of the Late Carboniferous comprises over 70 genera in 34 families, representing all of the Paleozoic orders.

In the succeeding Permian Period, the Paleozoic amphibians reached their greatest diversity, with nearly 100 genera known in 40 families. However, an interesting change occurred in the amphibian fauna during the 40-odd million years of the Permian.

The amphibians of the Early Permian are known best from the Red Beds of Texas. These seem to have been laid down in a flood-plain or delta environment, similar to that around the Mississippi River today. The amphibians shared this environment with the pelycosaurs, early types of mammal-like reptile (see pp.186–188).

At this time, the amphibians made a decisive shift to the land. About 60 percent were terrestrial, another 15 percent were semi-terrestrial, and only 25 percent were exclusively aquatic.

This, however, was to be the peak of achievement for the amphibians in their conquest of the land. The Late Permian Karroo Beds of southern Africa reveal an amphibian fauna in which terrestrial and aquatic types are now equal in diversity, and most of the terrestrial forms have a protective body armour. This change was due to the rise of the therapsids, the mammal-like reptiles (see pp.188–193), which ousted amphibians from most of their recently acquired, land-based niches.

Demise of the ancient amphibians

The Triassic Period saw the final exclusion of the ancient amphibians from the land. Although over 80 genera are known, these belong to only 15 families, and all are temnospondyls. Almost without exception, they were aquatic, but some were of considerable size. The largest known amphibian, *Parotosuchus*, from southern Africa, was probably over 13 ft/4 m long.

The long existence of the fossil amphibian groups was now almost over. Only two genera are known in the Jurassic, one in Australia and the other in China. By this time, the ancestors of today's moist-skinned amphibians had already appeared. The first frog, *Triadobatrachus*, is known from the Early Triassic of Madagascar; bones of the first urodele (the group to which modern newts and salamanders belong) are found in Jurassic rocks. The other order of modern amphibians, the caecilians (Gymnophiona), are almost unknown in the fossil record.

FROM FLESHY-LOBED FIN TO FORELEG

RHIPIDISTIAN FISH (EUSTHENOPTERON)

DIPNOAN FISH (DIPTERUS)

The ancestor of the land animals was one of the lobe-finned fishes. It may have been one of the rhipidistians, such as Eusthenopteron, or it may have been one of the dipnoans, represented today by the lungfish. The internal skeleton of the pectoral fin of both types of fish is shown here.

EARLY TETRAPODS

The first tetrapods to colonize dry land most probably evolved from the first aquatic tetrapods. By Carboniferous times, the existence of new terrestrial habitats with well-established vegetation, inhabited by numerous arthropods, opened up new possibilities for land-going amphibian tetrapods.

Classically, these animals were subdivided into the labyrinthodonts, which had large bodies and conical teeth with infolded (labyrinthine) enamel; small lepospondyls which had simple teeth; and the modern lissamphibians, such as the frogs and salamanders of today. But research has made it clear that the labyrinthodonts and lepospondyls contain unrelated groups with different origins. The classification has been modified.

So far there is but a single genus in this family – *Acanthostega*. Hovewer, the characters of this primiative tetrapod are sufficiently different from those of *Ichthyostega* to be placed in a separate family. The presence of two pairs of well-developed limbs denotes that tetrapod status had evolved in these animals, but analysis of the articulation of the limbs and the presence of internal gills showed that they were still fundamentally aquatic.

NAME *Acanthostega*

TIME Late Devonian

LOCALITY Greenland

SIZE 2ft/60cm long

New fossils of *Acanthostega* found in the 1980's revolutionized ideas about the earlier tetrapods. They had weak wrists and ankles and the hind limbs were posteriorly orientated and adapted for swimming rather than walking. *Acanthostega* had eight fingers rather than five, which was believed to be basic to vertebrates. *Acanthostega* retains some fish-related characteristics, such as the flattened tail and lateral line system. It did not have well-developed ribs, but it did have internal gills.

The jaws had an array of sharply-pointed teeth which imply that *Acanthostega* was an active predator that fed on fish.

Family Ichthyostegidae

The fossil remains of early tetrapods are so rare that at the moment most species are placed in their own families. Additionally, their inter-relationships are unknown so there is no higher classification. Fossil remains of ichthyostegids have only been found in rocks of Late Devonian age in Greenland so far.

NAME *Ichthyostega*

TIME Late Devonian

LOCALITY Greenland

SIZE 3ft 3in/1m long

Ichthyostega is one of the earliest tetrapods. It was a large, aquatic animal, bigger than any of its fish ancestors, with a long deep body and a heavy skull of solid bone. Its four limbs were well-developed but not suitable for movement on land, as previously thought. The hind limbs were directed backwards, like those of a seal, and were better adapted for a paddling mode of swimming than for walking. The feet had seven toes. It is not known how many digits were on the forelimbs. If they were like those of the contemporary tetrapod *Acanthostega*, they would have had more than five digits and would have been adapted for holding onto submerged vegetation in fast-flowing rivers and grubbing around in sediment for arthropod and molluscan food.

The fish-like tail of this creature was laterally flattened and had a delicate fin more suited for swimming than moving around on land. The ribs were flattened, giving the body a deep profile. There was a lateral line system, which is a sensory system similar to that used by fish for detection of vibration, but effective only in water.

Ichthyostega's skull is dorsally flattened, with the eyes placed high on the skull roof, giving a field of view similar to that of living aquatic crocodiles. Its wide mouth was full of small, sharp, conical teeth. The palate was also studded with teeth, some of them long and fang-like, similar to the teeth of the rhipidistian fishes, and well-adapted for a mode of life as an active predator.

The new understanding of *Ichthyostega* and the other early tetrapods suggests that they were not land-going as previously thought, but well-adapted for aquatic life in the shallow, fast-flowing rivers of the late Devonian continents.

An early Carboniferous family of tetrapods are characterized by key-hole shaped eye sockets with unusual pointed openings at the front that may have housed a special gland.

NAME *Eucritta*

TIME Lower Carboniferous

LOCALITY Scotland

SIZE 10 in /25cm

This newly-described (1998) fossil from 334 million-year-old Scottish rocks combines features usually associated with different groups of tetrapods. The skull is amphibian-like, the palate is reptile-like and the eye socket baphetid-like. It supports the view that the separation of living amphibians and reptiles was not present when the early tetrapods arose.

Eucritta melanolimnites, ('creature from the black lagoon') inhabited a shallow lake surrounded by active volcanoes.

ORDER UNCERTAIN

The remains of about five genera of Carboniferous tetrapods have been found in Europe and North America. They can be grouped in families, but do not fit any of the known orders.

NAME *Crassigyrinus*

TIME Early Carboniferous

LOCALITY Europe (Scotland)

SIZE 6ft 6in/2m long

Crassigyrinus had a fish-like body tapering into a long tail, with tiny fin-like limbs. Its head was about 1ft/30cm long, and the teeth-filled jaws could probably open wide. Its close-set eyes were particularly large. These unusual features suggest that *Crassigyrinus* had lost the use of its limbs, and reverted to an aquatic life. Its teeth are those of a fish-eater, and the streamlined body indicates a fast-moving predator. The large eyes may suggest that it hunted in the dark, murky Carboniferous swamps.

NAME *Greererpeton*

TIME Early Carboniferous

LOCALITY North America (West Virginia)

SIZE 5ft/1.5m long

Although *Greererpeton* evolved amongst the first land-living temnospondyls it soon reverted to a fully aquatic life. Its slim body shape would have been ideal for moving through water with sinuous undulations. The low flat head was about 7in/18cm long. The elongated body (which had 40 vertebrae, about twice the usual number) ended in a long tail. The legs were short, each with five toes for steering and braking.

Open grooves along the sides of *Greererpeton*'s skull are a sign of its fish ancestry. They mark the position of sensory lateral line canals, which was used to detect water-borne vibrations. *Greererpeton*'s ear structure was poorly developed, unlike that of land-living amphibians.

Colosteids have been placed with the temnospondyls in some classifications and with the anthracosaurs in the others, though the skull is different from most members of that group.

ORDER TEMNOSPONDYLI

The temnospondyls are undoubted amphibians which evolved at the end of the Early Carboniferous Period (Late Mississippian), about 330 million years ago.

Over the following 120 million years, they developed into many varied, often very large, terrestrial forms. With the rise of the terrestrial mammal-like reptiles (see pp.182–193) in the early Permian Period, however, competition for resources on land increased and the temnospondyls were forced back to the damp places from whence they came. The temnospondyls had become extinct by the Early Jurassic times, but not before some of their members had given rise to the proanurans, the ancestors of the modern frogs and toads (see pp.56). Representatives of the main temnospondyl families are described.

EARLY TETRAPODS CONTINUED

NAME Eryops

TIME Late Carboniferous to Early Permian

LOCALITY North America (New Mexico, Oklahoma and Texas)

SIZE 6ft 6in/2m long

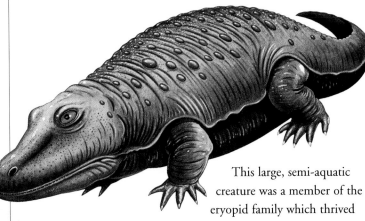

This large, semi-aquatic creature was a member of the eryopid family which thrived in North America from Late Carboniferous (Pennsylvanian) times through to the end of the Permian Period.

Eryops' thick-set body and large head were supported by sturdy, short limbs. Bony plates covered its back, perhaps to help support *Eryops'* body when it came out of the water onto land.

The size of the head and the position of the jaw hinge suggest that *Eryops* probably fed in water. The physiology indicates that the large mouth could probably not have been opened on land without lifting its head clear of the ground.

Eryops was one of the top carnivores in its biota. It was truly amphibious and it fed on smaller tetrapods and fish.

NAME Cacops

TIME Early Permian

LOCALITY North America (Texas)

SIZE 16in/40cm long

Cacops was a member of the dissorophids. This diverse family of temnospondyls arose slightly later than the eryopids, and became extinct in the Early Triassic. Many dissorophids were fully-adapted land-living amphibians.

Cacops and its relatives, along with some of the eryopids, were quick to adapt to the drier Carboniferous climate. *Cacops* was well-adapted to life on land. Bony plates covered its body, and a row of thick armour ran down the backbone. Its legs were well-adapted for walking, and were almost reptile-like in structure. A broad opening (the otic notch) behind each eye was covered by a taut membrane which acted as an eardrum.

NAME Platyhystrix

TIME Early Permian

LOCALITY North America (Texas)

SIZE 3ft 3in/1m long

Platyhystrix was more heavily armoured than its close relative, *Cacops*. It had a more pronounced covering of armour plates on its back to protect itself against predators. Certain carnivorous pelycosaurs, such as the sphenacodont *Dimetrodon* (see p.187), lived in the same area and would have preyed on *Platyhystrix* and its terrestrial relatives.

Platyhystrix's most arresting feature was the spectacular 'sail' on its back, made of tall spines that grew up from the vertebrae. Blood-rich skin may have covered the whole structure. Contemporary pelycosaurs, *Dimetrodon* and *Edaphosaurus*, also had great sails. It is thought that the sails served as a device to help these cold-blooded reptiles regulate their body temperature.

NAME Peltobatrachus

TIME Late Permian

LOCALITY Africa (Tanzania)

SIZE 2ft 3in/70cm long

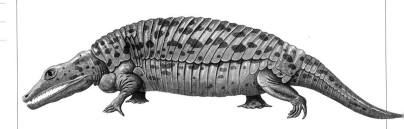

Peltobatrachus was a slow-moving, fully terrestrial amphibian. Its body was enclosed in heavy armour like that of an armadillo, which served as protection against the dominant carnivores of the day – the gorgonopsian therapsids with their enormous canine teeth (see p.189).

Peltobatrachus' bony armour-plating was arranged in broad shields over the shoulders and behind the hips, and in close-fitting bands across the body. The teeth of this amphibian have not been found, but it probably ate insects, worms and snails, just as armadillos do today.

NAME *Paracyclotosaurus*

TIME Late Triassic

LOCALITY Australia (Queensland)

SIZE 7 ft 5 in/2.3 m long

By Triassic times, two groups of mammal-like reptiles, the dicynodonts and cynodonts, dominated the land. *Paracyclotosaurus*, and other amphibians of the capitosaur family, had been forced to return to the water. A general adaptation among these Triassic water-dwellers was toward a general flattening of the body. The head of the bulky *Paracyclotosaurus* was flat-topped and almost 2 ft/60 cm long. The point of articulation with the neck was almost on the same plane as the jaw hinge. As a result, the mouth could be opened easily by raising the head.

NAME *Gerrothorax*

TIME Late Triassic

LOCALITY Europe (Sweden)

SIZE 3 ft 3 in/1 m long

The general trend toward flattening the body reached its climax among the plagiosaurs, such as *Gerrothorax*. This large amphibian probably lay quite still on the stream or lake bed, camouflaged among the sand and pebbles, watching for fish with its upwardly directed eyes. It may even have attracted prey with a fleshy, brightly coloured lure dangling inside its open mouth. Once the prey was within easy reach, *Gerrothorax* would have swiftly closed its gaping jaws, trapping the victim.

Gerrothorax could live permanently in water because it still retained the three pairs of feathery gills that it possessed as a larva. So, this ancient creature clearly proves that fossil amphibians, like their modern counterparts, went through an aquatic, gill-breathing, larval stage before developing into a four-legged, lung-breathing adult.

ORDER ANTHRACOSAURIA

The anthracosaurs (also known as batrachosaurs) were amphibian tetrapods that arose during the Carboniferous and survived until the middle of the Permian. They were not so numerous or diverse as the temnospondyls. Among their members were the ancestors of the reptiles, and they are generally referred to as reptiliomorphs.

NAME *Eogyrinus*

TIME Late Carboniferous

LOCALITY Europe (England)

SIZE 15 ft/4.6 m long

Eogyrinus was a long-bodied aquatic predator which probably lived an alligator-type life in the deltas and swamps of the Carboniferous coal forests. It swam after its fish prey using powerful strokes of the long tail, its body stabilized by the tall, fish-like dorsal fin on its back.

NAME *Seymouria*

TIME Early Permian

LOCALITY North America (Texas)

SIZE 2 ft/60 cm long

Specimens of this seymouriamorph were found in the Red Beds of Texas. It was a well-adapted land-dweller, with many reptilian features (such as the structure of its hip and shoulder girdles).

In fact, *Seymouria* was originally thought to be an early reptile, until fossilized juveniles were found. Their skulls clearly showed the marks of fish-like, lateral line canals, whose only function is to detect water-borne vibrations.

LEPOSPONDYLS

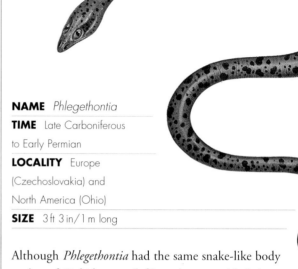

Contemporary with the large, bulky temnospondyls (see pp.51–53) and reptiliomorphs (see pp.57, 62) were a group of smaller, insectivorous amphibians, classically grouped together as the 'lepospondyls'. It is now known that these include at least two unrelated groups: the extinct batrachomorphs and the living lissamphibians. These amphibians evolved in the Carboniferous Period and survived until the end of the Permian.

During this span of some 100 million years, a variety of small batrachomorphs evolved, which tended to look like salamanders or snakes. They can be grouped into three major orders – the aïstopods, nectrideans and microsaurs.

ORDER AÏSTOPODA

The earliest group of batrachomorphs, the aïstopods, were the most specialized of all amphibians. They first appeared in the Early Carboniferous (Mississippian) – about 20 million years after the first tetrapods, the ichthyostegids (see p.50), had set foot on land. Presumably the aïstopods evolved from a four-legged ancestor, but almost immediately they lost their legs, and became snake-like, burrowing amphibians.

Obviously, this specialized way of life had its advantages, since the aïstopods were a long-lived group, surviving for almost 80 million years, until the middle of the Permian Period.

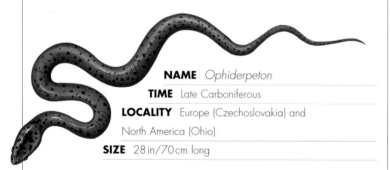

NAME *Ophiderpeton*
TIME Late Carboniferous
LOCALITY Europe (Czechoslovakia) and North America (Ohio)
SIZE 28 in/70 cm long

About 230 vertebrae made up the body of this snake-like aïstopod. There is no trace of limbs within the skeleton. The eyes were large, and placed forward on the skull, which was about 6 in/15 cm long and similar in structure to that of a primitive tetrapod, although no definite connection has been found between the two groups.

Ophiderpeton must have led the life of a burrower. Such a lifestyle would have paid dividends during the Late Carboniferous, when vast amounts of rotting vegetation were accumulating on the forest floor and in the swamps – the coal beds of today. Insects, worms, centipedes, snails and other invertebrates lived and fed on this debris, providing *Ophiderpeton* with a rich source of food.

NAME *Phlegethontia*
TIME Late Carboniferous to Early Permian
LOCALITY Europe (Czechoslovakia) and North America (Ohio)
SIZE 3 ft 3 in/1 m long

Although *Phlegethontia* had the same snake-like body as that of *Ophiderpeton* (left), and presumably led a similar burrowing life, its skull was quite different in structure. Large openings, separated by narrow bones, made it a lightweight structure (fenestrated like that of a modern snake).

ORDER NECTRIDEA

The nectrideans were four-legged amphibians. They were newt-like in appearance and with long, flattened tails to provide the propulsion when swimming. Exclusively aquatic in lifestyle, they evolved during the Late Carboniferous, and survived until the end of the Permian Period.

Early nectrideans had a skull structure very like that of an early tetrapod. Their limbs were well-developed, with five toes on each. The later members of the group tended to have small forelimbs, and a toe had been lost from each. The snout also became greatly elongated in some of the later nectrideans.

NAME *Keraterpeton*
TIME Late Carboniferous
LOCALITY Europe (Czechoslovakia) and North America (Ohio)
SIZE 1 ft/30 cm long

The tail of *Keraterpeton* was more than twice the length of the animal's body and head combined. It was flattened sideways, and would have provided the propulsive force that pushed the animal through the murky waters of the coal swamps in which it

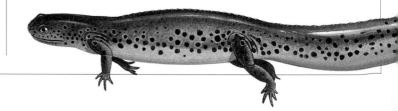

lived. The five-toed hind legs were longer than the four-toed forelegs. The short and rounded skull had eyes set far forward.

Despite its long, slender body, *Keraterpeton* had no more trunk vertebrae than usual (15–26 on average), unlike other long-bodied amphibians, such as the anthracosaur *Eogyrinus* which had 40 vertebrae in front of the hips (see p.53).

NAME *Diplocaulus*

TIME Early to Late Permian

LOCALITY North America (Texas)

SIZE 3 ft 3 in/1 m long

Diplocaulus had a distinctive flattened, triangular-shaped head, rather like a boomerang. Two of the bones at the back of the skull had become greatly elongated on each side to form the points of the triangle.

The body was short, and the limbs weak. *Diplocaulus'* tail, too, was quite short, unlike the tails of other nectrideans, a physical feature that has led some paleontologists to think that this amphibian probably moved through the water by undulating its flattened body in an up-and-down motion rather than using its tail in the usual manner.

Diplocaulus may have lived on the bottom of ponds and streams. The triangular 'wings' on either side of the creature's head may have acted like hydrofoils, allowing the animal to swim above the river bed facing into the current. Alternatively, perhaps the odd shape of the creature's head made *Diplocaulus* an awkward mouthful to swallow, and so acted as a deterrent to such local predators as the thick-set, semi-aquatic temnospondyl *Eryops* (see p.52).

ORDER MICROSAURIA

The microsaurs, or 'small lizards', were the most varied group of 'lepospondyls', with terrestrial types that lived like lizards, burrowing types with legs, and aquatic types that kept their larval gills into adult life. Notwithstanding this diversity, all microsaurs had small legs and short tails.

The group evolved late in the Carboniferous Period, and survived into the Early Permian. They may have been the ancestors of the newts and salamanders.

NAME *Microbrachis*

TIME Late Carboniferous

LOCALITY Europe (Czechoslovakia)

SIZE 6 in/15 cm long

This tiny microsaur had the typical elongated body of an aquatic animal, made up of more than 40 vertebrae. Its legs were tiny, and played no part in swimming, which was achieved instead by sideways undulations of the body and slender tail. This amphibian probably fed on small shrimp-like invertebrates among the freshwater plankton.

Microbrachis was a Peter Pan among the batrachomorphs, since the adult retained the three pairs of feathery gills it had as a larva. This phenomenon is called paedomorphosis, and is seen in several modern salamanders, such as the cave-dwelling olm of Europe and the North American mudpuppy. The Mexican axolotl also retains the tadpole tail of its youth.

NAME *Pantylus*

TIME Early Permian

LOCALITY North America (Texas)

SIZE 10 in/25 cm long

A great head on a small, scaly body characterized this microsaur. It was a well-adapted land animal, moving about on short, sturdy limbs. It probably lived like a modern lizard, scuttling about after insects and other small invertebrates, which were crushed by the numerous large, blunt teeth.

LEPOSPONDYLS CONTINUED

ORDER ANURA

As adults, the anurans – frogs and toads – are the most specialized of all vertebrates, with the shortest backbones in the animal kingdom and powerful jumping legs. Anurans undergo a profound transformation from limbless, herbivorous, swimming tadpole with a long tail, to jumping, insectivorous, tailless adult.

Paleontologists are fairly certain that today's frogs and toads arose from among the land-living temnospondyls, possibly from eryopid-types (see p.52). The first amphibian to resemble a modern frog dates from Early Triassic times (below).

NAME *Vieraella*

TIME Early Jurassic

LOCALITY South America (Argentina)

SIZE Just over 1 in/3 cm long

After *Triadobatrachus*, there is a frustrating gap of about 30 million years in the fossil record of the anurans. Then, the first true frogs appear in the Early Jurassic. *Vieraella* is the oldest-known frog. In all respects its anatomy is essentially the same as that of a modern frog, with the characteristic lattice-work skull, long hip girdle (which is shaped rather like a three-pronged fork) and long jumping legs.

NAME
Triadobatrachus

TIME Early Triassic

LOCALITY
Madagascar

SIZE 4 in/10 cm long

This tiny creature lived about 240 million years ago. Its hip structure suggests that it swam by kicking out with its short hind legs. This vigorous motion may have evolved over millions of years into the jumping action of modern frogs.

Triadobatrachus' skull is strikingly similar to that of a modern frog. It would have been able to hear well on land, because the bony parts of the ear were well-developed, and there

was a broad eardrum on either side to pick up air-borne sounds.

Triadobatrachus had a relatively short body, with 14 back vertebrae as opposed to the usual 24 vertebrae of primitive amphibians, but a long one relative to the five to nine back vertebrae of the modern frog. It also had a short tail, which has been lost in modern anurans.

Triadobatrachus represents an intermediate stage in the evolution of the anurans, sufficiently different from its descendants to be placed in a distinct order (Proanura) and family of its own.

NAME *Palaeobatrachus*

TIME Eocene to Miocene

LOCALITY Europe (Belgium and France) and North America (Montana and Wyoming)

SIZE 4 in/10 cm long

An offshoot from the main line of frog evolution, *Palaeobatrachus'* remains have been preserved in large numbers within the freshwater sedimentary deposits of Early Tertiary Europe. Even fossilized specimens of *Palaeobatrachus'* tadpoles have been discovered.

Palaeobatrachus probably looked and behaved like a modern African clawed toad (*Xenopus laevis*). It would have been an adept swimmer, as fast as any fish, with a streamlined body and powerful, webbed feet.

ORDER URODELA

Newts and salamanders, which are grouped together as urodeles, first appeared in Late Jurassic times. Their modern descendants are the least specialized of living amphibians – they do not have the shortened backbone or powerful jumping legs of the anurans. Unlike frogs and toads, they do not undergo a complicated metamorphosis, because the larvae and adults live similar lives: both are long-tailed, swimming insectivores.

The ancestors of the urodeles remain a mystery. They may have had a common ancestor with the anurans (which are suspected to have descended from the temnospondyls, see pp.51–53). Or they may have arisen from among the microsaurs (see p.55). No linking fossils have yet been found, however.

NAME *Karaurus*
TIME Late Jurassic
LOCALITY Asia (Kazakhstan)
SIZE 8 in/20 cm long

Salamanders seem to have changed little over the known 150 million years of their evolution. The structure of the oldest-known salamander, *Karaurus*, is practically the same as that of modern forms. Its lifestyle was presumably similar too – it would have been a good swimmer and a voracious predator of snails, worms, crustaceans and insects.

ORDER UNCERTAIN

Some of the Late Carboniferous and Early Permian land-living tetrapods were very close in evolutionary terms to the origin of the amniote reptiles. They are generally referred to as reptiliomorphs and are characterized by a mobile braincase which can rotate against the bones of the palate.

NAME *Diadectes*
TIME Early Permian
LOCALITY North America (Texas)
SIZE 10 ft/3 m long

This creature was one of the bulkiest land animals alive in Early Permian times. Its skeleton was like that of a reptile, and well-adapted to life on land. But certain features of the skull prove that it was not a member of that group.

Diadectes had a specialized skull, with a secondary bony palate (a feature found in advanced reptiles which allowed them to chew and breathe at the same time, see p.185), though this was only partially developed. It had stout grinding teeth in its short, strong jaws.

It is possible that *Diadectes* ate shellfish, but its bulky body suggests that it ate plants. If so, it was the first amphibian herbivore, and lived at the same time as the first reptilian herbivore, *Edaphosaurus* (see p.188).

CONQUERORS OF THE LAND

Within the unfolding history of the vertebrates, each new group has been hallmarked by some new feature, or number of features, that allowed it either to survive more efficiently in the environment of its ancestors, and thus to replace them, or to move on and conquer new environments.

The egg that revolutionized life

Below a certain size, a vertebrate would find life on land impossible. Its weight would be too great for its frail limbs to bear or propel, and it would rapidly lose its body moisture and dry out. Amphibians solve this problem by dividing growth into two phases. The egg first develops into an aquatic larva; this feeds and grows into a miniature adult, which then leaves the water and emerges onto land. Reptiles, have found another solution. The evolution of a shelled egg was the innovation that allowed the reptiles to quit the water, and to step out on land, equipped for terrestrial life. They could dispense with the aquatic larval phase that was, and still is, obligatory for amphibians.

A reptile's egg is similar to that of a bird, except that the shell is usually leathery and not hard, and the egg contains less-watery albumen. The shell protects the developing embryo from drying out, and from predators. Safe within its egg, the developing reptile can sustain a longer period of growth; it emerges only when it has reached a size at which it is already competent to survive on land.

The egg's shell inevitably cuts off the developing reptile from the surrounding world. The embryo must, therefore, be self-sufficient throughout its term of development. This is achieved by a food source, the yolk, and a series of ingenious membranes – the amnion, allantois and chorion – that transform the egg into an independent, life-support unit.

Millions of Years Ago

142

JURASSIC

205

TRIASSIC

248

PERMIAN

290

CARBONIFEROUS

354

AMNIOTES

SYNAPSIDS

SAUROPSIDS

PELYCOSAURS DINOCEPHALIANS DICYNODONTS THEROCEPHALIANS CYNODONTS MAMMALS MESOSAURS MILLERETTIDS

The eggs of modern reptiles show the same pattern of membranes, and biologists are confident that a single, ancestral group of original reptiles possessed this new, complicated type of 'amniotic' egg, and that all later groups of vertebrates evolved from this basal stock.

Land adaptations for adult reptiles

Although protection of the developing embryo from drying out was a great step forward in the conquest of the land, two other innovations were necessary before that conquest was complete. First, reptiles had to be protected from desiccation after they emerged from the egg. This was achieved by evolving a horny layer that covered their scales or armour, making them impermeable to water loss.

Second, in order to remain active, reptiles had to develop a more efficient breathing method than that of their amphibian ancestors. Amphibians ventilate their lungs by means of a throat, pump, which forces air into the lungs. Reptiles developed a new system, in which the rib cage was expanded and contracted, resulting in air being sucked into the lungs, and then expelled. The capacity of this system

was limited only by the volume of the lungs, not merely by the volume of the mouth.

However, even with all these adaptations, living reptiles are still, like amphibians, limited in one respect. They are 'cold-blooded'- that is, they obtain nearly all of their energy from the heat of the sun. When the weather or climate becomes cooler, their body temperature is lowered, and they become inactive. The physiology of reptiles is, therefore, geared to a low and varying body temperature, and they cannot sustain prolonged periods of activity.

In contrast, 'warm-blooded' birds and mammals obtain their energy from their food, and have a high, constant body temperature, independent of their surroundings, which allows them to sustain a high rate of activity for longer periods. Paleontologists are currently debating whether dinosaurs were cold or warm-blooded.

Like their amphibian ancestors, and the fish before them, reptiles move by lateral flexure of their bodies. The upper parts of a reptile's limbs project laterally from the body, since the length of each stride depends on the distance across the body from one knee or elbow joint to the other. The feet are also angled somewhat to the side, to resist

The reptiles evolved from the amphibians during the Late Carboniferous. The anapsid reptiles were the first to appear, and are represented today by the turtles and tortoises. The anapsids gave rise to the synapsid reptiles, the ancestors of the mammals, and to the diapsid reptiles, including the modern sphenodonts, lizards and snakes. Many groups of reptile have become extinct, including the great marine reptiles, the ichthyosaurs and plesiosaurs. One of the diapsid groups, the protorosaurs, gave rise to the dinosaurs and the other ruling reptiles.

ANAPSIDS

EUREPTILES

DIAPSIDS

PROCOLOPHONIDS PAREIASAURS TESTUDINES CAPTORHINIDS PROTOROTHYRIDIDS PETROLACOSAURUS PROTOROSAURUS ARCHOSAURS LEPIDOSAURS the lateral forces produced by this type of movement. Toes have to be different lengths if they are to leave the ground at the same time, so that they share weight of the body evenly.

As a result of all these adaptations, both structural and physiological, reptiles were able to colonize the land to the full, living even in the hottest deserts. The peak of their evolutionary development was reached in the form of the great dinosaurs, which grew to sizes that even their successors, the mammals, were unable to rival.

Radiation of the reptiles

The reptiles evolved from the early tetrapods some time in the Late Carboniferous (Pennsylvanian) period. The earliest-known reptile is *Hylonomus* (see p.62), preserved in the Late Carboniferous rocks of Nova Scotia. These rocks are about 300 million years old – 60 million years after the early tetrapods started the invasion of the land.

From *Hylonomus*, many different types of reptile evolved. Like the early amphibians, all of the early reptiles seem to have been confined to the ancient continent of Euramerica. Most of these different lineages of reptile can be distinguished by the pattern of openings in the skull .

EGG SHELL

YOLK SAC

EMBRYO

AMNION

AMNIOTIC CAVITY

CHORION

ALLANTOIC CAVITY

There are four membranes inside the shelled egg of a reptile – the amnion, chorion, allantois and yolk sac. Each plays a particular role to enable the embryo – in this case a turtle – to develop to maturity within its protective egg, independent of its surroundings. The developing embryo is suspended in a fluid-filled cavity surrounded by the amnion. It receives nourishment from the surrounding yolk sac through blood vessels connected to its gut. Waste products are excreted into the allantoic cavity. Oxygen enters the egg via the chorion, which lies just beneath the egg's porous shell.

REPTILIAN BEGINNINGS

The reptiles are one of the most successful groups of vertebrates on Earth. Despite the loss of all the dinosaurs and their numerous distant relatives in the K/T extinction, reptiles (over 6500 living species) are still more numerous than mammals (some 4000 living species). Today most reptiles are relatively small lizards and it is perhaps ironical that the whole group began its extraordinary success from an apparently unpromising beginning, a small lizard-like creature.

Evidence shows that Hylonomus (below), from the late Carboniferous strata of Nova Scotia, is the earliest known true reptile. Older reptile-like forms such as Westlothiana, from Scotland show a mixture of early tetrapod and reptilian characters and are regarded as 'reptiliomorphs'.

In addition to skull structure, evidence for the interrelationships of reptiles can be seen in the structure of their ankles and major blood vessels. In some reptiles, one of the ankle bones is hooked, and provides extra leverage for one of the foot muscles (just as our projecting heel bone provides leverage for the Achilles tendon). This type of ankle is found in all lizards and chelonians (including modern turtles and tortoises), as well as in the 'ruling reptile' lineage – the crocodiles, dinosaurs and their relatives.

The living representatives of all these groups also have an unusual arrangement of the major blood vessels near the heart. These twist around one another in a spiral fashion.

For all these reasons – skulls, ankles and blood vessels – paleontologists are confident that these groups of reptile are closely related to each other.

Skull patterns

In the earliest reptiles, as in their amphibian ancestors, the skull was a box of bone, without any openings except for those of the eyes and nostrils. The muscles of the jaws were attached to the underside of the bony roof of the skull.

In most of the later reptiles, the weight of the animal's skull was reduced by the development of areas in which the bone was replaced by a sheet of lighter, elastic, tendon-like material. This material decays and does not fossilize, but the areas in which it was located appear in a fossilized skull as holes (called temporal openings) between the bones. These openings not only serve to lighten the skull, but also provide additional attachment points to which the jaw muscles can attach, thereby increasing the bite-power of the jaws.

The presence or absence of these temporal openings in the skull form the basis for grouping reptiles into major groups, but recently doubts have been cast on their validity. The earliest reptiles (such as *Hylonomus* and other protorothyridids) had no temporal openings, and their skulls are called anapsid.

The ruling reptiles – including the dinosaurs, pterosaurs and crocodiles – have diapsid skulls, with two pairs of openings behind the eyes on each side. The primitive lizards, the sphenodonts (which today are represented by the sole surviving member, the tuatara), also have a diapsid skull. Later lizards have made the skull even lighter and more flexible, by losing the bar of bone below the lower opening on each side. Snakes have taken this evolutionary tendency even further, by dispensing with the bar of bone between the upper and lower openings.

Other groups of reptiles are not so easily defined. The extinct marine reptiles, the nothosaurs and plesiosaurs, for example, developed a skull pattern (sometimes called euryapsid) similar to that of most lizards. These groups would also seem to have evolved from diapsid ancestors. Two other groups of extinct marine reptiles, the ichthyosaurs and placodonts, also have a euryapsid type of skull. But these animals are very different from one another and also from the plesiosaurs. Each reptile group may have evolved from diapsids, but there is no evidence to detail their precise lines of ancestry. A similar uncertainty surrounds the origin of the diapsid, herbivorous rhynchosaurs, which are also extinct.

HOW A REPTILE MOVES

The legs of a typical reptile, such as a lizard, are splayed out to the side of its body. This results in a sprawling gait, with the whole body being twisted from side to side at each step. Here the backbone and limb girdles are emphasized to illustrate this bending of the body.

EARLY REPTILES

REPTILIOMORPHS

Reptiliomorphs are those vertebrates which have an incomplete number of reptilian characteristics. They are not fully developed reptiles. They may be a transitionary form between the early tetrapods and true reptiles.

NAME *Westlothiana*

TIME Lower Carboniferous

LOCALITY Scotland

TIME 11 in/30cm

Westlothiana was first found in 1984, and was nick-named 'Lizzie the lizard'. It hit the headlines as the oldest known reptile or amniote, capable of laying shelled eggs and therefore being independent of water for breeding like amphibians. 'Lizzie' is about 26 million years older than the previously 'oldest' reptile *Hylonomus* from Joggins, Nova Scotia. Detailed analysis of the skull and post-cranial skeleton of *Westlothiana* shows a mixture of reptilian features with primitive tetrapod ones so that it is now considered to be a 'stem amniote' or reptiliomorph.

SUBCLASS ANAPSIDA

The most primitive reptiles, the anapsids, all shared a common characteristic – the skull was a heavy, solid box of bone, with no openings apart from the sockets to accommodate the animals' eyes and nostrils (see p.61). The muscles that controlled the jaws were confined within this strong, bony box; a position which limited their size and length, and meant that the mouth could not be opened very wide or closed with any force.

In more advanced reptiles, openings developed in the skull that allowed for more efficient jaws. Such 'diapsid' reptiles and their descendants had much greater bite-power, and could open their jaws wider which enabled them to tackle larger prey (see p.82).

Only one order of anapsid reptiles has survived – the chelonians, (the turtles and tortoises, see pp.66–69).

The other two orders of primitive reptiles, the captorhinids and the mesosaurs, became extinct over 250 million years ago.

ORDER CAPTORHINIDA

The captorhinids (which are also sometimes called the cotylosaurs) are the earliest and most primitive of all reptiles. The evolved from the amphibians during the Late Carboniferous Period, 300 million years ago but had become extinct by the end of the Triassic, about 90 million years later.

Two major evolutionary lines arose from the captorhinid order: one led to the evolution of mammals, and the second to the ruling reptiles (see pp.88–169).

Family Protorothyridae

The Protorothyridae family contains the earliest known reptiles. The family first appeared in the Late Carboniferous Period, and survived into Mid-Permian times, a span of 50 million years. Protorothyridids were the basal stock from which many specialized groups may have evolved. Their descendants included the ruling reptiles (see pp.88–169).

NAME *Hylonomus*

TIME Late Carboniferous

LOCALITY North America (Nova Scotia)

SIZE 8 in/20cm long

Hylonomus is the earliest-known, fully adapted terrestrial vertebrate. It closely resembled a modern lizard and probably ate insects and other invertebrates, crushing them with its conical teeth. The teeth were simple and unspecialized, but some of the front ones were longer than the rest – a feature usually found in the more advanced reptiles.

Hylonomus was preserved in the coal beds of Nova Scotia, perishing in the holes left by rotted giant club mosses, where they had ventured in search of invertebrate food.

Family Captorhinidae

The Captorhinidae family of primitive reptiles lived through the Permian Period, surviving for almost 40 million years before their extinction. They lived in Africa, Asia, India and North America.

Although the captorhinids were primitive creatures, they were more advanced than their protorothyridid ancestors. Their skulls were much stronger, with the braincase now firmly attached to the skull roof and cheeks, and the multiple rows of teeth in their jaws were capable of dealing with tough plants or hard-shelled animals.

NAME *Labidosaurus*

TIME Early Permian

LOCALITY North America (Texas)

SIZE 2 ft 5 in/75 cm long

This primitive, heavily built reptile was squat with a large head and a short tail. Its shape suggests that it was at home on land.

A typical captorhinid, *Labidosaurus* had several rows of teeth in the jaws, all of which would have been functional at the same time. The rows in *Labidosaurus'* mouth provided a broad surface on which shelled invertebrates, such as insects and snails could be crushed, or tough plant material ground down.

Family Procolophonidae

This family ranged throughout the world from Late Permian times to the end of the Triassic. Early members were small and lightly built. The members of the family were probably quite agile creatures, which chased, caught and crushed insects and other invertebrates with the many small, peg-like teeth.

Later members, however, from the Mid-Triassic onward, were larger creatures with a very different dentition. Their broad cheek teeth suggest that they probably ate plants.

Strange bony spikes grew outward from the sides of their skulls, presumably as a means of defence for these heavy, slow-moving herbivores.

NAME *Hypsognathus*

TIME Late Triassic

LOCALITY North America (New Jersey)

SIZE 13 in/33 cm long

One of the later members of the family, *Hypsognathus* had many features that indicate it was a plant-eater. Its wide, squat body suggests that it was not agile and its broad cheek teeth were suitable for grinding up tough plant material. Spikes around its head were probably for defence. .

Family Pareiasauridae

The pareiasaurs were the largest of the early, primitive reptiles, reaching lengths of up to 10 ft/3 m. These massive herbivores had sturdy limbs, which in later members tended to be placed beneath the body allowing them to walk in a more upright way.

Pareiasaurs appeared in southern Africa during the Mid-Permian, and spread to Europe and Asia in large numbers. At the end of that period they became extinct.

NAME *Pareiasaurus*

TIME Middle Permian

LOCALITY Southern and eastern Africa, and eastern Europe

SIZE 8 ft/2.5 m long

This animal was a typical member of the family. *Pareiasaurus'* back was protected by bony plates embedded in its skin. Its thick and strong legs splayed out in typical reptilian fashion, supporting the animal's huge body. The skull was heavy and solid and studded with spikes and warty lumps.

The teeth were small and leaf-shaped, with serrated edges in order to deal with the tough plants that the animal ate. Even its palate had teeth to grind its food.

EARLY REPTILES CONTINUED

NAME *Scutosaurus*

TIME Late Permian

LOCALITY Eastern Europe

SIZE 8 ft/2.5 m long

NAME *Elginia*

TIME Late Permian

LOCALITY Europe (Scotland)

SIZE 2 ft/60 cm long

The typical features of the pareiasaur family – a massive body, a heavy, spiked head and bony armour – had become developed to an extreme extent in *Scutosaurus*.

This later member of the pareiasaur family had also developed a more upright gait than its relatives. Its legs were drawn in, and held more directly beneath the animal's body in order to support its great weight. This evolutionary trend was to be perfected later among the later ruling reptiles, the dinosaurs (see pp.88–169).

The presence of such large plant-eaters as *Pareiasaurus* and *Scutosaurus* throughout eastern Europe during Permian times could suggest that the climate in that region was quite warm and stable at the time, because such heavy, slow-moving reptiles as these would not have been able to migrate in order to avoid cold conditions, nor would they have been able to hibernate through the winter months.

This creature was one of the last of the pareiasaurs. *Elginia* was also one of the smallest. Its head was decorated with the bony head spikes which were typical of the family, but they were developed into an incredible array on *Elginia*'s small skull. Their purpose was probably more for display than for defence – perhaps this diminutive reptile shook its elaborately decorated head to and fro in order to threaten a rival male, or perhaps to attract the attention of a female.

Family Millerettidae

The millerettids were a family of anapsid reptiles with a pair of openings in the skull behind the eyes. This characteristic is unusual in the anapsid order, which were the group of reptiles characterized generally by an absence of openings in their skulls, apart from the eyes and nostrils.

Despite this contradictory evidence, the other features of their skulls place the millerettids firmly within the anapsid group. It is most likely that this family represented a specialized side branch of the main reptilian family tree, and evolved these skull openings independently.

The millerettids were all small insectivores that lived from the Middle to Late Permian Period in southern Africa and so far, their remains have not been discovered elsewhere.

NAME *Milleretta*

TIME Late Permian

LOCALITY South Africa

SIZE 2 ft/60 cm long

The *Milleretta* was a small, lizard-like creature which was quick and agile enough to chase after fast-moving insects.

Because of the pair of openings in its skull, some paleontologists used to hold the theory, which has now been disproved, that *Milleretta*, or a closely related member of its family, may have been ancestral to the more advanced group of reptiles, the diapsids, which had two pairs of openings on either side of the skull (see p.65). The diapsid group includes nearly all the modern reptiles and the extinct dinosaurs and pterosaurs.

However, the remains of the earliest-known diapsid, the araeoscelid *Petrolacosaurus* (see p.82), date from the Late Carboniferous Period – more than 40 million years before the evolution of the millerettids.

ORDER MESOSAURIA

The mesosaurs were early aquatic reptiles, the first group to return to the water since their ancestors had adopted a land-living existence. They appeared at the beginning of the Permian Period, and died out relatively soon after. Their remains have only been found in the southern hemisphere.

Family Mesosauridae

This is the only family of mesosaurs. Its members were all fully aquatic, swimming by means of a long, broad tail and long hind legs, and steering with the forelimbs. The mesosaurs probably sieved plankton from the water through the fine, pointed teeth in their elongated jaws.

NAME *Mesosaurus*

TIME Early Permian

LOCALITY Southern Africa and South America (Brazil)

SIZE up to 3 ft 3 in/1 m long

This creature was one of the first reptiles to revert to a water-dwelling existence. It had many adaptations to an aquatic life. Its long tail was flattened from side to side, possibly with a fin running along its length, top and bottom. Its hind legs were long, and the elongated foot-bones were splayed and probably webbed. The shorter forelegs also had broad, webbed feet. The tail and hind legs propelled the animal, and the forelegs steered it.

Mesosaurus could bend easily from side to side, as seen in the flexible structure of the backbone, though it could not twist its body. The ribs were greatly thickened – an aquatic adaptation also seen in the modern sirenians, or sea cows.

Mesosaurus' head was long and narrow, with the nostrils high on its snout near the eyes. It had only to break the surface of the water to breathe and see. An array of long, delicate teeth armed the elongated jaws. Each tooth fitted into its own socket – a feature of meat-eating animals. Yet the teeth would have been too fine for capturing prey. Instead, they probably formed a kind of sieve through which small shrimp-like animals were filtered from the water – similar to how a modern flamingo feeds with its comb-like bill.

The evolutionary importance of *Mesosaurus* does not derive from its aquatic adaptations, but from its geographical distribution. Remains have been found in southern Africa and eastern South America. This distribution was one of the earliest pieces of evidence for continental drift (see p.11). The animal could not have swum across the South Atlantic; the only explanation, for its peculiar distribution is that these two continents had not yet split apart when *Mesosaurus* was alive.

TURTLES, TORTOISES AND TERRAPINS

ORDER TESTUDINES (CHELONIA)

Turtles, tortoises and terrapins are the only surviving members of this ancient group of reptiles, the testudins or chelonians. They differ from all other reptiles in having their bodies, except for the head, tail and legs, enclosed within a shell, above and below. Many of them can pull their heads and legs into the shell for total protection.

Even the earliest chelonians, dating from the Late Triassic, had a shell; in fact, today's turtles and tortoises have hardly changed since those times, over 200 million years ago.

Like other anapsids (see pp.62–69), chelonians have solidly roofed skulls, with no openings in them save for the eyes and nostrils. They are classified for convenience in the anapsid subclass, but some paleontologists believe that their anatomy is so specialized, and their lifestyle so different from other reptiles', that they should be put in an order (Testudines) of their own.

There are two distinct suborders of chelonian, which include the 230 species of living turtles, tortoises and terrapins. They are distinguished from each other by the way in which the animal retracts its head into its shell – either by bending the neck sideways (*Pleurodira*) or by bending it back vertically (*Cryptodira*). The members of a third suborder (*Proganochelydia*) are all now extinct, but they were the ancestors of the chelonian group (below).

SUBORDER PROGANOCHELYDIA

The proganochelids were land-living, tortoise-like reptiles with shells encasing their bodies. They began to evolve in Late Triassic times, some 215 million years ago, and were most probably the stock from which today's land tortoises and aquatic turtles arose. But the ancestry of the proganochelids themselves is not known. Most paleontologists believe it to lie among one of the early groups of anapsid reptiles, perhaps the pareaisaurs or procolophonids (see pp.63–64).

Family Proganochelidae

Most of the early tortoises belong to this family, and date from the Late Triassic Period. The best-preserved skeletons have been found in Germany although others have come from Southeast Asia, North America and southern Africa. Many of the characteristic features seen in modern tortoises were developed at this early stage in their evolution.

NAME	*Proganochelys*
TIME	Late Triassic
LOCALITY	Europe (Germany)
SIZE	3 ft 3 in/1 m long

This is the most primitive chelonian known, but the typical tortoise shape and structure were already well-established. In fact, *Proganochelys* was remarkably similar to a modern land-living tortoise, except that it could not retract its head or legs into its shell.

The body of this ancient tortoise was short and broad, with only ten elongated vertebrae making up the backbone. This is also a feature of modern chelonians and, except for frogs, gives them the shortest backbones among vertebrate animals. *Proganochelys*' short neck (made up of only eight vertebrae) and head were armed with bony knobs.

Proganochelys had a broad, domed shell (known as the carapace) covering its back, and flat, bony plates (the plastron) protected its underside. About 60 plates of various sizes made up the shell, and they were solidly fused to the underlying vertebrae and ribs. Their arrangement was essentially the same as that found in the shells of modern turtles and tortoises. Unlike its modern relatives, however, *Proganochelys* had a number of extra plates around the margin of its shell. These projected outward, and gave the legs some protection.

In life, the shell would have been completely scaled over with plates of smooth horn – the beautiful 'tortoise shell' from which combs and other ornaments are made. (The horn itself does not fossilize, but marks on the bones indicate its presence.)

The only teeth in *Proganochelys'* mouth were on its palate. Otherwise, it had the typical toothless, horny beak characteristic of modern tortoises. Like them, *Proganochelys* probably spent most its time cropping low-growing vegetation.

SUBORDER PLEURODIRA

A few members of this group of aquatic chelonians survive today, and are known as the 'side-neck' turtles, because of their peculiar method of retracting their head inside their shells. This is done with a sideways-flexing of the short neck, and is made, possible by the jointing system between the vertebrae.

Pleurodires date from Jurassic times and were once abundant in the rivers and lakes of the world. Today, only 49 species survive, grouped in two families – the Pelomedusidae (below) and the Chelidae. All are restricted to the fresh, waters of the southern continents.

Family Pelomedusidae

These aquatic turtles were the most prolific of all the pleurodires during Late Cretaceous and Early Tertiary times. There are only 19 living species – in the rivers and lakes of tropical Africa, Madagascar and South America.

NAME *Stupendemys*
TIME Early Pliocene
LOCALITY South America (Venezuela)
SIZE 6 ft 6 in/2 m long

This turtle (left), extinct for some three million years, was a giant among the pleurodires; in fact, it was the largest fresh-water turtle that has ever existed. None of its modern relatives come close to it in size – the largest living species is the Arrau Turtle of the Orinoco and Amazon rivers of South America (*Podocnemis expansa*), and it only grows up to 2 ft 6 in/75 cm in length.

The heavy shell that covered *Stupendemys'* back was immensely broad and over 6 ft/1.8 m long. Its weight would have allowed the animal to stay submerged for fairly long periods, while it cropped the prodigious quantities of weeds needed to fuel its body.

SUBORDER CRYPTODIRA

The cryptodires were the most successful group of chelonians, and survive to this day – most modern turtles and tortoises belong to this group. Many of them can retract their heads into the shell by lowering the neck and pulling it back vertically.

As a group, the cryptodires evolved along with their pleurodire cousins during Jurassic times. But by the end of that period they had become enormously diverse, and replaced the pleurodires in the seas, rivers and lakes of the world. New forms developed on land.

Family Meiolaniidae

The land tortoises of this family appeared in the Late Cretaceous Period, and only became extinct relatively recently in the Pleistocene, less than two million years ago. Although unable to retract their heads into their shells, they were well-protected in other ways.

NAME *Meiolania*
TIME Pleistocene
LOCALITY Australia (Queensland, New Caledonia and Lord Howe Island)
SIZE 8 ft/2.5 m long

Apart from its great size, the most remarkable feature of this well-armoured tortoise was the flamboyant ornamentation on its head. It was surmounted by great spikes, two of which stuck out on either side, giving the head an overall width of some 2 ft/60 cm. Their presence makes it highly unlikely that *Meiolania* could have withdrawn its head into the shell in times of attack. However, the shell protected the back, and the tail was encased in rings of bony armour, and ended in a spiked club.

TURTLES, TORTOISES AND TERRAPINS CONTINUED

Family Testudinidae

Modern land tortoises belong to the Testudinidae family, the most successful of the cryptodires. They appeared in modern form during Eocene times some 50 million years ago, and have remained practically unchanged since.

All tortoises have high, domed shells in order to accommodate the capacious gut which is needed to digest their plant food. The shell also offers protection from attack since the animal can withdraw its head and elephantine legs inside.

NAME	Testudo atlas
TIME	Pleistocene
LOCALITY	Asia (India)
SIZE	up to 8 ft/2.5 m long

Testudo atlas was the largest land tortoise ever to have existed. Sometimes it is called *Colossochelys*, which means, 'colossal shell'.

This mighty creature weighed about 4½ US tons/4 tonnes. Its elephantine legs sprawled out at the sides of its body in the typical reptilian fashion, and supported the massive protective shell which was carried on its back. Cushioned pads on the soles of *Testudo atlas'* compact feet spread the animal's considerable weight evenly over the five, heavy-nailed toes of each foot – an arrangement similar to that seen in modern elephants.

Testudo atlas probably fed exclusively on plants, as do most of its modern relatives (though some are known to eat slugs and worms). It would have spent its time browsing and cropping leaves with its sharp, toothless beak, without fear of being attacked. Because if a predator, such as one of the sabre-toothed cats, did try to attack, *T. atlas* would have pulled its head and legs back into its shell, and presented a solid, bony box, which would have been almost impossible to move or turn over.

The modern counterpart of this extinct tortoise, in terms of size and weight, is the Galápagos giant tortoise, *Geochelone elephantopus,* found on the Galápagos Islands, off the coast of Ecuador. But even this large animal is only 4 ft/1.2 m long – half the length of *T. atlas* – and weighs a mere 500 lb/225 kg.

Family Protostegidae

The protostegids numbered among their members some of the most spectacular sea turtles that ever lived. All species are now extinct, but they thrived during the Late Cretaceous Period. By the Late Cretaceous the protostegids had developed the two main features that distinguish all sea turtles from their land and river-based relatives.

First, since there were fewer predators in the sea than on land, the sea turtles did not need to carry such heavy armour on their backs, and so the shell was reduced to a much lighter structure, which also made the turtles more manoeuvrable than their land-living relatives. Second, the toes of the front and back limbs were greatly elongated, and modified into broad flippers which gave greater propulsion when swimming.

Today, only seven species of sea turtle survive, grouped in two families. All of the species are endangered due to man's interference with their habitats, especially their nesting beaches. The green turtle and the great leatherback turtle, both of which inhabit warm seas, are the most familiar members of the families. No sea turtle, either extinct or modern, has the ability to retract its head or legs into the shell.

NAME *Archelon*

TIME Late Cretaceous

LOCALITY North America (Kansas and South Dakota)

SIZE 12 ft/3.7 m long

This giant turtle which inhabited the seas of the Cretaceous Period did not have the heavy, many-plated shell that was characteristic of its land and freshwater relatives. Instead, the shell of *Archelon* was reduced to a framework of transverse struts, made from the bony ribs that grew out from its backbone. Most probably, the ribs were covered by a thick coat of rubbery skin (as seen in the modern leatherback turtle), rather than by the usual plates of horn.

The limbs of this ancient sea turtle were transformed into massive paddles that would have cleaved the water in powerful, vertical strokes – the method is comparable to the underwater flight of penguins, which propel themselves along by flapping their wings. The front flippers of *Archelon* were well-developed, and would have provided the main propulsive force.

Like the modern leatherback turtle, *Archelon* probably fed on a diet of jellyfish, whose soft bodies were easily dealt with by the reptile's weak jaws and toothless beak.

Family Trionychidae

This family of soft-shelled turtles first appeared, along with the sea turtles, in the Late Jurassic Period. They were an early group of specialized cryptodires, and a relatively successful one, since over 30 species survive today, in the freshwaters of North America, Africa and Asia.

The shells of trionychids are low and rounded, and have lost the horny covering that usually protects the underlying bony plates. Instead, a layer of soft, leathery skin covers the shell, hence the name of the family.

NAME *Palaeotrionyx*

TIME Paleocene

LOCALITY Western North America

SIZE 18 in/45 cm long

This extinct, freshwater turtle was a specialized cryptodire. Unlike most of its relatives, it had a long, mobile neck, only three toes on each foot, and a skin-covered shell, rather than the usual coat of horny plates.

Palaeotrionyx was probably similar in appearance and lifestyle to its living cousins, the soft-shelled turtles (*Trionyx* species) of North America and Africa. Like them, it was probably omnivorous, using its sharp beak to crop water weeds and snap up insects, molluscs, crayfish and even small fish.

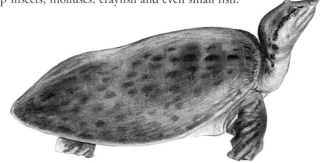

SEMI-AQUATIC AND MARINE REPTILES

During the Mesozoic Era, several groups of reptiles returned to the sea, and became adapted to a marine life. The ichthyosaurs, or 'fish lizards', and the long-necked plesiosaurs were the most successful of these groups, and they dominated the seas of the world for more than 100 million years.

The relationship of these marine reptiles to other reptilian orders, and even to each other, is still unclear. But they are sufficiently alike in one respect to be grouped together conveniently, their common feature is a pair of openings in the skull, behind the eyes and below the cheekbones.

There are four distinct types of marine reptile, each of which shows a different degree of adaptation to life in the marine environment. The least specialized were the placodonts of the Triassic Period (below). The nothosaurs, also of the Triassic, were more adapted to aquatic life (see p.72), and their relatives, the plesiosaurs (see pp.74–77), ranged the open seas throughout Jurassic and Cretaceous times (see pp.78–81). The ichthyosaurs shared the Jurassic seas with the plesiosaurs, and were the most specialized group of marine reptiles.

ORDER PLACODONTIA

The placodonts were the least specialized swimmers among the marine reptiles. They appeared and disappeared in the Triassic Period, and during this span of some 35 million years, many types evolved. But they never became fully adapted to life in the open seas. Placodonts were confined to the shallow, coastal waters of the Tethys Sea, which existed at the time between the northern landmass of Laurasia and the southern landmass of Gondwanaland (see p.11). Many placodonts had turtle-like shells protecting their backs and undersides from predators.

Family Placodontidae

This group of semi-aquatic reptiles was equally at home walking along the seashore or swimming in the coastal shallows. Both areas provided them with rich feeding grounds for their preferred diet of shellfish, which were crushed between the placodont's broad teeth.

NAME	*Placodus*
TIME	Early to Middle Triassic
LOCALITY	Europe (Alps)
SIZE	6ft6in/2m long

The skull of *Placodus* shows that this reptile was a specialized feeder. Its teeth were fully adapted to a shellfish diet. An array of blunt teeth protruded at the front of the jaws, and were used to pluck shellfish – bivalves and brachiopods – off the rocks. The back teeth were broad and flat, for crushing the shells (hence the name of the family, Placodontidae, meaning 'flat-plate tooth'.) Even the palate was covered with large, crushing teeth.

This formidable battery of teeth was powered by massive jaw muscles, which could extend through the pair of openings on each side of the creature's skull to provide the jaws with great bite-power.

Some modern sharks (such as the Port Jackson shark, *Heterodontus portusjacksoni*) that eat such hard-shelled animals as molluscs, crustaceans and sea urchins have the same kind of specialized teeth. So similar are they that when the teeth of *Placodus* were originally found, paleontologists thought that they belonged to ancient sharks.

Placodus was hardly modified at all for its aquatic lifestyle and it was anything but streamlined. Its body was stocky, its neck short, and its limbs sprawled out to the sides of its body like those of early, land-living reptiles. Its only swimming aids were the webs of skin between the five toes of each foot, and the long, slender tail, which was flattened from side to side and may have had a fin running along its length,

Like all placodonts, the underside of *Placodus'* body was protected by a strong armour of belly ribs. A row of bony knobs was raised above the backbone, and provided some protection for this otherwise defenceless animal. Body armour was developed to a much greater extent in later placodonts.

Family Cyamodontidae

This group of placodonts had developed turtle-like shells on their backs. They evolved in the Mid-Triassic and survived to the end of that period.

These shelled placodonts assumed a more completely aquatic lifestyle than *Placodus* (left), and began to look and behave more like modern turtles, although they were unrelated. The phenomenon of unrelated animals evolving similar characteristics is known as convergent evolution.

NAME	*Placochelys*
TIME	Middle to Late Triassic
LOCALITY	Europe (Germany)
SIZE	3 ft/90 cm long

This small reptile was well-adapted to an aquatic lifestyle in the seas of the Middle to Late Triassic Period. The slender body of *Placodus* had been replaced by a broad, flat, turtle-like body in *Placochelys* and a tight mosaic of tough knobby plates covered the creature's back, forming a protective body armour. *Placochelys'* tail was short, and its limbs had evolved into elongated paddles which provided the animal with propulsion in the water.

Placochelys' head, however, was that of a specialized shellfish-eater. It had lost the protruding front teeth seen in *Placodus* and in their place was a horny, toothless beak. However, this was still strong enough to enable it to pluck shellfish from the rocks. Like *Placodus*, strong muscles provided the jaws with great bite power. The jaws were equipped with broad, crushing teeth along the sides and on the palate to cope with the shells of its prey.

Family Henodontidae

These armoured placodonts evolved in the Late Triassic Period. The similarity to modern turtles, which was first developed among the cyamodonts, was developed to an extreme in members of the Henodontidae family. The henodontids had developed a great, bony shell that covered their backs and undersides, and they had lost most of their teeth, which had been replaced with a horny beak similar to those of modern turtle species.

NAME	*Henodus*
TIME	Late Triassic
LOCALITY	Europe (Germany)
SIZE	3 ft 3 in/1 m long

The body of *Henodus* was as broad as it was long – the same shape as that of a modern turtle. Its back and belly were covered in an irregular mosaic of many-sided, bony plates. These formed a defensive shell to protect it from attack by other marine reptiles, such as the ichthyosaurs, in the Triassic seas.

Many more plates made up the shell of *Henodus* than are present in the shell of a modern-day turtle. But as in a modern turtle, the shell was completely covered by plates of horn.

Henodus' head was peculiarly square and box-like. There were no teeth in its jaws; instead, there was probably a horny beak, similar to that of a modern turtle, which could be used effectively to both dislodge and crush the shellfish on which it lived.

SEMI-AQUATIC AND MARINE REPTILES CONTINUED

ORDER UNCERTAIN

The claudiosaurs were marine reptiles that evolved in the Late Permian Period. Their classification is uncertain as yet, but they may represent a transition group between the land-living eosuchian reptiles (see p.84–85) and the later, more advanced aquatic reptiles, the nothosaurs and their relatives, the plesiosaurs.

Only one genus of claudiosaur has been found to date – a semi-aquatic, lizard-like animal named *Claudiosaurus*, which is placed in its own family, the Claudiosauridae.

NAME	*Claudiosaurus*
TIME	Late Permian
LOCALITY	Madagascar
SIZE	2 ft/60 cm long

Claudiosaurus was a long-necked, lizard-like animal, whose lifestyle could be compared to that of the modern marine iguana. *Claudiosaurus*, probably spent much of its time resting on rocky beaches, warming up its body so that it could go foraging. It would have fed underwater, poking its long, flexible neck and small head in among the seaweed to find edible plants and animals. When it swam, its legs would have been folded against the body to give a more streamlined shape, and offer less resistance to the water. The main propulsive force came from sideways undulations of the rear body and long, narrow tail.

There was quite a lot of cartilage in the skeleton of *Claudiosaurus*. This suggests that the animal relied on the buoyancy of the water to give it support. Also, the breastbone, or sternum, was neither well-developed nor ossified, as it is in true terrestrial animals, where it braces the ribs apart on the underside of the body as an adaptation to walking. The sternum in *Claudiosaurus* suggests that its limbs were not well-adapted for moving on land.

ORDER NOTHOSAURIA

Nothosaurs were streamlined, fish-eating marine reptiles. Their necks, bodies and tails were long, their feet were webbed, and they had many sharp teeth in the narrow jaws. Their forelegs were much sturdier than their hind legs, which suggests that they were more actively used for propulsion.

Like the placodonts, nothosaurs evolved and died out during the Triassic Period. Some paleontologists believe that they may be a halfway stage between the land-living reptiles and the aquatic plesiosaurs. However, certain features in the palate and shoulder girdles show that the nothosaurs were not the direct ancestors of the plesiosaurs, rather an offshoot of their ancestors.

Family Nothosauridae

There are several families of nothosaurs, but the best-known representatives belong to the family Nothosauridae. They have been found in the marine sediments of Europe and Asia.

NAME	*Nothosaurus*
TIME	Early to Late Triassic
LOCALITY	Asia (China, Israel and Russia), Europe (Germany, Netherlands and Switzerland) and North Africa
SIZE	10 ft/3 m long

This typical nothosaur probably lived as modern seals do, fishing at sea and resting on land. It had few adaptations to aquatic life. The feet had five long toes, and several well-preserved specimens show that these were webbed. The body, neck and tail were long and flexible. The length of the spines on the vertebrae of the tail suggest that it probably had a fin. The jaws of *Nothosaurus* presented a formidable fish trap – long and slim, with sharp, interlocking teeth.

NAME *Lariosaurus*

TIME *Middle Triassic*

LOCALITY *Europe (Spain)*

SIZE 2 ft/60 cm long

Lariosaurus was one of the smaller nothosaurs, though not the smallest – some of them were only 8 in/20 cm long. It possessed a number of primitive features, including a short neck and short toes. The webs of skin between the toes would therefore have been small in area, and not much use for swimming. This reptile probably spent much of its time walking about on the seashore or paddling around in the coastal shallows, feeding on small fishes and shrimps.

NAME *Ceresiosaurus*

TIME Middle Triassic

LOCALITY Europe

SIZE 13 ft/4 m long

The toes of *Ceresiosaurus* were much longer than those of most other nothosaurs. In fact, the animal exhibited the phenomenon of hyperphalangy, in which the number of bones (phalanges) in each toe is increased. Longer toes mean longer feet, and *Ceresiosaurus* had two pairs of paddle-like flippers. These would have been efficient swimming organs, and anticipated the great, oar-like limbs of the advanced swimmers of the Jurassic Period, the plesiosaurs (see pp.74–77).

Ceresiosaurus swam by undulating its long, sinuous body and tail from side to side. The bones of the forelegs were more massive than those of the hind legs, suggesting that the front flippers played more of a role in swimming, maybe for effective steering and braking.

Family Pistosauridae

The close relationship between the nothosaurs and plesiosaurs is revealed in the characteristics of the sole member of the Pistosauridae family. Most of the skeleton of *Pistosaurus* is similar to that of a typical nothosaur (particularly the body), but the creature's skull also displays many plesiosaur features, as does its backbone.

NAME *Pistosaurus*

TIME Middle Triassic

LOCALITY Europe (France and Germany)

SIZE 10 ft/3 m long

This marine reptile may represent an intermediate stage between the nothosaurs and the plesiosaurs, since it possessed features from both of these groups. Its plesiosaur-type head still had the palate of a nothosaur. And its nothosaur-type body still had the stiff backbone typical of the plesiosaurs, which meant that most of the propulsion came from the creature's paddle-like limbs. This was in contrast to the swimming method of the nothosaurs and other earlier marine reptiles, which used lateral undulations of the body and tail as the chief propulsive force to move them through the water.

Pistosaurus had a mouthful of sharp, pointed teeth. It would have been an efficient fish-eater – a way of life shared by both the nothosaurs and the plesiosaurs.

MARINE REPTILES CONTINUED

ORDER PLESIOSAURIA

The great ocean-going reptiles of the Mesozoic Era were the plesiosaurs. Some of these marine creatures were huge – reaching lengths of up to 46 ft/14 m. The plesiosaurs had become adapted for life in the sea by evolving their limbs into long, narrow flippers which made swimming through the water more efficient. Instead of there being only five or fewer bones in each finger or toe, there were up to ten in each. The plesiosaurs had sturdy, deep bodies and relatively short tails.

At one time, paleontologists believed that the plesiosaurians had used their flippers like enormous oars – moving their limbs backward and forward in order to 'row' themselves through the water. However, a more recent theory suggests that the plesiosaurs' flippers were moved in great vertical strokes, rather like the wings of a bird, and that plesiosaurs in fact 'flew' along in the water, beating their limbs in slow, steady rhythm.

The flippers were hydrofoil shaped, like aeroplane wings – with rounded leading edges and tapering rear ends. Their shape is comparable to the wings of modern penguins or the flippers of sea turtles, both of which swim in a kind of 'subaqueous flight'.

These specialized limbs of the plesiosaurs required modifications in the animals' limb girdles, and their structure was unique to this group of marine reptiles. The collar bones and two of the three hip bones were massive, and formed broad plates on the underside of the animal's body. The powerful muscles that operated the limbs were attached to these great, bony plates.

A dense series of belly ribs connected the bones of the shoulder and hip girdles on the animal's underside. This made the short body more rigid, and provided a strong, solid arrangement against which the great flippers could work. The belly ribs would also have protected the animal when it had to leave the water in order to lay its eggs. Just as modern sea turtles have a belly armour of bony plates, so the belly ribs of plesiosaurs would have protected their undersides as they dragged themselves ashore and crawled laboriously up the beach, pushing their bodies along with their powerful flippers.

There is no evidence to show that the plesiosaurs gave birth to live young, as the ichthyosaurs did (see pp.78–81). It is likely that they came ashore and laid their eggs in nests dug out of the sand, just as sea turtles do today. However, the plesiosaurs would probably have been even more clumsy when they came onto land than turtles because of their unwieldy long necks. They would have been highly vulnerable to attack by predators at such times. Like modern baby turtles, the newly-hatched young would have faced a dangerous trek down the beach to the sea.

The ancestry of the plesiosaurs is not known. Paleontologists used to think that they had probably evolved directly from one of the well-known nothosaurs, but they now recognize a more likely candidate in the Mid-Triassic reptile *Pistosaurus* (see p.73), whose physical structure seems to be intermediate between the two groups – *Pistosaurus* had the body of a nothosaur and the skull of a plesiosaur.

There were two major groups (or superfamilies) of plesiosaurian. The main differences between the members of the two groups was in the lengths of their necks and the nature of their feeding habits. The plesiosaurs had long necks and short heads, and fed on smaller sea creatures. The pliosaurs had short necks and large heads which enabled them to bite and swallow larger prey. Because of these different characteristics the two groups probably did not compete with one another or with their cousins the ichthyosaurs or 'fish lizards' (see pp.78–81) for food although they shared the same seas for many millions of years. Both the plesiosaurs and the pliosaurs survived to the end of the Cretaceous Period.

SUPERFAMILY PLESIOSAUROIDEA

The early members of this group of long-necked marine reptiles were the basal stock from which all other plesiosaurs later developed. The Plesiosauroidea superfamily first appeared in Early Jurassic times, and flourished throughout that period. One family, the elasmosaurs (right), continued to the very end of the Cretaceous Period, and were the last of the group to survive.

The general evolutionary trend among the various families of plesiosaur was toward the development of longer necks and limbs. This reached an extreme in later members of the group, some of which had necks as long as their bodies and tails combined. They also had huge, paddle-like flippers that would have swept them inexorably through the water.

The forelimbs of these plesiosaurs were always somewhat larger than the hind limbs.

The plesiosauroids fed on modest-sized fishes and squid. Their long necks enabled these great creatures to raise their heads high above the surface of the sea and scan the waves in search of potential prey.

Family Plesiosauridae

This group has small skulls and moderately long necks. They are mainly known from fossils found in Europe dating from the Early Jurasssic Period.

NAME *Plesiosaurus*

TIME Early Jurassic

LOCALITY Europe (England and Germany)

SIZE 7 ft 6 in/2.3 m long

Plesiosaurs seem to have changed little during their 135 million years of evolution. The earliest member of the group, *Plesiosaurus*, had already developed all the main structural features that characterize these marine reptiles.

There were several species of the genus *Plesiosaurus*. *Plesiosaurus macrocephalus*, for example, had a larger head than most species, but in other respects its structure sets the pattern for all its relatives.

A plesiosaur was built for manoeuvrability, rather than speed. Its fish-hunting habits would have required quite precise movements. For example, a forward stroke by the flippers on one side of the body, coupled with a backward stroke by the flippers on the other side, would have turned the animal's short body almost on the spot. Its long neck could then dart out swiftly to catch fast-swimming prey.

Family Cryptoclididae

The cryptoclidids tended to have long necks made up of some 30 vertebrae. The skull had a long snout with the nostrils set back from the tip. Their geological range extended from the Late Jurassic to the Late Cretaceous.

NAME *Cryptoclidus*

TIME Late Jurassic

LOCALITY Europe (England)

SIZE 13 ft/4 m long

Cryptoclidus and other members of its family retained the same moderately long neck proportions as *Plesiosaurus*. But they evolved a large number of very sharply-pointed curved teeth which intermeshed when the jaws were closed. This arrangement formed a fine trap for holding very small fishes or shrimps.

Like other Late Jurassic plesiosaurs, *Cryptoclidus* had perfected the transformation of the limbs into flippers by greatly increasing the number of bones in each of the five digits to produce a long, flexible paddle.

Family Elasmosauridae

A long-ranging group which arose in the Early Jurassic and increased in diversity during the late Jurassic and Cretaceous. Some of the Late Cretaceous forms had extremely long necks with up to 76 vertebrae.

NAME *Muraenosaurus*

TIME Late Jurassic

LOCALITY Europe (England and France)

SIZE 20 ft/6 m long

The most successful family of plesiosaurs were the elasmosaurs, of which *Muraenosaurus* is an early member. They evolved in the middle of the Jurassic Period and survived to the end of the Cretaceous. Elasmosaurs had the longest necks of all plesiosaurs.

The neck of *Muraenosaurus* was as long as its body and tail combined and was supported by 44 vertebrae. The head, perched at the end of this crane-like neck, was tiny – only about one-sixteenth of the total body length.

The typically short, stiff plesiosaur body had become quite stout and inflexible in *Muraenosaurus*. This rigidity would have helped to make the flippers more effective propulsion organs.

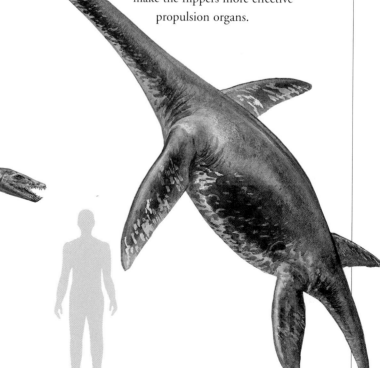

MARINE REPTILES CONTINUED

NAME *Elasmosaurus*

TIME Late Cretaceous

LOCALITY Asia (Japan) and North America (Kansas)

SIZE 46ft/14m long

SUPERFAMILY PLIOSAUROIDEA

Pliosaurs first appeared in the Early Jurassic, alongside their ancestors, the plesiosauroids. They became the tigers of the Mesozoic seas, chasing and overpowering the large sea creatures such as sharks, ichthyosaurs and even their relatives, the plesiosauroids. They evolved a large head with very strong teeth and jaws, powered by huge jaw muscles. Some pliosaurs had heads almost 10ft/3m long. Their bodies were streamlined for speed by progressively shortening the neck. Some had as few as 13 vertebrae, compared to at least 28 in the shortest-necked plesiosaur. They also became larger, to tackle even larger prey.

NAME *Macroplata*

TIME Early Jurassic

LOCALITY Europe (England)

SIZE 15ft/4.5m long

This early pliosaur had a slender crocodile-like skull which was only a little larger proportionally than that of early plesiosaurs. It still had quite a long neck, with 29 slightly shortened vertebrae, which was twice the length of its head.

The pliosaurs progressively improved the limbs into powerful paddles, with a great increase in the number of bones in the digits. But the hind limb, not the forelimb, became the larger, implying a difference in the use of the limbs in the two groups.

'Snakes threaded through the bodies of turtles'– was the description of the plesiosaurs coined by Dean Conybeare, a nineteenth-century English paleontologist who did much of the initial work on these reptiles. *Elasmosaurus*, was the longest known plesiosaur. More than half of its total length was neck – 26ft/5m out of a total of 46ft/14m.

Elasmosaurus had 71 vertebrae – more than the earliest plesiosaurs, which had about 28 neck vertebrae. The structure would have enabled *Elasmosaurus* to curl its neck around sideways, making almost two full circles on each side of its body. It would have been only half as flexible in the vertical plane. However, had *Elasmosaurus* swung its neck around underwater while swimming, it would have met great water resistance.

Some paleontologists suggest, therefore, that the habit of such long-necked reptiles was to paddle along on the surface, their necks held clear of the water. When fish or other prey were spotted from this vantage point, the long neck was plunged into the sea, and the prey snapped up. The modern anhinga, or snake bird, has a long neck, and hunts in much the same way.

NAME *Peloneustes*

TIME Late Jurassic

LOCALITY Europe (England and the former USSR)

SIZE 10ft/3m long

Although smaller than *Macroplata*, this pliosaur (below) shows an advance in the trend to a larger head and shorter neck. It had only about 20 neck vertebrae and its head and neck were of almost equal length. *Peloneustes'* more streamlined shape enabled it to swim rapidly after its fast-moving prey and its long head gave it the reach that its short neck did not allow. Its teeth were adapted to its diet, being fewer and less sharp than those of the fish-eating plesiosaurs, and better for catching soft-bodied squid and crushing the hard shells of ammonites.

NAME *Kronosaurus*

TIME Early Cretaceous

LOCALITY Australia (Queensland)

SIZE 42 ft/12.8 m long

The Australian *Kronosaurus* is the largest-known pliosaur. Its skull was flat-topped and massively long, measuring 9 ft/2.7 m – almost a quarter of the total body length, and therefore substantially larger and more powerful than that of the greatest carnivorous dinosaur, *Tyrannosaurus* (see p.121).

Throughout the Triassic and Jurassic periods, the modern continent of Australia had been dry land, but in the early part of the Cretaceous, the seas submerged many areas. The environment was warm and the seas shallow, and these conditions would have supported large populations of fish and their cephalopod predators. *Kronosaurus* and other short-necked pliosaurs were highly manoeuvrable swimmers, and they would have found rich feeding grounds in these shallow seas.

NAME *Liopleurodon*

TIME Late Jurassic

LOCALITY Europe (England, France, Germany and the former USSR)

SIZE 39 ft/12 m long

This large pliosaur was typical of the later members of the family. It was whale-like in appearance, with a heavy head, short, thick neck and a streamlined body. From the structure of the limb girdles, it is evident that this pliosaur was highly manoeuvrable and could swim at all depths.

The front flippers were used in an up-and-down motion, like those of the plesiosaurs. The strong downward stroke would have pushed water to the rear, so propelling the animal forward. On the recovery stroke, the flippers would have been lifted up automatically by the passage of water over their hydrodynamic shape.

The hind flippers would have thrust back against the water in a powerful kicking motion, and then been turned, to offer the least resistance to the water on the recovery stroke.

This combination of movements would have made for efficient, fast, long-distance swimming. This, in turn, enabled the pliosaur to sustain the chase after its fast-moving cephalopod prey.

MARINE REPTILES CONTINUED

ORDER ICHTHYOSAURIA

The ichthyosaurs were the most specialized of marine reptiles. Their name means 'fish lizards', and describes them well, since they ate fish, and were shaped like fish (though, of course, they were air-breathing reptiles). In fact, their overall body shape was like that of a modern mackerel or tuna – a highly streamlined form that allowed these living fish to reach swimming speeds of over 25 mph/40 kmph.

Unlike their contemporaries, the plesiosaurs (see pp.74–77), ichthyosaurs did not rely on their paddle-like flippers for swimming. Instead, they developed a fish-like tail, the lateral movements of which provided the animal's main propulsive force, just like the tail of a modern shark or tuna.

So fully adapted were the ichthyosaurs to a marine life that they could no longer come ashore to lay eggs, in the same way as the sea turtles and plesiosaurs. Instead, ichthyosaurs gave birth to live young at sea. In fact, some of the most remarkable of fossil finds show adult female ichthyosaurs with young babies just emerging from their bodies – preserved forever in the process of birth.

As a group, the ichthyosaurs occupied the same ecological niche as today's dolphins. They were wide-ranging and highly successful for about 100 million years. These aquatic creatures cruised the open seas of the world from Early Triassic times, and reached their peak of diversity in the Jurassic Period. Thereafter, they declined until, by the mid-Cretaceous, they were all but extinct. The demise of this group could be related to competition from the advanced sharks, which had evolved into their modern form by this time, and were the dominant carnivores of the Late Mesozoic seas (see pp.26–28).

The origin of the ichthyosaurs is not known. The only certainty is the fact that they descended from some terrestrial group of reptiles, rather than evolving from one of the known types of aquatic reptile.

Family Shastasauridae

The shastasaurs were among the earliest ichthyosaurs to appear, in Mid-Triassic deposits, mainly in those from North America. (Older types are known from Japan and China, dating from the Early Triassic Period.) At this early stage of their evolution the shastasaurs moved in an eel-like fashion. However, by the end of the Triassic Period, they had evolved the fish shape characteristic of the ichthyosaur group and swam in a manner more like modern fishes.

NAME *Cymbospondylus*
TIME Middle Triassic
LOCALITY North America (Nevada)
SIZE 33 ft/10 m long

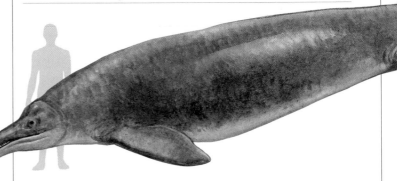

This large ichthyosaur was one of the least fish-like of the group. The body and tail made up most of its length. There was no fin on its back nor on its tail, features that were to develop in later ichthyosaurs. However, it did have the typical long, beak-like jaws, armed with pointed teeth – the sign of a fish-eater.

The limbs of *Cymbospondylus* were short, and looked more like the fins of fish than the paddles of later ichthyosaurs. They would not have been effective for swimming, so they were probably used to control steering and braking. The main propulsive force in swimming must, therefore, have been provided by lateral undulations of the animal's long body.

NAME *Shonisaurus*
TIME Late Triassic
LOCALITY North America (Nevada)
SIZE 49 ft/15 m long

Shonisaurus is the largest-known ichthyosaur, and the only almost-complete skeleton known from Late Triassic rocks. It had developed the fish-like shape characteristic of the group and its enormous length was divided approximately into equal thirds – the head and neck, the body, and the tail.

The backbone of *Shonisaurus*, too, had started to include a typical feature of later ichthyosaurs – it bent downward into the lower lobe of the tail.

It seems likely that *Shonisaurus* was an independent, specialized offshoot from the main line of ichthyosaurs. It had a number of structural peculiarities. For example, its jaws were greatly elongated, and had teeth only at the front.

Its limbs were also extended into extra-long, narrow paddles. This was not a typical feature of the ichthyosaurs. Not only were the paddles unusually long, but the fact that they were of equal size was also unusual – the front pair of limbs in most ichthyosaurs were generally longer than the hind pair.

Family Mixosauridae

The mixosaurs had developed a stabilizing fin on the back (like the dorsal fin of a fish) – a swimming aid which was present in all later ichthyosaurs. But the mixosaurids did not have the typical fish-like tail, with two equal lobes, that made their later relatives such powerful swimmers.

In mixosaurs, the end of the backbone was not bent sharply down into the tail, as it was in later ichthyosaurs; instead, the vertebrae were extended upward, probably to support a low fin on top of the tail.

NAME	*Mixosaurus*
TIME	Middle Triassic
LOCALITY	Asia (China and Timor, Indonesia), Europe (Alps), North America (Alaska, Canadian Arctic and Nevada) and Spitsbergen
SIZE	3 ft 3 in/1 m long

Mixosaurus seems to have been intermediate in appearance between the early, primitive ichthyosaurs, as exemplified by *Cymbospondylus* (left), and the later, more advanced types. For example, *Mixosaurus* had a fish-like body with a dorsal fin on its back, and probably also the beginnings of a fin on the top of its tail. Its limbs had become transformed by the evolutionary process into short paddles, the front pair being longer than the hind pair. Each paddle consisted of five toes, which were greatly elongated by the addition of many small bones (hyperphalangy). The long, narrow jaws were equipped with sharp teeth, adapted for catching and eating fish.

Family Ichthyosauridae

The most typical fish lizards belong to this large family, which flourished throughout the Jurassic Period and into the Cretaceous. The Ichthyosauridae family are known from some remarkably well-preserved fossil specimens, which show them to have been highly specialized marine-living animals.

The ichthyosaurs had developed a streamlined body, torpedo-shaped, with a stabilizing dorsal fin on the back; short, paired paddles which were used for steering; and a strong, fish-like tail with two equal lobes which produced the propulsion for swimming. Ball-and-socket joints between the tail vertebrae allowed for powerful sweeping strokes from side to side. The powerful tail, together with the great flexibility of the backbone, propelled the animal rapidly through the water – the swimming method which is also used by modern-day, fast-moving fishes.

Fossil ichthyosaurids were first found at the beginning of the 19th century by the Anning family in the Jurassic limestones of Lyme Regis, on the southern coast of England.

MARINE REPTILES CONTINUED

NAME *Ichthyosaurus*

TIME Early Jurassic to Early Cretaceous

LOCALITY Europe (England and Germany), Greenland and North America (Alberta)

SIZE up to 6ft 6in/2m long

Ichthyosaurus is one of the best-known prehistoric animals, since a graphic record of its remains are preserved in the shales of southern Germany, near Holzmaden. These rocks were laid down in shallow waters during the Early Jurassic. Several hundred complete skeletons of *Ichthyosaurus* have been found, their bones still articulating with each other. The tiny bones of their young were also found inside the bodies of several adults. This – combined with some specimens where the young is preserved actually emerging from the body of the adult (tail-first, as in modern whales) – shows without a doubt that these marine reptiles gave birth to live young at sea.

The find in Germany also yielded a unique picture of how the animals looked in life. A thin film of carbon had been laid down around many of the specimens, outlining the exact shape of their bodies when the flesh was still on the bones. The characteristic features of a typical ichthyosaur can be clearly seen – the high dorsal fin on the back; the half-moon shape of the tail (caudal) fin, with the backbone angled down sharply into its lower lobe; and the short, hydrofoil-shaped paddles that enclosed the elongated toes of the limbs, the front pair longer than the hind pair.

The nostrils of *Ichthyosaurus* were set far back on its snout near the eyes, so the animal only had to break the surface of the water to breathe. The bones of the ear were massive, and probably transmitted mined vibrations from the water to the inner ear, so that the direction of potential prey could be judged. But *Ichthyosaurus'* main sense for locating its prey would have been sight – its eyes were large and, most probably, extremely sensitive.

Even fossil droppings (called coprolites) and stomach contents of these marine reptiles have been preserved in the rocks. They confirm that fish was the bulk of the diet, but that cephalopods were also eaten.

The remains of pigment cells have also been preserved, and analysis of these suggests that the smooth, thick skin of *Ichthyosaurus* was a dark reddish-brown.

NAME *Ophthalmosaurus*

TIME Late Jurassic

LOCALITY Europe (England and France), North America (Western USA and Canadian Arctic) and South America (Argentina)

SIZE 11ft 6in/3.5m long

Ophthalmosaurus was even more streamlined than its contemporary, *Ichthyosaurus*. Its body was shaped almost like a teardrop – massive and rounded at the front, and tapering toward the rear to culminate in the great, halfmoon-shaped caudal fin. Its front limbs were much more developed than the hind limbs, indicating that the front paddles did most of the steering and stabilizing work, with the tail propelling the body from the rear.

The most remarkable feature of *Ophthalmosaurus* was its huge eyes. Their sockets are about 4in/10cm in diameter, and occupy almost the whole depth of the skull on each side. A ring of bony plates (sclerotic ring) surrounded each eyeball, to prevent the soft tissues from collapsing under the external water pressure, and to help with focusing. (The eyes of all ichthyosaurs had these sclerotic rings, but they are particularly noticeable in *Ophthalmosaurus*.)

The super-large eyes of this ichthyosaur suggest that it was a night-feeder. It probably hunted close to the surface, feeding on squid, which in turn were feeding on the plankton-eating fish.

Family Stenopterygiidae

During the Jurassic Period, two distinct types of ichthyosaur evolved, differing in the shape of their paddle-like limbs. *Ichthyosaurus* and members of its family had short, broad paddles, with more toes than the normal five – sometimes up to nine toes in each limb. The stenopterygiids, in contrast, had longer, narrow paddles, each made up of five toes but with an increased number of bones in each toe.

NAME   *Stenopterygius*

TIME   Early to Middle Jurassic

LOCALITY   Europe (England and Germany)

SIZE   10 ft/3 m long

A find of ichthyosaur skeletons near Holzmaden in Germany includes well-preserved specimens of *Stenopterygius*. *Stenopterygius* was similar in build to *Ichthyosaurus*, but had a smaller head and the narrow paddles characteristic of its family. Five toes made up each paddle, many more bones gave them their narrow shape.

Family Leptopterygiidae

This family contains the last surviving members of the ichthyosaurs before they became extinct at the base of the Late Cretaceous. Like the earlier stenopterygiids (above), the leptopterygiids had narrow paddles, with a great number of bones in each of the five toes.

NAME   *Eurhinosaurus*

TIME   Early Jurassic

LOCALITY   Europe (Germany)

SIZE   6 ft 6 in/2 m long

This extraordinary-looking ichthyosaur, was unlike any other known member of the group. Its upper jaw was twice the length of its lower jaw, giving it the appearance of a modern sawfish. Teeth stuck out sideways along the length of the blade-like projection. The function of this strange structure is not known for certain, just as the purpose of the saw of the modern sawfish also remains somewhat mysterious. *Eurhinosaurus* could have used it to probe around in the sand or mud of the seabed, or among seaweeds and rocks, to flush out flatfish, shrimps or octopus. Perhaps it was also swung rapidly from side to side as *Eurhinosaurus* swam through a shoal of fish, stunning and wounding them as it passed.

NAME   *Temnodontosaurus*

TIME   Early Jurassic

LOCALITY   Europe (England and Germany)

SIZE   30 ft/9 m long

This large creature (sometimes known as *Leptopterygius*) must have cruised the warm waters of the shallow Jurassic seas looking for food, its movements finely controlled by the long, narrow paddles at the front of its body. Propelled through the water by its great tail, *Temnodontosaurus* would have preyed upon large squid and ammonites.

EARLY DIAPSIDS

SUBCLASS DIAPSIDA

Most modern reptiles belong to the diapsids, an ancient group that first appeared in Late Carboniferous times, more than 300 million years ago. The skulls of these animals are distinctive because they have a pair of openings on either side of the skull behind the eye (see p. 61).

The muscles of the jaws are attached to ligaments that stretch across these holes, and endow their owners with stronger jaws, which can be opened wide and closed forcefully to deal with large prey.

The diapsids are not only an ancient group. They are also an important group in evolutionary terms, because from them came the ancestors of most modern reptiles (lizards, snakes and tuataras), and the ancestors of the ruling reptiles (the extinct dinosaurs and pterosaurs, and the modern crocodiles).

ORDER ARAEOSCELIDIA

The earliest and most primitive of the diapsid reptiles were the small, lizard-like araeoscelids, with long necks and slim running legs. Only about four genera are known, classed in two families. They date from the Late Carboniferous Period to the middle of the Permian – a span of less than 40 million years.

NAME	*Petrolacosaurus*
TIME	Late Carboniferous
LOCALITY	North America (Kansas)
SIZE	16 in/40 cm long

The earliest-known diapsid reptile, with the characteristic pair of openings on either side of its skull, looked much like a modern lizard, but with longer legs and a tail as long as its body and head combined. *Petrolacosaurus* probably also behaved like a modern lizard. It would have been an active hunter, chasing

around after insects and other small invertebrates. Its home was the dry, upland areas of what is now Kansas, above the swampy marshes where coal was forming during the Late Carboniferous (Pennsylvanian) Period.

The jaws of this early reptile were equipped with many sharp, pointed teeth, including an upper pair of canines. This arrangement is reminiscent of that of *Hylonomus*, the most primitive reptile known (see p.62).

Despite the newly evolved openings in its diapsid skull, the jaws of *Petrolacosaurus* were not very strong. The openings probably served to lighten the skull, rather than to provide attachment points for the jaw muscles – which was their function in later diapsids.

NAME	*Araeoscelis*
TIME	Early Permian
LOCALITY	North America (Texas)
SIZE	2 ft/60 cm long

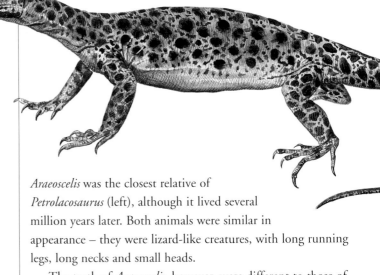

Araeoscelis was the closest relative of *Petrolacosaurus* (left), although it lived several million years later. Both animals were similar in appearance – they were lizard-like creatures, with long running legs, long necks and small heads.

The teeth of *Araeoscelis*, however, were different to those of its earlier relative, and indicate that this creature may have been a more specialized feeder. Instead of the sharp, pointed teeth of *Petrolacosaurus*, *Araeoscelis* had fairly massive, blunt, conical teeth which would have been ideal for crushing the tough chitinous covering of insects such as beetles.

Associated with this specialized diet there was a structural change in the skull of *Araeoscelis*. One of the two pairs of openings in its otherwise-typical diapsid skull had been closed over with bone. This feature was probably an adaptation to strengthen the skull, so that the animal could develop a more powerful bite, which would enable it to deal with its tougher food source.

ORDER UNCERTAIN

There is no fossil record of diapsid reptiles during the Mid-Permian Period. So far, no traces have been found to indicate the course of their evolution during this time. However, in the Late Permian a number of specialized groups appear, which cannot be related to each other with any certainty.

The weigeltisaurid family is one such specialized group, with only a few members known from Madagascar and Europe.

Family Weigeltisauridae

NAME *Coelurosauravus*

TIME Late Permian

LOCALITY Madagascar

SIZE 16 in/40 cm long

This early reptile was highly adapted for gliding through the air, and probably looked similar to the modern lizard known as the flying dragon, *Draco volans*, of Southeast Asia.

The ribs of *Coelurosauravus* were greatly elongated on each side of its short body. Flaps of skin would have connected the ribs, to form a pair of 'wings' with a total span of about 1 ft/30 cm. This reptile probably lived in forests, like the modern flying dragon, and glided from tree to tree, feeding on insects. Its legs would have been held out from its body as it glided, its feet spread wide to offer resistance to the air, and hence slow its descent.

The skull of *Coelurosauravus* was lighter than that of other early diapsids. The openings for the eyes were huge, and there was a wide frill developed from the bones at the back of its head, presumably to make it more aerodynamic.

ORDER THALATTOSAURIA

The thalattosaurs were another specialized group of early diapsid reptiles that lived during the Triassic Period. They were adapted to a marine way of life, probably spending most of their time at sea, and only coming ashore to lay their eggs.

The few thalattosaurs known from Europe and western North America are classed in three families, of which the Askeptosauridae is the best known.

NAME *Askeptosaurus*

TIME Middle Triassic

LOCALITY Europe (Switzerland)

SIZE 6 ft 6 in/2 m long

As with many animals adapted to an aquatic way of life, the neck and body of *Askeptosaurus* were long and slim. Its tail was greatly elongated and almost ribbon-like, and accounted for about half the body length. Sinuous movements of the body and tail would have propelled the animal, eel-style, through the water. Its feet, too, would have helped in swimming – they were broad and webbed, and were probably used to control direction and speed by steering and braking.

Askeptosaurus had long jaws, armed with many sharp teeth. It probably dived deep after its fish prey. This is deduced from two features: its eyes were large, for seeing in the ocean's twilight zone, and they were strengthened by a ring of bony plates, in order to prevent the eyeballs collapsing under the great water pressure at depth.

EARLY DIAPSIDS CONTINUED

ORDER CHORISTODERA

A strange assemblage of crocodile-like reptiles diverged from the main diapsid line during the Early Cretaceous Period, some 140 million years ago. The Choristodera lived in the freshwaters of North America, Europe and eastern Asia until well into the Tertiary – becoming extinct during the Eocene Epoch, some 50 million years ago.

NAME *Champsosaurus*

TIME Late Cretaceous to Eocene

LOCALITY Europe (Belgium and France) and North America (Alberta, Montana, New Mexico and Wyoming)

SIZE 5 ft/1.5 m long

Champsosaurus lived in the rivers and swamps of Europe and western North America throughout Late Cretaceous and Early Tertiary times. With its long, narrow jaws, which were filled with fine, pointed teeth, *Champsosaurus* could easily have been mistaken for a close relative of the crocodile – the modern gavial of India. However, although both animals are diapsid reptiles, they are not closely related to each other. Their similarity can be explained instead by the phenomenon of convergent evolution, in which adaptation to life in a particular environment leads unrelated animals to adopt the same body shape, and often the same behaviour.

Champsosaurus probably swam using lateral undulations of its sinuous body and tail to propel itself while holding its legs tight against the flanks to give itself a more streamlined shape – the same swimming method can be seen in modern crocodiles and marine iguanas.

This reptile was a fish-eater with extremely powerful jaws. The great width of the *Champsosaurus'* skull behind the eyes would have provided a large surface area to which jaw muscles could have been attached, to give great bite-power.

ORDER EOSUCHIA

The lizard-like eosuchians are thought to be close to the ancestry of the later, advanced diapsid reptiles, many of which survive today in the form of snakes and lizards (see pp.86–87).

Eosuchians first appeared in Late Permian times, and continued until the middle of the Triassic. They are grouped into four families, all of whose members were apparently confined to southern and eastern Africa, and Madagascar. The family Tangasauridae contains two representative members (below).

NAME *Thadeosaurus*

TIME Late Permian

LOCALITY Madagascar

SIZE 2 ft/60 cm long

The tremendously long tail of the land-living *Thadeosaurus* measured about 16 in/40 cm – making up two-thirds of the animal's total length. The five clawed toes of each foot were greatly elongated, and so arranged that the longer toes were on the outside. This characteristic had the advantage of allowing most of the animal's toes to remain in contact with the ground as the foot was lifted, giving a strong push off the surface with each step taken and facilitating a more powerful stride. The sternum, or breastbone, was massively developed, a feature which helped to increase the stride of the forelegs.

NAME *Planocephalosaurus*

TIME Late Triassic

LOCALITY Europe (England)

SIZE 8 in/20 cm long

This lizard-like animal was among the earliest of the sphenodonts to evolve. Its skeleton is almost identical to that of the modern tuatara of New Zealand. But its skull is primitive – its teeth are fused to the jaw, rather than attached to grooves in the jaw bones as in advanced lizards.

The teeth of *Planocephalosaurus* were strong, and its jaws could have delivered a powerful bite. It would have crushed insects between its teeth, supplementing its diet with worms and snails, and probably the occasional small lizard.

NAME *Hovasaurus*

TIME Late Permian

LOCALITY Madagascar

SIZE 20 in/50 cm long

The most striking feature of this aquatic lizard-like reptile was its tail. Not only was it twice the length of the rest of the animal's body; it was also deep and flattened from side to side. Each of the tail vertebrae was extended above and below the midline. The result was a tail that formed a broad, stiff paddle, allowing *Hovasaurus* to swim efficiently.

Another unusual feature of *Hovasaurus* is the mass of pebbles found in the abdominal cavities of most of the specimens recovered. Evidently, these reptiles swallowed stones as ballast, to help them sink quickly in the water when diving for their fish prey, or to keep them submerged when feeding.

SUPERORDER LEPIDOSAURIA

The evolutionary line leading to the surviving lepidosaurs – the 6000 species of modern snakes and lizards – arose from an eosuchian-type ancestor some time during the Late Permian Period. A third group of lepidosaurs, the sphenodonts, did not meet with such success (below).

ORDER SPHENODONTIDA

The sphenodonts (also called rhynchocephalids) are an ancient group of lepidosaurs. They are an offshoot from the main evolutionary line of diapsids leading to true lizards and snakes.

Once a diverse group, sphenodonts appeared in the Late Triassic, over 200 million years ago, and many families evolved during the subsequent Jurassic Period. Thereafter, their members began to decline, perhaps due to competition from the true lizards, which were well-established at that stage.

The sole surviving member of the whole sphenodont order is the tuatara, *Sphenodon punctatus*, found only in New Zealand.

NAME *Pleurosaurus*

TIME Late Jurassic to Early Cretaceous

LOCALITY Europe (Germany)

SIZE 2 ft/60 cm long

Pleurosaurus was a member of the pleurosaur family – a group of specialized sphenodonts that evolved on land, but returned to the water during Early Jurassic times. The only specific aquatic adaptation among the pleurosaurs seems to have been a great elongation of the body – up to 57 vertebrae in some types, about twice the typical sphenodont number.

Snake-like movements of the long, sinuous body and tail moved *Pleurosaurus* rapidly through the water. Its nostrils were set far back on its snout, near to the eyes. Its legs were much shorter than those of land-living sphenodonts, and played no role in swimming.

SNAKES AND LIZARDS

ORDER SQUAMATA

The most successful group of reptiles today comprises the lizards and snakes. There are some 6000 species of walkers, gliders, crawlers, swimmers, climbers and burrowers, living in every continent of the world except Antarctica. They are descended from an ancient lineage of diapsid reptiles, most probably the lizard-like eosuchians, stretching back over 250 million years, to Late Permian times (see pp.84–85). The other living reptiles – the turtles, tortoises and crocodiles – evolved along quite different lines (see pp.66–69, 98–101).

The chief feature that distinguishes the lizards and snakes from all other diapsid reptiles (including their closest relatives, the sphenodonts, see p.85), is the great flexibility and power of their jaws. Two structural changes brought this about. First was the loss of the lower arch of bone that enclosed the lower pair of openings in the skull. This gave more room for larger muscles to develop to operate the jaws. Second, a movable hinge joint developed within the skull, which provided even more flexibility in the movements of the jaws.

SUBORDER LACERTILIA

Lizards are a much more ancient group than snakes. The earliest known lizard-like reptiles were small insectivores that inhabited southern Africa during the Late Permian Period. Few fossils remain to trace the course of their evolution during the first half of the Mesozoic Era. However, at the end of the Jurassic Period the group seems to have undergone a burst of evolutionary development, and primitive members of all the major modern groups had suddenly appeared – including geckos, skinks, iguanas, slow worms and monitors.

Besides the changes in the skull that produced more efficient jaws, other structural changes gave lizards better hearing and better articulating surfaces in the joints of their limbs for improved walking. All these features combined to make lizards fast, efficient hunters, able to deal with comparatively large prey, such as other reptiles.

Family Kuehneosauridae

Members of this family are among the earliest-known lizard-like reptiles. They are often placed in the lepidosauromorphs because their relationships may be closer to the sphenodonts than the lacertilians. Early though they were, they had a specialized lifestyle – that of gliding through the air on outstretched, wing-like membranes.

NAME	*Kuehneosaurus*
TIME	Late Triassic
LOCALITY	Europe (England)
SIZE	26 in/65 cm long

This long-legged lizard could glide through the air on a pair of membranous 'wings' which spanned more than 1 ft/30 cm and projected out from each side of its body between the front and hind limbs.

Greatly elongated ribs formed the framework for the skin-covered gliding membranes. – the same arrangement developed by the gliding *Coelurosauravus* (see pp.83) and the living flying dragon *Draco volans*, of Southeast Asia.

Family Ardeosauridae

The Gekkota or geckos were among the earliest of the modern groups of lizard to appear, in the Late Jurassic Period. The only surviving family, the Gekkonidae, evolved relatively recently – in the Late Eocene, some 40 million years ago. It contains more than 670 species, which have spread throughout the warm tropical zones of the world.

NAME	*Ardeosaurus*
TIME	Late Jurassic
LOCALITY	Europe (Germany)
SIZE	8 in/20 cm long

This early gecko had the flattened head and large eyes typical of its modern relatives. Like them, it was probably a night-hunter, agile enough to snap up insects, spiders and smaller lizards with its powerful jaws. Whether it had the 'friction pads' of today's geckos is not known; these are specialized scales under the toes which enable the animal to climb up smooth, vertical surfaces.

Family Varanidae

The anguimorphs or monitors are the largest of all land lizards. They appeared in the Late Cretaceous Period, more than 80 million years ago, and have changed little since. They were large, heavy, active hunters. The forked tongue acts as an organ of smell. Modern representatives include the Komodo dragon.

NAME *Megalania*

TIME Pleistocene

LOCALITY Australia (Queensland)

SIZE up to 26 ft / 8 m long

This relative of the Komodo dragon, *Varanus komodensis*, of Indonesia, hunted on the plains of Australia less than 2 million years ago, ambushing large marsupials, such as kangaroos, grazing there. It would have torn off chunks of flesh with its powerful jaws and long, sharp teeth, serrated along their edges.

Family Mosasauridae

This successful, though short-lived, offshoot from the monitor lizard group was fully adapted to a marine life, during the Late Cretaceous Period.

NAME *Platecarpus*

TIME Late Cretaceous

LOCALITY Europe (Belgium) and North America (Alabama, Colorado, Kansas and Mississippi)

SIZE 14 ft / 4.3 m long

Platecarpus swam in the seas some 75 million years ago. Its tail was as long as its body, and was probably flattened from side to side, with a broad, vertical fin running along its length, above and below. Snake-like undulations of the long, sinuous body, combined with the finned tail, would have propelled *Platecarpus* forward, while the short legs and broad, webbed feet were used to steer.

This marine lizard would have eaten fish and soft-bodied cephalopods, snapping them up in its long, pointed jaws, which were equipped with many sharp, conical teeth.

Platecarpus would also have tackled the ammonites, whose soft bodies were enclosed within a hard, coiled shell.

NAME *Plotosaurus*

TIME Late Cretaceous

LOCALITY North America (Kansas)

SIZE 33 ft / 10 m long

Plotosaurus was a giant among mosasaurs. About 50 vertebrae made up its body and neck, with at least the same number again making up the long tail. The rear of its tail was expanded into a vertical fin.

Its limbs were developed into short flippers, with the front pair longer than the hind pair due to a greater number of bones in each toe. Impressions preserved in the chalk near the bones of the limbs suggest that *Plotosaurus* was covered in a scaly skin, like a modern snake.

SUBORDER SERPENTES

Modern snakes developed during Miocene times some 20 million years ago. But the oldest-known snake is over 100 million years old, and comes from Early Cretaceous rocks in North Africa. It has many of features of the modern groups – elongation of the body; loss of limbs, bony arches above the two lower openings in the skull; and flexibility of the jaw hinges. Snakes are believed to have evolved from a type of burrowing lizard, or from an aquatic, monitor-type lizard.

NAME *Pachyrhachis*

TIME Early Cretaceous

LOCALITY Asia (Israel)

SIZE 3 ft 3 in / 1 m long

The aquatic reptile *Pachyrhachis* had the long body of a snake and the large head of a monitor lizard. The limbs and shoulder girdles had disappeared, but there were still traces of the hip bones. The ribs were broad and evidently *Pachyrhachis* swam by snake-like undulations.

DINOSAURS AND THEIR KIN

The dinosaurs and their kin – the crocodiles and flying pterosaurs – dominated the air, land and waters of the Earth during the Mesozoic Era. This 'Age of the Ruling Reptiles' began more than 200 million years ago, and ended some 65 million years ago. During this time, some of nature's most awesome beasts evolved. The carnivorous dinosaurs stood 20 ft/6 m tall, the plant-eating dinosaurs were some 85 ft/26 m long, and pterosaurs had a wingspan of some 40 ft/12.2 m. The sole surviving members of this great assemblage of 'ruling reptiles' (the archosaurs) are today's crocodiles.

The first step in the evolution of the ruling reptiles was taken in the Late Permian Period, some 250 million years ago. A new line of small, diapsid reptiles evolved, and from them radiated a variety of reptiles, which have been called the thecodontians, but are now known to include several unrelated groups. Now generally referred to as the basal archosaurs, they thrived during the subsequent Triassic

Period, and some of their members became progressively more skilled at walking upright on two legs. The dinosaurs (see pp.106–169), crocodiles (see pp.98–101) and probably also the flying pterosaurs (see pp.102–105) evolved from these basal archosaurs of the Triassic.

Past masters of the world

The first-recorded dinosaur bones were found in England. They belonged to the giant carnivore *Megalosaurus* (see p.116) and the giant herbivore *Iguanodon* (see p.143) and were described to the scientific community in 1824 and 1825. Over a decade passed before Sir Richard Owen, the English anatomist, realised that they were representatives of an extinct group of reptiles. It was he who, in 1842, coined the name *Dinosauria* for them, meaning 'terrible lizards'.

Over the next 50 years, many dinosaurs were discovered in Europe and North America. Various systems of classification were proposed, but it was not until 1887 that another English anatomist, Harry Seeley, recognized that there were two distinct types of hip girdle or pelvis (see p.90). In some dinosaurs, the pelvis was of a normal reptilian build; Seeley called this group the Saurischia, or 'lizard-hipped' dinosaurs. In others, the pelvis resembled that of modern birds; he called these the Ornithischia, or 'bird-hipped' dinosaurs.

Both groups may have evolved independently from the thecodontians, but it is also possible that the 'bird-hipped' species evolved from an early 'lizard-hipped' dinosaur.

Dinosaur finds

The first traces of dinosaurs in North America were found in the Triassic rocks of the Connecticut Valley in 1835. They were footprints, recording the passage of great, two-legged creatures 220 million years ago. Edward Hitchcock, Professor of Theology and Geology, and later President, in Amherst College in Massachusetts, described the footprints in 1848; concluding that enormous birds had made them. The first description of dinosaur bones from North America was made by Dr Joseph Leidy of the Academy of Natural Science in Philadelphia in 1856. He described dinosaur teeth from Montana and two years later the first skeleton of a North American dinosaur, (*Hadrosaurus* see p.147).

An immense wealth of dinosaurs was soon to be revealed in the American Mid-West, among the great Jurassic and Cretaceous deposits laid down over 65 million years ago. The driving force for their discovery lay in the rivalry between two leading paleontologists, both wealthy men: Othniel Charles Marsh, of Yale University, and Edward Drinker Cope, of the Academy of Natural Science in Philadelphia.

The first bones of dinosaurs that lived in the Late Jurassic, 150 million years ago, were discovered in 1877 in the Morrison Formation of Colorado, and later in Wyoming. Samples found their way to both Marsh and Cope, and the 'dinosaur wars' began. Rival teams of fossil hunters went west. Marsh financed six years of excavation at Como Bluff in Wyoming, where many bones were collected. Cope, too, sent parties to that region, as well as to Colorado.

The 'Age of the Ruling Reptiles' spanned the Jurassic and Cretaceous periods, when the great dinosaurs dominated the land, the pterosaurs ruled the skies, and the crocodiles flourished in the seas and rivers. The ancestor of all these reptiles was a small archosaur. With the exception of the crocodiles, all these ruling reptiles had perished by the end of the Cretaceous Period – the close of the Mesozoic Era. The birds probably evolved from among the theropod dinosaurs.

ORNITHISCHIANS

EROPODS   SAURISCHIANS

DINOSAURS

MEGALOSAURS   AVES   THECODONTOSAURUS   PLATEOSAURUS   RIOJASAURUS   SAUROPODS   HETERODONTOSAURIDS   HYPSILOPHODONTIDS   IGUANODON   HADROSAURS   PACHYCEPHALOSAURS   CERATOPIANS   ANKYLOSAURS   STEGOSAURS

From these Late Jurassic sites, many now-famous dinosaurs were described by both men, including *Allosaurus* (see p.117), *Ceratosaurus* (see p.106), *Camarasaurus* (see p.128), *Diplodocus* and *Apatosaurus* (popularly known as *Brontosaurus,* see pp.130–131), *Camptosaurus* (see p.142) and *Stegosaurus* (see p.154).

The richest treasure house of dinosaurs was found in the Late Cretaceous rocks of Montana and Colorado, laid down toward the end of the Mesozoic Era, between 100 and 65 million years ago. Due to the rivalry between Marsh and Cope many creatures were discovered, among them *Ornithomimus* (see p.109), *Nodosaurus* (see p.158) and *Triceratops* (see p.166).

Canada, too, has contributed its share of dinosaurs to the world's museums (see p.305). The Late Cretaceous deposits of Red Deer River Valley, Alberta, were discovered and explored cooperatively by parties from both the American Museum of Natural History in New York, and the National Museum of Canada and the Royal Ontario Museum. The valley yielded a rich variety of dinosaurs, especially during the years 1910 to 1917, among them the tyrannosaur *Albertosaurus* (see p.119), the duckbilled dinosaur *Corythosaurus* (see p.151) and the horned ceratopian *Styracosaurus* (see p.166).

The Gobi Desert of Outer Mongolia, central Asia, was first explored by expeditions from the American Museum of Natural History during the years 1922 to 1925. Ironically, it was the search for fossil humans, rather than fossil reptiles, that led to the exploration of the region, which yielded an array of Late Cretaceous beasts, including *Protoceratops* together with its nests and eggs (see p.164), and the saurischian dinosaurs *Oviraptor* (one specimen preserved with a clutch of *Protoceratops'* eggs, see p.100), *Velociraptor* and *Saurornithoides* (see p.111).

Dinosaurs have been found in South America, Africa, Australia, New Zealand and Antarctica. The dinosaur localities of the southern hemisphere are increasingly important, with remarkable new finds being made in Argentina.

Perhaps the most famous African locality is Tendaguru in Tanzania, East Africa, where a wealth of Late Jurassic dinosaurs was found, similar to those of the Morrison Formation in the western USA.

Another African site, discovered in 1987 in Niger, south of the Sahara, promises to be a rich source of dinosaur remains. Initial work has unearthed the bones of *Camarasaurus*, one of the giant, plant-eating sauropods, and a giant tyrannosaur *Carcharodontosaurus*.

A worldwide distribution

Although the dinosaurs of the southern hemisphere are less well-known than those of the north, there is little doubt that, in reality, they were just as diverse. Both 'lizard-' and 'bird-hipped' dinosaurs evolved in the Triassic, when all the continents of the

world were still joined together in one super-landmass called Pangaea. Any land animal, including dinosaurs, could have spread throughout the world.

The continents were still joined throughout the Jurassic, and it was not until the Late Cretaceous that there is evidence of different, isolated dinosaur faunas. By then, there were two separate areas of land in the northern hemisphere – Euramerica

DINOSAUR HIPS

When dinosaurs evolved an upright, two-legged posture, they had to evolve a new attachment site for the muscles that swung the powerful hindlimbs forward. Lizard-hipped dinosaurs evolved a downward and forward extension of the pubic bone to which the muscles attach. In bird-hipped dinosaurs, the muscles were attached to either a forward extension of the ilium, or, in later types, to a new 'pre-pubic' extension of the pubis.

LIZARD-HIPPED DINOSAUR (*MASSOPONDYLUS*)

BIRD-HIPPED DINOSAUR (*MONTANOCERATOPS*)

and Asiamerica (see p.11). For some reason, many new types of Late Cretaceous dinosaur evolved in Asiamerica, including the hadrosaurs, ornithomimids, troodontids, tyrannosaurs and protoceratopsids. As a result, older types of dinosaur, such as the iguanodonts, persisted for longer in Euramerica, safe from the competition of their new relatives.

About 300 genera of dinosaur have so far been described, of which about 55 percent are 'lizard-hipped' saurischians, and the rest are 'bird-hipped' ornithischians. Only 7 percent of known dinosaurs come from Triassic rocks (nearly all saurischians), and 28 percent from Jurassic rocks. The remaining 65 percent come from Cretaceous rocks, and three-quarters of these have been found only in the Late Cretaceous. It is significant that at the end of the Cretaceous, the flowering plants underwent an explosive evolution, diversifying into many new types which adapted to niches all over the world. This new food source may well have led to the evolution of new dinosaur types.

Warm-blooded dinosaurs?

Biologists have long assumed that dinosaurs, like the living reptiles and the ancestral amphibians, were cold-blooded (ectothermal). But recently it has been suggested that they may have been warm-blooded (endothermal), like modern birds and mammals.

Cold-blooded animals rely mainly on the sun for heat and energy. Warm-blooded animals, in contrast, rely on energy from food. There are a number of lines of evidence which are claimed to support the argument for dinosaurs being warm-blooded (ectotherms). Measurements from their trackways has suggested that some were very active predators. Estimated running speeds of up to 40 km/h (30mph) suggest high metabolic rates. Dinosaur remains have been found within the Alaskan Arctic Circle of Cretaceous times and normally only warm blooded animals can tolerate such conditions. The detailed internal structure of dinosaur bones is in many ways more like that of mammals than reptiles. But, this may reflect a fast rate of growth.

It is possible that dinosaurs were intermediate – neither typically cold nor warm-blooded. Some may have been warm-blooded, but the ratio of body volume to surface area of some of the larger ones would have kept them at fairly constant temperatures anyway.

Mass-extinction of the dinosaurs

The disappearance of the dinosaurs worldwide at the end of the Mesozoic Era is the best-known mass-extinction event of the prehistoric world. But other extinctions took place at or about the same time. The flying pterosaurs, and also the marine ichthyosaurs, plesiosaurs and mosasaurs, all disappeared at or near the end of the Cretaceous. And several marine invertebrate groups suffered the same fate – ammonites, certain bivalves and many tiny organisms of the plankton.

Since modern methods of dating rocks are accurate only to within a few hundreds of thousands of years, it is difficult to be certain whether the terrestrial and marine extinctions of the Cretaceous took place at the same time. It seems that the vertebrate extinctions happened gradually. For example, the ichthyosaurs became extinct before the end of the Cretaceous, while the plesiosaurs, pterosaurs and dinosaurs may have been becoming less common toward the end of that period. These facts suggest some gradual change in the environment taking place worldwide, rather than the popular notion of a cataclysmic event that wiped out huge numbers of creatures.

Sea levels dropped comparatively rapidly during the Late Cretaceous. As a result, the average air temperature dropped, and the climate became more variable worldwide. This could have been the cause of the gradual decline of the pterosaurs and dinosaurs, especially if the dinosaurs depended on an equable environment to maintain their body temperature.

In contrast, the extinction of many types of microscopic marine invertebrates seems to have happened suddenly and simultaneously, at the end of the Cretaceous. They disappeared at precisely the time that the rocks show abnormally high concentrations of several normally rare metals, such as iridium, osmium and rhodium. This enriched layer has been found in some 50 localities, ranging from North America and Europe to New Zealand, and in deep-sea sediments of the Pacific.

The American scientists Luis and Walter Alvarez pointed out that these metals are present in the same proportions as in meteorites. In 1980 they suggested that a great meteorite, some 6ml/10km in diameter, hit Earth at the end of the Cretaceous Period, some 65 million years ago. An intense search for the impact crater ensued, and in 1991 a crater of the right order of size and age was located, buried under nearly half a mile (1 km) of younger sediments at Chicxulub in the Yucatan Peninsula, Mexico. Establishing the size of the crater and how much rock had been excavated by the impact proved difficult, but was eventually achieved by geophysical measurement in 1998.

The Chicxulub meteorite made a hole 5ml/12km deep and 60ml/100km wide and blasted some 38,400 cuml/50,000cukm of pulverized rock into the atmosphere. The rock dust, CO_2 and SO_2 released would have had a considerable impact on global weather; it may have produced an initial cooling followed by marked warming, and caused a breakdown in the food chain. This could well have finally driven vulnerable species, including dinosaurs, to extinction. The regional effect was devastating to the Americas. A tidal wave over half a mile (1 km) high swept all life from coastal areas and wildfire burned the forests further inland and all that lived in them. It probably took more than a million years for conditions to return to normal.

EARLY RULING REPTILES

INFRACLASS ARCHOSAUROMORPHA

Cladistic analysis has suggested that the amniotes can be divided into three groups – the diapsids and anapsids, which form the Eureptilia, and the synapsids. In the Late Permian, around 250 million years ago, diapsid reptiles divided into two groups that subsequently became of particular importance. The archosauromorphs (a name which means 'ruling reptile forms') gave rise to the dinosaurs, crocodilians and birds, and the lepidosauromorphs, which in turn led to the snakes and lizards.

The archosauromorphs include the rhynchosaurs, prolacertiformes and archosaurs. Of these, the prolacertiformes arose during mid Permian times, the archosaurs at the end of the Permian and the other two groups arose during the Triassic Period.

Most archosauromorphs were well-adapted land-living animals. The long legs of these creatures tended to be placed more directly under the body than is common in other reptiles, which made them more stable and faster moving. Associated with this evolutionary change were improvements in the feet, particularly the articulation of the ankle joints and flexibility of the first digit ('big toe') of the archosaur foot which improved their locomotion.

The Prolacertiformes include the carnivorous protosaurs (the earliest-known members of this infraclass), such as *Protosaurus* of late Permian times, and the plant-eating rhynchosaurs are represented by *Hyperodapedon* from the late Triassic Period.

The most important of the early archosauromorph groups were the Archosauria. The Triassic evolution of the Archosaurs was to change the history of life on land for nearly 200 million years. From the Archosauria radiated the dinosaurs, crocodiles, the flying pterosaurs and birds.

NAME	*Hyperodapedon*
TIME	Late Triassic
LOCALITY	Asia (India) and Europe (Scotland)
SIZE	4 ft / 1.3 m long

Hyperodapedon (below) was a member of the rhynchosaur group of early reptiles and was especially common in South America and Africa. These creatures were all heavy, barrel-shaped plant-eaters, which thrived from the Middle to Late Triassic. They were the most abundant reptiles of the day.

The success, though short-lived, of *Hyperodapedon* and its rhynchosaur relatives can be attributed to their teeth. There were two broad tooth plates on each side of the upper jaw. Each tooth plate was well-equipped with several rows of teeth, and a groove ran down the middle. The two single tooth rows of the animal's lower jaws fitted into this groove when the mouth was closed, to give a strong chopping action which was well-suited to the animal's vegetarian diet.

Rhynchosaurs would have feasted on seed ferns, which were abundant everywhere during the Triassic Period. But these plants died out at the end of that period, and were replaced by conifers. Rhynchosaurs died out too, and their herbivorous ecological niche was taken by the newly evolved, plant-eating dinosaurs. The 'Age of Ruling Reptiles' had begun.

ORDER PROLACERTIFORMES

Prolacertifomes appeared during the Mid Permian Period, but became abundant in the Triassic. Initially they looked like large lizards with long necks, but some developed this tendency to an extreme. They shared many characteristics with archosaurs, such as a long snout and narrow skull and backward curving teeth.

NAME *Protorosaurus*

TIME Late Permian

LOCALITY Europe (Germany)

SIZE up to 6 ft 6 in/2 m long

This lizard-type reptile is the earliest known archosauromorph. *Protosaurus* inhabited the deserts of Europe toward the end of the Permian Period, about 250 million years ago.

Protosaurus would have been an agile, speedy animal. Its long legs were tucked in under its body, allowing it to chase after fast-moving prey – mainly insects. Its neck was made up of seven large and greatly elongated vertebrae.

NAME *Tanystropheus*

TIME Middle Triassic

LOCALITY Asia (Israel) and Europe (Germany and Switzerland)

SIZE 10 ft/3 m long

The long necks which are characteristic of the protorosaurs reached an extreme in this member of the group. *Tanystropheus'* neck was longer than its body and tail combined. Yet, only 10 vertebrae made up the neck – only three more than in *Protorosaurus* – but each bone was greatly elongated. In fact, when these neck bones were first discovered, they were initially thought to be leg bones.

The shape of *Tanystropheus'* shape is so bizarre and unlikely that some paleontologists believe that this creature would have been unable to support its extremely long neck on land and must have lived in water. But *Tanystropheus* shows no specific adaptations to an aquatic life.

Perhaps it lived on the shoreline, dipping its head into the water after fish or shellfish, and crushing them with its peg-like teeth.

SUPERORDER ARCHOSAURIA

The archosaurs were the most spectacular group of 'ruling reptiles'. They dominated life on Earth during the Mesozoic Era, reigning for more than 180 million years. Flying reptiles, the pterosaurs, ruled the skies (see pp.102–105); dinosaurs ruled the lands (see pp.106–169); and crocodiles – the only surviving archosaurs – invaded the seas and freshwaters (see pp.98–101).

These diverse creatures all shared a common feature – a diapsid skull, with two openings behind each eye (see p.61).

The earliest archosaurs appeared in the Late Permian, more than 250 million years ago. They evolved rapidly into many diverse forms through the Triassic and became extinct by the end of that period. Their evolutionary history was brief (less than 40 million years) but successful and from them arose the ancestors of the ruling reptiles. There were some short lived forms in the Early and Mid Triassic before a major split occurred. One line led to the crccodiles and the other to the dinosaurs and birds.

The remaining Triassic archosaurs that do not belong to either of these groups were previously grouped as the thecodontians but they are now known to be a paraphyletic group from different origins. These basal archosaurs include Early Triassic forms such as the proterosuchids, which took over carnivorous niches which had been occupied in the Permian by animals such as the gorgonopsids. *Euparkeria*, the little archosaur from the Mid Triassic of South Africa is sometimes placed in the orhithosuchids or regarded separately, but it marks the beginning of the first major development of the archosaurs. The rauisuchids, phytosaurs and stagenolepidids have been recently the characterized as basal crutotarsans and grouped with the crocodylomorphs.

These early archosaurs show a general evolutionary trend toward a more upright stance, with the hind limbs in particular being progressively brought in from their former, sprawling position at the side of the body to be oriented more directly beneath the body. This trend was eventually perfected in the ornithosuchians, which could walk upright on two legs.

EARLY RULING REPTILES CONTINUED

Family Proterosuchidae

The proterosuchians were the earliest of the archosaurs to appear, and they are known from Late Permian times in Russia (about 250 million years ago). Some proterosuchians were aquatic, crocodile-like animals, while other members of the family were fully adapted land-dwellers. They spread throughout the world during the Triassic Period and died out at the end of that period (about 210 million years ago).

NAME *Chasmatosaurus*
TIME Early Triassic
LOCALITY Africa (South Africa) and Asia (China)
SIZE 6 ft 6 in/2 m long

Chasmatosaurus (formerly named *Proterosuchus*) is the earliest well known archosaur. It looked rather like a modern crocodile, and probably behaved in much the same way. Its robust limbs, each with five toes, were angled out horizontally from the body, resulting in a sprawling, lizard-like gait.

Although *Chasmatosaurus* could walk on land, it probably spent most of its time in rivers, swimming after its fish prey using sinuous movements of the long tail and body. Its jaws were well-equipped with sharp, backwardly curved teeth, each set in a shallow socket, the upper jaw turned down sharply at its tip. There were also teeth on the palate – a primitive feature, lost in later archosaurs.

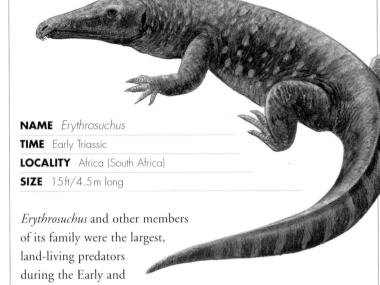

NAME *Erythrosuchus*
TIME Early Triassic
LOCALITY Africa (South Africa)
SIZE 15 ft/4.5 m long

Erythrosuchus and other members of its family were the largest, land-living predators during the Early and Middle Triassic Period (about 250–230 million years ago). Some of them reached a length of 16 ft/5 m. They must have exerted a profound, selective pressure on the evolution of other terrestrial reptiles. For example, several new types of thecodontian with protective body armour appeared around this time, such as the aetosaurs (Family Stagenolepididae) and phytosaurs.

Erythrosuchus had a large head, up to 3 ft 3 in/1 m long, and its powerful jaws were filled with sharp, conical teeth. It was a top predator which probably preyed on the large herbivorous dicynodonts of the time.

Its legs were held rather more directly beneath its bulky body than those of the sprawling *Chasmatosaurus*, suggesting that this active predator could move more effectively on land.

Family Rauisuchidae

This group of crocodile-like archosaurs were the major carnivorous land-dwellers of the time, some of them growing up to 20 ft/6 m long. They evolved in the Mid-Triassic and survived to the end of that period. They are known from the Americas, East Africa and western Europe.

Not only were the hind limbs of rauisuchids held more directly beneath the body, but an effective ankle joint had been developed, together with a heel that enhanced the leverage and flexure of the feet during walking.

NAME *Ticinosuchus*
TIME Middle Triassic
LOCALITY Europe (Switzerland)
SIZE 10 ft/3 m long

The back of this medium-sized rauisuchiad was lightly armoured, with a double row of small, bony plates; the long tail was also armoured, above and below. From the structure of the hips, and the ball-and-socket joints with which the thigh bones (femurs) connect, paleontologists can tell that the hind legs of *Ticinosuchus* were held almost directly beneath its body, unlike the sprawl position in earlier archosaurs.

In addition, the ankle joints of *Ticinosuchus* and other rauisuchids had become adapted for walking on land, and part of one of the foot bones had developed into a heel. This was an important innovation, since a strong tendon (the equivalent of our Achilles tendon) could attach to the heel, and serve as a lever to flex the foot.

Until the development of the heel, it had been the fifth, or outer, foot bone (metatarsal), together with the long fifth toe, that helped to lever the foot off the ground. Animals with heels could afford to reduce the length of the fifth toe. In some, it was lost completely; in others, it was shortened so that it did not reach the ground at all.

Family Phytosauridae

The phytosaurs were aquatic carnivores that are known only from the Late Triassic Period (about 210 million years ago).

With their heavily armoured, crocodile-like bodies, up to 16 ft/5 m long, it is likely that the phytosaur family were the dominant predators in the rivers of the northern hemisphere during this period.

Family Phytosauridae represents a classic case of parallel evolution with the true crocodiles; both types of reptile are descended from the same ancestral archosaur stock, and each assumed independently the same general structure in response to the same way of life and environmental factors. They differed from the crocodiles in having nostrils above the eyes instead of at the tip of the snout.

NAME *Rutiodon*
TIME Late Triassic
LOCALITY Europe (Germany and Switzerland) and North America (Arizona, New Mexico, North Carolina and Texas)
SIZE 10 ft/3 m long

Rutiodon (below) was a typical member of the phytosaur family. Its back, flanks and tail were heavily armoured with bony plates. It had a long snout like a modern gavial (a modern crocodile found only in Indian rivers), and its jaws were filled with sharp teeth, which would have been ideal tools for catching and eating fish. *Rutiodon* probably also ate other reptiles, since their remains have been found preserved in the body cavities of some fossilized phytosaurs.

Rutiodon and its relatives bore a striking resemblance to modern-day crocodiles. However, the immediate feature that distinguishes the *Rutiodon* from modern crocodiles is the position of the nostrils. In phytosaurs, the nostrils were elevated on a bony bump set far back on the animals' snout, near the eyes. However, in modern crocodiles the nostrils are positioned at the tip of the snout.

EARLY RULING REPTILES CONTINUED

Family Stagenolepididae

Unlike all their archosaur relatives, the stagenolepidids, or aetosaurs, as they are more commonly known, were plant-eating archosaurs. They had small, leaf-shaped teeth, and their deep, bulky bodies were encased in a heavy, bony armour. Looking like short-snouted crocodiles, aetosaurs were an offshoot from the main archosaur line, and are known only from the Late Triassic of Europe and North and South America.

NAME *STAGONOLEPIS*
TIME Late Triassic
LOCALITY Europe (Scotland)
SIZE 10 ft/3 m long

The deep body of *Stagonolepis* is typical of the herbivorous aetosaurs, and was developed to accommodate the longer intestines needed to digest plant food. A slow-moving browser, *Stagonolepis* also needed its heavy body armour to protect itself from attack by its agile, carnivorous, thecodontian relatives.

Stagonolepis had a small head for its size, only 10 in/25 cm out of a total length of 10 ft/3 m. It had no teeth at the front of its foreshortened jaws, but the peg-like teeth at the back would have dealt effectively with tough plants such as horsetails, ferns and the newly evolved cycads. The snout was flattened and almost pig-like, a good shape for rooting in the undergrowth.

NAME *Desmatosuchus*
TIME Late Triassic
LOCALITY North America (Texas)
SIZE 16 ft/5 m long

This large North American aetosaur had particularly heavy body armour. Quadrangular plates covered its back and tail and part of its belly, while long spines, up to 18 in/45 cm long, projected from its shoulders. It had a small head, pig-like snout and weak, peg-like teeth suited to plant-eating.

Family Ornithosuchidae

Paleontologists are undecided about the relation of ornithosuchids to dinosaurs. They share some characteristics of the limbs, but in other ways are closer to crocodiles and are therefore placed with them in the Crurotarsi. They are known from the Late Triassic in Scotland and South America.

NAME *Euparkeria*
TIME Early Triassic
LOCALITY Africa (South Africa)
SIZE up to 2 ft/60 cm long

The powerful hind legs and long tail that had evolved in the ancestral archosaurs gave rise to a new stance in their descendants, the ornithosuchians. *Euparkeria* was an early member of this group. It was a small, slimly built creature, with light bony plates down the centre of its back and tail. The hind legs were longer than the forelegs by about one-third.

Although it spent most of its time on all-fours, this ornithosuchid was capable of rising up on its hind legs to run away from danger. Its long tail, which made up about half of the total body length, would have been stretched out behind to balance it at the hips as it ran. This two-legged (bipedal) stance was to become the norm among the carnivorous dinosaurs that made their first appearance at the end of the Triassic (see pp.106–109).

Euparkeria's skull was large, but its weight was reduced by several wide openings between the bones. Its teeth were well-suited to a carnivorous diet – long and sharp, curved slightly backward and serrated along the edges.

NAME *Ornithosuchus*

TIME Late Triassic

LOCALITY Europe (Scotland)

SIZE 13 ft / 4 m long

At one time, *Ornithosuchus* was regarded by some paleontologists as a primitive dinosaur. However, it is now thought to be more closely related to the crocodiles.

One feature of *Ornithosuchus* that led to its misidentification as an early dinosaur was its stance. This was certainly dinosaur-like – its hind legs were held vertically beneath its body, a position that allowed it to walk upright. Moving about on all-fours was probably its more usual method of locomotion, however; the faster upright stance would have been reserved for a speedy escape in case of emergency, as with *Euparkeria*.

The primitive features of *Ornithosuchus* include a double row of bony plates down its back; a short, broad pelvis, which was attached to the backbone by a weak arrangement of only three vertebrae; and five toes on each hind foot. However, its skull is advanced, and strikingly similar in structure to that of the large theropods, such as *Tyrannosaurus*.

NAME *Lagosuchus*

TIME Middle Triassic

LOCALITY South America (Argentina)

SIZE 1 ft / 30 cm long

The diminutive *Lagosuchus* and its relatives are the most dinosaur-like of all the known ornithosuchids. The resemblance is based mainly on the structure of its hip bones and ankle joints and on the long, slim hind legs, in which the shin bones are almost twice the length of the thigh bones.

This structure of the leg bones is a feature of fast-running animals, which can be particularly well-seen in the bipedal dinosaurs. Like the other ornithosuchids, *Lagosuchus* would have been capable of rising up on its hind legs. It is no longer believed, however, as it once was, that *Lagosuchus* is the most likely ancestor of the dinosaurs.

Family Uncertain

The single species *Longisquama insignis*, first described in 1970, has some unusual features, which distinguish it from any named family. Paleontologists are reluctant to name a new family for a single species and would rather wait for further information and specimens before making a taxonomic judgement.

NAME *Longisquama*

TIME Early Triassic

LOCALITY Asia (Turkestan)

SIZE 6 in / 15 cm long

A curious, lizard-like creature, *Longisquama* was a tiny ornithosuchid. It cannot be placed in any of the known suborders or families of the group. Its body was covered in overlapping, keeled scales. A remarkable row of tall scales, stiff and V-shaped in cross-section, rose from the back. Their function is unknown. They could have been display structures, used either for attracting a mate or for warning away rivals. Other suggestions are that they could have been used for gliding through the air, or as heat-exchange devices; they may even have been an early stage in the evolution of feathers.

CROCODILES

SUPERORDER CROCODYLOMORPHA

The crocodiles and their close relatives are the only representatives of the archosaurs, or ruling reptiles, alive today. Remarkably consistent in structure throughout their evolution, crocodiles have changed little since they first appeared in Mid-Triassic times, some 230 million years ago.

The crocodiles probably evolved from an ornithosuchian type of archosaur (see pp.96–97). Although modern crocodiles are more at home in water than on land, they evolved as small, terrestrial carnivores, capable of running upright on their long, slim hind legs, unlike the short limbs of their modern relatives.

Crocodiles have long, low, massive skulls, to resist the pressure created by the powerful snapping of their jaws. The muscles attach far back on the skull, allowing the jaws to open wide. A secondary palate of bone separates the mouth from the nasal passages, allowing the animal to breathe while eating.

Family Sphenosuchidae

The sphenosuchians are the earliest known crocodiles, making their appearance in the middle of the Triassic Period. So similar are they to the lightly built ornithosuchians (see p.96–97) that they were long regarded as belonging to that group. These early crocodiles were built for a life on land.

NAME *Gracilisuchus*
TIME Middle Triassic
LOCALITY South America (Argentina)
SIZE 1 ft/30 cm long

This tiny creature was classified with the ornithosuchians until the early 1980s. Like them, it had a lightly built body and a disproportionately large head, and it could run erect on its slim hind legs. However, the structure of its skull, neck vertebrae and ankle joints place it firmly among the crocodiles.

Gracilisuchus was a well-adapted land animal, protected by a double row of bony plates that interlocked down the length of its backbone, to the tip of the tail. It probably chased after small lizards on its long hind legs, despatching them in its powerful jaws, armed with sharp, recurved teeth.

Family Saltoposuchidae

Although true crocodiles did not appear until the early Jurassic, there were some close relatives in the Late Triassic Period, all of which are now placed in the Superorder Crocodylomorpha. Some of these close relatives, such as the saltoposuchids, appear at first to be most unlike crocodiles. However, they do have in common some important features which are considered to be diagnostically crocodilian.

NAME *Terrestrisuchus*
TIME Late Triassic
LOCALITY Europe (Wales)
SIZE 10 in/50 cm long

Terrestrisuchus was smaller and much more delicately built than *Gracilisuchus* (left). Its body was also shorter, with extremely long, slim limbs and greatly elongated foot bones in the hind legs. The tail was almost twice the length of the body and head combined. Its head was more crocodile-like – longer and lower – than that of its earlier relative.

From its light build – almost like that of a greyhound, although it was completely unrelated to that mammal – it seems that *Terrestrisuchus* must have sprinted over the dry landscape of Late Triassic Europe, snapping up insects and small lizards in its elongated jaws. It probably ran mostly on four legs, but could easily have risen upright to move even faster, using its long tail to help it keep its balance.

ORDER CROCODYLIA

Today, crocodiles are a small group of eight genera, comprising crocodiles, alligators and gavials, all found in the tropics – a tiny vestige of a once abundant and highly successful group. Marine forms were particularly successful in the Jurassic when they competed with other marine reptiles. In the Tertiary, some became fully terrestrial, competing with mammals and giant birds for the top carnivore niches in South America.

Family Protosuchidae

Although their skulls were slightly more crocodile-like in appearance, the protosuchians were long-legged land-dwellers like the sphenosuchians. Some may have developed a secondary palate separating the mouth and nasal passages, but made of a fleshy membrane, not the bony palate of later crocodiles.

NAME *Protosuchus*

TIME Early Jurassic

LOCALITY North America (Arizona)

SIZE 3 ft 3 in / 1 m long

This terrestrial crocodile's skull was more crocodile-like than that of the earlier sphenosuchids. The short jaws broadened out at the base of the snout into a fairly wide area at the back of the skull, providing a large surface to which the jaw muscles could attach. This increased the gape and the force with which the jaws could be closed. A pair of canine-like teeth at the front of the lower jaw fitted into notches on either side of the upper jaw when the mouth was closed – as seen in modern crocodiles.

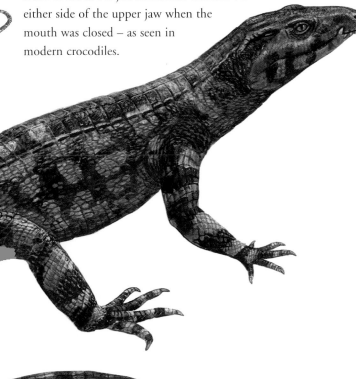

DIVISION MESOEUCROCODYLIA

Most of the fossil crocodiles belong to this group, though they include some that are not closely related, which is recognized by their being placed in this division along with the eusuchians.

They evolved in the Early Jurassic, most probably from the protosuchids (left); the last known member of the division dates from the relatively recent Miocene Epoch, 15 million years ago. Most of them were either fully adapted land-dwellers, like their predecessors, or semi-aquatic in their habits.

One terrestrial family, the sebecids, inhabited South America during Early Tertiary times. Their teeth were saw-edged and compressed into long blades, like those of large carnosaur dinosaurs. This has led some paleontologists to speculate that they were the dominant predators of the day, since no large, carnivorous mammal had reached South America at the time.

Only four families had a fully aquatic lifestyle, of which the teleosaurs and metriorhynchs are probably the best known.

NAME *Teleosaurus*

TIME Early Jurassic

LOCALITY Europe (France)

SIZE 10 ft / 3 m long

Teleosaurus was a member of one of the four families of Mesozoic crocodiles that adopted the sea as their home and shared the seas of the world with the ichthyosaurs and plesiosaurs throughout the Jurassic Period and into the Cretaceous. It probably looked similar to the modern gavial of India's northern rivers.

The body of this ancient marine crocodile was long and slim, its back heavily armoured like that of a modern crocodile. Its powerful jaws were tremendously narrow and elongated, in comparison with those of its land-living relatives, and lined with numerous sharp teeth. These interlocked when the mouth was closed, to form an ideal trap for catching slippery fish or squid.

Teleosaurus' forelegs were particularly short – only half the length of the hind legs – and were probably held flat against the flanks during swimming to give a more hydrodynamic shape. Sinuous movements of the body and long, narrow tail would have moved *Teleosaurus* rapidly through water, like a modern aquatic lizard.

CROCODILES CONTINUED

NAME *Bernissartia*

TIME Early Cretaceous

LOCALITY Europe (Belgium and England)

SIZE 2 ft/60 cm long

NAME *Metriorhynchus*

TIME Middle to Late Jurassic

LOCALITY Europe (England and France) and South America (Chile)

SIZE 10 ft/3 m long

This crocodile was tiny in comparison with its relatives. It lived along the shores of the shallow Wealden Lake that stretched from southeast England into Belgium during Early Cretaceous times, some 130 million years ago.

Bernissartia led a semi-aquatic life, judging by the two types of teeth in its jaws. Those at the front were long and pointed, as if for catching fish, while those at the back were broad and flat, as if for crushing shellfish, or even the bones of dead animals.

Metriorhynchus and other members of the metriorhynch family were the most specialized of all the aquatic crocodiles. They had dispensed with the heavy back armour of their relatives, because such protection was unnecessary in their aquatic environment.

The loss of the armour had the additional advantage of making them more manoeuvrable, allowing the sinuous movements of the body which were necessary for swimming. *Metriorhynchus'* limbs were transformed into paddle-like flippers, the hind pair longer than the front pair. And their tails had developed a large, fish-like fin which could be moved from side to side in order to propel the animal smoothly through the water. This fin was supported by the sharply downturned tip of the animal's backbone. Exactly the same adaptations were developed independently by the ichthyosaurs (see pp.78–81), a group of fish-like reptiles.

Geosaurus was another member of the metriorhynch family, found in Late Jurassic and Early Cretaceous sediments in South America and Europe. It was about the same length as its relative *Metriorhynchus*, but even more streamlined in shape. One excellent fossil specimen of *Geosaurus* from southern Germany was outlined by a fine film of carbon. This provided invaluable information for paleontologists, showing the shape of the fleshy limbs in life. The front flippers were considerably shorter than the hind pair, and the tail fin was particularly large. The tip of the backbone bent even more sharply into the lower lobe than did the backbone of *Metriorhynchus*.

SUBORDER EUSUCHIA

This group of true crocodiles includes the 21 living species of modern crocodile, the seven species of alligator and caiman, and the single species of gavial. Crocodiles and alligators appeared in their modern forms in the Late Cretaceous. But their ancestors evolved at least 80 million years before that, in the Late Jurassic. They probably descended from among the semi-aquatic mesoeucrocodylians.

The eusuchians were once a much more abundant and widespread group than they are today. They lived in the swamps, rivers and lakes of the late Mesozoic Era. They were contemporaries of the great dinosaurs, and most probably preyed on them when they strayed too close to the water's edge.

Sturdy, well-armoured bodies, massive heads, powerful jaws and meat-shearing teeth – these weapons of the crocodile would have been used to overpower even a large dinosaur. Once it had been dragged into the water, the crocodile could have held it under in a vice-like grip; the secondary bony palate allowed the crocodile to open its mouth without inhaling water.

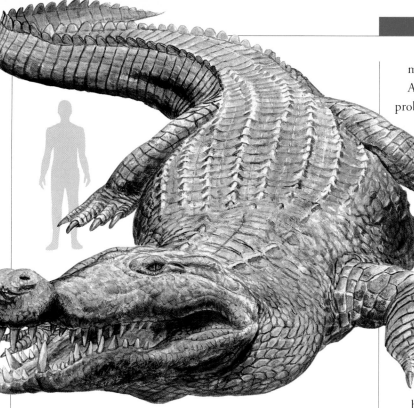

mouths underwater to seize prey without swallowing water. Also in common with its modern counterparts, *Deinosuchus* probably swallowed stones. These would have remained in the stomach to act as stabilizing ballast in the water.

Some paleontologists, however, dispute this account of *Deinosuchus'* lifestyle. They suggest that *Deinosuchus* was smaller than the measurements of it skull seem to suggest and was in fact a short-bodied, long-legged predator that lived on land. Until more fossil remains of the skeleton are found, the way of life of this gargantuan crocodile will remain uncertain.

Gigantic crocodiles were not confined to the Mesozoic Era. *Rhamphosuchus* was a gavial known from the Pliocene deposits of India. Only part of its jawbone has been found, but on the basis of this find it is estimated that this creature may have been the same size as *Deinosuchus*.

NAME	*Deinosuchus*
TIME	Late Cretaceous
LOCALITY	North America (Texas)
SIZE	possibly 49 ft/15 m long

Only the skull of this immense crocodile (above) has been found, and this alone measured more than 6 ft 6 in/2 m in length. Assuming *Deinosuchus* had the same body proportions as those of other crocodiles, its overall length is judged to be just under 50 ft/15.2 m – several times bigger than most of its relatives. The name *Deinosuchus* reflects this imposing size: it means 'terrible crocodile'. It is also sometimes known as *Phobosuchus*, meaning 'horror crocodile'.

Deinosuchus lived in the swamps of Texas toward the end of the Cretaceous Period. For food it probably ambushed passing dinosaurs, lying very still and grabbing its prey in the same way that the modern Nile crocodile seizes mammals and birds that come to the water's edge to drink. Unlike earlier crocodylians, all eusuchians such as *Deinosuchus* had a secondary bony roof (palate) to the mouth. This advanced feature is clearly advantageous to aquatic predators because it allows them to open their

NAME	*Pristichampsus*
TIME	Eocene
LOCALITY	Europe (Germany) and North America (Wyoming)
SIZE	10 ft/3 m long

A number of heavily armoured eusuchians lived on land during Tertiary times. *Pristichampsus* (below) was typical of these terrestrial crocodiles. It had long legs well-suited to running and its feet had hooves instead of claws – an additional adaptation to its terrestrial lifestyle. It would have fed on the abundant mammals that had recently evolved, and that had replaced the dinosaurs throughout the world.

Pristichampsus' fearsome teeth were well-suited to its carnivorous diet: they were sharp and flattened from side to side with saw-edges, rather like steak knives. Such teeth were almost identical to those of the largest carnivorous dinosaurs, such as *Tyrannosaurus* or *Albertosaurus*. When isolated teeth of *Pristichampsus* were found in Tertiary deposits, paleontologists at first thought they belonged to such theropod dinosaurs, and mistakenly took them as evidence that these great creatures had survived into Tertiary times.

FLYING REPTILES

ORDER PTEROSAURIA

The first group of vertebrates to take to the air as a way of life were the pterosaurs. These flying reptiles flew on 'wings' made of skin, which were attached along the length of the greatly elongated, fourth fingers of each hand, and rejoined the body at thigh-level.

These flying reptiles evolved in Late Triassic times, some 70 million years before the first-known bird, *Archaeopteryx*, appeared (see p.174). They thrived throughout the Jurassic and early part of the Cretaceous, diversifying into many forms, among them the largest flying creatures of all time. Then the group began to decline, its last members becoming extinct at the end of the Mesozoic Era. Pterosaur remains have been found all over the world, except in Antarctica, mostly in marine deposits.

There are two suborders of pterosaur (below). The earliest and most primitive types are the rhamphorhynchs; the later types include the more familiar flying reptiles – the pterodactyls.

SUBORDER RHAMPHORHYNCHOIDEA

The earliest-known pterosaurs were already advanced flyers by the Late Triassic Period, 190 million years ago. They flourished worldwide until their extinction at the end of the Jurassic.

NAME *Eudimorphodon*
TIME Late Triassic
LOCALITY Europe (Italy)
SIZE 2 ft 5 in/75 cm wingspan

Eudimorphodon is well-known from remains preserved in marine rocks of northern Italy. It was a typical rhamphorhynch, with a short neck and a bony tail, which made up about half the animal's length of 2 ft 4 in/70 cm. The head was large, but lightweight, owing to the two pairs of openings in its diapsid skull.

The membranous flaps of skin that made up *Eudimorphodon*'s wings were attached to the enormously elongated fourth finger of each hand. This finger was composed of four extra-long finger bones (phalanges), and was attached to the wrist by an elongated hand bone (metacarpal). The wings joined the body on each side at the thighs. Another small flying membrane also ran from the bones of each wrist to the base of the animal's neck.

Eudimorphodon was evidently an active flyer, capable of flapping its wings like a modern bird. The sternum, or breastbone, was developed into a broad, flattened plate, to which the powerful flight muscles attached, although the keel was low in comparison to the great keel of modern flying birds.

The long tail would have been held out rigidly during flight, its vertebrae lashed together by bony tendons into an inflexible rod, which counterbalanced the animal's comparatively heavy forequarters. As in many other rhamphorhynchs, there was a vertical, diamond, shaped flap at the tip of the tail, which most probably functioned as a rudder during flight.

The short jaws of *Eudimorphodon* were armed with two kinds of teeth. There were long, peg-like teeth at the front of the mouth, and short, broad teeth at the back. This pterosaur probably flew low over the sea, its large eyes trained on the surface to spot its fish prey.

NAME *Dimorphodon*
TIME Early Jurassic
LOCALITY Europe (England)
SIZE 4 ft/1.2 m wingspan

Dimorphodon had the disproportionately large head typical of the rhamphorhynchs. It measured about 8 in/20 cm long, about a quarter of the total body length. But it had a remarkable puffin-like shape, deep and narrow, unlike that of its relatives. There seems to be no structural reason for this, since the teeth show that the jaws were simple. Perhaps the shape of the head represents some type of display structure for territorial or courtship behaviour, like the showy heads of modern hornbills or toucans.

The walking method of pterosaurs has long been debated. Based on studies of *Dimorphodon*'s hips and legs, some paleontologists believe that they had an erect, bird-like stance, with the legs directly under the body, so that they could run on their toes quite quickly.

But finds of other types of pterosaur in 1986 indicate that perhaps *Dimorphodon* was an exception. These recent finds show that the upper leg bones splayed out sideways from the hips, which could only have resulted in a clumsy, sprawling, bat-like gait. It has been suggested that pterosaurs spent much of their time hanging from cliffs and branches, using their clawed fingers and toes to reach these vantage points, from which they could then launch themselves.

NAME *Rhamphorhynchus*
TIME Late Jurassic
LOCALITY Europe (Germany) and Africa (Tanzania)
SIZE 3 ft 3 in/1 m wingspan

This pterosaur is particularly well known because it was preserved in the fine-grained limestones of Solnhofen in southern Germany which also yielded specimens of the earliest known bird, *Archaeopteryx*, complete with impressions of its feathers (see p.174).

Similarly, the fine structure of *Rhamphorhynchus'* wings, made of membranous skin, has been preserved in these limestones. Microscopic study reveals that thin fibres ran from the front to the back of the wings, strengthening them – a comparable structure to the radiating fingers that support the wings of a modern bat.

Rhamphorhynchus had long, narrow jaws filled with sharp teeth that pointed outward, like the barbs on a fishing spear. Fish remains have been found in the crop and stomach of some specimens; its habit was probably to skim over the water, its long tail held out for stability, snapping up fish in its jaws.

NAME *Scaphognathus*
TIME Late Jurassic
LOCALITY Europe (England)
SIZE 3 ft 3 in/1 m wingspan

Scaphognathus, although similar to *Rhamphorhynchus* has a shorter head, long teeth and a

blunter tip to its jaws. It is not clear whether it was an insect feeder or a fish catcher.

The skull of one specimen of this typical rhamphorhynch is sufficiently well-preserved for the brain cavity to be studied by scientists. The size of the brain cavity revealed that *Scaphognathus* had a much larger brain in comparison to that of other similar-sized reptiles. Its brain was almost as large as that of a modern bird.

Paleontologists have studied the relative sizes of the areas of the brain that controlled various senses. They conclude that *Scaphognathus*, and presumably all its relatives, had excellent eyesight, but a poor sense of smell.

The cerebellum and associated lobes in the brain were highly developed, indicating agility of movement, which supports the theory that small pterosaurs made active flapping movements, like small modern birds.

NAME *Sordes*
TIME Late Jurassic
LOCALITY Asia (Kazakhstan)
SIZE 1 ft 6 in/50 cm wingspan

For a long time paleontologists have argued about whether carnivorous dinosaurs and pterosaurs were endothermic or warm-blooded. The active, predatory life of both these types of ruling reptile would suggest that they had a high metabolic rate, and could control their body temperature.

To support this theory, some paleontologists have suggested that both dinosaurs and pterosaurs were covered in an insulating layer of down or hair, as an aid to regulating their body temperature. In the case of dinosaurs, no such evidence has ever been found. However, a find in 1971 seemed to confirm the theory for the pterosaurs. A specimen of *Sordes pilosus* was discovered, southeast of the Ural Mountains. The creature's body appeared, from the impressions in the fine-grained deposits, to be covered in a pelt of dense fur while the tail and wings were naked.

Although the exact nature of the hair that covered *Sordes pilosus* has not yet been confirmed, presumably it is different from mammalian hair in detail, but performed a similar function – to act as an insulation and keep the body warm. Like bird feathers, the pterosaur hair probably evolved from reptile body scales.

FLYING REPTILES CONTINUED

NAME *Anurognathus*

TIME Late Jurassic

LOCALITY Europe (Germany)

SIZE 1 ft/30 cm wingspan

This comparatively small rhamphorhynch had a deep, narrow head with short jaws, which were filled with strong, peg-like teeth, suited to crushing and grinding. This structure could suggest that *Anurognathus* probably lived on a diet of insects.

Unlike other rhamphorhynchs, *Anurognathus* had a short tail, and this feature, combined with the small body size, would have made it highly manoeuvrable when in flight chasing after its fast-moving prey.

SUBORDER PTERODACTYLOIDEA

The pterodactyls are the most familiar of the flying reptiles. They were already established in Late Jurassic times, when their relatives, the rhamphorhynchs, became extinct. The pterodactyls continued through the Cretaceous, although only a few types survived to the end of that period.

These pterosaurs had the same general structure as the earlier rhamphorhynchs, but the tail was shorter, the neck longer and the skull more elongate.

The suborder Pterodactyloidea ranged from some of the smallest known pterosaurs to some of the largest flying vertebrates that ever lived.

NAME *Pterodactylus*

TIME Late Jurassic

LOCALITY Africa (Tanzania) and Europe (England, France and Germany)

SIZE up to 2 ft 5 in/75 cm wingspan

Pterodactylus demonstrates all of the typical pterodactyl features. It had a short tail and a long neck, and greatly elongated hand bones (metacarpals), which, with the long fourth fingers, supported the creature's broad wings.

Many species of *Pterodactylus* have been discovered, each species varying in the size and shape of the head. The species illustrated here, *Pterodactylus kochi*, had long, narrow jaws, which were lined with sharp teeth with which it devoured the fish that were its habitual prey.

NAME *Pterodaustro*

TIME Late Jurassic

LOCALITY South America (Argentina)

SIZE 4 ft/1.2 m wingspan

The most remarkable feature of *Pterodaustro* was its extraordinary jaws. They were elongated, slender and curved upward, accounting for most of the length of the creature's small skull, which measured about 9 in/23 cm long in total. The lower jaw bristled with thousands of long, fine, densely packed teeth and there were also tiny teeth in the upper jaw.

This pterosaur probably fed by skimming along the surface of the sea with its mouth open. As the water flowed through its jaws, the tiny animals of the plankton would have been enmeshed on the sieve-like teeth – a feeding method which can be compared with that of a modern baleen whale.

NAME *Cearadactylus*

TIME Early Cretaceous

LOCALITY South America (Brazil)

SIZE 13 ft/4 m wingspan

Cearadactylus' jaws were expanded at the tip (rather like those of the modern gavial crocodile), and several large teeth protruded around the edges. These teeth interlocked when the mouth was closed, forming a trap in which *Cearadactylus* could tightly hold its slippery fish prey, which was then easily dealt with by the numerous conical teeth that lined the jaws.

NAME *Dsungaripterus*

TIME Early Cretaceous

LOCALITY Asia (China)

SIZE 10ft/3m wingspan

Dsungaripterus had a peculiar bony crest running along its snout, and long, narrow jaws that curved upward to a fine point at the tip. These forceps-like jaws could have been used to prise shellfish off rocks or out of crannies on the seashore. The flattened teeth at the back of the jaws crushed the shells.

NAME *Pteranodon*

TIME Late Cretaceous

LOCALITY Europe (England) and North America (Kansas)

SIZE 23ft/7m wingspan

NAME *Quetzalcoatlus*

TIME Late Cretaceous

LOCALITY North America (Texas)

SIZE possibly up to 39ft/12m wingspan

Only fragments of this immense pterosaur have been discovered, found preserved in non-marine sediments, but they indicate a creature with enormously long, narrow wings and a weight of some 190lb/86kg. Should these findings prove to be correct, *Quetzalcoatlus* will have been the largest flying vertebrate of all time.

Quetzalcoatlus was probably an accomplished glider. It lived far inland, unlike its marine pterodactyl relatives, and would have used its immense wings to soar high above the ground on rising thermals. Like a modern vulture, its keen eyes would have spotted carrion from afar, and the long neck and toothless jaws could have probed far inside the carcase of a decaying dinosaur. However, the structure of the neck vertebrae shows that it was quite inflexible.

One of the longest-winged pterosaurs known, *Pteranodon* was most probably a glider. Its short, tailless body was relatively heavy, at about 37lb/17kg and would have been highly manoeuvrable in the air (like a modern, short-tailed fighter jet), and it probably relied on rising, hot-air currents to keep it aloft in soaring flight over the ocean.

The function of the great crest on the back of *Pteranodon*'s head, often as long as the skull itself, is unknown. It could have been an aid for flight, perhaps acting as a stabilizer. It may have been used to steer or brake, or it could simply have acted as an aerodynamic counterbalance to the heavy, elongated head.

The jaws were unusual for a pterosaur in being devoid of teeth. It is likely that *Pteranodon* fed like a modern pelican, scooping up fish in its jaws and swallowing them whole.

CARNIVOROUS DINOSAURS

SUBORDER THEROPODA

The great reptilian order of 'lizard-hipped' dinosaurs, the Saurischia, can be divided into two distinct groups (suborders) on the basis of what they ate. The plant-eaters belong to the Sauropodomorpha (see pp.122–133) and the flesh-eaters belong to the Theropoda.

INFRAORDER CERATOSAURIA

Traditionally, carnivorous theropods were subdivided (into infraorders) according to size: large, massively-built predators (see pp.114–121); medium-sized carnivores with a killing claw on each foot (see pp.110–113); and small, lightweight hunters, the ceratosaurs, with thin-walled, hollow bones that made up not only their tails, but most of their delicately built bodies. Their inter-relationships, however, are not at all clear, and different classifications have been produced.

Family Ceratosauridae

A small horn on the snout characterizes this family. They lived in North America and East Africa in Late Jurassic times. Similarities to megalosaurs have led to debate about their classification. They are sometimes included with the carnosaurs.

NAME *Ceratosaurus*
TIME Late Jurassic
LOCALITY North America (Colorado and Wyoming)
SIZE 20ft/6m long

The function of the horn on the snout is unclear. It may have been for defence or sexual display. *Ceratosaurus* was an active predator. Its massive jaws had sharp, curved teeth. The short arms had four clawed fingers. Each foot had three clawed toes. A row of bony plates forming a serrated crest down its back may have been a temperature control device.

Footprints of *Ceratosaurus* in the rocks of the Morrison Formation in the western USA suggest that they moved in groups, and may have cooperated to kill large prey.

Family Podokesauridae

The earliest and most primitive of the small carnivorous theropods were the podokesaurids, which were around for some 50 million years – from the Late Triassic to the Early Jurassic.

They were little different from their immediate ancestors, the early archosaur reptiles (see p.93). They were fast, active predators (possibly hunting in packs) and ran on long legs, with necks and long tails outstretched for balance. Arms were shorter than the legs. The head was wedge-shaped, with many sharp, pointed teeth in the jaws.

NAME *Procompsognathus*
TIME Late Triassic
LOCALITY Europe (Germany)
SIZE 4ft/1.2m long

This rapacious little beast was one of the earliest dinosaurs. It lived in the deserts of northern Europe during Triassic times. It would have chased its prey, which was small lizards and insects, on its long legs, running with only three of its four toes touching the ground.

Each hand had five fingers, which is a primitive feature, since the trend was toward fewer fingers and toes.

NAME *Saltopus*
TIME Late Triassic
LOCALITY Europe (Scotland)
SIZE 2ft/60cm long

Saltopus is one of the smallest and lightest dinosaurs discovered. It was similar to its relative *Procompsognathus*, but was much smaller and lighter. It was shorter than a domestic cat, and probably weighed as little as 2lb/1kg.

Saltopus still had the primitive feature of five fingers on each hand, although the fourth and fifth digits were tiny. But it was more advanced than *Procompsognathus* in its hip/backbone arrangement. Four of the spine's sacral vertebrae were fused to its hips (rather than only the three of its relative), and this formed a fairly solid anchor for its long, agile legs.

NAME *Coelophysis*

TIME Late Triassic

LOCALITY North America (Connecticut and New Mexico)

SIZE 8–10ft/2.4–3m long

The appearance of this comparatively large ceratosaur is well known from a find made in 1947 at Ghost Ranch in New Mexico. A number of skeletons of different sizes were massed together, about a dozen of them complete. There were very young individuals (maybe just hatched) and adults, ranging in length from 3–10ft/1–3m. The find suggests that they lived as a group, and must have all died at the same time.

This dinosaur must have been a ferocious hunter – it was built for speed. Its slender, hollow-boned body probably weighed less than 50lb/23kg. The neck, tail and legs were long and slim, the tail making up about half the body length. The long, narrow head was armed with many sharp teeth, each with a cutting, serrated edge. The bird-like feet had three walking toes with sharp claws. There were four fingers on each hand, though only three were strong enough to grasp prey.

Coelophysis probably roamed the upland forests, hunting in packs close to streams and lakes. Their prey would have included small, shrew-like mammals.

Two of the adult skeletons found in New Mexico contained the bones of tiny *Coelophysis* in their body cavities. Initially, paleontologists thought that this meant *Coelophysis* gave birth to live young, rather than laying eggs like most other reptiles. But the hip bones proved too narrow for this to be the case. The conclusion seems to be that this dinosaur was cannibalistic.

DIVISION MANIRAPTORA

This group of theropods shares a number of characteristics with the birds, especially, as the name suggests, in the hand. Indeed, in some modern classifications, the division includes the birds. Other features are also shared, such as modified tail vertebrae and a downwardly directed pubis.

Family not named

NAME *Protarchaeopteryx*

TIME Late Jurassic/Early Cretaceous

LOCALITY China

SIZE 3ft 3in/1m long

One of the most remarkable recent discoveries has been the Chinese find of small bipedal theropods that were feathered but could not fly. In skeletal structure *Protarchaeopteryx* is a typical coelurid dinosaur, but it is similar in form to the earliest true bird *Archaeopteryx*. *Protarchaeopteryx* has a short skull and teeth that retain primitive serrations. The skeleton has light hollow bird-like bones, a 'wishbone' and shorter forelimbs than hind limbs. The hand is elongate with sharp curved claws and the tail had 28 vertebrae. Most important, is the remarkable preservation of small down feathers (about 1 inch/2-3cm long) on the chest, tail and upper legs. Clusters of large symmetrical feathers (6in/10cm long) are attached to the end of the tail and the arms.

Family Coeluridae

Coelurids flourished worldwide from the Late Jurassic to the Early Cretaceous. They were lightweight, active predators, running about on long legs, and grasping prey with their three strong, clawed fingers on each hand.

NAME *Coelurus*

TIME Late Jurassic

LOCALITY North America (Wyoming)

SIZE 6ft 6in/2m long

Coelurus had a small, low head (only about 8in/20cm long), and the hollow, bird-like bones that characterized early dinosaurs. This active predator lived in the forests and swamps of North America. Its hands, with their three clawed fingers, were long and strong, to grasp the flesh of its small animal prey.

CARNIVOROUS DINOSAURS CONTINUED

Family Compsognathidae

There is only one known member of this family. It was a contemporary of the coelurids, and closely resembled them.

NAME *Compsognathus*

TIME Late Jurassic

LOCALITY (Germany and France)

SIZE 2 ft/60 cm long

This tiny, chicken sized, two-legged creature probably weighed up to 8 lb/3.6 kg. *Compsognathus* must have been a swift hunter. It was designed for speed with hollow bones; a long neck; a long tail for balance; short arms with two pincer-like fingers; slender, long-shinned legs; and bird-like feet with three clawed toes. (A tiny fourth toe pointed backwards.)

Compsognathus is similar to *Archaeopteryx* (see p.174). Both inhabited the Late Jurassic wooded islands and lagoons of southern Germany.

NAME *Sinosauropteryx*

TIME Late Jurassic/Early Cretaceous

LOCALITY China

SIZE 4 ft/1.2 m long

First discovered in the same region of China as the *Protarchaeopteryx* and *Caudipteryx* in 1996, *Sinosauropteryx* was the first of the feathered dinosaurs. This chicken sized theropod had a long tail, short and stout forelimbs with a very specialized hand. It was an effective predator; fossilized stomach remains include a lizard and a small mammal. For the first time, eggs have been found in the body cavity of a female dinosaur. The distribution of the fossil eggs suggests the presence of typically reptilian paired oviducts rather than a single avian-type oviduct.

A hair-like feathery fringe or crest some 2 in (4 cm) high

probably ran from the top of the skull to the tail. These protofeathers were nothing to do with flight and may have had a role in camouflage, display or species recognition.

Sinosauropteryx is closely related to and similar in appearance to the coelurid theropod *Compsognathus*.

Family Ornithomimidae

The so-called 'bird mimics' were a specialized offshoot of the coelurosaurs. About the same height and proportions as an ostrich, except with long arms with three powerful fingers, they seem to have had a similar lifestyle to that bird, hence the popular name of the group: 'ostrich dinosaurs'. They were widespread in North America and East Asia in Mid Cretaceous times, but seem to have died out before the end of that period.

All were large, long-legged sprinters. It has been estimated that some of them could run at speeds of 22–37 mph/35–60 kmph. They probably travelled the plains in groups, looking after their young while on the move.

Unlike other dinosaurs, instead of teeth the ornithomimids had a horny, bird-like beak, which was used to snap up small animals and insects. Other special features were exceptionally large eyes and big brains. Both features would have made them well-coordinated, efficient and intelligent hunters.

NAME *Elaphrosaurus*

TIME Late Jurassic

LOCALITY Africa (Tanzania)

SIZE 11 ft 6 in/ 3.5 m long

Only one skeleton of *Elaphrosaurus* has been found and, unfortunately, the skull was missing. Since the characteristic feature of the ornithomimids was that they had no teeth, it is impossible to say whether *Elaphrosaurus* belonged to this family. Loose teeth have been found in the same sediments, and these may belong to this dinosaur.

The rest of the creature's skeleton, however, seems to be intermediate in structure between the Jurassic coelurids and the later, Cretaceous ornithomimids. It may be that *Elaphrosaurus*, or a close relative, was the ancestor of the ostrich dinosaurs.

NAME *Dromiceiomimus*

TIME Late Cretaceous

LOCALITY North America (Alberta)

SIZE 11 ft 6 in / 3.5 m long

Ornithomimids had long, slender legs. The shin bone (tibia) was about 20 percent longer than the thigh bone (femur) – a sure sign of a sprinter. *Dromiceiomimus'* particularly long shins indicate that it was a very fast runner indeed.

Dromiceiomimus' brain cavity and eye sockets indicate that it had an exceptionally large brain, and huge eyes (proportionally larger than those of any modern land animal). *Dromiceiomimus* most probably hunted after dark, chasing small mammals and lizards through the deciduous woods in which it lived.

NAME *Ornithomimus*

TIME Late Cretaceous

LOCALITY North America (Colorado and Montana) and Asia (Tibet)

SIZE 11 ft 6 in / 3.5 m long

This ostrich dinosaur was the typical ornithomimid. It had a small, thin-boned head with a large brain cavity, no teeth and beak-like jaws.

Ornithomimus would have sprinted along with its body parallel to the ground, balanced by its extra-long, outstretched tail. This was kept stiff by strong ligaments that lashed the vertebrae together to form a rigid structure. Its neck would have curved upward in an S-bend, holding the head high allowing the best use of its large eyes. The arms dangled above the ground, with the dextrous, clawed fingers ready to grasp potential food.

Like other ornithomimids, *Ornithomimus* was probably omnivorous, eating leaves, fruit, insects and small animals, such as lizards and mammals. It may even have raided the nests of other dinosaurs and eaten their eggs. If caught by a parent, it would have employed its only means of defence – running away at a speed, it is estimated, of up to 30 mph / 50 kmph.

NAME *Struthiomimus*

TIME Late Cretaceous

LOCALITY North America (Alberta and New Jersey)

SIZE 11 ft 6 in / 3.5 m long

For years after its discovery in 1914, *Struthiomimus* (below) was thought to be the same animal as *Ornithomimus*. More research in 1972 showed that they were different, albeit in small ways.

Struthiomimus had longer arms than its relative, and stronger, curved claws on its fingers. It also existed slightly earlier than *Ornithomimus*, in the Late Cretaceous, and individuals probably hunted along riverbanks in more open country, in contrast to the dense cypress swamps and forests inhabited by *Ornithomimus*.

NAME *Gallimimus*

TIME Late Cretaceous

LOCALITY Asia (Mongolia)

SIZE 13 ft / 4 m long

This is the largest known ostrich dinosaur (below). It had a long snout ending in a broad, flat-tipped beak, and its spade-like hands seem poorly designed for grasping. Perhaps it was a specialist feeder, using its hands to unearth other dinosaurs' eggs.

In 1965, the remains of much larger bird-like dinosaurs were found in Late Cretaceous deposits in the Gobi Desert. The find, named *Deinocheirus*, consisted of a pair of shoulder bones and arms. Each arm measured 8 ft / 2.5 m from the shoulder to the tip of the three powerful, clawed fingers. Each claw bone was about 10 in / 25 cm long, and would have had an even longer nail. No other parts of the skeleton have been found, so it is impossible to say whether this animal was ain a family of its own until it can be classified with more certainty.

CARNIVOROUS DINOSAURS CONTINUED

Family Oviraptoridae

This small family of toothless theropods lived in Late Cretaceous times in eastern Asia, and were named the 'egg thieves' because of their suspected eating habits. They had large heads and short, deep beaks – quite unlike the long, narrow skulls and pointed beaks of their relatives, the ornithomimids, known as the 'ostrich dinosaurs' (see pp.108–109).

NAME *Oviraptor*

TIME Late Cretaceous

LOCALITY Asia (Mongolia)

SIZE 6 ft / 1.8 m long

This 'egg thief', after whom the family is named, had a distinctive skull, different from that of any other dinosaur. The head was almost parrot-like – short and deep, with a stumpy beak and no teeth. Powerful muscles operated the curved jaws, and gave the beak enough power to crush objects as hard as bones. There was also a small, horn-like crest above the snout.

Oviraptor's body, however, was typical of the small, flesh-eating maniraptorans (see pp.107–113). There were three grasping fingers on each hand, with strongly curved nails (each about 3 in/8 cm long). The animal walked upright on long, slender legs, each with three clawed toes. The body was balanced by the long, outstretched tail.

When the first specimen of *Oviraptor* was found in 1924, it was preserved with a clutch of eggs, which were thought to have been laid by the herbivorous dinosaur *Protoceratops* (see p.164). The inference was that the 'egg thief' had been caught in the act of raiding a nest and overcome by a sandstorm which entombed it. Now that an *Oviraptor* embryo has been found in one of the eggs, however, it appears that this dinosaur was completely misnamed. Seemingly it died while refusing to abandon its nest and unhatched eggs.

Family Dromaeosauridae

Members of this family must have been among the most fearsome predators of the Cretaceous Period in North America and Asia. They had the light, speedy body of a coelurosaur, and the large head of a carnosaur. Although they were no larger than many of the other meat-eaters around at the time, dromaeosaurs were formidable predators. They had a lethal weapon in the form of a large, sickle-shaped claw on the second toe of each foot. They were also armed with sharp, pointed teeth and clawed, grasping hands. They had large brains, and were intelligent enough to have hunted in packs. They shared these characteristics with the maniraptorans and birds.

NAME *Deinonychus*

TIME Early Cretaceous

LOCALITY North America (Montana)

SIZE 10–13 ft / 3–4 m long

The discovery of *Deinonychus* in 1964 in the claystones of Montana is one of the most exciting finds in the recent history of paleontology. Well-preserved skeletons revealed a dinosaur built for the chase and the kill – a fast, agile, intelligent predator.

Deinonychus had the lightweight body characteristic of the coelurosaurs, from which it probably evolved. It was, on average, 10 ft/3 m long, stood about 6 ft/1.8 m tall, and weighed some 150 lb/68 kg. The large head was equipped with many meat-shearing teeth, which were curved backward to allow great chunks of flesh to be torn from the prey. The arms were quite long for a theropod (though still much shorter than the legs), and hung from sturdy shoulder girdles. Each hand had three grasping fingers with long, strongly curved claws.

The legs were slender, with long shin bones and four clawed toes on each foot. The first toe was residual, as in most of the later theropods; the third and fourth toes carried the whole weight of the body.

But it was the remarkable adaptation of the second toe that gave *Deinonychus* its most offensive weapon – and its name, which means 'terrible claw'. The second toe on each foot had a large, sickle-shaped claw, 5 in/13 cm long. This would have been used like a dagger, to slash through a victim's flesh as *Deinonychus* stood on one leg and lashed out with the other.

NAME *Dromaeosaurus*

TIME Late Cretaceous

LOCALITY North America (Alberta)

SIZE 6ft/1.8m long

This dromaeosaur was the first of the sickle-clawed dinosaurs to be discovered, in Canada in 1914, and gave its name to the whole family. However, it was not until *Deinonychus* was unearthed in 1964 that the true nature and significance of *Dromaeosaurus* was assessed. Up until then, it was regarded as either a large coelurosaur or a small carnosaur. The new find made it apparent that the creature belonged to an intermediate group, and shared features with both types of theropod.

Dromaeosaurus is only known from its skull and some odd bones. But from such meagre finds, paleontologists can piece together a picture of a dinosaur smaller than *Deinonychus*, intelligent and agile, a rapacious predator with large, killing claws on its toes, though not as large as those of *Deinonychus*.

When *Deinonychus* ran, the sickle-clawed toes were flicked back and held clear of the ground. The body was held horizontally and balanced by the long, outstretched tail. This was kept rigid by bundles of bony rods that grew out from the vertebrae, and formed a supporting framework to stiffen the tail along most of its length. When *Deinonychus* was standing on one foot and attacking with the other, balance was essential and a tail like a ramrod would have made the pose easier to hold. The big brain (evident from the size of the skull's brain cavity) would have coordinated a finely-tuned nervous system to control such complex movements.

One of the finds in Montana revealed five complete skeletons of *Deinonychus* lying by the body of a large, plant-eating dinosaur called *Tenontosaurus*, which measured some 24ft/7.3m long (see p.140). This assemblage of bodies was most probably brought together by chance after death, washed down by a flood into a hollow or river basin.

But one could, perhaps, reconstruct the scene that may have taken place some 140 million years ago. A small pack of *Deinonychus* surrounded the plant-eater. Some may have leapt on its back, and held on with their clawed hands, while slashing

NAME *Velociraptor*

TIME Late Cretaceous

LOCALITY Asia (Mongolia and China)

SIZE 6ft/1.8m long

through its thick hide by repeated kicks of the dagger-like killing claws on their feet. The plant-eater may have wounded or even killed some of its attackers by lashing out with its long, heavy tail or rearing up on its hind legs to crash down on their bodies. But, perhaps in the end, it succumbed and bled to death, while the pack of carnivores waited nearby.

The active, predatory lifestyle suggested by the anatomy of *Deinonychus* is seen by some paleontologists as strong evidence that it was an endothermic ('warm-blooded') creature, and could control its body temperature, as do modern birds and mammals (see p.91).

A dramatic find in Mongolia in 1971 revealed two fossilized skeletons – *Velociraptor* locked in combat with the horned dinosaur *Protoceratops* (see p.164). A great struggle had obviously taken place, since *Velociraptor* had died grasping the head shield of *Protoceratops* with its hands, while ripping into the belly with its sickle-clawed feet. *Protoceratops* had caved in the chest of *Velociraptor*, possibly with its horny beak, before it, too, died. The scene was indicative of the ferocious lifestyle of the dromaeosaurs in general, and *Velociraptor* in particular.

The long, low, flat-snouted head of *Velociraptor* is the main feature that distinguishes it from other dromaeosaurs, which typically had short, deep heads. In other respects, it was similar to them, although its sickle claws were relatively small.

CARNIVOROUS DINOSAURS CONTINUED

NAME *Saurornitholestes*

TIME Late Cretaceous

LOCALITY North America (Alberta)

SIZE 6 ft / 1.8 m long

In 1978, the skull and some arm bones and teeth of this dinosaur were found. It is not clear whether it was a dromaeosaur or one of the 'bird-lizards', the saurornithoidids (below).

The scanty remains suggest that *Saurornitholestes* had a larger brain than was usual among the dromaeosaurs (but not among the saurornithoidids), and that it possessed powerful hands adapted for grasping. The restoration shown above is based on the evidence available, but remains highly speculative.

Family Saurornithoididae

Like the dromaeosaurs, these 'bird-lizards' were fast, intelligent, rapacious predators, though smaller and lighter in build. They also had a sickle-shaped, killer claw on each foot.

But the skull of these saurornithoidids shows the greatest development. The brain cavity was large. Relative to body weight, it was about seven times the volume of the brain cavity of their modern relative, the crocodile. In addition to this well-developed nervous system, these dinosaurs had large eyes and it seems very likely that they had binocular vision.

Thus, the saurornithoidids of Late Cretaceous times – living in North America, southern Europe and Mongolia – were among the most efficient hunters of the carnivorous dinosaurs.

NAME *Saurornithoides*

TIME Late Cretaceous

LOCALITY Asia (Mongolia)

SIZE 6 ft 6 in / 2 m long

Although the skull was bird-like – long, low and light – it housed a large brain, giving its owner an intelligence far superior to that of most other dinosaurs around at the time. The eyes must have been huge relative to the head, judging from the size of their sockets. Moreover, their position suggests that these dinosaurs used binocular vision, allowing them to judge distances between objects.

Such large eyes suggest nocturnal habits. *Saurornithoides*, together with other members of its family, was probably active after twilight, dodging through the woods to hunt down small mammals and reptiles.

NAME *Stenonychosaurus*

TIME Late Cretaceous

LOCALITY North America (Alberta)

SIZE 6 ft 6 in / 2 m long

This was the 'brainiest' dinosaur of them all – the brain cavity in the skull is, relative to its body size, the largest so far discovered. Its brain was larger than that of a modern emu. Comparing its brain size to that of a modern mammal, scientists think *Stenonychosaurus* was about as intelligent as an opossum.

Only incomplete skeletons of this saurornithoidid have been found. It seems to differ little in structure from *Saurornithoides* (left), leading some paleontologists to think that it is actually the same animal. However, the clawed fingers of the *Stenonychosaurus* specimens seem longer and slimmer than those of *Saurornithoides*. Also, *Stenonychosaurus* was probably of a lighter overall build; it is estimated that its live weight would have been 60–100lb/27–45kg.

Like other members of its family, *Stenonychosaurus* possessed large eyes – each eye was about 2in/52mm across, the same size as that of a modern ostrich. The combination of large brain, large eyes, and slim build indicate that it was an agile night hunter, with fast reflexes and well-developed senses.

Family Baryonychidae

This family was created in 1986 to cover one member – *Baryonyx*, which has a narrow, crocodile-like skull, adapted for fish-eating. New spinosaurid remains from Africa show similar adaptations, and the two families may be closely related.

NAME	*Baryonyx*
TIME	Early Cretaceous
LOCALITY	Europe (England)
SIZE	20ft/6m long

Two unusual features made this large, theropod dinosaur quite distinct from any other. Its first singular characteristic was a huge, curved claw, about 1ft/30cm long – hence its scientific name *Baryonyx*, meaning 'heavy claw', and its popular nickname of 'Claws'. However, the claw was not attached to the animal's skeleton, so it is not known whether it was part of the forefeet or hind feet.

Paleontologists assume that the claw belonged to one of the forefeet, since the forelimbs of this dinosaur were unusually thick and powerful compared to those of other theropods, and would therefore have been able to carry such a large weapon. In addition, the great size of the *Baryonyx* would have made the large claw difficult to wield if it had been located on one of the animal's hind feet.

The second peculiar feature of *Baryonyx* was its skull, which was long and narrow, rather like that of a crocodile. The jaws were armed with a great number of small, pointed teeth, twice as many as a theropod usually possessed. There was also a bony crest on top of the head. The neck was not as flexible as that of other theropods, and could not have been carried in their characteristic S-shaped curve.

The habits of this mysterious beast may be surmised from these two distinctive features and some fish remain that were found with the skeleton. It is possible that *Baryonyx* hunted on all-fours along riverbanks, hooking fish out of the water with its long, gaff-like claws on the front legs – a hunting technique that grizzly bears can be seen employing on riverbanks today.

CARNIVOROUS DINOSAURS CONTINUED

INFRAORDER CARNOSAURIA

Some of the largest terrestrial carnivores that have ever existed belong to this group of theropod dinosaurs – the carnosaurs or 'flesh lizards'. The taxonomic basis of this group has been questioned recently since many of the characteristics may well be size-related convergences. *Tyrannosaurus* is the most familiar member of the group. They were massively built animals, and dominated life in Jurassic and Cretaceous times.

Their efficiency as predators is, however, debatable. In reality, the largest of them, such as *Tyrannosaurus* and *Tarbosaurus*, could have been part-time scavengers. They may have been the 'hyenas' of the dinosaur world rather than the 'lions'. It is likely that their sheer bulk would have precluded any sustained chase. But they could have ambushed prey, attacking in short bursts of speed, like a modern tiger.

There were also other smaller carnosaurs that were lighter and more agile than their giant contemporaries.

Family Megalosauridae

The earliest and most familiar carnosaurs belong to this family of 'great lizards'. Their remains have been found in North America, Africa and Europe, and as a group they span a period of 140 million years – from the Early Jurassic Period to the end of the Cretaceous.

All were enormous, big-boned creatures. The large head was high and narrow, equipped with powerful jaws and many sharp, saw-edged teeth. The arms were short but strong. The legs were long and massive enough to support the great body weight on the three spreading, clawed, toes of each foot (a tiny fourth toe was also present), yet light enough to allow the creature to amble along quite quickly.

NAME *Teratosaurus*
TIME Late Triassic
LOCALITY Europe (Germany)
SIZE 20 ft / 6 m long

This is a puzzling beast among the dinosaurs. From fragments of its skeleton, mostly teeth, paleontologists have tentatively constructed a picture of *Teratosaurus* as a primitive carnosaur.

It was a large, two-legged creature, with a heavy head and many sharp, curved teeth. Its body was also heavy, with a short neck and long, stiffened tail. Sturdy legs ended in three powerful, clawed toes, for walking and ripping flesh. (A fourth toe was present, but it was tiny.) The short, strong arms had grasping fingers with curved claws.

From the remains of *Teratosaurus*, and fragments of related beasts found in southern Africa, some paleontologists postulate that a group of large, meat-eating theropods may have existed some 60 million years before the main stock of carnosaurs appeared, in Early Jurassic times. *Teratosaurus* may, therefore, be the earliest-known relative of the megalosaur family.

However, other paleontologists are of the opinion that *Teratosaurus* may be an early member of the prosauropod group of dinosaurs (see pp.122–125) or even a large representative of the thecodontians, from which group arose the ancient ancestors of the dinosaurs (see p.123).

NAME *Proceratosaurus*
TIME Middle Jurassic
LOCALITY Europe (England)
SIZE 16 ft / 5 m long

This early carnosaur is known only from a single skull. Although longer than average, the skull shows the same general features as other primitive carnosaurs. But there is one atypical feature – a small horn above the snout. This suggests that this creature may have been an ancestor, or even an early member, of the ceratosaurs, those theropods characterized by a nose horn (see pp.106–107). The restoration shows *Proceratosaurus* as a typical carnosaur – large head, short neck, heavy body, long tail, short arms with clawed fingers, and long legs for running, each foot bearing three toes.

NAME *Dilophosaurus*

TIME Early Jurassic

LOCALITY North America
(Arizona)

SIZE 20ft/6m long

Found in Early Jurassic strata, *Dilophosaurus* is the earliest known large carnivorous dinosaur. The broad range of animal remains found in the strata indicates that these carnosaurs were part of quite cosmopolitan communities, including sauropods and theropods of various sizes. First discovered in 1942 by an expedition from the University of California, *Dilophosaurus* seems to have been a lightly built carnosaur. This sounds like a contradiction, but it was intermediate in structure between the carnosaurs and the coelurosaurs. Its head was large (a typical carnosaur feature) but light-boned, while its neck, tail and arms were long and slender (typical coelurosaur features, see pp.106–113).

The skull of *Dilophosaurus* was unusual for any group. A pair of semicircular bony crests rose vertically on either side of the skull. Although the crests were wafer-thin in places, they were strengthened by vertical struts of bone. At the back of the head, the tip of each crest narrowed into a spike.

The function of these head crests remains a mystery. Some paleontologists think that they could have been used for sexual display, and that only the males had them – a theory supported by the fact that not all specimens found had the crests. Indeed, there were none on the first few skeletons unearthed, and the animals were thought to have been a species of *Megalosaurus* (see p.116). The crests have never been found actually attached to the skull, but lying nearby, so there is a certain amount of guesswork about their position in life, and there is even the possibility that they belonged to another dinosaur.

The jaws of *Dilophosaurus* give a clue to its lifestyle. The lower jaw was strong and full of long, sharp, thin teeth. The upper jaw, however, had a cluster of teeth at the front, separate from the rest of the teeth – similar to the arrangement in the jaws of a modern crocodile.

Although *Dilophosaurus* had a large head and strong jaws, it probably did not kill its victims by biting them: the thin teeth and delicate head crests would have been too vulnerable. It is more likely that it caught and ripped its prey apart with the clawed feet and hands. Or, like many of its relatives, it could have been a scavenger, feeding on the kills of stronger carnosaurs.

NAME *Eustreptospondylus*

TIME Middle Jurassic to Late Cretaceous

LOCALITY Europe (England)

SIZE 23ft/7m long

Until the discovery of a nearly complete skeleton of this early megalosaur in southern England, and its description in 1964, *Eustreptospondylus* remains were identified as *Megalosaurus*. The skeleton which revealed that this was in fact a separate animal, despite its similar build to *Megalosaurus,* is now mounted in the University Museum of Oxford, and although parts of its skull are missing, it remains the best-preserved specimen of any European carnosaur.

CARNIVOROUS DINOSAURS CONTINUED

NAME *Megalosaurus*

TIME Early Jurassic to Late Jurassic

LOCALITY Europe (England and France) and Africa (Morocco)

SIZE 30 ft/9 m long

Megalosaurus, or 'great lizard', may not be the biggest or heaviest dinosaur, but it can claim a number of 'firsts'. The first dinosaur bone on record, discovered in England in 1676, probably belonged to *Megalosaurus*. It was the first dinosaur to be scientifically named and described in the 1820s, and it was one of the three fossils that prompted the English paleontologist Richard Owen in 1842 to coin the name for the whole group: he chose 'Dinosauria', meaning 'terrible lizards'.

With an overall length of 30 ft/9 in, a height of 10 ft/3 m, and an estimated weight in life of 1 US ton/900 kg, *Megalosaurus* was a massive creature. A short, muscular neck carried the large head, with its powerful, hinged jaws armed with curved, saw-edged fangs. Its fingers and toes were strong and clawed. With such weapons, *Megalosaurus* was well-equipped to attack and kill large, long-necked, plant-eating dinosaurs (see pp.126–133).

Trackways of *Megalosaurus* footprints are seen in the limestone rocks of southern England, and show how these bulky bipeds walked upright on two legs, their toes pointing slightly inward, and their long tails probably swinging from side to side at each step acting as a counterbalances to their heavy bodies.

Family Allosauridae

Allosaurs were similar in build to megalosaurs, but even larger. They were the largest carnosaurs around during Late Jurassic times, and lumbered through every continent in the world. But they were soon to be rivalled by even bigger creatures – the tyrannosaurs of the Cretaceous Period (see pp.119–121).

NAME *Yangchuanosaurus*

TIME Late Jurassic

LOCALITY Asia (China)

SIZE up to 33 ft/10 m long

The skeleton of this large carnosaur was discovered in Sichuan (Szechuan) Province of eastern China, and described in 1978. It is now on display in the Natural History Museum in Beijing (Peking).

It was a typical allosaur, with a huge head and powerful jaws, equipped with sharp fangs that curved backward and were serrated along their edges like steak knives. The neck was short and thick but flexible. The long tail made up about half the total body length. It was flattened from side to side and held out stiffly to balance the deep, narrow body of the animal as it strode along on its huge, pillar-like legs. Three great, clawed toes bore the whole weight of the body. (As usual, there was a small first toe that pointed backwards.) Short arms ended in three powerful, clawed fingers.

The skull of *Yangchuanosaurus* differs from that of other allosaurs in having more teeth at the front of the jaws, and a bony hump above the snout.

NAME *Allosaurus*

TIME Late Jurassic to Early Cretaceous

LOCALITY North America (Colorado, Utah and Wyoming), Africa (Tanzania) and Australia

SIZE up to 39ft/12m long

This enormous carnosaur, the largest member of the family Allosauridae, would probably have been the most fearsome predator of the Late Jurassic Period. *Allosaurus* would have weighed between 1–2 US tons/1–2 tonnes, and must have stood some 15 ft/4.6 m tall.

In appearance, *Allosaurus* was a bigger version of its close relative and contemporary *Megalosaurus* (opposite), although it had a few peculiarities of its own. The head, for example, had two bony bumps above the eyes, and a narrow bony ridge running from between the eyes down to the tip of the snout, giving it a distinctive shape. An opening in the side of the skull around the snout area is thought to have housed a salt gland. *Allosaurus* had five pairs of teeth in the upper jaw, compared to four in *Megalosaurus*.

The skull was massive in size, but not in weight. This was due to several large openings ('windows' or fenestrae) between various bones of the skull that reduced its solid structure to an intricate network of bony struts, so lessening its weight. The bones themselves were only loosely articulated with one another (a feature also seen in the skulls of other large carnosaurs, such as *Ceratosaurus*, see p.106). This resulted in a degree of flexibility, which added to the strength of the lightly built skull.

Allosaurus' efficiency as a hunter is a matter of debate among experts. Some paleontologists believe that it was too heavy and clumsy to have run down prey, and therefore probably fed on carrion. Others believe that it was quite an agile creature for its size, and may even have hunted in packs to bring down the giant, plant-eating dinosaurs of the day, such as *Apatosaurus* (*Brontosaurus*) and *Diplodocus*. Bones of *Apatosaurus* have, in fact, been found in western North America bearing the marks of teeth resembling those of *Allosaurus*. Similar broken teeth have also been found scattered around other specimens of this plant-eater.

A single site in Utah discovered in 1927, the Cleveland-Lloyd Dinosaur Quarry, has revealed thousands of dinosaur bones including the remains of 44 individual *Allosaurus*. The remains include individuals which range in size from 10ft (3m) long juveniles to fully grown adults. the accompanying remains give a reasonable insight into the diversity of dinosaurs at the time and include ornithopods, stegosaurs, ankylosaurs, sauropods and another theropod, *Ceratosaurus*.

CARNIVOROUS DINOSAURS CONTINUED

Family Spinosauridae

The spinosaurids were a specialized group of large Cretaceous theropods. Some had backbones elongated into a tall crest or 'sail', like that of the 'fin-backed' pelycosaurs and perhaps with a similar thermo-regulatory purpose.

The discovery of a new spinosaurid from Africa (*Suchomimus*) with a long crocodile-like snout suggests a close relationship between the spinosaurids and *Baryonyx*. If this surmise is correct, it also suggests a connection across the seaway from Africa to Europe in Early Cretaceous times.

NAME *Acrocanthosaurus*

TIME Early Cretaceous

LOCALITY North America (Oklahoma)

SIZE 43 ft / 13 m long

In 1950, several skeletons of this enormous, flesh-eating dinosaur were found in North America. The name *Acrocanthosaurus* means 'top spiny lizard', and refers to the elongated spines (up to 1 ft/30 cm long) that grew up from the animal's backbone. These spines would have been covered by a web of skin, to form a pronounced ridge or crest running down the length of the back.

The crest of *Acrocanthosaurus* was low in comparison to that of some of its relatives living in other parts of the world. For example, *Altispinax* of western Europe had spines that were about four times the length of the vertebrae from which they grew, while *Spinosaurus* of Africa had a 'sail' over 6 ft/1.8 m high on its back (right).

NAME *Spinosaurus*

TIME Late Cretaceous

LOCALITY Africa (Egypt and Niger)

SIZE 39 ft / 12 m long

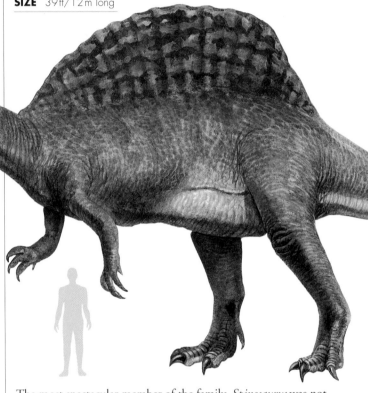

The most spectacular member of the family, *Spinosaurus* was not only enormous – ranking with the largest of the carnosaurs – but also had an extravagant 'sail' on its back, taller than a modern man. Broad, club-shaped spines, 6 ft 6 in/2 m long, projected upward from the backbone, and would have been covered with a layer of skin. The whole arrangement was reminiscent of the tall fin on the back of the pelycosaur *Dimetrodon* (see p.187).

The function of this strange, and highly vulnerable, structure is not known for certain. One theory is that the sail acted as a crude device to regulate body temperature. When the animal stood with the sail turned sideways, towards the sun's rays, its large surface area, which was amply supplied with blood vessels, would absorb heat rapidly.

The warmed-up blood would then be carried all over the body. To lower its body temperature, the animal would angle its sail into the wind, so dissipating heat.

The advantage to *Spinosaurus* would be that it could warm up quickly in the early morning, and be prepared for hunting well in advance of its cold, sluggish prey, which was mostly composed of other reptiles.

An alternative theory is that the sail was brightly coloured, and was used for sexual display by the males to attract the attention of the females. Males could also have used their sails to threaten each other during the ritualistic fights engaged in to establish dominance.

There is no reason why both theories cannot apply, with the sail being used as a heat exchanger and as a sexual ploy.

At about the same time that *Spinosaurus* inhabited western Africa, a large, two-legged, plant-eating dinosaur, *Ouranosaurus* also lived in the region. It, too, had a high sail on its back (see pp.144–145). There is therefore good reason to believe that some environmental or climatic factor influenced the development of these structures.

The bony sail would have increased *Spinosaurus'* weight considerably. The total body weight is estimated to have been some 7 tons/6 tonnes – close to that of *Tyrannosaurus*, the largest carnosaur of them all (see p.121).

The arms of *Spinosaurus* were larger than is usual among large theropods, and it is possible that it spent some of its time on all-fours, which was an unusual posture among the two-legged carnosaurs. Its teeth were also different from those of other carnosaurs: they were straight rather than curved.

Family Tyrannosauridae

The largest terrestrial carnivores that ever lived belonged to this family of 'tyrant lizards'. It was a small, specialized group, with less than a dozen types (genera) identified to date. Yet its members have inspired the popular notion of what flesh-eating dinosaurs looked like and how they behaved.

The evolutionary relationships and taxonomic position of the tyrannosaurids have been questioned by some dinosaur experts recently. On the basis of certain specialized structures in the ankle, it is suggested that they are more closely related to the ornithomimids (see pp.108–109) and troodontids, and should therefore be placed with them within the Subdivision Arctrometatarsalia.

The remains of tyrannosaurs have been found in Asia and western North America. As a group they were short-lived, appearing in Late Cretaceous times and disappearing at the end of that period in the mysterious mass extinction of all the dinosaurs. Their existence, spanning less than 15 million years, was only a 'moment' in terms of the evolution of life.

Tyrannosaurs had a well-developed second set of ribs on the underside of the body. A possible explanation for these extra ribs and the short arms could be that when a tyrannosaur rested it lay on its belly, the innards would have been supported by the extra ribs, and not crushed by the great weight of the body. When the animal got up, its tiny arms stopped the bulky frame from sliding forward, and steadied it as it rose to its feet.

There is also a suggestion that the tiny arms were used by the males to hold on to the females while mating.

NAME	*Albertosaurus*
TIME	Late Cretaceous
LOCALITY	North America (Alberta)
SIZE	26 ft/8 m long

This 'small' tyrannosaur shows all the features common to the family. It was massively built, with a big head and short body, balanced at the hips by a long, strong tail. Pillar-like legs, with three-toed, spreading, feet supported the great body weight.

Albertosaurus and other members of its family were specialized theropods. Their arms were puny in comparison to the size of the body – they were so short that they could not have reached up to the mouth. There were only two fingers on each hand, which would not have been very effective for grasping prey. And although the jaws could be opened wide, the bones of the skull were rigidly fixed, without the same degree of flexibility as seen in the skulls of the allosaurs (see pp.116–117).

CARNIVOROUS DINOSAURS CONTINUED

NAME *Alioramus*

TIME Late Cretaceous

LOCALITY Asia (Mongolia)

SIZE 20ft/6m long

A group of Asiatic tyrannosaurs, represented by *Alioramus*, differed from 'typical' tyrannosaurs in the shape of their skulls. Whereas most members of the family had deep skulls with short snouts, *Alioramus* and its relatives had shallow skulls with long snouts. There were also some bony knobs or spikes on the face between the eyes and the tip of the snout. These may have been display features that distinguished the sexes – perhaps with the males having larger structures than the females for use in courting displays or to threaten other males.

Alioramus and its tyrannosaur relatives lived in Asia and western North America during the Late Cretaceous Period. At that time, the modern continents of Asia and North America were joined into one enormous landmass; the Bering Strait that separates them today was then dry land (see pp.11). But the North American part was divided in two by a shallow sea that ran north to south, with 'Asiamerica' to the west, and 'Euramerica' to the east.

Animals, including the great tyrannosaurs, would have been able to migrate freely between Asia and western North America, but relatively few seem to have managed to cross the great divide over to the eastern half of the landmass. However, the remains of one tyrannosaur, similar to *Albertosaurus* (see p.119), have been found in the eastern USA.

NAME *Tarbosaurus*

TIME Late Cretaceous

LOCALITY Asia (Mongolia)

SIZE up to 46ft/14m long

This giant carnosaur lumbered around the lands of central Asia, eating anything it came across, whether dead or alive. Its skills as a hunter are suspect, because of its sheer bulk. It could have preyed on the herbivorous duckbilled and armoured dinosaurs that lived in its environment. It could also have supplemented its diet with the kills of other carnosaurs. It was probably big enough to scare off even the most tenacious predator.

Many *Tarbosaurus* skeletons have been unearthed in Mongolia, some complete. Its structure was almost identical to *Tyrannosaurus*, but it was more lightly built with a longer skull. It has been possible to analyse the upright posture of this tyrannosaur. The back would have been held almost horizontal, with the body balanced at the hips. The long, flexible neck curved abruptly upward from the body, with the heavy head held almost at right angles to it in a bird-like pose. In the fossil finds, *Tarbosaurus'* head was pulled right back, toward its shoulders. This often happens when an animal dies, because the ligaments of the neck dry out and shrink, pulling the head backward into an unnatural position.

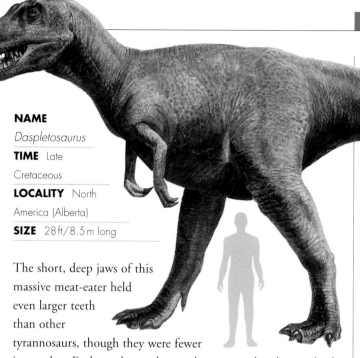

NAME
Daspletosaurus

TIME Late
Cretaceous

LOCALITY North
America (Alberta)

SIZE 28 ft/8.5 m long

The short, deep jaws of this
massive meat-eater held
even larger teeth
than other
tyrannosaurs, though they were fewer
in number. Each tooth was dagger-sharp, curved and saw-edged.
Formidable jaws, clawed feet and sheer bulk (a body weight of
up to 4 US tons/3.6 tonnes) were the weapons used by
Daspletosaurus. It was capable of killing the large, horned,
dinosaurs that browsed the forests of northern North America.

NAME *Tyrannosaurus*

TIME Late Cretaceous

LOCALITY North America (Alberta, Montana, Saskatchewan, Texas and
Wyoming) and Asia (Mongolia)

SIZE up to 49 ft/15 m long

This awesome theropod was the largest of the carnosaur dinosaurs
– the largest known terrestrial carnivore.

On average, *Tyrannosaurus* was 39 ft/12 m long, up to 20 ft/6 m
tall, and weighed about 8 US tons/7 tonnes (heavier than a
modern, adult African bull elephant). Its head alone was over
4 ft/1.25 m long, and was armed with fangs, each some
6 in/15 cm in length.

No complete skeleton has yet been
found, although
many bones and
teeth have surfaced since it was first discovered in the USA in
1902. Early reconstructions were often inaccurate; mounted
skeletons often show the animal propped up on a whip-like tail,
its body sloping backward at an angle of 45°. But since the
skeletons of other tyrannosaurids have been unearthed, such as
Tarbosaurus in Mongolia, we now have a more accurate idea of the
stance of these dinosaurs.

Investigations of *Tyrannosaurus'* structure have triggered some
debate over whether it really was a fearsome predator. The
animal's hips and legs seemed to indicate that *Tyrannosaurus* may
have been no more than a slow-moving scavenger, only able to
take small, clumsy steps.

Calculations have also suggested that the animal's weight and
height were so great that if it fell while running, the impact would
have been enough to break its skull. The tiny forearms would not
have broken the force of the impact.

However, some paleontologists believe that the purpose of the
unusually wide area of the skull behind the eyes was to anchor
extremely powerful jaw muscles. Taken together with other
features – such as the robust, saw-edged teeth; the strong, flexible
neck; the large areas of the brain associated with sight and smell;
and the possibility of binocular vision – the findings argue in
favour of an active, predatory lifestyle.

It is surmised that *Tyrannosaurus'* diet could have consisted
primarily of the duckbilled dinosaurs, or hadrosaurs, that browsed
the hardwood forests of North America (see pp.146–153). These
animals lived in herds, and sprinted away on two legs when
danger threatened. So it is likely that *Tyrannosaurus* hid among
the trees, ambushing its prey with a short burst of speed as it held
its mouth open wide. The force of any impact would have been
absorbed by its strong teeth, sturdy skull and powerful neck.

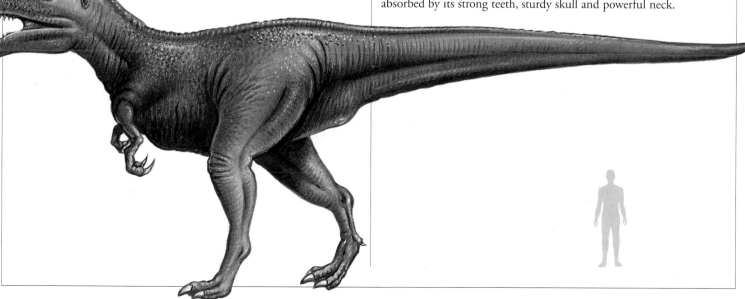

EARLY HERBIVOROUS DINOSAURS

SUBORDER SAUROPODOMORPHA

The lifestyle of the sauropodomorph dinosaurs was completely different from that of their contemporaries, the theropods. Although both were saurischians, or 'lizard-hipped' dinosaurs, the theropods were two-legged carnivores (see pp.106–121), whereas the sauropodomorphs were, in the main, four-legged herbivores. The differences in gait are reflected in the bones of the feet. Yet their lives were inextricably linked, since the sauropodomorphs were probably the chief prey of the larger predatory theropods.

INFRAORDER PROSAUROPODA

Like the theropods, the sauropodomorphs can be grouped according to their size. There were gigantic types, with long necks and tails, placed in the Infraorder Sauropoda (see pp.126–133). *Apatosaurus* (previously known as *Brontosaurus*) is the most famous sauropod (see p.131).

There were also smaller sauropodomorphs (though some were still fairly large, at over 30 ft/9 m), which are grouped in the Infraorder Prosauropoda. As their name implies, they were 'before the sauropods', and lived during Late Triassic times. Current theory rejects the once-held notion that the prosauropods were the direct ancestors of the sauropods. They are now generally regarded as a side branch of the sauropod family tree – a branch that got fatally pruned in the Early Jurassic Period.

Prosauropods themselves are thought to have evolved from theropod-type ancestors. The remains of two likely candidates have been found, both from South America. *Staurikosaurus* is the only known dinosaur from the Mid-Triassic Period, and was about 6 ft 6 in/2 m long; *Herrerasaurus*, from the Late Triassic, was 10 ft/3 m long. Both seem to have been active, two-legged flesh-eaters, with large heads and long tails.

Family Anchisauridae

This family comprises most of the earliest prosauropods, which were among the first dinosaurs to appear. Members of the family were all fairly small creatures (reaching less than 10 ft/3 m in length), with long, lightly-built bodies, slim limbs, small heads and long necks and tails.

Anchisaurs seem to represent an early experiment in plant-eating among dinosaurs. Their teeth were cylindrical and blunt, with file-like serrations along the edges – like the teeth of some modern herbivorous lizards such as the land iguanas of South America. The serrations would have helped shred plant material and thereby aid digestion. The arms were only slightly shorter than the legs, which suggests that the animal probably spent much of its time on all-fours. This stance would have made it easier to reach plants growing at ground level. But the ankle joint was strong and well-developed too, indicating that the animal could also stand up on its hind legs, and use its hands to pluck off higher vegetation.

Some paleontologists believe that anchisaur-type prosauropods may have been the ancestors of the bird-hipped dinosaurs, the ornithischians (see pp.134–169). Certain features of *Anchisaurus* (below), in particular, seem similar. Its long, slender neck, the structure of its shoulders and forelimbs, and details of its hip bones and ankle joints – all these structures are similar to those of some of the early ornithopods, such as *Heterodontosaurus* (see p.135).

NAME	*Anchisaurus*
TIME	Early Jurassic
LOCALITY	North America (Connecticut) and southern Africa
SIZE	7 ft/2.1 m long

This early dinosaur was probably typical of the small prosauropods. It had a small head, tall, flexible neck and long, slim body. The arms were shorter than the legs, by about a third. Each hand had five fingers, though the two outer ones were quite short. The first finger, or 'thumb', was equipped with a large claw, which may have been used for rooting up plants or perhaps for fighting.

The round, blunt teeth suggest that *Anchisaurus* ate plants.

Ferns and horsetails flourished in damp places at the time, and conifers and palm-like cycads grew in drier, upland areas. But all plant-eaters, including modern ones, need a larger digestive system than meat-eaters, since tough, fibrous plant material takes longer to break down than flesh. So, a capacious stomach and long intestines would have been found in *Anchisaurus'* long body, accommodated in front of the hips. This mass of innards would have unbalanced a two-legged animal so, it is argued, *Anchisaurus* and its relatives had to take up a four-legged stance most of the time for stability.

All the continents of today's world were fused together into one great landmass in Jurassic times, some 200 million years ago, when *Anchisaurus* was alive. To find its remains in such divergent places as the eastern seaboard of North America and in southern Africa is therefore not surprising, and is further evidence for the theory of plate tectonics.

NAME *Thecodontosaurus*
TIME Late Triassic to Early Jurassic
LOCALITY Europe (England) and southern Africa
SIZE 7 ft/2.1 m long

Thecodontosaurus was similar in build to *Anchisaurus*, but with a shorter neck and more teeth. It was first named in 1843 from remains discovered near Bristol in southwest England. The bones were found in Triassic deposits that had been laid down in gullies and caves eroded out of limestones that had been formed in earlier, Carboniferous times. During the desert-like climate that prevailed in Europe during Late Triassic times, when *Thecodontosaurus* was living, these limestones would have formed high, parched plateaus.

Piecing together such climatic and rock evidence suggests that *Thecodontosaurus* lived in dry, upland areas, possibly in or

near the entrance to the limestone caves; when it died, it was covered over by later, Triassic deposits. Alternatively, its bones could have been washed into the caves and gullies by torrents during the rainy seasons.

Thecodontosaurus has many features of a basic sauropodomorph and is sometimes placed with other genera in a separate family of thecodontosaurids.

NAME *Efraasia*
TIME Late Triassic
LOCALITY Europe (Germany)
SIZE 8 ft/2.4 m long

Discovered in 1909 by E. Fraas and named after him, *Efraasia* was slightly larger than its prosauropod relatives, but otherwise similar in build. Like them, it had multipurpose hands. Its long fingers could have grasped small plants and bundles of leaves, with the help of its mobile 'thumbs'. The wrist joint was also well-developed, so the palm of the hand could be pressed to the ground easily, enabling the animal to walk on all-fours.

Efraasia had a primitive feature, however; only two sacral vertebrae joined the hips to the backbone, which made for a rather weak arrangement of the hindquarters. All the other 'lizard-hipped' dinosaurs had at least three vertebrae linking the hips to the spine.

Efraasia was just one of several prosauropods which appear in abundance in the Late Triassic of Germany. Others include *Plateosaurus*, *Sellosaurus* and *Thecodontosaurus* and they are accompanied by theropods, phytosaurs, rauisuchids and aetosaurs. It is thought that they migrated into the area from elsewhere as yet unknown.

EARLY HERBIVOROUS DINOSAURS CONTINUED

Family Plateosauridae

These heavy, large, stout-limbed prosauropods were bigger versions of their contemporaries, the anchisaurs. The proportions of their bodies are reminiscent of the giant sauropods, such as *Apatosaurus* (*Brontosaurus*) that thrived later, in the Late Jurassic and Cretaceous periods (see p.131).

NAME *Massospondylus*
TIME Late Triassic
LOCALITY Africa (South Africa and Zimbabwe) and North America (Arizona)
SIZE 13 ft/4 m long

This was the most common prosauropod in southern Africa. It was named in 1854 by the English paleontologist Richard Owen from a few large vertebrae found in South Africa. On the basis of these bones, he called the dinosaur *Massospondylus*, which means 'massive vertebra'.

Massospondylus had a tiny head perched on a particularly long and flexible neck. Its five-fingered hands were massive and had a great span; they could have been used for walking or for grasping hold of food. Each 'thumb' had a large, curved claw.

Polished stones have been found in the stomach cavities of some skeletons. When *Massospondylus* swallowed these stones they would have had rough edges and would have helped the dinosaur to grind up the tough plant material that it ate. Many modern birds retain stones in their gizzards for just the same purpose. Since *Massospondylus* probably spent most of its time eating, in order to maintain its great body mass, the surface of these stones would have been polished smooth in a short time, and been of no further use. Then they would have been regurgitated and replaced with fresh, rough-edged stones.

NAME *Plateosaurus*
TIME Late Triassic
LOCALITY Europe (England, France, Germany and Switzerland)
SIZE up to 23 ft/7 m long

Plateosaurus is the best known of the prosauropods. Dozens of well-preserved skeletons have been unearthed in Triassic sandstones all over western Europe. In some locations, groups of complete individual fossils have been found. Mass burials of this kind suggest that the *Plateosaurus* was a gregarious creature. Herds travelled together through the Triassic desert landscape of Europe, searching for new feeding grounds. An alternative explanation for the groups of fossils, however, is that solitary individuals inhabited dry, upland areas. When they died, their bodies would have been washed away in the periodic flash floods that are typical of desert environments even today. Many individual corpses could have piled up at the end of well-worn flood channels formed at the edge of desert basins.

Plateosaurus was a large animal, its tail making up about half its length. It had a stronger, deeper head than most prosauropods. Its many small, leaf-shaped teeth, and the low-slung hinge of its lower jaw (to give the muscles greater leverage) suggest that it fed exclusively on plants.

Plateosaurus would have moved about on all-fours most of the time, occasionally rearing up and stretching out its long neck to browse at higher levels. The foliage of trees such as cycads and various conifers, which flourished in Late Triassic Europe, would have featured in its diet.

Similar herbivorous dinosaurs to *Plateosaurus* lived in other parts of the world. In southern China there was the 20 ft/6 m-long *Lufengosaurus*, and in South America there was the smaller, 13 ft/4 m-long *Coloradia*. The presence of these animals, with similar builds and lifestyles, in such widely-spaced parts of the globe is further evidence to support the theory that all continents were fused together into one gigantic landmass (Gondwanaland) in those days.

NAME *Mussaurus*
TIME Late Triassic to Early Jurassic
LOCALITY South America (Argentina)
SIZE possibly 10 ft/3 m long

When paleontologists unearthed a group of tiny, perfectly-formed dinosaurs in southern Argentina in 1979, it seemed as though they had discovered the smallest ever type of dinosaur and they promptly called it 'mouse lizard'. However, the skeletons had been found in a nest alongside two small, almost intact eggs, each measuring only 1 in/25 mm on the longest axis. The largest skeleton was only 8 in/20 cm long. It had a large head, with big eyes, and a short neck – features you would expect to find in a young animal, not yet fully developed. Paleontologists now think that the adult *Mussaurus* could have grown up to 10 ft/3 m in length, with the body proportions of a typical prosauropod.

Family Melanorosauridae

This family contains the largest prosauropods. Some experts think that they may even have been early representatives of the giant, plant-eating sauropods.

Melanorosaurs walked exclusively on four legs, unlike their smaller, more lightweight contemporaries, the anchisaurs (see pp.122–123), which could also walk on two.

NAME *Riojasaurus*
TIME Late Triassic to Early Jurassic
LOCALITY South America (Argentina)
SIZE up to 33 ft/10 m long

The limb bones, and the shoulder and hip girdles of this large prosauropod, were more massive than those of its relatives, the plateosaurs (opposite). This indicates that it had to walk on four legs to support its weight. The skeleton was modified accordingly. The limb bones were thick and solid, and held vertically under the body. The hips were fused to the backbone by three vertebrae, giving a solid attachment for the legs. The vertebrae had extra articulating surfaces to keep the backbone rigid.

Riojasaurus was named after the northwestern Argentinian province of La Rioja where it was found along with another basal prosauropod, the plateosaur *Coloradisaurus*. *Mussaurus* was another South American prosauropod from Patagonia.. Together, they show that there was a rapid and considerable increase in abundance and body size (at least for some of them) in Late Triassic prosauropods. Other large prosauropods, similar in build and structure, lived in southern Africa at about the same time – *Roccosaurus* and *Thotobolosaurus* of the Late Triassic, and *Vulcanodon* of the Early Jurassic. This last animal exhibits a mixture of features. Some of them were 'primitive' prosauropod characteristics, while others were 'advanced' sauropod traits. *Vulcanodon* may, therefore, have been closely related to the giant, long-necked browsers of the Mesozoic Era, the sauropods.

LONG-NECKED BROWSING DINOSAURS

INFRAORDER SAUROPODA

Between 65 and 200 million years ago, the largest herbivores – in fact, the largest land animals ever to have lived – were the giant, long-necked, four-legged sauropods. As a group, they survived for some 50 million years. They evolved in the Late Triassic or Early Jurassic, reached their peak in the Late Jurassic, and became extinct by the end of the Cretaceous. Even in the early stages of their evolution, most sauropods were huge – well over 50 ft/15.2 m long.

The body plan of all sauropods was structurally similar. There was a small head on top of an extra-long neck; a long, deep body to accommodate an enormous gut; thick, pillar-like legs with five-toed, spreading feet; and a long, thick tail that tapered gradually to a whiplash.

Two special adaptations of the skeleton were evident, even in the earliest sauropods. First, great cavities were hollowed out of the vertebrae: this helped to lighten the load of the animal considerably, while still retaining the structural strength of its skeleton. This hollowing-out became more extreme as the sauropods evolved, so that bone was developed only along the lines of stress (comparable to the steel struts in a crane jib).

The second special skeletal feature was that the massive hip girdle was firmly fused to the backbone by four (and in later types, five) sacral vertebrae, which formed a solid support for the heavy body and tail.

Family Cetiosauridae

The earliest sauropods lived worldwide during the Jurassic Period and into the Cretaceous. Their name means 'whale lizards', referring to their great size.

Two primitive features remained in members of the cetiosaur family. First, their vertebrae were only partially hollowed out. And second, the hips were attached to the backbone by four sacral vertebrae, a weaker arrangement than in later sauropods. They may be close to the origins of the giant sauropods of the Late Jurassic. Nevertheless, this is still a poorly defined group.

NAME	
Barapasaurus	
TIME	Early Jurassic
LOCALITY	Asia (India)
SIZE	49 ft/15 m long

A field in central India yielded the only sauropod to be found on that subcontinent to date, and also the world's oldest known sauropod. *Barapasaurus* probably lived alongside the later prosauropods.

In build, *Barapasaurus* followed the general sauropod plan, like *Vulcanodon*, its contemporary from Southern Africa and the only other Triassic sauropod known. Only the neck and some of the back vertebrae were hollowed out, as a weight-saving adaptation. Its teeth were spoon-shaped and saw-edged, ideal for eating plants.

NAME	*Cetiosaurus*
TIME	Middle Jurassic to Late Jurassic
LOCALITY	Europe (England) and Africa (Morocco)
SIZE	up to 60 ft/18.3 m long

Bones of this huge sauropod were discovered in 1809 in Oxfordshire in southern England, 32 years before anyone had heard of 'dinosaurs'. People thought the bones belonged to some great marine animal, hence the name *Cetiosaurus*, or 'whale lizard'. Others thought the bones came from some huge crocodile. It was not until the remains of a similar sauropod, *Haplocanthosaurus*, were found in the Late Jurassic rocks of Colorado in western North America, that the true nature of the beast was appreciated.

Cetiosaurus was massively built, but with a shorter neck and tail than usual among sauropods. It may have weighed over 10 US tons/9 tonnes. The backbone was a solid mass, since the vertebrae were hardly hollowed out at all.

A skeleton of *Cetiosaurus* that was unearthed in Morocco in 1979 revealed the size of the animal. The animal's thigh bone alone measured over 6 ft/1.8 m long, and one of the shoulder blades measured over 5 ft/1.5 m in length. The amount of plant food needed to power such great limbs must have been enormous.

Family Brachiosauridae

Members of this family were the giants of the sauropod group. They ranged through North America, Europe and eastern Africa during Mid-Jurassic to Early Cretaceous times. All had a similar structure – small heads perched on extra-long necks, deep bodies and shortish tails. They differed from all other sauropods in that their front legs were longer than their hind legs, so that the body sloped down from the shoulders, like that of a modern giraffe.

Until recently, brachiosaurs could claim to have included not only the most massive dinosaur ever to have lived, but also the largest creature ever to have walked on land. This was *Brachiosaurus* (right). But recent finds in North America show that there were even larger sauropods. In the 1970s, massive bones from two sauropods were found in Colorado, and unofficially called *Supersaurus* and *Ultrasaurus*. In 1986, even larger bones were unearthed in New Mexico, and provisionally named *Seismosaurus*. Some of the remains are enormous, and suggest creatures more than 100 ft/30 m long. There is a shoulder blade 8 ft/2.4 m long, and individual vertebrae 5 ft/1.5 m long.

NAME	*Brachiosaurus*
TIME	Late Jurassic
LOCALITY	North America (Colorado) and Africa (Tanzania and Algeria)
SIZE	75 ft/23 m long

Of all the land animals for which a complete skeleton exists, *Brachiosaurus* is the largest and most massive. A complete specimen of *Brachiosaurus* is displayed in the Paleontological Museum at Humboldt University in East Berlin. It is the largest mounted skeleton in existence. Its bones were found in Tanzania, East Africa, by a university expedition in 1908–12.

Brachiosaurus was, on average, 75 ft/23 m long, and 41 ft/12.6 m tall. Its shoulders were 21 ft/6.4 m off the ground: the upper arm bone, or humerus, alone accounted for 7 ft/2.1 m of this height. It weighed 89 US tons/80 tonnes – almost three times the weight of that other well-known giant sauropod *Apatosaurus* (*Brontosaurus*), or the equivalent of 12 modern, adult African bull elephants.

The secret of supporting such a massive body lay in the construction of *Brachiosaurus'* backbone. Great chunks of bone were hollowed out from the sides of each vertebra, to leave a structure, anchor-shaped in cross-section, made of thin sheets and struts of bone. The resulting skeleton was a masterpiece of engineering – a lightweight framework, made of immensely strong, yet flexible, vertebrae, each articulated to provide maximum strength along the lines of stress.

Brachiosaurus had a deep, domed head, with a broad, flat snout. The head was tiny in comparison with the creature's body, and the brain cavity was equally small.

LONG-NECKED BROWSING DINOSAURS CONTINUED

Pointed, peg-like teeth lined the jaws. Two great nasal openings (external 'nostrils') were on top of the head above the eyes, as in all other sauropods.

The position of the nasal openings originally led paleontologists to think that *Brachiosaurus* and its other massive relatives spent most of their time submerged in water, browsing on soft weeds, with their nostrils above the surface, breathing in air. But it is now recognized that the pressure exerted by the great depth of water needed to cover the animals would have made breathing difficult, if not impossible. Footprints and trackways left by these giant sauropods confirm that they were not aquatic but terrestrial plant-eaters.

An animal's fleshy nostrils may not necessarily be close to its external nasal openings. Modern elephants, for example, have nasal openings on the upper part of the skull, but they breathe through the fleshy nostrils at the tip of their trunks. This raises the question, did some sauropods have trunks?

Another possible function of the large nasal openings of sauropods involves heat regulation; the openings may have been lined with moist, blood-rich skin that helped to keep the animal's brain cool in hot weather.

Brachiosaurus' neck was extremely long, making up about half of its height. There were no more neck vertebrae than usual among sauropods (between 12 and 19), but each was elongated to three times the length of the vertebrae of the back.

An unusual feature among sauropods – but a characteristic of the brachiosaur family – was that the front legs were longer than the back legs. So, the whole body sloped down from its highest point at the shoulders, as in a modern giraffe, giving the animal's long neck an even greater reach to tree-top foliage that was beyond the reach of other dinosaurs.

Family Camarasauridae

Members of this family were much smaller than their contemporaries, the brachiosaurs and diplodocids. Their necks and tails were shorter, and their skulls were higher, with blunter snouts. The teeth, too, were quite different from those of other sauropods; they were long, spoon-shaped and forward-pointing. All these features suggest that the camarasaurs ate different plants from the larger sauropods in the locality, and so did not compete with them for food.

NAME *Camarasaurus*

TIME Late Jurassic

LOCALITY North America (Colorado, Oklahoma, Utah and Wyoming)

SIZE up to 59 ft / 18 m long

This ubiquitous sauropod probably roamed in herds over the moist, tropical plains that covered western North America during the Jurassic Period. Its heavy, spoon-shaped teeth could have dealt with fibrous plants, such as ferns and horsetails, and it could have reached up to the lower branches of conifer trees, tearing away great mouthfuls of tough, needle-like leaves.

Camarasaurus had enormous nasal openings on top of its skull. Their size, together with the animal's short face, has led some paleontologists to speculate that this sauropod had a trunk, like that of a modern elephant, which it used in the same way. However, other scientists think that the large nasal openings acted as a cooling device for the brain (see *Brachiosaurus*, pp.127–128).

The remains of juveniles have been found with adult *Camarasaurus* in the same sequence of rocks (known as the Morrison Formation) in the western USA. This suggests that the young travelled with the herd, maybe on long migrations in search of food. Periodic droughts typical of this tropical Jurassic land could have made such migrations necessary.

Another clue to lifestyle is found in the isolated heaps of polished pebbles preserved in the same rocks. These could be the regurgitated stomach stones. Many sauropods, including *Camarasaurus*, swallowed rough-edged stones as an aid to grinding up their tough plant food. (Many modern birds also swallow stones for the same reason.) When the stones became so worn as to be of little use as digestive aids, they were regurgitated and replaced with new rough-edged stones.

NAME *Euhelopus*
TIME Late Jurassic or Early Cretaceous
LOCALITY Asia (China)
SIZE 49ft/15m long

Although *Euhelopus* and *Camarasaurus* lived on opposite sides of the world, the two sauropods were closely related and of similar build. There were some differences, however. For example, *Euhelopus* had a much longer neck, made up of 17–19 elongated vertebrae (*Camarasaurus* had a short neck, with only about 12 vertebrae). In addition, *Euhelopus* did not have the 'pug nose' of its relative; its head was longer, with a more pointed snout. But like *Camarasaurus*, it possessed the same heavy, spoon-shaped teeth, and large nasal openings on top of its head.

NAME *Opisthocoelicaudia*
TIME Late Cretaceous
LOCALITY Asia (Mongolia)
SIZE possibly 40ft/12.2m long

The exact size and appearance of this sauropod can only be guessed at, since the one skeleton unearthed in the Gobi Desert of Mongolia was missing its neck and head. However, the rest of the body was well-preserved, and seems to be that of a typical, though relatively small and streamlined, camarasaur.

It is the way in which the tail vertebrae lock together that sets *Opisthocoelicaudia* apart from all other known sauropods. Usually, a sauropod's vertebrae are hollowed out on their front ends (i.e. concave toward the animal's head), and they lock together in a forward-pointing arrangement. The tail vertebrae of *Opisthocoelicaudia*, however, are concave on their rear faces, and lock together in a backward-pointing direction, towards the tip of the tail. This feature gives the animal its name, which means 'tail bones hollow at the back'.

The peculiar articulation of *Opisthocoelicaudia*'s tail formed a powerful and rigid arrangement. Some paleontologists have suggested that the tail was used as a prop to steady the animal when it reared up on hind legs to feed on the topmost branches of trees. Other sauropod dinosaurs, such as the diplodocids (see pp.130–132) and the titanosaurs (see p.133), seem to have used their tails to prop themselves up in the same way.

LONG-NECKED BROWSING DINOSAURS CONTINUED

Family Diplodocidae

Diplodocids were sauropod dinosaurs with enormously long necks and even longer tails. Their bodies and limbs were slender, and their heads tiny. But despite their great length, these giant plant-eaters were lightweights in comparison to their relatives, the bulky brachiosaurs (see pp.127–128). This was because the vertebrae of diplodocids had been reduced to a complex latticework of bony struts, designed to save weight, and yet be able to take maximum stress.

The diplodocid family thrived worldwide during the Late Jurassic Period and into the Cretaceous. But toward the end of that period, the group seems to have gone into decline, with only a few representatives restricted to eastern Asia.

NAME	*Diplodocus*
TIME	Late Jurassic
LOCALITY	North America (Colorado, Montana, Utah and Wyoming)
SIZE	85 ft/26 m long

Diplodocus was a huge animal, some specimens reaching lengths of 100 ft/30 m, although the average individual was 85 ft/26 m long. Most of its length was accounted for by the long neck (about 24 ft/7.3 m), and the extra-long tail (about 46 ft, 14 m). The high, narrow body was only about 13 ft/4 m long, and the tiny head measured just over 2 ft/60 cm in length.

Despite its great size, *Diplodocus* weighed only 11 US tons/10 tonnes – about one-eighth the weight of *Brachiosaurus* (see pp.127–128), and one-third that of *Apatosaurus* (also known as *Brontosaurus*, opposite), neither of which were as long as *Diplodocus*. The

reason for this was in the lightweight structure of the animal's vertebrae, which were so hollowed out as to be almost cavernous. But the bony struts that remained were strong enough to support the animal's great frame.

The name *Diplodocus* means 'double beam', and refers to a pair of anvil-shaped bones, or skids, that grew from the underside of each vertebra of the tail. These would have protected the delicate blood vessels and tissues on the underside of the tail as it was dragged over the rough ground.

A well-preserved skeleton of *Diplodocus* was found in Wyoming at the turn of the century by an expedition financed by the American steel millionaire, Andrew Carnegie. Several casts were made of this skeleton and distributed to eight museums throughout the world. Unfortunately, the original Wyoming specimen was incomplete – the bones of the front feet were never found. But in order to complete the casts, the feet were modelled – inaccurately, as it turned out – on the feet of *Camarasaurus (see p.128–129)*, a sauropod that lived in Wyoming at the same time as *Diplodocus*. The mistake can be seen in the front feet – *Diplodocus* had only one clawed toe on each foot, not three as portrayed.

The hind legs of *Diplodocus* were longer than the front legs – as was usual among the sauropods (except for the brachiosaur family). The animal's body sloped downward from the high hips. The vertebrae of the lower back, hips and upper tail had developed tall, vertical spines, and these would have formed attachment points for strong muscles to operate the enormous neck and tail.

It was probably *Diplodocus*' habit to rear up on its hind legs, bending the tail around to form a 'third leg' for balance. Stretching up with its long neck, the animal could browse on the uppermost cones and leaves of the coniferous trees that dotted the Jurassic landscape. Just like today in parts of Africa where herds of giraffes gather, the trees of 150 million years ago would have had a distinctive 'browsing line', below which level most of the leaves would have been stripped away. But instead of the modern-day browsing line at a height of about 20 ft/6 m, the Jurassic line would have been 49 ft/15 m above the ground.

The only predators big enough to attack *Diplodocus* would have been members of the allosaur family, such as *Allosaurus*, which weighed up to 2 US tons/2 tonnes (see p.117). *Diplodocus*' only weapons against such powerful carnivores were its tail and forelegs, combined with its bulk. The long, flexible tail, powered by great back muscles, could have swept clear a large area around the animal, and the whip-like tip could have stunned a predator. Another ploy could have been to rear up on hind legs and bring the stout forelegs crashing down on its attacker.

NAME *Apatosaurus* *(Brontosaurus)*

TIME Late Jurassic

LOCALITY North America (Colorado, Oklahoma, Utah and Wyoming)

SIZE up to 70 ft/ 21.3 m long

The giant, plant-eating dinosaur *Apatosaurus* was once known by the more familiar and evocative name of *Brontosaurus*. This means 'thunder lizard', and could be a reference to the noise its 33 US ton/30 tonne bulk must have made as it walked through its homeland in today's western USA. But *Brontosaurus* was the second name allocated to remains of the beast. So, according to strict scientific convention, it is more properly called by the first name given to it – *Apatosaurus*.

Up until 1975, the skull of *Apatosaurus* was unknown, although the rest of its skeleton had been discovered about 100 years before. The head of this giant sauropod was tiny in comparison with its body – a mere 22 in/55 cm long out of a total body length of over 65 ft/20 m. Although it was not as long as *Diplodocus*, *Apatosaurus* was simply a bulkier version of it. Both animals had long, slender peg-like teeth that grew only at the front of their jaws. The teeth were clearly not very strong and were replaced by new ones as they became worn. There are gaps between them and strange outward facing wear marks on the cutting ends. Such large bulky animals are always herbivores and have to spend much of their lives eating to get enough low-energy plant material to survive. Until recently the feeding habits of peg-toothed sauropods has been something of a mystery. Now research shows that the wear was produced by the action of stripping foliage from branches, using the 'gappy' teeth as rakes.

Both animals could rear up on their hind legs to crop the highest vegetation – though this would have been much more of an effort for *Apatosaurus* since it weighed three times as much as *Diplodocus*. However, *Apatosaurus*' great weight could have been used effectively against a predator such as *Allosaurus*. The plant-eater could have reared up and then brought its heavy forelegs down to crush its enemy. It seems that this ploy did not always work, since many bones of *Apatosaurus* have been found scored with tooth marks similar to those of *Allosaurus* (see p.117). But it could be that the carnivore did not overcome *Apatosaurus*, but came across dead specimens and fed off their corpses.

Apatosaurus had a longer tail than *Diplodocus*, made up of no less than 82 interlocking vertebrae (as compared with 73 in *Diplodocus*). Like *Diplodocus*, it had pairs of bony skids on the underside of the tail vertebrae, which would have helped to protect the soft tissues of the tail.

Apatosaurus could have used its heavy tail as a great whiplash to deter attackers. The tail was powered by strong back muscles, which were anchored to tall spines projecting from the vertebrae of the lower body.

Like *Diplodocus*, *Apatosaurus* had five short toes on each foot, with one claw on the 'big toe' of each front foot, and three claws on each back foot. There were thick wedges of weight-bearing cartilage in the ankle joints (as in those of modern elephants), for flexibility and to spread its weight.

LONG-NECKED BROWSING DINOSAURS CONTINUED

NAME *Dicraeosaurus*

TIME Late Jurassic

LOCALITY Africa (Tanzania)

SIZE 41 ft/12.6 m long

NAME *Mamenchisaurus*

TIME Late Jurassic

LOCALITY Asia (Mongolia)

SIZE 72 ft/22 m long

Not all diplodocids were giants. *Dicraeosaurus* (right) was a relatively small member of the family. It was different in other ways, too – its neck was shorter, its head larger and its tail lacked the whiplash end.

The tall spines that projected from the vertebrae, and provided muscle-attachment points, were not straight as in *Diplodocus* and *Apatosaurus*. Each spine was forked at the top, like a 'Y', and this feature gives *Dicraeosaurus* its name – 'forked lizard'. These tall spines were not confined to the lower back and upper tail as they were in other diplodocids. They ranged along the whole length of the back and even up into the neck. Perhaps they carried strong ligaments, which linked several vertebrae at a time to give extra strength to the backbone.

The remains of *Dicraeosaurus* were found in the fossil-rich rocks of Tendaguru Hill, in modern Tanzania. These Late Jurassic rocks yielded many other dinosaurs, including the giant sauropod *Brachiosaurus* (see p.127–128) and the plated dinosaur *Kentrosaurus (see p.156)*, a relative of *Stegosaurus* (see pp.154–155). All these plant-eaters lived together peacefully on the tropical river plains of eastern Africa, browsing on different plants that grew at different levels, thereby avoiding competition with each other.

This animal (below) had the longest neck of any known dinosaur – of any known animal, in fact. Its neck is so unusual in structure that many paleontologists place *Mamenchisaurus* in a family of its own.

The neck accounted for almost half the animal's total length. It consisted of 19 vertebrae, each elongated to over twice the length of the 12 back vertebrae. Slender, bony struts grew out from each neck vertebra and overlapped the one behind, to provide greater strength and support.

As the animal walked, its stiff neck must have been held out almost horizontally from the body. All movement would have been restricted to the flexible joint between the neck and head, plus a swinging motion from the shoulders. Presumably, this super-long neck gave *Mamenchisaurus* an advantage over other long-necked sauropods in the locality. When it reared up on hind legs, it was able to reach a new food source – the fresh growth at the very tips of the uppermost branches of conifers.

In 1986, the bones of a mighty sauropod were unearthed in Late Jurassic deposits in New Mexico. These have yet to be studied and formally described, but their owner has been tentatively given the name *Seismosaurus* ('earthquake lizard') to reflect its possible size. Initial calculations put this beast at 130 ft/40 m long. Its proportions seem to be like those of *Diplodocus*, but the forelegs were longer. If the early findings prove correct, *Seismosaurus* will hold the record for the world's largest-ever land animal.

Family Titanosauridae

This was the latest family of sauropods, surviving right to the end of the Cretaceous Period. The group was widespread, ranging all over the world, especially in the southern continents, and survived for about 80 million years. Not all members of this family were 'titans' (the mythical giants of Greek legend), as their name implies. Most averaged 40–50 ft/12.2–15.2 m long, which was small in comparison to some of the brachiosaurs and diplodocids.

To date, only fragmentary remains of titanosaurs have been found, not complete skeletons. They seem to have been like *Diplodocus* in structure, but with a shorter neck and a high skull that sloped steeply down to the snout. But unlike *Diplodocus* and other large sauropods, titanosaurs had solid vertebrae; their bones were not hollowed out as a weight-saving adaptation. In addition to this solid skeleton, some animals also had bony armour covering their backs – a unique feature in sauropods.

NAME *Saltasaurus*

TIME Late Cretaceous

LOCALITY South America (Argentina)

SIZE 39 ft/12 m long

The remains of this medium-sized sauropod came as a surprise to paleontologists when discovered in Salta Province of northwest Argentina in 1970. Lying around a group of skeletons were thousands of bony plates. Most of these were tiny, about ¼ in/5 mm across; others were larger, about 4½ in/11 cm across, and may have borne horny spikes.

Dinosaur skin is not normally preserved, so we have little or no evidence of its nature, beyond an expectation that it was scaly because they were reptiles. But here there is good evidence

that in life, these bony plates would have studded the thick skin of the animal's broad back and sides, forming a protective armour for the otherwise defenceless plant-eater against the flesh-eating carnosaurs of the day (see pp.114–121). The tail was flexible and could have supported the body when the animal reared up to reach high vegetation.

The fact that these unique armoured sauropods were confined largely to South America indicates that the continent could have been separate, in Mid Cretaceous times, from the great northern landmass that included North America and Eurasia. Present-day Central America was under water in the Mid Cretaceous. So the South American fauna would have developed in isolation, removed from evolutionary changes.

NAME *Alamosaurus*

TIME Late Cretaceous

LOCALITY North America (Montana, New Mexico, Texas and Utah)

SIZE 69 ft/21 m long

Alamosaurus was among the last sauropods to live before the mass extinction of the dinosaurs at the end of the Cretaceous Period, 65 million years ago. During Late Cretaceous times, there had been a dramatic climatic change in many parts of the world. Much of lowland North America had turned into moist, swampy jungle, which was the domain of the ornithopod dinosaurs – two-legged sprinters with bird-like feet (see pp.134–153). But there were still some high, dry places where the sauropods could live.

It is appropriate that this section on the great saurischian dinosaurs should end with *Alamosaurus*. It was one of the last dinosaurs to survive, and, perhaps coincidentally, is named after the Alamo, that famous fortress in San Antonio where the Texans made their last stand in 1836 against the Mexicans.

FABROSAURS, HETERODONTOSAURS AND PACHYCEPHALOSAURS

INFRAORDER ORNITHOPODA

Members of the great reptilian order of 'bird-hipped' dinosaurs, the Ornithischia, were all plant-eaters. The cheek teeth of most ornithischian dinosaurs were set slightly in from the edges of the jaws. The space lateral to the teeth was probably enclosed by fleshy cheeks which prevented food from falling out of the sides of the mouth during the lengthy process of chewing. These cheeks may have been the reason for the great success of the small to medium-sized (up to 33ft/10m long) plant-eating dinosaurs of the Jurassic and Cretaceous periods. Linked to this success was the extinction of their early, cheekless rivals, the prosauropod saurischians of the Triassic (see pp.122–125).

Ornithischian dinosaurs fall into several groups, some of which consist of four-legged creatures that were armed in various ways. The stegosaurs had bony plates down their backs (see pp.154–156). The ankylosaurs had armour-plated skins and 'clubs' at the end of their tails (see pp.147–161). The ceratopsids had horns on their heads and bony neck frills (see pp.162–169).

The ornithopods, or 'bird feet', walked on two legs, and may have been the ancestral group from which the other ornithischian dinosaurs evolved. They varied in size, habits and distribution, but structurally they were all similar. A highly successful group, they survived for 148million years, spanning the whole of the Jurassic and Cretaceous periods.

Family Fabrosauridae

The earliest-known ornithopods belong to this family and date from the Early Jurassic Period, some 200million years ago. This was the heyday of the fabrosaurs, and they spread throughout the world. In appearance, they were small and lizard-like, but they ran upright on long, slender legs. Superficially, they looked like small, carnivorous theropod dinosaurs (see pp.106–121). In some classifications they are placed apart from the ornithopods but still within the ornithischians.

NAME *Lesothosaurus*
TIME Early Jurassic
LOCALITY Africa (Lesotho)
SIZE 3ft 3in/1m long

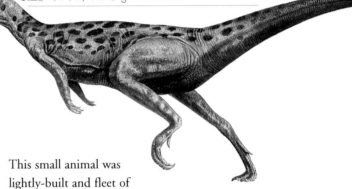

This small animal was lightly-built and fleet of foot, well-suited to sprinting over the hot, dry plains of southern Africa. Its long legs, short arms, flexible neck and slender tail set the general pattern for all subsequent ornithopods. Its skull was small, short and flat-faced, rather like that of a modern iguana. The pointed teeth had grooved edges: during chewing, its upper teeth fitted alternately between the lower ones, producing a chopping motion which would have dealt with tough plants.

A pair of *Lesothosaurus* skeletons found together in southern Africa were curled up and surrounded by worn, discarded teeth, although the skulls of both animals contained a full set of teeth. On the basis of this find, some paleontologists think that they may have slept through the hottest, driest months of the year underground, as do many modern desert creatures. The worn teeth could have been shed during sleep, while new ones grew.

Another find in Lesotho consisted of a jawbone and some teeth. These scanty remains were called *Fabrosaurus*. It is possible that this animal and *Lesothosaurus* were the same creature.

NAME *Scutellosaurus*
TIME Early Jurassic
LOCALITY North America (Arizona)
SIZE 4ft/1.2m long

Scutellosaurus was an armoured fabrosaur – the only one known. Rows of bony studs covered its back and flanks, forming a kind of skin armour. Perhaps to compensate for this extra weight, *Scutellosaurus'* tail was particularly long, about half the total body length. It would have been held out stiffly behind the body to help the animal balance on its hind legs when it needed to run away from an attacker.

The arms, too, were longer than those of other fabrosaurs, suggesting that *Scutellosaurus* probably browsed and rested on all-fours, relying on its armour as its first means of defence.

NAME *Echinodon*
TIME Late Jurassic or Early Cretaceous
LOCALITY Europe (England)
SIZE 2ft/60cm long

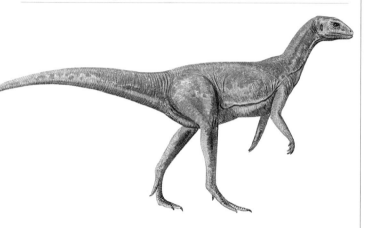

Only the jaw bones of this small fabrosaur have been found. But they provide enough evidence to tell paleontologists that *Echinodon* had a shorter head than *Lesothosaurus*, and that it also possessed unusual teeth. Most reptiles have teeth all of the same size and shape, but *Echinodon* had paired canine-type teeth at the front of its jaws, long and sharp, like the 'eye teeth' of modern cats and dogs. Such teeth were also a feature of a group of contemporary ornithopods – the heterodontosaurs.

Family Heterodontosauridae

Members of the heterodontosaur family looked very much like fabrosaurs and lived at the same time, but they are distinguished from members of that family by their teeth, which were quite different. In fact, the dental arrangement of the Heterodontosauridae family was unique among dinosaurs, and indeed among most other reptiles as well.

Heterodontosaurs were among the first dinosaurs to have developed cheeks, to retain food within the mouth during chewing. They also had three kinds of teeth in their jaws, each of which performed a different function (see *Heterodontosaurus*, right). The family's name reflects this distinctive feature – 'varied-toothed lizards'.

NAME *Heterodontosaurus*
TIME Early Jurassic
LOCALITY Africa (South Africa)
SIZE 3ft/90cm long

The rabbit-sized skull of *Heterodontosaurus* was discovered in 1962 in South Africa's Cape Province, and a complete skeleton has since been found. In build it was like a fabrosaur – a small lightweight, two-legged plant-eater.

Heterodontosaurus was, however, remarkable because of its teeth. Usually, a reptile's teeth are all the same size and shape. But *Heterodontosaurus* had three kinds of teeth – a dental pattern that is reminiscent of a mammal's, although *Heterodontosaurus* had no connection with the mammalian line of evolution.

At the front of the upper jaw there were some small, pointed teeth (like a mammal's incisors). There were no opposing teeth at the front of the lower jaw; instead, the chin bone carried a horny beak. This bone (known as the predentary) was unique to the ornithischian dinosaurs. No other reptile, or indeed any backboned animal, has this bone: usually, the two dentary bones that make up the lower jaw meet in the centre to form the chin.

Behind the upper teeth and lower beak, *Heterodontosaurus* had two pairs of large, canine-type teeth (like the canines of a mammal). The lower pair fitted into a socket in the upper jaw. Behind these canines were the back teeth – tall, chisel-like teeth with cutting edges (comparable to a mammal's molars).

Each type of tooth performed a different job. The pointed ones at the front combined with the beak to nip off leaves; the back teeth cut the leaves up with a scissor-like motion and ground them into small pieces.

Nobody knows the function of this animal's canine teeth. Carnivorous mammals have canines for tearing apart flesh, but *Heterodontosaurus* was a plant-eater. Some skulls have been found that had no canines, or even sockets that would have contained them. This has led some paleontologists to suggest that only the males had canines, and that they used them for fighting each other. According to this theory, skulls without canines would have belonged to females.

FABROSAURS, HETERODONTOSAURS AND PACHYCEPHALOSAURS CONTINUED

NAME *Pisanosaurus*

TIME Late Triassic

LOCALITY South America (Argentina)

SIZE 3 ft/90 cm long

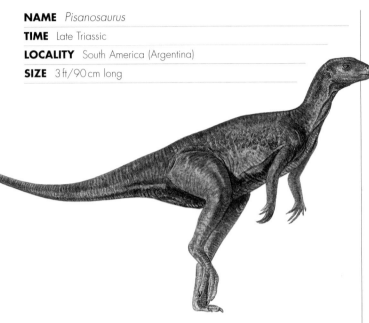

Pisanosaurus has the distinction of being the oldest-known of the successful and long-lived order of ornithischian dinosaurs. It lived during Late Triassic times, several million years before any other 'bird-hipped' dinosaur appeared.

Although its fossil remains are scanty, paleontologists think that *Pisanosaurus* belongs to the heterodontosaur family. The fact that all members of this family discovered to date lived in southern Africa or South America is taken as strong evidence that these southern continents were still joined together during Late Triassic times.

INFRAORDER PACHYCEPHALOSAURIA

The skulls of the so-called 'thick-headed lizards', or boneheads, were dome-shaped, giving their owners a bizarre appearance. The pachycephalosaurs had high foreheads and thick skull caps, made up of enormously thickened bones. Some species also had bony frills, knobs and spikes on the back and sides of their heads, and sometimes on their snouts.

Most paleontologists believe that these boneheaded dinosaurs had a lifestyle similar to that of modern mountain goats. Like these mammals, they would have lived together in herds, and the males would most likely have engaged in competitive, head-butting fights to establish a pecking order.

In other respects, pachycephalosaurs were like ornithopods – two-legged plant-eaters, with five-fingered hands, three-toed feet (with a tiny first toe), and a long, heavy tail. As a group they

were rare, known mainly from Late Cretaceous times in North America and central Asia. But one bonehead, called *Yaverlandia*, has been found earlier than this – dating from Early Cretaceous rocks in southern England.

Family Pachycephalosauridae

The pachycephalosaurid family have the characteristic thick, high-domed skulls of this infraorder, which probably denotes a competitive head-butting habit.

NAME *Stegoceras*

TIME Late Cretaceous

LOCALITY North America (Alberta)

SIZE 6 ft 6 in/2 m long

The whole body of this boneheaded dinosaur seems designed to provide the power behind the ramming head. When an animal charged a rival, its head would have been lowered at right angles, and its neck, body and tail held out stiffly in a horizontal line, balanced at the hips. The skull cap was thickened into a high dome of solid bone, and the small brain was well-protected inside. This domed area would have absorbed the main impact of the blow as the animal crashed head-on against its opponent. A full-grown *Stegoceras* could have weighed 120 lb/54.4 kg.

The 'grain' of the bone in the dome was angled perpendicularly to the surface, and this orientation would have made it capable of withstanding great impact.

Stegoceras, like other pachycephalosaurs, had small, slightly curved and serrated teeth that were highly effective for shredding plant material. Their life habits were probably similar to those of modern wild sheep and goats.

NAME *Prenocephale*

TIME Late Cretaceous

LOCALITY Asia (Mongolia)

SIZE 8 ft/2.4 m long

A truly bulbous dome surmounted the head of *Prenocephale*, and a row of bony spikes and bumps surrounded back and sides of the solid skull. It is probable that the females had smaller, thinner skulls than the males, just as the females of the modern big-horned sheep of the Rocky Mountains in the USA have smaller horns than the males.

Like other boneheaded dinosaurs, *Prenocephale* probably had large eyes and a keen sense of smell. It lived in upland forests, browsing on leaves and fruits.

NAME *Pachycephalosaurus*

TIME Late Cretaceous

LOCALITY North America (Alberta)

SIZE 15 ft/4.6 m long

Pachycephalosaurus was a giant among boneheads. Although it is known only from its skull, this measured 2 ft/60 cm in length. The enormous dome on top of the head was made of solid bone, some 10 in/25 cm thick. Like a great crash helmet, the thick skull could have absorbed tremendous impact as rival males butted each other, head-on.

Pachycephalosaurus was not only the biggest member of the bonehead family, it was also the last member to exist before all its plant-eating relatives and its carnivorous cousins became extinct at the end of the Cretaceous Period.

Family Homalocephalidae

This family of pachycephalosaurs have low, domed skulls. Paleontologists believe that the homalocephalids used their skulls for for a head-pushing, rather than butting, habit.

NAME *Homalocephale*

TIME Late Cretaceous

LOCALITY Asia (Mongolia)

SIZE 10 ft/3 m long

Homalocephale means 'even head', and refers to the fact that this pachycephalosaur did not have a dome on top of its skull. It had a rather flat, wedge-shaped head, although the bones of the skull cap were greatly thickened. There were numerous pits and bony knobs scattered all over the head. This has led some paleontologists to think that rival male *Homalocephale* fought the same kinds of ritualistic, head-butting battles as do the modern marine iguanas of the Galápagos Islands.

Homalocephale had broad hips, and paleontologists interpret this in different ways. Some suggest that the hips could have absorbed the impact when rival males fought. Others postulate that the hips indicate this bonehead gave birth to live young.

HYPSILOPHODONTS

FAMILY HYPSILOPHODONTIDAE

Hypsilophodonts were the 'gazelles' of the dinosaur world. They probably lived in social herds, like modern deer, and would have been continually alert. When danger threatened, they sprinted off at high speed, their lightweight bodies and long, running legs facilitating a fast retreat.

Hypsilophodonts were among the most successful of the dinosaurs. As a group they flourished for about 100 million years, from the Late Jurassic to the end of the Cretaceous, and spread to every continent in the world except Asia.

They are also an important group in the evolution of the dinosaurs. Paleontologists believe that the hypsilophodonts gave rise to two other major groups of ornithopods – the familiar iguanodonts (see pp.142–145) and the abundant 'duckbills' or hadrosaurs (see pp.146–153).

The herbivorous lifestyle of hypsilophodonts was similar to that of the fabrosaurs see p.134–135), the group of earlier Jurassic ornithopods that became extinct at about the same time the hypsilophodonts began their rise. In fact, the chronological evidence combined with several similarities has led some paleontologists to believe that the fabrosaurs were the direct ancestors of the hypsilophodonts.

Structurally, the fabrosaurs and hypsilophodonts were similar. But the hypsilophodonts had several anatomical modifications. For example, they had developed the retaining cheeks that prevented food from falling out of the sides of the mouth. And their upper and lower teeth met, or occluded, as regular rows, rather than interlocking alternately as those of fabrosaurs. This would have given a better chewing and grinding surface.

The hips of hypsilophodonts were also more advanced than those of the fabrosaurs. Part of the pubis bone (known as the pre-pubic process) projected forward, and provided an extra area to which the muscles of the hind legs could attach (see p.90). This resulted in greater running power. But this extra bone was still small enough to leave room for the plant-eater's capacious gut, which was accommodated, in the usual arrangement, in front of its hips.

From the Late Cretaceous rocks of Montana comes possible evidence of how hypsilophodonts lived. Ten dinosaur nests were unearthed there in 1979. Each nest contained about 24 small, ellipsoidal eggs, arranged in a circular pattern, all with the pointed ends downward. The remains of young hypsilophodonts were also discovered in the same area. From this indirect evidence, paleontologists have surmised that the young left the nest immediately on hatching, but remained in the same area for a time, being cared for by their parent or parents. The fact that the eggs were so precisely arranged in the nests suggests that there was certainly some parental care, at least before birth. Modern turtles and alligators also lay their eggs carefully in well-concealed nests in a similar manner, though turtles then vacate the nesting site, leaving their young to take their chances alone.

In contrast, when the eggs of sauropod dinosaurs have been found, they are always laid out in lines, as though the female dropped them while on the move rather than collecting them together in a nest. This suggests that the sauropod eggs were probably left unguarded or cared for and that the offspring were on their own after they hatched out.

NAME *Dryosaurus*

TIME Late Jurassic to Early Cretaceous

LOCALITY North America (Colorado, Utah and Wyoming), Africa (Tanzania). Possibly Australia and Europe (England and Romania)

SIZE up to 10 ft/3 m long

Dryosaurus (also known as *Dysalotosaurus*) was one of the largest of the hypsilophodonts. Although it was also one of the earliest members of the family, its anatomy was advanced in several ways. For example, each of its long, slender legs had only three toes. And there were no teeth in the front part of the upper jaw. Instead, the horny beak at the front of the lower jaw met with a tough, toothless pad opposite on the upper jaw – an efficient arrangement for cropping vegetation.

Like other members of this family of long-legged sprinters, *Dryosaurus'* shin bones were much longer than its thigh bones. The animal's running power came from the heavy leg muscles, which were concentrated around the short thigh bones, and the lower leg. The creature's long feet were operated by light but powerful tendons.

With these characteristics the leg works somewhat like a long pendulum which has a great deal of length but only a small weight on the end. As a consequence of these proportions it has a short swing-time or 'period'. When the animal is running the hind leg moves backwards and forwards very quickly – an obvious advantage for creature that needs to be able to move at great speed.

A further and very necessary aid to speed is a tail to counterbalance the forward weight of *Dryosaurus'* large gut and body. The effectiveness of the tail as a counterbalance is increased by its stiffness. This is achieved by ossified ligaments which link the vertebrae of the tail together. This arrangement gave *Dryosaurus* extra speed and it is exactly the same as the pattern possessed by modern deer and gazelle.

Dryosaurus was obviously a wide-ranging ornithopod, with remains occuring as far apart as western North America and East Africa. In Jurassic times, these continents had begun to separate, but only the initial stretch of the North Atlantic Ocean separated them from each other, and it would still have been possible for animals to migrate across land by way of Europe (where remains of what may be dryosaurs have also been found) and via Siberia and Alaska, which were still linked. This migration explains why the dinosaur remains found in the fossil-rich beds of the Morrison Formation in the western USA are so similar to those that have been discovered in Tendaguru Hill of Tanzania.

Dryosaurus would, therefore, have shared its world with giant plant-eating dinosaurs such as *Apatosaurus* (=*Brontosaurus*), *Diplodocus* and *Brachiosaurus*; small, rapacious carnivores such as the coelurosaurs *Coelurus* and *Elaphrosaurus*; and large carnosaurs such as *Allosaurus* and the horned *Ceratosaurus*.

NAME	*Hypsilophodon*
TIME	Early Cretaceous
LOCALITY	Europe (England and Portugal) and North America (South Dakota)
SIZE	5 ft/1.5 m long

About 20 perfect skeletons of this small hypsilophodont were found in one particular bed of Lower Cretaceous rocks in the Isle of Wight, just off the coast of southern England. This find probably represents a herd of animals that lived and died together, perhaps overwhelmed by the rising tide of the shallow seas that lay over northern Europe some 120 million years ago.

Hypsilophodon is the classic representative of the family, and has given its name to the whole group. Its name means 'high ridge tooth', and refers to the tall, grooved cheek teeth. The upper and lower teeth met to form a flat surface ideally suited to chewing and grinding up tough plant food. These teeth are are typical feature of all hypsilophodonts.

Oddly enough, in comparison with its earlier relatives of the Late Jurassic (see *Dryosaurus*, p.138–139), *Hypsilophodon* had certain primitive features. For example, it had four toes on each foot, and there were incisor-type teeth at the front of the upper jaw. When these were closed on the toothless, horny beak of the lower jaw, they formed an effective device for cropping vegetation (compare *Heterodontosaurus*, p.135).

Hypsilophodon may also have been armoured, with two rows of thin, bony scales running down either side of its back. But paleontologists are uncertain about this feature.

The study of *Hypsilophodon* since its discovery in the 19th century is a classic story of paleontological research and shows how, even with perfect fossil remains, paleontologists also have to rely on analogies with living creatures to infer the lifestyles of new discoveries. When *Hypsilophodon* was first described by Thomas H. Huxley in 1870, paleontologists of the day were struck by the similarity of its build to that of a modern tree kangaroo. For almost a century, classic illustrations of *Hypsilophodon* showed it perched, bird-like, in a tree, with three of its four toes gripping the branch, and the fourth toe directed backward. This reconstruction neatly filled an ecological niche not yet occupied by any dinosaur and so, the idea of a tree-dwelling, plant-eating ornithopod was conceived.

It was not until 1974 that the skeleton of *Hypsilophodon* was reassessed. Paleontologists concluded that there was no evidence to show that it lived in trees. In fact, it was a perfectly-adapted terrestrial animal, capable of running rapidly on two legs.

HYPSILOPHODONTS CONTINUED

NAME *Othnielia*

TIME Late Jurassic

LOCALITY North America (Utah and Wyoming)

SIZE 4 ft 6 in/1.4 m long

This dinosaur is named after the famous 19th-century American fossil-hunter and professor at Yale University, Othniel Charles Marsh (see pp.89–90). He had originally given it the name *Nanosaurus* in 1877, but it was renamed exactly 100 years later, in 1977, to commemorate his prolific and pioneering fieldwork in the study of dinosaurs.

Othnielia was a typical hypsilophodont, with long legs and tail, a lightweight body, and short arms with five-fingered hands. Only its teeth differed. They were proportionally smaller than those of other hypsilophodonts, and were completely covered in enamel, not just on their grinding faces.

It is possible that *Othnielia* ate tougher plants than usual, which would explain the presence of the protective tooth enamel to avoid excessive wear. A tough, fibrous diet would also have meant that *Othnielia* had to grind its food down more finely before it could be digested. As an aid to this, *Othnielia*, like all its relatives, had cheeks that retained the food in the mouth while it was being chewed.

NAME *Tenontosaurus*

TIME Early Cretaceous

LOCALITY North America (Arizona, Montana, Oklahoma and Texas)

SIZE 24 ft/7.3 m long

This dinosaur is so uncharacteristically large compared with other hypsilophodonts that some paleontologists class it with the iguanodonts (see pp.142–145). Indeed, its skull is very similar in shape to that of an iguanodont, but its teeth and their arrangement in the jaws place it firmly in the hypsilophodont family.

Over half the total length of *Tenontosaurus* was made up of the tail, which was enormously thick and heavy. The animal is estimated to have weighed about 1 US ton/900 kg, and probably spent much of its time on all-fours. Its arms were much longer and stouter than those of other hypsilophodonts.

A remarkable find in the rocks of Montana consisted of a skeleton of *Tenontosaurus* surrounded by five complete specimens of *Deinonychus*, a ferocious predator of the day (see pp.110–111). Although these bodies were most likely brought together by chance after death, perhaps in a flash flood, it is interesting to speculate that this mass-burial could have been the outcome of an encounter between the bulky plant-eater and a pack of predators.

Although *Deinonychus* was only about 10 ft/3 m long, it had sharp, meat-shearing fangs, and great, dagger-like claws on its feet. The bulky *Tenontosaurus* could have put up a good fight, kicking out with its heavy-clawed feet or using its great tail as a whiplash. But these were paltry defences when compared with the lethal weapons of the agile carnivores.

NAME *Thescelosaurus*

TIME Late Cretaceous

LOCALITY North America (Alberta, Montana, Saskatchewan and Wyoming)

SIZE 11 ft 6 in/3.5 m long

NAME *Parksosaurus*

TIME Late Cretaceous

LOCALITY North America (Alberta)

SIZE 8 ft/2.4 m long

Thescelosaurus was discovered in the topmost rocks of the Late Cretaceous Period in western North America. It was bulkier and bigger-boned than its closest relatives, the typically small, lightweight hypsilophodonts. It is possible that *Thescelosaurus* is not a hypsilophodont, but a member of the iguanodont family.

Several features distinguish *Thescelosaurus* from other hypsilophodonts. It had teeth in the front of its upper jaw. It had five toes on each foot (hypsilophodonts had three or four). And its thigh bones were as long as its shin bones (the shins of the hypsilophodonts were longer than the thighs).

The structure of the legs strongly suggests that *Thescelosaurus* was not a gazelle-type sprinter but a slower-moving creature. Although it was not built for speedy escape, rows of bony studs set in the skin of its back would have offered it some protection.

Parksosaurus was one of the last of the long-lived hypsilophodont family still surviving at the time of the mass-extinction of the dinosaurs at the end of the Cretaceous Period. It was similar in build to all other hypsilophodonts with short arms, long shins and feet for sprinting and a stiffened counterbalancing tail. It also has a relatively small head with ridged cheek teeth and a horny beak replacing the front teeth, but there were minor differences in the skull, notably its large eyes. *Hypsilophodon* (see p. 139) from the Early Cretaceous appears to be most closely related to *Parksosaurus*.

Parksosaurus probably foraged close to the ground, snuffling about among the low-growing undergrowth, and selectively nipping off its preferred food with its narrow, beaked jaws.

IGUANODONTS

FAMILY IGUANODONTIDAE

The iguanodonts evolved in the Mid Jurassic, about 170 million years ago, and spread throughout the world. *Iguanodon* is the most popular and familiar member of this family of large, plant-eating, ornithopod dinosaurs. They have even been found within what is now the Arctic Circle, although these lands would have been ice-free all those millennia ago. Iguanodonts reached their peak of diversity and abundance by the end of the Early Cretaceous. Thereafter they declined, and finally died out at the end of that period.

Unlike their ancestors – the gazelle-like hypsilophodonts (see pp.138–141) – iguanodonts did not evolve as running animals. Their bodies were bulky and big-boned; the thigh bones were longer than the shin bones (the relative lengths are reversed in sprinting animals); and both the fore- and hind feet had heavy, hoof-like nails. Iguanodonts, therefore, were probably fairly slow-moving animals that spent most of their time on all-fours, browsing on low-growing plants such as horsetails. The beak-like jaws would nip off the leaves, and the rows of high, ridged cheek-teeth would then grind them down to a pulp. These dinosaurs could also rear up on their hind legs to reach higher vegetation and to escape from predators.

The stance of these reptiles has undergone several stages of reinterpretation since they were first found in the early 19th century. To begin with, they were seen as quadrupeds, based on an assumed similarity to living reptiles such as the iguana. However, when more complete specimens were found at the end of the century, it was realized that there was a considerable disparity in size between the forelimbs and hind limbs. This, plus the large tail, was compared with the anatomy and habits of the mammalian kangaroo. It was imagined that the iguanadonts used their large muscular tails for support when reaching to browse in high canopy vegetation. More recently, it was discovered that the tail vertebrae have ossified ligaments interconnecting and stiffening them. It now appears that the tail was used more as a counterbalance to the heavy body and that the iguanodonts probably had a semi-quadrupedal gait – like, indeed, some kangaroos. They could have moved either quadrupedally or bipedally.

NAME	*Callovosaurus*
TIME	Middle Jurassic
LOCALITY	Europe (England)
SIZE	11ft6in/3.5m long

Known only from a single thigh bone, *Callovosaurus* was unlike its contemporary relatives, the hypsilophodonts. It was, in fact, the earliest-known member of the iguanodonts, and presumably was similar in structure and appearance to the later *Camptosaurus* (below).

NAME	*Camptosaurus*
TIME	Late Jurassic
LOCALITY	Europe (England and Portugal) and North America (Colorado, South Dakota, Utah and Wyoming)
SIZE	20ft/6m long

Like *Callovosaurus*, *Camptosaurus* was a primitive member of the iguanodont family. The many skeletons found – particularly in the dinosaur-rich beds of the Morrison Formation in the western USA – suggest that it was an abundant dinosaur.

The skull of *Camptosaurus* was very different from that of its hypsilophodont ancestors. It was long, low and broad; it was also heavy, since some of the gaps between the bones had been closed up. The snout was elongated, and the jaws formed a toothless beak at the tip. A bony palate separated the breathing passages from the eating area of the mouth. This allowed the animal to breathe and chew at the same time – an important development for all herbivores, since they had to spend most of their time eating in order to fuel their massive bodies. *Camptosaurus'* legs were long and powerful, each with three hoofed toes. The thigh bones were massive and slightly curved. The arms were much shorter than the legs, but also equipped with small hoof-like nails, so that the animal could use its hands as feet.

NAME	*Iguanodon*
TIME	Early Cretaceous
LOCALITY	Europe (eg England, Belgium and Germany), North America (Utah), Africa (Tunisia) and Asia (Mongolia)
SIZE	30 ft/9 m long

Iguanodon deserves its place in dinosaur lore. It was the second dinosaur to be discovered, although the word 'dinosaur' had yet to be invented (see pp.17, 88). Part of its great shin bone was found in southern England in 1809, and then some teeth and other bones were discovered in 1819. Scientists of the day regarded the teeth as belonging to some giant mammal. But Gideon Mantell, a geologist and keen fossil collector, saw that the teeth were reptilian, and that they resembled those of the modern iguana of Central and South America. He named the animal *Iguanodon*, and described it in 1825 to the scientific community. Mantell attempted a restoration, but with the sparse information available, it was speculative. He reconstructed *Iguanodon* as a dragon-like beast, with a heavy tail and small, lizard-like head. He placed a short horn – actually one of the animal's 'thumbs' – on the snout.

It was not until 1877 that the true nature of *Iguanodon* became apparent. During that year, in the small town of Bernissart in Belgium, the massive bones of what turned out to be 31 *Iguanodon* were found by workers tunnelling through coal deposits. These spectacular skeletons are now on display in the Royal National Institute of Natural Sciences in Brussels.

Iguanodon stood 16 ft/5 m tall, measured 30 ft/9 m in length, and probably weighed about 5 US tons/4.5 tonnes. Herds of *Iguanodon* would have roamed the tropical Cretaceous landscape, browsing on ferns and horsetails near rivers. Although usually on all-fours, they could also walk upright, using their long outstretched tails to balance.

The head of this great dinosaur ended in a prominent snout and powerful, beak-like jaws. The cheek teeth would have provided a strong, grinding action, because the bones of the upper jaw could move apart when the lower jaw was raised up between them. The banks of cheek teeth then moved past each other, pulverizing the plant food.

The legs were long and pillar-like, each with three stout toes, ending in heavy, hoof-like nails. Each short arm had a five-fingered hand, which could be splayed wide, and used for walking when the animal was on all-fours. Three of the fingers had hoof-like nails. The fifth, or 'little', finger was flexible enough to have been used for grasping or hooking down leaves to the mouth. The first finger, or 'thumb', was developed into a prominent spike, which stuck out sideways from the hand. In 1825, Mantell had found only one of these thumb spikes and, not knowing which part of the animal it came from, placed it, incorrectly, on the snout as a horn.

The function of these thumb spikes is not known. They could have been used to tear down foliage, as defence against attacks from contemporary predators like *Megalosaurus* (see p.116). Or, perhaps, the spikes were sexual display structures used in courtship and mating.

Like *Megalosaurus*, *Iguanodon* has left its footprints in the rocks of southern England. Great trackways suggest that the animals were walking upright at the time they passed, and were travelling in a herd. Similar footprints, though no actual bones, have also been found in South America and in Spitzbergen, north of today's Arctic Circle, which shows how widespread *Iguanodon* must have been 100 million years ago.

IGUANODONTS CONTINUED

NAME *Vectisaurus*

TIME Early Cretaceous

LOCALITY Europe (England)

SIZE 13 ft/4 m long

NAME *Ouranosaurus*

TIME Early Cretaceous

LOCALITY Africa (Niger)

SIZE 23 ft/7 m long

Vectisaurus was a close relative of *Iguanodon*, living in the same place at the same time. Indeed, some paleontologists think it was simply a species of *Iguanodon*.

Unlike its famous relative, only scanty remains have been found of *Vectisaurus*, on the Isle of Wight, off the southern English coast. The only difference between it and *Iguanodon* was the height of the spines that grew upward from its backbone. These spines were long enough in *Vectisaurus* to have formed a prominent ridge down the animal's back. This feature has led some paleontologists to think that *Vectisaurus* may represent an early stage in the evolution of the 'fin-backed' ornithischian dinosaurs, such as *Ouranosaurus* (right).

Vectisaurus belongs to the Wealden fauna of southern England, which is the most varied Early Cretaceous dinosaur assemblage in Europe. The animals include several other ornithopods such as *Hypsilophodon* and *Valdosaurus*; several species of *Iguanodon*; the nodosaurids *Hylaeosaurus* and *Polacanthus*; the early pachycephalosaurid *Yaverlandia*; several sauropods (including a brachiosaurid, titanosaurid and possibly a diplodocid); and finally several theropods.

Two complete skeletons of *Ouranosaurus* were found in 1965, in the southern Sahara of northeastern Niger. Although the remains were identified as belonging to an iguanodont, it was an unusual-looking member of the family. It had a tall wall of spines running down the centre of its back, from the shoulders to halfway along the tail. These spines were outgrowths from the vertebrae of the back, and would have been covered with skin to form a prominent 'fin' or 'sail'.

Another group of dinosaurs, the saurischian spinosaurs, also sported such a fin on the back (see pp.118–119). In fact, one of their members, the large, carnivorous *Spinosaurus*, lived in Niger at about the same time as *Ouranosaurus*.

The function of the fin in the saurischian and ornithischian dinosaurs is not known for certain, but many researchers believe that it was used by these dinosaurs as a mechanism to regulate their body temperature. Such large, bulky animals as *Spinosaurus* and *Ouranosaurus* could easily have become overheated in the hot conditions that prevailed in West Africa during the Cretaceous Period. When the fin was turned toward the sun's rays, its large surface area would have absorbed heat. When it was turned away from the sun, it would have lost heat. Such tall, vertebral spines would have made the body and tail of *Ouranosaurus* quite rigid. But this rigidity was compensated for by the extreme flexibility of the neck. Some paleontologists have proposed that the tall spines actually supported a muscular hump on the back of *Ouranosaurus*, rather like that of a modern American bison. *Ouranosaurus*' skull was also unlike that of other iguanodonts. It was long and low, and sloped gently down to a wide, flat, snout.

The overall appearance of *Ouranosaurus*' skull is reminiscent of a later group of ornithischian dinosaurs, the 'duckbills' or hadrosaurs, that evolved in Late Cretaceous times (see pp.146–153). A pair of bony bumps on the skull increased *Ouranosaurus'* likeness to those hadrosaurs with low crests on their heads.

In other respects, *Ouranosaurus* was like *Iguanodon*. It had five-fingered hands, although they were much smaller and the fingers much shorter than those of *Iguanodon*, and only the second and third fingers had 'walking hooves'. The three-toed feet had heavy, hoof-like nails, as in *Iguanodon*, and the neck was short but flexible.

All in all, *Ouranosaurus* lived like other members of its family. It was probably a slow-moving browser that spent most of its time on all-fours, cropping leaves, fruits and seeds with its horny, duck-like beak.

NAME	*Muttaburrasaurus*
TIME	Early Cretaceous
LOCALITY	Australia (Queensland)
SIZE	24 ft/7.3 m long

Although Australia reputedly has few dinosaur fossils, the last few years have seen a considerable increase in the rate of discovery especially in Queensland. Two kinds of sauropod are known from the Cretaceous deposits of the region but the most common dinosaurs appear to have been the ankylosaurs (*Minmi*) and large ornithopods – *Muttaburrasaurus*. Both of the latter are quite distinct and probably represent endemic lineages, suggesting that during the Early Cretaceous, the continent of Australia was isolated.

Muttaburrasaurus was unearthed in 1981 from what are now the grasslands of central Queensland. In structure, this creature was similar to *Iguanodon*. Only the skull exhibited minor differences. There was a bony bump on the snout in front of the eyes. It is thought by paleontologists that this could have been a sexual display structure, and it was similar in appearance to the crests possessed by some of the later hadrosaurs, such as *Kritosaurus* (see p.147).

Also, there is evidence that the external nostrils were greatly enlarged, indicating that the sense of smell was extremely important to these creatures.

NAME	*Probactrosaurus*
TIME	Early Cretaceous
LOCALITY	Asia (China)
SIZE	20 ft/6 m long

By the end of the Early Cretaceous Period, about 100 million years ago, iguanodonts had reached their peak both in terms of abundance and diversity, and they had spread all over the world. They began to decline from the Mid-Cretaceous Period onward, and very few remains are found in the Late Cretaceous. *Probactrosaurus* of eastern Asia and *Muttaburrasaurus* of Australia were among the few iguanodonts to survive to the end of the Mesozoic Era.

The demise of the iguanodonts was probably linked with the rise of a most successful group of plant-eating ornithopods. These were the duckbilled dinosaurs, or hadrosaurs, that were already common by Late Cretaceous times (see pp.146–153). Like the West African *Ouranosaurus* (opposite), the anatomy of *Probactrosaurus* has several features akin to the hadrosaurs, but the skull is only incompletely known. It could, therefore, have been close to the ancestry of that group, or it may even have been an early member of it.

DUCKBILLED DINOSAURS

FAMILY HADROSAURIDAE

The hadrosaurs were the most common, varied and well-adapted group of ornithopod dinosaurs. Theirs is a real success story in the history of the ruling reptiles. The group probably evolved in central Asia, and by Late Cretaceous times it had spread all over the lands of the northern hemisphere – migrating eastward into North America across the land bridge that existed at the time. From there the group moved eastward again, into Europe.

The spread of the hadrosaurs however was inhibited somewhat by the fact that the southern landmass of Gondwanaland had broken up by Late Cretaceous times and the continents were drifting apart. No hadrosaurs have been found in Africa, India or Australia. But some obviously managed to reach South America, because the remains of a primitive, flat-headed hadrosaur, called *Secernosaurus*, were discovered in Late Cretaceous rocks in southern Argentina. These animals probably crossed over into South America from North America via the chain of volcanic islands that existed where Central America now lies.

Superficially, hadrosaurs looked quite different from each other – with many variations of crests and bumps on their heads. Structurally, however, they were all the same. The most obvious feature that united them as a group was the way the front of the face was elongated into a broad, flattened snout with a toothless beak. This beak looked rather like the bill of a modern duck, and it is this feature that has given the group its popular name of 'duckbilled' dinosaurs.

Although there were no teeth in the front of a hadrosaur's mouth, there were batteries of cheek teeth arranged in rows in the upper and lower jaws. New teeth continually grew to replace old, worn ones (see *Edmontosaurus*, p.149) which had been worn down or damaged due to the hadrosaurs' tough plant diet. This was a unique development among dinosaurs, and was probably a major factor in the success of the group.

Another likely reason for the hadrosaurs' success was that the flowering plants (angiosperms) had evolved during the Cretaceous Period, and toward the end of that period had multiplied over all the surface of the earth. So, as well as plant foods such as ferns, horsetails, cycads and conifers, hadrosaurs were now able to add a profusion of flowering plants to their diet. Competition from the successful hadrosaurs could well have been an important factor in the decline of the other types of plant-eating dinosaurs – the iguanodonts and giant sauropods – which were not able to compete for resources with these versatile newcomers.

All hadrosaurs had long hind legs and shorter forelegs, both equipped with hoof-like nails for walking. It is likely that they spent most of their time browsing on all fours, but when they had to escape from predators, they would have been able to rear up on their hind legs and sprint away, using their long tails to maintain their balance as they ran.

The hadrosaur family is divided into two distinct groups (subfamilies), categorized according to the type of crest. The first group of animals had flat heads surmounted with solid, bony crests – some even had no crests at all. This flat-headed group is called the hadrosaurine duckbills. They were the most successful, long-lived and wide-ranging members of the family, being among the last dinosaurs to survive.

The second group of hadrosaurs had high, domed heads, surmounted by flamboyant, hollow crests. This second group are called the lambeosaurine duckbills (see pp.151–153). They seem to have evolved in North America, and been largely confined to that continent.

NAME	*Bactrosaurus*
TIME	Late Cretaceous
LOCALITY	Asia (Mongolia and China)
SIZE	13 ft/4 m long

The earliest-known hadrosaur and one of the smallest members of the family, *Bactrosaurus* seems to have been intermediate in structure between the two types of duckbills. It had a low, flat head with no crest, and a narrow bill (both features of the hadrosaurine duckbills), but in build it was like a lambeosaurine duckbill. It had the characteristic dentition of the hadrosaurs, with batteries of cheek teeth; these were set well back in the mouth and were capable of grinding tough plant material. *Bactrosaurus* most probably represents an ancestral stage in the development of the group. It could have evolved from one of the iguanodont family, such as *Probactrosaurus* of China (see p.145).

NAME *Kritosaurus*

TIME Late Cretaceous

LOCALITY North America (Alberta, Montana and New Mexico)

SIZE 30ft/9m long

Kritosaurus was a typical member of the flat-headed group of duckbilled dinosaurs. Although this creature did not have a crest on its head, the structure of its skull does reveal the beginnings of one – developed as a large, bony hump on the snout in front of the eyes.

The function of this hump of solid bone is not known. It could have been a sexual display structure, perhaps possessed by the males of the species only, and used in courtship and mating. Alternatively, it is possible that the bony hump had the same purpose as the thickened skull caps of the pachycephalosaurs (see pp.136–137). In these creatures the strengthened skull caps served to absorb the impact when rival males crashed head-on in their ritualistic, head-butting battles. These battles probably took place at the beginning of each season to decide leadership of the herd, and control of the harem.

Like most hadrosaurs, *Kritosaurus* had five or six paired rows of grinding cheek teeth, in both the upper and lower jaws. The rows of teeth grew from inside the jaws progressively towards the wear surfaces. Only the uppermost rows of teeth were in use at any one time.

Some paleontologists believe that *Kritosaurus* and *Hadrosaurus* were not in fact separate genera, but merely different species of the same animal.

NAME *Hadrosaurus*

TIME Late Cretaceous

LOCALITY North America (Montana, New Jersey, New Mexico and South Dakota)

SIZE 30ft/9m long

Hadrosaurus, meaning 'big lizard', has the distinction of being the first dinosaur to be discovered in North America. Its bones were found in New Jersey, and it was reconstructed and named in 1858 by the American professor of anatomy, Joseph Leidy, of the University of Pennsylvania. Joseph Leidy recognized that *Hadrosaurus* was structurally related to *Iguanodon*, the remains of which had first been discovered in southern England, and described in 1825 (see p.143).

Leidy was able to avoid the errors of Mantell who made the early, inaccurate reconstructions of *Iguanodon* as a four-legged, dragon-like creature. Leidy had the benefit of more complete skeletal material to work with and was an anatomist by training. By comparison, Mantell's fossils were very incomplete and, although a medical doctor, Mantell had no special training in vertebrate anatomy.

Leidy was able to infer from the structure of *Hadrosaurus* that it could rise up on its hind legs. He showed it in a running pose as a bipedal animal – standing upright on two legs, its short arms dangling and its body bent horizontal to the ground, balanced by the long, outstretched tail.

Hadrosaurus was the typical member of the duckbill family. Like *Kritosaurus*, it did not have a crest on its long, low head, but there was a large hump on its snout, which was formed from solid bone, and was probably covered with thick, hard skin. *Hadrosaurus'* bill, at the front of the jaws, had no teeth, but there were hundreds of teeth at the back of the jaws, and these would have been in a continual state of replacement with new teeth growing to replace those worn down by the animal's tough vegetarian diet.

Hadrosaurs could move their upper and lower jaws against each other in both a vertical and horizontal direction. This range of movement would have produced strong chewing and grinding actions, which would have thoroughly pulverized the food before it was swallowed, making it easier to digest.

DUCKBILLED DINOSAURS CONTINUED

NAME *Maiasaura*

TIME Late Cretaceous

LOCALITY North America (Montana)

SIZE 30 ft/9 m long

The discovery of *Maiasaura* in 1978 gave paleontologists a new insight into the family life of dinosaurs. In that year, a complete nesting site was found in Montana – the remains of an ancient nursery, some 75 million years old, where duckbills laid their eggs, and the young could develop in a safe and nurturing environment, protected from predators.

This exciting find consisted of the skeleton of an adult (the mother, presumably); several youngsters (each about 3 ft 3 in/1 m long); a group of hatchlings (each about 20 in/50 cm long) together in a fossilized nest; and several other nests complete with intact eggs, and pieces of broken shell lying around.

The nests themselves had been made of heaped-up mounds of mud – long since turned to solid rock – each about 10 ft/3 m in diameter and 5 ft/1.5 m high. In the centre of each mound was a crater-like depression, about 6 ft 6 in/2 m in diameter and 2 ft 6 in/0.75 m deep. The spacing between the nests was about 23 ft/7 m, indicating that the mothers nested fairly close to each other, since the average length of *Maiasaura* was some 26 ft/8 m.

The fossilized eggs found in the nests were obviously placed with care. They were arranged in circles within the crater, layer upon layer. The mother probably covered over each layer with earth or sand as she went, and then covered the whole nest with earth when she was finished. This would have kept the eggs warm while they hatched, and well-concealed from predators.

These duckbilled hadrosaurs were obviously social animals, as seen by this nursery site. The females nested in groups, probably even returning to the same site each year, as do some modern animals – seabirds, turtles and fish. The youngsters stayed with their mothers until they were mature enough to fend for themselves – also seen in many modern groups.

NAME *Shantungosaurus*

TIME Late Cretaceous

LOCALITY Asia (China)

SIZE 43 ft/13 m long

This massive, flat-headed duckbill was among the biggest of the hadrosaurs. An almost complete specimen was discovered in Shandong (formerly Shantung) Province of eastern China during the 1970s, and its reconstructed skeleton is now on display in Beijing's (Peking's) Natural History Museum.

Shantungosaurus had an extra-long tail, accounting for almost half its total body length. This was needed to counterbalance the animal's great weight – probably over 5 US tons/4.5 tonnes. When *Shantungosaurus* walked upright, the tail was held out behind, balancing the body at the hips.

This duckbill's tail was deep, and flattened from side to side – rather like the tail of a crocodile. Because of this structure, paleontologists originally thought that duckbills spent most of their time in water, and used their tails for swimming. However, the vertebrae of the tail were lashed together by bony tendons, making it much too inflexible to have acted as a paddle. In addition, the spines above and below the tail vertebrae sloped backward. In true aquatic animals, these spines are vertical, to provide attachment points for strong swimming muscles.

Shantungosaurus and its relatives most likely ventured into water only to escape predators.

NAME *Anatosaurus*

TIME Late Cretaceous

LOCALITY North America (Alberta)

SIZE 33 ft/10 m long

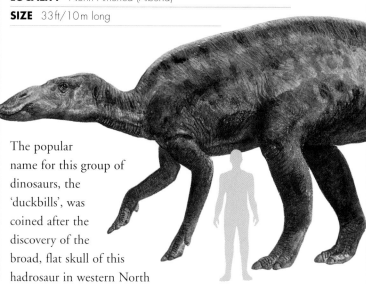

The popular name for this group of dinosaurs, the 'duckbills', was coined after the discovery of the broad, flat skull of this hadrosaur in western North

NAME	*Edmontosaurus*
TIME	Late Cretaceous
LOCALITY	North America (Alberta and Montana)
SIZE	43 ft/13 m long

America. The name *Anatosaurus*, in fact, means 'duck lizard', and refers to the animal's horny, toothless bill or beak. The fossil evidence for *Anatosaurus* is good, with several well-preserved skeletons of *Anatosaurus* having been found. From these specimens, paleontologists can tell that this duckbill was over 30 ft/9 m long, stood some 13 ft/4 m tall, and probably weighed about 4 US tons/3.6 tonnes. Two 'mummified' specimens were also found – a rare and highly informative discovery – with dried-up tendons and the contents of their stomachs intact. Analysis of the stomach contents revealed that the last meal eaten by these two individuals consisted of pine needles, twigs, seeds and fruits.

Impressions of the animals' skin were also preserved, stamped into the surrounding rocks. Though all the skin had long since rotted, these impressions show that *Anatosaurus* was covered in a thick, leathery hide.

The same mummified specimens appeared to have had webs of skin between the three main fingers of each hand. At first, this was taken as support for the theory that duckbills were aquatic animals, using their webbed hands and flattened tails for swimming. Closer examination, however, indicated that the hands could not be stretched widely, and it seems more likely that the webs of skin were the shrivelled remains of weight-bearing walking pads, calloused with wear like those on the feet of modern camels. Taken in conjunction with the presence of hoof-like nails on two of the main fingers of each hand, this interpretation of the 'webs' supports the current theory that duckbills were true land-dwellers that walked on all-fours.

Many skulls of this large, flat-headed duckbill have been found. The teeth are particularly well-preserved, and show the typical hadrosaur pattern of dentition. Behind the toothless beak, banks of tightly-packed teeth formed a veritable grinding pavement in both jaws. As those at the top were worn down and discarded, new teeth would have grown to replace them from beneath. At any one time, there may have been over 1000 teeth in *Edmontosaurus'* mouth.

The outer edge of each tooth was coated with hard enamel, which wore away more slowly than the dentine that made up the rest of the tooth. The result was that each tooth had a cutting ridge of hard, upstanding enamel. Packed so closely together in each jaw, the batteries of teeth presented a coarse, abrasive surface for pulverizing plant food.

The jaw structure of this creature was rather like that of *Iguanodon* (see p.143) in that the upper jaw could move over the lower jaw, so that the teeth ground against each other when the mouth was closed. This feature produced a shearing, grinding action between the tooth rows, capable of shredding the toughest of plant material. Indeed, *Edmontosaurus* and its relatives lived on coarse food, as the fossilized stomach contents of *Anatosaurus* showed.

Like other hadrosaurs, *Edmontosaurus* had a long tail that counterbalanced the weight of the front end of the animal's body when it rose up on its hind legs in order to run. The tail was also deep – like that of *Shantungosaurus* (opposite) – with long spines extending below the vertebrae, and could have been of some use in swimming when *Edmontosaurus* occasionally ventured into water.

DUCKBILLED DINOSAURS CONTINUED

NAME
Prosaurolophus

TIME Late Cretaceous

LOCALITY North
America (Alberta)

SIZE 26 ft/8 m long

Prosaurolophus was a
typical member of the
hadrosaurine group of
hadrosaurs – those
duckbills with solid, bony crests on their heads. Its skull was
similar to that of one of the flat-headed duckbills, such as
Anatosaurus (see pp.148–149), but the nasal bones were
extended into a low crest of bone that ran from the tip of the
broad snout to the top of the head, where it was developed into
a small, bony knob. Since this crest became more pronounced in
relatives of *Prosaurolophus*, this duckbill may have been ancestral
to later members of the family, such as *Saurolophus*.

NAME *Saurolophus*

TIME Late Cretaceous

LOCALITY North America (Alberta and California) and Asia (Mongolia)

SIZE 30 ft/9 m long

The face of this large duckbill swept upward in a curve, from
the broad, flattened snout to the tip of a solid, bony crest that
sloped backward from the top of its head. The Asian species had
a larger crest than its North American relative and a
correspondingly larger body, about 39 ft/12 m long.

The crest was an extension of the nasal bones, and the nasal
passages would have run
through it. This has
led some

paleontologists to think that there was a mass of
nasal tissue which could have been inflated, and used
to produce bellowing or honking sounds. The bony
crest would have acted as a support for this
inflatable sac, increasing its area and hence its
efficiency. Since hadrosaurs lived in herds, such
sounds would have been an effective means of
communicating, especially over a distance.

NAME *Tsintaosaurus*

TIME Late Cretaceous

LOCALITY Asia (China)

SIZE 33 ft/10 m long

A unicorn-type
horn grew from the
top of this Chinese
duckbill's head, giving
it a bizarre appearance
quite unlike that of any
of its relatives.

The tip of this column
of bone was expanded and
notched, and there was a
connection between the base of the
crest and the nostrils. These facts
have led some paleontologists to
believe that there may
have been a flap of
skin attached to the horn, or stretched between the
tip of the horn and the beak. This flap could have been
inflated like a balloon, and used as a signalling device, either
for courtship or for threatening rivals. It may have been brightly
coloured, and would have made a spectacular display.

Other paleontologists, however, think that the horn was
wrongly mounted in the reconstruction of the original specimen
of *Tsintaosaurus* and should point backward, as in *Saurolophus*.

NAME *Corythosaurus*
TIME Late Cretaceous
LOCALITY North America (Alberta and Montana)
SIZE 30 ft/9 m long

A spectacular semicircular crest decorated the head of this large, North American duckbill, which weighed almost 5 US tons/ 4.5 tonnes. The crest rose steeply from just in front of the animal's eyes into a tall, narrow fan shape (about 1 ft/30 cm high) that curved down to the back of the head.

Several sizes of crest have been found in different specimens of *Corythosaurus*. This could reflect different species of this duckbill or, more likely, the specimens may simply represent different growth stages of the same species, with juvenile specimens having much smaller crests than adults. There may even have been a size difference between the sexes, with full-grown males having the largest crests.

Corythosaurus was a typical member of the lambeosaurine group of hadrosaurs – those duckbills with hollow crests on their heads. (Solid head crests characterized the hadrosaurine duckbills, see pp.146–50) As a group, the hollow-crested types seem to have evolved in North America, and been largely confined to the western part of that continent. Some species have also been found in eastern Asia. These widely separated finds lend support to the theory that western North America and eastern Asia were joined together in Late Cretaceous times as one landmass, 'Asiamerica', which was surrounded by shallow continental seas.

The domed crest was made up of the greatly expanded nasal bones. The hollows inside the crest were the actual nasal passages, which ran up into the crest and looped back down into the snout. Several theories have been proposed for such an arrangement, some of them more likely than others. The old notion, for example, that hadrosaurs were aquatic animals, led to the belief that the crest, with its series of hollow tubes, was some kind of snorkel, which allowed the animal to breathe air while its mouth and nostrils were submerged. Another theory proposed that the crest acted as an air reservoir, so that the duckbill could draw on its supply while swimming or feeding underwater.

It is now known that the duckbills were well-adapted land animals. They were also gregarious and lived in herds, browsing in the forests on tough pine needles, magnolia leaves, seeds and fruits of all kinds. When threatened by predators such as *Tyrannosaurus*, they could sprint away on two legs. They may even have taken to water to escape.

Several more likely explanations exist for the hollow crest, and it is quite possible that it served some or all of the proposed functions. First, the hollow crest with its convoluted tube system could have been used as a vocal resonator – like the pipe of a trombone – to produce sounds that allowed communication with the rest of the herd. These sounds could have been made for a variety of purposes – to warn other members in the herd of danger, to win a mate or discourage a rival, and to facilitate species-recognition between groups.

The results of recent research in the USA seem to support this theory. An exact model of a lambeosaur's crest was constructed, and experiments show that these duckbills could have produced a kind of foghorn sound from such a structure. These booming, resonant notes would have been heard over wide distances, and provided these forest-dwellers with an effective means of communicating both within and between herds. The postulated inflatable nasal sacs on the faces of the flat-headed, solid-crested duckbills (in the hadrosaurine subfamily) probably served the same purpose.

Another theory proposes that the long air passage within the hollow crest could have served as a cooling system. Its surface may have been lined with a moist membrane, evaporation from which would have reduced the temperature of the surrounding tissue. This would have helped to cool down the animal when it was browsing in the open under the hot sun, or after a strenuous flight from a predator.

A third theory suggests that the hollow crest enhanced *Corythosaurus'* sense of smell, helping it to find food, detect the approach of danger and keep with the herd.

A primitive-looking crested duckbill was found in Montana after the discovery of *Corythosaurus*, and named *Procheneosaurus*. Its crest was much smaller than that of *Corythosaurus*, but it contained the same, typical S-shaped air passage. Some paleontologists think that this creature is possibly the most primitive of the hollow-crested duckbills. Others, however, believe it to be simply a juvenile specimen of *Corythosaurus* itself.

DUCKBILLED DINOSAURS CONTINUED

NAME *Hypacrosaurus*

TIME Late Cretaceous

LOCALITY North America (Alberta and Montana)

SIZE 30 ft/9 m long

Another duckbill with a prominent semicircular crest on its head was *Hypacrosaurus*. The crest was similar to that of *Corythosaurus*, but not so tall or narrow. Nor did it rise so steeply from the animal's face as that of *Corythosaurus*, but rather sloped upward in a gentle curve. Since *Hypacrosaurus* is found in slightly later rock deposits than *Corythosaurus*, it is possible that it evolved from the earlier duckbill.

Another difference between these two similar-sized duckbills was that the back vertebrae of *Hypacrosaurus* were extended upward into tall spines, which would have formed a prominent skin-covered ridge down the animal's back. The function of this ridge may have been to regulate the body temperature, operating in the same way as that proposed for other reptiles, such as the fin-backed pelycosaurs (see pp.186–188) or the carnivorous spinosaurs (see pp.118–119).

There is evidence from trackways which suggests that these large hadrosaurids were quadrupedal for most of the time.

ungainly, mounted as it was on the long, flexible neck.

Like all members of the duckbill family, *Lambeosaurus* moved about on all-fours while browsing on low-growing vegetation. The animal's flexible neck seems to have been an adaptation that allowed it to reach around its body easily and gather low-growing plants from a wide area without having to shift its position.

The Californian specimen of *Lambeosaurus* seems to have been a giant among duckbills. Although the remains are fragmentary, the size and weight of the bones found indicate that their owner may well have reached a length of 54 ft/16.5 m, making it the largest hadrosaur known.

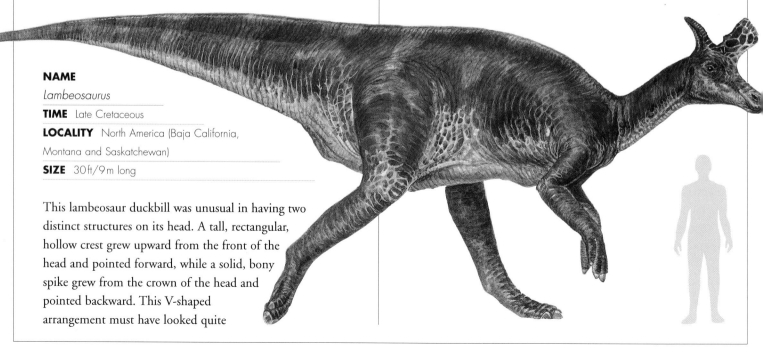

NAME

Lambeosaurus

TIME Late Cretaceous

LOCALITY North America (Baja California, Montana and Saskatchewan)

SIZE 30 ft/9 m long

This lambeosaur duckbill was unusual in having two distinct structures on its head. A tall, rectangular, hollow crest grew upward from the front of the head and pointed forward, while a solid, bony spike grew from the crown of the head and pointed backward. This V-shaped arrangement must have looked quite

NAME	*Parasaurolophus*
TIME	Late Cretaceous
LOCALITY	North America (Alberta, New Mexico and Utah)
SIZE	33 ft/10 m long

Like *Saurolophus* (see p.150), this duckbill had a shorter snout than other hadrosaurs, and a single backward-pointing, horn-like crest mounted on the top of its head. But there the resemblance ends, since the crest of the lambeosaurine *Parasaurolophus* was not solid like that of its hadrosaurine relative. Instead, it was constructed like a hollow tube, and was many times longer than that of *Saurolophus*. In fact, the great crest was up to 6 ft/1.8 m long. Inside, in an arrangement similar to that of *Corythosaurus*, the paired nasal passages ran from the nostrils right up to the tip of the crest, and then curved back down to the snout.

A skull with a much shorter crest and more tightly curved nasal passages was originally identified as a separate species of *Parasaurolophus*. But it is now regarded as belonging to a female of the long-crested type, in accordance with the theory that the sexes had crests of different sizes.

A unique feature of *Parasaurolophus* was a notch in its backbone which occurs behind the shoulders, just at the point where the tip of the crest would abut the back when the duckbill's neck was held in its natural, S-shaped pose. Some paleontologists have suggested that the crest fitted into this notch while the animal was running through dense undergrowth. Then, the crest would have acted like a deflector, sweeping low-hanging branches upward and away from the body. The head crest of the modern cassowary is often used to break a path in the same way.

The tail of *Parasaurolophus* was also unusual, in that it was particularly deep. This has led some researchers to think that it

may have been brightly patterned, and was used as a signalling device, perhaps during courtship or maybe to help the herd stay together as it moved through the forest. In addition, it has been suggested that there could have been a frill of skin at the back of the head, loosely connecting the crest with the neck. This frill could also have been brightly coloured, and may have served a similar display function.

If the theory is correct that the hollow crest was used as a vocal resonating chamber (see *Corythosaurus*, p.151) then one might suppose that the sounds produced through the long crest of *Parasaurolophus* were different from those produced, for example, by the high, semicircular crest of *Corythosaurus*. Indeed, the head-dresses of the lambeosaurine duckbills show such a variety in size and shape that it seems likely that different species had quite different calls.

The forests of North America in Late Cretaceous times must have reverberated with sounds – from the foghorn bellowings of the hollow-crested duckbills, to the honking and trumpeting that came from the nasal sacs of their neighbours, the solid-crested duckbills.

The skeleton is quite heavily built, especially in the shoulder region, hips and front legs. The increased musculature and robustness of the front end suggests that *Parasaurolophus* made a great deal of use of its front legs for walking. Likewise, the hip region has enlarged pelvic bones for increased muscle attachment and strength required to rear up on the hind legs.

The bulk of these hadrosaurids originate in the Middle Cretaceous and are well-distributed across the northern continents but are less well known from the southern continents. They were remarkably diverse and evolved rapidly into the Upper Cretaceous. Although there was some turnover in genera, within the dinosaurs as a whole, the group were one of the main victims of the end Cretaceous extinction.

ARMOURED DINOSAURS

SUBORDER THYREOPHORA

Recently the great order of ornithischian ('bird-hipped') dinosaurs has been divided into two suborders, the cerapodans and the thyreophorans. The latter suborder includes the stegosaurids and ankylosaurids as well as the more primitive scelidosaurids and are characterized by parallel rows of keeled bony scutes down the back and sides.

Family Scelidosauridae

The position of the scelidosaurs in the dinosaur array is controversial. Some paleontologists maintain that they were the ancestors of the stegosaurs, while others believe them to be ancestral ankylosaurs. Here, they are placed with both of those groups as a family of the Suborder Thyreophora.

NAME *Scelidosaurus*

TIME Early Jurassic

LOCALITY Europe (England)

SIZE 13 ft / 4 m long

Only two skeletons of *Scelidosaurus* have been found to date, both from the Early Jurassic of Dorset in southern England. The first specimen was discovered in about 1860 and the second almost a century later, in 1955.

Scelidosaurus seems to be one of the earliest and most primitive of the ornithischian dinosaurs. It had a small head (only about 8 m/20 cm long), a toothless beak and small, leaf-shaped teeth in its weak jaws. The body, however, was massive and stoutly armoured: the back was covered in bony plates, which were studded with parallel rows of spikes running from the neck to the tip of the tail and over the upper flanks. It is this arrangement of the armour that leads some paleontologists to believe that *Scelidosaurus* was a primitive type of ankylosaur, but this relationship is not universally accepted.

INFRAORDER STEGOSAURIA

The stegosaurs were a distinctive group of ornithischian, or 'bird-hipped', dinosaurs. Their small-headed, massive bodies were characterized by double rows of great, bony plates that extended down either side of the backbone. Their heavy tails were armed with pairs of long, sharp spikes.

Like their ornithopod relatives, such as the iguanodonts (see pp.142–145) and the duckbills (see pp.146–153), the stegosaurs were plant-eaters, and probably lived in herds. But unlike the more agile ornithopods, stegosaurs moved about exclusively on four legs, and were not capable of running on two legs to escape predators. Their body armour made up for this deficiency. When attacked, they would most likely have stood their ground, lashing out with the spiked tail, and protected to a certain extent by the bony plates on the back.

Family Stegosauridae

All the familiar stegosaurs belong to this family, including *Stegosaurus* itself. They evolved in Mid-Jurassic times, some 170 million years ago, and reached their peak of diversity by the end of that period. A wide-ranging group, they spread through western North America, western Europe, East Asia and East Africa. By Early Cretaceous times, the stegosaurs had started to decline, although it is quite possible that some species survived in isolated pockets until the end of the Cretaceous.

NAME *Stegosaurus*

TIME Late Jurassic

LOCALITY North America (Colorado, Oklahoma, Utah and Wyoming)

SIZE up to 30 ft / 9 m long

This armoured dinosaur is the state fossil of Colorado and the largest and most familiar of the stegosaurs. A double row of broad, bony plates, shaped like huge arrowheads, ran down either side of the backbone, from just behind its head to halfway along its tail. Some of the plates were over 2 ft/60 cm high.

The heavy tail was armed with pairs of vicious spikes, each about 3 ft 3 in/1 m long. The number of spikes varied between species: *Stegosaurus ungulatus* had four pairs, *S. stenops* had two.

No-one is certain exactly how the bony plates were arranged on the back of *Stegosaurus*. Although many well-preserved specimens have been found – one of the best is mounted in Colorado's Denver Museum of Natural History – the plates have never been found actually attached to the skeleton. Some paleontologists maintain that they lay flat in or on the skin, and formed a defensive armour over the back and upper flanks.

Most paleontologists, however, believe that the plates stood up almost vertically, and were arranged either in a zigzag pattern or opposite each other in pairs. They would have formed a spiky fence, protecting *Stegosaurus* from attack by such predators as the contemporary carnosaur *Allosaurus* (see p.117). They were probably covered in tough horn, like the horns of modern cattle.

Alternatively, a thin layer of blood-rich skin could have covered the plates. This theory has led some paleontologists to propose an entirely different function for the plates – that of heat exchangers, a crude but effective means of regulating body temperature. The near-vertical plates could have been arranged alternately down the back. Their large surface area and rich supply of blood would have enabled them to absorb heat rapidly when oriented toward the sun (thus raising the body's internal temperature), and to lose heat when turned away.

The long, sturdy spikes on the tail of *Stegosaurus* were probably covered in horn, and were undoubtedly used for defence. *Stegosaurus* could have swung its long, heavy tail from side to side, and inflicted great damage on an attacker.

On average, *Stegosaurus* was 20 ft/6 m long, and weighed up to 2 US tons/2 tonnes. The massive hind legs, with their heavy hooves, were over twice the length of the forelegs – a striking feature in this four-legged animal, since it meant that the body sloped forward from its highest point at the hips.

Tall spines projected upward from the vertebrae of the hips and base of the tail, probably acting as anchor points for strong back muscles. This arrangement suggests that *Stegosaurus* could have lifted its forelegs off the ground without much effort, allowing it to feed off the lower branches of trees.

The skull of this huge dinosaur was only about 16 in/40 cm long. The brain was correspondingly small, about the size of a walnut. *Stegosaurus* was not particularly well-equipped for chewing plant food: it had a toothless beak at the front of the jaws, and the cheek teeth were small and weak. In order to digest its food, it is likely that *Stegosaurus* swallowed stones (as did many of the herbivorous dinosaurs), and held them in its stomach, where they helped to grind down tough plant material.

An intriguing cavity in the hip vertebrae of *Stegosaurus*, above the hind legs and just at the point where the spinal cord would have passed in life, has led paleontologists to speculate that this site housed a 'second brain' that controlled the movements of the animal's hindquarters. This 'brain' would really have been a conglomeration of nervous tissue, situated where the nerves of the hips and hind legs met. In fact, all backboned animals have this extra 'brain', but its size is related to the size of the hips: in big-hipped animals, such as many of the dinosaurs, the hip's 'brain' was larger than that of the skull.

An alternative theory proposes that the cavity housed a gland that produced glycogen. Doses of this sugary substance could have been released to provide the animal's hindquarters with an extra boost of energy in times of stress.

ARMOURED DINOSAURS CONTINUED

NAME *Kentrosaurus*

TIME Late Jurassic

LOCALITY Africa (Tanzania)

SIZE 16ft/5m long

Well-preserved remains of this East African stegosaur – a contemporary of the *Stegosaurus* – have been found in modern Tanzania among the fossil-rich deposits of Tendaguru Hill.

Kentrosaurus was not as large as its North American relative, but it was at least as well armoured. A double row of narrow, triangular, bony plates rose on either side of the backbone, grouped in pairs along the neck, shoulders and front part of the back. Halfway along the back, the plates gave way to pairs of sharp spikes (some of them about 2ft/60cm long) that ran along the remainder of the backbone right to the tip of the tail. In addition, a pair of extra-long spikes stuck out at hip-level on each side, affording good protection should a predator attack from the side.

NAME *Tuojiangosaurus*

TIME Late Jurassic

LOCALITY Asia (China)

SIZE 23ft/7m long

Tuojiangosaurus is one of several armoured dinosaurs found in China. It was the first stegosaur to be discovered in Asia, and is known from an almost complete specimen. Structurally similar to *Stegosaurus*, it had a small, narrow head with low teeth and a heavily built body. Fifteen pairs of bony plates surmounted its back, becoming taller and more spike-like over the hips and down the tail. As in *Stegosaurus stenops*, there were two pairs of long spikes on the tail.

It seems that *Tuojiangosaurus* was not able to rear up on its hind legs, as was *Stegosaurus*. This is deduced from the fact that the tall spines that projected upward from the back vertebrae of *Stegosaurus* (to provide muscle-attachment points) are not present in either *Tuojiangosaurus* or *Kentrosaurus*. This suggests that they were ground-feeding animals.

NAME *Wuerhosaurus*

TIME Early Cretaceous

LOCALITY Asia (China)

SIZE 20ft/6m long

This Chinese stegosaur is known only from a few fragmentary remains of bones and scattered plates. The restoration here is therefore tentative. *Wuerhosaurus* is one of the few to have survived into Early Cretaceous times. However, another possible stegosaur, *Dravidosaurus*, has been found in India in Late Cretaceous beds. It is possible that India was an island continent at that time, isolated from the other landmasses, and a few species may have survived there, while the rest died out.

INFRAORDER ANKYLOSAURIA

The decline of the stegosaurs toward the end of the Jurassic Period may be linked to the rise of another group of armoured dinosaurs, the ankylosaurs. They spread throughout the northern continents during Cretaceous times, and were particularly abundant in Asiamerica (see p.11) toward the end of that period.

Like the stegosaurs, ankylosaurs were heavily-built, four-legged plant-eaters. They were also armoured, but with a different, and more effective, kind of defensive plating than that of the stegosaurs. The neck, back, flanks and tail were entirely covered in a mosaic of flat, bony plates, which were embedded in the thick, leathery skin, and covered in horn. Spikes and knobs of various sizes studded the bony armour.

There were two distinct families of ankylosaur. The nodosaurs had narrow skulls, armoured backs and rows of long spikes projecting from their flanks. The ankylosaurs themselves had broad skulls and a heavy 'club' of solid bone at the end of their tails (see pp.160–161).

Family Nodosauridae

The nodosaurids were the earlier and more primitive of the two families of ankylosaur, and ranged throughout the northern hemisphere during the Cretaceous Period. Some paleontologists think that they may have evolved in Europe during the Late Jurassic, and then spread to the other northern continents. Some types at least also reached the southern hemisphere – *Minmi* is a recent discovery from Australia.

The nodosaurids had narrow skulls, longer than they were wide. Solid, bony plates covered the body from neck to tail, and long spikes guarded the flanks.

There is considerable uncertainty about nodosaurid inter-relationships and future finds will doubtless necessitate reassessment of the classification of the group.

NAME *Hylaeosaurus*
TIME Early Cretaceous
LOCALITY Europe (England)
SIZE 20 ft/6 m long

Hylaeosaurus is the earliest creature that can definitely be identified as a nodosaur. Its remains were first found in Sussex in southern England in the late 1820s, and named by that English pioneer of paleontology, Gideon Mantell, in 1832. To this day, its bones are still imprisoned in the slab of rock in which they were fossilized, but there are now plans to extract the skeleton

with the use of acetic acid. This dissolves away the mineral calcite, which cements together the particles of rock, and will therefore release the fossilized bones.

Until new evidence is available, the restoration of *Hylaeosaurus* shown here must remain speculative. The narrow head, armour-plated body and tail, and the outwardly projecting spikes on the flanks were typical nodosaur features.

NAME *Polacanthus*
TIME Early Cretaceous
LOCALITY Europe (England)
SIZE 13 ft/4 m long

This 'many-spined' nodosaur was a contemporary of *Hylaeosaurus*. Indeed, some paleontologists are of the opinion that the two animals are the same. The remains of *Polacanthus* consist of the bones of the sturdy hind legs and some solid armour plates and spines.

Because of the incomplete nature of the remains, it is not known exactly how the armour was arranged on the body. The restoration shown here is the traditional view of the animal. Pairs of heavy, vertical spines protected the shoulders and upper back; a shield of fused bone covered the hips; and two lines of small, vertical spines ran down to the tip of the deep, heavy tail.

ARMOURED DINOSAURS CONTINUED

NAME *Sauropelta*

TIME Early Cretaceous

LOCALITY North America (Montana)

SIZE 25 ft/7.6 m long

Sauropelta, from the western USA, is the largest known member of the nodosaur family of ankylosaurs, the armoured dinosaurs of Cretaceous times. It is estimated to have weighed over 3 US tons/3 tonnes.

Its massive body was encased in a bony armour. Bands of horn-covered plates with raised keels ran transversely over the body from the neck to the end of the long, tapering tail. The plates were embedded in the skin to form a strong flexible, covering all over the back. Attacks from the side were deterred by a row of sharp spikes along each flank. This slow-moving herbivore would have needed such protection against the attacks of the carnivorous dinosaurs of the day.

NAME *Silvisaurus*

TIME Early Cretaceous

LOCALITY North America (Kansas)

SIZE 11 ft/3.4 m long

Silvisaurus was covered in the heavy bony armour characteristic of the nodosaurs. Thick plates encased the animal's neck, a more open arrangement of plates lay across the back and tail, and heavy spikes flanked the body. *Silvisaurus* is, however, considered to be a primitive member of the family. Most nodosaurs had toothless beaks at the front of their jaws, but *Silvisaurus* retained teeth in its upper jaw. Some paleontologists therefore believe that it may be ancestral to some of the later nodosaurs.

As in most of the nodosaurs and later ankylosaurs, the amount of bone in the skull of *Silvisaurus* was much reduced, so that it was lightweight and full of cavities and air passages. These could have been used to produce sounds for communicating with other members of the species. Such vocalization was not unknown among dinosaurs: for example, the gregarious duckbills had inflatable nasal sacs or hollow crests on their heads, through which the animals probably produced sounds for social communications among the herd (see pp.146–153).

NAME *Nodosaurus*

TIME Late Cretaceous

LOCALITY North America (Kansas and Wyoming)

SIZE 18 ft/5.5 m long

Nodosaurus is the typical nodosaur, and has given its name to the whole family). Its body armour was arranged from neck to tail in transverse bands: narrow, rectangular plates covered the ribs, alternating with broad plates that occupied the spaces in between. Hundreds of bony nodes studded the broad plates, hence the animal's name – *Nodosaurus*, meaning 'node lizard'.

The skull of *Nodosaurus* was small, long and narrow, and the teeth were weak – typical features of the family. The shoulders and hips were powerfully developed to carry the great weight of the body armour, as were the strong, stout legs, which had broad, hoofed feet. The bones of the hips were so modified as weight-bearing structures that they no longer resembled the typical ornithischian, or 'bird-hipped', pattern (see pp.134–169).

The skeletons of several nodosaurs, all lying on their backs, were found in Kansas in marine sediments of Late Cretaceous age. They may represent a small herd of animals that were overcome and washed down to the sea; alternatively, these individuals could have come together after death by chance.

In either case, as they were swept along in the river, the decaying organs would have generated gases that bloated the body. This, combined with the weight of the armour on the back, would have made them top-heavy, and so they would have flipped over and floated downstream on their backs. Eventually, they would have sunk into the mud of the seabed, belly-side up, in which position they were preserved.

NAME	*Struthiosaurus*
TIME	Late Cretaceous
LOCALITY	Europe (Austria, France, Hungary and Romania)
SIZE	6 ft 6 in/2 m long

Struthiosaurus is the smallest known member of the nodosaur family, and of the whole ankylosaur group. This has led to the suggestion that it may have evolved on islands. Many large animals develop dwarf species when confined to isolated habitats – an adaptation to limited food resources. In Tertiary times, for example, species of dwarf elephant and hippopotamus evolved on the Mediterranean islands. A modern example is provided by the ponies of the Shetland Islands off northern Scotland.

In Late Cretaceous times, some 80 million years ago, most of modern Europe was covered by shallow seas. Islands were the only dry land. Perhaps groups of *Struthiosaurus* got marooned on various of these islands, and evolved as smaller species just as the fauna of today's Galápagos Islands is thought to have developed.

Whatever the circumstances of its development, *Struthiosaurus* retained its body armour. A variety of armour covered its back. There were plates around the neck; small bony studs covered the back and tail; and spikes guarded each flank.

Struthiosaurus fossils are still poorly understood and various different names have been given to fragmentary specimens.

NAME	*Panoplosaurus*
TIME	Late Cretaceous
LOCALITY	North America (Alberta, Montana, South Dakota and Texas)
SIZE	15 ft/4.4 m long

The latest of the nodosaurs to arise, and the last known, *Panoplosaurus* was a medium-sized animal in comparison to some of its relatives. But it was massively built, and encased in a heavy body armour. It is estimated that it could have weighed as much as 4 US tons/3.6 tonnes.

Panoplosaurus' body armour consisted of broad, square plates with keels, arranged in wide bands across the neck and shoulders. The rest of the back was covered in smaller, bony studs. Massive spikes, angled to the side and front, guarded each flank, especially on the shoulders.

Even *Panoplosaurus'* head was protected with thick, bony plates. These are fused so solidly to the underlying skull bones that their boundaries cannot be seen. But on the inside, this solid, bony box was full of cavities and air passages, with a bony palate separating the nasal system from the mouth. This would have enabled the animal to eat and breathe at the same time. The snout was narrow, which could suggest that *Panoplosaurus* rooted about among the ground vegetation to find the plants that it preferred as food.

It is likely that *Panoplosaurus* actively defended itself against attack, unlike many of its relatives, which would probably have squatted down on the ground and relied on their armour plating to protect them. *Panoplosaurus* could have charged, directing one of its spiked shoulders toward the attacker. Its forelegs were strongly built, and especially well-endowed with muscles in the elbow area. This suggests that the animal was quite manoeuvrable, and could move its forequarters nimbly in reaction to its enemy's tactics. A charging rhinoceros is the most apt, modern comparison.

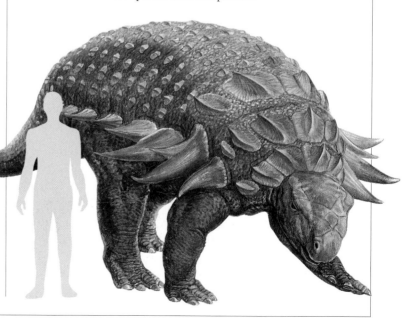

ARMOURED DINOSAURS CONTINUED

Family Ankylosauridae

This family of armoured dinosaurs became abundant toward the end of the Cretaceous Period, and largely replaced their relatives, the nodosaurs, in western North America and East Asia. Like the nodosaurs, they were heavily armoured on the back with thick plates and spikes. But the head armour was more extensively developed, and there was a unique weapon at the tip of their tails: a large ball of fused bone, which could be swung like a club with potentially lethal effect on an attacker.

These ankylosaurs were built like military tanks, and some species were about the same size. They were shorter and stockier than the nodosaurs, with massive-boned hips and hind legs to support the heavy, clubbed tail. The hips were fused to the backbone by at least eight sacral vertebrae, forming a super-strong anchor for the hindquarters. The hip bones themselves had degenerated into a shapeless mass, with no obvious trace of the bird-like arrangement so characteristic of the ornithischian dinosaurs.

NAME *Talarurus*
TIME Late Cretaceous
LOCALITY Asia (Mongolia)
SIZE 16 ft/5 m long

Talarurus shows the typical features of the family. The armoured skull broadened out at the back into a pair of bony spikes, which gave this dinosaur the appearance of having ears. Another pair of spikes projected from the cheeks. There was a toothless beak at the front of the jaws and small weak teeth in the back.

The barrel-shaped body was armoured with thick plates, and fringed with spikes on the flanks. The club at the end of the tail was formed from three masses of fused bone, and welded to the tail vertebrae. Bony tendons lashed the vertebrae together, so that when the animal walked, its tail was held off the ground. The base of the tail was supple and well-muscled.

When *Talarurus* was threatened by, for example, a contemporary tyrannosaur like *Tarbosaurus* (see p.120), it would have swung its clubbed tail at the attacker. The ramrod stiffness of the tail would have increased the force of the mass at its tip.

NAME *Euoplocephalus*
TIME Late Cretaceous
LOCALITY North America (Alberta)
SIZE 18 ft/5.5 m long

Most of our knowledge of ankylosaurs is based on studies of this animal, carried out in the 1970s and 1980s. Bands of armour were embedded in the skin of the back, and dotted with huge bony studs. Heavy plates covered the neck, and large, triangular spines protected the shoulders and base of the tail.

Externally, the head was a heavy box of bone, covered in plates that were fused to the skull bones. Inside was the complex of chambers and air passages that characterized both the ankylosaurs and nodosaurs. Thick spines protected the sides of the face. Even the eyelids were armoured, forming shutters that could descend to guard the eyes when danger threatened. These bony eyelids were only accessory structures: the real eyelids would have consisted of the usual delicate membranes. There was a horny, toothless beak at the front of the broad face.

It may be that *Euoplocephalus* was an indiscriminate eater, cropping any vegetation that presented itself. Its nodosaur relatives had narrow snouts, and probably were more selective in what they ate.

NAME *Saichania*

TIME Late Cretaceous

LOCALITY Asia (Mongolia)

SIZE 23 ft/7 m long

The massive head of *Saichania* was armoured with great bony nodules that stuck out in high relief. Spikes swept outward from each flank, and the whole of the back and tail were protected by rows of knobbly plates.

Inside the skull, the air passages were more complex than those of other ankylosaurs, and were probably more effective in cooling and moistening inhaled air before it reached the lungs. The bony palate, separating the nasal tubes from the mouth, was also stronger than in other ankylosaurs, perhaps allowing the animal to eat tougher plants. And there is some evidence to show that there may have been a salt gland associated with *Saichania*'s nostrils.

Taken together, all these features could suggest that *Saichania* lived in a hot, arid environment, unlike the cold climate that prevails in modern Mongolia's Gobi Desert where the remains of this ankylosaur were found.

NAME *Ankylosaurus*

TIME Late Cretaceous

LOCALITY North America (Alberta and Montana)

SIZE up to 33 ft/10 m long

Ankylosaurus was one of the last of the armoured dinosaurs to survive, right to the end of the Cretaceous Period. The largest of the ankylosaurs, it gives its name to the family. It was a massively built animal, and probably weighed a good 4 US tons/3.6 tonnes. *Ankylosaurus*' skull was about 2 ft 5 in/76 cm long and its body was broad (16 ft/5 m at the widest point) and squat. It was supported on strong, stumpy legs set directly beneath the body.

Thick bands of heavy armour ran across *Ankylosaurus*' back, from the top of the head to near the tip of the tail. The tail ended in the great, bony club that is the distinguishing feature of this dinosaur family. The creature's armour consisted of hundreds of oval-shaped plates set close together, and embedded in the leathery hide. This open arrangement would have given great flexibility to the armour plating, combining strength with manoeuvrability.

Ankylosaurus had a blunt snout, a broad face and a toothless beak. A pair of spikes stuck out on either side at the back of the head, and two more spikes projected from the cheeks.

When attacked, *Ankylosaurus* would probably have stood its ground, well-protected by its body armour. When the predator got within range, the heavy, clubbed tail would have been swung sideways with great force and if it hit its target, the attacker would have been severely wounded.

HORNED DINOSAURS

INFRAORDER CERATOPSIA

This infraorder is now placed under the Suborder Cerapoda – along with the pachycephalosaurs and ornithopods – on the basis of a number of shared characteristics. All of its members have five or fewer premaxillary teeth and a gap between the premaxilla and maxilla teeth.

The horned ceratopians were the last group of ornithischian, or 'bird-hipped', dinosaurs to evolve before the whole assemblage of these ruling reptiles suffered mass extinction at the end of the Mesozoic Era.

The ceratopians (also sometimes called ceratopsians) evolved late in the Cretaceous Period. As a group, they existed for a mere 20 million years before becoming extinct, but in that short time, geologically speaking, they established themselves all over western North America and central Asia.

They were well-armoured dinosaurs, although their weaponry was confined to the head, unlike the heavy armour plating that covered the backs of the ankylosaurs (see pp.157–161). The advanced ceratopians had massive heads, armed with a sharp, parrot-like beak at the front; long, pointed horns on the brow or snout, sometimes both; and a great sheet of bone, the 'frill', which grew from the back of the skull and curved upward, to protect the neck and often the shoulders too.

The success of the ceratopians can be related to their efficient chopping teeth and powerful jaws. These dinosaurs could eat even the toughest of plant foods, including a relatively new source – the shrubby flowering plants, similar to magnolia, that had begun to thrive worldwide in Late Cretaceous times. Ceratopians probably lived in herds in the upland forests, browsing on low-growing trees and ground vegetation.

Family Psittacosauridae

The 'parrot' dinosaurs were a rare group of ornithischian dinosaurs, found only in the Early Cretaceous rocks of East Asia. Their skulls show many features that suggest that they were the ancestors of the horned dinosaurs, or ceratopians. Their long-tailed and relatively lightly-built bodies, however, were similar to those of the gazelle-like hypsilophodonts, from which stock they probably arose (see pp.139–141).

Like the hypsilophodonts, the parrot dinosaurs could rise up on two legs to run away from predators. The suggestion, therefore, is that the early ceratopians, descended from the parrot dinosaurs, were also bipedal, and only reverted to a four-legged stance later in their evolution.

NAME	Psittacosaurus
TIME	Early Cretaceous
LOCALITY	Asia (China, Mongolia and Siberia)
SIZE	up to 8 ft/2.5 m long

A square skull and a horny, toothless curved beak are the features that have given this Asian dinosaur its name – *Psittacosaurus*, meaning 'parrot lizard'.

A thick ridge of bone on the top of the skull squared off the head at the back. This ridge served as an anchor point for the muscles of the powerful lower jaws. Over millions of years, it was to develop into the characteristic great, bony neck frill of the later ceratopians. The cheek bones of *Psittacosaurus* were drawn out into a pair of horn-like projections – the forerunners of the horny spikes that grew out from each side of the head shield of later ceratopians. *Psittacosaurus* had a long flexible neck, four blunt claws on each hand, long hind limbs and short forelimbs. Its long tail helped it to maintain its bipedal stance.

The ancestor of the ceratopian group is believed to be among the parrot dinosaurs. However, it is unlikely to have been *Psittacosaurus* itself, since this animal had only four fingers on each hand, while the ceratopians had five. Also, *Psittacosaurus* had no teeth in its beak, while the early ceratopians, the protoceratopids, had teeth in the upper beak.

Several juvenile *Psittacosaurus* have been found, one of which at only 24 cm/12 in long is the smallest dinosaurs known.

Family Protoceratopsidae

The protoceratopids constitute the early, primitive horned dinosaurs, although only some had horns. They evolved in Asia, in the same region as the parrot dinosaurs (from which stock they probably evolved), but lived there many millions of years later, in the Late Cretaceous. They also spread to western North America.

Like the earlier parrot dinosaurs, the protoceratopids could walk upright, although it is likely that they spent most of their time browsing on all-fours, and only rose up on two legs when they had to run away from predators.

The protoceratopids were much smaller than their later relatives, the ceratopids. They shared the characteristic parrot-like beak of the psittacosaurs, but unlike them they had teeth in the upper beak: this is considered a primitive feature, lost in the more advanced ceratopids.

The protoceratopids had no horns on their heads, or else only rudimentary ones. However, they did have the beginnings of the neck frill that was to become so prominent in the later ceratopids.

NAME *Microceratops*

TIME Late Cretaceous

LOCALITY Asia (China and Mongolia)

SIZE 2 ft/60 cm long

This creature is the smallest horned dinosaur known. It was probably not a direct ancestor of the later ceratopids, but rather an early, specialized offshoot of the main group.

Microceratops was a lightly-built, two-legged runner, as evidenced by the length of its shin bones – almost twice as long as the thigh bones, the sign of a sprinting animal. Its front legs, however, were also quite long in comparison to other bipedal dinosaurs, so it probably moved about mainly on four legs, only rising upright to escape from danger. Its lifestyle would have been similar to that of such ornithopods as the gazelle-like hypsilophodonts of North America.

NAME *Leptoceratops*

TIME Late Cretaceous

LOCALITY North America (Alberta and Wyoming) and Asia (Mongolia)

SIZE 7 ft/2.1 m long

Leptoceratops is one of the few protoceratopids known from North America: most of the family lived in Asia. In appearance, it was intermediate between the lightly-built parrot dinosaurs and the heavier, early

horned dinosaurs. It could probably walk on two legs as easily as on four. *Leptoceratops'* hind legs were built for running, as evidenced by the long shin bones. The five clawed fingers of each hand could be used to grasp bundles of leaves, and pass them to the mouth.

The bones at the back of *Leptoceratops'* skull were expanded upward into a tall peak. This was an intermediate stage in development between the muscle-attachment ridge of the parrot dinosaurs and the neck frill of the horned dinosaurs.

NAME *Bagaceratops*

TIME Late Cretaceous

LOCALITY Asia (Mongolia)

SIZE 3 ft 3 in/1 m long

This small protoceratopid represents another specialized offshoot from the main evolutionary branch of the horned dinosaurs. It had a squat, heavy body and long tail, supported on solid legs, five-toed at the front and four-toed at the back.

Bagaceratops possessed several of the features that were to be developed in the later horned dinosaurs. There was a prominent bony ridge at the back of its skull (the precursor of the ceratopids' neck frill); a pair of leaf-shaped projections on either cheek (part of the ceratopids' head shield); and a definite, though short, horn halfway along its snout (anticipating the great horns of the ceratopids). In addition, it had lost its teeth in the upper beak; other members of its family retained these teeth, which is considered a primitive feature. But despite these advanced characteristics, *Bagaceratops* was probably not the direct ancestor of the horned dinosaurs.

HORNED DINOSAURS DINOSAURS

NAME	*Protoceratops*
TIME	Late Cretaceous
LOCALITY	Asia (Mongolia)
SIZE	up to 9 ft/2.7 m long

The average adult of this early horned dinosaur (right) measured about 6 ft 6 in/2 m long, and weighed almost 400 lbs/180 kg. It had a well-developed broad neck frill at the back of its large, heavy skull. This would have provided anchoring points for the powerful muscles of the toothed, beaked jaws.

Although *Protoceratops* had no horns, it did have a prominent bump midway along its snout – more of a crest than a horn. This bump seems to have been larger in older male specimens, suggesting that it may have been used for ritual head-butting fights between rival males.

Protoceratops almost certainly spent most of its time on all-fours. However, the hind legs were still long in comparison to the forelegs, so it seems probable that this animal could also run upright, as did its likely ancestors, the parrot dinosaurs.

In the 1920s, the first dinosaur eggs and nests were discovered in Mongolia. They belonged to *Protoceratops*. The nests, dug in the sand over 70 million years ago, contained clutches of eggs, as many as 18 in some nests. Each egg was sausage-shaped, about 8 in/20 cm long, with a thin, wrinkled shell, only a fraction of an inch thick. The eggs were carefully laid in three-tiered spirals. Astonishingly, some of the eggs were still intact, and inside were found fragments of fossilized bones from tiny *Protoceratops* embryos.

Plant-eating dinosaurs, such as *Leptoceratops* and *Triceratops*, were thought to have muscular cheeks to keep food in their mouths while chewing. However, no evidence for such cheeks has been found. They probably had stiff horny coverings to the jaws, which would have been less efficient. It may be necessary to remodel the way we think these dinosaurs fed.

the ceratopids. However, *Montanoceratops* had the typical primitive features of the protoceratopid family – teeth in the upper beak, and claws on its feet, rather than hooves.

The tail of this medium-sized ceratopian was unusually deep due to the presence of tall spines that jutted upward from the vertebrae along its length. The fossil evidence also suggests that the tail was also extremely flexible, and could be moved easily and rapidly from side to side. A possible explanation for these features could be that the tail – which may have been brightly coloured – was used as a sexual signal during the mating season, or for recognition of its own species.

Family Ceratopsidae

The most abundant large herbivores of the Late Cretaceous period in western North America were the great horned dinosaurs of this family. Their fossil remains have been found nowhere else in the world.

Exclusively four-legged, these herbivores were well-protected from attack by contemporary, bipedal carnosaurs, such as *Tyrannosaurus* (see p.121) and *Albertosaurus* (see p.119). Long, sharp horns grew from their massive heads, and a large bony frill,

NAME	*Montanoceratops*
TIME	Late Cretaceous
LOCALITY	North America (Montana)
SIZE	10 ft/3 m long

This North American dinosaur (right) was similar in appearance to *Protoceratops* (above), with the notable exception of having a definite horn on its snout. This has led some paleontologists to regard it as an early member of the more advanced family of horned dinosaurs, developed from the rear skull bones, guarded their necks. The head was relatively large and heavy in proportion to the body size. Pillar-like legs, with their heavy, hoofed feet, supported a stocky body that was covered in thick hide. There was also safety in numbers, and the horned dinosaurs moved in great herds through the upland forests, foraging for plant food and chopping off vegetation with their sharp, toothless beaks.

The family of horned dinosaurs is divided into two evolutionary lines. Some members of the family had short neck frills and great horns on the snout, while others had long neck frills and great horns on the brow.

NAME *Centrosaurus*

TIME Late Cretaceous

LOCALITY North America (Alberta and Montana)

SIZE 20ft/6m long

This horned dinosaur was a typical member of the short-frilled group. (It used to be known by the name *Monoclonius*.) A long horn surmounted the snout of *Centrosaurus,* giving it an appearance somewhat like that of the modern rhinoceros, (in some species, this horn curved forward), and two short horns rose above its eyes from the brow.

The neck frill stood up from behind the head, and its wavy edge was fringed with spines. There were two large openings on either side of the frill, which in life were covered over with skin, as was the rest of the frill. These holes reduced the weight of the bony structure, and their edges provided additional attachment points for the powerful jaw muscles. A strong ball-and-socket joint connected the head to the neck.

This was placed well-forward in the skull, about under the eye region, so that the weight of the heavy frill at the back of the head was balanced by the great horn on the front. This mobile joint ensured that *Centrosaurus* could turn its massive head easily and quickly. This was important for such a slow-moving animal, since its head weapons were its only defence. Some of the neck vertebrae were fused together, to increase its strength, and the muscles of the forequarters were powerfully developed.

As with all of the ceratopids, *Centrosaurus*' tail was relatively short in comparison to those of the protoceratopids, with only its tip resting on the ground. Unlike their proteceratopid relatives, these four-legged animals did not rise up on their hind legs and so did not need a long tail to balance their body weight.

NAME *Pachyrhinosaurus*

TIME Late Cretaceous

LOCALITY North America (Alberta)

SIZE 18ft/5.5m long

So far only two skulls of *Pachyrhinosaurus* have been found, and it seems to have been an unusual 'horned dinosaur' because it apparently had no horns. Instead, there was a large, thick pad of bone above the eyes where the brow horns were usually found.

There are two theories to account for this strange bony pad. Some paleontologists equate its function with the thickened skull caps of the boneheaded dinosaurs – for in-fighting among male members of the herd. Other paleontologists, however, believe that the bony pad simply represents scar tissue where the brow horns had fallen off. Supporters of this theory expect that eventually specimens will be discovered with their brow horns intact, settling the argument once and for all.

HORNED DINOSAURS CONTINUED

NAME *Styracosaurus*

TIME Late Cretaceous

LOCALITY North America (Alberta and Montana)

SIZE 17 ft/5.2 m long

One of the most spectacular of the short-frilled family of horned dinosaurs was the well-armed *Styracosaurus*. It had an enormous, straight horn on its snout, directed upward and forward. Two smaller horns grew above the eyes. The remarkable neck frill, like an oriental dancer's head-dress, had six main spikes arrayed around its top, some as large as the nose horn. A number of smaller spikes made up a defensive fringe.

As in other short-frilled ceratopids, there were two large, skin-covered openings in the frill, which reduced the weight of this great bony structure considerably.

Styracosaurus could certainly have defended itself well. Charging head-down, rhinoceros-style, at an attacking *Tyrannosaurus*, for example, the herbivore's great nose horn could have ripped open the carnivore's soft belly, and the bony frill would have presented a formidable array of spikes to protect its neck from the carnivore's powerful jaws.

The spikes on the frill probably also provided a highly effective defensive display. If *Styracosaurus* stood head-on to an enemy, or even a rival male in its own herd, the spikes would have stood out from around its face, making the animal look sufficiently fearsome to deter most attackers. Modern African elephants hold their great ears out at the sides of the head to intimidate others in the same way.

NAME *Triceratops*

TIME Late Cretaceous

LOCALITY North America (Alberta, Colorado, Montana, South Dakota, Saskatchewan and Wyoming)

SIZE 30 ft/9 m long

Triceratops is the most familiar of the horned dinosaurs. It was also the most abundant of the group, as well as the largest and the heaviest. It is thought to have weighed up to 11 US tons/10 tonnes – heavier than a modern, adult African bull elephant. Its skull alone, with the short neck frill, was over 6 ft 6 in/2 m long.

Great herds of these imposing horned dinosaurs lived throughout western North America toward the very end of the Late Cretaceous Period, some 70 to 65 million years ago. They were the most common of the ceratopids, and the last member of the short-frilled group to survive.

The name *Triceratops* means 'three-horned face'. Although this dinosaur belonged to the short-frilled group – in which the nose horn was typically longer than the brow horns – the arrangement of horns on the face of *Triceratops* was more like that of the long-frilled types (see *Chasmosaurus*, right) for example). It had a short, thick nose horn and two long brow horns, each over 3 ft 3 in/1 m long. In some species, the brow horns could have been even longer, reaching beyond the snout.

Also unlike other members of its group, *Triceratops'* neck frill was a solid sheet of bone. The fact that there were no openings in it suggests that its main function was to act as a defensive shield, rather than as an anchoring plate for the jaw muscles. In some species, there were pointed knobs, like great barnacles, set all around the edge of the frill, offering further protection.

Because of the massive, solid structure of *Triceratops'* skull, it was more likely to survive through fossilization than other, less robust, dinosaur skulls. Hundreds of well-preserved specimens have been found over the years in the western states of North America. Othniel C. Marsh, the famous American fossil-hunter, first named the beast in 1889. By the turn of the century, another American fossil-hunter, Barnum Brown, is supposed to have discovered over 500 skulls.

Today, more than 15 species of *Triceratops* are recognized, all distinguished by differences in the structure of the skull. However, some of these may in fact represent different sexes and growth stages in individuals of a much smaller number of species.

Many of the skulls, horns and neck frills have been found to be damaged and scarred. This suggests that individual *Triceratops* often sparred with one another, possibly by locking horns and shoving with the head shield, rather than doing any actual damage with the sharp horns. The full potential of these weapons was probably reserved to inflict damage on a real enemy, such as one of the large, contemporary tyrannosaurs – *Tyrannosaurus* or *Albertosaurus.*

NAME	*Chasmosaurus*
TIME	Late Cretaceous
LOCALITY	North America (Alberta)
SIZE	17 ft/5.2 m long

Chasmosaurus was a typical long-frilled type of horned dinosaur. Its skull was quite long and narrow, with a pair of long, upwardly curved horns on the brow and a single, shorter horn on the snout. The bony frill, however, was enormous, stretching from the back of the skull to cover the neck and upper shoulders. Its margin was elaborated with bony spikes and knobs. The two openings on either side of the frill were so large that the frill itself provided a mere framework surrounding these great holes. So, although the bony frill was a vast size, it was lightweight, and allowed the head to be moved easily.

This spectacular frill was undoubtedly a display structure and may have been brightly coloured. The great head area that it presented would have acted as a warning to attackers, whether predators or rival males, or as a sexual signal to females, especially when the head was moved about. It is possible that all the males in a herd would cooperate in a display of threat, forming a ring around the young in times of danger, and shaking their great heads and neck frills at the enemy.

Some paleontologists think that these horned dinosaurs could run quite quickly when necessary. This is suggested by certain features of their anatomy. The shoulder blades, for example, were not firmly fixed to the rest of the skeleton, and there were no collar bones to keep them in place. So, the whole shoulder girdle would have moved back and forth with the forelegs, helping the animal to run quickly.

In contrast, the hips were firmly fixed in position, attached to the backbone by eight sacral vertebrae, which provided a strong, solid anchor for the heavy hindquarters.

HORNED DINOSAURS CONTINUED

NAME *Arrhinoceratops*

TIME Late Cretaceous

LOCALITY North America (Alberta

SIZE 18 ft/5.5 m long

NAME *Anchiceratops*

TIME Late Cretaceous

LOCALITY North America (Alberta)

SIZE 20 ft/6 m long

The long-frilled *Anchiceratops* lived near the very end of the Late Cretaceous Period, later than its relative *Chasmosaurus*. In fact, it has been suggested by some paleontologists that *Anchiceratops* could have been a descendant of that dinosaur.

Although it was somewhat larger than its relative *Chasmosaurus*, *Anchiceratops* was more streamlined in build. Its bulky body was longer, with a shorter tail, and the tall neck frill was considerably narrower. Two long, narrow horns curved forward from the creature's heavy brow, and a shorter nose horn pointed directly ahead.

Anchiceratops' frill was divided along the midline by a strong ridge. On either side of the ridge there were medium-sized openings in the bone. A pair of horn-like protuberances pointed forward at the top-rear edge of the frill.

The remains of *Anchiceratops* have been unearthed from deposits laid down in deltas, mixed with beds of coal, and dating from the topmost rocks of the Late Cretaceous Period. The location of the fossil finds of *Anchiceratops* suggests that this dinosaur may have inhabited swamps or the surrounding areas. It would probably have fed, using its sharp beak and shearing cheek teeth, on the abundant vegetation that grew in this waterlogged environment – such plants as swamp cypresses, ferns, giant redwoods and cycads.

The name *Arrhinoceratops* means 'no nose-horned face' and was given to the animal by its discoverer William Parks (who excavated it from the Red Deer River, Alberta in 1925) because he thought that it lacked a nose horn. Parks believed that there should be a separate bone to support a nose-horn, but this is now known to be incorrect. *Arrhinoceratops* has a distinct bony knob where the horn should be and modern interpretation regards this as sufficient evidence for the presence of a horn. However, because the internationally recognised laws of biological nomenclature are based on historical priority, this dinosaur has to keep its completely inappropriate name.

Arrhinoceratops was a close relative of the long-frilled dinosaur *Chasmosaurus* (see previous page). But it resembled the short-frilled *Triceratops* in having a short face, and well-developed brow horns that curved forward over the snout. There was also a modest-sized nose horn.

Round openings cut through the bone of *Arrhinoceratops'* neck frill, thereby reducing its weight. The frill itself was a large one, as in *Chasmosaurus*, and had a deeply scalloped margin, which was set with great bony knobs at wide intervals.

The remains of this North American horned dinosaur are not as common as many others of its family. This may be due to the fact that the animal itself was not abundant, or to its favoured habitats: perhaps it inhabited dry, upland areas where it was less likely to become fossilized.

NAME *Pentaceratops*

TIME Late Cretaceous

LOCALITY North America (New Mexico)

SIZE 20ft/6m long

Like *Anchiceratops*, *Pentaceratops* may well have been a descendant of *Chasmosaurus*, which lived earlier in Late Cretaceous times. It, too, had a huge neck frill, its margin fringed with small spines. In some species, the frill stretched halfway along the back, and as many as four large openings punctured the bony surface, reducing its weight.

When *Pentaceratops* was discovered, the scientists reckoned that they had found an unusual dinosaur with five horns on its face, hence its name. In fact, *Pentaceratops* had the usual three-horned face: there was a short, stout horn on its snout and a pair of long horns that curved forward from the brow. The two remaining 'horns' were merely outgrowths of the cheek bones, and were not unusual features among the long-frilled ceratopids.

NAME *Torosaurus*

TIME Late Cretaceous

LOCALITY North America (Montana, South Dakota, Texas, Utah and Wyoming)

SIZE 25ft/7.6m long

This horned dinosaur, whose name means 'bull lizard', is found in the topmost beds of the Late Cretaceous. It was the largest, and the last, of the long-frilled group and a contemporary of the short-frilled *Triceratops*, the largest of all the horned dinosaurs. Herds of both types of horned dinosaur would probably have roamed together through the North American landscape some 70 million years ago.

The skull of *Torosaurus* is the largest known from any land-living animal, either modern or extinct, with a length of 8ft 5in/2.6m. The enormous neck frill extended along half this length, rising from the back of the head in a hollowed-out sheet, with the usual pair of large openings. The margin was smooth, lacking the usual array of bony knobs.

Two great horns surmounted the brow of *Torosaurus*, and a shorter horn grew from its snout, above the massive, sharp beak. All three horns were straight and pointed forward.

Few predators would have risked attacking such a formidable animal as *Torosaurus*. Weighing some 9 US tons/8 tonnes and

moving at a fair pace on its stout legs, its head armed, its neck and upper back protected by the great frill and the rest of its body covered in thick hide – this horned dinosaur could have done battle with the largest of carnivorous dinosaurs.

However, by the end of the Cretaceous Period the days of the dinosaurs were numbered. The 'Age of Dinosaurs' ended some 65 million years ago, with a worldwide mass-extinction. Several other major groups disappeared at about the same time – the plesiosaurs, ichthyosaurs and ammonites in the sea, and the pterosaurs in the air. No trace of any of these groups has been found in the rocks of the subsequent Tertiary Period.

Dozens of theories have been put forward in the past to account for this mass extinction. Hypotheses, such as virus attack from outer space, temperature change, producing juveniles of one sex only and egg shells too thick for the embryos to break out of, range from the peculiar to the plainly eccentric. It is now generally accepted that there was a major impact event and a major change in sea-level at the end of the Cretaceous, both of which would have had a severe effect on the global food chain (see p.91). However, there are still many unanswered questions about why some organisms should have survived and others have become extinct.

MASTERS OF THE AIR

The conquest of the air was the last great opportunity for the vertebrates, demanding dramatic modifications of both structure and physiology. Such modifications have evolved independently within mammals and reptiles, who have evolved powered flight. Arguably, the most successful of the reptilian fliers were the birds.

Flight engineering

The birds are the acknowledged masters of the air. Their abundance and diversity, both past and present (with some 166 families of living birds), exceeds that of any other flying creature. Their success lies in

the development of a structure unique in the animal world – feathers. These aerodynamic structures, developed from reptilian scales. They are lightweight and easily replaced if damaged, in contrast to the vulnerable skin-wings of pterosaurs and bats.

By evolving feathered wings, birds acquired the enlarged surface area needed to support the body in the air. Their modified forelimbs were wholly devoted to flight, folding away on land. The hind limbs became adapted for walking upright.

The power for flapping flight comes from large muscles that make up 15 to 30 percent of a bird's body weight. They stretch down from the wings and attach to the pectoral, or shoulder, girdle.

The sternum (breast bone) is greatly enlarged, and bears a prominent keel (carina) down the middle; both surfaces provide a large area to which wing muscles attach. They also attach to the fused clavicles (collar bones), which form the wishbone (furcula), and to a membrane connecting the wishbone and sternum.

To provide length and space for these muscles, the shoulder joints have moved upward, to a position level with the backbone. And to resist the powerful forces produced when the flight muscles contract, the sternum is braced away from the shoulder joints and backbone.

For a bird to launch itself, the hind legs must be long and powerful so the bones of the lower leg, and some of the bones of the ankle, to add a new section (the tarso-metatarsus) are elongated. The powerful muscles needed to swing the legs forward and backward are attached to the modified pelvic, or hip, girdle, whose bones have become elongated. The ilium projects far forward from the hip joint, and is strongly attached to the backbone by between 11 and 23 vertebrae (compared with only two or three in most reptiles). The pubis and ischium both project backward from the hip joint.

A bird's body is short to balance it while walking and it has moved back between the legs to bring the centre of gravity to a point above the feet. The enlarged sternum lies between the knees.

The wings propel and guide the bird, so a long tail is not needed for stability and has been reduced to a short 'pygostyle'. The tail feathers can be erected to form a fan that acts as a brake.

Archaeopteryx, the earliest-known bird, appeared in the Late Jurassic. The Cretaceous Period saw an explosive evolution of the birds, with many new groups, and most modern groups had appeared by the end of that period or by the Eocene.

Since the fragile bones of birds are rarely fossilized, this evolution chart is based on recent studies, carried out in the USA by Sibley and his colleagues, on the genetic material of modern birds.

Only a proportion of the 27 or so orders of modern birds are shown here. Relatively few groups have become extinct over their 140 million years of evolution.

NEOGNATHAE

DUCKS, CHICKENS

GREBES, PENGUINS, PELICANS

CRANES, SHOREBIRDS, PIGEONS

STORKS

FALCONS, OWLS

NIGHTJARS, SWIFTS

KINGFISHERS, WOODPECKERS, SONGBIRDS

Fuelling the changes

A bird's physiology had to change in order to cope with the energy demands of flight. The respiratory system became more efficient. A unique arrangement of numerous air sacs off the main respiratory passage ensures that air passes through a bird's lungs in a continual stream. Birds are warm-blooded, so their levels of energy do not vary with the environmental temperature. Insulation is provided by the feathers.

Archaeopteryx: the first bird

A modern bird's skeleton is so different from that of any reptile, so the origins of birds could not be deduced with certainty until *Archaeopteryx* was discovered in Late Jurassic limestones. It is an intermediate, in time and structure, between reptiles and birds.

Archaeopteryx was fossilized in such fine-grained sediments that the clear impression of its feathers can be seen around the skeleton. The feathers and the shape of the wings, are exactly like those of living, flying birds. It also had a wishbone, which forms an attachment site for flight muscles. The wing feathers of *Archaeopteryx* are remarkably modern, fully developed with asymmetrical flight feathers with downy elements near the base.

Archaeopteryx had small, sharp teeth in its jaws, replaced in later birds by a horny, toothless beak. It had three clawed fingers on each forelimb, each distinct from the others (unlike their partly fused arrangement in modern birds). And it had a long, bony tail, fringed on either side by long feathers to provide uplift.

Archaeopteryx probably lived in trees, eating the insects there, and using both flapping and gliding flight to get from tree to tree. From time to time, it would have landed on the ground, and used its sharp, clawed fingers to climb back into the trees.

Apart from the proportions of its wings, the skeleton of *Archaeopteryx* is strikingly similar to that of a small, bipedal dinosaur, such as the coelurosaur *Compsognathus*. Most paleontologists believe that it evolved from just such a dinosaur.

The problem of the evolution of feathers has intrigued scientists for many years since the first fossil feather was found in the late Jurassic strata of Solenhofen in Bavaria in 1861. There are two main kinds of feathers; the long tough flight feathers and the smaller fluffy body and down feathers. Fight feathers are characteristically asymmetric. However, feathers must have initially evolved for some other purpose – organisms cannot develop a structure before its use.

The main possibility seemed to be body insulation, which is of particular importance for small animals, without much in the way of defence

mechanisms, which need to be constantly active and alert to predators. Birds are warm blooded and the feathers both conserve heat and shield the animal from high temperatures.

Until recently, feathers have also been thought to be unique to birds. But, the discovery of feathered dinosaurs in China has shown that they are not. The Chinese dinosaurs (see p.108) also raise interesting questions about the pre-adaptive role of feathers. These dinosaurs were not capable of flight since the feathers are restricted to bunches of long symmetric feathers on their hands and long bony tail. Some have a crest of feather-like structures running from the head down the neck and along the back. The body was also covered with small down feathers.

There is clearly an function as insulation, but the hand and crest feathers must have had other uses. The most obvious is for sexual display and perhaps species recognition.

Further new finds from Las Hoyas in central Spain are also helping to fill in some of the large gaps in the fossil record. The Las Hoyas site was an ancient lake and filled with very fine grained calcareous mud deposits in the early to mid Cretaceous, which preserve very detailed structures. The Spanish deposits promise to give insights into the early evolution of the birds. One new form, called *Iberomesornis*, seems to help bridge the gap between *Archaeopteryx* and the first of the Enantiornithes.

The 'missing link' controversy

As a link between reptiles and birds, *Archaeopteryx* is a major piece of evidence for Darwin's theory of evolution. Its importance was recognized when it was discovered in 1861. *Archaeopteryx* has, therefore, always been a target of attack for those who question the theory of gradual evolutionary change. In 1985, the British astronomers Fred Hoyle and N.C. Wickramasinghe suggested that many evolutionary innovations were the result of a shower of extra-terrestrial viruses, which infected organisms with new characteristics. They suggested that birds and mammals evolved, and the dinosaurs became extinct due to such a virus shower, at the end of the Cretaceous.

Archaeopteryx, one of the most important fossils ever found, has features that link it incontrovertibly with reptiles and birds.

Archaeopteryx, dating from over 80 million years before the Late Cretaceous, is a fatal weakness in this virus-shower theory. So Hoyle and Wickramasinghe suggested that the specimens of *Archaeopteryx* were fakes. However, the *Archaeopteryx* fossils have been shown to be genuine.

The evolution of birds

Between *Archaeopteryx* and the diverse fossil record of living bird groups there is a time gap representing most of the Cretaceous (some 70 million years). It is partly filled with a sporadic record of archaic toothed birds which have little or no known relationship with modern birds. Two unusual groups (subclasses) existed in the Cretaceous Period. One group, the Enantiornithes, were discovered in Argentina, and described in 1981. Still only poorly known, certain features of their legs, upper arm bones and shoulder girdles distinguish them from all other birds.

Another Cretaceous group, the Odontornithes provide the next major window on bird evolution. These early seabirds had teeth in their jaws. Some had lost the power of flight; others still had wings, and were probably more like modern terns.

Several types of birds have lost the ability to fly. This seems to happen when there are no active predators, as at the end of the Cretaceous, when the dinosaurs disappeared, and mammalian carnivores, had not yet appeared. Flightless birds evolved in the relative safety of, for example, South America.

Modern flightless birds (the ostrich, emu, kiwi, cassowary and rhea), and the extinct moas and elephant birds, are grouped as Ratites. They all have the bony palate and shoulder girdle, which may suggest that they descended from flying birds.

Living birds and their fossil representatives are grouped in the subclass Neornithes. They share a common, complicated structure of the bony palate, and this fact leads paleontologists to believe that they have descended from a common ancestor.

There is considerable argument about the origin of the modern birds. Some experts claim that a few pre-Tertiary fossil birds belong to modern groups such as the charadriiforms (shorebirds) and gaviiforms (ducks). Others say that few bird lineages survived the Cretaceous extinction.

There is a lack of abundant bird fossils. Birds are not easily preserved. In the next decade or so, more and better-preserved fossil birds will probably be found.

Birds have retained essentially the same skeletal structure. The fossil record reveals little about the interrelationships of the modern birds. Since the record is so patchy, and impressions of feathers are rarely fossilized, no-one can be certain what prehistoric birds looked like. The reconstructions here are mainly the traditional view of these birds, based on the known fossil names and a degree of guesswork from studies of modern, related species.

FROM REPTILE TO BIRD

DINOSAUR (COMPSOGNATHUS)

WISHBONE

EARLIEST-KNOWN BIRD (ARCHAEOPTERYX)

MODERN BIRD OF PREY (CARACARA FALCON)

PYGOSTYLE (TAIL)

KEELED STERNUM (BREAST BONE)

Birds evolved, so paleontologists believe, from small carnivorous dinosaurs that could run upright on their long, slim hind legs. The skeleton of the dinosaur Compsognathus(top) is strikingly similar to the skeleton of the earliest known bird, Archaeopteryx (middle). Both animals had long running legs, long bony tails, bird-like feet, clawed fingers, and sharp, pointed teeth. However, Archaeopteryx had feathers – unmistakable bird characteristics – which were preserved as impressions in the rocks. Its collar bones also formed a distinct bird-like wishbone.

A modern flying bird (right) has a short, compact body, centred over the legs for balance. The breast bone has developed into a large, keeled sternum, to which the flight muscles attach. The tail is reduced to a stump (pygostyle) and the jaws are toothless.

EARLY AND FLIGHTLESS BIRDS

CLASS AVES

This large group of highly successful flying vertebrates contains nearly 9000 living species arranged in some 160 families, of which 134 have fossil representatives. There are a further 77 extinct families. Despite significant advances in recent years, major difficulties remain in understanding bird phylogeny, with molecular and morphological evidence indicating very different relationships.

Family Archaeopterygidae

This group of 'ancient birds' currently contains one genus – *Archaeopteryx* – and perhaps only one species. This is the earliest-known bird, and it occupies a special place in evolutionary history, since it shows in its structure the link between two major groups – the reptiles and the birds.

NAME	*Archaeopteryx lithographica*
TIME	Late Jurassic
LOCALITY	Europe (Germany)
SIZE	14 in / 35 cm long

The discovery of *Archaeopteryx* is a classic in the history of paleontology. In 1861, blocks of fine-grained limestone were being cut in a quarry at Solnhofen, southern Germany. These rocks are of Late Jurassic age, some 150 million years old: one split slab revealed the almost perfect skeleton of *Archaeopteryx*, the first-known bird. Not only were most of its delicate bones intact, but the impression of its feathers was stamped in the rocks, preserved in their natural positions on the wings and tail. A glass-fibre cast of this specimen is displayed in London's Natural History Museum.

A second, more complete specimen was discovered from the same site in 1877, and this slab of rock, together with its priceless occupant, is now housed in Berlin's Humboldt University Museum. Four more specimens are now known.

These fossil finds reveal a creature about the size of a modern pigeon, with a small head and large eyes, pointed teeth in its jaws and a long bony tail. Its limbs were long and slender, with three clawed digits on each elongated hand, and it had typical bird feet. *Archaeopteryx* lower-leg bones were long, and indicate a running animal.

This description does not wholly fit in with the picture of most modern birds, but *Archaeopteryx* had two unmistakable bird features. It had a well-developed wishbone (formed by the union of the two collar bones) and the typical feathers of a bird, attached to its long arms and tail.

Were it not for these bird-like characteristics, *Archaeopteryx* could easily be mistaken for one of the coelurosaurs small, two-legged, carnivorous dinosaurs (see pp.106–109). Indeed, one of the most recent *Archaeopteryx* specimens, discovered in Germany in 1951, was attributed to the coelurosaur *Compsognathus* until the early 1970s, when impressions of its feathers were noticed.

Most paleontologists believe that *Archaeopteryx* was an insectivorous creature that inhabited open forests, and could fly or glide from tree to tree. It may have caught insects on the wing as it flew, or perhaps it swooped down in surprise attacks on ground-living invertebrates. Its clawed hands and feet could have been used to haul it up the trunks of trees and to clamber among the branches, in order to launch itself on the next flight.

The sternum, or breastbone, of *Archaeopteryx* appears to have been tiny, unlike the great, keeled sternum of modern birds, which provides the main site for the attachment of powerful wing muscles. Some paleontologists have suggested that the feathers of *Archaeopteryx* were merely for insulation, rather than for flight. This ancestral bird was almost certainly warm-blooded, like its modern relatives. By controlling its body temperature, it could have led a more active, predatory life.

However, *Archaeopteryx's* feathers are so similar in structure and arrangement on the wings to those of modern birds that it is almost certain they were used for flying, even if this was less powerful than the flight of modern birds.

SUBCLASS ODONTORNITHES

This group of 'toothed birds' lived throughout the Cretaceous Period. The Odontornithes subclass were similar to modern birds, except that they possessed small, pointed teeth set in sockets in their jaws.

They had developed (though some had already lost) the main structural feature necessary for sustained flight: a broad, keeled sternum to which the powerful wing muscles could attach. They had lost the long bony tail of their ancestors.

ORDER ICHTHYORNITHIFORMES

Members of this group of primitive, probably fish-eating, seabirds are common in marine deposits of Late Cretaceous age in North America. They were good flyers, to judge from the strong, keeled sternum.

NAME *Ichthyornis dispar*
TIME Late Cretaceous
LOCALITY North America (Kansas and Texas)
SIZE 8 in/20 cm tall

First discovered in the 1870s, the toothed jaws of this ancient bird were originally thought to belong to a mosasaur – a contemporary, fish-eating marine lizard (see p.87). This reptile was preserved in the same rocks, and had similar jaws and teeth to those of *Ichthyornis*.

Ichthyornis dispar and others of its genus had a general structure like that of a large, modern sea tern, but with a proportionally bigger head and bill. The large sternum suggests strong flight.

ORDER HESPERORNITHFORMES

This Cretaceous group of toothed birds were specialized diving seabirds that had lost the power of flight. Although they had a well-developed sternum, the keel was reduced, and the wings had degenerated. These birds seem to have fished the shallow waters that covered much of central North America during Cretaceous times, and would have nested on low shores.

NAME *Hesperornis regalis*
TIME Late Cretaceous
LOCALITY North America (Kansas)
SIZE 6 ft/1.8 m tall

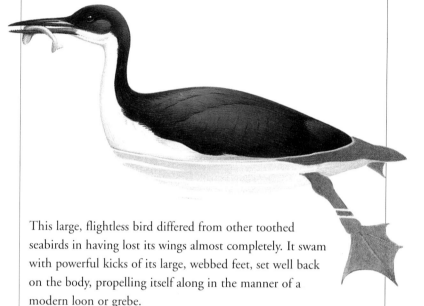

This large, flightless bird differed from other toothed seabirds in having lost its wings almost completely. It swam with powerful kicks of its large, webbed feet, set well back on the body, propelling itself along in the manner of a modern loon or grebe.

Hesperornis regalis could have chased fast-moving fish and squid underwater, holding such slippery prey in its long bill, equipped with sharp, pointed teeth. It probably nested at the water's edge, like a modern loon, and it would have been clumsy and vulnerable while on land.

SUBCLASS NEORNITHES

This group of 'new birds' encompasses all recent species. They began to adapt to varied environments in the Early Cretaceous, and representatives of most of the modern groups had appeared by the Early Eocene, some 50 million years ago.

A number of extinct groups and species are known, of which the following are some of the more striking.

ORDER STRUTHIORNITHIFORMES

The typically large, long-legged flightless birds, collectively known as the Ratites, belong to this order. All have small or tiny wings, and the sternum has lost the keel that provides the attachment site for the wing muscles of flying birds.

Ratites first appeared during the Cretaceous or Early Tertiary, and different types evolved on the separating continents. Today, the only survivors of the group are the emus and cassowaries of Australia and New Guinea, the kiwis of New Zealand, the rheas of South America, and the ostriches of Africa (which were formerly also in Eurasia).

Two spectacular groups have become extinct only recently – the elephant birds of Madagascar and the moas of New Zealand.

EARLY AND FLIGHTLESS BIRDS CONTINUED

NAME *Aepyornis titan*

TIME Pleistocene to Recent

LOCALITY Madagascar

SIZE up to 10 ft / 3 m tall

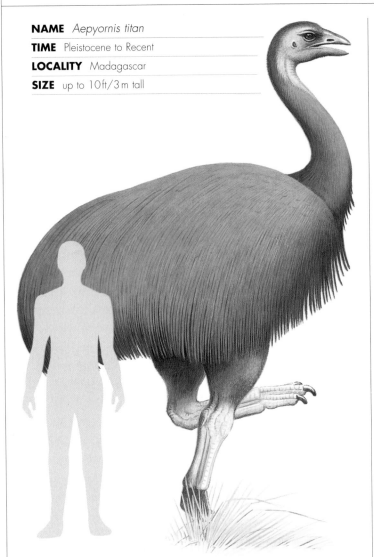

NAME *Dinornis maximus*

TIME Pleistocene to Recent

LOCALITY New Zealand

SIZE up to 11 ft 6 in / 3.5 m tall

Dinornis maximus was the tallest bird that ever existed – taller than the great elephant bird of Madagascar, but of a much lighter build. It was one of about a dozen types of flightless moa that survived in New Zealand until recent times.

Man came to the New Zealand islands in about the 10th century, and over the next 800 years destroyed most of the forests by burning them for agriculture, and hunted the moas relentlessly, causing their extinction by the year 1800.

All moas were bulky, heavy-legged, long-necked birds. In the absence of large carnivores and herbivores, these slow-moving birds had taken the place usually occupied by browsing mammals, feeding off the rich supplies of seeds and fruits.

This species is the largest of the extinct genus *Aepyornis* and weighed up to ½ ton/500 kg. The common name – elephant birds – stems from Arabian tales of the 'rukhkh', that could carry off an elephant.

Aepyornis' legs ended in three widely spread, stumpy toes. The elongated, thick thigh bones are evidence that it was not a runner.

Aepyornis eggs were over 1 ft/30 cm long, could hold 19 pints/9 litres and may have weighed 20 lb/10 kg.

Aepyornis bird had no special defences – no teeth, no talons and no wings. Size and strength were protection against predators. When man arrived in Madagascar, less than 1500 years ago, species of *Aepyornis* were still alive. It may have become extinct in the 17th century.

NAME *Emeus crassus*

TIME Pleistocene to Recent

LOCALITY New Zealand

SIZE 5 ft / 1.5 m tall

This moa, only half the height of *Dinornis*, was peculiar in having massive lower legs, which were out of all proportion to its body size. Its feet were also enormously broad. It must have been a painfully slow-moving animal, providing easy prey for the moa-hunters. The modern kiwi, the bird which is the emblem of New Zealand, is regarded by some paleontologists as a highly specialized moa. The three living species are tiny in comparison to their extinct relatives, being less than 2 ft/60 cm tall.

ORDER COLUMBIFORMES

Modern pigeons have changed little since their first appearance in the Late Cretaceous or Early Tertiary. Larger types of Columbiformes evolved on warm islands, which were free of predators, especially during Pleistocene times when several large, and often flightless, forms inhabited the Mascarene Islands of the Indian Ocean.

NAME	*Raphus cucullatus*
TIME	Pleistocene to Recent
LOCALITY	Mauritius
SIZE	3 ft 3 in/1 m tall

Raphus cucullatus, commonly known as the dodo, was a giant, terrestrial pigeon that became another casualty of man's habit of destruction. Flightless and slow-moving, it was easy prey to sailors who stopped off on islands in the Indian Ocean to restock their larders.

The dodo was about the size of a modern turkey, and was covered in soft, downy feathers. It had a fat body (weighing some 50 lb/23 kg), a large head and a bald face. It had a massively strong, hooked bill and a curly, tufted tail. Its wings were tiny and useless, and it had a ponderous gait, waddling about on stout, toed feet, feeding on low-growing plants, seeds and fallen fruits.

There were no natural predators on the island of Mauritius to disturb the dodo's slow progress or to endanger it which left the dodo so ill-equipped to defend itself against large predators that it did not even flee the hungry sailors. *Raphus cucullatus* was not only easy prey for the people landing on the island, but also for the animals (pigs and dogs, for example) which were introduced to the island. This had caused the extermination of the dodo by the 17th century – less than 200 years after it had first been discovered.

ORDER CICONIIFORMES

This large order includes the modern shorebirds – the wading water birds (other than waterfowl, see p.181), the seabirds and the typical birds of prey. Most of the Ciconiiformes evolved and diverged to occupy different habitats toward the end of the Cretaceous Period. Birds of prey, such as the eagles, were widespread from Eocene times onwards.

NAME	*Harpagornis moorei*
TIME	Pleistocene to Recent
LOCALITY	New Zealand
SIZE	possibly 3 ft 6 in/1 m tall

This eagle may not have been much larger than many of its modern relatives, the eagles and Old World vultures, but it was stronger and more heavily built. The legs of *Harpagornis moorei* were stout and equipped with heavy talons, the beak was deep and sharply hooked, and the bird's powerful and impressive wings spanned some 7 ft/2.1 m.

Harpagornis moorei coexisted with moas in New Zealand, and became extinct at about the same time – perhaps as recently as the 17th century. Since there were no other large predators on the New Zealand islands, this bird may have fed on the smaller moas, *Emeus crassus* for example, and on other birds which have also since become extinct, such as the flightless goose.

Moas would have been bulky prey to attack, but their probable slowness of movement, together with their relatively small heads and their long necks, could have made them vulnerable to aerial attack. Certainly, the moa chicks would have provided easy prey for these powerful raptors.

WATER AND LAND BIRDS

NAME *Palaelodus ambiguus*

TIME Late to Early Oligocene

LOCALITY Europe (France)

SIZE 2 ft/60 cm tall

This medium-sized, long-legged shorebird is related to the modern wading and water birds, seabirds and birds of prey (grouped in the Order Ciconiiformes, see p.177).

It is often suggested by paleontologists that *Palaelodus* and its relatives represented early flamingos. But recent assessment instead suggests that they were more likely to be of shorebird origin and that they branched off fairly late from the main shorebird assemblage, and lived from the Late Oligocene to the Early Pliocene in Europe, North Africa and North America.

Paleontologists really know very little about what the head and bill of *Palaelodus* would have looked like; the reconstruction (above) is the traditional view of the bird. However, the structure of its legs suggests that rather than wading in shallow water it may have dived and swum underwater to feed, behaving in a way similar to a modern diving duck.

NAME *Pinguinus impennis*

TIME Pleistocene to Recent

LOCALITY Small islands off western Europe (British Isles), Greenland, Iceland and North America (Maine to Labrador)

SIZE 20 in/50 cm tall

Another member of the ciconiiformes, the great auk, *Pinguinus impennis*, lost its final battle against extinction on a small island off Iceland in 1844. For years, it had been relentlessly hunted by sailors for its flesh, its eggs and the layer of insulating fat beneath its skin, which was used to provide oil for lamps.

Despite its name, the great auk was not a large bird, being only about half as tall again as the razorbill, the modern auk that it most resembled. It differed only in that it had become flightless. *Pinguinus impennis* was a well-adapted seabird, like all modern auks, propelled by its webbed feet when on the surface, and using its small wings for propulsion when swimming underwater after its fish prey.

The legs of the great auk were set well back on its body, allowing it to walk upright on land, although it would have moved in a slow and awkward way. It nested in colonies on islands where it could get ashore easily, and incubated its single egg on bare ground. These nesting colonies, however, were highly vulnerable, and the birds were either killed on the spot by sailors or herded live into boats, like sheep.

The great auk evolved in the Pleistocene epoch, some 2 million years ago. Other members of the auk family, however, date back to Miocene times, and probably even earlier. During the ice ages of the Pleistocene, great auks swam southward, and they are known from the Mediterranean and Florida.

Although unrelated to the modern penguins of the southern hemisphere, the great auk was their northern counterpart in lifestyle and appearance. In fact, *Pinguinus impennis* was the original 'penguin', being given this name by early mariners. Today's penguins are named after it.

NAME *Argentavis magnificens*
TIME Late Miocene
LOCALITY South America (Argentina)
SIZE 5 ft / 1.5 m tall

NAME *Limnofregata azygosternum*
TIME Early Eocene
LOCALITY North America (Wyoming)
SIZE up to 1 ft / 30 cm tall

Limnofregata azygosternum appears to have been an ancestral form of the modern frigatebirds. Today, these are specialized marine birds, related to pelicans, and almost wholly adapted to an aerial existence over the sea. But 50 million years ago, they were only just evolving, and *Limnofregata* may be a halfway stage in their development.

Limnofregata's general structure was similar (although a less extreme adaptation to its lifestyle) to that of modern frigatebirds. Its legs and feet, although reduced in size, were larger and longer than those of modern species. Its wings, too, were proportionally shorter, with a span of about 3 ft 3 in / 1 m (compared with the long wings of the modern frigatebirds, which can reach up to 8 ft / 2.5 m wingspan in the largest species). Its bill was shorter, more tapering and less hooked than that of living species.

However, unlike the modern frigatebirds, *Limnofregata azygosternum* did not glide on thermals over the ocean. Instead, it flew by flapping its wings, and its habitat was large, freshwater lakes, far inland. It was probably more like a gull in appearance and feeding method, than frigatebirds and it was more likely to land on water than its modern relatives, which snatch up fish and squid without alighting on the water surface.

Argentavis magnificens had huge wings compared with its body size. Although only some of its bones have been found, estimates place its wingspan at about 24 ft / 7.3 m – twice the wingspan of the longest-winged living bird, the wandering albatross.

A bird of this size did not fly by flapping its wings. It would have conserved its energy by gliding from one food source to another, using as few wingbeats as possible. Launching itself from high places, it used the rising thermal currents of warm air during the day to keep it aloft. As with the modern albatross, its initial take-off technique was probably awkward.

Argentavis was most probably a scavenger, like its modern relatives; the New World vultures. Its deep, hooked beak would have been used to tear through the tough hide of dead animals, rather than used to attack live prey. The large, herbivorous mammals that grazed the open plains of Argentina during the Miocene provided a rich food source. But such a large bird was vulnerable to changes in food supply or climate. *Argentavis'* fate would have been closely linked to that of the early mammals of South America (see pp.246–253).

Argentavis was more closely related to storks than to other birds of prey; in fact, they share a common origin with the storks, diverging from them very early in the Tertiary Period.

WATER AND LAND BIRDS CONTINUED

NAME *Osteodontornis orri*

TIME Late Miocene

LOCALITY North America (California)

SIZE 4 ft/1.2 m tall

Osteodontornis orri is one of the 'bony-toothed', gliding seabirds. They combine pelican and petrel/albatross characteristics. They probably arose from a common ancestor in the Late Cretaceous and by the Late Paleocene, they were highly developed. They were the largest seabirds during the Tertiary, perhaps preventing the evolution of larger albatrosses.

Osteodontornis' body was heavily built, with legs and feet like a huge petrel. The long, narrow wings, designed for constant gliding flight, had a wingspan in some of the larger species of up to 20 ft/6 m, and would have been held out stiffly. They were probably not much use for strong or rapid manoeuvres.

The head, with its heavy, long, pelican-like bill, probably rested back on the shoulders in flight, like a modern heron or pelican. Its bill was as long as that of a modern pelican, but stouter and more rounded, with a hook at its tip. Large and small tooth-like outgrowths projected along the edges of both jaw bones. When the bill was closed, those of the lower jaw fitted into deep grooves on the palate inside the upper jaw.

The wing structure suggests that it may have snatched prey from at, or just below, the water surface. The bony spikes on the bill would have been ideal for gripping slippery fish or squid. The slanting roof of the throat suggests that there was an elastic pouch along the neck, used as a temporary fish larder.

Nothing is known of the nesting habits of these birds. They probably chose level-topped islands, which would have provided a good runway for easy take-off. Constant, but not violent, breezes were essential for their gliding flight. Perhaps stormier, more varied weather during the Pleistocene caused the demise of these birds, some 2 million years ago.

ORDER GRUIFORMES

The Gruiformes evolved in Late Cretaceous times, 90 million years ago, and rapidly diversified into a great assemblage, ranging from small, strong flyers to giant, flightless forms. Most of today's Gruiformes are aquatic birds, such as the long-legged cranes and rails, moorhens and coots. There are also some ground-living species, such as the bustards and trumpeters.

NAME *Phorusrhacus inflatus*

TIME Early to Middle Miocene

LOCALITY South America (Patagonia)

SIZE 5 ft/1.5 m tall

Phorusrhacus inflatus was a medium-sized member of a family of flightless birds that became the dominant predators in South America during the Tertiary Period. All the phorusrhacids had strong running legs, small, useless wings and large heads, equipped with great, eagle-like beaks. Some species were giants, and stood 10 ft/3 m tall: the head of one species was over 1 ft 6 in/50 cm long.

In the Early Tertiary, South America had become an island continent. The dinosaurs had died out, and no large carnivores had evolved to take their place. *Phorusrhacus* and its relatives filled this vacant niche. Some paleontologists have suggested that phorusrhacids were also carrion-eaters, using their deep, hooked beaks for tearing at the flesh of dead animals, as well as for seizing prey.

These formidable birds were extinct by the Early Pleistocene. But their nearest modern relatives may be the two species of seriema that live in the grasslands of South America today. These small, ground-living birds can fly, but prefer to run.

NAME *Neocathartes grallator*
TIME Late Eocene to Early Miocene
LOCALITY North America (Wyoming)
SIZE 18 in/45 cm tall

Originally thought to be a New World vulture modified for running, *Neocathartes* appears to be a flesh-eating member of another group of gruiform ground birds, the bathornithids. It was slimly-built and capable of flight, although from its structure it is likely that it spent most of its time hunting on the ground.

Chasing after prey on its long legs, in the manner of a modern secretary bird, *Neocathartes'* clawed feet and hawk-like beak would have coped easily with small rodents and reptiles.

NAME *Diatryma gigantea*
TIME Early Eocene
LOCALITY Europe (Belgium, England and France) and North America (New Jersey, New Mexico and Wyoming)
SIZE 7 ft/2.1 m tall

Diatryma gigantea was a giant flightless birds that lived in North America and western Europe during the Paleocene and Eocene when the continents were joined together.

Like other members of its family, it was heavily built with tiny wings, incapable of flight. Its stout legs were armed with strong, clawed feet. The bird's large head (with its massive, hooked beak) was almost the size of that of a modern horse.

Some paleontologists suggest that the diatrymids became the dominant carnivores in the northern hemisphere because there were no other large predators around at the time. So, like the later phorusrhacids in South America, the diatrymids may have been the dominant predators.

Other paleontologists, however, have suggested that the diatrymids were actually herbivorous creatures that used their heavy, sharp-edged beaks to shear through tough vegetation, such as tussocks of grass or rush-like growth.

ORDER ANSERIFORMES

The ancestors of today's waterfowl the ducks, geese and swans – belong to this order. They diverged from other birds early in the Cretaceous Period.

NAME *Presbyornis pervetus*
TIME Late Cretaceous to Early Eocene
LOCALITY Europe (England), North America (Utah and Wyoming) and South America (Patagonia)
SIZE 3 ft 3 in/1 m tall

Presbyornis was a typical member of its family – a long-legged, long-necked bird, so slenderly-built that paleontologists first thought it was a flamingo, until it was discovered that its head and bill were similar to those of modern ducks.

From the abundant remains of both bones and eggs, it seems that *Presbyornis pervetus* flocked together on the shallow margins of lakes. They nested in great, open colonies, and would have waded in the shallows, sifting the water with their broad, flattened bills to remove tiny animals and plants – a method used by modern dabbling ducks.

ANCESTORS OF THE MAMMALS

In the warm, moist, tropical forests that covered Nova Scotia in the Late Carboniferous Period, more than 300 million years ago, there lived two types of reptile. Both looked much the same – small and lizard-like, with legs and feet that sprawled out to the sides of their bodies. One, *Hylonomus*, scuttled about after insects, and tried to avoid being eaten by the other – the larger, predatory *Archaeothyris*, with its powerful, snapping jaws and sharp, pointed teeth.

While *Hylonomus* (see p.62) was the earliest known reptile, *Archaeothyris*, an ophiacodontid, was the first of a long line of reptiles that were to dominate the land for the next 80 million years, throughout the Permian and much of the Triassic. These were the mammal-like reptiles, so-called because their evolutionary history culminated in the mammals – the most varied and successful group of vertebrates alive today (see pp.194–297).

At first, the mammal-like reptiles gave no hint of any unusual potential. Only a feature of their skulls betrays their ultimate affinities with the mammals. A pair of openings, set low behind each eye socket, distinguishes them from all other reptiles. The same structure – known as 'synapsid' – is seen in mammals, although the design is modified with much larger openings. Other reptiles fit into the anapsid group (no skull opening) or diapsid group (two skull openings), their living descendants being, respectively, the turtles and tortoises, and the lizards, snakes and crocodiles.

The development of stronger jaws among the mammal-like reptiles and their descendants, the mammals, is believed to have been the direct result of the evolution of the synapsid type of skull. Related to this was the development of a new type of dentition – the typical mammalian pattern, with teeth of different sizes and shapes for different purposes: sharp-edged incisors for cutting, pointed canines for tearing and cheek teeth with a crushing surface for chewing.

Rise of the mammal-like reptiles

The earliest synapsid reptiles to evolve were the pelycosaurs (see pp.186–188). From such little creatures as *Archaeothyris* a great variety of large reptiles evolved, both carnivorous and herbivorous. Their heyday was during the early part of the Permian Period, when they constituted some 70 percent of the terrestrial fauna. Their remains are particularly common in Texas. Some 280 million years ago, the warm, tropical humid, delta floodplains of this region would have swarmed with a variety of early amphibians and fishes, all of them prey to the powerful jaws of the dominant predators of the day, the land-living pelycosaurs.

Toward the middle of the Permian Period, a more advanced group of mammal-like reptiles arose from the pelycosaurs, and ultimately replaced them. These were the therapsids, the direct ancestors of the mammals. Their fossil remains are first found in rocks of European Russia at the base of the Late Permian; their sudden appearance in the fossil record suggests that they may have evolved earlier in more upland areas (where fossilization is less likely).

During the Late Permian Period, these therapsids spread to the great southern landmass of Gondwanaland. Many types are found in the Karroo rocks, laid down in the lowland basin of southern Africa. Others are found in European Russia, in the sediments eroded from the newly formed Ural Mountains. Later still, in the Early Triassic Period, the therapsids spread to Asia, South America, India and even Antarctica, all of which were joined together at the time into the supercontinent Pangaea (see p.11).

The therapsids enjoyed domination of the land until the middle of the Triassic Period, and successfully adopted the diverse lifestyles of carnivores, herbivores and insectivores. At that point, however, two new groups of terrestrial reptiles surged into their ecological niches – the early, carnivorous ruling reptiles (see pp.106–121) and the herbivorous rhynchosaurs (see p.92).

Thereafter, the therapsids began their slow decline; 55 million years later, by Mid-Jurassic times, the last group (the tritylodont cynodonts, see p.193) finally became extinct. But not before its members had given rise to the first mammals – tiny, shrew-like creatures that were to wait for more than 150 million years before they entered the limelight of vertebrate history.

Through these insignificant little creatures, the synapsid reptiles had the last laugh over their dinosaur usurpers, when those great creatures lay dead at the end of the Cretaceous Period, their reign over, and the mammal-like reptiles survived to inherit the earth in the form of their mammalian descendants.

Vital steps toward warm-bloodedness

The main advance of mammals over reptiles is their ability to regulate their body temperature. Mammals are warm-blooded, or endotherms; reptiles are cold-blooded, or ectotherms (see p.91). But there is little doubt that the early mammal, like reptiles, were still cold-blooded creatures, relying on the sun as their prime source of body heat. Strong evidence for this is provided by the remains of the early synapsids, such as the sphenacodont pelycosaurs. Some of these animals had great skin-covered sails on their backs, the function of which must have been to control body temperature – to absorb heat when cold, and radiate it when warm (see *Dimetrodon*, p.187).

Pelycosaurs without such obvious regulatory devices, and early therapsids such as the dinocephalians, probably controlled their body temperature simply by virtue of their greater body size. A larger, bulkier body retains a greater amount of heat than a small one, providing a thermal reservoir that reduces the effects of fluctuations in the environmental temperature.

However, the later therapsid reptiles developed other features that would finally end their dependence on the sun as a source of energy. By eating more food more frequently, and by digesting and metabolizing it more quickly and efficiently, they could now rely on food as a major energy source.

This new method of controlling body temperature required many changes, including better jaws and teeth, better locomotion, better breathing control, and better external insulation to maintain the body's internal temperature.

Dental developments

An innovation among the mammal-like reptiles was the evolution of teeth of different sizes and shapes (called a 'heterodont' dentition). Even the earliest pelycosaurs had three distinct kinds of teeth in their jaws. The food-grasping incisors at the front were separated from the biting cheek teeth at the back by several long, stabbing canines.

In normal reptilian fashion, all of these teeth were renewed periodically by waves of replacement along each jaw and the old, worn teeth discarded; the even-numbered teeth were replaced in one wave,

and the odd-numbered teeth in the next. The more advanced therapsids, however, had departed from this reptilian 'all-change' method of tooth replacement. Instead, the teeth were replaced only a few times during the animal's life.

This new pattern of tooth replacement was a major development, because it meant that each tooth could remain in the jaws for a longer period. As a result, the opposing crowns of the upper and lower teeth could develop a complex pattern of crests and valleys. These could then meet in a precision bite, and presented a rough pavement on

The mammal-like reptiles appeared during the Late Carboniferous Period in the form of the pelycosaurs, all of which were well-adapted land animals. It is believed that some of them, including the edaphosaurs, could control their body temperature by means of a large, heat-regulating 'sail' on their backs.

The sphenacodonts were the ancestors of the advanced mammal-like reptiles, the therapsids. Many of these were ferocious carnivores, which dominated land life during the Late Permian. Others, such as the dicynodonts, were large plant-eaters.

which food could be cut, crushed and ground to a pulp before being swallowed. The well-chewed food could then be digested more quickly and easily, which resulted in a more rapid release of the vital nutrients needed to fuel the body.

The jaws and skull of the mammal-like reptiles also changed. First, the size of the synapsid openings in the skull increased, allowing longer jaw muscles to develop. Second, the back of the skull became longer, and the sides bowed out, to produce more space for the jaw muscles. Both of these developments allowed for stronger jaw muscles resulting in a more powerful bite.

Third, there was an improvement in the structure of the lower jaw. Previously, some of the jaw muscles were attached to the large dentary bone at the front of the jaw, while others were attached to a number of smaller bones at the back. These smaller bones were progressively reduced in size among the therapsids (and finally lost completely from the jaws of mammals, so removing a potential weakness in the junction between the bones of the lower jaws. The dentary bone itself also developed a high flange (the coronoid process) at the back, and this provided an additional attachment point for larger, more powerful jaw muscles.

Another small change in connection with the jaw bones of mammal-like reptiles had the spectacularly important result of providing better hearing in mammals. The two bones that had formed the joint between the skull and the lower jaw in the mammal-like reptiles gradually retreated into the middle ear of mammals. Here, they linked up with the already present stapes ('stirrup') bone, to form a chain of three bones (called the hammer, anvil and stirrup because of their shapes). Sound is transmitted along this chain from the outer eardrum to the fluid-filled canals of the inner ear.

The progressive integration of these three small bones into the ear can be traced in the remains of therapsids from the Triassic Period. In fact, these changes can still be observed, dramatically telescoped in time, during the development *in utero* of a modern mammal embryo. They provide as good a proof of evolutionary change as that provided by *Archaeopteryx* for the link between reptiles and birds (see p.174).

Mammals also developed a pair of fleshy ear-flaps on either side of their heads. It is not certain precisely when these external ears evolved, but they have been shown on some of the later therapsids illustrated on p.193.

Limb improvements

While all these changes were occurring in the jaws and teeth of the mammal-like reptiles, other changes in the skeleton were taking place that made the limbs of these creatures more efficient. The primitive pelycosaurs of the Late Carboniferous Period, such as *Archaeothyris*, still moved in the old reptilian fashion – bending the body from side to side, with the limbs sprawled out horizontally.

By the Early Permian, sphenacodonts, such as *Dimetrodon*, had evolved a new and better type of locomotion. The shape of the bones in the hips and hind limbs, and of the joints between the vertebrae, show that the stride of the hind limbs was accompanied by an up-and-down flexure of the backbone.

From *Dimetrodon* onward, the evolutionary story of the mammal-like reptiles is of a steady and rapid increase in this flexing of the limbs and body in the vertical, rather than the 'old-fashioned' horizontal, plane.

In addition, the feet changed position relative to the legs, from projecting to the sides to pointing forward, and the toes became shorter and of similar lengths.

This whole system of locomotion had far more potential for fast movement, since a longer stride and a faster swing of the legs could now be achieved simply by elongating various bones of the limbs and feet.

AN ADVANCED MAMMAL-LIKE REPTILE (*THRINAXODON*)

Thrinaxodon walked like a mammal, with its legs directly beneath its body. Its teeth and jaws were powerful, with a high coronoid process on the lower jaw for strong muscle attachment. The rib cage was probably closed off by a muscular diaphragm, which allowed the lungs to expand and contract for efficient breathing.

Better breathing

Other features of the advanced therapsid reptiles strongly suggest that they were warm-blooded, like their descendants, the mammals. For example, the abrupt reduction in the extent of the ribs in such cynodonts as *Thrinaxodon* suggests that the whole front part of the body cavity, which houses the vital organs, the lungs and heart, had been closed off by a muscular sheet of tissue, the diaphragm. This development set off a chain of events. It allowed larger lungs to be filled and emptied more rapidly and more frequently, which, in turn, resulted in more oxygen entering the bloodstream. This permitted the tissues to use oxygen faster – to speed up digestion or to increase muscular exertion, when, for example, chasing prey or avoiding predators.

Because the tissues of a warm-blooded animal require a constant supply of oxygen, it cannot stop breathing for more than a short time. This need conflicts with the need to keep food in the mouth while it is being chewed up. This problem was solved in some of the advanced therapsids (the therocephalians and the cynodonts) by the development of a secondary palate – a shelf of bone that separated the air passage from the mouth, allowing them to breathe and chew at the same time. The existence of such a structure provides further support for the theory that these mammal-like reptiles were already warm-blooded.

Insulation for survival

There is no way of knowing whether the mammal-like reptiles were covered in hair or fur. Such insulation is not necessary in larger animals (and many of the therapsids were large), since they have a proportionately smaller surface area through which to lose heat. It is significant, however, that the final transition between the mammal-like reptiles and the mammals, at the end of the Triassic, was accompanied by a marked reduction in size.

The first mammals, such as *Megazostrodon* (see p.198) were tiny, shrew-like creatures. It is likely that they were hairy and fully endothermic (warm-blooded), and possessed mammary glands – that is, they possessed those features that characterize true mammals. It is also likely that they were nocturnal burrowers, but there is no direct fossil evidence for any of this. What is known is that they had enlargements of the brain associated with hearing and smell, both of which are particularly useful for nocturnal animals. Their teeth indicate that they were insect-eaters and it would have been advantageous for them to be nocturnal to avoid having to compete with insect-eating birds and lizards. A nocturnal burrowing habit would also have helped them keep out of the way of the abundant reptilian predators and may well have helped them survive the extinction at the end of the Cretaceous.

FROM MAMMAL-LIKE REPTILE TO MAMMAL

PELYCOSAUR (VARANOSAURUS)

DENTARY · EYE SOCKET · SYNAPSID OPENING

PRIMITIVE THERAPSID (PROCYNOSUCHUS)

DENTARY · EYE SOCKET · SYNAPSID OPENING

EARLIEST MAMMAL (MORGANUCODON)

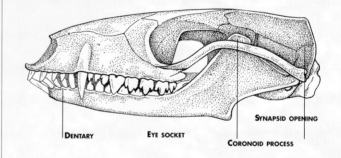

DENTARY · EYE SOCKET · SYNAPSID OPENING · CORONOID PROCESS

A mammal's strong, biting jaws resulted from progressive changes in the skull and lower jaws of their ancestors. In the earliest mammal-like reptiles, the pelycosaurs, the lower jaw was made of several bones, the dentary being the largest. In the more advanced therapsids, the skull was higher and the synapsid opening larger, for longer jaw muscles. The dentary bone was also larger. In the mammals, the eye socket and synapsid opening merged, and the lower jaw was formed entirely of the dentary. this had a high coronoid process which formed an extra site for muscle attachment. The small bones at the rear of the therapsid's lower jaw had moved into the mammal's middle ear, to form part of a chain along which sound was transmitted.

PELYCOSAURS AND THERAPSIDS

SUBCLASS SYNAPSIDA

The reptilian ancestors of the mammals – the pelycosaurs and therapsids – and the mammals themselves all share the same type of synapsid skull (see p.61) The single, large opening behind each eye socket allowed the development of longer jaw muscles, which resulted in stronger jaws that could be opened wide and closed forcefully, to deal with large prey.

ORDER PELYCOSAURIA

Pelycosaurs were the earliest of the synapsid (mammal-like) reptiles to evolve. They first appeared during the Late Carboniferous Period, some 300 million years ago when reptiles were first colonizing the land. Like the early reptiles, the pelycosaurs started as small, lizard-like creatures. But they evolved into many different types, of a much heavier build and with strong jaws and teeth of different sizes and shapes.

The ophiacodont family were the earliest and the most primitive pelycosaurs, and were the ancestors of the other three families. Carnivorous sphenacodonts were the most important group in evolutionary terms because they were the direct ancestors of the therapsid reptiles and indirectly, of mammals.

The edaphosaurs were large plant-eaters, related to the sphenacodonts, but with a very different skull and dentition. The caseids were also herbivorous, and the latest, and last, of the pelycosaurs to evolve.

Family Ophiacodontidae

This group of six or seven genera ranging from the Late Carboniferous to the Mid Permian includes the earliest and most primitive known of the pelycosaurs.

NAME *Archaeothyris*
TIME Late Carboniferous
LOCALITY North America (Nova Scotia)
SIZE 20 in/50 cm long

This small, lizard-like ophiacodont is the earliest-known pelycosaur. Its remains were found in the same Late Carboniferous (Pennsylvanian) locality as those of

the first-known reptile, the anapsid *Hylonomus*. These rocks indicate a warm, tropical, humid climate, with great forests of conifers and a rich undergrowth of ferns and club mosses. In the lowland swamps, masses of decaying vegetation would have accumulated (giving rise to the coal beds of today), providing food and breeding grounds for insects and other invertebrates. They, in turn, attracted insectivorous reptiles, such as *Hylonomus*, which were probably preyed upon by the larger, newly evolved synapsid reptiles, such as *Archaeothyris*.

Archaeothyris was already more advanced than the other early anapsid reptiles. Its jaws were strong, and could be opened wide and snapped shut. Although its teeth were all the same shape – sharp and pointed – they were of different sizes, including a large pair of canines at the front of the jaws. Such teeth suggest a varied, carnivorous diet.

NAME *Ophiacodon*
TIME Early Permian
LOCALITY North America (Texas)
SIZE up to 12 ft/3.6 m long

Ophiacodon shows the rapid evolution of features within the pelycosaur group. Its skull had changed from the small, low shape of its earlier relative *Archaeothyris* (left) to a deep, narrow shape. This allowed more space for longer jaw muscles to develop. Its hind limbs were longer than the forelimbs, and set somewhat more directly beneath the body. So, although it still sprawled like a typical reptile, *Ophiacodon* was probably a better runner than *Archaeothyris*.

Ophiacodon was considerably larger than the earlier pelycosaurs, and this factor may have helped it to control its body temperature. It is estimated to have weighed between 66 lb and 110 lb/30 kg and 50 kg. To support this considerable weight, it is likely that it spent some of its time in water, scuttling about floodplains or swamps, catching fish and amphibians in its elongated jaws, and despatching them with its sharp teeth.

Family Varanopseidae

This group includes four or five small pelycosaurs, all early Permian and all found in North America. With long limbs and light skeletons, they have been interpreted as active carnivores.

NAME *Varanosaurus*
TIME Early Permian
LOCALITY North America (Texas)
SIZE 5 ft / 1.5 m long

Varanosaurus lived in the same place at the same time as *Ophiacodon* (left), and probably competed with it for fish in the same swamps. Its skull was also deep and narrow, the jaws somewhat elongated and armed with small, spiky teeth. It had the build of a modern monitor lizard.

Family Sphenacodontidae

The largest group of bigger pelycosaurs, this family comprises eight carnivorous genera including *Dimetrodon*, one of the best known of the 'sail-finned' pelycosaurs.

NAME *Sphenacodon*
TIME Early Permian
LOCALITY North America (New Mexico)
SIZE 10 ft / 3 m long

This large sphenacodont is typical of the family, with a deep, narrow skull, massive jaws and varied teeth: long canines, dagger-like incisors and small, cutting cheek teeth. The sphenacodonts were the first animals to develop such specialized teeth, and were the first large terrestrial carnivores.

The vertebral spines of *Sphenacodon*'s backbone were long, and acted as attachment points for massive back muscles, allowing it to lunge powerfully at its prey. In other members of the family, these spines were elongated, and supported a huge fin or 'sail', probably for regulating body temperature.

NAME *Dimetrodon*
TIME Early Permian
LOCALITY North America (Oklahoma and Texas)
SIZE 10 ft / 3 m long

The spectacular 'sail' on the back of *Dimetrodon* has earned it the popular name of the 'finback', and is believed to be an early method of controlling body temperature.

The framework for the sail was provided by the elongated spines of the animal's back vertebrae, which were up to 3 ft 3 in / 1 m long in the centre. In life, a sheet of skin covered the spines, and this was probably richly supplied with blood vessels.

Dimetrodon's likely routine would have been to stand with its sail oriented toward the sun in the early morning. Like a solar heater, the sail would have absorbed heat and warmed the blood, which then coursed through the body, raising the reptile's temperature so it could begin its daily hunt for food. To cool down, after a strenuous chase, for example, *Dimetrodon* angled its sail away from the sun and into the wind, dissipating heat.

An interesting example of convergent evolution is seen between these synapsid sphenacodonts and the unrelated diapsid reptiles, the dinosaurs. Two dinosaurs, *Spinosaurus* (see pp.118–119) and *Ouranosaurus* (see pp.144–145) – both living in West Africa during the Cretaceous – had also developed solar-heating sails on their backs.

According to calculations, a *Dimetrodon* weighing about 440 lb / 200 kg would have taken about an hour and a half to raise its body temperature from 79°F to 90°F (26°C to 32°C). Without the sail, the same animal would have needed to bask in the sun for more than three and a half hours to achieve the same rise in temperature.

The massive canines and well-developed shearing teeth of *Dimetrodon* confirm that it was a formidable predator: its name means 'two kinds of teeth'. Its prey would have included other pelycosaurs, which without the advantage of a sail would have remained slow and sluggish until the sun warmed them sufficiently to allow activity.

PELYCOSAURS AND THERAPSIDS CONTINUED

Family Edaphosauridae

This group of 'sail-finned' pelycosaurs ranged from Late Carboniferous to Mid Permian in age. They show several adaptations for a herbivorous habit, such as palatal teeth forming a broad crushing area.

NAME *Edaphosaurus*
TIME Late Carboniferous to Early Permian
LOCALITY Europe (Czechoslovakia) and North America (Texas)
SIZE 10 ft/3 m long

Edaphosaurus had a large sail on its back, similar to that of *Dimetrodon*. It differed in that the extended vertebral spines of *Edaphosaurus* had cross-pieces of bone along their length. As well as serving to regulate body temperature, it is possible that the sail could also have served for display purposes – either of courtship or of threat – and it may have been brightly coloured.

This bulky pelycosaur was not an active creature, nor was it built for speed. Its body was long and barrel-shaped to accommodate the large gut, its limbs were short and stocky, and it had a sprawling gait not suited to running. Its teeth were those of a plant-eater. As well as the closely packed, peg-like teeth which lined the jaws, there were also teeth on the palate, which formed a broad, chewing pavement, ideal for chopping and grinding plant material.

Family Caseidae

These Mid Permian pelycosaurs included both large and small forms, which have been found in North America and Europe. Their teeth show adaptations for a herbivorous diet, and such a lifestyle is also suggested by the barrel-shaped ribcage, which would have contained the enlarged stomach necessary for a massive plant-digesting gut.

NAME *Casea*
TIME Early Permian
LOCALITY Europe (France) and North America (Texas)
SIZE 4 ft/1.2 m long

The caseids, represented by *Casea*, were the last family of pelycosaurs to evolve, in Early Permian times. They became the most abundant of the plant-eating pelycosaurs, and thrived almost to the end of the Permian.

Casea was one of the smaller members of the family; some of its more imposing relatives reached lengths of 10 ft/3 m and weights of more than 1320 lb/600 kg. All of the caseids had deep, bulky bodies, in which the rib cage was enormously expanded in order to accommodate the long, plant-digesting gut. Their square-shaped heads were tiny, with enormous synapsid openings at the back and large nasal openings at the front.

The caseids were unique among pelycosaurs in having no teeth in the lower jaw. Those in the upper jaw were thick, blunt pegs with wavy edges, like those of modern herbivorous lizards. Numerous small teeth studded the palate. This dentition suggests that they lived in a diet of tough plants, such as ferns and horsetails, which would have needed grinding and chewing.

ORDER THERAPSIDA

The therapsids were advanced synapsid reptiles, descendants of the carnivorous sphenacodonts and the direct ancestors of the mammals. Although the remains of the first therapsids are found at the base of the Late Permian, they had diverged from the sphenacodont pelycosaurs more than 20 million years before, probably during the Early Permian. They spread rapidly to all parts of the world, including Antarctica.

The therapsids are grouped into several suborders (see pp.302), only one of which, the cynodonts (see pp.192–193), survived into the Jurassic Period.

NAME *Phthinosuchus*

TIME Base of Late Permian

LOCALITY Europe (USSR)

SIZE 5 ft/1.5 m long

Only the skull of this primitive therapsid is known. It is strikingly similar to that of a sphenacodont, but with larger synapsid openings behind the eyes and more prominent canine teeth. Paleontologists believe it to be intermediate in structure between the pelycosaurs and the therapsids.

NAME *Titanosuchus*

TIME Late Permian

LOCALITY Africa (South Africa)

SIZE 8 ft/2.5 m long

Titanosuchus was a member of the large-skulled dinocephalians or 'terrible heads'. It was carnivorous, with sharp incisors and fang-like canines at the front of the jaws, and meat-shearing teeth at the back. Its main prey would have been its herbivorous relatives.

NAME *Moschops*

TIME Late Permian

LOCALITY Africa (South Africa)

SIZE 16 ft/5 m long

The Karroo Beds of South Africa have yielded many therapsids, among them this plant-eating dinocephalian (right), with a massive skull and deep body. The bones of its forehead were greatly thickened, suggesting that it engaged in head-butting battles for dominance – as did the boneheaded dinosaurs or pachycephalosaurs (see p.136–137).

Moschops had sturdy, sprawling forelegs; the longer hind legs were placed directly under the hips. Its short jaws had numerous chisel-edged teeth for cropping vegetation.

NAME *Lycaenops*

TIME Late Permian

LOCALITY Africa (South Africa)

SIZE 3 ft 3 in/1 m long

Lycaenops, or 'wolf face', was a small, lightly-built carnivore, with long running legs. It was a member of the gorgonopsians, the dominant predators of the Late Permian in southern Africa and European Russia. It may have hunted in packs, and probably preyed on large, plant-eating therapsids, such as *Moschops*. The canines were particularly long, and the front part of the skull was deeper than normal to accommodate their roots.

NAME *Galechirus*

TIME Late Permian

LOCALITY Africa (South Africa)

SIZE 1 ft/30 cm long

This tiny lizard-like reptile is thought to be an early member of the dicynodonts (see pp.190–191) – the most abundant and successful group of the plant-eating therapsids. However, *Galechirus'* teeth suggest that it was actually an insectivore. Many paleontologists think that *Galechirus* simply represents the juvenile form of an adult therapsid.

THERAPSIDS

SUBORDER DICYNODONTIA

The dicynodonts were the most successful and wide-ranging group of plant-eating therapsids, or mammal-like reptiles. They evolved during the Late Permian Period, and survived to the end of the Triassic Period – a span of almost 50 million years. The only group of therapsids that outlived the dicynodonts were the cynodonts (see pp.192–193), which were the direct ancestors of the mammals (see pp.194–297).

The advanced development of the dicynodonts' skulls and jaws was the main factor in the animals' success. The synapsid openings at the back of the skull (see p.61) were greatly enlarged in dicynodonts, so as to allow for longer, stronger muscles to operate the creatures' jaws. The hinge between the lower jaw and the skull also permitted the jaws to move forward and backward with a strong, shearing action, ideal for grinding up vegetation. And the dentition of these reptiles was unique. These adaptations equipped the dicynodonts to cope with all kinds of tough plant material.

NAME *Robertia*

TIME Late Permian

LOCALITY Africa (South Africa)

SIZE 18 in/45 cm long

Although *Robertia* was among the first dicynodonts to evolve, it had already evolved the specialized dentition characteristic of its later relatives. There was a horny, turtle-like beak at the front of its jaws, and the only teeth that remained were a pair of tusk-like canines in the upper jaw (an arrangement reflected by the name dicynodont, which means 'two dog teeth').

In the case of *Robertia*, there was a notch in the jaw immediately in front of the canine teeth, into which tough stems, twigs and roots could presumably be inserted, then severed by the sharp beak.

NAME *Cistecephalus*

TIME Late Permian

LOCALITY Africa (South Africa)

SIZE 13 in/33 cm long

Dicynodonts adapted to many lifestyles. Some were semi-aquatic, while others browsed in the coniferous forests. Some, such as *Cistecephalus*, lived underground.

This creature had a wedge-shaped, flattened head, a short body and strong, stumpy forelimbs with broad toes, like those of a modern mole. It probably used its powerful limbs to dig into the soil to find worms, snails and insects.

NAME *Dicynodon*

TIME Late Permian

LOCALITY Africa (South Africa and Tanzania)

SIZE 4 ft/1.2 m long

Dicynodon had the characteristic pair of canine tusks in its upper jaw, which gives the dicynodont group its name, 'two dog teeth'. It may have used these strong tusks to root up plants.

Another group of herbivorous reptiles, the pareiasaurs, were contemporaries of *Dicynodon*. Some of these were elephantine beasts, heavily armoured and with a full set of leaf-shaped teeth in their jaws. This was quite a different dentition to that of the horny-beaked, virtually toothless dicynodonts. These two types of unrelated reptile avoided competition with each other by eating different plants.

NAME *Lystrosaurus*

TIME Early Triassic

LOCALITY Africa (South Africa), Antarctica, Asia (China and India) and Europe (former USSR)

SIZE 3 ft 3 in/1 m long

The remains of *Lystrosaurus* were found in Antarctica in the late 1960s. The wide distribution of this sturdy, herbivore provides further evidence that, during Late Permian and Triassic times, India and all the southern continents were united as one landmass, Gondwanaland (see p.11, 299).

Lystrosaurus used to be regarded as a kind of reptilian 'hippopotamus' which wallowed in shallows, browsing on water weeds. New analysis shows that it probably fed on more resistant vegetation and may have burrrowed Both habits are more likely for an animal adapting to an increasingly semi-arid climate.

NAME *Kannemeyeria*

TIME Early Triassic

LOCALITY Africa (South Africa), Asia (India) and South America (Argentina)

SIZE up to 10 ft/3 m long

A skull bone of the ox-sized *Kannemeyeria*, or a close relative, was found in Australia in 1985, adding to the mass of biological evidence for Gondwanaland. This dicynodont was a well-adapted land-living herbivore. Its limb girdles formed massive plates of bone, to support the heavy, bulky body.

Kannemeyeria's massive head was lightweight, due to the great size of the openings for the eyes, nostrils and jaw muscles. Mouthfuls of leaves and roots would have been torn up by the powerful, horny beak and ground down by the shearing action of the toothless jaws.

SUBORDER THEROCEPHALIA

The Late Permian rocks of European Russia and southern Africa reveal the remains of advanced mammal-like reptiles, the therocephalians. They are also known from eastern Asia and southern and eastern Africa. They survived until the middle of the Triassic Period.

NAME *Ericiolacerta*

TIME Early Triassic

LOCALITY Africa (South Africa)

SIZE 8 in/20 cm long

This lizard-like creature was an active insectivore, judging from its small teeth and long, slim limbs.

The abundant plant life of early Triassic Africa – horsetails, ferns, conifers and early cycads – that supported the great populations of dicynodonts also provided home and food for many insects and other invertebrates. These, in turn, were a source of suitable prey for small therocephalians such as *Ericiolacerta*.

THERAPSIDS CONTINUED

SUBORDER CYNODONTIA

The cynodonts, or 'dog teeth', were the most successful group of therapsid reptiles. Not only were they the longest-lived group, surviving for some 80 million years, from Late Permian times to about the middle of the Jurassic. They were also the direct ancestors of the world's most successful modern group of animals – the mammals.

The first fossil cynodonts are found in the Late Permian rocks of European Russia and southern Africa. They show many advanced mammalian characteristics. For example, they had fewer bones in the lower jaw, a secondary bony palate and a complex pattern on the crowns of their cheek teeth.

Such advanced features suggest that these reptiles had evolved much earlier, probably during the early part of the Permian. Their ancestors were most probably among the carnivorous sphenacodont pelycosaurs (see p.187), which had already evolved a crude method of temperature control.

Although there is no trace in the fossil record, the cynodonts may well have been covered with hair, which would have insulated them and helped to maintain a high body temperature.

NAME *Procynosuchus*

TIME Late Permian

LOCALITY Africa (South Africa)

SIZE 2 ft/60 cm long

Although not a typical cynodont, *Procynosuchus* is interesting because, although it is one of the earliest and most primitive members of the group, it was specialized for living in water.

The rear of its body and tail were more flexible than was usual among cynodonts, and could obviously be flexed from side to side, in a crocodile-style swimming motion. The tail vertebrae were flattened, to increase the surface area, making the tail a more efficient swimming organ. And the limbs were paddle-like, similar to those of a modern otter.

Despite these specialized features, *Procynosuchus* is thought to be close to the ancestor of all the cynodonts.

NAME *Thrinaxodon*

TIME Early Triassic

LOCALITY Africa (South Africa) and Antarctica

SIZE 20 in/50 cm long

Thrinaxodon was much more mammal-like than its earlier relative, *Procynosuchus*. It was a small, solidly-built carnivore, probably capable of running quite fast due to the erect posture of its strong hind legs. The body was long and distinctly divided (for the first time among vertebrates) into a chest (thoracic) and lower back (lumbar) region. The division was marked by the extent of the ribs: only the thoracic vertebrae bore ribs, and these formed a distinct cage, which housed the vital organs.

As in living mammals, there was probably a sheet of muscular tissue, the diaphragm, that closed off the rib cage in *Thrinaxodon*. As the animal breathed, the movement of the diaphragm would have filled and emptied its lungs efficiently – an essential development in the evolution of body temperature control (see p.182–183). Another indication that *Thrinaxodon* could control its body temperature is the presence of a secondary bony palate, which completely separated the breathing passage from the mouth. This development allowed the animal to breathe at the same time as retaining food in its mouth for longer periods, chewing it up into small pieces for quicker digestion.

Many other structural changes had occurred in *Thrinaxodon*'s skeleton. For example, one of the foot bones had developed a heel which, with the help of strong tendons, would have levered the foot clear of the ground. The toes were of equal length, allowing the body weight to be evenly distributed.

Another mammalian trend is seen in the lower jaw of *Thrinaxodon*. The teeth on either side were set into a single bone, the dentary, which had become larger at the expense of the smaller bones at the back of the jaw. The effect of this trend among cynodonts, toward a single lower jaw bone, was to make the jaws stronger.

function as in living rodents and rabbits. These animals can nip in their cheeks to keep the food in the back of the mouth while it is being chewed.

The precise matching of the cheek teeth, and the advantage of concentrating chewing in the back of the mouth, would have made *Massetognathus* and its relatives efficient plant processors.

NAME *Cynognathus*

TIME Early Triassic

LOCALITY Africa (South Africa) and South America (Argentina)

SIZE 3 ft 3 in / 1 m long

The jaws of *Cynognathus* show without doubt that it was a ferocious predator. It was one of the largest cynodonts, strongly built, with its hind limbs placed directly beneath its body. Its head was more than 1 ft / 30 cm long.

Practically the whole of the lower jaw on each side was made up of a single bone, the dentary, into which the teeth were set – cutting incisors, stabbing canines and shearing cheek teeth. A great bony flange (the coronoid process) at the back of the dentary articulated with the skull, and enabling the jaws to open wide. It also provided an area to which extra jaw muscles could attach, giving the jaws tremendous bite-power.

NAME *Massetognathus*

TIME Middle Triassic

LOCALITY South America (Argentina)

SIZE 19 in / 48 cm long

Of the dozen or so cynodont families, only three included herbivores. The traversodonts, represented by *Massetognathus*, were plant-eaters, with a distinctive dentition. The cheek teeth were greatly expanded and the crowns were patterned with a series of crests and valleys. The teeth of the lower jaw fitted into those of the upper jaw. There was also a gap between the cheek teeth and the small canines toward the front of the jaws which probably had the same

NAME *Oligokyphus*

TIME Early Jurassic

LOCALITY Europe (England)

SIZE 20 in / 50 cm long

Oligokyphus and other members of its herbivorous family, the tritylodonts, were the last group of cynodonts to appear, in the Late Triassic. They were the longest-lived group of all therapsids, and the only mammal-like reptiles to endure into the Jurassic.

Oligokyphus was like a modern weasel in appearance, with a long, slim body and tail. Its forelegs, as well as its hind legs, were placed directly beneath the body, as they are in mammals. This little cynodont had achieved a fully upright, four-legged posture, unlike all other therapsids, which had sprawling forelimbs.

The dentition of the plant-eating *Oligokyphus* was also significantly different from that of other cynodonts. It had no canines, and the front pair of incisors were greatly enlarged, like those of a gnawing mammal such as a beaver. Like *Massetognathus*, a large gap separated the incisors from the square-shaped cheek teeth.

The cheek teeth in the top jaw had three rows of cusps running along its length, with grooves between: the lower teeth had two rows of cusps which fitted into the grooves, allowing the teeth to meet in a precision bite.

Oligokyphus is so like a mammal that paleontologists believed it to be a member of that group for years. But the small bones at the back of the lower jaw betray its reptilian affinities.

THE EVOLUTION OF VERSATILITY

The word mammal comes from the most important and unique characteristic of all species in this class of vertebrates, including humans: the presence in females of mammary glands, which produce milk to feed the young. Even the egg-laying mammals – the echidnas and platypus – have mammary glands.

The evolutionary implications of this milk-feeding strategy are enormous. The mother can leave her offspring in a den or nest while she goes foraging or hunting; she is then able to produce milk and so provide her young with a regular supply of this highly nutritious food. With nothing to do but sleep and suckle, the infants can grow fast.

The second most important mammalian characteristic is the presence of hairs, which usually form a dense fur coat. The prime purpose of the fur is to retain body heat, for mammals are warm-blooded. Most mammals keep their bodies at a constant temperature,

which is usually well above that of the environment. Humans, for example, have a body temperature of about 98.6°F/37°C; if the air temperature is lower, then we shiver and must put on clothes to keep warm; if it is higher, then we sweat to lose heat.

By maintaining this regular temperature, mammals can be very active for long periods, regardless of external conditions. But they pay a high price for this benefit; mammals must eat a great deal of food to produce the energy needed for such a high level of activity.

The earliest known mammals appeared in Late Triassic times, about 220 million years ago. Throughout the Jurassic and Cretaceous, mammals remained only minor elements in the world land faunas, which were dominated by reptiles, and in particular by dinosaurs.

Mesozoic mammals were all small shrew- or vole-sized creatures. They lived by scavenging small animals. Other early mammals, such as multituberculates, probably ate plant matter, as do the voles today.

With the close of the Mesozoic Era, the world changed. On land, the major development was the disappearance of the dinosaurs. The succeeding Cenozoic Era began 65 million years ago, and the dominant forms of life on land since then have been flowering plants, insects, birds and mammals.

The rise of the mammals

The emergence of tropical rainforests, temperate woodlands, savannah and prairie grasslands, provided new habitats for mammals to exploit. Mammals have inhabited all continents, most large islands and the oceans worldwide. Today, Antarctica is the only large landmass without resident mammals, save for the sealions on its shores. However, back in Eocene times, 50 million years ago, Antarctica had a wooded landscape in which lived marsupial mammals.

Mammals enjoyed their maximum diversity about 15 million years ago, during the Miocene. Since then, world climates have deteriorated, culminating in the Great Ice Age of the Pleistocene, which began about 2 million years ago. Diversity is always greatest in the tropics, and the shrinkage of tropical habitats is largely responsible for the decline in the number of mammal species. But alternate cold and warm periods of the Ice Age encouraged the evolution of remarkable large mammals, such as the woolly mammoth, giant deer and ground sloths – all of which disappeared within the last 12,000 years.

An active lifestyle calls for a high degree of control over the nervous system, so mammals have a large and complex brain capable of rapidly processing information fed to it from the eyes, nose and ears.

Limb adaptations

As the small, shrew-like early mammals evolved into large forms, they extended their range from the undergrowth up into the trees and out into the scrublands; some took to the water and others took to the air.

The mammals arose during the Late Triassic Period. Primitive members, represented today by the echidna and platypus, betray their reptilian ancestry by laying eggs. But the ancestry of all the later mammals is still quite obscure and hidden among the various groups of primitive mammals of Jurassic and Cretaceous times. Subsequently, two major groups arose: the marsupials, or pouched mammals, and the placental mammals, which dominate today. The inter-relationships of living mammals have been thrown into confusion due to conflicting evidence from DNA obtained from tissues compared with evidence from bones.

ARTIODACTYLS · CONDYLARTHRANS · LITOPTERNS · NOTOUNGULATES · CETACEANS · DINOCERATES · PERISSODACTYLS · HYRACOIDS · PROBOSCIDS · SIRENIANS · DESMOSTYLIANS · TUBULIDENTATES · MULTITUBERCULATES · DOCODONTS · SYMMETRODONTS · TRICONODONTS · MONOTREMES

All these exploitations of different environments required the evolving mammals to develop adaptations in their limbs. Shrews have basically primitive five-toed, or pentadactyl, feet. Those of fast-running predators, such as domestic cats, are essentially large-scale versions of this plan, with the loss of the inner toe. Mammals that climb and brachiate (swing from branch to branch) evolved elongated arms and legs with long fingers.

Mammals that graze the prairies and tropical savannahs have long slender legs with hoofed feet; in these 'ungulate' mammals, the legs have only one purpose – to move the animal. The ability to turn the feet sideways is lost, and the lateral digits also disappear until only two toes (as in cattle) or a single toe (as in horses) remain. Carnivores cannot pursue this economical course, since they must use their limbs for various purposes – walking, running, crawling, digging, climbing and swimming, as well as for seizing, holding and tearing into their prey. Their limbs retain the primitive structure for a multipurpose life.

Seals and sealions swim using highly modified limbs; the upper part of the limb is short, and the foot elongated and webbed to form a paddle. In whales, by contrast, the main power is provided by up-and-down movements of the tail fin. The forelimbs, modified into fins, are used mainly to control direction, and the hind limbs are totally absent.

Bats make use of another sort of modification of their forelimbs as 'wings', by elongating three fingers which radiate out like the spokes of an umbrella to provide support for the flight membrane, or patagium, made of a thin layer of skin.

Mammals basically have three different types of horny outgrowths at the end of their digits: nails, claws and hooves. Nails are found in primates, elephants and rhinoceroses. Claws are best developed in carnivores, but also occur in digging animals such as anteaters. Hooves characterize mammals, such as horses and antelopes, which live on grass-covered plains and scrub. They are also found in mountain goats and desert camels.

So, by elongating or shortening parts of the primitive pentadactyl limb, and sometimes by losing bones and digits, the basic cat-like leg has become modified to enable mammals to move in virtually all types of environments.

Mammal teeth

The ability to move efficiently through a great range of different habitats enables mammals to exploit a wide range of food. This, in turn, requires a dentition adapted for obtaining the food in the first place, and then reducing it to an easily swallowed mass. A mammal also needs an efficient digestive system, which can process the food to extract the maximum amount of nutrients.

Mammals are classified primarily on the basis of the structure and arrangement of their teeth and their limbs: that is, on how they feed and how they move. Since they have to move to obtain their food, these two functions are intimately related.

Teeth are made of tough calcium phosphate, so they fossilize well and outlast every other part of a mammal's body. After death it is teeth which are most likely to endure the centuries and even millennia.

During its lifetime, a mammal has two sets of teeth: the first dentition erupts after weaning and lasts only a short time, allowing the animal to feed while growing rapidly. The second, permanent set erupts to replace this. In an unspecialized, primitive mammal it comprises 44 teeth. These teeth are arranged in a distinct series, with different shapes and functions: three incisors, one canine, four premolars and three molars make up a total of 11 teeth in each half of each jaw. Few mammals exhibit this 'primitive' pattern without modification; some teeth have been lost, and those that remain are further specialized.

The incisors are sited at the front of the jaws; they usually have a chisel edge, and are used for holding and tearing. Specializations include the loss of two incisors, with the remaining one becoming a tusk or a cutting tool.

The canine (or dogtooth) is a small tusk-like tooth used by carnivores to pierce and hold their prey; in some it becomes greatly enlarged to form a sabre-tooth. In most herbivores, such as rabbits, cattle and horses, the canine is lost or is at most vestigial.

The incisors and canines are often separated, especially in herbivores, by a gap (the diastema) from the premolars and molars – the 'cheek teeth'. This allows their different functions to proceed simultaneously.

Like the incisors and canines, the premolars are often simple in shape, with only a single 'cusp' (projection) on their biting surface, but they have two roots instead of one. The premolars are often reduced in number, and may be specialized. In the hyenas, for example, premolars are thick, low cones used to crush bones, while they have become 'molarized' in many herbivores, taking on the form and grinding function of the molar teeth.

The molars are usually the most complex of the teeth. They have no precursors in the milk dentition, and erupt last. The molars are usually multicusped and multirooted. The cusp patterns are constant for each mammal family and genus, and are of enormous value in identification and classification.

In primitive mammals, the cusps on the molar teeth are arranged in reverse triangles. These interlocked as the jaws closed to give a series of zigzag cutting edges to pierce soft food, such as worms or insects. Full closure of the jaw cut up the food fully.

Carnivores have refined the cutting action, and evolved scissor-like blades – 'carnassial teeth' for slicing meat. In herbivores, the addition of a fourth cusp changed the triangle into a square. This provides a solid platform, so that when the upper and lower teeth meet as the jaws close, the food is crushed. Sideways, front-to-back or circular movements can then break up the food ready for swallowing.

ADAPTATIONS OF MAMMALS (*EUSMILUS*)

Mammal teeth and feet are well-adapted for particular lifestyles. Most mammals have four kinds of teeth – incisors, canines, premolars and molars – whose functions vary with diet.

In a carnivore, such as a dog, prey is killed with the canines and skinned with the incisor teeth. Molars and premolars cut flesh. A herbivore such as a horse crops grass with strong incisors and grinds it with molars and premolars. The canines have been lost or are reduced. The gap (diastema) between the front and back teeth separates the cropping and grinding actions of the jaws. An

insectivore such as a hedgehog seizes prey with its incisors; molars pierce and cut soft food.

Carnivores use their limbs for capturing prey and for locomotion. They are essentially primitive and unspecialized. Herbivore feet are, by contrast, specialized for movement over the ground, with the lateral toes reduced as in Parahippus (above). Insectivores have five-toed, lightly built unspecialized feet which perform a variety of functions digging, grasping, climbing, swimming and running.

Reproduction and classification

Mammals are reproductively highly sophisticated. This has traditionally been the basis for their classification into the major groups, the egg-laying Prototheria and the live-bearing Theria.

The Prototheria represent a more primitive group and are thought to include extinct groups such as the multituberculates as well as the living monotremes. However, there is no direct proof that the extinct groups were egg-laying. Indeed, there are good arguments that some of them may not have been. Many are very small animals with pelvic openings smaller than any living egg-laying animals. It may be that such morphological constraints may have promoted the development and bearing of live though very immature young, similar to those of marsupials today. Monotremes survive today only in Australasia as the echidnas (spiny anteaters) and a single species of platypus. There is a considerable problem in identifying fossil monotremes, and the relationships of the few known extinct forms with the living monotremes is highly problematic.

Marsupials, or pouched mammals, have little or no placenta and are grouped as the Metatheria. The young are born in a far less advanced state than Eutherian mammals (also called the

Placentalia), and continue their development after birth by crawling into their mother's pouch and attaching themselves to a nipple. Molecular data suggest that the marsupials are more primitive than the placentals and are more closely related to the monotremes. Their fossil record through the Tertiary into the Cretaceous is well-established, but the origin of the group is not.

In the advanced Eutherian mammals, the fetus develops within a uterus, or womb, where it is nourished through the placenta by its mother's bloodstream. Again, there is a vast fossil record throughout the Tertiary, with the majority of groups still having at least some living representatives. However, there are a number of extinct groups, such as the condylarthrans and creodonts. Their inter-relationships and origins are largely unresolved. The problems of classification have been exacerbated by contradictions between the molecular and morphological evidence for affinity. And, of course, the biomolecule markers – the DNA proteins that are analysed for evidence of genetic make-up – are unknown for most of the extinct groups, except for those that have only recently become extinct, such as the quagga and the mammoth. (Frozen mammoth and bison tissue from the Siberian and Alaskan permafrost is sufficiently well-preserved to yield molecular evidence).

PRIMITIVE MAMMALS

SUBCLASS PROTOTHERIA

The most primitive mammals belong to this group of 'first mammals'. Some modern classifications make a greater separation between the living mammal groups (the therians) and the extinct groups. Most of the latter are placed in the Subclass Mammaliaformes, which is nearly equivalent to the prototherians. However, recent discoveries of fragmentary fossil remains from the Late Triassic rocks of Texas (*Adelobasileus*) and Early Jurassic of China (*Sinocodon*) cannot yet be fitted into even this classification. Furthermore, the inter-relationships between the primitive mammal groups are far from clear, largely because so much of the fossil material just consists of teeth remains. Nevertheless, it is still thought that they all evolved from the cynodonts (see pp.192–193), a group of synapsid reptiles , during the late Triassic Period, some 220 million years ago.

The only surviving 'prototherians' are the monotremes – the echidnas, or spiny anteaters, and the duckbilled platypus, all of which are found only in Australasia. The reproductive method of the monotremes still reflects their reptilian ancestry – they all lay eggs. However, the newly-hatched young then suckle milk from their mothers, as all other mammals do.

Family Morganucodontidae

As an extinct group, the morganucodonts – thought to represent the earliest true or modern mammals – are not accessible to molecular assessment. For the time being, they are probably best placed along with the other extinct primitive groups, such as the kuehneotheriids and dryolestids, outside the associations of living mammal groups.

These earliest well-known mammals inhabited the desert environments during the Late Triassic Period. They were very small furry creatures, only about 5in/12cm long – as tiny as some of the smallest living mammals. They looked similar to modern shrews, but in many respects they still resembled the ancestral group of advanced mammal-like reptiles, the therapsids (see pp.188–193).

Their mode of locomotion was mammalian and possibly quite rapid, but may not have been able to sustain running for any great length of time. Well-developed and pointed cutting teeth suggest a carnivorous diet of insects. They were capable of a fairly complex chewing motion, in which the jaws could move sideways to a limited extent. This means that food could be digested quickly in order to release the vital energy needed to maintain both the high rate of metabolism which is typical of warm-blooded mammals and a predatory lifestyle. Like small modern mammals, the morganucodonts would have had to spend most of their waking hours eating and they were probably nocturnal.

Fossils of the morganucodonts have been discovered in Europe, southern Africa and eastern Asia.

NAME *Megazostrodon*
TIME Late Triassic to Early Jurassic
LOCALITY Africa (Lesotho)
SIZE 5in/12cm long

The morganucodont *Megazostrodon* looked similar to a modern shrew, and may have behaved in a similar way too. However, its limbs stuck out from its body to some extent, which implies that it probably had a more sprawling and less efficient gait than modern shrews.

Megazostrodon probably hunted for insects and other small invertebrates among the leaf litter and undergrowth, probably during the night, when it was less likely to fall prey to carnivorous dinosaurs.

Its body shape is well known from an almost complete skeleton found in Lesotho, while remains of closely-related animals have been found in China and Britain. The skeleton is very similar to that of primitive mammals.

Family Haramiyidae

This little-known group of primitive mammals with broad cheek teeth originated in the Late Triassic and extended through into the Mid Jurassic Period. The Haramiyidae family may be related to the ancestors of the multituberculates.

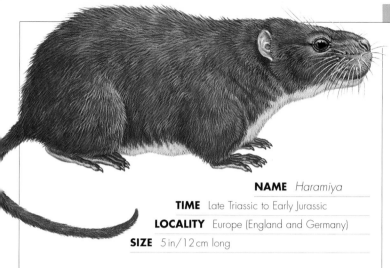

Megazostrodon (opposite). The multituberculates show no close affinity with any of the other mammal groups, and it is possible that they evolved independently from the mammal-like reptiles.

New discoveries from the Late Cretaceous of Mongolia of virtually complete skeletons promise to increase our understanding of this group and its relationships to the other primitive mammals.

Family Ptilodontidae

The Ptilodontidae family consists of animals with long tails. The tails were prehensile, serving as a fifth limb which could be used for grasping branches of the trees in which they probably lived. Their feet also show adaptations for climbing: like squirrels, ptilodonts could point their toes backward, due to a highly mobile ankle joint, an adaptation which enabled them to run down a tree trunk headfirst. They could also spread their big toes wide, to give a sure grip, aided by sharp claws. Their remains have been found mainly in North America.

NAME *Ptilodus*

TIME Early to Late Paleocene

LOCALITY North America (the Rockies, New Mexico to Saskatchewan)

SIZE 20 in/50 cm long

Apart from its long, prehensile tail, *Ptilodus* was similar to a modern squirrel in appearance, and may have lived in a similar way – scampering about in the branches of trees.

The lower premolar teeth were very large and blade-like, and *Ptilodus* may have used them to strip the husks from tough nuts and seeds.

NAME *Haramiya*

TIME Late Triassic to Early Jurassic

LOCALITY Europe (England and Germany)

SIZE 5 in/12 cm long

Haramiya is known from only a few isolated teeth. This fragmentary evidence suggests that it was somewhat like a miniature vole, and crushed its food with its broad cheek teeth. It may have lived on low-growing vegetation, possibly on the fruits of cycad-like plants.

ORDER MULTITUBERCULATA

The multituberculates were the earliest of the plant-eating mammals, evolving during the Late Jurassic and Early Cretaceous, with some groups surviving into the Oligocene. They were the largest group of Mesozoic mammals and ranged from mouse-sized creatures to animals the size of a modern beaver (very large for a primitive mammal). They were distinctly rodent-like in appearance, although they were in no way related to these animals. The similarity, especially of the tooth arrangement, is simply an adaptation to the same lifestyle and feeding habits.

Like rodents, the multituberculates had gnawing incisor teeth at the front of their jaws and grinding premolar and molar teeth at the back. The two types of teeth were separated by a gap called a diastema, which enabled them to be used independently. The array of grinding cheek teeth had many cusps (projections) to break up tough vegetation, as in many rodents.

The jaws worked with an up-and-down action, without the sideways movement of the early insectivorous mammals, such as

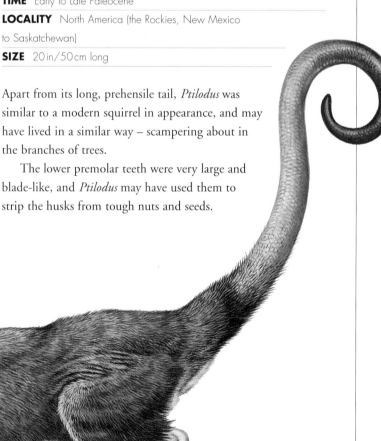

PRIMITIVE MAMMALS CONTINUED

Family Dryolestidae

The dryolestids probably represent an offshoot of the evolutionary line that eventually led to the modern mammals. The family members are known only from the remains of a few teeth and jaw bones. The remains show that the mammalian jaw hinge had fully evolved in this group. Three bones that had been part of the jaw in the reptiles were now incorporated into the middle ear, as the hammer, anvil and stirrup bones. These tiny bones form part of a chain of communication along which sound is transmitted to the inner ear.

NAME	Crusafontia
TIME	Early Cretaceous
LOCALITY	Europe (Portugal)
SIZE	4 in/10 cm long

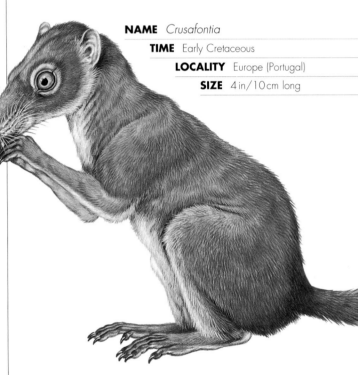

The dryolestid *Crusafontia* is known only from a few teeth. The reconstruction (above) is based on a relatively complete skeleton of another member of the family from the Late Jurassic Period of Portugal.

Paleontologists believe that *Crusafontia* probably resembled a tiny squirrel, living in trees and feeding on fruit, nuts and seeds. The creature's long tail may have been prehensile.

The bones of *Crusafontia*'s hip girdle suggest that it may have reproduced the way a marsupial does – giving birth to very immature young then suckling them in a pouch for the first few weeks of their lives.

SUBCLASS THERIA

This great group includes the majority of fossil mammals and their living relatives. The subclass is subdivided into three major orders – the pantotheres, which were restricted to the Mesozoic Era; the marsupials, or pouched mammals, which still survive in Australasia and America; and the eutherians, or placental mammals, which include all other living mammals and many extinct ones, too.

INFRACLASS METATHERIA

The two major subgroups of the subclass Theria – the Metatheria and Eutheria – diverged from a common ancestor early in the Cretaceous Period. The Metatheria contains only one order, the Marsupialia, or pouched mammals. This group is dealt with in detail on pp.202–205, but a primitive member is described here as a comparison with other primitive mammals.

NAME	Alphadon
TIME	Late Cretaceous
LOCALITY	North America (Alberta to New Mexico)
SIZE	1 ft/30 cm long

Primitive marsupials such as *Alphadon* were probably very similar to modern opossums. They were omnivores, and ate a wide range of foods, including insects, small vertebrates and fruit. They were probably also tree-dwellers, able to climb well, using feet equipped with opposable toes, which could be brought together to give a good grip, and prehensile tails. Their small size and tree-dwelling habits would have meant that they did not compete directly for food with the Late Cretaceous dinosaurs, and so were able to survive alongside them.

INFRACLASS EUTHERIA (PLACENTALIA)

The placental mammals, or eutherians, give birth to well-developed young after nurturing them for some time inside a womb. They make up the vast majority of modern mammals, and are grouped into about 24 orders (see pp.302–303).

One of the earliest families known, the *Zalambdalestidae* (below), may represent a side-branch from the main evolutionary line rather than a direct stage in the evolution of later placentals.

NAME *Zalambdalestes*

TIME Late Cretaceous

LOCALITY Asia (Mongolia)

SIZE 8 in/20 cm long

Zalambdalestes looked very much like the modern elephant shrew. It had a long upturned snout and powerful little legs, the back pair being longer than the front. The legs had greatly elongated foot bones. The fingers could not be brought to meet each other (they were not opposable), which is a development that is essential for giving a good grip, so *Zalambdalestes* is unlikely to have been a tree climber.

The animal's brain was quite small and the eyes large. *Zalambdalestes* may well have behaved in a similar way to the modern elephant shrews, running and jumping through the undergrowth after insects, and catching them with its long incisor teeth.

ORDER PRIMATES

It is possible that the primates are the most ancient order of placental mammals and date back as far as Late Cretaceous times – some 70 million years ago. The more advanced members of the primate group are dealt with on pp.286–297, but a primitive form, which provides the basis for the claimed longevity of the order, is described here in order to give a comparison with contemporary mammals.

The Family Paromomyidae consisted of small creatures quite similar in many ways to modern tree shrews, which may have been the ancestors of the later lemurs, monkeys and apes.

However, some paleontologists do not regard the Family Paromomyidae as members of the Primate order at all, but place them instead in a group of their own called the Primatomorpha.

NAME *Purgatorius*

TIME Late Cretaceous and Early Paleocene

LOCALITY North America (Montana)

SIZE possibly 4 in/10 cm long

Little is known about this small animal except for what can be deduced by paleontologists from the single molar tooth which was discovered in Late Cretaceous rocks in Montana. However, even such a tiny piece of evidence as this single tooth is important because it belonged to the earliest-known primate. The tooth resembles the molars of a modern lemur.

More complete sets of teeth from a slightly later, but related, creature from the Early Paleocene Period indicate that *Purgatorius* may have been omnivorous. However, the creature's diminutive size – it probably weighed no more than about ¾ oz/20 g – suggests that it was most probably an insect-eater first and foremost.

MARSUPIALS

ORDER MARSUPIALIA

The marsupials – including the familiar kangaroos and koalas of Australia, and the opossums of America – are among the most ancient of all of the orders of mammals. They evolved during the Late Cretaceous, between 100 and 75 million years ago.

The unique feature of marsupials is their method of reproduction. Placentals (the vast majority of mammals, including humans) nurture their young via a placenta within a womb, and do not give birth until the young have reached a relatively advanced stage. But marsupials give birth to very small and immature young – little more than embryos. These are then suckled, usually in a pouch on the belly, and grow to maturity outside the mother's body.

Recent molecular data puts greater weight on the differences between the marsupials and the placentals than traditional morphological methods. The marsupials are more closely associated with the primitive egg-laying monotremes.

The marsupials seem to have evolved in North or South America, and one group migrated via Antarctica (then much warmer than it is today) to Australia. A further group of marsupials moved via North America into Europe. The closeness of the drifting continents to one another in Late Cretaceous times enabled them to do this (see pp.11, 299). The marsupials flourished in isolation in South America during the Tertiary, where they developed before the placental mammals, and in Australia, where they have their stronghold today.

Another group of marsupials moved into Europe via North America during the Early Eocene, and in the Oligocene reached North Africa and central Asia. These were the didelphids, represented today by the opossums. They are thought of as the most primitive of the marsupials, and are the group to which the earliest-known marsupials belong.

By the Early Miocene, didelphid marsupials had become extinct in North America, and they disappeared from Europe, too, by Middle Miocene times. Although they never returned to Europe, the modern genus *Didelphis* (the Virginia opossum) re-entered North America from South America some 3 million years ago, via the newly-formed Panama land bridge.

However, the South American marsupials are nearly all gone, wiped out by invasions of placental mammals from North America. This happened when, during the Pliocene, a Central American land bridge was formed between these two great continents. This bridge was a tenuous one, however, and was not 'permanent' until the Panama connection was created.

The Australian marsupials still flourish today, despite competition from placentals. The reason may be that Australia had been moving northward by the slow process of continental drift during the Tertiary. This drift was relatively rapid, and the Australian climate changed from temperate conditions to tropical rainforest in a few tens of millions of years. The marsupials there had to evolve to keep up with this change, resulting in genetically strong stock. However, some have been much reduced in numbers (such as koala bears) or have become extinct (such as the Tasmanian 'wolf', or thylacine) as a result of human activities.

In contrast, South America has remained stationary during the same period. The animals did not need to evolve so much so placental invaders found a relatively primitive and genetically weak fauna population there, which was easy to replace.

Family Borhyaenidae

This family evolved from didelphid ancestors, and consists entirely of extinct carnivorous South American marsupials. Although completely unrelated to placental mammals of other continents, the borhyaenids have short limbs and rather dog-like skulls. Thus they evolved body shapes and lifestyles similar to those of cats, dogs, bears and other placental carnivores. This is a superb example of convergent evolution.

NAME *Cladosictis*
TIME Late Oligocene to Early Miocene
LOCALITY South America (Patagonia)
SIZE 2 ft 6 in/80 cm long

Cladosictis was a primitive carnivorous marsupial which may have resembled an otter in shape and size, with a long body and tail and short limbs. It probably scampered through the undergrowth, seeking out, chasing and catching small mammals and reptiles, and swam in rivers after fish. It may even have eaten reptiles' or birds' eggs and insects. The tooth pattern was similar to that of carnivorous placental mammals. The teeth consisted of incisors at the front for holding prey, followed by pointed canines for killing it, and meat-shearing (carnassial) premolars and molars at the back.

NAME	*Borhyaena*
TIME	Late Oligocene to Early Miocene
LOCALITY	South America (Patagonia)
SIZE	5 ft/1.5 m long

Some borhyaenids were rather bear-like, with heavy bodies and flat feet. The wolf-sized *Borhyaena* was typical of this group, but other closely related types ranged from fox-sized creatures to animals as big as bears.

These were the main predators of the day. Their prey would have included the plant-eating hoofed mammals (see pp.246–253) that were restricted to South America. The short limbs suggest that *Borhyaena* itself was not much of a runner, but probably ambushed its prey. It may also have been a scavenger.

Family Thylacosmilidae

In this group of large predatory marsupials, the skull became very similar to that of the placental sabre-tooth cats. The incisor teeth were lost, and very long upper canine teeth developed, which grew continually. These were formidable weapons.

NAME	*Thylacosmilus*
TIME	Late Miocene to Early Pliocene
LOCALITY	South America (Argentina)
SIZE	4 ft/1.2 m long

Thylacosmilus, like the sabre-tooth cats of North America and Europe (see pp.222–224), sported a pair of upper canine teeth that had evolved into long, stabbing sabres projecting down well below the creature's mouth-line. In both of these unrelated creatures, the musculature of the neck and jaws allowed the sabre-teeth to be driven downward with a tremendous killing force. The powerful jaws were capable of a gape that would leave the teeth clear to do their work.

Unlike the sabre-tooth cats, *Thylacosmilus* had no incisor teeth or scabbard-like tooth-guards on its lower jaw. Also the sabre-teeth grew continuously throughout life, rather like the incisors of rodents.

The victims of *Thylacosmilus* may have been large, slow-moving hoofed mammals that could not be killed rapidly with a quick bite to the neck. The sabre-teeth would have inflicted deep wounds and the prey presumably bled to death.

Family Argyrolagidae

The Argyrolagidae family consists of animals very similar to the kangaroo rats and jerboas of today, but they are completely unrelated to them. Like such rodents, they may have lived in arid desert environments and have been mostly nocturnal animals. They would have moved swiftly over the open ground by a series of prodigious leaps, and fed on the shoots and roots of desert plants.

NAME	*Argyrolagus*
TIME	Late Miocene to Late Pliocene
LOCALITY	South America (Patagonia)
SIZE	16 in/40 cm long

Just like modern kangaroo rats and other desert rodents (to which it is no relation), *Argyrolagus* moved quickly over open country on its slim, two-toed hind legs, balanced by its long heavy tail. The head was somewhat rodent-like, but it had a pointed snout. Enormous eye sockets, which suggest that the animal foraged only at night, were situated far back in the skull. The teeth suggest that it ate desert plants.

MARSUPIALS CONTINUED

Family Necrolestidae

This family has a single member, the extinct *Necrolestes* (below), so specialized that it can be classed with no other animal. However, its jaws and teeth do show some resemblance to those of the living golden moles of Africa. However, the golden moles are themselves a highly problematic group which are currently placed in the Insectivora.

NAME *Necrolestes*
TIME Early Miocene
LOCALITY South America (Patagonia)
SIZE possibly 6 in/15 cm long

All that is known of this little creature is a single specimen of the tip of the jaws with an oddly upturned snout. This may have ended in fleshy folds, possibly serving as sensitive organs of touch that helped the animal to find its food, like the complex fringe of tentacles surrounding the nostrils of the living star-nosed mole.

From its many fine teeth, paleontologists think that *Necrolestes* ate insects or worms. It may have lived as a burrower, – hence its ghoulish name, which means 'grave-robber'.

Family Thylacoleonidae

This family of lion-like marsupials lived in Australia in Pliocene and Pleistocene times. They probably hunted on the Australian grasslands. Research suggests that they may be related to living phalangeroid possums and kangaroos.

NAME *Thylacoleo*
TIME Pleistocene
LOCALITY Australia (New South Wales, Queensland, Western and South Australia)
SIZE 5 ft 6 in/1.7 m long

This 'marsupial lion' had a short, cat-like face. Projecting front incisors were modified into killing teeth, and looked rather like the canines in the placental carnivores – the canines themselves were insignificant. The back teeth formed powerful meat-shearing blades.

Thylacoleo was once believed to have used its unusual front teeth to break open nuts and fruit. However, recent studies have shown that wear on the teeth is consistent with a meat-eating diet, and the animal probably preyed on the giant kangaroos and wombats of the time.

Family Diprotodontidae

This major group of Australian marsupials includes mostly herbivorous animals. Diprotodonts have a single pair of lower incisors, which point forward. They have between one and three pairs of upper incisors, no canines, and a long gap (diastema) between their incisors and cheek teeth, as in rodents. The second and third toes of their hind feet are greatly reduced in size and are bound within a single sheath of tissue – a specialization used for grooming.

The diprotodontids evolved during the Mid Miocene and survived through into the Holocene, and it is possible that they were hunted to extinction by the early Australian aborigines. At present the group is thought to be related to the living wombats (vombatoids).

NAME *Diprotodon*
TIME Pleistocene
LOCALITY Australia (South Australia)
SIZE 10 ft/3 m long

The grazing marsupials attained their greatest size in *Diprotodon* and its relatives. In appearance *Diprotodon* was rather like a rhinoceros-sized wombat.

This impressive creature probably fed on a particular species of salt-bush, which it could scrape out of the ground with its paws. Remains of this bush have been found in the stomach cavities of several fossil specimens.

The body, head and neck of *Diprotodon* were massive, and the animal's limbs were strong. The feet were plantigrade, or flat-footed, so that the considerable weight was borne on the palms and the soles, in the same way as in a bear, rather than on the toes. Unlike the feet of other mammals, the outer ('little') toe of this animal was the longest – a peculiar feature with no apparent function.

Complete *Diprotodon* skeletons have been found preserved in lake muds. In the dry climates in which these animals lived, salt crusts may have formed over the local lakes of the open landscape. The heavy *Diprotodon* would easily have fallen through and become entombed in the mud beneath.

Family Palorchestidae

This family of large herbivores inhabited Australia from Miocene to Pleistocene times. The Family Palorchestidae may have been the marsupial equivalents of the placental ground sloths (see pp.206–207).

NAME	*Palorchestes*
TIME	Miocene to Pleistocene
LOCALITY	Australia
SIZE	8 ft/2.5 m long

The arrangement of the nasal bones in the skull of this animal suggests that it probably had some sort of trunk. In that case *Palorchestes* would have looked like a giant marsupial tapir.

Palorchestes' front legs were strong, and each had five toes equipped with huge claws. This characteristic has led experts to believe that this creature may have fed by pulling down branches in order to reach the leaves.

Family Macropodidae

The most familiar of the modern marsupials, eleven genera of kangaroos and wallabies, are included in the family Macropodidae, which is distributed throughout Australia and New Guinea.

The kangaroos arose in early Miocene times and developed larger forms in the Pliocene. They became adapted to a wide range of habitats: plains, mountainsides and forests (even developing some arboreal species).

Even though the Pleistocene extinction greatly reduced this overall diversity of this family, the macropodid kangaroos still represent the largest radiation of marsupials, with 14 living species of *Macropus*.

NAME	*Procoptodon*
TIME	Pleistocene
LOCALITY	Australia
SIZE	10 ft/3 m long

Extinct kangaroos tended to be generally larger than the modern forms, and had some different features. *Procoptodon* was the largest of these kangaroos, and was distinctive because of the short face. It was also set apart from the modern kangaroos by the fact that each hind foot had only a single long, functional toe (the fourth), with mere nailless stumps on either side. However, *Procoptodon* was probably just as capable of fast hopping as modern kangaroos, which can reach up to 31 mph/50 kmph over short distances.

Procoptodon was a grazing kangaroo, which fed on grass and low-growing vegetation, like most modern forms. Other extinct kangaroos, however, were browsers, using their great height to reach up into trees to feed off leaves.

GLYPTODONTS, SLOTHS, ARMADILLOS AND ANTEATERS

COHORT EDENTATA

The edentates are represented today by the anteaters, tree sloths and armadillos. The name of the cohort (a grouping of many orders) means 'without teeth', but in fact only the anteaters are completely toothless. The other members of the Edentata cohort have teeth, although these have become reduced to just a few rudimentary pegs, often without roots or a protective enamel covering.

The edentates comprise some of the world's most bizarre mammals. As well as the living anteaters with their greatly elongated snouts, the armadillos with their flexible suits of armour, and the proverbially slow sloths, the edentates include several strange, extinct groups. There were the tank-like glyptodonts with solid, immovable body armour, and the giant ground sloths, up to 6ft/1.8m high. Both these prehistoric animals ranged widely throughout North and South America during Pleistocene times.

The anteaters and armadillos became highly-adapted for feeding on ants and termites. Glyptodonts, ground sloths and tree sloths are vegetarian.

The edentates first appear in the Early Tertiary, but their evolutionary origins are obscure. Molecular data from living forms is not as complete as for many other mammals, but it does seem to indicate a surprising closeness to the carnivores, whales and even-toed ungulates. The group has had a remarkable history which is not in the least evident from the few remaining living forms.

Family Metacheiromyidae

These earliest and most primitive of the edentates, have uncertain relationships with other edentate groups. The Metacheiromyidae family may be the ancestors of the scaly anteaters or pangolins.

NAME *Metacheiromys*

TIME Middle Eocene

LOCALITY North America (Wyoming)

SIZE 18 in/45 cm long

With its short legs, sharp claws and long, heavy tail, *Metacheiromys* may have resembled a modern mongoose. However, it had a long, narrow, head, more like that of an armadillo. It had strong canines, but had lost almost all of its cheek teeth. Horny pads grew in their place, which the animal doubtless used to crush its prey.

Metacheiromys' habitat was the dense, subtropical forests that covered parts of the western USA during the Eocene. The claws on its forefeet were much larger than those on its hind feet, so *Metacheiromys* probably dug for its food, rooting out ants, beetles and grubs buried in the soil.

ORDER XENARTHRA

The name Xenarthra refers to the extra joints between the vertebrae which are a characteristic of this group. Their presence may have enabled animals as diverse as glyptodonts and armadillos to support the weight of a heavy suit of armour, or the giant ground sloths to haul their huge bodies into a near, vertical position in order to feed on leaves from branches at considerable heights.

The xenarthrans evolved in South America during the Paleocene, some 60 million years ago. They flourished on their island continent, isolated from predators and evolutionary changes. Then, in the Early Pliocene, about 5 million years ago, the land bridge that had once connected the two Americas during Early Tertiary times was re-established and glyptodonts, ground sloths and armadillos lumbered across it, heading north.

Families Mylodontidae, Megatheriidae and Megalonychidae

Today's tree sloths of Central and South America look and behave quite differently from their ancestors, the extinct ground sloths. Many of these creatures were so large that they could never have hauled their bulk up into the trees, and so were permanently grounded. One of the largest, *Megatherium*, was some 10 times bigger than its living relatives.

Ground sloths were slow-moving creatures and strict vegetarians. They appeared in Early Oligocene times, some 35 million years ago, and survived up to recent times.

NAME *Hapalops*

TIME Early to Middle Miocene

LOCALITY South America (Patagonia)

SIZE 30 cm/1 m long

NAME *Glossotherium*

TIME Pliocene to Pleistocene

LOCALITY North America (California)

SIZE 13 ft/4 m long

By Miocene times, some 20 million years ago, ground sloths had become well-established in South America. *Hapalops* was an early Miocene member of the group, and it was small in comparison with its later relatives.

Its short head, stout body and long tail were supported on long, slender forelegs and even longer, heavier hind legs. The long, curved claws on its toes must have forced this sloth to walk on the knuckles of its front feet, rather like a modern gorilla.

Being of fairly light build, *Hapalops* could have spent some of its time in trees, clinging on with its sharp-clawed feet and using its long legs to hook down succulent leaves and fruit.

Like all the edentates, *Hapalops* had very few teeth, only four or 5 pairs of cheek teeth remaining in its jaws.

NAME *Megatherium*

TIME Pleistocene

LOCALITY South America (Patagonia, Bolivia and Peru)

SIZE 20 ft/6 m long

This gigantic creature is the largest, known ground sloth. It probably weighed as much as 3 US tons/3 tonnes. Its head was deep and bear-like, and its jaws were equipped with strong muscles for grinding up its plant food between the few remaining, peg-shaped cheek teeth.

Although this giant ground sloth was as large as a modern elephant, it would have been able to rear up on its sturdy hind legs, supported on its thick tail. (Such a two-legged pose is reminiscent of the great herbivorous dinosaurs, such as *Apatosaurus*, see pp.131). In this position, *Megatherium* could browse near the treetops, hooking down branches with its three-clawed forefeet.

The Rancho La Brea tar pits in Los Angeles have yielded excellent specimens of this great ground sloth, which travelled up from South America, some 3 million years ago, over the newly reformed land bridge. There it met its fate in the sticky pools of crude oil that had seeped up to the surface and lay covered by water.

Glossotherium was a bulky creature, with a large head and heavy tail. Its long, clawed feet were turned inward, as they are in its relatives, so it walked on its knuckles, gorilla-style. *Glossotherium* could rear up on its hind legs, and used the long claws to bring food to its mouth. It seems to have lived on desert shrubs, to judge by the plant remains found preserved in its fossil droppings.

The giant ground sloths died out only 11,000 years ago. It is still not clear whether humans were responsible for their demise.

GLYPTODONTS, SLOTHS, ARMADILLOS AND ANTEATERS CONTINUED

Family Glyptodontidae

The glyptodonts were gigantic, armadillo-like creatures, which can be thought of as the mammalian equivalent of the heavily armoured dinosaurs called ankylosaurs (see pp.157–161). Some 50 genera evolved from the Early Miocene, about 20 million years ago, reaching their peak of success on the grasslands of South America and southern North America during the Pliocene and Pleistocene Epochs, between about 5 million and 3 million years ago. The glyptodonts survived until historical times, and feature in the legends of Patagonian Indians.

Glyptodonts were grazing animals, lacking teeth in the front of their mouths, but equipped with powerful grinding teeth at the back of the mouth. They had massive, deep jaws with downward-pointing projections of their cheekbones, which provided a site for the attachment of the powerful muscles that the animals needed in order to chew up the grasses and other tough vegetation on which they lived.

Some glyptodonts became very large: one of the biggest, *Glyptodon*, which lived in Argentina during the Pleistocene, between 2 million and 15,000 years ago, was the size of a small car and as formidably armoured as a military tank (5 ft/1.5 m tall and 10 ft 6 in/3.3 m long). The glyptodonts evolved from armadillo-like animals with armour arranged in rings.

By the end of the Pliocene, about 2 million years ago, the armour had become fused to form a rigid bony dome-shaped 'shell' made up of a mosaic of polygonal bony plates that enclosed the animal's back, a helmet above its skull, and a series of rings or a solid tube of bone around the tail. This armour accounted for 20 percent of the animal's weight (the tusks of an elephant account for only 3 percent).

NAME	*Doedicurus*
TIME	Pleistocene
LOCALITY	South America (Patagonia)
SIZE	13 ft/4 m long

As well as being protected by an armoured suit, *Doedicurus* possessed a powerful defensive weapon at the end of its tail – a bony club covered in spikes and borne at the end of a stiff

shaft. This remarkable structure bore a striking resemblance to the maces carried by medieval knights and, like them, was probably used by its owner to flail out at enemies – such as the carnivorous borhyaenids (see pp.202–203).

Family Dasypodidae

The armadillos first appeared in Argentina in Late Paleocene times, about 60 million years ago. By the Late Oligocene, some 30 million years ago, several forms had evolved the characteristic articulated armour seen in the living armadillos, which are essentially very similar and are included in the same family. Armadillos have always remained restricted to the Americas: the 20 modern species are almost all found in South and Central America, though one has recently extended its range into the southern part of the United States.

NAME	*Peltephilus*
TIME	Oligocene to Miocene
LOCALITY	South America (Patagonia)
SIZE	20 ft/6 m long

The armour of *Peltephilus*, like that of other armadillos, developed from its skin, and consisted of tough bony plates, or 'scutes', covered with horn. These were arranged in bands around the armadillo's body, and were connected to the underlying skin, making for a flexible protective 'shell'.

On the snout of *Peltephilus* a pair of long scutes was modified into a pair of horn cores, covered in life with horn. Unlike the true horns of cattle, sheep or antelope, the bony core was not an outgrowth of the skull bones. *Peltephilus* may also have borne a second, smaller pair of horns farther forward on its snout. Because it is peculiar among the edentates in having large canine-like teeth, *Peltephilus* may possibly have been a carnivore or carrion-eater.

Family Myrmecophagidae

The myrmecophagids, or 'true anteaters' (to distinguish them from the completely unrelated marsupial anteaters such as the modern numbat *Myrmecobius*) are highly specialized for exploiting a diet of ants and termites. They have a very poor fossil record and as a result their evolution is little known. An early form, *Protamandua*, from the Early Miocene about 20 million years ago, was already a typical anteater.

NAME *Eurotamandua*
TIME Middle Eocene
LOCALITY Europe (Germany)
SIZE 3 ft/90 cm long

Until recently, when a fossil anteater was discovered in deposits of oil shale near Frankfurt in Germany, and named *Eurotamandua*, paleontologists thought that anteaters were confined to South America. With its long tubular snout, weak toothless jaws and powerful forelimbs armed with huge claws, this was undoubtedly an anteater, and seems to have been very similar to the modern collared anteater *Tamandua*.

The fossil record of anteaters is poor, so it is not known how this exciting European find fits into the overall evolutionary history of the group. Evidence of *Eurotamandua's* typical anteater diet is provided by the fossilized ants found at the German site. It has been claimed that *Eurotamandua* is not a myrmecophagid, but an unrelated ant-eating placental mammal which has evolved and adapted to a similar lifestyle (a phenomenon known as convergent morphology).

Family Manidae

Manidae is the sole family in the Order Pholidota. The members of the family are the pangolins – curious mammals which are covered in protective horny, overlapping scales made up of densely fused hairs. This peculiar armour gives them the appearance of giant, animated pine cones. When the animal curls up in a ball it forms an almost impenetrable shield. Pangolins have stout limbs, which are well-adapted for unearthing their insect prey, and which are used in some cases for digging out burrows to sleep in.

Pangolins have often been grouped together with the anteaters and armadillos because of their very similar lifestyles: they all feed largely on ants and termites, which they pick up with their narrow, sticky tongues. However, this grouping is probably an arrangement of convenience rather than a reflection of any close relationship.

The extreme specializations of all of these creatures make it difficult to determine their true relationships. However, molecular data suggests, somewhat surprisingly, that like the other edentates, pangolins are closely associated with the Carnivora. All seven living species of pangolins are placed in the single genus *Manis*. They are found in tropical Africa and Southeast Asia.

NAME *Eomanis*
TIME Middle Eocene
LOCALITY Europe (Germany)
SIZE 20 in/50 cm long

The earliest known pangolin, *Eomanis* is represented by a well-preserved fossil from the same oil shale deposits that yielded the skeleton of *Eurotamandua*. Even the scales were preserved, and it is quite obvious that *Eomanis* looked very much like the pangolins of today. The animal may have been able to close its eyes, ears and nostrils as a protection against ant stings, as the modern species is also able to. From the fossilised remains of *Eomanis'* stomach, it is clear that its diet consisted of both plant matter and insects.

INSECTIVORES AND CREODONTS

A wide range of orders of both living and fossil animals have traditionally been placed within the superorder Insectivora. The group was based on an understanding of the morphology of the living hedgehogs, shrews and moles. The extinct anagalids are an example of a group which was thought to be within the insectivores but is now associated with the elephant shrews. Likewise, the dermopterans (including the extant flying lemurs) and chiropterans (including the extant bats) are grouped together outside the insectivores.

Molecular data shows that the relationships of the Insectivora with the Carnivora and other living groups are problematic. Consequently the status of the Insectivora as a natural unit is in doubt and it is now considered to be something of a taxonomic 'wastebin'. Nevertheless, it is still regarded as a primitive group and placed at the base of the placental mammals, with the hedgehog as the oldest of living placental groups.

ORDER ANAGALIDA

The anagalids were rabbit-like, digging mammals, known from the Early Tertiary rocks of eastern Asia. Once believed to be related to the elephant shrews, anagalids are now considered to have more in common with the rodents and rabbits.

NAME	*Anagale*
TIME	Early Oligocene
LOCALITY	Asia (Mongolia)
SIZE	1 ft/30 cm long

Anagale may have looked similar to a modern rabbit in some respects, but it had a long tail and, probably, short ears. It also ran about, rather than jumping rabbit-style. This pattern of behaviour and movement is conjectured from the proportions of the bones in the animal's hind legs.

Anagale's hind legs were a little longer than the forelegs, and they were equipped with spade-like claws on the feet. *Anagale* probably searched through the soil for beetles, grubs, worms and the like. The fact that the teeth in many specimens found are thoroughly worn down suggests that it also ate the soil – perhaps the easiest way of extracting food from it.

ORDER DERMOPTERA

The dermopterans constitute the group of 'flying lemurs' – a somewhat confusing name since the dermopterans are neither lemurs, nor are they capable of flight. Only two species have managed to survive until today – the Malayan and Philippine colugos (*Cynocephalus variegatus* and *C. volans*) of Southeast Asia. Both creatures are strict vegetarians.

These modern animals, less than 1 ft/30 cm long, can glide as far as 450 ft/137 m from tree to tree on outstretched skin membranes. It is assumed, though there is no direct evidence for this, that Mid-Paleocene and Early Eocene dermopterans could do likewise.

There is a gap in the colugo's fossil record from the Miocene to the living forms. There is some evidence that dermopterans are closely related to bats, tree shrews and primates, and that they all share a common ancestry with insectivores. However, this relationship is by no means certain: the similarities displayed may simply be a result of convergent evolution of unrelated groups. The molecular evidence supports the association with the tree shrews and bats.

NAME	*Planetetherium*
TIME	Late Paleocene
LOCALITY	North America (Montana)
SIZE	10 in/25 cm long

Planetetherium's remains have been found in beds of coal formed over many millions of years from dense lakeside forests of cypress trees.

As in the colugos, each incisor was divided to make a forward-pointing comb, with about five 'teeth' arising from each root. Their function is unknown – they may have been used for grooming, or for scraping and straining food.

ORDER CHIROPTERA

These are the bats – the only mammals to have evolved true, powered flight. The order Chiroptera have achieved this feat by modifying their forelimbs into flapping wings, made of a thin membrane (the patagium) and supported by four greatly elongated fingers.

Most modern bats use echolocation to detect obstacles, prey and predators in the darkness of night and the gloom of their roosting haunts. The bat emits high-frequency sounds which bounce off objects in its path and are picked up by the sensitive ears of the bat. The bat then analyses and acts on the information it receives.

The development of this extraordinary natural radar system involved extensive modification of the bat's larynx, nose, ears and brain. However, it is impossible to trace the course of this evolution because the parts of the body which are concerned do not fossilize.

There are two distinct suborders of living bats. The Microchiroptera (or microbats) are by far the most numerous, with some 780 species alive today. They are found the world over, except for the Arctic and Antarctic regions and on the highest mountains. Most microbats are small nocturnal animals with tiny eyes and large, often complex, extremely sensitive ears. Many microbats also have specialized outgrowths of the nose which are used for echolocation.

The nature and arrangement of their teeth depends largely on their diet, but the great majority catch insects on the wing and have shearing ridges on their upper molars arranged in a W-shaped pattern. A few species are carnivorous.

The second suborder is the Megachiroptera (or megabats), with about 170 species alive today. These are the fruit bats and are restricted to the Old World tropics. They are large animals with fox-like faces, hence their alternative name of flying foxes. The megabats lack the large, complex ears and elaborate noses characteristic of the microbats.

Traditionally the bats are grouped with the 'flying lemurs' (dermopterans) and tree shrews (scandentians), but recent molecular data from a microbat has placed them closer to the carnivores.

NAME *Icaronycteris*

TIME Early Eocene

LOCALITY North America (Wyoming)

SIZE 5½ in/14 cm long, 14 in/37 cm wingspan

Icaronycteris must have been almost identical to a modern microbat, but still had a few very primitive features. Its wings were relatively short and broad, and its mouth contained a large number of teeth, arranged like those of an insectivore. The body was not quite as rigid as that of a modern bat, and the tail was long and not connected to the hind legs by a web of skin. The thumb and first finger each bore a claw – modern bats have a claw only on the thumb – for hanging vertically from cave walls or other supports. Even at this early stage in their evolution, bats roosted upside down.

Icaronycteris undoubtedly lived like the modern microbats, catching insects on the wing, probably while flying low over water in the evening when there were few birds around.

Some remarkably well-preserved bats are known from the Middle Eocene oil shale deposits of Messel near Frankfurt-am-Mein in Germany. Even the wing membranes are still visible, and remains found in the area of the bat's stomach confirm that it was an insect-eater.

INSECTIVORES AND CREODONTS CONTINUED

SUPERORDER INSECTIVORA

Fossil forms of the Insectivora are known from the Mid-Cretaceous, about 100 million years ago, which makes them the earliest known placental mammals. Although patchy, the fossil record includes about 150 genera throughout the northern hemisphere, in Africa, Southeast Asia and Central America. There is a single species of living shrew in South America.

Almost all insectivores are small, and nocturnal or crepuscular (active at dusk or dawn). They usually have poor vision but good senses of smell and hearing. Many species of shrews use echolocation. Because of their small size and high metabolic rate, they must feed more or less constantly.

Insectivores are a successful group of animals: they have colonized an impressive range of habitats and adopted a variety of lifestyles, from burrowing underground to a semi-aquatic existence. Their diet is equally varied: as well as insects, they eat worms, molluscs and other invertebrates, small fish, amphibians, reptiles, birds, mammals and small amounts of plant matter. To deal with this varied diet, the dentition in both fossil and living forms is usually quite complete.

The skeleton is generally little modified from the basic mammalian plan, with five digits on each foot and platigrade locomotion (palms and soles touching the ground). Moles and golden moles, however, have shortened and strengthened forelimbs for digging.

ORDER LEPTICTIDA

The leptictids were one of many primitive groups of shrew-like mammals known from the Late Cretaceous, about 70 million years ago. They became prolific in the early part of the Tertiary and appeared in North America, Asia, Africa and Europe.

NAME *Leptictidium*
TIME Middle Eocene
LOCALITY Europe (Germany)
SIZE 2 ft 6 in/75 cm long

Leptictidium probably resembled the modern elephant shrew, except for its longer hind legs and tail. It was a bipedal runner, like humans and some of the smaller flesh-eating dinosaurs. The hind legs were long, light and

bird-like, with most of the muscles concentrated around the thigh. The forelimbs were less than half the length of the hind limbs and were adapted for holding food. The body was very short and the long tail served as a balancing organ.

Leptictidium ate more than insects: some skeletons show the remains of small mammal bones, lizard bones and plant matter.

ORDER LIPOTYPHLA

The Lipotyphla includes five fossil and seven living families. The latter include hedgehogs, shrews and moles, as well as solenodons of the West Indies, golden moles of Africa, tenrecs of Madagascar and otter shrews of Central Africa.

NAME *Palaeoryctes*
TIME Early Paleocene to Early Eocene
LOCALITY North America (New Mexico)
SIZE 5 in/12.5 cm long

A well-preserved skull shows *Palaeoryctes* must have closely resembled a modern shrew in appearance, with a small sleek body and a pointed snout armed with little, insect-crushing teeth. Although it ate mostly insects, probably beetles and caterpillars, it may have taken a wide range of foods, including small vertebrates. Such a generalized feeder would have been in a good position to evolve into more specialized types, and *Palaeoryctes* or a close relative may have evolved into the great flesh-eating mammals of the Early Tertiary – the creodonts.

ORDER CREODONTA

The creodonts were the dominant flesh-eating mammals worldwide throughout the early part of the Tertiary, between about 60 and 30 million years ago, except in South America and Australia. Yet they had all disappeared by the Late Miocene, some 7 million years ago. Before doing so, they evolved a great number of forms ranging from stoat- to bear-sized, anticipating the members of the order Carnivora.

Main differences between the creodonts and the carnivores proper are the smaller brains of the creodonts, the lack of a bone enclosing the middle ear, their different foot bones (the wrist bones are not fused and the claw bones have a groove in them) and differences in the teeth, especially in those teeth which perform a carnassial function (the pairs of teeth, which are formed like scissor-blades to shear meat).

The 50 or so genera of creodonts are classified in 2 families – the Oxyaenidae and Hyaenodontidae. It used to be thought that the creodonts were ancestors of the modern carnivores. But recent analyses suggest that the creodonts are probably not a natural group but are derived from different origins.

NAME *Sarkastodon*

TIME Late Eocene

LOCALITY Asia (Mongolia)

SIZE 10 ft / 3 m long

Around 35 million years ago, during the Late Eocene, Central Asia boasted some huge mammals, notably brontotheres, chalicotheres, and rhinoceroses (see pp.258–265). To exploit such massive prey, the creodonts grew to a great size, too. *Sarkastodon* was one of the largest, bigger than the biggest bear. The teeth were large and heavy, and thick like those of a modern grizzly bear. *Sarkastodon* probably ate a wide range of foods.

Other oxyaenids living in the northern hemisphere during Paleocene and Eocene times, between about 55 million and 40 million years ago, included animals that resembled wolverines and cats.

NAME *Hyaenodon*

TIME Late Eocene to Early Miocene

LOCALITY Widespread over North America, Europe (France), Asia (China) and Africa (Kenya)

SIZE Up to 4 ft / 1.2 m long

The hyaenodonts, the later family of creodonts, were a larger group than the oxyaenids. They evolved in the Eocene and persisted to the Late Miocene, ranging from North America, to Asia, Europe and Africa.

Hyaenodon was a widespread and long-lived genus including many species, from animals the size of a stoat to species as large as a hyena. Its long, slim legs and digitigrade feet (only the toes touched the ground) indicate that *Hyaenodon* could run, though its spreading toes suggest that it would not have been very fast. *Hyaenodon* may have been hyena-like in habits, actively hunting down other animals, but also scavenging dead ones.

ORDER CARNIVORA

Cats, civets and mongooses, dogs, bears and pandas, stoats, weasels and otters, seals, sealions and walruses – all these mammals belong to the large order Carnivora. All of the animals in the order Carnivora are carnivores, meaning 'meat-eaters', and they all share a common feature relating to their teeth. Living carnivores have (and their ancestors also had) a pair of meat-shearing teeth, called carnassial teeth, which have become specialized for slicing up flesh. However, some members of the Carnivora order, such as seals, have lost these teeth, since they have developed and evolved to feed mainly on fish, and therefore no longer need them.

However, not all animals that eat meat are members of the order Carnivora. The toothed whales, for example, are not 'true carnivores', although one species which is part of the group, the killer whale, is a formidable predator and will eat other whales and seals and sea birds.

An extinct group of ferocious carnivores, the creodonts (see p.213), were not members of the order Carnivora, nor were the insatiable carnivorous dinosaurs. Conversely, not all members of the Carnivora only eat meat. Bears and badgers, for example, are omnivores, and consume a wide range of animal and plant food.

Besides the meat-shearing blades of the carnassial teeth, true carnivores are also distinguished by having small, sharp incisor teeth at the front of their jaws for holding prey and large, pointed canine teeth for delivering the killing bite (see p.196)

The order Carnivora has traditionally been divided into two major groups, the fissipeds (meaning 'split feet') and the pinnipeds (meaning 'fin feet'). However, it is now thought that the relationships within the order are more complicated was previously believed and this is reflected in more modern classifications. The extinct miacids are treated separately and the feliforms (cats and hyaenas) are distinguished from the caniforms (dogs, weasels, civets and bears). The pinnipeds, made up of the seals, sealions and walruses, are still grouped together. Molecular analysis now groups the Carnivora with the whales and even-toed ungulates.

Carnivores appeared during Late Cretaceous or Early Paleocene times, about 70–65 million years ago. The carnivores evolved from the same ancestors as did the insectivores (see pp.210, 212), but the carnivores remained relatively insignificant until Oligocene times, some 35 million years ago. At this time they began to replace the creodonts, which had been the dominant carnivorous land mammals up to that time.

Family Miacidae

The miacids were the earliest true carnivores to appear, during the Paleocene, 60 million years ago. This is an 'artificial' group, since it contains animals that were not closely related. However, it is a convenient classification that distinguishes these early carnivores from the more modern types. Miacids were mostly small mammals that lived in woodlands. The scant remains they have left indicate that they resembled the creodonts in many ways, although they were possibly more intelligent and had better-developed meat-shearing teeth.

NAME	*Miacis*
TIME	Paleocene to Middle Eocene
LOCALITY	Europe (Germany)
SIZE	8 in/20 cm long

Scampering through the branches, this animal must have looked like a modern pine marten (*Martes martes*). The shape of its limbs and its flexible shoulder and elbow joints indicate that it was well-adapted for moving through the trees of its native tropical swamp forest.

Miacis probably also lived in much the same way as a pine marten, hunting small mammals and birds on the ground and in the trees. It may also have eaten insects, birds' eggs and fruit. A primitive feature of *Miacis* was its full set of 44 teeth. This is the basic number of mammalian teeth, but the more advanced carnivores lost many of them during their evolution into more specialized forms.

Family Mustelidae

Mustelids probably evolved from the miacids in the Early Tertiary. Modern members of the family include weasels, stoats, badgers and otters, civets, genets and mongooses– all slim, long-bodied hunters.

NAME *Potamotherium*

TIME Early Miocene

LOCALITY Europe (France)

SIZE 5 ft / 1.5 m long

Potamotherium is the earliest-known otter, and like its modern counterpart it had a long, sinuous body and short legs. It probably ran through the riverside undergrowth in a series of leaps, with its back arched and its head close to the ground. *Potamotherium's* sense of smell was not well-developed, but its senses of hearing and sight seem to have been acute, helping it to hunt down its fish prey in the water.

Potamotherium was without a doubt an excellent swimmer. The creature's sleek, streamlined shape would have cut through the water, and its flexible backbone enabled it to dive and dart about easily underwater.

The otters are the only mustelids that are well-represented in the fossil record. This is probably because they lived near water, and so were more likely to become buried in sediments and subsequently fossilized. Paleontologists believe that the true seals, or phocids (see p.226), evolved from a mustelid ancestor.

Family Procyonidae

The procyonids, including the modern raccoons, pandas and coatis, first appeared in the Early Oligocene, about 35 million years ago. They had the typical meat-shearing blades on their premolar and molar teeth, the characteristic feature of the true carnivores. But this design has been lost in modern members of the family, and their premolars and molars have reverted to a purely grinding and crushing function.

This dentition suits the omnivorous diet of most modern procyonids. However, the diet of the giant panda, *Ailuropoda melanoleura*, consists almost exclusively of bamboo shoots, and it is probable that this animal is more closely related to the bears than to the raccoons.

NAME *Plesictis*

TIME Early Oligocene to Early Miocene

LOCALITY Asia (China), Europe (France) and North America (USA)

SIZE 2 ft 5 in / 75 cm long

This tree-living hunter had big eyes, perhaps for nocturnal hunting, and a long tail for balance. It was similar to the modern cacomistle (*Bassaricus sumichrasti*), and may have been its direct ancestor. It probably led much the same lifestyle, scampering through the trees.

Like other procyonids, the cusps of its teeth were blunt and the molars were square in cross-section, indicating that it was probably omnivorous, eating eggs, insects and plant matter, as well as hunting for small mammals and birds.

NAME *Chapalmalania*

TIME Late Pliocene

LOCALITY South America (Argentina)

SIZE 5 ft / 1.5 m long

The procyonids travelled south from North America via the Central American land bridge. Once in South America, they evolved into a number of specialized forms. *Chapalmalania* was a gigantic raccoon that must have looked rather like the modern giant panada. It was so large that its remains were at first thought to be those of a bear. Like the panda, it probably had a specialized diet, relying on some local plant on the mountainsides for much of its food.

MUSTELIDS AND BEARS CONTINUED

Family Amphicyonidae

The amphicyonids were a family of 'bear-dogs' that existed from the Eocene Epoch 50 million years ago to Miocene times, about 5 million years ago.

Amphicyonids were a varied and successful group of large hunting animals. They spread throughout Europe, Asia, and North America. When the creodonts declined, the amphicyonids replaced them in the ecosystems and were then themselves replaced by the 'true dogs' during Pliocene times (some 5 million years ago).

The amphicyonids' common name 'bear-dogs' refers to their similarity to both of these creatures. The amphicyonid's body was bear-like in shape and bulk. They walked with the whole foot placed on the ground (known as plantigrade locomotion, and the same method that is used by bears and humans), rather than just the toes (known as digitigrade locomotion, and the same method used by the fleet-footed cats and dogs). The shape of the head and the arrangement of the teeth, however, were more dog-like.

NAME	*Amphicyon*
TIME	Middle Oligocene to Early Miocene
LOCALITY	Europe (France and Germany) and North America (Nebraska)
SIZE	6 ft 6 in/2 m long

Amphicyon was a typical 'bear-dog'. It probably looked like a large bear with the strong, sharp teeth of a wolf. It had a thick neck, strong legs and a heavy tail. It may have led a similar life to that of a modern brown, or grizzly, bear, eating a wide range of plant and animal foods, and killing its prey with powerful blows from its strong forefeet.

Amphicyon must have been a fearsome adversary for any other creature living on the plains of the northern hemisphere in Mid-Tertiary times, about 30 million years ago. One fossil species, *Amphicyon giganteus*, from the Miocene of Europe, was about the same size as a modern tiger.

Family Ursidae

The Ursidae family comprises the bears. Taxonomically, the bears are associated with the dogs (canids), raccoons (procyonids) and weasels (mustelids) as caniforms.

The ursids occur later in the fossil record than many other carnivores, having first appeared in Europe during Oligocene times. Since their first appearance they have spread throughout most of the world.

Although there are no bears native to Africa today, there are two separate records of bears having inhabited that continent in the past. The primitive *Agriotherium* (below) lived in southwestern Africa during the Pliocene, some 5 million years ago, and brown bears are known to have lived in the Atlas Mountains of northern Africa during the Pleistocene Epoch, even surviving into recent times.

Bears are omnivorous creatures, consuming anything that they can catch, from small mammals to fish and insects. They also forage for fruit, eggs, nuts and, of course, honey. They generally search for food by day and their eyesight and hearing are quite poor, though their sense of smell is very acute.

Their pattern of dentition reflects their catholic diet. Bears have unspecialized incisors, long canines, reduced or absent premolars (with no meat-shearing blades) and broad, flat molars with rounded cusps. The molars are probably the most used of this animal's teeth, being used to crush up the tough plant food that makes up the major part of a bear's diet.

The modern Kodiak bear (*Ursus arctos middendorffi*) which is found in the forests of Kodiak, Afognak and Shuyak islands on the northwest coast of the USA, is the world's largest living land carnivore.

NAME *Agriotherium*

TIME Late Miocene to Pleistocene

LOCALITY Africa (Namibia), Asia (China) and Europe (France)

SIZE 6 ft 6 in/2 m long

Although bears are no longer found in Africa, they were in the past. *Agriotherium* lived in southwestern Africa *Agriotherium* was a very large bear, even larger than the Kodiak bear. It was also very primitive, and looked like a dog in some ways. However, its teeth had developed the typical bear pattern, so it is safe to assume that it was omnivorous.

NAME *Hemicyon*

TIME Early to Late Miocene

LOCALITY Asia (Mongolia), Europe (France and Spain) and North America (USA)

SIZE 5 ft/1.5 m long

Despite its great size, *Hemicyon* was lightly built for a bear. Indeed, it was more like a heavy dog, and its name means 'half-dog'. It was probably more carnivorous than most other bears, and so was likely to have been an active

hunter. It had powerful legs, and the structure of its feet indicates that it ran on its toes (digitigrade) rather than with the whole foot pressed to the ground (plantigrade) as in modern bears. This digitigrade structure of the foot is an adaptation for swift running. These features suggest that *Hemicyon* was a hunter of the open plains, possibly roaming about in packs.

NAME *Ursus spelaeus*

TIME Pleistocene to Recent

LOCALITY Europe (Austria, Germany, Netherlands, Spain, UK and former USSR)

SIZE 6 ft 6 in/2 m long

The genus *Ursus* is represented today by the brown, or grizzly, bear, the polar bear and the American black bear. But in Pleistocene times, the cave bear, *Ursus spelaeus*, was a particularly numerous and impressive species.

Ursus spelaeus lived in Europe during the height of the last Ice Age, and often escaped the worst of the winters by hibernating in Alpine caves. Many bears seem to have congregated together for this long, annual sleep, to judge from the heaps of fossil bones that have been found together.

One cave, the Drachenhohle, or 'Dragon's Cave', in Austria for example, contains the remains of more than 30,000 cave bears. And many of them seem to have died in their sleep, possibly during their period of hibernation.

Despite its great size and fearsome appearance, the cave bear was probably a vegetarian. It was hunted by Neanderthal people (see p.297), and its bones were important in their rituals.

DOGS AND HYENAS

FAMILY CANIDAE

The canids – including the modern foxes, jackals, coyotes, wolves and dogs – are a successful group of 'all-rounders'. With an evolutionary history of some 40 million years, they have become adapted to an enormous range of habitats and a wide variety of diets. As members of the order Carnivora (see p.214), the Canidae family are related to the otters and weasels, cats and mongooses, and to the seals, sealions and walruses.

First known from Late Eocene times, about 40 million years ago, the earliest canids were relatively short-legged animals that resembled mongooses and civets more than modern dogs. They were almost entirely restricted to North America, the centre of canid evolution; the family did not colonize other continents until the end of the Miocene, as recently as 6 million years ago.

From a mere five genera in the Early Oligocene (35 million years ago), the canids had evolved and diversified to 42 genera by the Late Miocene (10 to 6 million years ago). This was their heyday and they have since declined to the 12 modern genera alive today, which includes the domestic dog.

The teeth of canids have contributed much to their versatility of habitat and diet. As well as the large, pointed canine teeth (the word canine simply means 'dog-like') and well-developed meat-shearing (carnassial) teeth, they also possess powerful crushing molars at the back of the jaws. So they are omnivorous – eating anything from bones and flesh, to insects and fruit.

Canids have also evolved a superb sense of smell, good vision and acute hearing. Their long limbs and great stamina, combined with their style of running on the tips of their toes (called digitigrade locomotion), allow them to chase swift-moving prey for considerable distances, until they succumb through exhaustion.

Intelligence and social living, as seen today in hyenas and wolves, also enhance their ability to catch prey, avoid predators, rear young successfully and colonize new habitats.

NAME	*Phlaocyon*
TIME	Early Miocene
LOCALITY	North America (Nebraska)
SIZE	2 ft 6 in / 80 cm long

Just as *Hesperocyon* superficially resembled a member of the cat family (felids), so *Phlaocyon* looked more like a member of the raccoon family (procyonids, see p.215). However, several features of its skull suggest it did belong to the dog family (canids), though it was a very primitive member.

Phlaocyon probably lived much like a modern raccoon. Although its feet were distinctly dog-like, its limbs were adapted for climbing trees rather than for running. It had a short, broad head with the eyes set well-forward.

The lower jaw of *Phlaocyon* was curved, similar to the lower jaw of a raccoon, and the premolars and molars were all grinding teeth. The creature's dentition did not include the meat-cutting blades which are so typical of dogs. The pattern and type of teeth suggest that *Phlaocyon* was probably omnivorous, feeding on a mixed diet of seeds, fruit, insects and birds' eggs, as well as small mammals and birds.

NAME	*Hesperocyon*
TIME	Early Oligocene to Early Miocene
LOCALITY	North America (Nebraska)
SIZE	2 ft 6 in / 80 cm long

An active little animal, looking like a mongoose or civet, *Hesperocyon* was one of the earliest members of the canid family to appear. With its long flexible body and tail, and its short, weak legs and spreading five-toed feet, it may not have looked much like a dog. However, the structure of its ear bones and the arrangement of its teeth show without a doubt that it was a primitive canid.

Fossils of the creature's skull show that parts of the inner ear were enclosed in bone rather than in cartilage (gristle) – a dog-like feature that distinguishes *Hesperocyon* from more primitive carnivores, such as *Miacis* (see p.214).

The teeth of *Hesperocyon* show that the last molar tooth was missing from each side of the upper jaw, giving a set of 42 teeth rather than the usual complement of 44. The last upper premolar tooth and the first lower molar tooth on each side were modified into meat-cutting (carnassial) blades, typical of dogs and most other true carnivores (that is, those grouped in the order Carnivora).

NAME *Cynodesmus*

TIME Late Oligocene to Early Miocene

LOCALITY North America (Nebraska)

SIZE 3 ft 3 in / 1 m long

Cynodesmus was one of the first canids that actually looked like a modern dog. It was roughly the size and shape of the coyote, *Canis latrans,* of today's North and Central America. Its face, however, was shorter (the long snout of typical dogs was to develop much later in their evolution), and its body was still quite long, with a heavy tail.

Cynodesmus' legs were quite dog-like, but they were not yet as efficient for running as those of modern dogs. The open grasslands of North America had not formed at this time; their development encouraged the evolution of fast-moving grazing

mammals, which in turn led to the rapid evolution of swift-footed hunters such as dogs.

There were still five toes on each of *Cynodesmus'* feet, although the first toes were smaller than the rest. Its claws were narrow and partially retractable, like those of a cat, rather than the thick, blunt, weight-bearing structures that developed in later dogs. It was probably *Cynodesmus'* habit to ambush its prey, cat-style, rather than running it down, dog-style.

NAME *Cerdocyon*

TIME Pleistocene

LOCALITY South America (Argentina)

SIZE 2 ft 6 in / 80 cm long

The dog family evolved in North America throughout the Tertiary Period. The animals that belonged to this group could not reach South America because the two continents were separated by a sea. Then, toward the end of the Tertiary, in Pliocene times (about 5 million years ago), the Central American land bridge was re-established, and animals could migrate southward. The dogs crossed into South America in the Early Pleistocene, some 2 million years ago, and the early fox *Cerdocyon* was among the invaders in this trek southward.

Two million years later, *Cerdocyon* lives on in the form of the common zorro or crab-eating fox, *Cerdocyon thous,* which is found from Colombia to northern Argentina.

Crabs are only part of the diet of this omnivorous night-hunter. Depending upon seasonal availability it also eats rats, mice, frogs and insects using its keen sense of hearing when hunting in the dark, and employing both stealthy and 'dash and grab' hunting techniques to catch its quarry. The crab-eating fox will also consume fruit and carrion, and any creature's eggs that it can find. Its Pleistocene relative probably pursued much the same opportunistic lifestyle.

DOGS AND HYENAS CONTINUED

NAME *Osteoborus*
TIME Late Miocene to Early Pleistocene
LOCALITY North America (Nebraska)
SIZE 2 ft 6 in/80 cm long

NAME *Canis dirus*
TIME Pleistocene to Recent
LOCALITY North America (California)
SIZE 4 ft 6 in/1.5 m long

The genus of dogs called *Canis* includes the nine living species of wolves, coyotes, jackals and dogs – both wild dogs and every domestic breed, from Great Dane to Chihuahua. Many more species existed in the past, one of the best known being *C. dirus*, the dire wolf. In appearance, this prehistoric wolf was much like its modern counterpart, but it was more heavily built. It was probably a scavenger rather than a hunter filling the niche of borophagines, such as *Osteoborus*, after their extinction in the Early Pleistocene.

The remains of more than 2000 dire wolves have been excavated from the tar pits of Rancho La Brea, where the city of Los Angeles stands today. About 25,000 years ago, crude oil seeped to the surface here, and evaporated away, leaving behind pools of sticky tar. These pools trapped unwary animals, such as ground sloths and elephants. The dying animals attracted carnivores, such as the dire wolf which also became stuck.

Their fossilization took place have left a detailed record of life in Pleistocene times. The dire wolves and sabre-tooths fought, since their bones are often covered with scars from each other's formidable teeth.

More intelligent, active hunters, such as the contemporary lions and dogs, were rarely trapped. It seems that they could more readily appreciate the danger of the pools.

Osteoborus was a member of the borophagines, a group of scavenging dogs that first appeared in late Miocene times, about 8 million years ago.

Osteoborus' heavy build and rather bulbous, swollen forehead gave it a rather bear-like appearance, however, this creature's scavenging hyena-like habits were partly reflected by the huge, bone-crushing premolar teeth which lined its jaws. *Osteoborus'* skull had also developed a shortened form in order to accommodate the massive muscles that were needed to work the animal's powerful jaws. This rugged combination of strong jaws and crushing teeth enabled *Osteoborus* to chew and splinter the bones of carcasses in order to reach the soft and nutritious bone marrow inside.

Osteoborus was a widespread inhabitant of North America, where it probably occupied the same ecological niche as the contemporary hyenas in Europe, Asia and Africa, scavenging what it could from dead animals or robbing other predators of their kills. *Osteoborus'* scavenging role in the ecosystem was eventually taken over in North America by more typical dogs, such as *Canis dirus*.

Family Hyaenidae

The hyenas, also members of the order Carnivora, appeared only relatively recently, in Mid-Miocene times, about 15 million years ago. They probably evolved on the African continent, and then spread throughout the Old World. Nowadays, the hyaenids are grouped with the feliforms and are thought to have originated from the viverrids (civets and relatives).

The only hyena known from the New World is *Chasmaporthetes*, which lived in North America during the Pleistocene. It also lived throughout Africa, Asia and Europe. It was a fast-running hunter rather than a scavenger, and its legs and teeth were similar to those of the modern cheetah. Indeed, in Africa it had to compete with the true cheetahs, which also lived there during Pleistocene times.

The role of 'mammalian scavenger' in North America was played chiefly by the heavy-toothed borophagine dogs, such as *Osteoborus*. Their diet and lifestyle mirrored that of the hyenas elsewhere in the world.

Today, hyenas are restricted to the warmer areas of Africa and Asia. Although they are chiefly scavengers, they are also agile and intelligent hunters, running in packs to bring down swift-footed grazing mammals such as gazelle. They have heavy bone-crushing teeth, and their remarkably tough digestive system enables them to absorb the organic matter in bone, while indigestible bone fragments, hooves, horns, ligaments and hair are regurgitated as pellets.

NAME *Ictitherium*
TIME Middle Miocene to Early Pliocene
LOCALITY Africa (Morocco) and Europe (Greece)
SIZE 4 ft/1.2 m

Ictitherium was one of the earliest hyenas, and probably looked more like a civet (a relative of the mongooses and genets, see p.225) in build and appearance. It also had teeth similar to those of a civet, which were well-suited to an insectivorous diet, rather than the formidable bone-crunching teeth of hyenas.

Along with its primitive relatives, *Ictitherium* was among the most widespread hunters of its time. Indeed, at one stage during the Pliocene its fossil remains outnumber those of all other carnivores put together.

Groups of animals are often found fossilized together, which suggests that a flood may have swept them all away at the same time. It is likely that this early hyena had already evolved a relatively advanced social order and hunted down their prey in packs, as hyenas do today.

NAME *Percocruta*
TIME Middle to Late Miocene
LOCALITY Widespread in Africa, Asia and Europe
SIZE 5 ft/1.5 m long

Hyenas of the genus *Percocruta* were the largest hyenas that ever lived. One species, *P. gigantea* which was unearthed in China, was as large as a modern-day lion.

Despite its great size, *Percocruta* was very similar to the present-day spotted hyena, *Crocuta crocuta*, of the African grasslands. This creature was much more widespread in Pleistocene times than it is today; fossilized remains have been found throughout Africa, Europe and Asia.

Like its modern relative, *Percocruta* had a large head and thickset muzzle with extraordinarily powerful jaws, armed with great bone-crushing teeth which would have suited a scavenging lifestyle. It also had the typical sloping stance of its modern relatives, with power forequarters and shorter hind legs. It probably moved with a similar loping gait.

CATS AND MONGOOSES

FAMILY NIMRAVIDAE

The nimravids were the earliest cats to evolve, in the Early Oligocene Epoch, about 35 million years ago. They survived until Late Miocene times, about 8 million years ago. The members of the family Nimravidae are sometimes called false sabre-tooths to distinguish them from the true sabre-tooths, grouped in the family Felidae (below).

Nimravids had long, low bodies and long tails. Their prominent upper canine teeth (the 'sabres') were longer than those of modern cats, but shorter than those of the true sabre-tooths, whereas their lower canines were proportionally longer.

NAME *Nimravus*

TIME Early Oligocene to Early Miocene

RANGE Europe (France) and North America (Colorado, Nebraska, North and South Dakota and Wyoming)

SIZE 4 ft/1.2 m long

Even as long ago as the Early Oligocene, this false sabre-tooth was a contemporary of other sabre-tooths in Europe and North America, such as *Eusmilus*, and competed with them for food and habitat.

Nimravus, with its sleek body, was probably not unlike the modern caracal (*Felis caracal*) which occurs in Africa and Asia, although it had a longer back and more dog-like feet. The creature's head was short and the eyes were positioned so that

they could be directed forward. This is an important development for a hunting animal because it provides stereoscopic vision which allows the animal to accurately judge the distance between itself and its quarry.

Nimravus' claws were thin and very sharp, and they could be partially retracted in order to prevent them from becoming damaged while the animal was running.

Nimravus probably hunted small mammals and birds; these it caught by ambush, like most cats, rather than by swift pursuit, the typical method used by dogs.

Family Felidae

The modern cat family contains such familiar creatures as the lion, tiger, leopard, cheetah and domestic cat.

Felids are the most highly specialized of all mammalian hunters. When the grassland environments developed during the Mid Tertiary Period, some 15 million years ago, the cats and dogs evolved in response. They developed to hunt down the herbivores grazing on the great plains. In these open landscapes, any prey animal could see danger approaching from a long way off, and a successful predator had to be either a skilled stalker or a very fast runner. Cats have adopted the first approach, hunting by stealth. Dogs, however, employ the second hunting method, chasing down prey.

Some cats, such as tigers, evolved as solitary hunters that caught and killed their prey by stalking and ambushing it. However, other cats, such as lions, developed a social, cooperative lifestyle and stalked their prey in well-coordinated groups, called prides.

Cats also developed two chief methods of killing their prey once it had been caught. The first method was employed by the 'biting cats', including all the modern types. These species killed their victims by breaking their necks with one swift, powerful bite from their sharp canine teeth. The second method was specific to the sabre-tooth cats, all of which are now extinct. These species used their greatly developed canine teeth to inflict deep wounds on their quarry and would then simply have waited for it to bleed to death.

In addition to the true sabre-tooths, another group of felids also developed sabre-like teeth, just as the primitive nimravid cats had done. Sabre-tooth cats are often misnamed 'sabre-tooth tigers', but they are not closely related to those big cats.

The felids originated in the Early Oligocene Epoch having evolved from the viverrids.

NAME *Eusmilus*

TIME Oligocene

LOCALITY Europe (France) and North America (Colorado, Nebraska, North and South Dakota and Wyoming)

SIZE 8 ft/2.5 m

This leopard-sized cat was rather long-bodied and short-legged compared with a modern big cat. *Eusmilus* first appeared in Europe toward the very end of Eocene times, about 40 million years ago, and then spread eastwards across the Bering land bridge, which was in existence at the time, into North America during the Oligocene.

Eusmilus was typical of the group of false sabre-tooth felids. The animal's pair of upper canine teeth had become enlarged into well-developed, stabbing 'sabres'. The lower canines, however, were insignificant, and many of the other teeth had been lost. *Eusmilus* had only 26 teeth in its jaws, a relatively small number compared with the maximum of 44 found in some carnivores.

The jaw hinge was modified to open to an angle of 90°, which allowed the great sabre teeth to do their work. The lower jaw had bony guards that lay along the length of the sabres, protecting them from damage when the animal's mouth was closed. In this respect *Eusmilus* resembled the marsupial sabre-tooth *Thylacosmilus* (see pp.203), although these mammals were not related. Their similarity is an example of similar environmental conditions resulting in the evolution of similar characteristics in unrelated animals, (a phenomenon known as convergent evolution).

Eusmilus and other false sabre-tooth cats inhabited the same parts of the world at the same time, and there is fossil evidence that their paths crossed. A skull of *Nimravus* found in North America is pierced in the forehead region, the hole exactly matching the dimensions of *Eusmilus'* sabre tooth. The wound was not fatal, however, for *Nimravus* survived the fight long enough to allow its wound to heal.

NAME *Megantereon*

TIME Late Miocene to Early Pleistocene

LOCALITY Africa (South Africa), Asia (India), Europe (France) and North America (Texas)

SIZE 4 ft/1.2 m long

Megantereon was an early true sabre-tooth cat, and it was probably ancestral to other forms of sabre-tooths. Its teeth were not quite long enough to be really sabre-like; they were more like daggers in size and shape, so *Megantereon* and its immediate relatives are often known as the dirk-tooth cats (from the Scottish word for dagger, 'dirk').

The development of long canine teeth enabled these powerful predators to hunt and kill the large, thick-skinned grazing mammals that shared their habitat. From stalking the prey, a short dash and leap would bring the animal down. Then neck bites would cause blood loss and shock, and a strangulation hold would soon kill the victim.

Megantereon flourished in the Mediterranean region during the Late Pliocene and Early Pleistocene, between about 3 and 2 million years ago. The genera also spread across Africa and North America from its centre of origin in northern India during Late Miocene times.

CATS AND MONGOOSES CONTINUED

NAME *Smilodon*

TIME Late Pleistocene

LOCALITY North America (California) and South America (Argentina)

SIZE 4ft/1.2m long

NAME *Homotherium*

TIME Early to Late Pleistocene

LOCALITY Africa (Ethiopia), Asia (China and Java), Europe (UK) and North America (Tennessee and Texas)

SIZE 4ft/1.2m

Besides sabre-tooth and dirk-tooth cats, there were also scimitar-tooth cats, so called because their death-dealing canines were shorter and flatter than those of the sabre-tooths. They also curved backward, like a scimitar's blade. The back teeth consisted of powerful, meat-shearing (carnassial) blades for slicing up flesh.

In profile, *Homotherium* must have had the sloping look of a hyena, since its forelegs were longer than its hind legs. When it walked, the whole foot was placed firmly on the ground, as in a bear or a human. This is called 'plantigrade' locomotion, and contrasts with most other cats, which walk on their toes (called 'digitigrade' locomotion).

Homotherium survived until the end of the advance of the ice in the Pleistocene, about 14,000 years ago. Scimitar-tooth cats probably preyed on mammoths, since in Texas the remains of young mammoths have been preserved alongside the bones of a family group of scimitar-tooths. *Homotherium* may have become extinct when its prey died out in the northern continents at the end of the Pleistocene ice age.

Smilodon was the classic sabre-tooth cat. Unlike most other cats, it had a short tail, like that of a modern bobcat. Its whole body was powerfully built, with the muscles of its shoulders and neck so arranged as to produce a powerful downward lunge of its massive head. The jaw opened to an angle of over 120°, to allow the huge pair of sabre teeth in its upper jaws to be driven into the victim.

The sabres were oval in cross-section to retain strength, but also to ensure minimum resistance as they were sunk into the prey. They were also serrated like steak-knives along their rear edges, so they pierced the victim's flesh more easily.

Smilodon probably preyed on large, slow-moving, thick-skinned animals, such as mammoths and bison. Unable to kill its prey with a quick bite to the neck, this sabre-tooth cat probably inflicted deep wounds in the victim's flanks or hindquarters, and then simply waited for it to bleed to death.

More than 2000 skeletons of *Smilodon* have been recovered from the Pleistocene tar pits of Rancho La Brea in Los Angeles, along with similar numbers of other carnivores, such as the dire wolf, *Canis dirus* (see pp.219). These animals had not yet developed the cunning of modern carnivores, and were lured into the tar by large animals already trapped there. The species of *Smilodon* found is *S. californicus*, and it has been adopted as the state fossil of California.

Another species of *Smilodon*, *S. neogaeus*, has been found in Argentina. It migrated from North America in Pleistocene times, once the land bridge between the two continents had been re-established at the beginning of the Pliocene Epoch, about 5 million years ago.

NAME *Dinofelis*

TIME Late Pliocene to Middle Pleistocene

LOCALITY Africa (South Africa), Asia (China and India), Europe (France) and North America (Texas)

SIZE 4 ft/1.2 m long

Dinofelis was a panther-sized cat, with flattened canines that were short compared with the sabre-tooths, scimitar-tooths or dirk-tooths, but longer than those of the biting cats. It is a matter of debate among paleontologists as to which subfamily of the felids *Dinofelis* belongs.

Dinofelis became extinct in Eurasia and North America during the Early Pleistocene, but survived in Africa until Mid-Pleistocene times. The Chinese species, *D. abeli*, (named in honour of an Austrian paleontologist, Professor Abel) is the largest-known form.

NAME *Panthera*

TIME Pleistocene to Recent

LOCALITY Africa (South Africa), Asia (India), Europe (England) and North America (California)

SIZE up to 11 ft 6 in/3.5 m long

Panthera leo, the modern lion, is found today in parts of Africa and in the Gir Forest of western India. A typical biting cat, its canine teeth (which are short compared with most extinct cats) are used to kill prey by biting through the neck and throttling it. The long, sharp claws can be fully retracted and tucked away beneath a sheath of skin, to prevent them becoming blunt.

There are two notable extinct subspecies of lion. *Panthera leo spelaea* was the cave lion of Europe. It was probably the largest cat that ever lived, being about 25 percent larger than the modern lion, and even bigger than the largest living cat, the Siberian subspecies of the tiger, *Panthera tigris altaica*. Cave paintings and other archeological discoveries indicate that the cave lion existed until historical times in southeastern Europe; its last stronghold seems to have been in the Balkans, up to about 2000 years ago.

The other subspecies of extinct lion was *Panthera leo atrox*, which ranged throughout North America and was also found in northern South America. This subspecies evidently crossed to North America by way of the Bering Strait during the last ice age, about 35,000 to 20,000 years ago.

Remains of this lion have been found in Alaska. But the most famous fossils come from the tar pits of Rancho La Brea in Los Angeles. They are scarcer than the remains of other carnivores, perhaps because the lion was intelligent enough to avoid the pits.

Family Viverridae

This family of small carnivores contains the modern civets, genets and mongooses. Viverrids are among the oldest of the carnivores, with ancestry dating back as far as the Middle Paleocene, about 60 million years ago. They are also among the most adaptable and least specialized of all carnivores. Early viverrids gave rise to the hyaenas in the Miocene and the cats (felids) in the early Oligocene.

Viverrids are mostly long-bodied, short-legged animals. Many are opportunistic omnivores, eating a great variety of food – from earthworms, molluscs, fish, birds and reptiles (including snakes in the case of mongooses), to eggs, carrion and fruit.

Despite the wide range of the group today – they are found throughout much of the Old World tropics (viverrids are the only group of carnivores in Madagascar) – the fossil record is poor.

NAME *Kanuites*

TIME Miocene

LOCALITY Africa (Kenya)

SIZE 3 ft/90 cm long

The viverrids have changed remarkably little during their evolution, and *Kanuites* probably looked similar to the existing genets (*Genetta*). It had a long tail and perhaps retractable claws like those of a cat. It was probably omnivorous and may have lived in trees as well as on the ground.

SEALS, SEALIONS AND WALRUSES

SUBORDER PINNIPEDIA

The order Carnivora includes not only the dominant carnivores of the land, the cats, dogs and bears, but also a successful group of marine carnivores, grouped together as the pinnipeds. They include the modern sealions and fur seals (Otariidae), walruses (Odobenidae) and the true seals (Phocidae). All have feet modified into flippers or pinnae.

The pinnipeds probably evolved in the northern hemisphere during the Late Oligocene, about 30 million years ago. They do not seem to have spread south of the equator until the Miocene, some 10 million years later. Although sealions and walruses were thought to have evolved from bear-like ancestors, and the true seals from otter-like carnivores, current opinion favours a single origin for the whole group from an ancestor among the mustelids (weasels, otters and their relatives, see pp.214–215).

Family Phocidae

Seals may not look much like dogs or cats, but they are nonetheless members of the order Carnivora. Grouped as phocids, they probably evolved from an otter-like mustelid, such as *Potamotherium* (see p. 215), in the Late Oligocene, some 30 million years ago. They appeared in European waters, and then spread north and south to the Arctic and Antarctic Oceans, and west to the Pacific, adapting to a marine, fish-eating life. However, they still leave the sea to breed on land.

The phocids are often called the 'true seals', to distinguish them from the otariids, or 'eared seals' (the sealions and fur seals). They are more abundant and varied today than the sealions, fur seals and walruses, but their fossil record is sparse.

NAME	*Acrophoca*
TIME	Early Pliocene
LOCALITY	South America (Peru)
SIZE	5 ft / 1.5 m long

Acrophoca may have been the ancestor of the modern leopard seal, *Hydrurga leptonyx*. It was a fish-eater, but it seems to have been less adapted to an aquatic life, and spent much of its time on or near the shore. Its flippers were not so well-developed, its neck was longer and less streamlined than that of a modern seal (more like that of its otter-like ancestor). Its snout was quite pointed.

Family Enliarctidae

The enaliarctids were the earliest members of the otariids to evolve, and were the ancestors of the modern sealions, fur seals and walruses. They lived during the Early Miocene, about 23 million years ago, and like the phocids, probably evolved from among the mustelids.

Later in the Miocene, about 18 million years ago, enaliarctids gave rise to another extinct family of early seals, the desmatophocids. Later still, about 15 million years ago, some of the enaliarctids evolved into the odobenids, or walruses. Another branch, which evolved in the Middle Miocene about 13 million years ago, led to the otariids, the sealions and fur seals.

NAME	*Enaliarctos*
TIME	Early Miocene
LOCALITY	North America (Pacific coast)
SIZE	5 ft / 1.5 m long

This primitive-looking sea mammal represents an early stage in the adaptation of a land-dwelling carnivore to a marine lifestyle. *Enaliarctos* is almost halfway between an otter and a sealion. Its cheek teeth still bore meat-shearing (carnassial) blades like those of a land-living dog. Its body was streamlined and rather otter-like, with distinct legs and a tail, although the feet were already modified into paddles.

Like the modern sea otter, *Enaliarctos* probably spent time on land as well as in the water, and eating a variety of marine animals, including fish and shellfish. Some sealion characteristics had already evolved, such as the large eyes, sophisticated senses associated with the whiskers, and the specialization of the inner ears for detecting the direction of sound underwater. These senses helped *Enaliarctos* to find its prey. Smell probably played a minor role in hunting, as in living pinnipeds.

Family Desmatophocidae

The desmatophocids were a family of primitive sealions. These carnivores are superficially similar to the seals of the family Phocidae, and they display the same adaptations to the same way of life.

The most obvious difference between the two groups is in the structure of their hind limbs. Sealions, fur seals and walruses can turn the hind flippers forward to help them move on land – something the true seals cannot do.

NAME	*Desmatophoca*
TIME	Middle Miocene
LOCALITY	Asia (Japan) and North America (California and Oregon)
SIZE	5 ft 6 in/1.7 m long

The typical streamlined shape of the modern sealion had begun to appear with *Desmatophoca.* As in its living relatives, its forelimbs were stronger than the hind limbs, and the feet were modified to form paddles, with the fingers elongated, splayed out and held together by webs of skin to produce a large surface area for swimming. All the bones in the limbs were shortened to make them stronger.

Although *Desmatophoca* still had a tail, in contrast to the sealions, this was greatly reduced, being only about the length of the animal's skull. Like its ancestor *Enaliarctos,* its eyes were enormous, which suggests that sight was its most important sense for hunting. Its hearing may not have been fully adapted for detecting underwater sounds, but it no doubt served the animal well on land.

Family Odobenidae

The walruses, or odobenids, differ from the sealions and fur seals in that they are adapted to feed on shellfish rather than on fish. Their upper canine teeth are enlarged into a pair of heavy tusks, in both sexes, and used to prise and probe their mollusc prey from the seabed.

By the Early Pliocene, about 5 million years ago, at least five genera of walrus, many of them looking rather like sealions, lived on the North Pacific coast. Some of the early walruses swam across the seaway that separated North America from South America in the Late Miocene, about 8 million years ago. By the Early Pliocene, about 3 million years later, they had moved northward to American and European North Atlantic coastal waters.

Later in the Pliocene, walruses became extinct in the Pacific, where they had originated. The North Atlantic populations flourished in the meantime, and groups eventually made their way back to the North Pacific by way of the Arctic Ocean about 1 million years ago.

The one remaining member of the genus – *Odobenus rosmarus* – inhabits the Arctic seas from East Canada and Greenland to Northern Eurasia and West Alaska. The walrus has long been a valuable source of food for the eskimo populations of the Arctic regions.

NAME	*Imagotaria*
TIME	Late Miocene
LOCALITY	North America (Pacific coast)
SIZE	6 ft/1.8 m long

Imagotaria is classed as a walrus, but it probably looked and behaved like a sealion. It may represent a transitional stage in the evolution of the walruses. The canine teeth, used by sealions to catch fish, had begun to enlarge, but had not yet formed the tusks used by walruses to dig up shellfish. The back teeth had not yet evolved into the broad shell-crushers of modern walruses so it probably ate fish and shellfish.

SEALS, SEALIONS AND WALRUSES CONTINUED

ORDER DESMOSTYLA

The desmostylians were a group of strange aquatic mammals that have been aptly described as 'seahorses'. Members of this order were about the size of a pony, and superficially similar in appearance: they lived along the coasts of the North Pacific in Miocene times, between about 25 and 5 million years ago.

The single record of a fossil from coastal Florida suggests that desmostylians found their way from the Pacific into the Atlantic via the narrow seaway that separated North and South America until the Pliocene, about 5 million years ago. However, the origin, relationships and diet of the desmostylians remain a mystery. Paleontologists generally believe that they are associated with the proboscids along with the sirenians.

NAME	*Desmostylus*
TIME	Miocene
LOCALITY	Asia (Japan) and North America (Pacific coast)
SIZE	6ft/1.8m long

Desmostylus was a typical member of the desmostylians. Built like a hippopotamus, and perhaps behaving in a similar way too, this creature had a thickset body and stout legs with broad feet, each with four hooved toes.

The bones of the lower foreleg were fused into a solid pillar, which meant that the foot could not be turned without turning the whole limb. Underwater, the animal probably poled itself along, in the same manner as a modern hippo 'walks' over the riverbed. However, on land, this construction would have meant that *Desmostylus* was quite clumsy.

The front parts of both the upper and lower jaws were elongated and carried an array of forward-pointing tusks, formed by the elongated incisors and canines. The animal's head must have looked similar to that of some of the shovel-tusked elephants that were in existence at the same time (see pp.239–242). *Desmostylus's* unusual back teeth formed clusters of upright cylinders.

Desmostylus must have had an amphibious lifestyle, paddling around in the coastal shallows and using its strong front tusks to prise shellfish from the rocks. It may also have sunk down to the seabed in search of food. Some paleontologists have also suggested that it grazed on the seaweeds that were left exposed between the tides.

ORDER SIRENIA

The sirenians, or sea cows, are the only group of mammals to have become fully adapted, aquatic herbivores. Today, they are represented by three species of manatee (*Trichechus*) and a single species of dugong (*Dugong dugon*). A fifth species in the order, Steller's sea cow, which had adapted to cold temperatures and fed on the kelp beds in the northern Pacific ocean, became extinct as recently as 1768.

All animals in the order are characterised by bulbous bodies, forelimbs modified into flippers, no hind limbs and a horizontally flattened tail, like that of a whale, which they use to propel themselves through the water at a leisurely pace.

The sirenians are known from the Early Eocene of Hungary. Their evolution is something of a mystery, but many paleontologists believe that they may have developed from a sea cow closely related to the ungulates and descended from an ancestor shared with the elephants. This evolutionary connection between sea cows and elephants has been supported by recent molecular analysis.

Throughout the Eocene, the climate was relatively warm, and vast meadows of seagrasses – the main food of the marine sirenians – grew in the shallow tropical waters of the Mediterranean and Caribbean. However, these seagrass beds retreated in the Oligocene when the climate cooled. The manatees adapted to feed on freshwater plants in the rivers along the coasts of South America. Teeth have to be continually replaced to compensate for the extensive wear which the tough grasses inflict upon them.

NAME *Prorastomus*

TIME Middle Eocene

LOCALITY West Indies (Jamaica)

SIZE possibly 5 ft/1.5 m long

Prorastomus is the most primitive sirenian known. Only its skull and parts of its backbone and ribs have so far been discovered. The restoration is therefore speculative.

Prorastomus skull indicates that it was not specialized for an aquatic lifestyle. It is quite likely that *Prorastomus* was still essentially a land-dweller. Its thick snout and double-crested cheek teeth suggest that is consumed a diet of soft vegetation.

NAME *Rytiodus*

TIME Miocene

LOCALITY Europe (France)

SIZE 20 ft/6 m long

By the Late Eocene, some 40 million years ago, dugongs were well-established and resembled their present-day forms.

Rytiodus was an enormous beast – about twice the size of the single remaining modern marine species. It possessed all the typical sirenian features. Its body was fat and smooth, its hind limbs had disappeared, but it had a powerful tail for swimming, and its forelimbs had developed into flippers. The animal's bones, particularly the ribs, were thick and dense, and acted as ballast, helping to give *Rytiodus* just the right buoyancy for its submerged existence. It grazed on shallow coastal seabeds, and the pair of sabre-like tusks in its upper jaw enabled it to root up seagrasses or seaweeds.

NAME *Hydrodamalis gigas*

TIME Pliocene to Recent

LOCALITY Arctic and North Pacific oceans

SIZE 26 ft/8 m long

This enormous sirenian, only recently extinct, was known as Steller's sea cow, named after Georg Steller, the German naturalist, who discovered it in 1741.

A former member of the dugong family, *Hydrodamalis gigas* evolved toward the end of the Pleistocene, about 200,000 years ago, but it became extinct (due to hunting by man) as recently as 1768. Its large size was probably an adaptation to life in the very cold waters of the creature's northern range. (A large animal retains heat better than a smaller one, which has a greater surface area relative to its size.)

Steller's sea cow had lost the thickened ribs of the other sirenians, and it had developed great layers of blubber, covered by a thick, bark-like skin, to serve as insulation against the cold waters of its habitat. As a result, the animal was probably too buoyant to dive.

Lacking teeth entirely, it fed on floating seaweed – a diet which is unique among mammals.

WHALES, DOLPHINS AND PORPOISES

ORDER CETACEA

The whales, dolphins and porpoises, sea creatures of magnificence and intelligence, are members of the only mammal order that have become thoroughly adapted to living their whole lives in the open oceans. The most specialized of all mammals, their sleek, streamlined bodies and fish-like shape allow them to swim with ease, but deny them any kind of life on land. However, they have retained the basic mammalian features of warm-bloodedness, the ability to suckle their young and the necessity to breathe air.

There are about 140 known genera of fossil cetacean. The 40 living genera are found throughout the oceans of the world, and there are also freshwater dolphins living in the rivers of South America, India and China. Many modern species are, however, threatened with extinction.

Cetaceans probably evolved from land-living early ungulates (see pp.234,254) at the very beginning of the Tertiary, about 65 million years ago. Recent molecular analysis supports this assumption and groups the cetaceans with the even-toed ungulates (artiodactyls such as cattle, deer and pigs) as the cetartiodactyls. This large group is in turn closely associated with the Carnivora and perissodactyls (horses). In detail the whales now seem to be most closely related to those aquatic ruminants, the hippos.

There are three suborders of whales: the primitive archaeocetes, all now extinct; the modern odontocetes, or 'toothed whales', including the great sperm whale and all the dolphins and porpoises; and the modern mysticetes, or 'baleen whales'. The baleen group includes the largest animal that has ever lived – the mighty blue whale, *Balaenoptera musculus*, which reaches a length of 100 ft/30 m and a weight of some 144 US tons/130 tonnes.

SUBORDER ARCHAEOCETI

The archaeocetes were the first cetaceans to appear, in the seas of the Early Eocene, about 54 million years ago. They evolved from amphibious mammals, and at first were small (never more than 10 ft/3 m long), four-legged, seal-like creatures with few specializations for life in water. But by the end of the Eocene, some 15 million years later, they had developed into enormous, serpent-like animals, highly adapted for a marine life.

NAME *Pakicetus*
TIME Early Eocene
LOCALITY Asia (Pakistan)
SIZE 6 ft/1.8 m long

Pakicetus is the earliest-known whale. Although only part of its skull has been found, this has such primitive features that it is safe to assume that the rest of its body had few adaptations to a marine existence.

Pakicetus probably looked quite different from the modern whales. Its teeth were similar to those of the mesonychids, such as *Andrewsarchus* (see p.234), and the cheek teeth had the same triangular arrangement of cusps. This suggests that *Pakicetus* had evolved from flesh-eating terrestrial ungulates only a short time previously.

Its ears were not particularly well-adapted for functioning underwater, so *Pakicetus* probably spent much of its time on land. Discoveries of other land-living animals in the same deposits as this early whale seem to confirm this.

Pakicetus was probably rather seal-like in general appearance. Its limbs were probably paddle-shaped, allowing it to move about awkwardly on land, but making it completely at home in the rivers and estuaries along the eastern shores of the Tethys Sea. This expanse of water still existed along the southern edge of Asia in Early Tertiary times, about 50 million years ago.

NAME *Protocetus*
TIME Middle Eocene
LOCALITY Africa and Asia
(Mediterranean area)
SIZE 8 ft/2.5 m long

Protocetus, which lived only some 8 million years after *Pakicetus*, had become much more whale-like in appearance. Its body was more streamlined, approaching the shape of modern whales. Its forelegs were flat and paddle-like, but the hind legs were greatly reduced, and while they may still have protruded outside the body, they would have been of little use in swimming.

A pair of horizontal lobes, called flukes, had probably developed on *Protocetus*' tail, to judge by the structure of the vertebrae in this area. Their up-and-down motion provided the propulsive force to drive the animal steadily through the sea.

The skull of *Protocetus* had become quite long, with a narrow snout. Its teeth were pointed and arranged in a zigzag pattern at the front of the jaws. These teeth held the prey, while the back teeth cut it up. *Protocetus* and other early whales doubtless hunted for fish in shallow coastal waters.

This whale's nostrils had begun to move back on the head, away from their position in earliest whales at the tip of the snout. *Protocetus* still had a good sense of smell, but vision was probably its most important sense for hunting prey. In contrast to *Pakicetus*, *Protocetus*' ears were adapted for underwater hearing, but it is unlikely that it had yet developed the sophisticated echolocation system used by modern whales.

NAME *Zygorhiza*
TIME Late Eocene
LOCALITY North America (Atlantic coast)
SIZE 20 ft/6 m long

Zygorhiza belonged to a family of early whales which developed extremely elongated, eel-like bodies. *Zygorhiza*, however, was more whale-like than most of its relatives. Its body was about six times the length of its skull – the same proportion as in a modern whale. Unlike modern whales, its head was attached to the body by a distinct, short neck, made up of the usual mammalian complement of seven vertebrae.

Its paddle-shaped forelimbs could probably have been moved from the elbow (unlike those of modern whales, which have their forearm bones fused to the upper arm), which would have helped to haul their bodies from the water. Early whales probably still mated and bred on land, like their amphibious ancestors.

NAME *Basilosaurus*
TIME Late Eocene
LOCALITY North America (Atlantic coast)
SIZE up to 82 ft/25 m long

When the remains of this remarkable early whale were first discovered in the 1830s, they were believed to belong to some kind of dinosaur. This creature, which belonged to the same family as *Zygorhiza*, must have looked like a great sea-serpent. Indeed its bones were used in a famous sea-serpent hoax about a century ago.

Basilosaurus' snake-like body was supported by a backbone of enormously elongated vertebrae. The ribs were short and confined to the front part of the body. The hip bones were still present, about two-thirds of the way down the animal, and the bones of the hind legs could still articulate with them. However, the limb bones were so small that it is difficult to imagine what use they would have been, or indeed if they showed outside the body at all.

Basilosaurus must have swum in the Eocene oceans by undulating its long body and tail. For the cylindrical body to have worked efficiently as a swimming organ, this whale most probably had tail flukes.

The head of *Basilosaurus* was typical of the early whales, although it was small in proportion to the body. The nostrils were high up on the animal's snout, and the teeth were of a variety of shapes and sizes. The front teeth were pointed and conical, while the back teeth were saw-edged. (An obsolete name for this animal is *Zeuglodon*, which means 'saw-toothed'.) The dentition of this creature indicates that these large early whales must have hunted fish and squid in deep waters, as do the larger species of modern toothed whale, such as the sperm whale.

WHALES, DOLPHINS AND PORPOISES CONTINUED

SUBORDER ODONTOCETI

The odontocetes – the toothed whales – probably evolved from the archaeocetes in late Eocene times, about 40 million years ago. Odontocetes make up the majority of the modern whales, including the sperm, beaked, pilot and killer whales, the belugas and narwhals, the dolphins and porpoises. All these modern species had appeared by Late Miocene times, some 10 million years ago.

The teeth of odontocetes tended to be simpler than those of the archaeocetes, losing their cusps and becoming rounded pegs or cones. Some odontocetes had several hundred teeth in their jaws, while others were almost toothless.

NAME *Prosqualodon*
TIME Oligocene to Early Miocene
LOCALITY Australia, New Zealand and South America
SIZE 7 ft 5 in/2.3 m long

Prosqualodon and its immediate family may have been ancestral to all the other toothed whales. It probably looked like a small modern dolphin, with a long, narrow snout armed with pointed, fish-catching teeth. But the teeth were primitive, since there were still triangular teeth at the back of the jaws, as there had been in the earlier whales, the archaeocetes.

Prosqualodon's skull had become lightweight as a result of several modifications to the animal's front end. First, the neck had become very short, and the back of the head blended in with the body and needed less support and protection. Second, the complex jaw structure of earlier whales had been greatly simplified, due to the purely fish diet. And thirdly, since the sense of smell was no longer the primary sense used in locating prey (sound having taken over), the complex olfactory apparatus was reduced.

In *Prosqualadon*, the nostrils were positioned on the roof of the head, between the eye sockets, where they formed a blowhole (as found in modern whales). The spent air which had accumulated during a dive was expelled explosively through the blowhole when the animal surfaced.

NAME *Eurhinodelphis*
TIME Middle to Late Miocene
LOCALITY Asia and North America
(Pacific coasts)
SIZE 6 ft 6 in/2 m long

The odontocetes diverged into a number of groups during the Oligocene Epoch, about 30 million years ago. *Eurhinodelphis* was a typical member of the rhabdosteid family of long-snouted porpoises. The structure of its ears had become much more complex than in earlier odontocetes, so it is likely that this whale had developed the complex echolocation system seen in modern toothed whales.

Living whales rely on a form of ultrasonic sonar to help them track down and catch their prey and to find their way about underwater – they emit high-frequency clicking sounds which travel through the water and bounce off objects, and the echoes are analysed by the animals' large brains to determine – with astonishing accuracy – the size, shape, distance and speed of the object and, of course, its edibility.

Like that of a modern dolphin, the skull of *Eurhinodelphis* had become somewhat asymmetrical, with structures on one side different from those on the other. This arrangement might have been associated with the development of new abilities to cope with the demands of the creature's lifestyle, such as chasing fast-moving prey and navigating with increasing accuracy.

The most distinctive feature of *Eurhinodelphis,* however, was its elongated snout. The snout was toothless at the tip, and may have been used in a way similar to the 'sword' of the modern swordfish, to strike at and stun its prey, which was then seized in the animal's jaws.

SUBORDER MYSTICETI

The mysticetes, or baleen whales, are first known from marine rocks in New Zealand dating from Early Oligocene times, some 35 million years ago. The fossils of their early forms occur along with rich deposits of plankton, the tiny creatures on which these huge creatures feed. The evolution of the baleen whales may have been triggered by the overall cooling of the southern oceans during the Early Oligocene, which encouraged the growth of the microscopic plants in the plankton and, in turn, the tiny, free-floating animals that feed on them. This rich food source is especially prolific in the southern oceans, where it is called krill. Despite the huge volume of water taken in and seived from each mouthful, these animals cannot swallow any large objects because the gullet is never any more than 22.5 cm/9 in wide, even in the largest of the baleen whales.

Baleen whales have evolved a unique method of feeding on the tiny, shrimp-like animals in the plankton or tiny crustaceans in the bottom sediments. They have no teeth in their jaws. Instead, the jaws have become greatly modified to support great plates of a fibrous, horny substance, known as whalebone or baleen. The baleen plates hang from their upper jaws on either side and form a huge natural sieve through which the whale is able to strain the ocean's waters or bottom sediments in order to catch the the abundant planktonic organisms and crustaceans living there

Only eight genera survive today, and most species are under severe threat from hunting by man. The grey whale is the sole remaining species in the eschrichteriid family whilst there are three species in the right whale family (the Balaenidae) and six species in the rorqual family (the Balaenopteridae). The right whales show the most extreme development of the baleen apparatus for filter feeding and the plates may be more than 4.5 m/15 ft long. However, the diverse rorquals, which have 300 or so baleen plates on each side of the jaws, include the magnificent giant blue whale. Some 30 m/100 ft in length and 144 tons/ 146 tonnes in weight, it is the largest mammal that ever existed. In the feeding season these ocean grazers consume up to 4 tons/4 tonnes of planktonic crustaceans each day from the nutrient rich waters of the polar oceans.

The radiation of the living families dates from Miocene times but their fossils are exceedingly rare until the Late Miocene, when the cetotheriids began to decrease in numbers. So it would appear that the living mysticetes replaced the cetotheriids.

NAME	*Cetotherium*
TIME	Middle to Late Miocene
LOCALITY	Europe (Belgium and former USSR)
SIZE	13 ft/4 m long

Cetotherium belonged to a family of early baleen whales which evolved in the Late Oligocene and reached their peak during the Miocene, some 15 million years ago. *Cetotherium* looked strikingly similar to the modern grey whale of the North Pacific, although it was less than a third of the grey whale's length. Its baleen plates were probably quite short, although this is difficult to determine, because baleen, like horn and hair, does not fossilize. The fossilized skulls retain the marks of blood vessels which would have kept the baleen supplied with blood during the creature's life, and much can be hypothesized from their traces.

Cetotherium and its relatives were probably preyed upon by a species of great white shark *Carcharodon* which, judging by the size of the teeth that are often found fossilized, reached a size approaching that of a small whale.

EARLY ROOTERS AND BROWSERS

Most ungulates ('hoofed animals') are large plant-eaters which root and browse among vegetation or crop grass. Early rooters and browsers were a diverse group of ungulates, most of which ate leaves, shoots and roots, though some evolved into scavengers. specialized grazers, such as horses, cattle and deer evolved from these early ungulates. They rose to dominance during the Miocene, moving from the forest to exploit the feeding opportunities in the developing grasslands.

Some early ungulates were once regarded as members of the primitive order of carnivorous mammals, the creodonts. This confusion indicates the generalized nature of the mammals at the end of the Cenozoic Era.

ORDER ARCTOCYONIA

The members of this abundant and varied group were mostly small mammals, little bigger than today's domestic dogs. They had long, low skulls, and a complete set of rather uniform teeth (evolved for crushing rather than biting).

Family Arctocyonidae

This is the earliest and most primitive family of the order, and may be close to the ancestors of the later hoofed animals. Arctocyonids were mostly short-limbed, rather clumsily-built animals, up to the size of small bears.

NAME	*Chriacus*
TIME	Early Paleocene to Early Eocene
LOCALITY	North America (Wyoming)
SIZE	3 ft/1 m long

This agile climbing animal may have scampered through the tropical forests of Early Tertiary North America, eating insects, small animals and fruit. It had powerful limbs, versatile joints, a semi-prehensile tail and plantigrade feet (the full foot was placed on the ground) and there were long claws. The forelimbs may have been used for digging, but the hind limbs were those of a climbing animal.

ORDER ACREODI

When plant-eating mammals (excluding multituberculates) first flourished at the start of the Paleocene, no carnivores preyed on them. By the Mid-Paleocene, however, over 60 million years ago, some primitive and generalized stock had developed into a new order, the Acreodi. This group of ungulates ranged from wolf-sized up to 15–24 ft/5-6 m long, far larger than any living terrestrial carnivore and matched in size only by the dinosaurs. Their closest affinities seem to be with the arctyocyonids and whales.

Family Mesonychidae

Among the Acreodi were mesonychids: wolf-like, hyena-like or bear-like omnivores able to take advantage of this new source of food. They ranged from the size of foxes to the immense *Andrewsarchus*. Mesonychids flourished until the Early Oligocene, some 35 million years ago, by which time the creodonts and then the true carnivores had become the dominant flesh-eaters.

Similarities in the arrangement of bones in the base of the skull and in the teeth suggest that, despite their radically different habitats and lifestyles, the mesonychids may have given rise to the whales and dolphins (see pp.230–233).

NAME	*Andrewsarchus*
TIME	Late Eocene
LOCALITY	Asia (Mongolia)
SIZE	13 ft/4 m long

With a gigantic skull nearly 3 ft/1 m in length, *Andrewsarchus* was the largest known terrestrial carnivorous mammal. The teeth were very large and adapted for crushing and tearing food. *Andrewsarchus'* lifestyle is still a mystery since complete skeletons have not been found. Comparison with its relatives suggests it was not a hunter, but a carrion-eater, like most hyenas today.

ORDER PANTODONTA

A diverse group of extinct Early Tertiary browsers that thrived in Paleocene and Eocene times from 60 million to 40 million years ago. In Asia, a few pantodonts survived until the Early Oligocene, some 35 million years ago. This order is divided into some ten families, which were widely dispersed throughout Asia and North America. They diversified to fill many of the available plant-eating niches. Their origins and relationships are not clear.

Family Coryphodontidae

Though some members of this family were as small as rats, they were mostly bulky animals, some as large as rhinoceroses. The coryphodontid family led a semi-aquatic lifestyle, feeding by rooting up tubers, roots and other vegetation.

NAME *Coryphodon*

TIME Late Paleocene to Middle Eocene

LOCALITY Widespread in North America, Europe and eastern Asia

SIZE 7 ft 6 in/2.25 m long

Coryphodon was a large animal with canine tusks rather like those of a hippopotamus. These were especially well-developed in the male. Like a hippopotamus, too, *Coryphodon* probably lived in swamps and marshes, where it may have uprooted plants with its tusks. The two prominent cross crests on its molar teeth suggest that *Coryphodon* browsed on jungle vegetation.

The upper section of the leg was longer than the lower, which would have provided the strength needed to support a massive body but could not have been suited to fast running.

Coryphodon's brain was very small and, at 3¼oz/90g per 1,100lb/500kg, probably represented the smallest ratio of brain to body weight in any mammal.

ORDER DINOCERATA

The largest mammals of the Early Tertiary were the dinocerates (meaning 'terrifying horns'), also known as uintatheres. The name refers to the three pairs of bony protuberances on the skulls of these animals. Males in particular were armed with a pair of long, sabre-like upper canine teeth.

Dinocerates were large, rhinoceros-like mammals from the late Paleocene and Eocene of North America and Asia, about 55 million years ago. Their evolution is something of a mystery.

Family Uintatheriidae

Except for one Mongolian genus, which had no skull protuberances or sabre-like canines, all members of the order Dinocerata are included in this family.

The uintatheres were the largest land mammals of their time, with massive bones, heavy limbs and broad, spreading feet. But their brains were very small – no larger in relation to body size than the brains of many of the dinosaurs. Uintatheres died out in the Oligocene, about 35 million years ago, and were replaced in their ecological niche as massive herbivores by the brontotheres (see pp.258–259).

NAME *Eobasileus*

TIME Late Eocene

LOCALITY North America (Wyoming)

SIZE 10 ft/3 m long; 5 ft/1.5 m high at the shoulder

Eobasileus looked rather like a rhinoceros with a pair of sabre-like canine tusks in its upper jaw and six bony protuberances on its head. These blunt 'horns' were probably covered with skin. It is likely that only the front pair on top of the nose were sheathed in 'horns' of matted hair, as in rhinoceroses (see pp.262–265).

Incisor teeth were very small in the lower jaw, and missing entirely from the upper, which suggest that the tongue and tusks were the most important food-gathering organs.

EARLY ROOTERS
AND BROWSERS CONTINUED

ORDER TILLODONTIA

The tillodonts were a small group of herbivores, about the size of modern bears, which have now become extinct.

The tillodonts may have been related to the pantodonts or to arctocyonids, but their origins and relationships to the other early mammals, and even their lifestyles, are still uncertain. However, paleontologists do know from fossil finds that they were once widespread across Paleocene and Eocene North America, eastern Asia and Europe.

Family Esthonychidae

The large, bear-sized esthonychids are believed to have been the sole family within the order Tillodontia. They were one of a number of families of herbivorous mammals which evolved and radiated rapidly in early Tertiary times. Within the brief span of the Paleocene to Eocene (30 million years) they spread throughout the warm interior continental basins of North America and Eurasia only to die out and be replaced by another mammalian radiation.

NAME *Trogosus*

TIME Early to Middle Eocene

LOCALITY North America (Wyoming)

SIZE 4ft/1.2m long

From a distance, the squat body, short head and the flat feet of this large animal would have given it the appearance of a modern bear. However, as soon as *Trogosus* opened its mouth, its huge chisel-like incisors would have made it appear more like a gigantic rat or rabbit. As among rodents, the incisors were adapted for gnawing: the front surfaces were coated with enamel and grew continuously throughout the animal's life. The grinding teeth to the rear of the jaw were constantly being worn away, which suggests that *Trogosus* ate abrasive plant material, perhaps roots and tubers clawed out of the ground.

ORDER TAENIODONTA

These were another small group of Early Tertiary herbivores, now extinct, which were rat- to bear-sized and have been found only in North America. As with the tillodonts, the origins and relationships of the order Teaniodonta with other mammals remains obscure.

The Taeniodonta order evolved quickly – in fact, faster than any other mammal group is ever known to have developed – during Paleocene times, and became quite specialized as digging animals.

Family Stylinodontidae

Stylinodontids form the only family within the order Taeniodonta. Like the esthonychids, they were one of a number of rapidly evolving ammmal families in early Tertiary (Paleocene–Eocene) times within North America.

NAME *Stylinodon*

TIME Early to Late Eocene

LOCALITY North America (Wyoming, Colorado and Utah)

SIZE 4ft 3in/1.3m long

With its short powerful digging forelimbs and strong claws, *Stylinodon* was probably bear-sized, with a body like an aardvark and a pig-like face.

The fossil remains uncovered have given a detailed picture of the dentition of this animal. *Stylinodon* had no incisor teeth in its massive jaws, but the canine teeth had become greatly developed into huge, rootless, gnawing chisels. The peg-like cheek teeth were equipped with enamel on their surfaces which was arranged in a narrow band (the word taeniodont means 'banded teeth'). The cheek teeth grew continuously throughout the animal's life, which suggests that *Stylinodon* had a diet of abrasive roots and tubers.

ORDER HYRACOIDEA

This order of herbivorous mammals was very diverse and abundant during the Early Oligocene Period, about 35 million years ago, having radiated from its origins in the Eocene into many ecological niches.

Some hyracoids looked similar to tapirs, some were similar to horses, while others resembled rabbits, as do modern hyraxes. Some grew as large as pigs, but most were smaller. The hyracoids seem to have declined as grazing animals expanded, and they are represented today by only seven species living in Africa and some parts of the Middle East. The most notable of these species is the rock hyrax.

The availability of living representatives of this group has allowed molecular analysis, which has shown that they are most closely related to the proboscids (elephants) and the sirenids (sea-cows).

Family Pliohyracidae

All the extinct forms of early Tertiary hyraxes are placed in this family. The later fossil hyraxes and all the living representatives of the order are placed in the family Procaviidae.

NAME	*Kvabebihyrax*
TIME	Late Pliocene
LOCALITY	Europe (Caucasus)
SIZE	5 ft 3 in / 1.6 m long

The great difference between the fossil types of hyrax and the modern animals can be seen in *Kvabebihyrax*. With its stout body and small eyes set high upon the skull, *Kvabebihyrax* must have looked more like a small hippopotamus than a hyrax. The snout was short, and a pair of very large incisor teeth projected downwards. The two pairs of lower incisors were flattened and horizontal, the upper pair of incisors fitting between their points when the animal's jaw was closed.

ORDER EMBRITHOPODA

The extinct embrithopods are an Early to Mid Tertiary group of herbivores which were widely distributed throughout Asia, eastern Europe and into North Africa. They do not easily fit anywhere into the evolutionary scheme and have no obvious ancestors or descendents, though the structure of their simple, small brains shows possible affinities with those of the elephants or sea-cows.

Family Arsinoitheres

The rhinoceros-like Arsinoitheres are the sole family in the order Embrithopoda.

NAME	*Arsinoitherium*
TIME	Early Oligocene
LOCALITY	Africa (Egypt)
SIZE	11 ft 6 in / 3.5 m long; 6 ft / 1.8 m high at the shoulder

Arsinoitherium's most memorable features were the two massive cone-shaped projections, fused at their bases, which covered the area from the nostrils to midway up its skull. In spite of its appearance, *Arsinoitherium* was only superficially like a rhinoceros. Its 'horns' were in fact hollow, and traces of blood vessels on their surface suggest that they were covered in skin, at least when the animal was young. There were two smaller knob-like projections higher on the head that must have looked like a giraffe's skin-covered ossicones.

With its complete set of 44 unspecialized teeth forming a continuous series from incisors to last molars, *Arsinoitherium* was obviously a plant-eater, and probably browsed in the riverside forests. However, the high cross crowns of its cheek teeth suggest it may also have been able to chew tougher vegetation. From an ecological point of view, *Arsinoitherium* may well have been the African equivalent of the North American uintatheres (see p.235) and brontotheres (see pp.258–259).

EARLY ELEPHANTS AND MASTODONTS

ORDER PROBOSCIDEA

The African and Indian elephants are the only two surviving species of a once diverse and widespread group called the proboscids. They are characterised particularly by developments of their teeth and adaptations of their limbs for supporting their increasing mass.

Recent analysis of elephant DNA has led to some significant changes in ideas about the affinities and relationships of the proboscids. Initially, the molecular data seemed to support the traditional grouping with the ungulates, but this has changed. Now the proboscids are grouped in a separate clade with just the sea-cows (sirenids) and hyraxes (hyracoids). It is thought that they evolved from a basal stock of primitive hoofed animals that also gave rise to the modern hyraxes (see pp.237) and the aquatic sirenians (the dugongs and manatees; see pp.228–229).

From their origins in northern Africa in the Eocene as pig-sized creatures, like *Moeritherium,* without tusks or trunks, proboscids had evolved by Pliocene times, 50 million years later, into giants that had spread over all continents with the exceptions of Australia and Antarctica.

Their evolution involved a progressive increase in the size of the animals, the development of long pillar-like legs to support the immense weight. Associated with this is the development of flattened soles to spread the animal's weight evenly across the ground. This is so successful that a modern elephant will leave almost no footprint when it walks over firm ground, despite its great weight. In addition there was an extension of a proboscis or trunk, accompanied by the massive enlargement of the head, and a shortening of the neck. There was also a reduction of the teeth to a few grinding molars. The second upper incisors, which became the specialized tusks in later forms, are enlarged. The lower canines and first premolars are absent whilst the molars progressively develop as broad teeth with thickened cusps and ridges for chewing and breaking down coarse vegetation. The trunk and tusks were originally adaptations that enabled a tall, short-necked animal to reach food on the ground or in the trees, but they also function in display and courtship.

By Pleistocene times, about 2 million years ago, mammoths and mastodonts flourished over the northern continents, only to suffer mass extinction with the advance of the ice age. In Siberia, some mammoths been discovered frozen in ice, with their flesh and fur perfectly preserved. The Elephantidae, the only family to survive, had already undergone rapid evolution in warmer climates to the south. Four families are known.

Family Moeritheridae

The name 'moerithere' is derived from the word Moeris – an ancient Greek name for the lake in Egypt's Fayum province where its remains were found. The moeritheriids are one of a number of short-lived families of proboscideans which reflect the initial divergence of the group in Mid Tertiary times.

NAME *Moeritherium*
TIME Late Eocene to Early Oligocene
LOCALITY Africa (Egypt, Mali and Senegal)
SIZE 2 ft/60 cm high

This pig-sized, low-slung animal resembled a tapir or a pygmy hippopotamus more than an elephant. The external nostrils were at the front of the skull, which implies that it did not even possess a trunk, though it may have had a broad thick upper lip that helped it to root about among swamp vegetation. *Moeritherium* would have weighed about 450 lb/200 kg. It was probably partly aquatic in its habits, like the modern hippopotamus. As with the hippopotamus, its eyes and ears were high up on the skull so that it could keep watch at the water's surface while wallowing in the swamps.

But *Moeritherium* also displays several features that clearly indicate the development of an elephant-like lifestyle. Its skull was long and low, with a large area at the back for the attachment of strong neck muscles, and the lower jaw was deep. The teeth were primitive – small and almost complete – yet there were no lower canines. Even at this early stage in the evolution of elephants, two of the incisors were already tusk-like.

Although it showed many primitive features, *Moeritherium* itself was probably not the ancestor of the rest of the proboscideans. It was a long-lived genus, surviving into Oligocene times when several more advanced elephants were also around.

Family Deinotheriidae

Deinotheres were very large elephants with down-curving tusks in the lower jaw. They probably evolved in the Early Miocene in Africa but they soon spread into central and southern Europe and southern Asia.

The Deinotheres thrived almost unchanged throughout the Pliocene but then retreated back to Africa. They vanished altogether about 2 million years ago.

NAME *Deinotherium*

TIME Miocene to Pleistocene

LOCALITY Europe (Germany and Bohemia), Asia (India) and Africa (Kenya)

SIZE 13 ft/4 m high

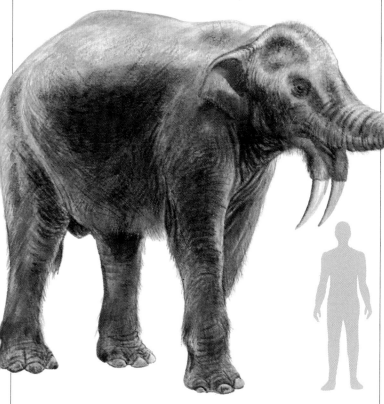

The most remarkable feature of this elephant was its tusks, the purpose of which is still a matter of debate amongst paleontologists.

Deinotherium had no tusks in the upper jaw, but the lower jaw was curved downward at a right angle and gave rise to two huge curved tusks. Such a structure and shape seemed so unlikely that when scientists in the 1820s attempted the first reconstructions of a *Deinotherium* skeleton, they attached the animal's jaw upside down. The animal may have used its bizarre tusks for foraging for food – stripping the bark from trees or digging up tubers.

Surviving almost unchanged for 20 million years, *Deinotherium* was clearly a very successful animal.

Family Gomphotheriidae

The gomphotheres are one of three families in the suborder Elephantoidea. One is the Elephantidae, the family that contains the mammoths and true elephants. The other two families are browsing mastodonts: the gomphotheres themselves, and the more advanced mammutids. Elephantoids evolved rapidly during the Early Miocene. Several divergent and distinctive groups occurred, but all died out in the Pliocene and Pleistocene. The mastodonts appeared in the Early Oligocene about 35 million years ago. The early forms had quite long upper and lower jaws. Advanced forms had either a shortened upper jaw and an extreme elongation of the lower jaw into 'shovel tusks', or a reduced lower jaw resembling that of modern elephants.

Gomphotheres were the dominant large mammals of the Miocene. They had spread from Africa into southern Europe and the Indian subcontinent by the Early Miocene, reaching North America by the Mid Miocene, and South America just before their extinction in the Pleistocene about 2 million years ago. Elephants gradually replaced them from about 5 million years ago.

NAME *Phiomia*

TIME Early Oligocene

LOCALITY Africa (Egypt)

SIZE 8 ft/2.5 m high

Phiomia evolved alongside its smaller, distant relative *Moeritherium*. *Phiomia* probably browsed in forests of the Fayum area, while *Moeritherium* wallowed in the swamps.

The upper and lower jaws were long, the flattened tusks of the lower jaw forming a spoon-shaped extension used for gathering food. The upper lip was probably extended to form a primitive trunk which worked in conjunction with this strange lower jaw apparatus. Shorter tusks in the upper jaw may have been used as defensive weapons.

EARLY ELEPHANTS AND MASTODONTS CONTINUED

NAME *Gomphotherium*

TIME Early Miocene to Early Pliocene

LOCALITY Europe (France), Africa (Kenya), Asia (Pakistan) and North America (Nebraska)

SIZE 10ft/3m high

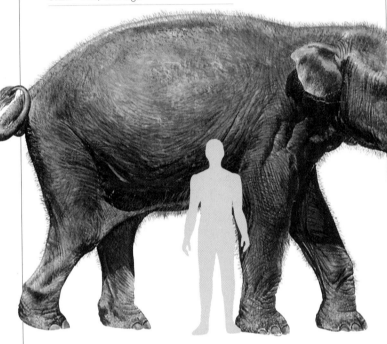

This four-tusked mastodont was wide-ranging, its fossilized remains have been discovered on four continents – Europe, Africa, Asia and North America. As a result of its occurrence in many places the same fossil animal has been given a variety of names by the people who unearthed it, including *Trilophodon* and *Tetrabelodon*.

The lower jaw of *Gomphotherium* with its parallel tusks, was greatly extended. The jaw was probably used in conjunction with an equally long trunk on the upper jaw for tearing and grasping leaves and other plant material.

Most members of the genus *Gomphotherium* ate the leaves from bushes, but one species was a swamp dweller and consumed soft water-plants.

As *Gomphotherium* evolved there was a progressive reduction in the number of teeth in the jaw, but those that remained developed a number of high ridges or cusps which served to increase the grinding area available in the animal's mouth.

This adaptation of the dentition was a necessary development to enable the teeth to cope with the large quantities of plant food that would have been required in order to maintain *Gomphotherium*'s immense bulk.

NAME *Platybelodon*

TIME Late Miocene

RANGE Europe (Caucasus Mountains), Asia (Mongolia) and Africa (Kenya)

SIZE 10ft/3m high

Platybelodon was another shovel-tusked browsing mastodont, similar to *Amebelodon*, which lived in Europe and Asia. The shovel arrangement of its tusks was shorter and broader than that of *Amebelodon*, and was indented at each side in order to make room for the tusks of the upper jaw.

Platybelodon evidently enjoyed much the same lifestyle as *Amebelodon*, wading through shallow rivers and dredging water weeds.

The fact that related types of proboscidean inhabited the continents of Eurasia and North America at this time suggests there was probably a migration route between the two landmasses – across a land bridge where the Bering Straits now lie.

The shovel-tuskers show an extreme specialization for a particular style of feeding. This means that, along with other highly specialized creatures, they were extremely vulnerable to environmental change because they were unable to adapt readily. As a consequence they were not a very long-lived group.

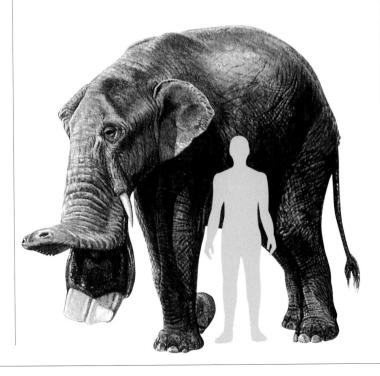

lower jaw lay side by side, forming a shovel or trough which projected more than 3 ft/1 m to a spade-like cutting edge.

The water plants on which *Amebelodon* fed would have been gripped between the flattened trunk and tusks and ripped from the mud of the river bottom, then pulled up the trough to the mouth by the trunk.

NAME	*Cuvieronius*
TIME	Pliocene to Recent
LOCALITY	North America (Arizona, Florida) and South America (Argentina)
SIZE	9 ft/2.7m high

Cuvieronius was named for the great French paleontologist and founder of comparative anatomy, Baron George Cuvier (1769–1832). A fairly small gomphothere, *Cuvieronius'* most remarkable feature was its tusks, which were spirally twisted like those of a narwhal.

We do not usually associate the South American continent with elephants. However, remains of *Cuvieronius* have been found in mountainous areas of both North and South America, a fact reflected in its synonym *Cordillerion* – 'the one from the mountain range'.

Cuvieronius evolved in western North America at the end of the Miocene, and migrated to South America during Pleistocene times, around 2 million years ago. It spread from the grassy pampas in the east to the heights of the Andes in the west, reaching as far south as Argentina. It was hunted to extinction, and probably died out as recently as AD 400.

NAME	*Anancus*
TIME	Late Miocene to Early Pleistocene
LOCALITY	Widespread in Europe and Asia
SIZE	10 ft/3 m high

With its short lower jaw and long, prehensile trunk, *Anancus* looked like a modern elephant; but it had shorter legs, and an extremely long pair of tusks which, at 10–13 ft/ 3–4 m, were almost as long as the rest of the animal.

Anancus seems to have adapted to woodland life. It could browse from high branches and root about among the leaf litter of the forest floor. It became extinct when grasslands replaced the woodlands.

NAME	*Amebelodon*
TIME	Late Miocene
RANGE	North America (Colorado, Nebraska
SIZE	10 ft/3 m high

Amebelodon roamed the prairies of North America during the Late Miocene. It evolved to feed off the water plants which flourished in the streams crossing the plains. In size and appearance, *Amebelodon* was similar to a modern elephant, but its skull and tusks were quite different. The flattened tusks of the elongated

MASTODONTS, MAMMOTHS AND MODERN ELEPHANTS

NAME *Stegomastodon*

TIME Late Pliocene to Pleistocene

LOCALITY North America (Nebraska) and South America (Venezuela)

SIZE 9 ft/2.7 m high

Stegomastodon is another gomphotheriid but this creature must have looked like a shorter, stockier version of a modern elephant. It had a short lower jaw, no lower tusks, and the upper tasks curved upward.

Stegomastodon's cheek teeth were even more elaborate than those of its forebears. With their convoluted pattern of enamel, which provided a wide abrasive surface and an efficient grinding action, it is possible that these adapted teeth enabled *Stegomastodon* to eat grass.

Stegomastodon was one of the few proboscideans that reached South America, having migrated there around 3 million years ago once the Central American land bridge had become established. This land bridge was formed and broken again several times during Pleistocene times before it reached its present proportions. Each time the continuous chain of volcanoes and fold mountains appeared above the ocean, the way was opened for a new influx of migrating animals.

Stegomastodon became extinct in North America about 1 million years ago, but survived in Venezuela in association with early humans.

Family Mammutidae

Despite their names, these were not mammoths but mastodonts. Their cheek teeth are characterized by having a simple pattern of low, flattish-sided cusps arranged to form transverse ridges with open valleys between. This contrasts with gomphotherid teeth, which have much more complex cusps in transverse rows, and many smaller cusps filling the valleys between.

NAME *Mammut americanum*

TIME Late Miocene to Late Pleistocene

LOCALITY North America (Alaska, New York, Missouri)

SIZE 10 ft/3 m high

The American mastodont, *Mammut americanum*, was one of the most common of the North American proboscideans. Like the woolly mammoth, it was a cold-climate animal, covered with a coat of long shaggy hair. Some of the hairy skin is sometimes found with the skeletons. Its remains have been found as far north as Alaska, and south to Florida.

The head was quite long and held low, with a pair of massive upward-curving tusks. It browsed in herds in spruce woodlands, and may have been a contemporary of modern humans. Like the woolly mammoth, *Mammut* became extinct less than 10,000 years ago. Other mastodonts are known from Africa, Europe and Asia, but these were not covered in hair.

Family Elephantidae

This is the family to which the modern elephants belong. They differ from their earlier relatives, the mastodonts, principally in the form of their teeth. True elephants have lost the tusks of the lower jaw, and this has enabled them to modify their method of mastication. Mastodonts ground up their food using a complex rotary motion, whereas elephants cut or shear it.

The change of chewing action has also affected the teeth, which are taller, with longer, more complex enamelled surfaces. In many species, there is only one grinding tooth at a time in each side, top and bottom.

Each of these four teeth has a series of up to 20 transverse loops of wrinkled enamel, infilled with softer dentine and separated from each other by thin bands of cement. The whole grinding surface thus forms a large, nearly flat area like the rasping surface of a file. The slight differences in hardness of the mineral phosphate between the enamel, dentine and cement result in variable rates of wear. Consequently the ridged and furrowed surface profile and its effectiveness in preparing plant material for digestion was maintained.

The mineral phosphate resists wear from grinding up the tough plant material which makes up the elephant's diet – hard and abrasive siliceous grasses, tree bark and tough twigs. Despite the structure, the teeth do get worn down by the wear of the animal's diet and need to be constantly replaced. Another tooth appears only when the earlier teeth have worn down.

The elephant's tusks are used for digging up roots while feeding or prising bark off trees, but they are also a weapon and in the males are used to display strength and size. The tusk themselves are greatly extended upper incisors and are made of a combination of dentine, cartilaginous material and calcium.

Several members of the elephantid family survived the end of the Ice Age but became extinct shortly afterwards, some possibly as the result of being hunted by early human populations. These extinct elephant species include the Eurasian woodland elephant, *Elephas antiquus*; the dwarf forms, such as *E. falconeri*, which lived on the Mediterranean islands; and two mammoths, *Mammuthus primigenius* and *M. jeffersoni*. Populations of mammoths also became stranded on islands off the shore of southern California and the arctic coast of Siberia. This isolation and the intense competition for dwindling resources resulted in a general reduction in the size of individuals. Their cousin, the American mastodont *Mammut americanum*, joined them in extinction at this time.

Only two species of elephants survive today. The smaller Indian elephants inhabit forests in the Indian subcontinent, Indochina, Malaysia, Indonesia and southern China. There are believed to be fewer than 50,000 remaining wild Indian elephants. The larger African elephant inhabits the grassland and forests of the African continent south of the Sahara. This species is the largest living land animal.

NAME	*Elephas antiquus*
TIME	Middle to Late Pleistocene
LOCALITY	Europe
SIZE	12 ft/3.7 m high

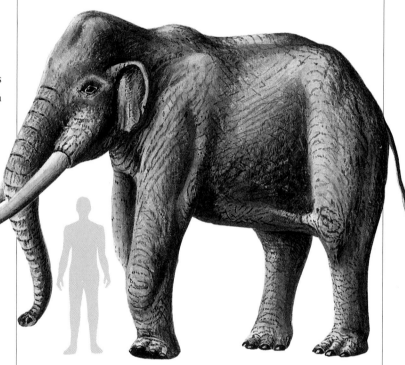

Elephas antiquus was a very large, long-legged and straight-tusked elephant. The tusks were long and straight, and slightly curved at the tip.

The bones of *Elephas antiquus* are relatively common in European Pleistocene deposits. During the Pleistocene Ice Age, the ice sheet advanced then retreated over large areas of the Northern Hemisphere. During the glacial retreats – periods of time known as the interglacials – the climate became much warmer. These interglacials tended to be warmer even than present-day climates, and subtropical conditions prevailed in places as far north as England. *Elephas antiquus* was one of the warm climate animals that frequented the lush woodlands that existed in these places at that time. The abundance of vegetation supported large populations of mammalian megaherbivores. The elephantids were accompanied by rhinoceroses, hippos, deer, horses and bison. The top carnivores, the big cats that preyed upon the herbivores, were also present. The scene would probably have resembled that of a modern African game park.

As each interglacial came to an end and the ice sheets advanced southward, *E. antiquus* moved southward as well. Its place in the northern lands was taken by the elephant group that was well-adapted to cold conditions – the mammoths.

MASTODONTS, MAMMOTHS AND MODERN ELEPHANTS CONTINUED

NAME *Elephas falconeri*

TIME Late Pleistocene

LOCALITY Mediterranean islands (Cyprus, Crete, Malta, Sicily, southern Calabria and some of the smaller Greek islands)

SIZE 3 ft/90 cm high

The genus *Elephas* includes the modern Indian elephant, *E. maximus*. The earliest members of the genus arose in Africa early in Pliocene times, about 5 million years ago, and radiated out into Europe and Asia. There are a number of interesting extinct dwarf elephants which may be separate species but were possibly varieties of their parent stock.

Elephas falconeri stood less than 3 ft/1 m in height and lived on the Mediterranean islands. Its ancestors, probably the European elephant *E. namadicus*, migrated out of Africa in the Early Pleistocene and spread west into central Europe and east to India and China, and even reached Japan.

During the lower sea-levels of the glacial periods, this elephant was able to reach Malta, Cyprus, Crete and Sardinia. With the rise of sea level as the glaciers melted in the interglacial periods, these areas became isolated as islands in the Mediterranean sea. In this isolation arose the dwarf form *E. falconeri*. Similar dwarf elephants arose on the Celebes Islands in Southeast Asia.

On islands such as these, natural selection would favour animals that made best use of smaller quantities of food, and dwarf varieties and species would evolve. A modern equivalent is the small Shetland ponies that have developed on the northern Scottish islands. There is a possible dinosaurian example, also, in the dwarf ankylosaur *Struthiosaurus* (p.159). The experience of very small animals such as rodents, however, is the exact opposite: rodents on the Mediterranean islands were often larger than elsewhere. In the absence of natural predators, there was little need to maintain a small and slender structure that could swiftly take refuge in holes and crevices.

NAME *Mammuthus meridionalis*

TIME Early Pleistocene

LOCALITY Europe (Spain)

SIZE Up to 15 ft/4.5 m high

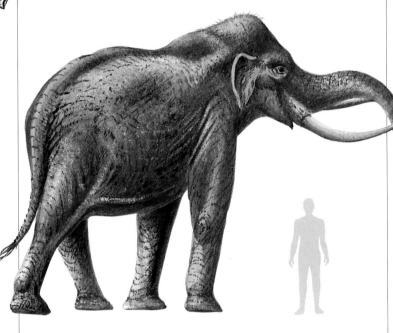

The mammoths were a wide-ranging group of herbivorous animals that developed adaptations to a cold climate, and which radiated from Africa to Eurasia and North America during the Early Pleistocene Period.

Mammuthus meridionalis was one of the first of the cold-adapted mammoths, evolving in the open woodlands of southern Europe, where the climates were cool, but not severe, around 2 million years ago.

The ancestors of this creature probably came from farther east, or from Africa.

Mammuthus meridionalis resembled the modern Indian elephant in general appearance, but it possessed much larger, more impressive tusks. It may have been the ancestor of a number of more specialized mammoths which developed later, including the European *M. primigenius* and the North American *M. imperator*.

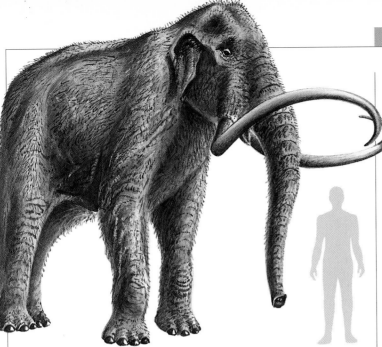

NAME *Mammuthus columbi*

TIME Late Pleistocene

LOCALITY North America (Carolina, Georgia, Louisiana, Florida)

SIZE 12 ft/3.7 m high

Mammuthus columbi was one of the American mammoths which migrated from Asia to North America, late in the Pleistocene, during a mild period, when it was possible to walk dryshod across the Bering Straits. *Mammuthus columbi* inhabited the warm grasslands in the south-eastern part of the continent and may even have moved as far south as Mexico.

Mammuthus columbi had twisted tusks, which perhaps distinguish it from the other American mammoth *M. imperator*, whose long tusks curled backward evenly. This latter species or subspecies had a more westerly range and its remains have been found in the tar deposits of Rancho La Brea, Los Angeles.

NAME *Mammuthus trogontherii*

TIME Middle Pleistocene

LOCALITY Europe (England, Germany)

SIZE 15 ft/4.5 m high

Mammuthus trogontherii was the steppe mammoth. It lived in the middle Pleistocene in central Europe, in much colder conditions than its ancestors, and because of this harsh environment *M. trogontherii* was probably the first to develop a hairy coat. It probably roamed in herds across the cold grasslands consuming the coarse grasses that grew there.

Mammuthus trogontherii was one of the largest mammoths. The spiral tusks, which were thicker in the males than in the females, were very long, some measuring about 17 ft/5.2 m.

NAME *Mammuthus primigenius*

TIME Late Pleistocene

LOCALITY Europe, Asia and North America

SIZE 9 ft/2.7 m high

Mammuthus primigenius, the woolly mammoth, is what most people think of as the typical mammoth. Relatively small for a mammoth, it was a cold-climate tundra-dweller, with a thick shaggy coat and a fatty hump.

Paleontologists are quite familiar with the animal's soft anatomy and appearance in life, since several well-preserved remains have been found buried in frozen mud in Siberia and Alaska. There are also the eye-witness reports from early people who painted and engraved images of the animal on cave walls in France and Spain.

The woolly mammoth's coat consisted of long black hair, not red as in most restorations. The red coloration, seen in specimens in which the hair is preserved, was due to a chemical reaction in the hair after death. There was an undercoat of fine hair and a thick layer of fat to help the insulation. Behind the domed head was a hump of fat, evidently used as a source of nutrition when times were hardest during the winter.

Scratches on the ivory suggest that the characteristic curving tusks were used for scraping away snow and ice from the low tundra vegetation on which it fed,

Mammuthus primigenius survived until about 10,000 years ago with a dwarf population surviving until 6000 years ago on Wrangel Island in the Arctic Ocean. The warming of the climate that accompanied the end of the last glaciation may have reduced its numbers. Overhunting by early humans probably hastened its extinction.

SOUTH AMERICAN HOOFED MAMMALS

During the Tertiary Era, South America supported as strange and unique a collection of mammals as Australia does today, and for many of the same reasons. Having once been part of a more or less unified landmass, continental drift and rising sea levels caused South America to become detached from North America and then from Africa and Antarctica. By early Tertiary times, roughly 50 to 60 million years ago, there was open sea, or possibly nothing more than a sporadic island chain, between North and South America.

At that time South America had three stocks of mammals on which evolution could act: marsupials (see pp.202–205), primitive edentates (anteaters, sloths and hairy armadillos, see pp.206–209), and some early rooting and browsing ungulates (see pp.234,254). But whereas North America subsequently acquired virtually all of the other evolving mammal stocks, due to its land connections with the Old World, South America gained only the rodents and primates.

For about 50 or more million years, from Paleocene until Pliocene times when the land bridge was re-established, the South American mammals were marooned on an island continent with no placental carnivores. As a result, the original stocks were given the opportunity to diversify into a variety of ecological niches which were filled elsewhere by other groups.

The animals described in the following pages are meridiungulates: the descendants of those stranded early rooters and browsers.

ORDER LITOPTERNA

Litopterns are mostly horse-like and camel-like animals. Their teeth are generally simpler than those of ungulates elsewhere in the world: their dentition remained more or less complete, and the gap (diastema) between front and cheek teeth was never as highly developed.

The legs and feet of the animals in this order are sometimes strikingly like those of the perissodactyls (the odd-toed ungulates, such as horses, tapirs and rhinoceroses; see pp.254–265). There is the same tendency to a reduction in the length of the upper limb and an elongation of the lower limb. The hoofed toes, too, have reduced to three or one, with the weight of the body being carried on the third digit.

There are differences, though. The radius/ulna and tibia/fibula bones of the forelimbs and hind limbs did not fuse, as they have done in the horse, and the ankle bones are less complex (their name means 'simple ankles').

Family Didolodontidae

It is not clear how this long-lived family should be classified. Some authorities place it with early rooting and browsing ungulates in the order Arctocyonia (p.234); other experts regard it as a litoptern. It is perhaps best considered as transitional between the two.

The earliest fossils are found from the Paleocene, around 60 million years ago, with examples still being found in the Mid-Miocene, 50 million years later.

NAME	*Didolodus*
TIME	Early Eocene
LOCALITY	South America (Argentina)
SIZE	Possibly 2 ft/60 cm long

The teeth of this creature were so much like those of the earliest hoofed animals that in life *Didolodus* may have resembled one closely.

A fleet-footed browser, which scampered through the undergrowth of the forests and ate the leaves of low-growing trees and bushes, *Didolodus* – or something closely related to it – may have been ancestral to most of the other hoofed South American mammals.

Family Proterotheriidae

The spread of the open grassy plains across the South American continent helped to induce the evolution of lightly-built running animals.

The proterotheres ('first creatures') were horse-like animals ranging from late Paleocene to late Pliocene times. Proterotheres appear to have undergone many of the same adaptive changes as the early horses in North America, sometimes in advance of developments elsewhere. It is unlikely that the proterotheres were able to graze, however, since their dentition remains that of browsing animals.

NAME *Diadiaphorus*

TIME Early Miocene

LOCALITY South American (Argentina)

SIZE 4 ft / 1.2 m

The graceful *Diadiaphorus* would have been very much like a short-necked antelope or a pony in appearance. It was about the size of a sheep, but it had the feet of a three-toed horse.

Although the paired bones of *Diadiaphorus'* lower limbs (ulna/radius and tibia/fibula) never fused as they did in the later true horses, the animal's legs were long and slender. The middle toe (the third) had become very large and bore the animal's entire weight, while the toes to each side (the second and fourth) had atrophied.

The head was relatively short and deep, and the brain case was quite large. The low-crowned teeth, however, were quite different from a horse's and suggest that *Diadiaphorus* probably lived by browsing on the softer vegetation, bushes and trees of Patagonia's plains.

NAME *Thoatherium*

TIME Early Miocene

LOCALITY South America (Argentina)

SIZE 2 ft 4 in / 70 cm long

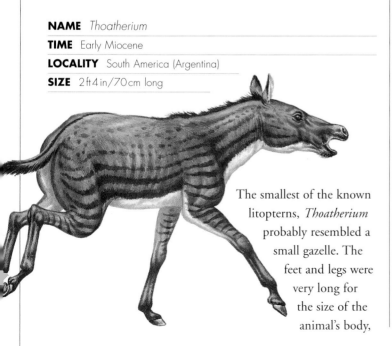

The smallest of the known litopterns, *Thoatherium* probably resembled a small gazelle. The feet and legs were very long for the size of the animal's body,

and it must have been a graceful runner. Although the paired bones of the lower limbs were reduced, they did not fuse. But the reduction of lateral toes which can be seen in both the true horses and in *Diadiaphorus* were taken to an extreme in *Thoatherium*. Indeed, the vestiges of its other two toes were even smaller than those of the single-toed horse of today. The dentition, too, remained primitive, so it can be assumed that *Thoatherium* lived on foliage rather than grasses.

Having achieved their greatest diversity in the early Miocene, the proterotheres became extinct in the Late Pliocene, about 3 million years ago.

Family Macraucheniidae

These curious camel-like litopterns, with rhinoceros-like feet, long necks and a proboscis, were once assumed to be extinct camels. This was not an unreasonable assumption because today the llamas and their close relatives in the camel family live in the same area (see pp.274–277). They are, however, quite distinct: any similarities that there are between the families are the result of evolutionary convergence – animals evolving in a similar way due to similar environmental pressures.

The macraucheniids were a long-ranging group and survived through much of Tertiary times and possibly the Pleistocene , only to become extinct in the last few thousand years.

NAME *Thesodon*

TIME Early Miocene

LOCALITY South America (Argentina)

SIZE 6 ft 6 in / 2 m long

Trotting across the Pampas plains, this browsing and grazing long-necked creature would have looked much like a modern guanaco. The main difference would have been in the feet, which in *Thesodon* were three-toed and hence rather heavier. The position of the nostrils in the skull of *Thesodon* suggests that a trunk was also present, but this may have been no more prominent than the one carried by the living saiga antelope.

The lower jaw was very slim and the mouth had a full set of 44 teeth – the maximum for a placental mammal which is unusual for a plant-eater at such a late date in the Tertiary.

SOUTH AMERICAN HOOFED MAMMALS CONTINUED

NAME *Macrauchenia*
TIME Pleistocene
LOCALITY South America (Argentina)
SIZE 10 ft/3 m long

Macrauchenia was a later and larger version of *Thesodon*, from which it may have evolved. The lifestyle of *Macrauchenia* ('large neck') is an enigma. It had certain camel-like features – including size, posture, small head and long neck. But its three-toed, hoofed feet were rhinoceros-like, and it probably bore a substantial trunk, too, since the nostrils enter the skull high up between the eyes.

Some paleontologists have suggested that signs of a trunk imply a semi-aquatic lifestyle. Others regard it as evidence that the nostrils were simply surrounded by lips which could be closed to keep dust out. The presence of a trunk allied to high-crowned cheek teeth also suggests that *Macrauchenia* may have been able both to browse and to graze.

The legs were long, and the front legs were much longer below the knee than above it – a common feature of running animals. But, *Macrauchenia* would probably not have been a fast runner since the proportions of the hind limbs were reversed, as in non-running animals.

ORDER ASTRAPOTHERIA

A small but well-represented order, the astrapotheres were low-bodied herbivores which survived from the Late Paleocene through to the Middle Miocene. Some were as large as rhinoceroses, and had tusks and a small trunk.

Family Astrapotheriidae

It has been possible to reconstruct many complete astrapotheriid skeletons. Yet their lifestyle and their relationship to the rest of the South America ungulates is puzzling.

NAME *Astrapotherium*
TIME Late Oligocene to Middle Miocene
LOCALITY South America (Argentina)
SIZE 8 ft/2.5 m long

Except for its greater size, *Astrapotherium* was typical of the family. The head was quite short, with a dome over the forehead created by enlarged air sinuses.

The canine teeth grew throughout life and formed four tusks. The larger top pair of tusks sheared against the lower pair. The broad lower incisors protruded, and probably worked against a horny pad in the upper jaw to crop plants.

Evidence for a trunk is contradictory. The nose bones were very short, and opened high on the forehead, which suggest a trunk. Yet there seems to have been no clear reason for a proboscis: *Astrapotherium*'s neck was not particularly short, and its head could easily have reached the ground. It is possible that the 'trunk' was really an inflated nose.

Astrapotherium had a long, low body with a weak back and legs, the hind legs feebler than the front ones. The feet were small and plantigrade (the weight borne on the flat of the foot).

The animal was probably largely aquatic, wallowing in shallow water and rooting about for water plants in a similar way to the amyndont rhinoceroses of the northern hemisphere (see p.264).

Family Trigonostylopidae

Paleontologists believe that the trigonostylopids may comprise a family of the astrapotherians, or that they may represent an order of their own. The principal resemblance of the trigonostylopids to the astrapotheres lies in their prominent canine tusks, but the remainder of the teeth suggest that they are more closely related to the litopterns.

NAME	Trigonostylops
TIME	Late Paleocene to Early Eocene
LOCALITY	South America (Argentina)
SIZE	Possibly 5 ft/1.5 m long

There are no remains of *Trigonostylops* other than its skull, so it is difficult to make any deductions about the animal's general appearance or its lifestyle.

The teeth are very primitive, but if *Trigonostylops* is an astrapothere – a deduction that is based on the large size of the lower canines – then the remainder of the body was probably something like that of *Astrapotherium*.

ORDER PYROTHERIA

The mammals of South America are excellent examples of convergent evolution – the development of similar structures and features among unrelated animals in response to similar environmental pressures. The pyrotheres were the South American 'equivalents' of the elephants, but it is not known from which group they evolved.

Family Pyrotheriidae

This was the principal family of the order. They ranged from Argentina to Brazil, Venezuela and Colombia, and are found from the Eocene to the early Oligocene.

NAME	Pyrotherium
TIME	Early Oligocene
LOCALITY	South America (Argentina)
SIZE	10 ft/3 m long

The remains of *Pyrotherium* were first found in the volcanic ash deposits of Deseado, Argentina: hence their name, which means 'fire animal'. Since that time, specimens have been discovered in many other parts of South America.

In life, *Pyrotherium* probably looked like the early elephant *Barytherium*, its African contemporary. *Pyrotherium* had a massive body supported on pillar-like legs, short broad toes, short thick neck, and a head equipped with a trunk and incisors enlarged to form tusks. There were two pairs of short, flattened tusks in the upper jaw and a single pairs of tusks in the lower jaw.

SOUTH AMERICAN HOOFED MAMMALS CONTINUED

ORDER NOTOUNGULATA

The notoungulates literally 'southern hoofed animals' were the largest order of South American ungulates. There are about 100 genera grouped into four suborders. The suborders may already have diverged by the time South America was detached from North America at the end of the Paleocene.

The isolation of South America allowed the separate evolution of its mammal groups, many of which diversified into ecological niches taken, elsewhere in the world, by other groups.

Many notoungulates were small animals which looked and lived much like rabbits or beavers. Other, larger species came to resemble sheep, wart hogs, horses, rhinoceroses and hippopotamuses. That they were related is confirmed both by the arrangement of cusps on the teeth and by ear bones, which are unique to the order.

Although most specimens are of South American origin, a few are also known from Late Paleocene and Early Eocene deposits in North America. The latter groups quickly died out, and from then the order existed only in South America.

The notoungulates achieved their greatest success as a group in the Oligocene, but they were still abundant early in the Miocene. Thereafter they declined. They have no surviving members. The last notoungulates became extinct in South America in the Pleistocene, about 1 million years ago, shortly after the emergence of the Panamanian isthmus opened the way to the invasion of mammal groups from the north.

SUBORDER NOTOPROGONIA

These are the most primitive notoungulates. When they first appear in the fossil record, members of all the suborders had primitive features. These include a complete dentition of all 44 teeth, low crowns to the teeth with little specialization, and no gap (diastema) between the front and cheek teeth.

The Notoprogonia were restricted to the Paleocene and Eocene: its members were extinct by about 45 million years ago.

Family Notostylopidae

Notostylopids were rodent-like, with prominent incisors at the front separated by a diastema from grinding premolars and molars at the back. However, the chisel-shaped incisors, which had roots and did not grow continually as those of a gnawing animal usually do, were adapted for nipping, not gnawing.

NAME	*Notostylops*
TIME	Early Eocene
LOCALITY	South America (Argentina)
SIZE	Possibly 2 ft 6 in/75 cm long

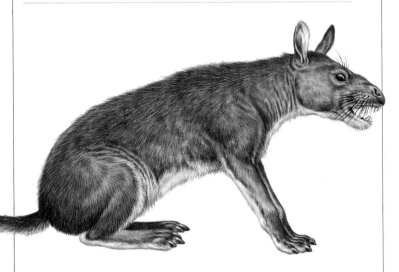

Notostylops was a rather rabbit-like animal which lived in the undergrowth, consuming herbaceous plants and other types of low-growing vegetation. The animal's body was probably fairly generalized with few adaptations to fit it for any particular ecological niche.

Notostylops would have had a short, deep face in order to accommodate the unusual rodent-like dentition that is characteristic of the family.

SUBORDER TYPOTHERIA

Typotheres have many features in common with rodents. Even their teeth are similar: the incisors and cheek teeth of advanced members of both groups are adapted for gnawing vegetation, and grow throughout life to compensate for the high rate of wear that the diet subjects them to.

Some members of the Typotheria suborder probably grew to about the size of the modern black bear, but most were smaller.

Family Interatheriidae

Most interatheriids were quite small, rodent-like mammals. They were a long-lived group, and fossil representatives have been found dating from Late Paleocene times through to the Late Miocene.

NAME *Protypotherium*
TIME Early Miocene
LOCALITY South America (Argentina)
SIZE 16 in/40 cm long

Protypotherium was about the size of a rabbit. It had a long tail and legs, and its rat-like head tapered to a pointed muzzle. All 44 teeth were present, and did not show specializations for any particular food. The neck was short and the body long, and there was a long and quite thick tail. The long, slender legs ended in paws which bore claws. *Protypotherium* probably ate leaves and scampered, rodent-like, over the Pampas.

SUBORDER HEGETOTHERIA

Like the typotheres suborder, in which they are often placed, hegetotheres include rabbit-like and rodent-like forms. They became effective gnawers. Later representatives have a diastema between incisors and cheek teeth. All teeth grew throughout life.

They emerged during the Middle Eocene, and did not become extinct until the Pliocene, about 3 million years ago.

Family Hegetotheriidae

Hegetotheriids include rabbit-like animals. Many members of the family had long hind limbs which would have enabled them to lope in the characteristic way.

NAME *Pachyrukhos*
TIME Late Oligocene to Middle Miocene
LOCALITY South America (Argentina)
SIZE 1 ft/30 cm long

Pachyrukhos shows certain similarities with the rabbits, whose ecological niche it filled in South America. It had a short tail, hind limbs that were considerably longer than its front limbs, and very long hind feet. It evidently moved about by hopping and leaping, like a rabbit.

The head was also rabbit-like, narrowing to a pointed muzzle. The teeth were adapted for a diet of nuts and tough plants. *Pachyrukhos* had a well-developed

hearing apparatus, which probably means that the ears were long, and large eye sockets. These features suggest that the animal was nocturnal.

SUBORDER TOXODONTA

The suborder Toxodonta was widespread and varied during the Eocene, Oligocene and Miocene (when some reached the size of horses or even rhinoceroses) and died out when the Central American landbridge was established.

The term 'toxodont' means 'bow tooth', a reference to a sideways curve in the cheek teeth. As in other notoungulate suborders, the teeth were low-crowned and complete in early genera, but became specialized later. The cheek teeth became large, and were coated in tough cementum. A diastema also appeared in many species.

Family Isotemnidae

The isotemnids evolved early and represent the most primitive family of toxodonts.

NAME *Thomashuxleya*
TIME Early Eocene
LOCALITY South America (Argentina)
SIZE 4 ft 3 in/1.3 m long

Thomashuxleya was named for the 19th century British naturalist and paleontologist, Thomas Huxley.

Robust and sheep-sized, *Thomashuxleya* appears to have been an unspecialized animal, with few adaptations to any particular way of life. The head was quite large in relation to the body, and all 44 teeth were present in the jaws.

The canine teeth, however, were enlarged into prominent tusks, so the animal may have rooted about in the undergrowth like a wart hog.

The strong limbs were like those of any primitive ungulate, and the relatively short feet were digitigrade – the weight was borne on the toes, not the soles. It is likely that *Thomashuxleya* was reasonably light on its feet, and perhaps not unlike a peccary (see pp.268–269).

SOUTH AMERICAN HOOFED
MAMMALS CONTINUED

Family Notohippidae

The term 'notohippid' means 'southern horse'. Yet although it was once thought to be an ancestor of the true horses, the similarities (which lie chiefly in the shape of the skull and the cropping incisors) are a result of convergent evolution – when unrelated animals develop in a similar way due to similar evolutionary pressures. In fundamentals, everything is notoungulate. This family, like several other groups of notoungulates and litopterns were abundant in early to mid Tertiary times in South America. The notohippids evolved in mid Eocene times (some 43 million years ago) and survived through to the mid Miocene (some 14 million years ago).

NAME	*Rhynchippus*
TIME	Early Oligocene
LOCALITY	South America (Argentina)
SIZE	3 ft 4 in/1 m long

Rhynchippus (the name means 'snout horse') presents a classic example of the convergent evolution of the South American ungulates with unrelated groups elsewhere in the world: in this particular case, with the horse. *Rhynchippus'* skeleton, with its deep body and its clawed toes, was not particularly horse-like, but the teeth were similar to those of a grazing animal such as a horse or a rhinoceros.

The animal's canine teeth did not form tusks, as they did in most of the other toxodonts. Instead they were the same size and shape as the incisors. These were tall and ideal for cropping vegetation. The large cheek teeth had a convoluted enamel surface, ideal for grinding up tough vegetation, and were coated in a cement.

Family Leontiniidae

The relationship of the Leontiniidae family to other groups is uncertain, but from the structure of the feet of the members it seems reasonable to include it among the toxodonts.

Leontiniids, were powerfully-built animals, and some may have had a rhinoceros-like horn.

NAME	*Scarrittia*
TIME	Early Oligocene
LOCALITY	South America (Argentina)
SIZE	6 ft 2 in/2 m long

Scarrittia is the only member of the Leontiniidae family that is known from a well-preserved skeleton.

In life, this bulky creature probably looked much like a lumbering, flat-footed rhinoceros. *Scarrittia* was a rather heavy animal with a long body and neck. It had stout legs, three-toed hoofed feet, and a very short tail. The tibia and fibula were partly fused at the top, which meant that the feet could not be turned sideways.

The animal's face was quite short and the jaws contained the full complement of 44 low-crowned, fairly unspecialized teeth.

Family Homalodotheriidae

A characteristic feature of the homalodotheriids is the presence of clawed toes. This characteristic is highly reminiscent of the chalicotheres which inhabited the Old World and North America (see p.260). The homalodotheriids , along with the loentiniids and toxodontids were abundant in mid to late Tertiary times in south America. The homalotheriids evolved in the early Oligocene and survived until late Miocene times.

NAME *Homalodotherium*

TIME Early and Middle Miocene

LOCALITY South America (Argentina)

SIZE 6ft 6in/2m long

The llama-sized *Homalodotherium* is the only well-known genus of the Homalodotheriidae family.

Unlike other notoungulates, *Homalodotherium* had a claw instead of a hoof on the four 'fingers' of each 'hand'. The animal's forelimbs were longer and heavier than the hind limbs; and whereas the hind foot was plantigrade (the weight was supported by the flat of the foot) the forefoot was digitigrade (the weight was supported on the digits). This characteristic would have made *Homalodotherium* higher at the shoulders than at the hips.

Such features made it likely that *Homalodotherium* was partly bipedal. It probably browsed on the leaves of low branches, rearing up on to its hind legs.

Family Toxodontidae

The toxodontids include animals, the teeth of which were exceptionally high-crowned and curved. They had open roots so the teeth grew all the time in order to compensate for the wear that resulted from feeding on the tough Pampas grasses. The animals themselves looked similar to rhinoceroses and some species even possessed a horn on the snout. The toxodontids evolved around 30 million years ago in Oligocene times and survived into the late Pleistocene.

NAME *Toxodon*

TIME Pliocene and Pleistocene

LOCALITY South America (Argentina)

SIZE 9ft/2.7m long

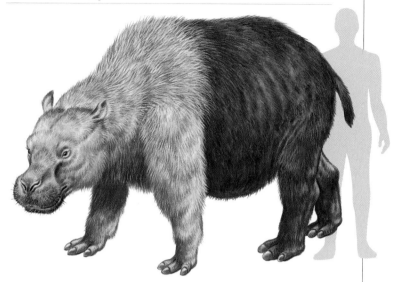

Toxodon was a rhinoceros-like animal, with a heavy barrel-shaped body supported on short stocky legs. The creature's three-toed, hoofed, plantigrade feet were rather small, however. Since the hind legs were longer than the front ones, the body sloped forward to the shoulders.

The front of the head was quite broad, and may have had a fleshy prehensile lip. Immediately behind the snout the skull narrowed, as in a rhinoceros, then widened again. Its teeth suggest that *Toxodon* was a mixed browser and grazer, chopping and chewing the hard Pampas grasses, but also taking foliage.

NAME *Adinotherium*

TIME Early to Middle Miocene

LOCALITY South America (Argentina)

SIZE 5ft/1.5m long

Adinotherium looked rather like a sheep-sized, and less ungainly, version of *Toxodon*. The front legs were relatively longer than in some toxodontids, so the shoulders were about the same height as the hips, and there was no hump.

Adinotherium also had a small horn on the skull. This was probably some kind of display structure.

HORSES

Ungulates – hoofed mammals – represent the main group of large plant-eating land animals living today. Their earliest representatives were early rooters and browsers (see pp.234–237), which had been dominant during Paleocene and Eocene times, about 50–60 million years ago. Many evolved to take advantage of the new opportunities presented by the formation of open grassy plains during the drier Miocene climates, about 20 million years ago.

Apart from the primitive rooters and browsers, ungulates can be divided into two great orders. The Perissodactyla or odd-toed ungulates (right) were represented by a large number of genera in the early Tertiary, but are now confined to horses, rhinoceroses and tapirs. The other great group of modern ungulates, the even-toed *Artiodactyla* (see pp.266–281), have far more representatives now than in any previous period, including deer, sheep, goats and cattle, pigs and peccaries, hippopotamuses, giraffes, and camels and llamas.

Unlike early rooters and browsers, most of the advanced ungulates are adapted for fast running: a crucial advance for small and medium-sized animals threatened by swift predators. The upper leg tends to be short, with long, thin, fused lower-leg and toe bones, enabling the animal to gallop without twisting its ankle or wrist joints. The muscles are concentrated around the upper bone and their power is transmitted to the rest of the leg by a series of tendons. The ankle joint tends to be rigid, and the animals walk up on their toes. The toes are generally elongated and reduced in number – another weight-saving feature – and the hoof itself is an enormously enlarged toe nail.

In the odd-toed Perissodactyla, where one or three toes are usual, most or all of the weight is taken on the middle digit. Among the even-toed Artiodactyla, the weight is divided between the toes, usually two or four in number.

Other ungulate developments associated with grazing include batteries of enlarged grinding teeth, a complex gut suited to the digestion of cellulose (the complex carbohydrate present in plant food), and living in large herds. Several groups have also developed skull outgrowths, made of horn, bone or even matted hair. The function of these growths varies, but includes defence and sexual display.

New molecular evidence for the affinities of the horses and other perissodactyls has produced another upset in the accepted view. Previously, the DNA data seemed to support a relationship of the perissodactyls with the hyraxes (hyracoids), elephants (proboscids) and sea-cows (sirenids). But they are now clustered with the cetartiodactyls (whales plus even-toed ungulates, such as pigs and cattle) and Carnivora. This association is better supported by the palaeontological evidence.

ORDER PERISSODACTYLA

The Perissodactyla order probably had its origins during Late Paleocene times about 55 million years ago.

There are three suborders. The Hippomorpha suborder contains the horses and the brontotheres (see pp.254–259), the Ancylopoda suborder (see p.260), and the Ceratomorpha suborder – the tapirs (see p.261) and rhinoceroses (see pp.262–265).

NAME	*Palaeotherium*
TIME	Late Eocene to Early Oligocene
LOCALITY	Europe
SIZE	2 ft 6 in/75 cm high at the shoulder

Palaeotherium was first described by the great French anatomist Georges Cuvier in 1804. It is placed in the family Palaeotheriidae, which were an early to mid Tertiary (Eocene–Oligocene) group of European perissodactyls.

The tapir-shaped *Palaeotherium* inhabited the tropical forests that covered Europe during early Tertiary times. The animal's short, stocky build was well-suited to a forest-browsing lifestyle, and it is one that evolved several times in the evolutionary record among different mammal groups.

The long head and short trunk enabled the animal to browse from low bushes, while the narrow body and long legs allowed it to run between close-growing trees.

Unlike the horses, the palaeotheres did not reduce the number of toes as they evolved: all palaeotheres have four toes on the front feet and three on the hind. These would have given the animal spreading feet suited to walking on boggy forest soil.

Palaeotheres probably moved about in herds – evidence for this is that large numbers are often found fossilized together. Some palaeotheres grew as large as a rhinoceros.

Family Equidae

Equids have their origins in small, scampering animals, no larger than small terriers, which browsed in the forests of Early Eocene times. With the arrival of the generally drier climate of the Miocene, around 20 million years ago, humid forests began to give way to more open country, and in some parts of the world, notably in North America, to vast grassy plains. It is to such conditions that the modern equids – horses, zebras and asses – are so well-adapted.

The evolution of the horses is often depicted as a straight line through time with increase in size, reduction in the number of toes and changes in tooth morphology. Many of these developments are associated with changes of habit and habitat, from the small forest and woodland browsers to the fast running grazers of open prairie.

The true picture, however, is far more complicated and interesting. Very many different perissodactyls evolved through Tertiary times and an overall view of their 'evolutionary tree' is much more like a many branched bush. There are as yet few clearly distinguishable 'lines of descent' but, as the fossil record of the horses is often quite good, it is highly likely that the picture will become clearer as research progresses.

NAME *Hyracotherium*

TIME Early Eocene

LOCALITY Widespread in Asia, Europe, and North America

SIZE 8 in/20 cm high at the shoulder

In spite of its name, *Hyracotherium* is not in fact a close relative of the hyraxes (see p.237) – this is the result of mistaken identification in the last century. A more evocative name, *Eohippus*, the 'dawn horse', has been suggested, but science retains the earlier term.

Hyracotherium, the earliest known equid, is believed to be ancestral to the rest of the horse line, and possibly to the palaeotheres as well.

This creature, however, was tiny compared to modern horses, only about 2 ft/60 cm in length. Its skull was elongated

and the mouth had a full complement of 44 teeth, indicating how primitive the animal was. The teeth were low-crowned and suitable only for chewing the soft leaves of tropical forest trees and shrubs.

As with *Palaeotherium*, *Hyracotherium* possessed four toes at the front and three at the back, making the feet large and unlike those of a horse. Most of the animal's weight was carried on the third toe, anticipating the evolutionary pattern to come.

The body was long and arched, an would have given the animal a hunched appearance.

The relative size and complexity of the brain suggests that *Hyracotherium* was alert and intelligent, and this may have been a factor in the survival of the horse line as a whole.

Hyracotherium was widespread during Eocene times, but when the horse line died out in Europe and Asia during the Early Oligocene around 35 million years ago, further evolution took place on the North American continent.

NAME *Mesohippus*

TIME Middle Oligocene

LOCALITY North America

SIZE 2 ft/60 cm high at the shoulder

In areas where the forests were giving way to more open country, the horses were no longer confined to scampering among the undergrowth and began to develop the capacity to trot and run.

About the size of a greyhound, with a body some 4 ft/1.2 m long, *Mesohippus* was larger than any of its predecessors, but it had rather lighter three-toed feet. The central toe was larger than the others.

The premolar teeth began to resemble the molars, which increased the chewing surface and hence their efficiency, but they were still low-crowned. Its feeding habits were similar to those of *Hyracotherium* and it probably browsed off leaves from bushes and low trees. Such teeth needed only a shallow jaw, so the head was quite long and pointed.

HORSES CONTINUED

NAME *Anchitherium*
TIME Early to Late Miocene
LOCALITY North America and later Asia and Europe
SIZE 2 ft/60 cm high at the shoulder

This latter change is highly significant. The newly-evolved grasses contained abrasive silica in their cell walls, which made them difficult to crop and masticate. Teeth would have worn down faster had it not been for the acquisition of hard-wearing 'cement' that coated their enamel crests and outer sides. It seems likely, therefore, that *Parahippus* ventured from the woodlands to take some advantage of the new source of nutrition – the spreading grasslands.

NAME *Merychippus*
TIME Middle to Late Miocene
LOCALITY North America (Nebraska)
SIZE 3 ft 3 in/1 m high at the shoulder

The evolution of the horse was not a simple 'straight line' affair, and a number of side-branches developed which have left no descendants today. *Anchitherium* represents a very successful, but conservative, offshoot.

Anchitherium evolved in North America in Early Miocene times, around 25 million years ago. A three-toed browsing horse, much like *Mesohippus* in size and shape, *Anchitherium* browsed the tender vegetation of humid forests. Crossing the Bering land bridge that once joined modern Alaska to Siberia, it spread across Asia and Europe. There, it survived long after it had been replaced in North America by the first grazing horses during the Mid Miocene, some 15 million years ago. *Anchitherium* did not become extinct in China until the end of Miocene times, some 5 million years ago.

Herds of *Merychippus*, the earliest horse to feed exclusively on grass, once roamed the prairies of what is now Nebraska.

Their teeth were tall-crowned – dental growth continuing for longer than had been the case hitherto – and interlined with cement. Continuing the development seen in *Mesohippus*, the premolars now had the same grass-grinding design as the molars. The tall teeth needed a deep jaw to contain them, so the head developed the heavy jawline of the modern horse.

Merychippus had a longer neck than its browsing ancestors, because it spent a great deal of its time with its mouth down in the grass. It also developed a strong ligament along the neck from the skull to the shoulder. The springiness of this ligament enabled the animal's heavy head to be raised with little effort, which

NAME *Parahippus*
TIME Early Miocene
LOCALITY North America
SIZE 3 ft 3 in/1 m high at the shoulder

Parahippus represents an intermediate stage in the evolution of the horse.

There were still three toes on the feet, and in appearance it was very similar to its ancestor *Mesohippus*. Its body was larger, though, as were its molars, which came to resemble millstones.

meant that *Merychippus* could stay alert to threats from swift predators, such as the early dogs and cats

Merychippus still had three toes but now only the middle toe was used to bear the animal's weight (the two side-toes did not reach the ground).

In addition, an elastic tendon in the leg linking muscle to bone acted like a spring, further increasing the efficiency of movement and making possible a progressively lighter foot and lower leg. The compression of this tendon absorbed the shock of each step, thus saving the ankle from damage, then released the energy stored up in the process to spring the foot up into its next stride.

NAME *Hipparion*

TIME Middle Miocene to Pleistocene

LOCALITY Widespread in North America, Europe, Asia and Africa

SIZE 4 ft 6 in/1.4 m high at the shoulder

Once the plains-living grazing horses had evolved they, too, radiated into many different types. Of these, all but the *Equus* species are now extinct.

Hipparion represents one of the many grazing horses that evolved during the Miocene, around 15 million years ago. It was a particularly successful genus, spreading during the Miocene from North America into Asia, Europe and Africa. In Africa, it survived until the Pleistocene about 2 million years ago.

This elegant creature resembled the modern horse, but like *Merychippus* had three toes, two of which were much reduced and did not touch the ground.

NAME *Hippidion*

TIME Pleistocene

LOCALITY South America

SIZE 4 ft 6 in/1.4 m high at the shoulder

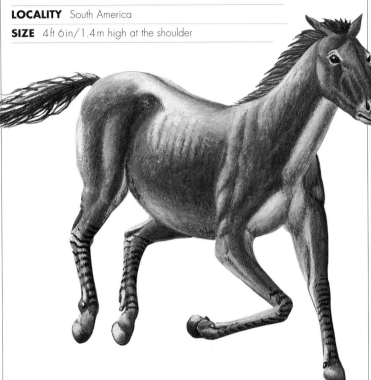

There seem to have been no horses in South America throughout the Tertiary Era. However, it cannot have been the environment that prevented their colonization of the region, since conditions in South America were able to support the evolution of horse-like litopterns such as *Diadiaphorus* (see p.247). When a land connection was re-established between North and South America during the Early Pliocene, 5 million years ago, horses were able to migrate to the south and thrive there.

Hippidion, which was probably a descendant of *Merychippus*, was one of these South American horses. It probably resembled a small donkey, with a fairly large head. However, its long, delicate nasal bones were quite distinct from those of other horses, suggesting that *Hippidion* continued to evolve in isolation from the mainstream of horse evolution in North America until it became extinct around 8000 years ago.

The modern genus *Equus*, which includes the zebras and asses as well as the wild and domestic horses, seems to have evolved about 4 million years ago in North America, from where it migrated to Asia, Africa and Europe.

Curiously, all the horses in North and South America died out about 8000 years ago, and did not reappear there until about 400 years ago – and then they appeared only as a result of deliberate introduction by human beings. Some paleontologists have speculated that the demise of the native American horse was caused by some devastating epidemic disease, possibly something similar to myxomatosis.

TAPIRS AND BRONTOTHERES

FAMILY BRONTOTHERIIDAE

Perissodactyls include two other groups of unusual extinct herbivores – the brontotheres and chalicotheres. The brontotheres are also called the titanotheres, or 'thunder beasts' due to their great size. This group of rhinoceros-like creatures evolved in the Early Eocene, about 50 million years ago, in North America and eastern Asia from small animals similar to the first horses. Although they existed for only about 15 million years, about 40 different types have been described.

Brontotheres browsed on soft forest vegetation. Some forms evolved massive horns and large canines, and there was a common tendency to hugely increased bulk. But although they are often referred to as 'horns', brontothere head growths did not contain any horn. Nor were they made of compacted hair, like those of rhinoceroses. They were more like the ossicones of giraffes: bony structures with a covering of thick skin. Since these knobs were larger in the males than the females, they were possibly used for display, or perhaps as weapons during fights.

Shortly after the brontotheres reached the peak of their monstrous development, climates became dryer and more open woodlands became plentiful. Evolution favoured more lightly-built animals that could graze and live on the plains. Brontotheres became extinct in the middle Oligocene and were replaced by the rhinoceroses.

NAME	*Eotitanops*
TIME	Early to Middle Eocene
LOCALITY	North America and Asia
SIZE	1 ft 6 in/45 cm high at the shoulder

If you could travel back through time to watch a group of *Eotitanops* scampering through the undergrowth of an Early Eocene forest, at a glance it would be impossible to tell *Eotitanops* from its distant cousin *Hyracotherium.* Both were small browsing mammals, with four toes on the front feet and three on the hind. *Hyracotherium* gave rise to the elegant horses, but *Eotitanops* evolved into the huge, small-brained, lumbering, brontotheres that failed to see out the Oligocene. It lived in North America in the early Eocene, but survived into the middle Eocene in Asia.

NAME	*Dolichorhinus*
TIME	Late Eocene
LOCALITY	North America
SIZE	4 ft/1.2 m high at the shoulder

In appearance *Dolichorhinus* resembled a small hornless rhinoceros with a particularly long head. Indeed, with its low-crowned teeth, which were only suitable for chewing soft forest leaves, it probably lived very much like one of the modern rhinoceroses. The four-toed front feet and three-toed hind feet of its ancestors were retained, as they were through the whole brontothere line. The type of feet adapted for swift running, with reduced toes, as seen in the horses and antelopes, were never evolved in the brontotheres.

NAME	*Brontops*
TIME	Early Oligocene
LOCALITY	North America
SIZE	8 ft/2.5 m high at the shoulder

As the Eocene passed into the Oligocene, the brontotheres became very large indeed – larger than any living rhinoceros – and developed the distinctive bony knobs on the snout.

Skeletons of *Brontops* have been found with partly-healed breaks in the ribs, a fact which lends support to the theory that the skull outgrowths were used in fights among males for dominance. The breaks suggest that the animal had received a heavy blow in the flanks from a rival, since no other animals of that time could have inflicted such damage. The movement of the ribs when breathing would have stopped broken bones healing properly.

One of the most famous skeletons of *Brontops* was discovered in rocks that had formed in a bog. The animal had evidently lived in swampy woodland, and had died by becoming swallowed up in the mud.

NAME *Embolotherium*

TIME Early Oligocene

LOCALITY Asia (Mongolia)

SIZE 8 ft/2.5 m high at the shoulder

The head of *Embolotherium* is typical of the grotesque shapes developed by the later brontotheres. From the back of the skull it swept forward in a deep hollow and then up to a massive single 'horn' on the nose. The eyes were situated well forward, just behind the nostrils and at the horn's base. The shallow skull left little room for much of a brain as in other large brontotheres, the brain was no bigger than a man's fist.

The occurrence of *Embolotherium* in the Gobi desert of Asia gives an indication of just how widespread and successful were the brontotheres in their heyday.

NAME *Brontotherium*

TIME Early Oligocene

LOCALITY North America

SIZE 8 ft/2.5 m high at the shoulder

The bones of this giant mammal are quite common in the Badlands of South Dakota and Nebraska. The local Sioux Indians had always associated them with the creatures of mythology – the great horses that galloped across the sky producing storms – and so the term 'brontothere', 'thunder beast', was born.

Brontotherium itself was one of the largest – larger than the living rhinoceroses. Its nasal horn was Y-shaped and swept upward higher than the back of the head.

The vertebrae at the creature's shoulders had enormous upward-projecting spines. These spines were evidently used to anchor powerful neck muscles that must have been needed in order to support the animal's heavy head with its huge, flamboyant ornamentation.

There may have been fleshy lips and a prehensile tongue, enabling *Brontotherium* to select and nibble the juiciest twigs and leaves from the bushes; the animal's teeth were of relatively simple design and were able to deal only with tender vegetation.

Brontotherium seems to have lived, like other brontotheres, in large herds that wandered through open scrubby woodlands. They roamed along the foothills of the rising Rocky Mountains – which was an intensely active volcanic area at that time. Every now and again a volcanic eruption would bury herds of *Brontotherium* in ash, and it is in these volcanic deposits that their fossilized skeletons are found today.

TAPIRS AND BRONTOTHERES CONTINUED

SUBORDER ANCYLOPODA

The second suborder of odd-toed ungulates, Ancylopoda, includes some bizarre animals, which have presented paleontologists with many enigmas.

There were two families within this suborder. The eomoropids were the first to evolve and generally resembled other primitive odd-toed ungulates. They lived in eastern Asia and North America during the Eocene and Early Oligocene, between 50 and 35 million years ago.

The second and most important family of ancylopods are the chalicotheres. They probably evolved in Eurasia during the Eocene and spread into Africa and North America during the Miocene. They survived until about 2 million years ago in eastern Asia and central Africa with little evolutionary change.

Family Chalcotheriidae

Whereas the rest of the ungulates have hooves on their toes, these animals evolved large claws instead and evidently would not have been able to run. The dentition and other features of some of the advanced chalicotheres, such as *Chalicotherium* from the Miocene of Europe, suggests that these animals were forest browsers, and may have been able to rear up onto their hind legs in order to feed on the succulent leaves of the trees and shrubs above their heads.

Although fossil evidence is sparse, chalicotheres seem to have been a remarkably successful group, which flourished for almost 50 million years.

Paintings of animals which resemble chalicotheres appear as decorations on Siberian tombs dating from the 5th century BC. Also, sightings are periodically reported in Kenyan forests of the so-called Nandi bear – a creature which allegedly has a gorilla-like stance, with forelimbs longer than its hind limbs, large bear-like claws, and with a horse-like face. It is little wonder, then, that claims are made that some chalicotheres still survive today.

NAME	*Moropus*
TIME	Early to Middle Miocene
LOCALITY	North America
SIZE	10 ft/3 m long

The chalicotheres have often been described as 'horses with claws'. The comparison is not a very apt one, however: although the head and body may have been somewhat horse-like, the limbs were heavy and not suited for running. The teeth were low-crowned, showing that it was a browser rather than a grazer, eating the soft leaves of trees rather than tough blades of grasses.

Moropus' back sloped upward to the shoulders from heavy hips, while its forelimbs were long and armed with three long claws. The three toes of the hind foot had shorter claws. When the claws were first discovered, without the rest of the skeleton, they were thought to have belonged to some kind of anteater.

The function of the claws is something of a mystery. They may have been used by the animal for digging roots and tubers out of the ground, but the teeth do not show enough wear for a diet of this kind of food. Alternatively, *Moropus* may have stood on its hind legs and hooked branches down from the trees, but its elbow joints do not seem to have been flexible enough for this method to have been habitual. It is possible that *Moropus* could have fed either way, and the claws may also have been used as defensive weapons.

SUBORDER CERATOMORPHA

The final suborder of odd-toed ungulates contains the tapirs and the rhinoceroses (see pp.262–265).

The tapirs were among the first of the perissodactyls to evolve, appearing during Early Eocene times, about 55 million years ago, at about the same time as the first chalicotheres (see left) and the horses (see pp.254–257).

Bulky tropical browsers with short trunks, tapirs were widely distributed throughout Europe, Asia and North America, but they were not discovered south of the equator until relatively recently. Tapirs managed to survive in the warmer areas of Europe, Asia and North America until the Late Pleistocene Epoch, about 10,000 years ago.

Tapirs are among the most 'conservative' of the mammals in terms of their evolution. In the 55 million years that they have been on Earth, the tapirs have changed remarkably little. Like the palaeotheres (see p.254), the tapirs evolved a body shape that is ideally suited to a life foraging around in the dense tropical forests. Indeed, this low, compact body shape has been so successful an adaptation that it has evolved separately in several very different groups, such as the peccaries (see pp.268–269) and capybaras.

Family Helaletidae

One of the earliest families of tapirs, the helaletids were much like today's species, but were smaller and more lightly built.

NAME *Heptodon*
TIME Early Eocene
LOCALITY North America (Wyoming)
SIZE 3 ft 4 in/1 m long

Heptodon, an early helaletid, had already evolved the characteristic tapir-shaped body but had no trunk. The short trunk that is such a distinctive feature of modern tapirs was just beginning to evolve as a fleshy outgrowth of the upper lip in *Helaletes*, a relative of

Heptodon that lived during the Middle and Late Eocene in North America and Asia. The trunk is a valuable evolutionary adaptation, which tapirs used as a sensitive tool for pulling food within reach and handling the twigs and leaves on which they feed.

Family Tapiridae

The family to which the modern tapirs belong, the Tapiridae, can be traced back as far as Early Oligocene times, about 40 million years ago.

The four species of living tapirs are all placed in the single genus *Tapirus*. Two species occur in Central America and northern South America and two in Southeast Asia: none remain in the group's original northern stronghold.

This scattered 'relict' distribution has often been cited by scientists as part of the evidence supporting the theory of the existence of the southern supercontinent of Gondwanaland. It is supposed that the animals reached their present, widely dispersed homes by migrating overland before the continents slowly drifted apart.

NAME *Miotapirus*
TIME Early Niocene
LOCALITY North America
SIZE 6 ft 6 in/2 m long

The characteristic tapir features – a heavy body, short legs and tail, a large head with a short flexible snout, and a short neck – appeared early in the evolution of perissodactyls and have remained unchanged ever since.

Miotapirus was probably nocturnal, as are members of the living species *Tapirus*, and may have been just as versatile, adapting to many different environments – fossils of *Miotapirus* have been discovered in a range of sites from sea level up to heights of 15,000 ft/4,500 m.

RHINOCEROSES

Rhinoceroses and their closest relatives are odd-toed ungulates, members of the Perissodactyla. Unlike the later horses, which have eliminated all the lateral digits and now have only one toe, most rhinoceroses have three toes, the axis of weight-bearing passing through the middle or third digit.

Family Hyrachidae

The hyrachyids mark the transition between the tapirs (see p.261) and rhinoceroses. The latter evolved from a tapir similar to *Hyrachyus* during Late Eocene times, about 40 million years ago.

NAME	*Hyrachyus*
TIME	Early to Late Eocene
LOCALITY	North America (Wyoming), Asia (China) and Europe (France)
SIZE	5 ft / 1.5 m long

Hyrachyus was generally a very similar creature to *Heptodon* (see p.261), but it was a little larger and more heavily built. It was a common and widespread animal. Many species have been discovered, ranging from the size of a modern tapir to that of a modern-day fox.

Hyrachyus appears to be ancestral to both the later tapirs and the rhinoceroses. Indeed, its resemblance to a primitive form of the latter group is so pronounced that it is often classed as rhinoceros, albeit a lightweight one.

SUPERFAMILY RHINOCERATOIDEA

Rhinoceratoids – literally 'nose horns', from the Greek – make up the largest superfamily of the suborder Ceratomorpha. In fact, only one family, the Rhinocerotidae, evolved 'horns', and even these are not true horns. In fact they are outgrowths composed of highly compacted hair.

Rhinoceratoids evolved in Middle Eocene times and adapted to the change in conditions as the worldwide forests gave way to grasslands. The inability of their cousins the brontotheres (see pp.258–259) to do likewise soon led to extinction. Nevertheless the rhinoceroses have now passed their peak, with only five species still managing to survive today.

The evolutionary history of the rhinoceratoids is quite complex: they are grouped into three families.

Family Hyracodontidae

The hornless hyracodont rhinoceroses, of which there are about a dozen genera, were the earliest and most primitive family of the group. They probably evolved from a tapiroid close to *Hyrachyus*.

Their large, efficient cheek teeth were similar to those of the tapirs, but their incisors and canines were modified in various ways. Earlier hyracodonts were quite horse-like in build, with slender, elongated limbs. Later members of the family developed a more robust build.

NAME	*Hyracodon*
TIME	Early Oligocene to Early Miocene
LOCALITY	North America (Saskatchewan, Dakota, Nebraska)
SIZE	5 ft / 1.5 m long

Hyracodon was a lightly-built fast-running animal, not unlike a pony. As with the horses, the number of its toes were reduced, so that the foot was lightened and could be moved quickly, and all the leg muscles were concentrated near the top. There were three toes on all feet.

The large and heavy head, however, seemed out of proportion to the body. No horns had evolved at this stage, and the only means of defence against such local meat-eaters as *Hyaenodon*, the last of the creodonts, or the early dogs would have been to flee. The back teeth were of a typical rhinoceros pattern, low-crowned and adapted for chewing leaves.

NAME	*Indricotherium*
TIME	Oligocene
LOCALITY	Asia (Pakistan and China)
SIZE	26 ft/8 m long

It seems quite impossible that an animal as small, lightweight and fleet-of-foot as *Hyracodon* could have evolved into the largest land mammal known to have lived, but all of the evidence points in that direction.

Indricotherium – also known as *Baluchitherium* after the state in Pakistan in which major specimens were discovered – was an immense animal. With an estimated weight of 33 tons/30 tonnes, it was twice the weight of the largest known mammoth and more than four times that of the heaviest modern elephant. The skull itself was 4 ft 3 in/1.3 m long, but this was relatively small compared to the overall body size.

The vertebrae of the back and the long neck were sculpted into hollows and struts, like those of the largest dinosaurs, which kept weight down while retaining the strength. The legs were elephantine, but the animal's entire weight would have been supported on only three toes – the normal rhinoceros pattern. Again, there was no horn; in fact, the nasal bones were quite weak.

The front teeth of the fossil rhinoceroses varied widely, but those of *Indricotherium* were very strange indeed. There were only two front teeth on top and two below: the upper pair pointing downward like tusks, while the lower pair pointed forward. Since there is some evidence that it had a large, flexible upper lip, such a construction would have enabled *Indricotherium* to browse giraffe-like from the tops of trees more than 26 ft/8 m from the ground.

Indricotherium probably lived in small family groups, taking advantage of the scattered trees found in dry open woodlands.

One skeleton was discovered in rocks formed from swamp mud. It is easy to imagine the difficulties such a huge creature would have had in a bog.

RHINOCEROSES CONTINUED

Family Amynodontidae

Amynodonts were a short-lived Eocene and Oligocene group of about 10 genera of hippopotamus-like, probably amphibious, animals with large bodies and short stout limbs. The canine teeth were short or absent in the two other rhinoceros families, but in the amynodontids they were huge, curved, and continually-growing.

It seems likely then that amynodontids took the place in this habitat of the aquatic pantodonts such as *Coryphodon* (see p.235), and were eventually replaced by aquatic species of the rhinocerotid family, such as *Teleoceras* (opposite).

NAME *Metamynodon*

TIME Late Eocene to Early Miocene

LOCALITY North America (Nebraska, South Dakota) and Asia (Mongolia)

SIZE 13 ft/4 m long

Remains of *Metamynodon* and its relatives are found in rocks that were formed from river sands and gravels, indicating that these beasts were mostly aquatic by nature. *Metamynodon* was like a hippopotamus in appearance. It had a broad, flat head, a short neck, a massive barrel-shaped body, and short legs. The front feet were unique among rhinoceroses in having four toes.

The crest up the middle of the skull ,may have anchored strong jaw muscles that evolved to cope with *Metamynodon*'s tough, woody diet.

The hippopotamus-like enlarged canine teeth may have been used for grubbing about in the mud at the bottom of a river. It is also likely that *Metamynodon* had prehensile lips.

Another adaptation to an aquatic lifestyle were the eyes. Set high up on the skull, they allowed the animal to see all around while it was almost totally submerged.

Family Rhinocerotidae

This is the family to which modern rhinoceroses belong. They evolved in Late Eocene or Early Oligocene times and thrived throughout North America, Asia, Europe and Africa. However, rhinoceroses began to decline during the Pliocene, and they had disappeared altogether from North America at the end of Miocene times, 5 million years ago.

Since this was about 2 million years before the Panama isthmus reformed, rhinoceroses never colonized South America. Neither did the woolly rhinoceros *Coelodonta* (opposite), which was once widespread throughout northern Eurasia, migrate across the Bering land bridge to reach North America.

Rhinocerotids adapted to a wide range of diets and habitats. Many were browsers, but some became specialized grazers. Some members of the family developed thick coats which enabled them to survive in northern regions even during the Pleistocene Ice Ages. Some also acquired 'horns' composed of matted hair, which have not fossilized.

It seems likely that the continued decline of these animals, now the largest land mammals after elephants, is associated with changing climate, but also with the rise of humans. Out of about 50 genera, only five species are still alive.

NAME *Trigonias*

TIME Early Oligocene

LOCALITY North America (Montana) and Europe (France)

SIZE 8 ft/2.5 m long

The earliest well-preserved example of a rhinocerotid is *Trigonias*. It was already similar to the modern rhinoceroses in its general appearance, but *Trigonias* had no horn on the snout. There were also more teeth in the jaw than are found in the jaws of any modern rhinoceros, though the actual number seems to have varied between different species.

Trigonias' front feet had five toes, although the fifth was small and could not reach the ground. This suggests that the evolutionary line split away from the other rhinoceroses before the lightweight three-toed running forms developed.

wrinkled enamel. Such teeth are adapted to eating tough, abrasive grasses. As the teeth wore down, the wrinkled enamel produced ridges that provided additional grinding surfaces. The teeth had no roots but grew continually to counteract wear.

Because of the lack of hiding places a grassland animal either needs to be very swift of foot to escape its predators, or so big and so well-armoured that its predators are discouraged from attacking in the first place. As the largest known of the true rhinoceroses – it was almost as big as a modern elephant – *Elasmotherium* adopted the latter strategy.

Elasmotherium's 'horn' was a truly remarkable structure, 6 ft 6 in/2 m long. Most rhinoceroses have their horns growing from the snout. In *Elasmotherium*, however, it grew from the forehead. There was a large dome of bone here, which presumably provided a more secure anchor for the massive structure than any foundation at the tip of the nose.

NAME	*Coelodonta*
TIME	Pleistocene
LOCALITY	Europe (Britain) and Asia (eastern Siberia)
SIZE	11 ft/3.5 m long

Coelodonta had its origins in the Pliocene of eastern Asia, from where it migrated into Europe (but not into North America) and became the woolly rhinoceros of the Ice Age.

Coelodonta had a pair of huge horns on its snout, the front one growing to lengths of over 3 ft/1 m in old males.

Like the woolly mammoth (see p.245), *Coelodonta*'s massive body and shaggy coat allowed it to withstand the harsh conditions of the tundra and steppe that bordered the great glaciers of the Northern Hemisphere. Although normally hair does not fossilize, the presence of the shaggy coat is known because of corpses found preserved in frozen gravels in Siberia. There are eye-witness accounts too. Early humans hunted this great beast, and depicted it on the walls of caves in southern France 30,000 years ago.

NAME	*Teleoceras*
TIME	Middle to Late Miocene
LOCALITY	North America (Nebraska)
SIZE	13 ft/4 m long

Like the amynodontids, the rhinocerotids developed hippopotamus-shaped forms as well. *Teleoceras* was typical of these. It had a long and massive body but short and stumpy legs. *Teleoceras'* legs were so short, in fact, that the creature's body would at times have dragged on the ground. It is likely that the legs were used to 'pole' the animal along underwater rather than for walking on dry land.

The feature of this extraordinary animal that most distinguished it from the modern hippopotamus was the short conical horn on the nose. It is possible that this feature was confined to males, and was used for defence or display.

NAME	*Elasmotherium*
TIME	Pleistocene
LOCALITY	Europe (southern Russia) and Asia (Siberia)
SIZE	16 ft/5 m long

As the forests of the Early Tertiary gave way to the grasslands of the Late Tertiary, many animal families adapted accordingly. Among the rhinoceroses, *Elasmotherium* shows the result well.

Elasmotherium had no incisors, and would have used its lips to pluck grasses. The creature's cheek teeth were like those of a huge horse – tall-crowned, covered in cement, and with

SWINE AND HIPPOPOTAMUSES

ORDER ARTIODACTYLA

The artiodactyls are the even-toed ungulates, and are the most widespread and abundant of today's running, grazing animals. They differ from their distant relatives the perissodactyls (odd-toed ungulates, such as the horses) in that they usually have four or two, rather than three or one, weight-bearing toes on each foot that form a semicircular hoof, giving rise to the 'cloven hoof' typical of pigs, deer and cattle.

Artiodactyls first appeared as small rabbit-sized herbivores in Eocene times, about 50 million years ago, and developed more slowly than the perissodactyls (see pp.254–265). Most groups had emerged by the close of Eocene times about 37 million years ago, when they rapidly outstripped their rivals.

Over the last few years, molecular analysis has emphasized the close relationship of the artiodactyls with the whales (cetaceans). New analysis confirms this and combines the two groups as the Cetartiodactyla, which is clustered with the Carnivora and horses (perissodactyls).

With the exception of the suines (pigs, peccaries and hippopotamuses, below), the artiodactyls all ruminate: that is, they 'chew the cud' to improve the efficiency of digestion. The ruminant stomach is divided into three or four chambers, the first of which is the rumen. Food is swallowed and passes into the first and second chambers, where it ferments until it is regurgitated for further chewing. It is only when this by-now fully masticated food is swallowed again that it makes the journey down the entire alimentary canal.

This complex digestive system increased the nutritional yield of the tough plants that were evolving in Miocene times. These, in turn, increased the range of habitats open to the artiodactyls, contributing in part to their success.

The importance of the ungulates, particularly artiodactyls, to human evolution and social development cannot be ignored. They were hunted, then more recently, several species were domesticated, which added to the resources available to humans, including milk, wool, transportation, and a source of energy for powering agricultural machinery. When harnessed to tools and machinery, ungulates enlarged the possibilities for the cultivation of crops.

SUBORDER SUINA

The word 'suina', like swine, comes from the Latin for 'pig'. The suborder Suina includes the non-ruminant artiodactyls – the hippopotamuses, pigs, peccaries and a number of other extinct groups.

These are generally considered the most primitive of the suborders of even-toed ungulates. Most have the simplest, almost complete teeth, and the least sophisticated digestive systems. Although the stomach may have two or three chambers, suines do not chew the cud.

Family Dichobunidae

Dichobunids are a family of small, primitive animals which must have looked more like rabbits than ungulates. Their classification as even-toed ungulates might seem to be inappropriate, since many had five toes on each foot. However, certain features of the skeleton indicate that this was the group from which all the others evolved.

NAME	*Diacodexis*
TIME	Early Eocene
LOCALITY	Europe (France), North America (Wyoming) and Asia (Pakistan)
SIZE	20 in/50 cm long including tail

The earliest-known of the artiodactyls, *Diacodexis* had simple teeth, and all five toes were present (though as in most artiodactyls, the third and fourth were the longest). There may also have been small hooves on the toes. *Diacodexis* must have lived in forest undergrowth, browsing leaves from bushes.

Diacodexis had much the same shape and general appearance as a muntjac deer, but with short ears and a long tail. The legs, too, were relatively longer than a rabbit's, and the forelimbs and hind limbs were equal in length. Such a build implies that *Diacodexis* ran rather than hopped and jumped. Indeed, it is the most highly adapted running animal known from Eocene times – the joints restricted the feet to an up-and-down movement, and the foot and lower leg bones were longer than the upper, a characteristic feature of fast-running animals.

Family Entelodontidae

These large pig-like animals, which probably originated in Asia in Late Eocene times, became common throughout Europe and Asia, and spread into North America. They were at their most prolific during the Oligocene but some survived in North America until the early Miocene, about 20 million years ago. Some members of the family were massive, reaching the proportions of a hippopotamus.

A prominent feature of the entelodontids was the presence of two pairs of bony knobs protruding from the side of the lower jaw.

NAME *Archaeotherium*

TIME Early Oligocene to Early Miocene

LOCALITY North America (Colorado) and Asia (China, Mongolia)

SIZE 4 ft/1.2 m long

Archaeotherium would have looked something like a modern wart hog with a narrow, crocodile-like head. Its skull was remarkably elongated, with long knobs of bone beneath the eyes and on the lower jaw. These protrusions may have been ornamental, or they may have anchored particularly powerful jaw muscles, which were used for grinding up the animal's diet of tubers and tough roots. The arrangement of *Archaeotherium*'s teeth suggests that, like a modern pig, this animal could eat just about anything, even scavenging on the corpses of animals.

The animal's shoulders were high, owing to a series of long spines on the vertebrae. These spines anchored the strong neck muscles needed to support the heavy head.

The creature's brain itself was tiny, but it did have large olfactory lobes, the areas of the brain associated with the sense of smell. *Archaeotherium* probably spent much of its time with its head down, snuffling and grubbing about in the soil of the Oligocene scrub in search of food.

NAME *Dinohyus*

TIME Early to Late Miocene

LOCALITY North America (Nebraska and South Dakota)

SIZE 10 ft/3 m long

The entelodonts reached their maximum size in the omnivorous *Dinohyus* of North America. This animal was much like *Archaeotherium*, but about the size of a bull.

Although *Dinohyus'* bodily proportions were pig-like, the evidence of its long and heavy skull suggests that its face must have been quite different. For example, its nose was not flat, and the nostrils opened at the side of the muzzle rather than the front. Like *Archaeotherium*, it is thought that the long bony projections, on the zygomatic arch beneath the eye, and the bony knobs below the jaw were for the attachment of specialized muscles. These may have been for chewing but their function is not certain. What is certain is that like *Archaeotherium*, *Dinohyus* fed close to the ground, its long muzzle making up for its short neck.

SWINE AND HIPPOPOTAMUSES CONTINUED

Family Anthracotheriidae

The anthracotheres or 'coal beasts', named for the deposits in which many have been found, may be related to the hippopotamus family. They were basically an Old World group, with many members appearing in Asia from the Eocene right up to the Pleistocene. They also migrated to North America, where they are mainly found in Oligocene deposits.

Like the hippopotamuses, which many of them resemble, anthracotheres were probably chiefly aquatic animals. It is possible that the hippopotamuses replaced them in the same aquatic niche.

NAME *Elomeryx*
TIME Late Eocene to Late Oligocene
LOCALITY Europe (France) and North America (Dakota)
SIZE 5 ft/1.5 m long

The hippopotamus-like *Elomeryx* had a long body and short stumpy legs, with a head which was long and superficially resembled that of a horse. Its teeth, however, were quite different, with elongated canines well adapted to hooking up the roots of water plants, and spoon-shaped incisors ideally suited for digging in the mud.

Unlike other even-toed ungulates, in which the toes are usually reduced to two, *Elemeryx* possed five toes (the first a 'dew-claw') on its forefoot and four on its hind foot. Such broad feet would have been useful for walking on soft mud.

Family Hippopotamidae

The hippopotamus family is a recent group dating from the Late Miocene. They may have evolved from the anthracotheres (above), whose niche as swamp-living rooters they probably took over, or possibly from fossil peccaries.

The name of the family comes from the Greek for 'river horse', referring to the semi-aquatic lifestyle of most of the family. Some, however, like the living pygmy hippopotamus, were forest dwellers. The only other living species is the almost entirely aquatic *Hippopotamus amphibius*.

NAME *Hippopotamus*
TIME Late Miocene to Recent
LOCALITY Asia, Africa and Europe
SIZE 14 ft/4.3 m long

The only obvious differences between a *Hippopotamus gorgops* of Pleistocene East Africa and the living species *H. amphibius* were the great size and particularly prominent eyes of the former. These eyes probably protruded, periscope-like, above the skull on stalks, which would have afforded the animal good panoramic vision while it lay in the water with its whole body submerged and only its eyes, ears and nostrils visible.

These differences aside, *H. gorgops* had the same familiar shape as its modern counterpart, with a heavy body more at home buoyed up in the water than on land, short thick legs, and broad feet ideally suited for walking on mud. Its mouth, too, was wide, with the canine teeth forming the characteristic huge tusks used to dig up water plants.

Family Tayassuidae

The tayassuids, or peccaries, resemble their close relatives the pigs in so many ways that it is difficult to distinguish them in the fossil record. They are readily identifiable among living suines, however, because a peccary's canines do not protrude when its mouth is closed. Their feet, too, are different, having only two toes (with laterals reduced) in the place of a pig's four toes (with little reduction in the laterals).

Living peccaries are confined to South America and the south-western states of North America, but most of the fossil forms are found in North America, where the family evolved in the Oligocene. Fossil peccaries have also been discovered throughout Eurasia and Africa.

The tayassuids were, and continue to be, versatile creatures, successfully inhabiting a wide range of environments from virtual desert to tropical rain forest.

NAME *Platygonus*

TIME Pliocene to Late Pleistocene

LOCALITY North America (Great Plains) and South America

SIZE 3 ft 3 in/1 m long

Platygonus was larger than modern peccaries, and had longer legs. Like its modern relatives, it was primarily a forest animal. It also inhabited the more open Great Plains region, however, a fact which may help to explain its elongated limbs, which are suitable for running.

The nose was rather like a pig's snout, as in modern peccaries, consisting of a flat disk with forward-pointing nostrils. Such a nose was ideal for snuffling about on the ground looking for roots, grass or fruit on which to feed.

Platygonus was herbivorous, as evidenced by a complex digestive system more like that of a cud-chewing animal than a pig's. Despite its diet, the canine teeth were almost those of a carnivore – long, straight and needle-sharp. Such teeth could not have been necessary for a herbivorous diet, so it seems likely that they would have been used as weapons, perhaps for protection against attackers such as big cats.

Family Suidae

The suids, the pig family, evolved in the Old World, probably in Asia, in Oligocene times, and they appeared slightly later in Europe during the Miocene. The Suidae family, however, never colonized the Americas.

Although pigs are omnivores rather than herbivores, they seem to have filled the same ecological niches that were taken in the Americas by the peccaries. Fossil suids, like their living descendants, include animals which lived in a wide variety of habitats: from tropical rain forests to savannah woodlands, and even semi-aquatic environments.

Suid fossils are often relatively abundant and are of considerable use in helping geologists determine the relative age of terrestrial sediments. They have also proved of particular importance in matching and dating strata with fossil hominid remains in East Africa.

NAME *Metridiochoerus*

TIME Late Pliocene to Early Pleistocene

LOCALITY Africa (Tanzania)

SIZE 5 ft/1.5 m long

A contemporary of early humans, *Metridiochoerus* was a giant wart hog which inhabited eastern Africa.

Its head was large and heavy, and both its upper and lower canine teeth curled outward and upward to form great curved tusks. *Metridiochoerus'* cheek teeth were high with a complex pattern of cusps, indicating the omnivorous nature of this creature's diet.

OREODONTS AND EARLY HORNED BROWSERS

SUBORDER TYLOPODA

Tylopods – the word means 'padded foot' – are a broad grouping of artiodactyls (even-toed ungulates). The suborder Tylopoda includes Old World rabbit-like cainotheres, the New World pig-like merycoidodonts and the camelids.

In many important respects, they stand midway between the swines (pigs, peccaries and hippopotamuses; see pp.268–269) and the pecorans (giraffes, deer and cattle; see pp.278–281).

The tylopods first appeared in the Late Eocene, around 40 million years ago, and were common through the Oligocene and up to Late Miocene times, 5 million years ago. Only the camelids – the camels, llamas and their closest relatives – still survive (see pp.274–277).

Family Cainotheriidae

This is one of the most primitive families of the suborder. As in most primitive members of any group, the cainotheres were generalized animals, with few features to hint at the more specialized members that were to evolve.

Most members of the Cainotheriidae family were rabbit-like in size, appearance and in their bounding or leaping style of locomotion.

NAME	*Cainotherium*
TIME	Late Oligocene to Early Miocene
LOCALITY	Europe (Spain)
SIZE	1 ft/30 cm long

Cainotherium was a small rabbit-like animal, with hind limbs longer than the front limbs. The parts of the creature's brain that were associated with hearing and with smell were well-developed.

This feature implies that *Cainotherium* was probably equipped with long rabbit-like ears and probably had a sensitive nose as well. As well as looking a little like a rabbit this animal must have lived in a similar way to a rabbit, scampering and hopping through the undergrowth, where it browsed on a variety of vegetation.

Yet *Cainotherium* was clearly an even-toed ungulate. Even at this early stage in its evolution, the animal's limbs had become slender, with only two toes and reduced lateral toes which ended in hooves.

Also, unlike the rabbit, *Cainotherium* did not have particularly specialized teeth. The full number of mammalian teeth (44) were present in its jaw. The teeth formed an almost continuous series with no gap (called a diastema) between the front and cheek teeth. However, the back teeth were quite broad, with five cusps, and were well-adapted for chewing and grinding up vegetation.

Cainotherium and its relatives may have competed with, and eventually lost the evolutionary competition to, the early rabbits and hares for the same ecological niches (see p.285). They were restricted to Europe and left no descendants beyond early Miocene times.

Family Merycoidodontidae

The suborder Tylopoda may well have evolved from the suborder Suina. This relationship can be seen from the Merycoidodontidae family which seems to combine some features typical of pigs with those characteristic of camels. Typically they were rather heavily built animals with short limbs and four toes on each foot. The merycoidodonts (the name means 'ruminating tooth') are sometimes more euphoniously referred to as oreodonts – 'mountain tooth', a reference to the type of terrain in which their remains were discovered. The teeth have advanced features which indicate relationships with the ruminants. The tooth was unbroken, without diastema or loss of teeth. The upper canine was a stout, somewhat projecting, chisel shape. The lower canine was reduced to the size of the incisors and the specialised cheek teeth were strongly selenodont (with pairs of crescent-shaped ridges). These features produced long-lasting grinding surfaces which were effective for the side to side chewing of vegetation.

A highly successful group of woodland and grassland browsers, the merycoidodonts evolved in North America during the Late Eocene, around 35 million years ago. The evidence suggests that they were particularly abundant throughout the Oligocene and into Miocene times. They then died out around 5 million years ago.

Members of the family may have diversified and adapted for existence in a variety of habitats. Some fossil merycoidodonts have been found with long tails and clawed digits similar to those of tree-climbing animals; others have the hippopotamus-like high eyes and nostrils, characteristics suited to life in semi-aquatic environments.

NAME *Merycoidodon*

TIME Early to Late Oligocene

LOCALITY North America (South Dakota)

SIZE 4 ft 6 in / 1.4 m long

Merycoidodon, which was a typical member of its family, probably looked something like a pig or peccary, but with a longer body and shorter legs.

Paleontologists believe that *Merycoidodon* probably would not have been able to run particularly well because there was no fusion of its limb bones. Also, the lower section of the animal's limbs were about the same length as the upper part, and the feet each had four toes.

The head, too, was pig-like, but with a full complement of 44 teeth. A significant feature of the dentition is that the lower canines had taken on the appearance of incisors – a characteristic which would continue to appear in the later camels and deer.

Another curious feature in *Merycoidodon* was a pit in the skull just in front of the eye which may have contained some kind of a gland. In fact modern deer have a gland here which they use to mark out their territories with scent. One theory to explain the pit is that *Merycoidodon* may have been a similarly territorial animal.

Vast numbers of fossils of *Merycoidodon* have been preserved in the Oligocene beds of the Badlands of South Dakota. The presence and numbers of the fossils imply that *Merycoidodon* probably roamed the woodlands and grasslands of the area in large herds.

NAME *Brachycrus*

TIME Early and Middle Miocene

LOCALITY North America (Great Plains)

SIZE 3 ft 3 in / 1 m long

Brachycrus was a merycoidodont that appeared quite late in North America. Although in some respects it was similar to its relative *Merycoidodon,* it was somewhat smaller and considerably more specialized.

The animal's skull and jaw were short – indeed, practically ape-like – and the eye sockets faced forward. The nostrils were placed far back on the top of the skull, a feature which suggests that the animal had a short tapir-like trunk. *Brachycrus* may have used this trunk in sniffing out and manipulating food in the undergrowth.

NAME *Promerycochoerus*

TIME Early Miocene

LOCALITY North America (Oregon)

SIZE 3 ft 3 in / 1 m long

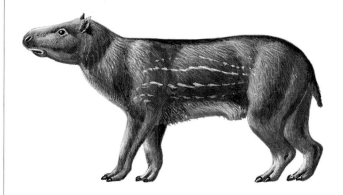

There are indications that some of the merycoidodonts were amphibious, pursuing a hippopotamus-like existence in the swamps and rivers of the time. *Promerycochoerus* may have been just such a semi-aquatic form since its body was particularly long and the limbs short and stumpy – features which often crop up in amphibious animals. There were two principal species: *P. superbus*, which had a long tapir-like face, and *P. carrikeri*, with a short, almost pig-like face.

OREODONTS AND EARLY HORNED BROWSERS CONTINUED

Family Protoceratidae

Protoceratids – the name means 'first horns' – were a family made up of about 10 genera of early animals that resembled modern deer but were actually more closely related to the camels. The Protoceratids inhabited the warmer, southern forests of North America for about 35 million years, from the Late Eocene to Early Pliocene times.

The most extraordinary features of these animals are their 'horns' (which are in fact, bony outgrowths rather than true horns), which were well-developed in males, but either reduced or absent in females.

Some species simply manifested a variety of bumps and knobs on the skull (ossicones), but others had developed complex forked structures (antlers). The relative lack of development among the female animals implies that such horns were probably organs used primarily for sexual display rather than as weapons, although later protoceratids doubtless 'sparred' with their rivals when competing for territory and/or mates.

The evolution of skull outgrowths in artiodactyls, whether horns, antlers or ossicones, relate to changes in body size, social behaviour patterns and territorial structures.

Early ruminants were small, feeding on soft vegetation for which they had to range widely. They used their enlarged canine teeth for defence when necessary.

The ruminants moved out of the forests into the new scrublands that were developing, and adapted to feeding on the tougher vegetation that grew there. With this change, the amount of territory that the animal required to obtain sufficient food for its existence diminished in area.

As territorial boundaries shrank, so the importance of defending them increased. This evolutionary pressure meant that the difference between the sexes became more pronounced. The larger, heavily-armoured males bearing antlers or horns defended a harem of females with many offspring, fighting off any challenges from outside. Protoceratids exhibit the beginning of these changes.

In some classifications, the ruminants are recognized as a distinct group and are given the same taxonomic ranking as the tylopods.

NAME	*Protoceras*
TIME	Late Oligocene to Early Miocene
LOCALITY	North America (South Dakota)
SIZE	3 ft 3 in / 1 m long

This graceful little deer-like animal inhabited the upland woodlands of western North America. It was an early member of the family and was still quite primitive in having four toes on the forefeet and the hind feet.

The most remarkable and least deer-like feature of *Protoceras*, and indeed all the protoceratids, was the arrangement of horns on the face. Unlike the ornamentation of deer, these were not antlers and were not shed annually. Nor could they be rightly termed 'horns', since they were not covered in horn. They were actually bony outgrowths that were probably covered with skin, like the ossicones of giraffes.

Protoceras had three pairs of knobs – one just behind the nostrils, one above the eyes, and one at the top of the skull. This arrangement was only present in the males. The females possessed only the top pair, and these were somewhat smaller than in the male. This arrangement of horns was evidently some kind of display structure for use in mating or for warning away rivals. These knobs would have probably been more effective seen from the side, rather than front on.

The earliest protoceratids retained the upper incisor teeth at the front of the jaw. However, by the time *Protoceras* had evolved, these teeth had been lost so that the lower cropping teeth worked against a bony pad in the upper jaw, just as in modern deer and cattle, to grind up the tough vegetation which made up its diet.

NAME *Syndyoceras*

TIME Early Miocene

LOCALITY North America (Nebraska)

SIZE 5 ft/1.5 m long

Syndyoceras was more deer-like than its predecessor *Protoceras* in that the elegant running legs now had only two toes, each with a narrow pointed hoof.

The shape of the nasal bones suggests that the animal may have had an inflated muzzle similar to that of a saiga antelope. As in the other advanced protoceratids there were no incisor teeth in the upper jaw.

There was, however, a pair of canine tusks and these may well have been used for grubbing about on the ground in the search for food.

The head had a pair of horns at the snout and another long pair above the eyes. The snout horns were united at the base but grew forward, diverging and curling up and back. The rear pair of horns curved upward like those of cattle. These would not have been true horns and were probably covered in skin.

Whereas the horn arrangement of *Protoceras* would have been seen to best advantage from the side, that of *Syndyoceras* and the other advanced protoceratids would have been more spectacular when seen from the front. This suggests that the growths were used for sparring as well as for display.

NAME *Synthetoceras*

TIME Late Miocene to Early Pliocene

LOCALITY North America (Texas)

SIZE 6 ft 6 in/2 m long

Synthetoceras was the latest and the largest of the family. Its long, shallow skull supported a pair of curving brow horns, similar to those of *Syndyoceras*. The horn at the animal's snout was long and Y-shaped. This flamboyant arrangement was only present in the males and was most probably used for sparring to protect mates and territory and for sexual display.

Synthetoceras browsed and grazed in herds.

Family Tragulidae

This family seems to link the suborder Tylopoda with the pecorans – the cud-chewing (ruminant) family that also contains the deer, the giraffes and the cattle (see pp.278–281). These animals possess four stomach chambers which allows the fermentation of vegetation, but it is not known whether the fossil forms possessed such a structure. Accordingly, there is much debate among paleontologists as to the true classification.

Always a rare group, the Tragulidae family consists of small, deer-like animals, which are hornless, but have strong upper canine tusks. Only two species survive today: *Hyemoschus*, the African water chevrotain which creeps though the undergrowth of the jungles of Central and West Africa, and *Tragulus* (spotted, lesser and larger mouse deer) the chevrotain which is found in tropical forests and mangrove swamps in south and east Asia.

Members of the family tend to be small and secretive and all of the living species are active only at night.

NAME *Blastomeryx*

TIME Early Miocene to Late Pliocene

LOCALITY North America (Nebraska)

SIZE 2 ft 6 in/75 cm long

This deer-like creature, which was not much bigger than a large rabbit, probably looked like and lived in a similar way to, the modern chevrotains. They were scampering, browsing forest animals, which were probably secretive in their habits. Their canine teeth had evolved into long sharp sabre-like tusks, useful for rooting up food or for self-defence.

Blastomeryx possessed no horns, as is characteristic of the whole family. However, a late species from the end of the Miocene did have bony bumps on top of the skull, suggesting that horns may have been evolving; they also showed a reduction in the size of the tusks. This development is consistent with the modern 'rule' that deer with tusks have no horns, and vice versa.

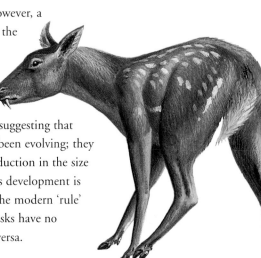

CAMELS

FAMILY CAMELIDAE

The modern camelids are found only where conditions are harsh. The camels are famed as 'ships of the desert' capable of covering immense distances across difficult terrain in the most inhospitable of climates. Thanks to their extraordinary physiology, they can live for up to two months on rough grazing alone, without additional water, and can endure great changes of temperature. The South American camelids – the llamas and their relatives – are also found in challenging habitats, including that of the high Andes.

Modern camels have evolved a whole array of adaptations for coping with hot, dry environments. Most other animals, including humans, lose water steadily in hot, dry weather by sweating, panting and breathing. As a result, their blood thickens, until eventually it circulates too slowly to remove heat from the body via the skin, and the animal suffers a sudden and dramatic rise in temperature which soon kills it. Camels avoid this danger by having unique blood that does not thicken. They also economize on water loss in a variety of ways.

Their thick coats protect them against becoming overheated and restricts water loss through evaporation from the skin. Their body temperature can fluctuate according to the outside temperature, so minimizing water loss through sweating. Camels also excrete very concentrated urine and dry faeces, which contain very little water, and they store fat in their distinctive humps, drawing on this food reserve in times of scarcity. As they process it, the fat releases extra water. Finally, camels are able to drink remarkably quickly; they can take in as much as 25 gallons/115 litres of water at a single session.

It is easy to think of camelids as specialized animals that can exist only in extreme environments, but modern camels are the remnants of a formerly widespread and diverse group. They first evolved in the Late Eocene, about 40 million years ago, not in Asia or Africa but in North America, and reached their peak in the Late Miocene, some 10 million years ago. It was not until the Pliocene, about 5 million years ago, that camels migrated into Eurasia and Africa, and llamas reached South America.

By the Pleistocene Ice Age, around 2 million years ago, the camelids ranged all over North America from Florida to Alaska. They had spread southward to South America across the Panama land bridge and eastward into Asia across the Bering land bridge.

Like some other animal groups that evolved chiefly in North America, such as the horses (see pp.254–257), the camelids survive today only on other continents – they became extinct in North America toward the end of Pleistocene times, about 12,000 years ago.

There are two living species of camel, the two-humped Bactrian camel and the one-humped Arabian camel or dromedary. Wild camels still inhabit the Gobi Desert, but the camels of Africa were introduced there by humans as recently as 2,500 years ago. Camels that are now feral in Australia were brought there just over 100 years ago. In South America the llama, alpaca, vicuna and guanaco are the only representatives of the second remaining group.

Camelids have no horns or tusks, and their jaws have a reduced number of upper incisors. The lower incisors are flattened and project forward horizontally. They have elongated facial bones, so there are wide spaces between the front teeth that are left, and a wide gap – the diastema – between the front and cheek teeth. The cheek teeth are formidably large and hypsodont – that is, they have short roots but high crowns, as in horses. Such spiky front teeth enable the camelids to rip and tear at tough vegetation, while their cheek teeth are well-suited to 'chewing the cud'.

Like many other artiodactyls, the camelids ruminate – a process which involves chewing the partly digested food (the 'cud') before swallowing it so that it undergoes a second digestion. The stomachs of camels are three-chambered, unlike those of more advanced ruminants, such as deer or sheep, which have four-chambered stomachs. The differences in the structure of their digestive systems suggest that they may have evolved the ruminant way of life independently from the other ruminants (convergent evolution). Another consequence of these differences is that the camelids are classified with the tylopods rather than the ruminants.

The camelids seem to have reduced the number of their toes much earlier than did most ungulate groups. Among the earliest camelids, the forelimbs had four toes, all of which touched the ground, but the second and fifth toes of the hind limbs were already vestigial (extremely reduced and insignificant). Indeed, the Late Miocene *Procamelus* already had legs that were probably almost identical to those of a modern member of the family. The shanks were long and thin, there were two spreading toes on each foot, and the two metapodials had become elongated and fused at the top like an upside-down 'Y' to form the cannon bone.

The later camelids thus walked in a characteristic way. Whereas other artiodactyls are unguligrade, walking on the tips of their hoofed digits, the later camelids are digitigrade: they have dropped down to walk on the entire underside of the splayed digits, and there is a tough pad beneath. Such developments have allowed modern camels to travel with ease across soft sand.

NAME *Protylopus*

TIME Late Eocene

LOCALITY North America (Utah and Colorado)

SIZE 20 in/80 cm long

As in most groups of ungulates, the first camelids were small, rabbit-sized animals. The simple, low-crowned teeth were arranged along the jaw without any breaks – a primitive feature and one that indicates that the animal's diet was the soft leaves of the forest vegetation.

The forelimbs, which were shorter than the hind limbs, had four toes, all of which touched the ground. The hind limbs also had four toes, but only the third and fourth were used to carry the animal's weight – the second and fifth toes were present as vestigial 'dewclaws'. The functional toes were pointed, which indicates that the early camels had narrow hooves rather than broad pads.

It is unlikely the *Protylopus* was a direct ancestor of later camels, but it probably closely resembled, and was contemporary with, the earliest camels.

NAME *Poebrotherium*

TIME Oligocene

LOCALITY North America (South Dakota)

SIZE 3 ft/90 cm long

By Oligocene times, around 35 million years ago, the dense forests that once covered Dakota had given way to more open woodlands. Camelids became plentiful and began to look more like modern camels. At about the size of a sheep, *Poebrotherium* was larger than *Protylopus*. Its head, with a distinctive narrow snout, was a smaller version of a llama's, and it may have had the llama's prominent ears as well.

Poebrotherium still had slightly longer hind legs than forelegs, and hoofed toes, yet its legs were clearly adapted for greater speed. These were relatively longer and more slender than those of *Protylopus*, they had lost their lateral toes, and the two central weight-bearing digits were beginning to diverge. *Poebrotherium*'s teeth, too, show an advance on *Protylopus*. Dentition is still complete but spaces were beginning to appear between the teeth. It seems likely that a number of different camelid lines radiated from *Poebrotherium*.

NAME *Procamelus*

TIME Late Miocene to Early Pliocene

LOCALITY North America (Colorado)

SIZE 5 ft/1.5 m long

Procamelus was either on the direct ancestral line to modern camels, or very close to it. It was much larger than any of the earlier camels, approaching the size of a modern llama. The head was very long but the braincase was quite small.

Procamelus still had incisors in the upper jaw, but only a single pair – and even these were reduced in size. Set in such a long jaw, the front teeth (one pair each of incisors and canines, and the first pair of premolars) had long gaps between them – a dentition that is adapted for tearing at vegetation. Crowns on the cheek teeth had grown to such an extent that they were now hypsodont, like those of a horse, and well-adapted for dealing with tough vegetation.

With *Procamelus*, the structure of the leg had almost reached that of the modern camel. The metapodials had partially fused and elongated to form a cannon bone, the shanks were long and thin, and there were two spreading toes. This splaying-out of the toes suggests that *Procamelus* may already have evolved a foot pad to spread the load when walking over soft terrain.

CAMELS CONTINUED

NAME *Titanotylopus*

TIME Pliocene to Pleistocene

LOCALITY North America (Nebraska)

SIZE 11 ft 6 in/3.5 m high at the shoulder

During Pliocene times, between 5 million and 2 million years ago, a number of very large camels evolved in North America. These huge camels were certainly closely related to *Procamelus* and may even have been derived from it.

Among them was *Titanotylopus*, which must have been taller than the elephants of the time (see pp.238–239, 243–244). However, in many other respects, this enormous creature was very similar to modern camels, with a narrow snout lacking upper incisors, a long neck and splayed two-toed feet.

Despite its similarities with its modern relation, however, one distinctive feature of modern camels was almost certainly not present in *Titanotylopus* – their fatty hump. The hump in modern camels is an adaptation which has evolved in order to

cope with the scarce supplies of food and water in the particularly hard environments inhabited by today's camels. Certainly the climate was cooling and becoming more dry throughout the Tertiary period in North America – climatic changes which caused forests to give way to scattered woodland and then to grasslands – but environmental conditions were still equable enough to relatively easily support a large number of different mammals. At this time, there was as yet no need for the development of such extreme food-storage devices as fatty humps and the camels' other moisture retentive physical adaptations.

NAME *Oxydactylus*

TIME Early Miocene

LOCALITY North America (South Dakota and Nebraska)

SIZE 7 ft 6 in/2.3 m long

Another offshoot from *Poebrotherium* was the line of giraffe-like camels with very long legs and necks – adaptations to browsing on high vegetation. The early Miocene landscape of central North America – grasslands with open scrub – must have been ideal for the evolution of such an animal. The toes were very narrow and bore slender antelope-like hooves, not the broad pads of the modern camels.

NAME *Camelops*

TIME Pleistocene

LOCALITY North America (California and Utah)

SIZE 6 ft 6 in / 2 m high at the shoulder

Camelops, which was another giant of the late Cenozoic Era and a contemporary of early humans, appears to have been the last camel to have survived on the North American continent.

It probably looked very much like the modern Asian camel, but certain parts of its anatomy indicate that it was more closely related to the South American llamas.

NAME *Stenomylus*

TIME Early Miocene

LOCALITY North America (Nebraska)

SIZE 3 ft / 90 cm long

A number of side-branches of the camel family evolved in the Miocene, but became extinct soon afterward. *Stenomylus* and its relatives were small gazelle-like animals. They must have lived

very much as African gazelles do today, browsing in herds on low vegetation and sprinting rapidly away from danger. The teeth of the lower jaw were unique in that the canines and the first premolars had taken the form of incisors, so the animal appeared to have 10 lower incisors. The neck was long and lightly-built, and the legs were slender. The two toes on each foot had small, deer-like hooves.

NAME *Aepycamelus*

TIME Middle and Late Miocene

LOCALITY North America (Colorado)

SIZE 10 ft / 3 m high at the head

The giraffe-like camel line reached its climax in *Aepycamelus*, formerly known as *Alticamelus* because of its extraordinary height. The legs were long and stilt-like, and the two toes had very small hooves. *Aepycamelus*, then, had lost the running hooves of its ancestors and put in their place the broad pads of modern camels.

The modern camel moves both legs on one side of the body in the same direction at the same time. This method of walking is known as pacing, and is confined to camels and giraffes. Pacing is a very efficient method of travelling great distances across open terrain. An extremely long-legged animal such as *Aepycamelus* must have moved with a similar gait. Indeed there is some direct evidence for this in camel-like footprints that have been discovered in Miocene deposits.

GIRAFFES, DEER AND CATTLE

FAMILY GIRAFFIDAE

Giraffes, like all other artiodactyls except the pigs and hippopotamuses (see pp.268–269) are cud-chewers, or ruminants. There are no incisor teeth at the top of the jaw, instead the lower incisors work against a bony pad at the front of the mouth. Having ripped off foliage from bushes and trees, the animal chews and then swallows it for the first time. The food then passes into the rumen, the first chamber of a complex, four-chambered stomach, where it is fermented by microorganisms. Once the food is partially digested, it is returned to the mouth and chewed again before its second journey back down the entire alimentary tract.

This method of digestion is very efficient at breaking down fibrous plant food, but the ruminant pays a price for this efficiency in that food takes a long time to pass through its gut, and it must spend a considerable proportion of each day chewing the cud.

There are two modern giraffes, both living in Africa, south of the Sahara. The more familiar is the tall, long-necked, long-legged giraffe *Giraffa* of the African savannah, which feeds from the tops of thorn trees. The other is the smaller, darker okapi, at home in the gloom of the African tropical forest.

With the exception of the camels, the ruminants typically have paired head ornaments. In the case of the giraffes these take the form of horn-like growths, called ossicones, which are covered in skin.

Both the giraffe and the okapi are two-toed browsers, the family having evolved before the grazing ungulates developed. The fossil record reveals a number of different forms, most of which were quite unlike the two surviving modern representatives of the family.

NAME	*Prolibytherium*
TIME	Early Miocene
LOCALITY	North Africa (Libya)
SIZE	6 ft/1.8 m long

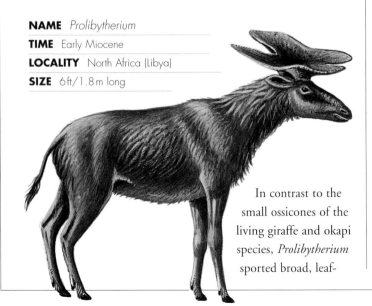

In contrast to the small ossicones of the living giraffe and okapi species, *Prolibytherium* sported broad, leaf-shaped ossicones that reached a span of about 14 in/35 cm.

Prolibytherium probably used the projections for display and in sparring contests between rivals, and it is possible that their covering of skin was shed annually. Apart from its flamboyant head ornamentation, *Prolibytherium* probably resembled the modern okapi.

NAME	*Sivatherium*
TIME	Pliocene to Late Pleistocene
LOCALITY	India (sub-Himalayas) and North Africa (Libya)
SIZE	7 ft/2.2 m high at the shoulder

Named in honour of Siva, or the Lord of the Beasts, who is one of the principal Hindu Gods, this massive animal would have appeared more like a moose than a giraffe.

The male of the species, at least, was ornamented with a pair of huge branched ossicones on the top of its skull, and a smaller pair of conical ones about the eyes – probably partly for display and defence. The body was quite stout, especially in the region of the shoulders, where strong muscles would have been needed to carry the animal's huge, heavy head.

Libytherium, which was a close relative of *Sivatherium*, lived in North Africa at the same time. Prehistoric human rock paintings that have been discovered in the Sahara Desert depict an animal that looks very much like *Libytherium*, so it is possible that sivatheres coexisted with early humans until as recently as about 8000 years ago.

Family Cervidae

Although the cervids, or true deer, were quite late to evolve they have become the principal browsing animals of the Northern Hemisphere and South America. Their diet includes leaves, grass, twigs, bark and moss.

A characteristic feature of all living cervids is the presence of antlers in the males (and in females of the reindeer *Rangifer*) of virtually all species. The exceptions are the hornless musk deer *Moschus* and Chinese water deer *Hydropotes*. Antlers are branched bony outgrowths of the head which are used chiefly in display or for ritual sparring. They differ from the ornaments of the other ruminants in that they are shed and regrown each year. There is a swollen 'burr' at the point at which they are shed. Each year the antler develops with another branch until the maximum for the species is reached.

NAME *Eucladoceros*
TIME Pliocene to Pleistocene
LOCALITY Europe (Italy)
SIZE 8 ft/2.5 m long

Some deer evolved huge, flamboyant antlers. One of the most spectacular examples was *Eucladoceros*, whose antlers, each with a dozen points, or tines, had a total span of 5 ft 6in/1.7m. Such a spread must have been something of a hindrance among the low branches of its forest home. As with *Megaloceros*, which had even bigger antlers, sexual selection probably sustained the development: the male that sported the most impressive antlers, and could spar most successfully in competitions for females during the breeding season, would have left the most offspring to continue his line.

NAME *Megaloceros*
TIME Late Pleistocene
LOCALITY Widespread in Europe and Asia
SIZE 8 ft/2.5 m long

Megaloceros is often called the giant Irish elk, but the name is doubly misleading. It is not an elk (or moose) but is more akin to the fallow deer. Also, *Megaloceros* was by no means confined to Ireland. Although many specimens have been unearthed in Ireland, with more than 80 found in a single bog near Dublin, *Megaloceros* ranged over the whole of the northern parts of the Old World, from the British Isles to Siberia and China.

The largest deer that ever lived, *Megaloceros* is chiefly known for its antlers. They were truly monumental, reaching a span of 12 ft/3.7 m and weighing over 100 lb/220 kg – about a seventh of the weight of the entire animal. Even more remarkable, perhaps, is that these horns were probably shed and regrown annually, as in all true deer. A male *Megaloceros* must have expended a great deal of energy growing such structures.

The *Megaloceros* herds reached their peak during the last interval between the cold spells of the Pleistocene Ice Age, and began to decline about 12,000 years ago. They died out in Ireland about 11,000 years ago, but may not have become extinct in Central Europe until

Evidence that early humans knew and hunted *Megaloceros* is provided by cave paintings depicting animals very like *Megaloceros* in Europe. One French cave painting shows the great deer with a small triangular hump on its back, like that of modern zebu cattle. This may have been a fatty structure, like a camel's hump, which was used as a food store during the harshest periods of the Ice Age winter.

Dwarf species of *Megaloceros* are also known, from Malta and the Channel Islands.

GIRAFFES, DEER AND CATTLE CONTINUED

Family Antilocapridae

The pronghorn *Antilocapra* of North America is the only surviving genus of this family, but Miocene and Pliocene times saw the evolution of a large number of different types of antilocaprids. The other ungulates that evolved in North America – the camels and the horses – spread across to Asia and to South America and became extinct in their homeland.

The antilocaprids, on the other hand, remained in North America and spread nowhere else, although they were a very successful and varied group during the Pliocene and Pleistocene.

Antilocaprid head ornamentation consisted of a horny sheath, usually branched, around an unbranched bony core. The sheath was shed annually but the core was retained.

Most species had a single pair of horns, but others had as many as five or six, and some were bizarre in shape. In the living pronghorn, males have longer horns, with forward-pointing prongs below backward, pointing hooked tips – hence the animal's common name.

Although most of the even-toed ungulates have only two functional toes, the others being greatly reduced and not touching the ground, it is only in the pronghorns that all vestiges of the other toes have finally disappeared, with not even bony splints remaining. Their evolution of long, pointed hooves at the end of long, slender legs has enabled the family to be fast runners, (sometimes managing to reach speeds of up to 55 mph/86 kmph when escaping from predators).

Their hooves have also developed cushioning which acts as a shock absorber, protecting the animal's legs against the impact of leaping up to 26 ft/8 m in a single stride.

NAME *Ilingoceros*
TIME Late Miocene
LOCALITY North America (Nevada)
SIZE 6 ft/1.8 m long

The various antilocaprids differ from one another in the shape and arrangement of the horns. *Ilingoceros*, which was slightly larger than the living pronghorn, had a pair of spirally-twisted horns which grew straight up and ended in a slight fork.

Other forms include *Osbornoceros*, with smooth, slightly curved horns; *Paracosoryx*, with flattened horns widening to a forked tip; *Ramoceros*, with extraordinary vertical fan-shaped horns; and the particularly well-endowed *Hayoceros*.

NAME *Hayoceros*
TIME Middle Pleistocene
LOCALITY Nebraska
SIZE 6 ft/1.8 m long

Hayoceros, which inhabited the grasslands of Nebraska in the Middle Pleistocene, was a particularly lavishly ornamented member of the Antilocapridae family. It had no fewer than four horns: one pair of broad, forked horns over its eyes, as in the pronghorn, and another much longer, narrower pair farther back at the top of its skull.

When two males were competing for mating partners, they probably adopted a sparring technique similar to that which is used by the living pronghorns. The competing males lock their forked horns and push until the weaker of the combatants withdraws. These ritualistic bouts, though they often appear to be quite violent, rarely seem to result in any permanent injury to either animal.

Family Bovidae

These are the true antelopes and the cattle. The head ornamentation of both males and females consists of bony horn cores covered with true horn that is not shed annually.

The bovids had evolved in the Old World by Miocene times around 20 million years ago but the older Mongolian genus *Hanhaicerus* from Oligocene deposits may also be a bovid. The earliest fossils, of gazelle-like bovids, have been found in France, the Sahara and Mongolia. By the Late Miocene, about 10 million years ago, there was a huge increase in bovid variety, with 70 new genera appearing. By the Pleistocene, there were more than 100 genera, about twice as many as exist today.

Bovids are grazing animals, with high-crowned teeth adapted for chewing grass. Their lifestyle contrasts with most other even-toed ungulates, which eat soft leaves. They spend a great deal of time feeding and their digestive system is adapted to extract the maximum nutrition from the grass on which they feed.

They were restricted to the Old World until as recently as the Mid Pleistocene, about 1 million years ago, when they migrated across the Bering land bridge that existed at the time to reach North America. There they survive today as bison, bighorn sheep and mountain goats. The vast majority of bovids, however, still live in the Old World, occupying a great range of habitats from forests and grasslands to swamps and even deserts.

NAME *Pelorovis*

TIME Middle to Late Pleistocene

LOCALITY East Africa

SIZE 10 ft / 3 m long

This massive animal was a close relative of the modern African buffalo. The main difference between *Pelorovis* and its modern counterpart, apart from its sheer size, was the enormous set of horns that the creature carried on its head. Since the bony cores of the horns alone had a span of 6 ft 6 in / 2 m, in life the horns

might have reached up to twice that size. (This has to be an estimate since horn itself decays rapidly after death and leaves behind no fossilized remains.)

Pelorovis survived in East Africa until as recently as about 12,000 years ago.

NAME *Bos*

TIME Pleistocene to Recent

LOCALITY Europe (Britain, Poland), Asia (India) and North Africa

SIZE 10 ft / 3 m long

This is the genus to which modern domestic cattle belong. It may have evolved from a rather slim and antelope-like ox, *Leptobos*, found in early Pleistocene deposits in Eurasia. The ancestor of most of today's cattle was *Bos primigenius*, better known as the aurochs. It was larger than most of today's breeds and was first domesticated about 6000 years ago, although it was known to humans much earlier. Cave paintings at Lascaux, in central France, include dramatic and beautiful representations of these great cattle.

The aurochs spread during Pleistocene times from its centre of origin in Asia. By the end of the last Ice Age it occupied a vast range in the Old World, from westernmost Europe to easternmost Asia, and from the Arctic tundras to North Africa and India. Despite their success, however, the aurochs eventually disappeared, succumbing to human hunting pressure. They became extinct in Britain by the 10th century AD, and the last surviving aurochsen died in Poland in 1627.

There are a number of surviving native species of *Bos* elsewhere such as the wild yak (*Bos grunniens*) of nothern India, Tibet and China.

RODENTS, RABBITS AND HARES

Traditionally, the rodents (guinea-pigs, rats and mice) have been thought by taxonomists to be closely associated with the lagomorphs (rabbits, hares, and pikas). Recent molecular analysis, however, has rejected this association, instead indicating a surprising relationship for the lagomorphs with the primates and tree-shrews (Scandentia).

As a result of this reassessment of their relationships with other orders the rodents, whose uniqueness as a group had been questioned, are now restored as a natural group, but separated from the lagomorphs. It is now generally believed by paleontologists that the rodents are a relatively early and primitive group in the evolution of the mammals, and that the lagomorphs branched off before the radiation of the primates, artiodactyls and Carnivora.

ORDER RODENTIA

The earliest-known rodents resembled small squirrels. They appeared in North America during the Late Paleocene, about 60 million years ago. Soon after their first appearance, the rodents diversified, adapting to take over the ecological niches abandoned by the similar-looking, although unrelated, multituberculates (see p.199), which were disappearing. The rodents have evolved into several major types, including squirrels, beavers, rats, mice, gophers, chinchillas, guinea pigs and porcupines.

The rodents are by far the largest order of mammals today, with about 2,000 species in 35 families, making up 40 percent of all known living mammals. There are almost as many fossil genera again, and another 12 families.

Rodents are a highly successful group. They have spread over every continent, except Antarctica, and conquered a huge range of habitats, making them ecologically very important. Rodents can be found everywhere from tropical forests to freezing Arctic tundras, and from the hottest, driest deserts to the mountain tops. Rodents frequently live in close association with humans.

Although they have not managed to invade the seas, there are some freshwater rodents, such as beavers and water-rats. There are many tree-dwellers, too, notably the tree squirrels. Most rodents are, however, primarily terrestrial.

Given their versatility and impressively rapid rate of reproduction, it is not surprising that rodents have had a major impact on human history. They consume millions of tons of food every year – both crops and stored food – and carry fatal diseases such as typhus. The most notorious pests are the rats, which are believed to have accounted for more human deaths than all the wars in history. In the Middle Ages, plague borne by

the black rat *Rattus rattus* killed around 25 million people – over a quarter of Europe's entire population.

The fossil record of the rodents is sparse, and much of what is known about their evolution is the result of studying tiny fossil teeth. Rodents were abundant throughout Tertiary times, and remains of their distinctive teeth can be used for dating and correlating continental sediments, just as the fossils of invertebrate shells are frequently used for dating and correlating marine sediments.

The chief distinguishing feature of rodents is their ability to gnaw using specially adapted front teeth. There is a single pair of large, curved incisors on the upper and lower jaws. These incisors are worn down with use but grow continuously from roots deep within the skull and mandible. Early members of the group had cylindrical gnawing teeth with enamel all round, but later forms had more triangular teeth with enamel confined to the front face. This keeps the edge sharp since the area behind wears down faster.

There are no canines, and even some of the premolars may be missing, so there is a large gap (diastema) between front and cheek teeth. The remaining cheek teeth form a battery of efficient grinding surfaces.

Rodents are generally small, the harvest mice being among the smallest of all mammals at 1½oz/40g. There are exceptions, however. The largest living rodent is the 110lb/50kg capybara which inhabits South America, but some extinct forms reached the size of a rhinoceros.

An interesting case study of gigantism among the rodents is provided by the giant Pleistocene dormouse *Leithia*, an inhabitant of several Mediterranean islands, including Malta and Sardinia. Except for its much greater size (10in/25cm long without tail), *Leithia* was indistinguishable from the modern dormouse *Muscardinus*.

Having been marooned on the islands when sea levels rose (possibly the result of the influx of the Atlantic into the Mediterranean basin or changing world temperatures during the Pleistocene Ice Age), the inhabitants of Mediterranean islands showed some unusual trends in body size. But whereas elephants (see pp.238–239, 243–244) and hippopotamuses (see p.268) became smaller, to make better use of the limited amount of food that was available, rodents such as *Leithia* became larger. In the absence of potential predators, the rodents had no reason to run and hide in cracks and crannies, as their smaller counterparts had to on the mainland.

The present classification divides the rodents into two suborders, differentiated by the arrangement of the bones and associated muscles of the lower jaw.

Suborder Sciurognathi

The sciurognaths (a name which means 'squirrel-jaws') have a deep lower jaw on which the chewing (masseter) muscles are attached. This is by far the larger of the two suborders of rodents, and possibly the more primitive. The suborder includes the present-day families of squirrels, beavers, pocket gophers, hamsters, rats and mice.

The sciurognath families seem to have diverged early in the evolutionary history of the rodents. Apart from their jaw and tooth structure, they have little else in common. Most are wholly vegetarian, but some are scavenging omnivores, and a few members of the Sciurognathi suborder eat insects.

A quarter of all mammal species today are rats, mice, and voles. Yet this immensely successful group only became ubiquitous at the beginning of the Pliocene, about 5 million years ago.

NAME *Ischyromys*

TIME Early Eocene

RANGE North America

SIZE 2 ft/60 cm long

Ischyromys is among the earliest known of the true rodents. Mouse-like in appearance, this creature had many of the typical rodent head features, including the characteristic pair of upper incisors. The rest of the body was that of a typical rodent as well, with versatile forelimbs, strong hind limbs and five clawed toes on each of its feet.

While many of the other early Tertiary mammals were occupying the terrestrial niches, all the evidence suggests that *Ischyromys* and its more squirrel-like relative *Paramys* were taking advantage of the possibilities presented by trees.

As the most advanced climbing animals of their time, they eventually displaced the primitive rodent-like primates which had existed there from Paleocene times.

NAME *Epigaulus*

TIME Miocene

RANGE North America (Great Basin)

SIZE 1 ft/30 cm long

Epigaulus is one of the oddest rodents known. It must have resembled a modern marmot, except that it possessed a pair of stout horns on the skull, small eyes and its clawed hands were broad and paddle-like. The powerful claws were long and compressed from side to side. Clearly they were well-adapted for digging and so it seems likely that *Epigaulus* lived underground in burrows. The small eyes support this interpretation because many modern burrowing animals, such as the mole, have reduced eyes and limited eyesight.

No other known rodent had horns like these, placed on the snout just in front of the eyes and their function is something of a mystery. They may have been used for protection, sexual display and combat between males. This interpretation is supported by the fact that not all fossils have horns; implying that those without were probably females. An alternative interpretation is that the horns may have assisted burrowing in some way.

Epigaulus and its closest relatives, the other primitive mylagaulids, died out when forests disappeared and were replaced by grassland in North America in Late Miocene times, about 5 million years ago.

RODENTS, RABBITS AND HARES CONTINUED

NAME *Steneofiber*

TIME Early Miocene

RANGE Europe (France, Germany)

SIZE 1 ft/30 cm long

Beavers are well-represented in the fossil record from as far back as the Early Oligocene, around 35 million years ago. The early Miocene beaver *Steneofiber* was small, and lived on and near freshwater lakes, much as most living beavers do today. It is unlikely, however, that it could have felled large trees, as its modern counterparts do.

Many early species were more terrestrial, however, and some even burrowed. The Miocene deposits of Nebraska show strange vertical corkscrew-shaped burrows, 8 ft/2.5 m deep, which have been given the name 'Daimonelix' or 'Devil's corkscrews'. These were excavated by the gopher-like beaver *Palaeocastor*, a close relative of *Steneofiber*.

Many beavers were giants, including the bear-sized *Castoroides* (7 ft 6 in/2.3 m long), found throughout North America during Pleistocene times.

Suborder Hystricognathi

This is thought to be the more advanced suborder of rodents, despite the fact that the earliest known rodent probably belongs to this group.

The hystricognaths or 'porcupine-jaws' have their chewing (masseter) muscles anchored on a bony flange which has developed from the lower jaw.

Although hystricognaths include some Old World species – for example porcupines, and the gundis and cane rats – most members of the suborder are natives of South America. No rodents have been found in South America prior to the Early Oligocene, when they occur in the far south of Patagonia.

South American hystricognaths include New World porcupines, cavies or guinea pigs, capybaras, pacaranas, chinchillas, agoutis and coypus.

NAME *Telicomys*

TIME Late Miocene to early Pliocene

RANGE South America

SIZE 7 ft/2 m long

Closely related to the guinea pigs and capybaras were the stout-tailed burrowing dinomyids ('terrible mice'), the pacarana family. The largest of these – indeed, probably the largest rodent which has ever lived – was *Telicomys*.

Teliocomys reached the size of a small rhinoceros, and would probably have looked rather like a hairy hippopotamus, or a giant capybara.

NAME *Birbalomys*
TIME Early Eocene
RANGE Asia (Pakistan)
SIZE 1 ft/30 cm long

Birbalomys is considered by some paleontologists to be the most primitive rodent, one which is probably close to the ancestry of the whole rodent group.

So little is known about *Birbalomys* that the restoration given (above) is highly speculative. *Birbalomys* may have resembled the North African gundis, creatures rather like guinea pigs which today inhabit desert or semi-desert habitats.

NAME *Eocardia*
TIME Miocene
LOCALITY South America
SIZE 1 ft/30 cm long

Cavioids are the most typical South American rodents and are closely related to the guinea pigs and the capybara.

Some cavioids became quite large. *Protohydrochoerus,* for example, was about the size of a tapir. However, *Eocardia* was more modest in size, reaching only 1ft/30 cm tall and resembling the present day guinea pig in appearance.

ORDER LAGOMORPHA

The lagomorphs – the pikas, rabbits, and hares – were once classed along with the rodents. Indeed, they seem to be very much like rodents, with their relatively small size and their continually growing, gnawing teeth.

The main difference between them lies in the fact that lagomorphs have two pairs of gnawing teeth in the front of the upper jaw, rather than the single pair found in rodents. These teeth have enamel all the way around them. Lagomorphs tend to have more cheek teeth than rodents (five or six, as opposed to five or fewer), and these are usually less ridged.

The chewing action is different too: lagomorph jaws work sideways, while those of rodents work backward and forward. The evidence that the lagomorphs are related to the rodents is ambiguous: their gnawing way of life might have developed through parallel evolution.

About 12 lagomorph genera survive today, although there have been four times that number since the order evolved. The earliest fossil representatives appeared possibly in eastern Asia, in the Late Paleocene or Early Eocene. Lagomorphs swiftly became a widespread vegetarian group, chiefly exploiting grassy plans and shrubs in rocky and desert areas.

Having been deliberately introduced in the 19th century into Australasia, where there were no natural predators, the rabbits' prodigious rate of reproduction and immense appetite for leaves and grain made it a serious pest.

NAME *Palaeolagus*
TIME Oligocene
RANGE North America
SIZE 10 in/25 cm long

The earliest lagomorph is *Eurymulus,* from the Late Paleocene of Mongolia. The separation of the group into the pikas on the one hand, and the rabbits and the hares on the other, had

already taken place by the early Oligocene. The pikas became compact animals with short legs and short ears, while the rabbits and hares developed longer legs and a running, then finally a hopping, locomotion.

The skeleton of *Palaeolagus* is similar to that of a modern rabbit. However, the hind legs are a little shorter, suggesting that is was not yet the leaping animal so familiar today.

LEMURS AND MONKEYS

PRIMATES AND PRIMATOMORPHS

For over 150 years it has been recognized that humans are related to the apes. More recently, it became evident that this relationship extended to the monkeys, lemurs and tarsiers, which are the survivors of a much more diverse group of fossil primates. The fossil record of the shared ancestry of humans and the primates is extremely patchy and fragmental. Consequently there is great difficulty in establishing relationships between the numerous groups and this is reflected in an often cumbersome, constantly changing and confusing classification.

The term primates – from the Latin word *primus*, meaning 'first' – has traditionally been used to group together lemurs (Lemuridae), monkeys, apes and humans (Anthropoidea), and their closest fossil ancestors. However, the recognition of the close association of the flying lemurs (called the Dermoptera and different from the Lemuridae) to the primates has resulted in the use of a wider definition under the term primatomorph, which is similar to an older classificatory term 'prosimians'. Several extinct fossil groups, such as the primitive form *Purgatorius* from the Late Cretaceous and the Plesiadapiformes, are also placed within this broader group of primatomorphs.

Molecular analysis broadens the morphological and palaeontological association of the true living primates with the tree-shrews (*Scandentia*), flying lemurs and bats (*Chiroptera*). With the exception of the bats, the morphologically based association of the living primates, tree-shrews, flying lemurs and their fossil ancestors is recognized as a superorder – the Archonta. But the exact nature of the relationships between all these groups is as yet unresolved.

ORDER DERMOPTERA

This group is based on the living flying lemurs. They do not fly but glide, using a membrane stretched between the limbs, body and tail. Until recently they had no fossil record, but recently an Eocene fossil flying lemur has been discovered in Thailand. The expanded concept of the order includes the extinct Plesiadapiformes, a fossil group of several families that radiated in the Early Tertiary of North America and western Europe.

Family Plesiadapidae

These are the best-known of the five families of Plesiadapiformes. Examples are plentiful from the Paleocene and Eocene of North America and Europe (roughly 65 million to 40

million years ago), a fact which indicates both a land connection between the continents and a uniformity of conditions between these areas at this time. It is possible that plesiadapids spread from North America to Europe via Greenland, which was at that time a warm, wooded 'land bridge'. Their features included a long tail, agile limbs with claws rather than nails, a long snout containing rodent-like jaws and teeth, and eyes placed on the sides of the head.

NAME	*Plesiadapis*
TIME	Late Paleocene to Early Eocene
LOCALITY	North America (Rocky Mountains) and Europe (France)
SIZE	2 ft 6 in/80 cm long

So many *Plesiadapis* remains have been found near Cernay in north-eastern France that it must have been a common animal at the time.

Plesiadapis was squirrel-like in build and about the size of a modern beaver. It may have spent much of its time on the ground; however it was also well-adapted for scrambling through trees, with hands and feet that could turn toward each other to grip branches, and long fingers and toes equipped with claws.

Nevertheless, the head of *Plesiadapis* was not that of a typical primate. The teeth resembled those of a rodent, with long gnawing incisors at the front, and a gap between them and the grinding molars in the cheek.

ORDER PRIMATES

The primates consist of some 200 living species, depending on how the order is defined. Modern humans are just one of these species. All primates are united by more than 30 characters that mostly relate to particular evolutionary adaptations for climbing in trees, prolonged parental nurture of offspring and high development of vision and intelligence.

Primates seem to have developed in a predominantly forested environment. In fact, many specific adaptations can be traced to the exacting demands of tree-dwelling, and to daylight living rather than nocturnal activity. Among these were interrelated developments in the enlarged, complex brain, the senses, and the limbs and digits. There was also a tendency toward a bipedal gait: the body became more erect, the feet and legs were specialized for movement, and the hands were adapted for holding and manipulating. Balance, touch and grasp all improved, and there were two great developments in vision: the ability to see stereoscopically and in colour.

Another critical development in such a precarious environment included a reproductive strategy that placed a premium on high parental involvement and protection and a small number of offspring.

The group includes a wide range of extinct and living forms from the fossil lemur-like adapids, to the lemurs (lemurids), lorises (lorisids), which are clustered as the lemuriformes. Also, there are the tarsiers (tarsiids) and extinct omomyids, which are clustered as tarsiiformes and finally the anthropoids – the monkeys, apes and their fossil ancestors.

Family Adapidae

The lemur-like adapids were abundant in Eocene times, but then declined, becoming extinct in the Late Miocene about 10 million years ago. They were mostly European, but some lived in Asia and North America.

Adapids had several features that were a distinct advance on those of the plesiadapids. Their backs were more supple, which increased their mobility in trees, as did their longer, more flexible limbs (whose digits bore nails rather than claws) and grasping big toes and thumbs. They had shorter snouts, with eyes that had moved round closer to the front of the face. Their brains, too, were relatively large. Although it is possible that adapids could only cling and leap, it seems likely that they were advanced enough to walk and run on top of branches.

The lemur-like adapids and lemurids are sometimes grouped together as the Strepsirhini ('twisted noses') because their moist noses are divided vertically and laterally by slits.

NAME	*Notharctus*
TIME	Early to Middle Eocene
LOCALITY	North America (Wyoming)
SIZE	16 in/40 cm long

This North American adapid was the last primate known from that continent. In appearance it was probably much like a modern lemur, and it was highly adapted for living in trees. It had eyes directed forward, which gave stereoscopic vision and

enabled it to judge distances accurately, long hind legs that allowed it to jump from branch to branch, and a long heavy tail to balance it in its acrobatics.

The first digit in the hand and on the foot formed a kind of thumb, a characteristic that enabled *Notharctus* to grasp both branches and food.

Family Lemuridae

Lemurs are similar to the adapids, but they have a long 'comb' derived from the front teeth in the lower jaw, which is used for grooming.

About 50 million years ago, lemurs and their close relatives were found throughout Africa, Europe and North America. Today, the lemurs, the Indri lemurs and the aye-ayes survive only in Madagascar.

NAME	*Megaladapis*
TIME	Recent
LOCALITY	Madagascar
SIZE	5 ft/1.5 m long

The largest-known lemur, with a massive body and short limbs, *Megaladapis* must have weighed about 110 lb/50 kg. Unlike its smaller relatives, it would not have been able to swing and leap about in the trees. It was probably a slow climber, clambering about in the tropical forest in search of leaves to eat. It was possibly finally wiped out by humans.

LEMURS AND MONKEYS CONTINUED

Family Omomyidae

This is the largest family of the tarsiers, and a group that still exists today (although in greatly depleted numbers) on some Southeast Asian islands, such as Sumatra and Borneo. The omomyids were abundant in Eocene times but declined during the Oligocene and had virtually died out by the beginning of the Miocene.

Tarsiers are grouped together as the Haplorhini (the 'whole noses') because their noses are undivided.

Some paleontologists have considered that the tarsiers were the common ancestors of the monkeys and apes, though this seems unlikely given their extreme specialization.

NAME *Necrolemur*

TIME Middle to Late Eocene

LOCALITY Western Europe

SIZE 10 in/25 cm long

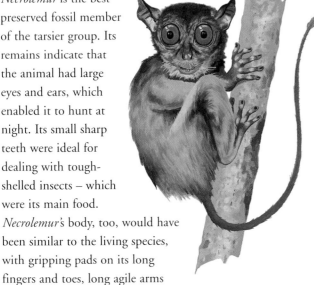

Necrolemur is the best preserved fossil member of the tarsier group. Its remains indicate that the animal had large eyes and ears, which enabled it to hunt at night. Its small sharp teeth were ideal for dealing with tough-shelled insects – which were its main food. *Necrolemur*'s body, too, would have been similar to the living species, with gripping pads on its long fingers and toes, long agile arms and legs, and a long tail that would have been used as a counterbalance when moving through the trees.

SUBORDER ANTHROPOIDEA

The suborder Anthropoidea contains two infraorders – the platyrrhines ('flat noses') or New World monkeys, and the catarrhines ('downfacing noses') or Old World monkeys, apes and hominids. They evolved in North America or Eurasia around 40 million years ago. The two lines diverged soon after when a land bridge that linked North with South America once more disappeared.

New World Monkeys

The New World monkeys are distinguished from the Old World monkeys partly by their nostrils, which are placed wider apart and face outward rather than downward. There are also several other distinguishing anatomical features, including distinctive skull joints, or sutures, and the possession of one more pair of premolars than their Old World relatives.

Some species have an additional 'limb' in the form of a prehensile tail – one that is able to support the body by coiling around branches. Curiously, this useful adaptation to tree dwelling never evolved in the Old World monkeys.

Modern representatives of this group include the delicate and often highly-coloured marmosets and tamarins, and the spider and howler monkeys. Together they constitute about one third of modern anthropoid genera.

NAME *Branisella*

TIME Early Oligocene

LOCALITY South America (Bolivia)

SIZE 16 in/40 cm long

This is the earliest-known monkey to have lived on the South American continent, but little can be said with confidence about *Branisella*'s lifestyle and relationships because the only fossil evidence of its existence are some fragments of jawbone.

The *Branisella*'s teeth were quite primitive, with many tarsier-like features. This would suggest that it evolved from the omomyids farther north. However, some other physical attributes seem to indicate that *Branisella* was quite close to the monkeys which were then living in Africa. So there is even the possibility that its ancestors may have reached South America by drifting across the Atlantic from west Africa on floating islands of vegetation.

NAME *Tremacebus*
TIME Late Oligocene
LOCALITY South America (Argentina)
SIZE 3 ft 3 in/1 m long

By the end of the Oligocene New World monkeys had become very much like the modern forms. *Tremacebus*, which is sometimes known as *Homunculus* because of its miniature humanoid form, must have resembled today's only truly nocturnal owl monkey, the *Douroucouli*.

Tremacebus is known from only a few specimens, including a skull, from Patagonia. The paucity of remains in this area suggests that the plains of Patagonia were as treeless then as they are now, so there was too small a woodland environment to support any greater monkey diversity.

Old World Monkeys

Old World monkeys, like apes and humans, differ from the New World monkeys in having nostrils that are close together and face downward, a bony canal leading from the exterior to the eardrum, and, in general, one fewer pair of premolar teeth.

Classed together in the family Cercopithecidae, these monkeys form the largest and most primitive group of catarrhines, and include among their modern representatives guenons, baboons, macaques, geladas, and the colobus monkey. Until recently the fossil record was confined to the last 10 million years. But now a 15 million year old, possible ancestor to the cercopithecines, called *Victoriapithecus*, has been found in Kenya which links these catarrhines with the much older *Aegyptopitheccus* (see p.291)

The tail is never prehensile, and may be greatly reduced or absent, especially in ground-living animals. The tail is useful for tree-dwellers, however, since it improves balance and may allow a change of trajectory in mid-jump.

NAME *Mesopithecus*
TIME Late Miocene to Late Pliocene
LOCALITY Europe (Greece) and Asia (Asia Minor)
SIZE 16 in/40 cm long

Mesopithecus, which is also known as the 'middle ape', was typical of the early cercopithecids. It was similar to the modern macaque monkey and was probably ancestral to the modern langur.

It was slim, had long muscular arms and legs, and long, nimble fingers and toes. Its limbs, like those of the modern macaque, could be used both for walking on the ground and for climbing in trees, which suggests that its environment was quite open.

Mesopithecus would have been active during the daytime rather than at night and would have eaten leaves and soft fruits.

NAME *Theropithecus*
TIME Middle Pliocene to Recent
LOCALITY South and East Africa
SIZE 4 ft/1.2 m long

The baboons are largely ground-dwelling monkeys that travel across open plains in family groups. They generally have dog-like faces and consume a wide range of foodstuffs. Although they tend to walk on all fours on the ground, baboons are still very adept at climbing, especially scrambling among rocks.

Theropithecus was a large baboon, the remains of which have been discovered in the Olduvai Gorge in Tanzania. For a baboon it had a short face, and there was a large crest of bone running along the top of its skull that must have held strong jaw muscles. It would probably have fed on tough dry-climate plant material.

APES

FAMILY OREOPITHECIDAE

The classification of the oreopithecids is problematical. Some paleontologists regard them as Old World monkeys related to *Mesopithecus*; but others point to their ape-like and even hominid-like attributes, such as their probable ability to brachiate (use their arms to swing from branch to branch) and even to walk upright. They are almost certainly an evolutionary blind alley, though, whose advanced features are a result of convergence. There is only one genus.

NAME	*Oreopithecus*
TIME	Late Miocene
LOCALITY	Europe (Italy)
SIZE	4 ft/1.2 m tall

Oreopithecus, the 'mountain ape', has been jocularly referred to as 'the abominable coalman' because the remains of this animal were found in the brown coal deposits of Tuscany in northern Italy, dated to about 14 million years ago and because some of its features were almost human.

Oreopithecus had a monkey's snout, ape-like brow ridges, and monkey-like ankle bones.

The face was flat and small, the canines conical, and the patterns on the molar teeth resembled those of hominids. This mixture of monkey and human characteristics may be best explained by considering oreopithecines an independent lineage.

Since its remains were preserved in beds of soft brown coal, *Oreopithecus* probably lived in forested, riverside swamps. It is likely that it survived on a diet of leaves, shoots and fruits of a wide variety of plants.

The animal's arms were rather longer than the legs, which indicates that it spent much of its time in the trees and probably moved about by swinging under branches. The spine and hip bones suggest that it was also able to walk, or at least to lope along in an upright stance.

SUPERFAMILY HOMINOIDEA

The only living hominoids – the word means 'resembling humans' – are the apes (pongids) and our own species, *Homo sapiens*. They differ from the Old World monkeys in having no tails, and arms and shoulder girdles that are designed for hanging and swinging from branches.

In addition to the gibbons (hylobatids) and humans plus great apes (hominids), the group includes extinct forms such as the pliopithecids, which are regarded as a subfamily (along with the living gibbons) within the family Hylobatidae.

SUBFAMILY PLIOPITHECINEA

Although pliopithecids possessed some primitive features, including a long snout, a small brain case, and in some cases a tail. They are the earliest well-defined family of true apes. Advanced characteristics include ape-like teeth, jaws and stereoscopic vision.

Pliopithecids almost certainly evolved in Africa, probably by the Early Oligocene, around 35 million years ago, and became extinct in the Miocene about 10 million years ago.

NAME	*Propliopithecus*
TIME	Middle Oligocene
LOCALITY	Africa (Egypt)
SIZE	16 in/40 cm long

In the Mid-Oligocene, over 27 million years ago, the Fayum region to the east of Cairo was not the dusty desert of today. The River Nile produced a swampy delta here, close to the shoreline of the now-vanished, Tethys sea. The forests of this delta once supported a large number of tropical animal types, including several primitive apes such as *Propliopithecus* and *Aegyptopithecus*. (It is possible that both names apply to the same creature, in which case the former has priority.)

Propliopithecus was basically a quadrupedal animal, the size of a small gibbon, which ran on all-fours along tree branches in much the same way as the macaques do today.

The eyes were set in well-developed sockets and pointed forward to give stereoscopic vision. The dentition was adapted for eating fruit and was ape-like. *Propliopithecus* probably also ate insects and even small vertebrates.

NAME	*Pliopithecus*
TIME	Middle to Late Miocene
LOCALITY	Europe (France and Czechoslovakia)
SIZE	1 ft/1.2 m tall

Opinions vary among paleontologists, but it now seems unlikely that *Pliopithecus* gave rise to the gibbons, as was once thought. Nevertheless, there are distinct similarities between the two creatures and they probably share a common ancestor in early Miocene times. The gibbon line may even extend back as far as *Propliopithecus* over 30 million years ago. *Pliopithecus* lived between 16 and 10 million years ago, when the Earth really was the 'planet of the apes', with some 30 different, but contemporaneous, species most of which are now extinct.

Pliopithecus was gibbon-sized, with a short face, large eyes and sharp canines. The body was long, and the limbs were equipped with long hands and feet. It may even have been able to brachiate. On the other hand, arms and legs were much the same length (the arms are much longer in gibbons), and there is evidence of a short tail, with 10 or more vertebrae. Its stereoscopic vision may not have been perfect either, because the orbits of the eyes were not directed fully forward.

NAME	*Dendropithecus*
TIME	Early to Middle Miocene
LOCALITY	East Africa (Kenya)
SIZE	2 ft/60 cm tall

It is now widely thought that it was not *Pliopithecus* but one of its earlier relatives, the small eastern Africa apes such as *Micropithecus*, *Limnopithecus* or *Dendropithecus* that was ancestral to the gibbons. Remains of the slimly built *Dendropithecus* ('tree ape') have been dated to middle and early Miocene times, about 15 million to 20 million years ago. Although it had shorter arms and a longer tail than *Pliopithecus*, and was probably no better at brachiating, *Dendropithecus* was more gibbon-like in other respects, including its diet. *Dendropithecus* almost certainly inhabited a densely-forested area and enjoyed fruit, leaves and flowers, just as the gibbon does today.

Family Hominidae

This family links humans (the subfamily Homininae) with the living great apes (the subfamily Ponginae) and their numerous fossil ancestors. Interrelationships within this broad group, however, are a matter of continuing development and debate as new fossil evidence begins to fill in what is still a very fragmentary fossil ancestry for both the humans and the great apes.

The family includes the largest of all primates at present, although in the past some other extinct primates, such as *Gigantopithecus*, have matched them for size. From fossil evidence and the molecular clock – a dating system based on the rate of genetic change – it is thought that the hominids originated at least 17 million years ago in Africa.

They subsequently diverged into two groups, one of which, the Ponginae, left Africa early in its development and migrated to Asia, where it is now represented by the still living but endangered orangutans. The other group, the Homininae, stayed in Africa until more recently.

APES CONTINUED

SUBFAMILY PONGINAE

The Ponginae family includes the fossil and living apes. They are semi-bipedal, sometimes walking on four feet and sometimes upright on two, and have no tail. Today, the pongines are restricted to tropical Africa and South-east Asia, where two species of chimpanzee, and a single species each of gorilla and orangutan, survive.

Pongines were once a much more diverse group both in terms of the number of genera and in their geographical distribution. The earliest members date from the Early Miocene, around 25 million years ago.

In the past, almost every new specimen of hominoid was treated as a separate genus, and given a new name. This became confusing, and certainly held back the understanding of the broad lines of hominoid evolution. It is now increasingly accepted that many of these 'near-people' were in fact closely related, in spite of subtle differences in their anatomies, and should perhaps be thought of as members of the same genus. (There are, after all, quite large anatomical differences among modern humans, too, yet we are one species.)

Until recent years, it was generally assumed that apes parted from the evolutionary line that resulted in australopithecines and humans around 15 to 20 million years ago. However, biochemical studies now suggest that this time period may be much too long.

Detailed investigations have been carried out into our mutual immune responses, and structural differences in DNA (the genetic material incorporated in every living cell) and complex proteins such as the haemoglobin in blood corpuscles. Given certain reasonable assumptions about the spontaneous rate of change of these molecules, it would seem that gibbons probably only split away from the ancestral line about 10 million years ago, with the orangutan parting shortly after.

Perhaps the greatest surprise, though, lies in what these studies imply about the relationship between modern humans and chimpanzees and gorillas. Although superficially we seem to be quite different from one another, in fact our biochemistry is too similar for much more than a period of between 5 million and 8 million years to have elapsed since we separated in evolutionary terms.

This theory about the interrelationships between the apes and man is still controversial, however, not least because fossil australopithecines have been discovered from as long ago as 3.5 million, and perhaps as long as 4 million to 5 million years ago. These seem too much like humans and too little like apes to be the product of only a few million years of evolution.

NAME *Dryopithecus*

TIME Early to Late Miocene

LOCALITY Europe (France and Greece), Asia (Caucasus) and Africa (Kenya)

SIZE 2 ft/60 cm long

The evolutionary lines that developed into the modern apes and *Homo sapiens* may have begun with the widespread *Dryopithecus* ('tree ape') which lived about 12 million to 9 million years ago.

Dryopithecus evolved in East Africa, where the earliest remains have been found, and migrated to Europe and Asia (especially around the eastern end of the Mediterranean) when the continent of Africa fused with that of Eurasia.

The chimpanzee-like limbs show that it would have walked mostly on all-fours but could also walk on two legs. Its wrist was more like a monkey's than an ape's, so it probably walked on the flat of its hand, rather than on its knuckles as chimpanzees do. Its head, too, was rather chimpanzee-like, but it lacked the heavy brow-ridges.

Dryopithecus was definitely a climbing, tree-living animal adapted to eating fruit, since its cheek teeth were too thinly enamelled to chew tougher food such as roots or grasses. However, the environment of the time was developing into woodland mixed with open grass land, so it seems likely that *Dryopithecus* may also have moved about on the grasslands, probably in groups.

NAME *Sivapithecus*

TIME Middle to Late Miocene

LOCALITY Southeast Europe, Asia and Africa (Kenya)

SIZE 5 ft/1.5 m tall

With its orangutan-like face, chimpanzee-like feet, and rotating wrists, *Sivapithecus* appears to be an ape in the transition period between life in the trees and life on the ground. This reconstruction showing a tail is speculative and that presented for the smaller *Ramapithecus* (which may be a sexual dimorph) is more accurate.

The evidence of its life habits are found in the dentition. The canine teeth were large and the molars had a thick covering of enamel – a dentition that is much more suited to the seeds, stems and roots that would have been found growing on the savannah than to the leaves and fruits of the forest.

It is clear that *Sivapithecus* ate drier, tougher foods than the dryopithecines could have managed. In fact, it is known that the climate was changing at that time, around 15 million to 7 million years ago. The forests were dwindling and the grasslands spreading, so it does seem likely that evolution would have promoted the animals that were adapting to these new environmental conditions.

Since important finds were made in India, *Sivapithecus* was named for Siva, one of the principal Hindu gods, sometimes known as Lord of the Beasts.

NAME *Gigantopithecus*

TIME Late Miocene to Middle Pleistocene

LOCALITY Asia (China, Pakistan, India)

SIZE 10 ft/3 m tall

This enormous creature was a veritable King Kong of the fossil apes. *Gigantopithecus* must have weighed something like 650 lb/300 kg. A close relative of *Sivapithecus*, it is known mostly from fragmental remains of its jaws and teeth, which were about twice the breadth of the teeth of a modern gorilla. They first came to the attention of scientists when a paleontologist saw four single molars in a Hong Kong drugstore in the 1930s.

Some complete lower jaws were discovered in the 1950s.

Gigantopithecus was a ground-dwelling ape, and was probably something like a gorilla in appearance, but with a shorter jaw and relatively small incisors and canines. It probably ate roots, tubers and seeds, but also small vertebrates.

Gigantopithecus certainly lived until Pleistocene times, about 1 million years ago, and perhaps until even more recently. Indeed, it has been surmised by some that *Gigantopithecus* is not extinct even today, but still survives in the remote foothills and mountain passes of the Himalayas, where it is occasionally sighted and identified as the Yeti.

NAME *Ramapithecus*

TIME Middle to Late Miocene

LOCALITY Asia (Pakistan) and Africa (Kenya)

SIZE 4 ft/1.2 m tall

Ramapithecus – named for Rama, the Hindu god of chivalry and virtue – was originally thought to be a close relative of *Sivapithecus*; but is a separate animal. The main distinguishing feature of its skeletal remains is that they are a little smaller in stature than *Sivapithecus*. They are now thought to be just sexual dimorphs, that is females of *Sivapithecus* and possibly some other similar genera.

Although the animal has elbows similar to those of modern apes, the arm bones are quite primitive and seem to indicate that movement by arm suspension was not a fundamental trait of the apes as has been thought. The face and skull share several features with the orang-utan which implies a developmental relationship between the two. If this is correct then this lineage has the potential to calibrate ape evolution.

The fossil evidence of the earliest occurrence of late Miocene Eurasian hominoids (such as *Sivapithecus* and *Dryopithecus*) is dated at around 12.5 million years in the Siwalik sedimentary sequence of Pakistan. Older strata show no evidence of any large hominoid so 12.5 million years is the minimum estimate for the timing of the orangutan lineage and its divergence from the African bipedal hominids and apes. This can be used to calibrate the molecular clock and the genetic distance between the orang-utan and the African ape/human lineages.

HUMANS

The key features of human evolution, or 'hominization', on which attention has focused include physical and cultural developments. As hominization has proceeded, differences in anatomy have been of less significance than changes in way of life, use of the environment, and interpersonal relations. Physical developments have included changes in locomotion and posture, notably an upright stance, bipedal locomotion, legs longer than arms and diminished big toes; the growth of the pelvis and of the birth canal to accommodate larger-brained babies; increased manual dexterity, due to lengthened thumbs and the 'precision grip' – the ability to hold small objects delicately between thumb and forefinger; and modifications of the head.

Compared with less evolved primates, hominids have smaller jaws and teeth, flatter faces and more thickly enamelled teeth. They have lost the ridges of bone over the eyes and the crest on the top of the skull, but their brains are larger relative to the rest of the body, and their brains are more complex.

Cultural developments have included the formation of groups, cooperative work, tool-making, the harnessing of fire, the making of sculpture and painting, and burial rites.

Each development should be seen as existing in a complex feedback relationship with the others. For example, the freeing of the hands from use in locomotion makes possible greater facility in the production of tools, which encourages increased hand-eye coordination and the development of the brain.

But tool-use also puts a premium on improvements in child-rearing, social organization and communication. A long-term social group which prolongs infant care and supports its members throughout adulthood is more capable of acquiring, sharing and accumulating experience. Groups that cooperate intimately are also likely to use tools better, and to improve their design and manufacture.

Many crucial cultural developments – such as language and social structure – do not fossilize, so paleontologists can only make guesses based on the activities which leave traces, for example evidence of burial rites. And precisely because we have such a selective record to go on, great caution must be exercised in interpretation.

It is easy to let prejudice colour the picture of the past. On the whole, it is only hard objects which survive, so a lot is known about stone tools but almost nothing about tools made of animal and plant materials, such as leather and plaited-fibre bags and baby slings. This type of bias in the fossil record could lead to misunderstanding, not only of the nature of our ancestors' diet but even their social life – if hunting is emphasized, for instance, and the possible significance of foraging for plants ignored.

SUBFAMILY HOMININAE

This subfamily unites humans and our fossil ancestors with the extinct group of australopiths, meaning 'southern apes'. This name reflects the discovery of these fossil hominids in southern Africa. Since the discovery of the first australopith in the 1920s by Raymond Dart, numerous other fossils have been found throughout southern and eastern Africa from Pliocene and early Pleistocene sediments. The fossil record from this area includes the earliest known hominines dating from around 4.4 million years ago, *Australopithecus ramidus*.

NAME *Australopithecus afarensis*

TIME Mid Pliocene

LOCALITY Africa (Ethiopia and Tanzania)

SIZE around 4 ft / 1.2 m tall

One of earliest known hominines, dating from around 3.5 million years ago, was *Australopithecus afarensis* – the 'southern ape from Afar'. The partial skeletons of this hominine, from the Afar Triangle in northern Ethiopia, match a slightly earlier series of footprints in volcanic ash near Laetoli in Tanzania. When it was excavated in 1974, the first skeleton was nicknamed 'Lucy' after a song by the Beatles.

The adults were small – not much larger in height and weight than a six-year-old child today. The skull and face were not unlike a chimpanzee's, with prominent brow ridges, but the brain was a little larger (about 400 cc). Lucy's teeth were chipped in front, probably the result of using them to grip with.

The hips were quite narrow – implying that babies had smaller heads relative to modern babies – but otherwise quite human-like. The legs, too, signify that Lucy was fully bipedal: she walked upright, albeit with a slight stoop, and with very little of the chimpanzee's lurching gait. The footprints confirm that the feet were essentially the same as modern human feet, but without a ball at the base of the big toe so that Lucy would have walked flat-footed, with the toes slightly curled in.

The combination of ape and human features makes *A. afarensis* a likely common ancestor of both modern humans and the robust australopithecines. Recent discoveries have, however, displaced *A. afarensis* as the oldest autralopithecine. In 1995 a new 4 million year old species, *A. anamensis* was described and in 1995 another *A. ramidus*, at around 4.4 million years old. It is now the most primitive, also having features linking it to the later hominds. Both new species were discovered the Turkana region of East Africa.

NAME *Australopithecus africanus*

TIME Late Pliocene

LOCALITY African (Ethiopia, Kenya, South Africa, Tanzania)

SIZE 4 ft 4 in / 1.3 m tall

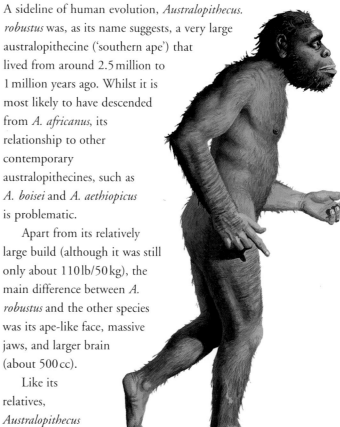

The skull of an infant specimen of *Australopithecus africanus* – 'southern ape of Africa' – was unearthed in the Transvaal in 1924. It was largely disregarded at the time because anthropologists thought that the story of human origins lay with a fossil found some years earlier in Piltdown in southern England which was later proved to be a fake.

Australopithecus africanus is now regarded as a hominine, which probably descended from *A. afarensis* and was ancestral to *A robustus.*

It lived around 3–2.5 million years ago. Even if *A. africanus* was not our direct ancestor, it was certainly very close. The brain was small by modern standards, being about the same size as a chimpanzee's (up to 400 cc), and the face still had heavy, ape-like jaws. The canine teeth were reasonably large, but in other respects the dentition was quite human.

Like *Australopithecus afarensis*, *A. africanus* was a slightly-built creature, probably weighing about 65 lb / 30 kg, which walked upright. More important than its overall appearance though, was its lifestyle. Some have claimed that *A. africanus* had moved from woodland to open savannah, and had already developed tools and cooperative hunting techniques, with a gang

of individuals hunting down and killing a single animal or chasing away another hunting animal from its kill. Others argue that the evidence is equivocal. The bone 'tools' are so ill-formed that they are probably nothing more than the remains of a hyena's meal.

Although hunting was probably significant in human evolution, it is likely that plants – including seeds, nuts, fruit, leaves, stems and roots – formed the major part of the diet.

NAME *Australopithecus robustus*

TIME Late Pliocene to Early Pleistocene

LOCALITY Africa (South Africa and Tanzania)

SIZE 5 ft 4 in / 1.6 m tall

A sideline of human evolution, *Australopithecus. robustus* was, as its name suggests, a very large australopithecine ('southern ape') that lived from around 2.5 million to 1 million years ago. Whilst it is most likely to have descended from *A. africanus*, its relationship to other contemporary australopithecines, such as *A. boisei* and *A. aethiopicus* is problematic.

Apart from its relatively large build (although it was still only about 110 lb / 50 kg), the main difference between *A. robustus* and the other species was its ape-like face, massive jaws, and larger brain (about 500 cc).

Like its relatives, *Australopithecus robustus* seems to have left the forests and taken up a plains-dwelling existence. Almost certainly exclusively vegetarian, the fossil evidence suggests that *A. robustus* would have been the hunted rather than the hunter, since most of the best-preserved skeletons come from carcasses that were killed by carnivores. For example, a broken skull of *A. robustus* has been found with teeth marks that match up exactly to the fossilized teeth of a leopard.

The very large jaws of *Australopithecus robustus* were powered by strong muscles anchored to a crest over the top of the skull, a physical characteristic which gave rise to one of the early vernacular names for this creature – 'nutcracker'.

HUMANS CONTINUED

Genus *Homo*

Fossil evidence from Africa shows that anatomical humans, placed in the genus Homo, emerged over 2 million years ago, either from *Australopithecus afarensis* or *A. africanus*. Stone tool making is the hallmark of these earliest humans and there were at least three contemporary tool making species of *Homo* living in Africa around that time, *H. rudofensis*, *H. ergaster*, *H. habilis* and possibly *H. erectus*. The emergence of modern humans took place over 0.5 million years ago, with *H. heidelbergensis* from whom firstly the Neanderthals came then *H. sapiens* about 40,000 years ago.

Analysis of DNA from all different groups of living humans shows that we are all integrally the same and originated from a common ancestor – probably an African *H. heidelbergensis*.

NAME *Homo habilis*

TIME Early Pleistocene

LOCALITY Africa (Ethiopia, Kenya, Tanzania, possibly South Africa) and possibly Southeast Asia

SIZE 4 to 5 ft/1.2 to 1.5 m

By about 2 to 1.5 million years ago, several hominines existed alongside one another in East Africa. Some were close enough to modern humans to be classed in the genus *Homo*. The relationship of *H. habilis* to the other *Homo* species is not clear.

Homo habilis was still quite short and light, with less massive jaws and brow ridges than its predecessors. Its head too was larger than that of its predecessors, as was its brain (up to about 800 cc). The brain was also more complex. There is even some evidence from the brain's structure that *H. habilis* would have been able to speak.

However, the distinctive feature of *H. habilis*, or 'handy human', is that it is one of the first hominines that is known to have fabricated and used tools. These tools mostly consisted of pebbles with a makeshift blade chipped out along one edge. There is also some evidence of the construction of simple shelters, scavenging and the hunting of game by *H. habilis*.

NAME *Homo erectus*

TIME Early to Middle Pleistocene

LOCALITY Africa (Tanzania, South Africa and Algeria), Europe (Germany, Spain, France, Greece and Hungary) and Asia (Java and China)

SIZE about 5 ft 4 in/1.6 m tall

Homo erectus (the name meaning 'upright human') was an outstandingly successful creature. Having evolved around 1.6 million years or more ago, it saw the extinction of all other hominids, including its possible ancestors. It survived until about 200,000 years ago and gave rise to our ancestor *H. heidelbergensis*.

In its bodily appearance, posture and gait, *Homo erectus* must have been very similar to a modern human, although a little shorter. At 950 to 1,200 cc, the brain volume, too, was approaching the modern size, and areas of the brain associated with speech were well-developed.

The head, however, still had heavy ape-like eyebrow ridges and protruding jaws. *H. erectus* was evidently a wandering gatherer and hunter, moving about in groups, but also creating settlements: a site in the south of France provides evidence of huts with brushwood walls supported on a framework of poles and anchored by stones. Tools found at the sites were sophisticated, and included spears, projectiles, blades, scrapers and choppers made from wood, stone, antler and bone. *H. erectus* is believed to have used fire for cooking and for defence.

About half a million years ago, *H. erectus* left its birthplace in Africa and spread throughout the tropical, subtropical and temperate parts of the Old World. Remains have been discovered in so many places that a multitude of confusing common and scientific names have been applied, including Java and Peking (Beijing) people, *Pithecanthropus* ('ape human') *Sinanthropus* ('China human') and *Palaeanthropus* ('old human'). All are now placed together in the same species.

NAME *Homo sapiens neanderthalensis*

TIME Late Pleistocene

LOCALITY Europe (Mediterranean region) and Asia (Israel)

SIZE up to 5 ft 7 in / 1.7 m tall

Homo sapiens neanderthalensis, the 'wise person from the valley of the River Neander', is named for a site in Germany where skeletons were discovered in 1856. However, it took more than 20 years for anthropologists to accept the significance of the find. Even when they did it was to portray the Neanderthals as very much 'subhuman', primitive beings with low intelligence. Now it is known that they were powerfully built intelligent people some 30 percent larger and heavier than modern humans, with males weighing in at some 198 lb/90 kg. Many fossils have been discovered from Gibraltar and North Africa in the west, throughout the Near East, and east to central Asia.

Neanderthal people evolved around 250,000 years ago. They were very successful during the warm periods toward the end of the Pleistocene Ice Age, but probably died out around 30,000 years ago. Until recently, it was thought that Neanderthals may have interbred with the later, more advanced migrants from North Africa. But it now seems more likely that the Neanderthals represent the most recent extinct side-branch of the human family. Samples of DNA taken from the original Neanderthal fossils have shown that modern humans have not inherited any Neanderthal genetic traits. Apparently, Neanderthals and Cro-Magnons, the modern humans that replaced them, did not interbreed although they co-existed in some places for around 10,000 years. The DNA data also shows that Neanderthals and modern humans diverged from a common ancestor (*Homo heidelbergensis*) around 500,000 years ago.

From north of the Pyrenees populations of Neanderthals seem to have adopted certain 'advanced' Cro-Magnon behavioural traits, whilst more southerly Spanish Neanderthals did not. They all became extinct between 34000 and 3000 years ago. It is not clear why.

Their bodies were short and powerfully built, and they had large hands and joints, a rather broad head, a flat or bulbous nose, and prominent eyebrows. The brain capacity, often in excess of 1,400 cc, was in fact on average greater than that of modern humans.

Neanderthal people were more sophisticated than previously thought, with a well-developed tool technology. They also show the beginnings of what has been thought of as a religious culture. For example, they buried the dead and clearly treated the cave bear, *Ursus spelaeus* (see p.217), with reverence.

NAME *Homo sapiens 'Cro-Magnon'*

TIME Late Pleistocene to Recent

LOCALITY Worldwide

SIZE 5 ft to 6 ft / 1.5 m to 1.8 m tall

The modern subspecies of *Homo sapiens* is well known throughout the world from about 35,000 years ago. Artefacts and cave paintings found in central France, dating from about 30,000 years ago, testify to their cultural sophistication.

These remains of 'Cro-Magnon people' suggest that they had a strong tribal system, made tools, gathered plant materials, hunted, fished and possibly herded animals, and built shelters and made clothing that enabled them to survive the last stages of the Pleistocene Ice Age. About 10,000 years ago, populations in many different parts of the world independently developed a farming lifestyle. Animals, such as pigs and sheep were domesticated, crops planted, a more sedentary lifestyle developed, and populations grew. The ability to modify the natural environment has led *Homo sapiens* to the dominant position that it currently enjoys.

GLOSSARY

ADAPTATION: modification in the structure, physiology, development or behaviour of an organism which makes it better able to follow a particular lifestyle.

ADAPTIVE RADIATION: divergence of an ancestral stock into forms (species, families etc) for distinct lifestyles or ecological niches. For example primitive shrewlike mammals evolved into organisms as varied as bats and whales.

ADVANCED (of a feature of an animal): more modified, specialized, complex forms.

ANAL: related to the anus.

ATROPHY: to wither away; become a useless.

BIPEDAL (locomotion): capable of standing, walking or running on two legs.

BRACHIATE: to swing through the trees moving from branch to branch using the hands.

CALCIFICATION: deposition of calcium minerals, which stiffen cartilage and form bone.

CANINE ('dog' or 'eye') tooth: conical mammal tooth between the incisors and premolars; well-developed and sharp for piercing prey. Absent or vestigial in many herbivores. There is a pair in each jaw in both the milk set of teeth and the adult set.

CARNASSIAL TEETH: upper and lower cheek teeth modified for meat-shearing.

CARNIVOROUS: animal that eats the flesh of vertebrate animals. See also scavenger, insectivorous.

CARPAL: see pentadactyl limb.

CARTILAGE: gristly, flexible material that makes up the skeleton in many fish. It is also present in more advanced animals in the embryo and in bone joints. May become stiffened by calcification.

CAUDAL: related to the tail.

CERVICAL: related to the neck.

CHEEK TEETH: teeth lying in the cheek region of the jaw. For example, mammalian molars.

CLASS: a high level grouping of similar organisms. A class contains one or more orders; similar classes form a phylum.

COLONIZATION: the 'invasion' of a new habitat or ecological niche. May displace existing animals.For example North American mammals caused extinction of many South American species when Panama landbridge was established.

CONTINENTAL DRIFT: see plate tectonics.

CONVERGENT EVOLUTION: the phenomenon whereby two distantly-related animals evolve similar structures in response to the same environmental pressures. For example, the wings of bats, birds and pterosaurs. Compare with parallel evolution.

COPROLITE: fossilized animal droppings.

CRANIAL: related to the skull.

CROWN: the exposed part of a tooth, normally coated with enamel.

CUSP: high point on a mammalian tooth. The number and pattern of cusps is characteristic.

DENTICLE: pointed scales of many cartilaginous, fishes; may be covered in enamel.

DENTITION: set of teeth.

DIAPHRAGM: sheet-like muscle and tendons separating the thorax from the abdomen; only found in mammals. Its movement helps draw air into the lungs and expel it.

DIASTEMA: a natural gap in a row of teeth; often seen in herbivores, such as that between the incisors and the cheek teeth of a rodent, where it separates functions of biting from chewing.

DIGIT: see pentadactyl limb.

DIGITIGRADE: walking on the underside of fingers or toes, as in a cat or dog, rather than flat of the hand/foot. See also plantigrade and unguligrade.

DISTAL: away from point of attachment, usually away from body. Opposite of proximal.

DORSAL: related or near to the back or upper part of the body.

ECOLOGICAL NICHE: a particular 'role' played, or position occupied, by an organism in its environment; determined by such factors as type of food, predators and tolerance of climatic conditions. Ecological niches tend to be exclusive, with no two closely-related species occupying the same niche in a particular area. The same niche in different areas may be filled by different species. See also adaptation.

ENAMEL: the hard layer that covers the crown of teeth and denticles; mostly calcium salts.

ENVIRONMENT: the sum total of all the factors – climatic, geological, biological etc – in which a creature lives.

FAMILY: a taxonomic grouping of similar organisms. A family contains one or more genera; similar families form an order.

FEMUR: See pentadactyl limb.

FIBULA: See pentadactyl limb.

GENERALIZED (Of an organism): showing few specific adaptations to a particular ecological niche. A generalized organism tends to be similar to its remote ancestors. See also primitive and advanced.

GENUS (plural, genera): a taxonomic grouping of similar organisms. A genus contains one or more species; similar genera form a family. The first of an organism's two scientific names refers to its genus, the second to its species. Eg the genus *Homo* includes species such as *Homo habilis* as well as the modern human *Homo sapiens*.

GONDWANALAND: see plate tectonics.

HERBIVOROUS: animal which eats plant matter only, vegetarian.

HOOF: massively-enlarged toenail adapted to take the weight of ungulates; made of keratin.

HORN: tough substance made of the protein keratin. A bony projection of the skull is properly called a horn if it is covered with horn (eg in cow), but those that lack a horny covering are called antlers (eg in deer) or ossicones (eg in giraffe). The 'horn' of a rhinoceros is made of compacted hair.

HYPERDACTYLY: condition in which there are more than the usual number of digits, as in an ichthyosaur's paddle.

HYPERPHALANGY: condition in which there are more than the usual number of joints in the digit, as in a plesiosaur's paddle.

ICE AGE: a period when climates are colder than usual and extensive areas of high latitude lowlands are covered by permanent snow and glaciers. The last Ice Age took place during the Pleistocene - in the last 2 million years or so - but several others have occurred

IGNEOUS: rock formed from molten material from within the Earth.

INCISORS: the cutting teeth at the front of a mammal's mouth.

INSECTIVOROUS animal which eats invertebrate animals.

KERATIN: strong fibrous protein, occurring in outermost skin layers of vertebrates. Forms nails, claws, hoofs, feathers, hair and horn.

LATERAL: related to the side of an organism.

LAURASIA: see plate tectonics.

LIGAMENT: An elastic fibrous tissue that joins bones together at a joint.

LITHOGRAPHIC LIMESTONE: fine-grained calcareous sediment of Jurassic age. found in southern Germany. Fossils preserved in it, such as *Archaeopteryx*, show minute detail such as feather impressions.

MOLARS: the back teeth of a mammal, usually adapted, eg for grinding, crushing or meat-shearing. Not present in milk dentition.

NATURAL SELECTION: since Darwin regarded as the principal mechanism of evolution. Emphasizes the importance of genetic mutation and hence variation in populations, and different rates of survival and reproduction consequent on possession of those variations. If a variation enables an organism to survive and leave more offspring, and the variation is inherited, the variation will tend to increase in the population.

OMNIVOROUS: animal able to eat material of plant or animal origin.

OPPOSABLE (of the thumb, etc): able to be brought up to meet or touch the tips of the rest of the digits; eg to grasp an object between big toe and other toes, as among chimps, or to grip an object between thumb and forefinger.

ORBIT: cavity in vertebrate skull which houses the eyeball.

ORDER: a taxonomic grouping of similar organisms. An order contains one or more families; similar orders form a class.

OSSICONE: 'horn' found among giraffes and possibly some fossil species, consisting of a bony core permanently covered in skin.

OSSIFICATION: formation of bone; a process thst involves calcification.

OVIPAROUS: animal which lays eggs. See also viviparous.

PALATE: the plate of bone roofing the mouth. See also secondary palate.

PALEONTOLOGIST: scientist who studies animal and plant life of the past.

PANGAEA: see plate tectonics.

PARALLEL EVOLUTION: the independent development of similar shapes or behaviour in closely related organisms in response to similar environmental pressures. See also convergent evolution.

PECTORAL: related to the shoulders.

PELVIC: related to the hips.

PENTADACTYL LIMB: (literally '5 fingers'); basic structure of forelimb and hind limb found among the tetrapods. Consists of single bone in upper limb (humerus or femur), two bones in lower limb (radius and ulna, or tibia and fibula), five joint bones in the wrist or ankle (carpals or tarsals), five rod-like bones in the palm or sole (metacarpals and metatarsals) tarsals) and digits (fingers or toes). Digits are made up of small bones arranged end-to-end, the phalanges. They may be modified to fewer or more

than five digits in course of adaptive radiation.

PHALANGES: see pentadactyl limb.

PHYLUM (plural, phyla): a high level grouping of similar organisms. A phylum contains one or more classes; similar phyla form a Kingdom.

PLACENTAL MAMMALS: the females of placental (eutherian) mammals nourish the fetus indirectly within their bodies, through a placenta; the blood systems of mother and fetus never mix. Describes all living mammals, except monotremes and some marsupials.

PLANTIGRADE: walking on the flat of the foot, as in humans. See also digitigrade and unguligrade.

PLATE TECTONICS ('continental drift'): the large-scale, slow movements of the Earth's surface crustal rocks, resulting from convection currents circulating heat outwards from its hot liquid core. Movement involves the generation and destruction of ocean floor rocks. It also causes the fragmentation of continental landmasses.

About 250 million years ago there was a single 'super continent' – Pangaea – which broke up into Laurasia and Gondwanaland. Laurasia, the northern landmass, further fragmented into North America, Europe and Asia (except India). Gondwanaland, the southern landmass, broke up into Africa, Antarctica, Australasia, South America and India.

Drifting landmasses collide and join up, throwing up mountain chains, eg the Himalayas, formed when the Indian subcontinent (from Gondwanaland) collided with Asia (from Laurasia).

PREMOLARS: mammalian teeth situated between the molars and the canines. May be enlarged or 'molarized' for grinding, or simplified for meat-shearing. Unlike molars, they are present in the milk teeth.

PRIMITIVE (of a feature of an animal): having changed little from the condition in its ancestor. Opposite of advanced.

PROBOSCIS: a tube-like muscular extension of the nostrils, eg elephant's trunk, adapted to forage, grasp, suck water etc.

PROXIMAL: situated on the same side as the point of attachment; usually towards the body. Opposite of distal.

QUADRUPEDAL: habitually walking on four legs. See also bipedal.

RADIUS: see pentadactyl limb.

SACRAL VERTEBRAE: vertebrae attaching the backbone to the hips.

SCAPULA: bone in the shoulder girdle, the shoulder blade.

SCAVENGER: animal that consumes the flesh of dead animals which it has not itself killed. See carnivorous.

SCUTE: a plate of bone or horn embedded in the skin.

SECONDARY PALATE: a sheet of bone separating the mouth and nasal passage.

SEDIMENTARY ROCK: rock that was originally laid down, usually by water or wind, composed of particles that were eroded from existing rocks. Sometimes sedimentary rock incorporates material of organic origin,such as shells. See lithographic limestone.

SPECIALIZED, SPECIALIZATION: to become adapted to a particular lifestyle and habitat; to become restricted to a specific ecological niche.

SPECIES: a group of organisms that can interbreed and produce viable, fertile young. Similar species form a genus.

STEREOSCOPIC VISION: ability to judge depth and distance; having both eyes pointed forward and able to focus on an object.

STERNUM: breast bone of vertebrates, to which most ribs are attached.

STRATUM (plural, strata): layer of sedimentary rock, distinct from adjacent layers.

SUPERCONTINENT: see plate tectonics.

TARSUS: See pentadactyl limb.

TENDON: a cord or band of strong tissue connecting muscle to bone or to other muscles.

TETRAPOD: four-footed animal; which evolved into amphibians, reptiles, birds and mammals, a tetrapod is characterized by two pairs of limbs.

THORAX, THORACIC: region of vertebrate body containing heart, lungs, etc; the 'chest'.

ULNA: See pentadactyl limb.

UNGULIGRADE: walking on the tips of the toes, which bear thickened hoof, as in horses or cattle. See also digitigrade and plantigrade.

VETRAL: related to the lower surface of an organism.

VERTEBRAL COLUMN, VERTEBRAE: chain of bones or cartilage surrounding spinal cord.

VESTIGIAL (of an organ): small, undeveloped, with little or no clear function; diminished from its former state. For example, the lateral toes of modern horses and the human appendix.

VIVIPAROUS: bearing live young that have been nourished by a placental connexion to the mother. See also placental mammal.

CLASSIFICATION OF VERTEBRATES

The fossil vertebrate animals described in this book are grouped in the following classification. They are not arranged in evolutionary sequence; see the evolutionary charts at the beginning of each main section in the book to see the relationships between groups. This classification is intended to show to which group a particular animal belongs. In most cases, the animals are classified to family level.

FISHES (see pp.18–45)

PHYLUM CHORDATA (vertebrate ancestors)

SUBPHYLUM CEPHALOCHORDATA (Acraniata): *Pikaia*

SUBPHYLUM VERTEBRATA (Craniata)

CLASS AGNATHA

SUBCLASS MYXINOIDEA (hagfish)

SUBCLASS PETROMYZONTIFORMES (lampreys)

SUBCLASS CONODONTA: *Promissum*

SUBCLASS UNNAMED

  ORDER HETEROSTRACI: *Arandaspis, Drepanaspis, Doryaspis, Pteraspis*

  ORDER THELODONTIDA: *Thelodus*

  ORDER GALEASPIDA

  ORDER OSTEOSTRACI: *Boreaspis, Dartmuthia, Hemicyclaspis, Tremataspis*

  ORDER ANASPIDA: *Jamoytius, Pharyngolepis*

CLASS CHONDRICHTHYES (cartilaginous fishes)

SUBCLASS ELASMOBRANCHII (sharks, skates and rays)

  ORDER CLADOSELACHIDA: *Cladoselache*

  ORDER SYMMORIIDA: *Cobelodus, Stethacanthus*

  ORDER XENACANTHIDA: *Xenacanthus*

  ORDER EUSELACHII: *Hybodus, Tristychius*

  ORDER NEOSELACHII: *Scapanorhynchus, Sclerorhynchus, Spathobathis*

SUBCLASS HOLOCEPHALI (chimaeras or ratfish)

  ORDER CHIMAERIDA: *Deltoptychius, Ischyodus*

CLASS ACANTHODII (spiny sharks)

  ORDER CLIMATIIFORMES: *Climatius*

  ORDER ACANTHODIFORMES: *Acanthodes*

CLASS PLACODERMI (armoured fishes)

  ORDER RHENANIDA: *Gemuendina*

  ORDER PTYCTODONTIDA: *Ctenurella*

  ORDER ARTHRODIRA: *Coccosteus, Dunkleosteus, Groenlandaspis*

  ORDER ANTIARCHI: *Bothriolepis*

  ORDER UNCERTAIN: *Palaeospondylus*

  ORDER ACANTHOTHORACANS

CLASS OSTEICHTHYES (bony fishes)

SUBCLASS ACTINOPTERYGII (rayed-finned fishes)

  ORDER PALAEONISCIFORMES: *Canobius, Platysomus, Cheirolepis, Moythomasia, Palaeoniscum, Saurichthys*

  ORDER PERLEIDIFORMES: *Perleidus*

  ORDER SEMIONOTIFORMES: *Dapedium, Lepidotes*

  ORDER PYCNODONTIFORMES: *Pycnodus*

  ORDER ASPIDORHYNCHIFORMES: *Aspidorhynchus*

  ORDER TELEOSTEI: *Berycopsis, Enchodus, Eobothus, Hypsidoris, Hypsocormus, Leptolepis, Pholidophorus, Protobrama, Sphenocephalus, Thrissops*

SUBCLASS SARCOPTERYGII (lobe-finned fishes)

INFRACLASS RHIPIDISTIA

  ORDER ONYCHODONTIFORMES: *Strunius*

  ORDER POROLEPIFORMES (rhipidistians): *Gyroptychius, Holoptychius*

  ORDER OSTEOLEPIFORMES (rhipidistians): *Eusthenopteron, Osteolepis*

INFRACLASS ACTINISTIA (coelacanths): *Macropoma*

INFRACLASS DIPNOIFORMES

  ORDER DIPNOI (lungfishes): *Dipnorhynchus, Dipterus, Griphognathus*

AMPHIBIANS (see pp.46–57)

CLASS AMPHIBIA

Family Acanthostegidae: *Acanthostega*

Family Ichthyostegidae: *Ichthyostega*

Family Baphetidae: *Eucritta*

ORDER UNCERTAIN: *Crassigyrinus, Greererpeton*

ORDER TEMNOSPONDYLI

Family Colosteidae

Family Eryopidae: *Eryops*

Family Dissorophidae: *Cacops, Platyhystrix*

Family Peltobatrachidae: *Peltobatrachus*

Family Capitosauridae: *Paracyclotosaurus*

Family Plagiosauridae: *Gerrothorax*

ORDER ANTHRACOSAURIA

Family Eogyrinidae: *Eogyrinus*

ORDER SEYMOURIAMORPHA

Family Seymouridae: *Seymouria*

SUBCLASS LEPOSPONDYLI

  ORDER AISTOPODA

  Family Ophiderpetontidae: *Ophiderpeton*

  Family Phlegethontiidae: *Phlegethontia*

  ORDER NECTRIDEA

  Family Keraterpetontidae: *Diplocaulus, Keraterpeton*

  ORDER MICROSAURIA

  Family Pantylidae: *Pantylus*

  Family Microbrachidae: *Microbrachis*

INFRACLASS LISSAMPHIBIANS

  ORDER PROANURA (early frogs and toads)

  Family Protobatrachidae: *Triadobatrachus*

  ORDER ANURA (modern frogs and toads)

  Family Ascaphidae: *Vieraella*

  Family Palaeobatrachidae: *Palaeobatrachus*

  ORDER URODELA (newts and salamanders)

  Family Karauriidae: *Karaurus*

  ORDER GYMNOPHIONA (caecilians)

REPTILIOMORPHS

Family uncertain: *Westlothiana*

ORDER DIADECTOMORPHA

Family Diadectidae: *Diadectes*

REPTILES (see pp.58–87)

CLASS REPTILIA

SUBCLASS ANAPSIDA

  ORDER CAPTORHINIDA

  Family Protorothyrididae: *Hylonomus*

  Family Captorhinidae: *Labidosaurus*

  Family Procolophonidae: *Hypsognathus*

  Family Pareiasauridae: *Elginia, Pareiasaurus, Scutosaurus*

  Family Millerettidae: *Milleretta*

  ORDER MESOSAURIA

  Family Mesosauridae: *Mesosaurus*

  ORDER TESTUDINES [CHELONIA] (turtles, tortoises and terrapins)

  SUBORDER PROGANOCHELYDIA

  Family Proganochelyidae: *Proganochelys*

  SUBORDER PLEURODIRA

  Family Pelomedusidae: *Stupendemys*

  SUBORDER CRYPTODIRA

  Family Meiolaniidae: *Meiolania*

  Family Testudinidae: *Testudo*

  Family Protostegidae: *Archelon*

  Family Trionychidae: *Paleotrionyx*

SUBCLASS UNCERTAIN

  ORDER PLACODONTIA

  Family Placodontidae: *Placodus*

  Family Cyamodontidae: *Placochelys*

  Family Henodontidae: *Henodus*

  ORDER UNCERTAIN

  Family Claudiosauridae: *Claudiosaurus*

  ORDER NOTHOSAURIA

  Family Nothosauridae: *Ceresiosaurus, Lariosaurus, Nothosaurus*

Family Pistosauridae: *Pistosaurus*
ORDER PLESIOSAURIA
SUPERFAMILY PLESIOSAURIDEA
Family Plesiosauridae: *Plesiosaurus*
Family Cryptocleididae: *Cryptoclidus*
Family Elasmosauridae: *Elasmosaurus,*
Muraenosaurus
SUPERFAMILY PLIOSAUROIDEA
Family Pliosauridae: *Kronosaurus, Liopleurodon,*
Macroplata, Peloneustes
ORDER ICHTHYOSAURIA
Family Shastasauridae: *Cymbospondylus,*
Shonisaurus
Family Mixosauridae: *Mixosaurus*
Family Ichthyosauridae: *Ichthyosaurus,*
Ophthalmosaurus
Family Stenopterygiidae: *Stenopterygius*
Family Leptopterygiidae: *Eurhinosaurus,*
Temnodontosaurus
SUBCLASS DIAPSIDA
ORDER ARAEOSCELIDIA
Family Petrolacosauridae: *Petrolacosaurus*
Family Araeoscelididae: *Araeoscelis*
ORDER UNCERTAIN
Family Weigeltisauridae: *Coelurosauravus*
ORDER THALATTOSAURIA
Family Askeptosauridae:*Askeptosaurus*
ORDER CHORISTODERA
Family Champsosauridae: *Champsosaurus*
ORDER EOSUCHIA
Family Tangasauridae: *Hovasaurus, Thadeosaurus*
SUPERORDER LEPIDOSAURIA
ORDER SPHENODONTIDA (tuataras)
Family Sphenodontidae: *Planocephalosaurus*
Family Pleurosauridae: *Pleurosaurus*
ORDER SQUAMATA (snakes and lizards)
SUBORDER LACERTILIA [Sauria] (lizards)
Family Kuehneosauridae: *Kuehneosaurus*
Family Ardeosauridae: *Ardeosaurus*
Family Varanidae: *Megalania*
Family Mosasauridae: *Platecarpus, Plotosaurus*
SUBORDER SERPENTES (snakes)
Family Dolichosauridae: *Pachyrhachis*

RULING REPTILES (see pp.88–169)
INFRACLASS ARCHOSAUROMORPHA
ORDER RHYNCHOSAURIA
Family Rhynchosauridae: *Hyperodapedon*
ORDER PROLACERTIFORMES
Family Protorosauridae: *Protorosaurus*
Family Tanystropheidae: *Tanystropheus*
SUPERORDER ARCHOSAURIA
Family Proterosuchidae: *Chasmatosaurus*
Family Erythrosuchidae: *Erythrosuchus*
Family Rauisuchidae: *Ticinosuchus*
Family Phytosauridae: *Rutiodon*
Family Stagonolepididae: *Stagonolepis*

Family Euparkertidae: *Euparkeria*
Family Ornithosuchidae: *Ornithosuchus*
Family Lagosuchidae: *Lagosuchus*
Family uncertain: *Longisquama*
SUPERORDER CROCODYLOMORPHA
ORDER CROCODYLIA (crocodiles)
Family Sphenosuchidae: *Gracilisuchus*
Family Saltoposuchidae: *Terrestrisuchus*
Family Protosuchidae: *Protosuchus*
DIVISION MESOEUCROCODYLIA
Family Teleosauridae: *Teleosaurus*
Family Metriorhynchidae: *Metriorhynchus*
Family Bernissartiidae: *Bernissartia*
SUBORDER EUSUCHIA
Family Crocodylidae: *Deinosuchus, Pristichampsus*
ORDER PTEROSAURIA (pterosaurs)
SUBORDER RHAMPHORHYNCHOIDEA
Family Dimorphodontidae: *Dimorphodon*
Family Eudimorphodontidae: *Eudimorphodon*
Family Rhamphorhynchidae: *Anurognathus,*
Rhamphorhynchus, Scaphognathus, Sordes
SUBORDER PTERODACTYLOIDEA
Family Dsungaripteridae: *Dsungaripterus*
Family Pterodaustriidae: *Pterodaustro*
Family Pterodactylidae: *Cearadactylus,*
Pterodactylus
Family Ornithocheiridae: *Pteranodon,*
Quetzalcoatlus
ORDER SAURUSCHIA ('lizard-hipped' dinosaurs)
SUBORDER THEROPODA
INFRAORDER CERATOSAURIA
Family Ceratosauridae: *Ceratosaurus*
Family Podokesauridae: *Procompsognathus,*
Saltopus, Coelophysis
DIVISION MANIRAPTORA
Family not named: *Protoarchaeopteryx*
Family Coeluridae: *Coelurus*
Family Compsognathidae: *Compsognathus,*
Sinosauropteryx
Family Ornithomimidae: *Dromiceiomimus,*
Elaphrosaurus, Gallimimus, Ornithomimus,
Struthiomimus
Family Oviraptoridae: *Oviraptor*
Family Dromaeosauridae: *Deinonychus,*
Dromaeosaurus, Saurornitholestes, Velociraptor
Family Saurornithoididae: *Saurornithoides,*
Stenonychosaurus
Family Baryonychidae: *Baryonyx*
INFRAORDER CARNOSAURIA
Family Megalosauridae: *Dilophosaurus,*
Eustreptospondylus, Megalosaurus,
Proceratosaurus, Teratosaurus
Family Allosauridae: *Allosaurus,*
Yangchuanosaurus
Family Spinosauridae: *Acrocanthosaurus,*
Spinosaurus
Family Tyrannosauridae: *Albertosaurus,*

Alioramus, Daspletosaurus, Tarbosaurus,
Tyrannosaurus
SUBORDER SAUROPODOMORPHA
INFRAORDER PROSAUROPODA
Family Anchisauridae: *Anchisaurus, Efraasia,*
Thecodontosaurus
Family Plateosauridae: *Massospondylus,*
Mussaurus, Plateosaurus
Family Melanorosauridae: *Riojasaurus*
INFRAORDER SAUROPODA
Family Cetiosauridae: *Barapasaurus,*
Cetiosaurus
Family Brachiosauridae: *Brachiosaurus*
Family Camarasauridae: *Camarasaurus,*
Euhelopus, Ophistocoelicaudia
Family Diplodocidae: *Apatosaurus*
(=Brontosaurus), Dicraeosaurus, Diplodocus,
Mamenchisaurus
Family Titanosauridae: *Alamosaurus,*
Saltasaurus
ORDER ORNITHISCHIA ('bird-hipped' dinosaurs)
INFRAORDER ORNITHOPODA
Family Fabrosauridae: *Echinodon, Lesothosaurus,*
Scutellosaurus
Family Heterodontosauridae:
Heterodontosaurus, Pisanosaurus
INFRAORDER PACHYCEPHALOSAURIA
Family Pachycephalosauridae: *Homalocephale,*
Pachycephalosaurus, Prenocephale, Stegoceras
Family Homalocephalidae: *Homalocephale*
Family Hysilophodontidae: *Dryosaurus,*
Hypsilophodon, Othnielia, Parksosaurus, Tenontosaurus,
Thescelosaurus
Family Iguanodontidae: *Callovosaurus,*
Camptosaurus, Iguanodon, Muttaburrasaurus,
Ouranosaurus, Probactrosaurus, Vectisaurus
Family Hadrosauridae: *Anatosaurus,*
Bactrosaurus, Corythosaurus, Edmontosaurus,
Hadrosaurus, Hypacrosaurus, Kritosaurus,
Lambeosaurus, Maiasaura, Parasaurolophus,
Prosaurolophus, Saurolophus, Shantungosaurus,
Tsintaosaurus
SUBORDER THYREOPHORA
Family Scelidosauridae: *Scelidosaurus*
INFRAORDER STEGOSAURIA
Family Stegosauridae: *Kentrosaurus,*
Stegosaurus, Tuojiangosaurus, Wuerhosaurus
INFRAORDER ANKYLOSAURIA
Family Nodosauridae: *Hylaeosaurus,*
Panoplosaurus, Nodosaurus, Polacanthus,
Sauropelta, Silvisaurus, Struthiosaurus
Family Ankylosauridae: *Ankylosaurus,*
Euoplocephalus, Saichania, Talarurus
SUBORDER CERAPODA
INFRAORDER CERATOPSIA
Family Psittacosauridae: *Psittacosaurus*
Family Protoceratopidae: *Bagaceratops,*

Leptoceratops, Microceratops, Montanoceratops, Protoceratops
Family Ceratopsidae: *Anchiceratops, Arrhinoceratops, Centrosaurus, Chasmosaurus, Pachyrhinosaurus, Pentaceratops, Styracosaurus, Torosaurus, Triceratops*

BIRDS (see pp.170–181)
CLASS AVES
SUBCLASS ARCHAEORNITHES
    Family Archaeopterygidae: *Archaeopteryx*
    Family Alvarezsauridae
    Family Iberomesomithidae
SUBCLASS ENANTIORNITHES
SUBCLASS ODONTORNITHES
    ORDER ICHTHYORNITHIFORMES: *Ichthyornis*
    ORDER HESPERORNITHIFORMES: *Hesperornis*
SUBCLASS NEORNITHES
DIVISION PALAEOGNATHAE
DIVISION NEOGNATHE
    ORDER STRUTHIORNITHIFORMES: *Aepyornis, Dinornis, Emeus*
    ORDER COLUMBIFORMES: *Raphus*
    ORDER CICONIIFORMES: *Argentavis, Harpagornis, Limnofregata, Osteodontornis, Palaelodus, Pinguinus*
    ORDER GRUIFORMES: *Diatryma, Neocathartes, Phorusrhacus*
    ORDER ANSERIFORMES: *Presbyornis*

MAMMAL-LIKE REPTILES
(see pp.182–193)
SUBCLASS SYNAPSIDA
    ORDER PELYCOSAURIA
    Family Ophiacodontidae: *Archaeothyris, Ophiacodon*
    Family Caseidae: *Casea*
    Family Edaphosauridae: *Edaphosaurus*
    Family Sphenacodontidae: *Sphenacodon, Dimetrodon*
    Family Varanopseidae: *Varanosaurus*
    Family Eothyrididae
    ORDER THERAPSIDA
    SUBORDER EOTITANOSUCHIA
    Family Phthinosuchidae: *Phthinosuchus*
    SUBORDER DINOCEPHALIA
    Family Titanosuchidae: *Titanosuchus*
    Family Tapinocephalidae: *Moschops*
    SUBORDER GORGONOPSIA
    Family Gorgonopsidae: *Lycaenops*
    SUBORDER DICYNODONTIA
    Family Galeopsidae: *Galechirus*
    Family Cistecephalidae: *Cistecephalus*
    Family Robertiidae: *Robertia*
    Family Dicynodontidae: *Dicynodon*
    Family Kannemeyeriidae: *Kannemeyeria*
    Family Lystrosauridae: *Lystrosaurus*

SUBORDER THEROCEPHALIA
Family Ericiolacertidae: *Ericiolacerta*
SUBORDER CYNODONTIA
Family Procynosuchidae: *Procynosuchus*
Family Galesauridae: *Thrinaxodon*
Family Cynognathidae: *Cynognathus*
Family Traversodontidae: *Massetognathus*
Family Tritylodontidae: *Oligokyphus*
SUBORDER BIARMOSUCHIA

MAMMALS (see pp.194–297)
CLASS MAMMALIA
SUBCLASS PROTOTHERIA
    Family Morganucodontidae: *Megazostrodon*
    Family Haramiyidae: *Haramiya*
    ORDER MULTITUBERCULATA
    Family Ptilodontidae: *Ptilodus*
    ORDER MONOTREMATA (platypus, spiny anteaters)
    ORDER DOCODONTA
    ORDER TRICONODONTA
    ORDER SYMMETRODONTA
    Family Dryolestidae: *Crusafontia*
SUBCLASS THERIA
INFRACLASS METATHERIA
    ORDER MARSUPIALIA (marsupials)
    SUBORDER DIDELPHOIDEA
    Family Didelphidae: *Alphadon*
    Family Borhyaenidae: *Borhyaena, Cladosictis*
    Family Thylacosmilidae: *Thylacosmilus*
    Family Argyrolagidae: *Argyrolagus*
    Family Necrolestidae: *Necrolestes*
    Family Thylacoleonidae: *Thylacoleo*
    Family Macropodidae: *Procoptodon*
    Family Diprotodontidae: *Diprotodon*
    Family Palorchestidae: *Palorchestes*
INFRACLASS EUTHERIA (placentals)
    Family Zalambdalestidae: *Zalambdalestes*
COHORT EDENTATA
    Family Metacheiromyidae: *Metacheiromys*
    ORDER XENARTHRA (armadillos, sloths, anteaters)
    Family Dasypodidae: *Peltephilus*
    Family Glyptodontidae: *Doedicurus*
    Family Megalonychidae: *Hapalops*
    Family Megatheriidae: *Megatherium*
    Family Mylodontidae: *Glossotherium*
    Family Myrmecophagidae: *Eurotamandua*
ORDER PHOLIDOTA
    Family Manidae: *Eomanis*
COHORT EPITHERIA
    SUPERORDER INSECTIVORA (hedgehogs, shrews, moles)
    ORDER LEPTICTIDA
    Family Pseudorhyncocyonidae: *Leptictidium*
    ORDER LIPOTYPHLA
    Family Palaeoryctidae: *Palaeoryctes*
    SUPERORDER ANAGALIDA

ORDER ANAGALIDA
Family Anagalidae: *Anagale*
SUPERORDER GLIRES
ORDER LAGOMORPHA (rabbits, hares)
Family Leporidae: *Palaeolagus*
ORDER RODENTIA (squirrels, rats, beavers)
SUBORDER SCIUROGNATHI
Family Paramyidae: *Ischyromys*
Family Mylagaulidae: *Epigaulus*
Family Castoridae: *Steneofiber*
SUBORDER HYSTRICOGNATHI
Family Ctenodactylidae: *Birbalomys*
Family Dinomyidae: *Telicomys*
Family Eocardiidae: *Eocardia*
SUPERORDER ARCHONTA
ORDER CHIROPTERA (bats)
Family Icaronycteridae: *Icaronycteris*
'PRIMATOMORPHS'
Family Paromomyidae: *Pargatorius*
ORDER DERMOPTERA (FLYING LEMURS)
Family Flagiomenidae: *Planetetherium*
SUBORDER PLESIADAPIFORMES
Family Plesiadapiae: *Plesiadapis*
ORDER PRIMATES (LEMURS, MONKEYS, APES AND HUMANS)
INFRAORDER ADAPIFORMES
Family Adapidae: *Notharctus*
INFRAORDER LEMURIFORMES
Family Lemuridae: *Megaladapis*
Family Lorisidae
DIVISION HAPLORHINI
Family Omomyidae: *Necrolemur*
Family Tarsiidae
SUBORDER ANTHROPOIDEA
INFRAORDER PLATYRRHINI
Family Cebidae: *Branisella*
Family Atelidae: *Tremacebus*
INFRAORDER CATARRHINI
SUPERFAMILY CERCOPITHECOIDEA
Family Cercopithecidae: *Mesopithecus, Theropithecus*
Family Oreopithecidae: *Oreopithecus*
SUPERFAMILY HOMINOIDEA
Family Hylobatidae (gibbons)
Family Pliopithecidae: *Dendropithecus, Pliopithecus, Propliopithecus*
Subfamily Ponginae (fossil and living apes): *Dryopithecus, Gigantopithecus, Ramapithecus, Sivapithecus*
Family Hominidae (humans and great apes): *Australopithecus, Homo*
Subfamily Homininae (humans and fossil ancestors)
SUPERORDER FERAE
ORDER CREODONTA (creodonts)
Family Hyaenodontidae: *Hyaenodon*
Family Oxyaenidae: *Sarkastodon*

ORDER CARNIVORA (true carnivores)

Superfamily Miacoidea

Family Miacidae: *Miacis*

Superfamily Feloidea (cats, mongooses)

Family Viverridae: *Kanuites*

Family Hyaenidae: *Ictitherium, Percrocuta*

Family Nimravidae: *Nimravus*

Family Felidae: *Dinofelis, Eusmilus, Homotherium, Megantereon, Panthera, Smilodon*

Superfamily Canoidea (dogs, bears, pandas)

Family Mustelidae: *Potamotherium*

Family Canidae: *Canis, Cerdocyon, Cynodesmus, Hesperocyon, Osteoborus, Phlaocyon*

Family Procyonidae: *Chapalmalania, Plesictis*

Family Amphicyonidac: *Amphicyon*

Family Ursidae: *Agriotherium, Hemicyon, Ursus*

SUBORDER PINNIPEDIA (seals, sealions, walruses)

Superfamily Phocoidea (eared seals)

Family Phocidae: *Acrophoca*

Superfamily Otarioidea (fur seals and sealions)

Family Enaliarctidae: *Enaliarctos*

Family Desmatophocidae: *Desmatophoca*

Family Odobenidae (walruses): *Imagotaria*

Family Otariidae

SUPERORDER UNGULATA (hoofed mammals or ungulates)

ORDER ARCTOCYONIA (condylarths)

Family Arctocyonidae: *Chriacus*

ORDER ACREODI

Family Mesonychidae: *Andrewsarchus*

ORDER TAENIODONTA

Family Stylinodontidae: *Stylinodon*

ORDER PANTODONTA

Family Coryphodontidae: *Coryphodon*

ORDER TILLODONTIA

Family Esthonychidae: *Trogosus*

ORDER DINOCERATA

Family Uintatheriidae: *Eobasileus*

ORDER ARTIODACTYLA (even-toed ungulates)

SUBORDER SUINA (pigs, peccaries, hippopotamuses)

Family Dichobunidae: *Diacodexis*

Family Entelodontidae: *Archaeotherium, Dinohyus*

Family Suidae: *Metridiochoerus*

Family Tayassuidae: *Platygonus*

Family Anthracotheriidae: *Elomeryx*

Family Hippopotamidae: *Hippopotamus*

SUBORDER TYLOPODA (oreodonts, camels)

Family Merycoidodontidae: *Brachycrus, Merycoidodon, Promerycochoerus*

Family Cainotheriidae: *Cainotherium*

Family Protoceratidae: *Protoceras, Syndyoceras, Synthetoceras*

Family Camelidae: *Aepycamelus, Camelops, Oxydactylus, Poebrotherium, Procamelus,*

Protylopus, Stenomylus, Titanotylopus

SUBORDER RUMINANTIA (deer, giraffes, cattle)

Family Tragul: *Blastomeryx*

Family Cervidae: *Eucladoceros, Megaloceros*

Family Giraffidae: *Prolibytherium, Sivatherium*

Family Antilocapridae: *Hayoceros, Illingoceros*

Family Bovidae: *Bos, Pelorovis*

ORDER CETACEA (whales, dolphins, porpoises)

SUBORDER ARCHAEOCETI

Family Protocetidae: *Pakicetus, Protocetus*

Family Basilosauridae: *Basilosaurus, Zygorhiza*

SUBORDER ODONTOCETI (toothed whales)

Family Squalodontidae: *Prosqualodon*

Family Eurhinodelphidae: *Eurhinodelphis*

SUBORDER MYSTICETI (baleen whales)

Family Cetotheriidae: *Cetotherium*

ORDER TUBULIDENTATA (aardvarks)

ORDER PERISSODACTYLA (odd-toed ungulates)

SUBORDER CERATOMORPHA (tapirs, rhinoceroses)

Family Helaletidae: *Heptodon*

Family Hyrachyidae: *Hyrachyus*

Family Tapiridae: *Miotapirus*

Family Hyracodontidae: *Hyracodon, Indricotherium*

Family Amynodontidae: *Metamynodon*

Family Rhinocerotidae: *Coelodonta, Elasmotherium, Teleoceras, Trigonias*

SUBORDER ANCYLOPODA

Family Chalicotheriidae: *Moropus*

SUBORDER HIPPOMORPHA (horses, brontotheres)

Family Palaeotheriidae: *Palaeotherium*

Family Equidae: *Anchitherium, Hipparion, Hippidion, Hyracotherium, Merychippus, Mesohippus, Parahippus*

Family Brontotheriidae: *Brontotherium, Brontops,Dolichorhinus, Embolotherium, Eotitanops*

SUPERORDER MERIDIUNGULATA (South American hoofed mammals)

ORDER LITOPTERNA

Family Didolodontidae: *Didolodus*

Family Proterotheriidae: *Diadiaphorus, Thoatherium*

Family Macraucheniidae: *Macrauchenia, Theosodon*

ORDER NOTOUNGULATA

SUBORDER NOTIOPROGONIA

Family Notostylopidae: *Notostylops*

SUBORDER TOXODONTA

Family Isotemnidae: *Thomashuxleya*

Family Homalodotheriidae: *Homalodotherium*

Family Leontiniidae: *Scarrittia*

Family Notohippidae: *Rhynchippus*

Family Toxodontidae: *Adinotherium, Toxodon*

SUBORDER TYPOTHERIA

Family Interatheriidae: *Protypotherium*

SUBORDER HEGETOTHERIA

Family Hegetotheriidae: *Pachyrukhos*

ORDER ASTRAPOTHERIA

Family Astrapotheriidae: *Astrapotherium*

Family Trigonostylopidae: *Trigonostylops*

ORDER PYROTHERIA

Family Pyrotheriidae: *Pyrotherium*

ORDER HYRACOIDEA

Family Pliohyracidae: *Kvabebihyrax*

SUPERORDER TETHYTHERIA

ORDER EMBRITHOPODA

Family Arsinoitheriidae: *Arsinoitherium*

ORDER PROBOSCIDEA

Family Moeritheriidae: *Moeritherium*

Family Deinotheriidae: *Deinotherium*

SUBORDER ELEPHANTIODEA (elephants, mastodonts, mammoths)

Family Gomphotheriidae: *Amebelodon, Anancus, Cuvieronius, Gomphotherium, Phiomia, Platybelodon, Stegomastodon*

Family Mammutidae: *Mammut*

Family Elephantidae: *Elephas, Mammuthus*

ORDER SIRENIA (dugongs, manatees)

Family Prorastomidae: *Prorastomus*

Family Dugongidae: *Rytiodus, Hydrodamalis*

ORDER DESMOSTYLA

Family Desmostylidae: *Desmostylus*

BIBLIOGRAPHY

GENERAL

Benton, M. J. editor (1988) Phylogeny of the Tetrapods Oxford, UK

Benton, M. J. (1990) The Reign of the Reptiles Kingfisher, UK

Benton, M. J. editor (1993) The Fossil Record 2 Chapman & Hall, UK, USA

Benton, M. J. (1997) Vertebrate Palaeontology Chapman & Hall, UK, USA

Benton, M. J. and R. Osborne (1996) Atlas of Evolution Viking, UK, USA

Benton, M. J. and D. A. T. Harper (1997) Basic Palaeontology Addison Wesley Longman, UK

Buffetaut, E. (1987) A Short History of Vertebrate Palaeontology Chapman & Hall UK

Carroll, R. L. (1988) Vertebrate Paleontology and Evolution Freeman, USA

Carroll, R. L. (1997) Pattern sand Processes of Vertebrate Evolution, Cambridge University Press UK, USA

Gould, S. editor (1993) The Book of Life Ebury UK

Hublin, J. (1982) The Hamlyn Encyclopaedia of Prehistoric Animals Hamlyn, UK & USA

McFarland, W. N., Pough, F. F. H., Cade, T. J., Heiser, J. B. (1979) Vertebrate Life Collier Macmillan, l UK; Macmillan, USA

McGowan, C. (1991) Dinosaurs, Dragons and Spitfires Harvard University Press USA

Patterson, C. (1978) Evolution British Museum (Natural History), UK

Romer, A. S. (1974) The Vertebrate Story University of Chicago Press, USA

FISHES

Janvier, P. (1996) Early Vertebrates Oxford UK

Long, J. A. (1995) The Rise of the Fishes Johns Hopkins University Press, USA

Maisey, J. G. (1996) Discovering Fossil Fishes Henry Holt, USA

REPTILES

King, G. (1996) Reptiles and Herbivory Chapman & Hall UK

Rowe, S. R., Sharpe, T., Torrens, H. S. (1981) lchthyosaurs: A History of Fossil Sea Dragons National Museum of Wales, Cardiff, I UK

Wellnhofer, P. (1991) The Illustrated Encyclopedia of Pterosaurs Crescent USA

RULING REPTILES

Alexander, R. McN. (1979) Dynamics of dinosaurs and other extinct giants Columbia University Press, USA

Alvarez, W. (1997) T. rex and the Crater of Doom Princeton USA

Bakker, R. T. (1986) The Dinosaur Heresies Morrow, USA; Penguin, UK

Carpenter, K., Hirsch, K. F. and J. R. Horner editors (1994) Dinosaur Eggs and Babies Cambridge University Press, UK

Charig, A. J. (1979) A New Look at the Dinosaurs Heinemann, UK

Colbert, E. H. (1986) Dinosaurs: An Illustrated History Hammond, USA

Currie, P. J. and K. Padian editors (1997) Encyclopedia of Dinosaurs Academic Press UK, USA

Czerkas, S. J. and E. C. Olson (1987) Dinosaurs Past and Present Natural History Museum of Los Angeles County USA

Glut, D. (1982) The New Dinosaur Dictionary Citadel, USA

Lambert, D. (1983) Collins Guide to Dinosaurs Collins, UK;

Norman, D. (1985) The Illustrated Encyclopaedia of Dinosaurs Salamander, UK

Norman, D. (1991) Dinosaur! Boxtree UK

Russell, D. (1989) An Odyssey in Time: The Dinosaurs of North America University of Toronto Press Canada

Thulborn, R. A. (1990) Dinosaur Tracks Chapman & Hall UK

Weishampel, D. B., H. Osmolska and P. Dodson (1990) The Dinosauria University of California Press, USA

Wilford, J. N. (1985) The Riddle of the Dinosaurs Faber & Faber, UK

MAMMAL-LIKE REPTILES

Hotton, N. III, P. D. Maclean, J. J. Roth and E. C. Roth editors (1986) The Ecology and Biology of Mammal-like Reptiles Smithsonian Institution Press USA

Kemp, T. S. (1982) Mammal-like Reptiles and the Origin of Mammals Academic Press, UK & USA

King, G. (1990) The Dicynodonts: A Study in Palaeobiology Chapman & Hall Uk

BIRDS

Dingus, L. and T. Rowe (1998) The Mistaken Extinction: Dinosaur Evolution and the Origin of the Birds W. H. Freeman USA

Feduccia, A. (1996) The Origin and Evolution of Birds Yale University Press USA

Shipman, P. (1998) Taking Wing: *Archaeopteryx* and the Evolution of Bird Flight Weidenfeld & Nicolson, UK

MAMMALS

Aiello, L. (1982) Discovering the Origins of Mankind Longman, UK

Benton, M. J. (1991) The Rise of the Mammals The Apple Tree Press, UK

Clutton-Brock, J. (1981) Domesticated Animals from Early Times Heinemann/ British Museum (Natural History), UK

Halstead, L. B. (1978) The Evolution of the Mammals Peter Lowe, UK

Jones, S., R. Martin and D. Pilbeam editors (1992) The Cambridge Encyclopedia of Human Evolution Cambridge University Press, UK

Lambert, D. (1987) The Cambridge Guide to Prehistoric Man Cambridge University Press, UK

Leakey, R. E. (1981) Human Origins Hamish Hamilton, UK

Lewin, R. (1984) Human Evolution: An Illustrated Introduction Blackwell Scientific Publications, UK

Lillegraven, J. A. S, Kielan-Jaworowska and W. A. Clemens (1979) Mesozoic Mammals University of California Press, USA

Lister, A. and P. Bahn (1994) Mammoths Macmillan USA

MacFadden. B. J. Fossil Horses (1992) Cambridge University Press

Napier, J. R. & P. H. (1985) The Natural History of the Primates British Museum (Natural History), UK

Reader, J. (1988) Missing Links, the Hunt for Earliest Man Penguin UK

Savage, R.J.G and Long, M. R. (1986)Mammal Evolution: An Illustrated Guide British Museum (Natural History), UK

Scott, W. 0. (1967) A History of Land Mammals in the Western Hemisphere Mac, Macmillan, USA

Simpson, G. C. (1980) Splendid Isolation: The Curious History of South American Mammals Yale University Press, USA

Stringer, C. B. and R. McKie (1996) African Exodus: the Origins of Modern Humanity Cape UK

Szalay, F. S., Delson, E. (1979) Evolutionary History of the Primates Academic Press, UK & USA

Szalay, F. S., M.J. Novacek, and M. C. McKenna (1993) Mammal Phylogeny Springer-Verlag, Germany, USA

Tattersall, I., E. Delson and J. Van Couvering editors (1988) Encyclopedia of Human Evolution and Prehistory Garland USA

INTERNATIONAL MUSEUMS

The museums listed below are among those that contain outstanding collections of fossils of the prehistoric creatures described in this book.

ARGENTINA Buenos Aires: Museo Argentino de Ciencias Naturales La Plata; Museum of La Plata University

AUSTRALIA Brisbane, Queensland: Queensland Museum
Sydney, New South Wales: Australian Museum

AUSTRIA Vienna: Natural History Museum

BELGIUM Brussels: Royal Institute of Natural Sciences

BRAZIL Rio de Janeiro: Museo Nacional

CANADA Calgary, Alberta: Zoological Gardens
Drumheller, Alberta: Tyrrell Museum of Paleontology
Edmonton, Alberta: Provincial Museum of Alberta
Ottawa, Ontario: National Museum of National Sciences
Patricia, Alberta: Dinosaur Provincial Park
Quebec: Redpath Museum
Toronto, Ontario: Royal Ontario Museum

CHINA Beijing (Peking): Beijing Natural History Museum; Institute of Vertebrate Palaeontology and Palaeoanthropology
Beipei, Sichuan: Beipei Museum

FRANCE Paris: National Museum of Natural History

GERMANY Berlin: Natural History Museum Humboldt University Darmstadt: Hesse State Museum
Frankfurt-am-Main: Senckenberg Natural History Museum
Munich: Bavarian State Institute for Paleontology and Historical Geography
Stuttgart: State Museum for Natural History
Tubingen: Institute and Museum of Geology and Paleontology

GREECE Athens: Department of Geology and Paleontology, University of Athens

INDIA Calcutta: Geology Museum, Indian Statistical Institute

ITALY Bologna: Q. Capellini Museum
Genoa: Civic Museum of Natural History
Milan: Civic Museum of Natural History
Padua: Museum of the Institute of Geology
Rome: Museum of Paleontology; Institute of Geology
Venice: Museo Civico di Storia Naturale di Venezia

JAPAN Osaka: Museum of Natural History
Tokyo: National Science Museum

KENYA Nairobi: Kenya National Museum

MEXICO Mexico City: Natural History Museum

MONGOLIA Ulan-Bator: State Central Museum

MOROCCO Rabat: Museum of Earth Sciences

NIGER Niamey: National Museum

POLAND Chorzow, Silesia: Dinosaur Park
Warsaw: Institute of Palaeobiology

RUSSIA Leningrad: Central Geological and Prospecting Museum; Museum of Geology
Moscow: Paleontology Museum

SOUTH AFRICA Capetown: South Africa Museum
Johannesburg: Bernard Price Institute of Palaeontology

SWEDEN Uppsala: Paleontology Museum, Uppsala University

UNITED KINGDOM
Birmingham: Birmingham Museum
Cambridge: Sedgwick Museum, Cambridge University
Cardiff, Wales: National Museum of Wales
Edinburgh, Scotland: Royal Scottish Museum
Elgin, Scotland: Elgin Museum
Glasgow, Scotland: Hunterian Museum
Leicester: The Leicestershire Museums
London: British Museum (Natural History); Crystal Palace Park
Maidstone: Maidstone Museum
Oxford: University Museum
Sandown, Isle of Wight: Museum of Isle of Wight Geology

UNITED STATES OF AMERICA
Boulder, Colorado: University Natural History Museum
Buffalo, New York State: Museum of Science
Cambridge, Massachusetts: Museum of Comparative Zoology, Harvard University
Chicago, Illinois: Field Museum of Natural History
Cleveland, Ohio: Natural History Museum
Denver, Colorado: Denver Museum of Natural History
Jensen, Utah: Dinosaur National Monument
Los Angeles, California: Los Angeles County Museum of Natural History
New Haven, Connecticut: Peabody Museum of Natural History
Yale University, New York, New York State: American Museum of Natural History
Pittsburg, Pennsylvania: Carnegie Museum of Natural History Princeton, New Jersey: Museum of Natural History, Princeton University
Salt Lake City, Utah: Utah Museum of Natural History Washington DC: National Museum of Natural History, Smithsonian Institute

ZIMBABWE Harare: National Museum of Harare

INDEX